Employment Law Handbook

A Guide for Michigan Employers

Authors

James B. Thelen
Editor

Kevin M. McCarthy, McCarthy Smith Law Group, PLC
Contributor

Michigan Chamber of Commerce
Publishers

Copyright 2009 © Miller, Canfield, Paddock and Stone, P.L.C.

All rights reserved. No part of this book may be reproduced or copied in any form without written permission from the publisher.

This publication presents a summary of information that is intended to be accurate and authoritative. The publisher and authors, however, cannot be responsible for any errors, omissions, or changes in the material presented, nor for any administrative or adjudicative body's interpretation or application of the legal premises upon which this material is based.

ISBN 1-893318-21-4

This publication is available from:
The Michigan Chamber of Commerce
600 South Walnut Street
Lansing, Michigan 48933
(800) 748-0344
www.michamber.com

About this book

This publication is designed to provide accurate and authoritative information in regard to the subject matter covered. However, a reference book on employment law, and sample forms or policies, cannot substitute for review of your particular circumstances by an experienced labor attorney. The appropriateness of particular policies or recommendations frequently depends on your company's history, objectives, and conditions in the workplace. Because the law of employment relations continues to develop rapidly, employers facing business decisions about legal issues involving employment, labor, or personnel relations questions should seek the advice of legal counsel for the company's particular situation. Therefore, this book is sold with the understanding that neither the authors nor the publisher is rendering legal, accounting, or other professional services. The publisher and authors disclaim any responsibility for errors, omissions, or changes in the material presented, or for any administrative or adjudicative body's interpretation or application of the legal premises upon which this material is based. This book is of a general educational nature and warranties of merchantability or fitness for a particular purpose are specifically excluded.

About the Authors

Miller, Canfield, Paddock and Stone, P.L.C. www.millercanfield.com

This book has been prepared by the Labor and Employment Group and the Employee Benefits Group of the law firm of Miller Canfield.

Miller Canfield traces its history to 1852 when it opened a practice on Detroit's Jefferson Avenue. Today, with seven offices in Michigan, Miller Canfield has the most lawyers in Michigan and one of the nation's leading firms in its specialty areas. We have grown to a legal staff of almost 400 lawyers and over 50 legal assistants.

The Labor and Employment and Employee Benefits Groups provide a full range of employment law, employment litigation, and employee benefit services to private and public sector clients. The Labor and Employment Group has a long standing policy of only representing management clients. Attorneys in both groups have extensive experience representing employer clients in service areas including municipal, state, and federal administrative proceedings; affirmative action plans; alternative dispute resolution (ADR); arbitration; audits; collective bargaining; disability law; drug testing and employee privacy issues; EEO litigation and advice; ERISA; NLRB; OFCCP; OSHA and MIOSHA; plant closings; retirement programs and reductions in force; public employer labor relations; Railway Labor Act; strikes and lockouts; tort law; union election campaigns; wage and hour issues; workers' compensation; wrongful discharge; and all aspects of employee benefit plan construction and advice, including tax implications.

Attorneys who currently practice in the above areas include the following individuals, listed with their principal office locations:

Michael A. Alaimo (Detroit)	Leonard D. Givens (Detroit)	Kalyn D. Redlowsk (Kalamazoo)
Timothy L. Andersson (Detroit)	Gary R. Glenn (Detroit)	Ryan J. Riehl (Detroit)
Tim A. Attalia (Detroit)	Linda O. Goldberg (Ann Arbor)	Jennifer L. Sabourin (Detroit)
Vernon Bennett III (Kalamazoo)	Kalman G. Goren (Troy)	Kenneth J. Sachs (Troy)
Lisa M. Berden (Detroit)	Leigh R. Greden (Ann Arbor)	Saura James Sahu (Detroit)
Andrew T. Blum (Grand Rapids)	Michael J. Hodge (Lansing)	Leigh M. Schultz (Kalamazoo)
Orin D. Brustad (Detroit)	John M. Jedlinski (Windsor)	Brian Schwartz (Detroit)
Beverly Hall Burns (Detroit)	Dawn E. Marshall (Detroit)	Richard J. Seryak (Detroit)
Douglas A. Callander (Kalamazoo)	Susan M. McBride (Windsor)	Kurt N. Sherwood (Kalamazoo)
Carolyn P. Cary (Saginaw)	Kurt P. McCamman (Kalamazoo)	Doreen E. Snelling (Windsor)
Geoffrey M. Chinn (New York)	Christopher A. McMican (Detroit)	Loretta Stoyka (Windsor)
Justin M. Crawford (Kalamazoo)	David M. McNevin (Windsor)	James B. Thelen (Lansing)
Douglas W. Crim (Lansing)	Charles S. Mishkind (Grand Rapids)	Deborah W. Thompson (Detroit)
Michelle P. Crockett (Detroit)	Megan P. Norris (Detroit)	Christopher M. Trebilcock (Detroit)
Donna J. Donati (Detroit)	Bruce D. Olson (Grand Rapids)	Joseph W. Uhl (Detroit)
Scott R. Eldridge (Lansing)	Charles T. Oxender (Detroit)	Richard W. Warren (Detroit)
Pamela C. Enslen (Kalamazoo)	Marianna J. Perakis (Detroit)	Jerome R. Watson (Detroit)
Adam S. Forman (Detroit)	Diane K. Phelps (Lansing)	John H. Willems (Detroit)
Brant A. Freer (Detroit)	J. David Reck (Detroit)	Robert T. Zielinski (Chicago)

We are the designated state of Michigan representative and a founding member of the Employment Law Alliance, the world's largest national and international network of labor and employment lawyers. For more information about the ELA, see *www.employmentlawalliance.com*.

If you have any general questions about the firm, you may contact the firm's Chief Executive Officer, Michael W. Hartmann, at 313-963-6420. If you have any questions about the firm's employment services, you may contact the Leader of the Labor and Employment Practice Group, Megan P. Norris (norris@millercanfield.com), at 313-496-7594; or the editor of this book, James B. Thelen (thelen@millercanfield.com), at 517-483-4901. Editorial assistance was provided by Rhonda R. Miller in Lansing.

Miller Canfield has offices in Ann Arbor, Detroit, Grand Rapids, Kalamazoo, Lansing, Saginaw, and Troy, Michigan. Other offices are located in Windsor and Toronto, Ontario, Canada; Naples, Florida; New York, New York; Chicago, Illinois; Cambridge, Massachusetts; Shanghai, China; and Gdynia, Warsaw, and Wroclaw Poland. You may also visit the firm's Web site at *www.millercanfield.com*.

Miller Canfield in Michigan
101 North Main Street, 7th Floor
Ann Arbor, MI 48104
Phone: 734-663-2445

150 West Jefferson, Suite 2500
Detroit, MI 48226
Phone: 313-963-6420

99 Monroe Avenue NW, Suite 1200
Grand Rapids, MI 49503
Phone: 616-454-8656

277 S. Rose Street, Suite 500
Kalamazoo, MI 49007
Phone: 269-381-7030

One Michigan Avenue, Suite 900
Lansing, MI 48933
Phone: 517-487-2070

4800 Fashion Square Blvd., Suite 120
Saginaw, MI 48604
Phone: 989-791-4646

840 West Long Lake Road, Suite 200
Troy, MI 48098
Phone: 248-879-2000

Miller Canfield in Florida
801 Laurel Oak Drive, Suite 705
Naples, FL 34108
(239) 596-1975

Miller Canfield in Illinois
225 W. Washington, Suite 2600
Chicago IL 60606
(312) 460-4200

Miller Canfield in Massachusetts
One Broadway, 6th Floor
Cambridge, MA 02142
(617) 679-5200

Miller Canfield in New York
500 Fifth Avenue, Suite 1815
New York, NY 10110
Phone: 212-704-4400

Miller Canfield in Canada
161 Bay Street, 27th Floor
Toronto, Ontario
Canada M5J 2S1

443 Ouellette Avenue, Suite 300
Windsor, Ontario
Canada N9A 6R4
Phone: 519-977-1555

Miller Canfield in China
29/F Shanghai Kerry Center
1515 Nanjing West Road
Shanghai, China 200040
Phone: 8621-6103-7000

Miller Canfield In Poland
ul. Batorego 28-32
81-366 Gdynia
Poland
Phone: (48-58) 782-0050

ul. Nowogrodzka 11, 5th Floor
00-513 Warsaw
Poland
Phone: (48-22) 447-4300

Pl. Stregomski 2-4
53-611 Wroclaw
Poland
Phone: (48-71) 337-6700

McCarthy Smith Law Group, PLC   www.mccarthysmithlaw.com

McCARTHY SMITH LAW GROUP, PLC is a Kalamazoo based law firm that specializes in the representation of employers throughout Michigan and in 45 other states. The principal and founder of the firm is Kevin M. McCarthy, who has 30 years of experience representing employers in all areas of labor and employment law.

Among the services provided by McCarthy Smith Law Group on a personalized, quality, and timely basis are:

- Day-to-day advice on labor and employment matters
- Negotiation of collective bargaining agreements
- Arbitration, mediation and other forms of ADR
- Compliance advice regarding federal, state and local employment laws
- Legal and "best practices" compliance audits
- Maintenance of a union-free workplace
- Drafting of handbooks and personnel policies
- Training programs
- Representation before administrative agencies
- Defense of employment claims and lawsuits
- Crisis management

The firm represents all types of organizations, ranging from large national and international firms to small companies, both public sector and private sector organizations, and both unionized and non-unionized entities.

McCarthy Smith Law Group was created to provide employers access to professional legal counsel that is forward-thinking and proactive. It is set up to respond quickly to clients' needs in a professional, cost-effective manner.

The lawyers and staff of McCarthy Smith Law Group may be reached at:

McCarthy Smith Law Group, PLC
550 W. Centre Avenue
Portage, MI 49024
(269) 488-6330 – phone
(269) 488-6333 – fax
mccarthy@mccarthysmithlaw.com
beuker@mccarthysmithlaw.com
stclair@mccarthysmithlaw.com

The firm's website can be found at www.mccarthysmithlaw.com

TABLE OF CONTENTS

CHAPTER 1: INTRODUCTION TO THE 2009 EMPLOYMENT LAW HANDBOOK 1

WHAT'S NEW FOR 2009 3
SOME BASIC GENERAL LIABILITY AVOIDANCE ADVICE 4
    Outplacement 4
    Releases 5
    Alternative Dispute Resolution 5
    Insurance Covering Employment Claims 6
    Preventive Audits 6

CHAPTER 2: PRE-HIRE EMPLOYMENT POLICIES 7

MEANS OF PROPERLY SCREENING JOB APPLICANTS 7
    Job Application Forms 7
    Job Interviews 8
    Reference Checks 11
    Criminal Record Checks 12
    Fair Credit Reporting Act 13
    Drug and Alcohol Testing 14
    Aptitude, Personality, and Honesty Testing 15
    Pitfalls to Avoid in the Hiring Process 16
    Theories of Negligent Hiring and Negligent Retention 22
    Liability Concerns in Providing References 24
NEW HIRE REPORTING REQUIREMENTS 25
SUMMARY 25

CHAPTER 3: EMPLOYMENT STATUS 27

AT-WILL EMPLOYEES 27
JUST-CAUSE EMPLOYEES 28
SATISFACTION EMPLOYEES 28
TERM CONTRACT EMPLOYEES 29
INDEPENDENT CONTRACTORS 30
IRS REVENUE RULING 87-41 31
LEASED OR TEMPORARY EMPLOYEES 35
MIXING EMPLOYMENT STATUSES 36
IMPLIED EMPLOYMENT LIABILITY—THE TOUSSAINT 36
DOCTRINE 36
    Reducing Your Risks 37
HUMAN RESOURCES AUDITS 38
PREVENTIVE LEGAL AUDITS 38
THE DANGER OF AUDITS 43

CHAPTER 4: DISCRIMINATION & HARASSMENT 45

DISCRIMINATION 46
    Elliott-Larsen Civil Rights Act – State Law 46
    Disparate Treatment Discrimination 47
    Intentional Discrimination 48
    Adverse Impact Discrimination 49
    Bona Fide Occupational Qualification 49
    Marital Status Discrimination 50
    Retaliation Prohibitions 50
    Avoiding Discrimination Liability—Elliott-Larsen 51
TITLE VII AND THE AGE DISCRIMINATION IN EMPLOYMENT ACT 51
    Title VII 51

    Age Discrimination in Employment Act 52
PREGNANCY ISSUES 54
GENETIC INFORMATION NON-DISCRIMINATION ACT (GINA) 54
AVOIDING DISCRIMINATION LIABILITY 55
HARASSMENT 57
    Sexual Harassment 57
    Quid Pro Quo 58
    Hostile Environment 58
    Favoritism 59
    Same Sex Harassment 60
DESIGNING A SEXUAL HARASSMENT POLICY 60
RACIAL HARASSMENT 62
HARASSMENT INVESTIGATIONS 64
AVOIDING HARASSMENT LAWSUITS 66
RECORDKEEPING REQUIREMENTS OF ANTI-DISCRIMINATION LAWS 66
    Records to be Kept by All Employers 67
    Records to be Kept by Employers Subject to OSHA 68
    Personnel Files and the Bullard-Plawecki Right-to- Know Act 68
ALTERNATIVE DISPUTE RESOLUTION OF EMPLOYMENT DISCRIMINATION CLAIMS 70
    Drafting or Adopting an Enforceable ADR Procedure 73
    Right of Representation 75
    Mediator and Arbitrator Qualifications 75

CHAPTER 5: DISABILITY DISCRIMINATION 77

EMPLOYERS SUBJECT TO ADA AND MPWDCRA 77
INDIVIDUALS PROTECTED BY ADA AND MPWDCRA 78
    Disability Defined 78
    Otherwise Qualified for the Position 81
    Able to Perform Essential Functions 81
    Drug and Alcohol Use 81
    Genetic Testing 82
PROHIBITED DISCRIMINATORY ACTS 82
MEDICAL INQUIRIES AND EXAMS 83
REASONABLE ACCOMMODATION: ADA AND MPWDCRA 84
    Undue Hardship 88
SAFETY OF SELF OR OTHERS 90
    Food Handling and Communicable Diseases 91
    AIDS Issues 91
CONFLICTS WITH OTHER FEDERAL LAWS: ADA AND MPWDCRA 92
    Notification of Need for Accommodation 92
    Remedies Under ADA and MPWDCRA 93

CHAPTER 6: AFFIRMATIVE ACTION 95

CONSIDERATIONS IN DEVELOPING AND MANAGING 95
DIVERSITY INITIATIVES 95
PLANNING AND IMPLEMENTING DIVERSITY INITIATIVES 96
EVALUATION AND ASSESSMENT OF DIVERSITY INITIATIVES 98
    Key Steps in a Program Evaluation Process 98
AFFIRMATIVE ACTION PLANS 100
    Voluntary Affirmative Action Plans 101
    Mandatory Affirmative Action Plans 102
    Legal Standards for Affirmative Action Plans 103
EMPLOYER'S SELF-ANALYSIS 106
    EEOC Suggestions for Employers 106
GUIDELINES FOR AFFIRMATIVE ACTION PLANS 107
    Content Requirements for Federally-Required Affirmative Action Plans 108
DURATION OF EXEMPTIONS GRANTED BY THE OFCCP 113

  Record Retention 113

CHAPTER 7: IMMIGRATION REFORM AND CONTROL ACT 115

 Verification and Form I–9 Requirements 115
  New I-9 Forms 117
 Penalties for Violating IRCA 117
  Avoiding Employer Sanctions—IRCA 117
 Antidiscrimination Provisions of IRCA 118
  Avoiding Discrimination Liability—IRCA 118
 U.S. Bureau of Immigration and Customs Enforcement Audits 118
  Notice of ICE Inspection 118
  Preparing for an ICE Inspection 119
  During an ICE Inspection 120

CHAPTER 8: WAGE AND HOUR ISSUES 121

 Michigan Wage and Fringe Benefits Act 121
  Employers Subject to MWFBA 121
  Purpose of the MWFBA 121
  Payment of Wages 122
  Payment of Wages Upon Termination 123
  Deducting Wages 123
  Overpayment of Wages or Fringe Benefits 124
  Employee Contributions to Political Committees 125
  Recordkeeping Requirements of MWFBA 125
  Retaliation Prohibitions—MWFBA 126
  Disclosure of Wages 127
  Enforcement of MWFBA 127
  Penalties for Violating MWFBA 128
  Debarment Penalties 128
  Reciprocity with Other States and Canada 129
 Fair Labor Standards Act 129
  Employers Subject to FLSA 129
  Employees or Independent Contractors? 130
  Employees or Trainees? 131
  Recordkeeping Requirements of FLSA 132
  Posting Requirements of FLSA 133
  Hours Worked 133
  Minimum Wage under FLSA and State Law 137
  Overtime under FLSA 139
  Regular Rate of Pay under FLSA 139
  Bonuses 141
  Per-visit or Flat-rate Pay 141
  Executive Exemption 142
  Administrative Exemption 143
  Professional Exemption 143
  Computer Software Employees 144
  Wage and Hour Interpretive Guidance 144
  Outside Salesperson Exemption 145
  General Considerations for Exemptions 145
  Salary and Pay Practices 146
  Enforcement of FLSA 147
 Michigan Minimum Wage Law of 1964 149
  Employers Subject to MMWL 149
  Independent Contractors 149
  Leased Employees 150
  Special Requirements of MMWL 150
  Recordkeeping Requirements of MMWL 153
  Enforcement and Sanctions under MMWL 154
  Non-Application of MMWL 154

    Retaliation Prohibitions Under MMWL 154
    Equal Pay 155
MICHIGAN YOUTH EMPLOYMENT STANDARDS ACT 155
    Employers Subject to MYESA 155
    Minimum Age Under MYESA 156
    Hour Restrictions Under MYESA 156
    Meals and Rest Periods 157
    Adult Supervision Required 157
    Restricted Occupations under MYESA 158
    Work Permits 158
    Deviations from Provisions 159
    Recordkeeping Requirements of MYESA 159
    Enforcement and Sanctions under MYESA 160
FEDERAL CHILD LABOR LAWS 160
    Employers Subject to Federal Child Labor Laws 160
    General Restrictions Under Federal Child Labor Laws 161
    Minimum Age Under Federal Child Labor Laws 161
    Restricted Occupations Under Federal Child Labor Laws 161
    Hour Restrictions under Federal Child Labor Laws 162
    Special School Programs 163
    Penalties for Violating Federal Child Labor Laws 163

CHAPTER 9: EMPLOYEE BENEFIT LAW 165

EMPLOYEE RETIREMENT INCOME SECURITY ACT 165
    Agency Responsibility under ERISA 165
    ERISA Key Definitions 165
    Reporting and Disclosure Rules 167
    Participation, Vesting, and Accrual 168
    Minimum Funding 169
    Fiduciary Responsibilities 170
    Interference with Protected Rights 172
    Enforcement of ERISA 172
    ERISA Jurisdiction 173
    Preemption under ERISA 173
TAX-QUALIFIED RETIREMENT PLANS 173
    Governing Rules for Retirement Plans 174
    Vesting in Retirement Plans 176
    Qualified Joint and Survivor Annuity Requirements 176
    Top-Heavy Rules for Retirement Plans 177
    Qualification of a Retirement Plan 177
CAFETERIA PLANS 177
    Types of Cafeteria Plans 178
    Cafeteria Plan Benefit Types 179
    Legal Operating Rules for Cafeteria Plans 180
FLEXIBLE SPENDING ACCOUNTS 181
    Use-It-or-Lose-It Rule for FSAs 181
    Coverage Period of FSAs 182
    Special Rules for Healthcare FSAs 182
    Nondiscrimination Rules for Cafeteria Plans 183
CONSOLIDATED OMNIBUS BUDGET RECONCILIATION ACT (COBRA) 184
    Notification Obligations under COBRA 185
    Extended Coverage Option 186
    Types of Benefits under COBRA 187
    Continuation Coverage Length 187
    Penalties for Violating COBRA 188
AVOIDING BENEFIT LIABILITY 189

CHAPTER 10: HEALTH INSURANCE PORTABILITY AND ACCOUNTABILITY ACT 195

PRE-EXISTING CONDITION LIMITS 195
CREDITED PERIODS OF PRIOR COVERAGE 198
- Types of Creditable Coverage 199
- Administrative Demands of Crediting Coverage 200
- Special Enrollment Periods 202
- Limits on Evidence of Insurability 203

LONG-TERM CARE 204
MEDICAL SAVINGS ACCOUNTS 204
ACCELERATED LIFE INSURANCE PAYMENTS 205
DISCLOSURE REQUIREMENTS OF HIPAA 205
HIPAA PRIVACY AND SECURITY REQUIREMENTS 205
DISCLOSURES TO HHS FOR COMPLIANCE REVIEW 211
- Effect on Employers *as* Employers 211
- Effect on Employers as Sponsors of Health Plans 217

DISTINCTION BETWEEN CERTAIN INSURED AND SELF-INSURED GROUP HEALTH PLANS—DUTIES UNDER THE RULES' "ADMINISTRATIVE REQUIREMENTS" 223
- Additional Requirements: Disclosures of Protected Health Information to Parties Other Than the Plan Sponsor 226
- Individual Rights 227
- Upcoming Amendment to the Privacy Rule 230
- Overview of Security Rule: Purpose and Scope 231
- Fundamental Obligations of a Covered Entity 231
- Electronic Protected Health Information 232

PROCEDURAL APPROACH TO COMPLIANCE 237

CHAPTER 11: FAMILY AND MEDICAL LEAVE ACT 241

EMPLOYERS COVERED BY THE FMLA 241
- Joint Employers 242
- Successor Employers 242

EMPLOYEES ELIGIBLE FOR FMLA LEAVE 243
CONDITIONS FOR WHICH FMLA CAN BE TAKEN 244
- Serious Health Condition 244
- Serious Health Condition Of A Parent, Spouse, Or Child 247
- Birth Or Adoption Of A Child 248
- Leaves Regarding Covered Service Members 248

DURATION AND CONDITIONS OF FMLA LEAVE 251
- Duration Of Leave 251
- Pay During Leave 252
- Continuation Of Benefits During Leave 253

RETURN-TO-WORK RIGHTS UNDER FMLA 255
- Equivalent Position 256
- Restoration of Benefits 256
- Key Employees 257

POSTING AND NOTICE REQUIREMENTS OF FMLA: COMMON QUESTIONS 257
- Employer Requirements 257
- Employee Requirements 259

REMEDIES 260
FMLA INTERPLAY WITH OTHER LAWS 260
- The United States Constitution 260
- State Workers' Compensation and Family and Medical Leave Laws 260
- The Americans with Disabilities Act 261
- Collective Bargaining Agreements 262
- The Uniformed Services Employment and Reemployment Rights Act of 1994 262

CHAPTER 12: WORKERS' DISABILITY COMPENSATION 263

EMPLOYERS AND EMPLOYEES COVERED BY THE MWDCA 263
- 1. Independent Contractors 264

  2. Farm workers 264
  3. Partnerships and Small Businesses 264
  4. Family Employees 264
  5. Real Estate 264
  6. Subcontractors and General Contractors 264
  7. List of Employers Who Must Carry Workers' Compensation Coverage. 265
INJURIES AND ILLNESSES COVERED 265
ARISING OUT OF AND IN THE COURSE OF EMPLOYMENT 266
 On-premise Injuries 266
 Off-premise Injuries 267
 Non-compensable Injuries 267
DISABILITY UNDER MWDCA 268
WORKER'S DISABILITY COMPENSATION BENEFITS 268
 Special Benefits 268
 Wage-Loss Benefits 268
 Medical Benefits 269
 Vocational-Rehabilitation Benefits 269
 Death Benefits 269
THE EXCLUSIVE REMEDY PROVISION OF THE MWDCA 270
 Claims allowed by statute 270
 Intentional torts 270
 Third-party claims 270
 Public-policy tort claims 270
MWDCA PROCEDURE 271
 Discovery 271
 Trial 272
 Settlement 272
MWDCA INSURANCE REQUIREMENTS 273
 Requirements for Workers' Compensation Coverage 273

CHAPTER 13: NATIONAL LABOR RELATIONS ACT 275

ELECTION CASES 275
 Election Petitions 275
 Pre-election Hearings 276
 Voluntary Election Agreements 278
 Campaigns 279
 Elections 283
 Objections to Elections 284
 Voluntary Recognition and Neutrality Agreements 284
 Decertification and Deauthorization Elections 284
UNFAIR LABOR PRACTICE CASES 285
 NLRB Procedures in Unfair Labor Practice Cases 287
 Remedies Against Unfair Labor Practices 288
COLLECTIVE BARGAINING 288
EMPLOYEE PARTICIPATION COMMITTEES 289
EMPLOYEE REPRESENTATION IN DISCIPLINE SITUATIONS 290
NO-SOLICITATION RULES 290
 Beck Rights 291
 A Word of Caution about Relying on NLRB Decisions 291
EMPLOYEE FREE CHOICE ACT 291

CHAPTER 14: MILITARY DUTY AND EMPLOYMENT RIGHTS 293

INTRODUCTION 293
IS YOUR COMPANY COVERED BY USERRA? 293
WHAT LEGAL RIGHTS DO EMPLOYEES HAVE UNDER USERRA? 294
HOW LONG DO EMPLOYEES HAVE RIGHTS UNDER USERRA? 295
IS THERE ANY TYPE OF MILITARY SERVICE THAT IS NOT PROTECTED BY USERRA? 296
IS AN EMPLOYEE'S STATE NATIONAL GUARD SERVICE SUBJECT TO USERRA? 296

ARE THERE ANY CIRCUMSTANCES UNDER WHICH AN EMPLOYEE ON MILITARY LEAVE WOULD LOSE HIS OR HER USERRA RETURN-TO-WORK RIGHTS? 297
WHAT NOTICE MUST THE EMPLOYEE GIVE OF THE NEED FOR MILITARY LEAVE? 297
HOW IS THE EMPLOYER TO TREAT THE EMPLOYEE'S TIME ON LEAVE? 298
WHEN DO EMPLOYEES HAVE TO RETURN TO WORK? 302
CAN THE EMPLOYER REQUIRE DOCUMENTATION UPON THE EMPLOYEE'S RETURN? 303
WHAT POSITION IS AN EMPLOYEE ENTITLED TO UPON HIS OR HER RETURN FROM LEAVE? 304
    Service of 90 Days or Less 306
    Service of More than 90 Days 306
    Accommodations for Disabilities Incurred in, or Aggravated by, Military Service 307
IS AN EMPLOYEE RETURNING FROM MILITARY LEAVE PROTECTED AGAINST DISCHARGE? 308
CAN THE EMPLOYER USE TEMPORARY WORKERS TO FILL IN FOR EMPLOYEES ON MILITARY LEAVE? 308
ARE THERE ANY POSTING OR OTHER NOTICE REQUIREMENTS THAT EMPLOYERS MUST PROVIDE TO EMPLOYEES? 309
HOW ARE LEGAL COMPLAINTS HANDLED UNDER USERRA OR MICHIGAN LAW? 309

CHAPTER 15: MISCELLANEOUS EMPLOYMENT LAWS 311

MICHIGAN LAW RECOGNIZES FOUR TYPES OF INVASION OF PRIVACY. 311
    Intrusion 311
    False Light 312
    Public Disclosure of Private Facts 312
    Appropriation 312
    Defenses to Invasion of Privacy Claims 312
    Guidelines for Personnel Record Contents 313
    Protecting Employee Privacy 315
EMPLOYER SEARCHES 317
DEFAMATION 317
    Types of Defamation 318
    Elements of a Defamation Claim 318
    Defenses to Defamation Claims 318
    Defamation when Investigating an Employee 319
    Defamation when Terminating an Employee 320
    Defamation when Communicating to Outside Parties 321
    Defamation in Written Information 322
MICHIGAN'S SOCIAL SECURITY NUMBER PRIVACY ACT 322
    Policy Requirement 322
    General Prohibitions 323
    Public Employers 323
    Financial Institutions 324
    Limited Exceptions 324
    Penalties for Violations 325
WORKPLACE SMOKING BANS 325
PRIVACY PROTECTION ACT 327
MONITORING TELEPHONES AND COMPUTERS 327
VIDEO SURVEILLANCE 328
E-MAIL MONITORING 328
SUBPOENA OF EMPLOYEE RECORDS 329
REGULATION OF POLYGRAPHS 330
    Prohibited Employment Practices 330
    Testing Requirements of PPA 331
    Penalties for Violating PPA 331
    Remedies under PPA 332
FEDERAL EMPLOYEE POLYGRAPH PROTECTION ACT 332
    Posting Requirements of FEPPA 333
    Enforcement of FEPPA 333
    Non-application of FEPPA 334
    Exemptions under FEPPA 334

Pretest Conditions 336
During a Polygraph Test 337
Polygraph Examiner Qualifications 337
Disclosure of Information Obtained by Polygraph 337
WHISTLEBLOWERS' PROTECTION ACT 338
Protected Activities 338
Proving Violations of the WPA 339
Enforcement of WPA 340
Remedies under WPA 340
GARNISHMENTS AND THE CONSUMER CREDIT PROTECTION ACT 341
Definition of Earnings 341
Restrictions on Garnishments 342
Michigan Provisions for Garnishments 343
Multiple Garnishments 343
Enforcement of Garnishment Laws 343
Penalties for Violating Garnishment Laws 344
NONCOMPETE COVENANTS IN MICHIGAN 344
Frequently Asked Questions 344
MICHIGAN'S CONCEALED WEAPONS LAW 350
EMPLOYMENT LAWS INFLUENCED BY WORLD EVENTS 351
Patriot Act of 2001 352
Bioterrorism Response Act of 2002 – "Select Agents" 352
Bioterrorism Response Act of 2002 – "Food Facilities" 353
Fair Credit Reporting Act Considerations 353

CHAPTER 16: EMPLOYEE LAYOFFS 355

AVOIDING LIABILITY FOR REDUCTIONS-IN-FORCE 355
DOCUMENTING LAYOFF DECISIONS 358
Good Documents 358
Bad Documents 359
WORKER ADJUSTMENT AND RETRAINING NOTIFICATION ACT (WARN) 360
Employers Subject to WARN 360
Rolling Layoffs – Aggregation 361
Employer Notification Obligations under WARN 361
Purchase and Sale of Business 363
Enforcement and Penalties Under WARN 363

CHAPTER 17: MAKING GOOD DISCIPLINE AND DISCHARGE DECISIONS 365

THE (WRITTEN) FOUNDATION FOR DISCIPLINE AND DISCHARGE 365
IMPOSING DISCIPLINE PROPERLY 369
HAS DISCIPLINE BEEN CONSISTENTLY IMPOSED FOR THE INFRACTION AT ISSUE? 370
MAKING DEFENSIBLE DISCHARGE DECISIONS 371
Boundaries of Just Cause 374

CHAPTER 18: UNEMPLOYMENT BENEFIT ISSUES 379

BASIC PROVISIONS 379
Coverage Under MESA 379
Covered Employment 380
Definition of "Unemployed" 380
The Difference Between Reimbursing and Contributing Employers 380
The Unemployment Insurance Tax 381
Determination of Tax Rates 381
The Charging of Benefits Against Employer Accounts 381
Record-Keeping and Filing Requirements for Covered Employers 382
Employment of Seasonal Workers 382
Pregnant Workers on Leave of Absence 382
Claims for Benefits and Qualifying Requirements 382
Claimants' Eligibility Requirements 383

    The Determination of Benefits 384
    Coordination of Unemployment and Workers' Compensation Benefits 384
    Appeal to the Unemployment Insurance Agency ALJ 384
PREPARING A CASE FOR THE ALJ 384
RECOMMENDATIONS FOR ALJ HEARINGS 387
APPEALING AN ALJ DECISION 391
NOTABLE RECENT STATUTORY AMENDMENTS 391
SUTA "DUMPING" PREVENTION 393

CHAPTER 19: SAFETY AND HEALTH ISSUES 395

FEDERAL OCCUPATIONAL SAFETY AND HEALTH ACT 396
    Federal Agencies Created by the OSH Act 397
    Enforcement of the OSH Act 397
    Occupational Safety and Health Review Commission 398
    National Institute for Occupational Safety and Health 398
    Employers Subject to the OSH Act 399
    Employers Subject to Other Regulations 400
    State Plans for Occupational Safety and Health 403
MICHIGAN OCCUPATIONAL SAFETY AND HEALTH ACT 407
    General Rights and Duties under MIOSHA 407
    General Duty Clause in MIOSHA 408
    Employer Obligations under MIOSHA 408
    Employee Obligations under MIOSHA 409
    Safety Standards 409
OCCUPATIONAL INJURY AND ILLNESS RECORDKEEPING RULE 411
    Employers Subject to Rule 411
    Consultation Education and Training 417
    MIOSHA Enforcement Approach - "Focused Inspections" for General Industry/Manufacturing 418
LOCKOUT/TAGOUT STANDARDS 419
    Part 85 Exclusions/Exceptions 419
    Minor Tool Changes & Servicing 420
    Cord and Plug Connected Equipment 420
    Hot Tap Operations 420
    Part 85 Energy Control Program 420
    Locks v. Tags 424
    Affected Employee 425
REQUESTS FOR WORKPLACE INSPECTIONS BY EMPLOYEES – COMPLAINT INSPECTIONS 427
    Workplace Enforcement Inspection 428
    Employer Appeals According to MIOSHA 432
HANDLING HAZARDOUS MATERIALS 433
    History of Hazardous Substances Regulation 434
    Hazard Communication 435
CHEMICAL CONTAMINATION PLANS AND TITLE III 453
    Emergency Planning 453
    Emergency Releases 454
    Chemical Inventories 455
    Routine Releases 456
    Air Contaminant Standards 456
    Employee Medical Records and Exposure Studies 457
GUIDELINES FOR AVOIDING WORKPLACE VIOLENCE 458
    New Employees 458
    Retaining Current Employees 458
    Threat Assessment and Response Team 459
    Educate Employees to Contact Human Resources 459
    Take Immediate Action Once a Problem Comes to Light 459
    Michigan Stalker Statutes 460
    If the Investigation Reveals Discharge Is Appropriate 461
SAMPLE LOCKOUT/TAGOUT PROCEDURE 462

EMPLOYMENT LAW CONTACT INFORMATION—FEDERAL 465

EMPLOYMENT LAW CONTACT INFORMATION—MICHIGAN 466

APPENDIX 469

INDEX 473

Glossary of Acronyms and Abbreviations

ADA	Americans with Disabilities Act
ADEA	federal Age Discrimination in Employment Act
AIDS	Acquired Immune Deficiency Syndrome
BFOQ	Bona Fide Occupational Qualification
CCPA	Consumer Credit Protection Act
CCW	Carry a Concealed Weapon permit
COBRA	Consolidated Omnibus Budget Reconciliation Act
DOL	Department of Labor
EEOC	Equal Employment Opportunity Commission
EGTRRA	Economic Growth and Tax Relief Reconciliation Act
EPA	Environmental Protection Agency
ERISA	Employee Retirement Income Security Act
FCRA	Fair Credit Reporting Act
FEPPA	Federal Employee Polygraph Protection Act
FLSA	Fair Labor Standards Act
FMLA	Family and Medical Leave Act
FSA	Flexible Spending Account
HCS	Hazard Communication Standard
HIPAA	Health Insurance Portability and Accountability Act
HIV	Human Immunodeficiency Virus
INS	Immigration and Naturalization Service
IRCA	Immigration Reform and Control Act
JCWAA	Job Creation and Worker Assistance Act
MBSR	Michigan Bureau of Safety and Regulation

MDCR	Michigan Department of Civil Rights
MESC	Michigan Employment Security Commission *(now the Michigan Unemployment Agency)*
MHCRA	Michigan Handicappers' Civil Rights Act *(now the Michigan Persons With Disabilities Civil Rights Act)*
MIOSHA	Michigan Occupational Safety and Health Act
MMWL	Michigan Minimum Wage Law of 1964
MPWDCRA	Michigan Persons With Disabilities Civil Rights Act
MPWFBA	Michigan Payment of Wages and Fringe Benefits Act
MSD	musculoskeletal disorders
MSDS	Material Safety Data Sheet
MUA	Michigan Unemployment Agency
MWDCA	Michigan Workers' Disability Compensation Act
MYESA	Michigan Youth Employment Standards Act
NLRA	National Labor Relations Act
NLRB	National Labor Relations Board
OSHA	Occupational Safety and Health Administration
OSH Act	Occupational Safety and Health Act
OWBPA	Older Workers' Benefit Protection Act
PPA	Michigan Polygraph Protection Act
PWBA	Pension Welfare Benefit Administration
REACT	Retirement Equity Act
SEP	simplified employee pension
SPD	summary plan descriptions
USERRA	Uniformed Services Employment and Reemployment Rights Act of 1994
WARN Act	Worker Adjustment and Retraining Notification Act (also known as the Plant Closing Act)
WPA	Whistleblowers' Protection Act

CHAPTER 1: Introduction to the 2009 Employment Law Handbook

Whether large or small, if your company does business in Michigan, you need to be informed about the laws and regulations that govern employment practices in our state. This book is intended to be a layperson's guide to those laws, presented in an easy-to-read fashion and geared to the small-to-mid-size business owner or human resources professional.

Your Company is Covered Even if You Only Have One Employee!

Even the smallest employer, with but a single employee, is required to comply with a number of state and federal laws covering the employment relationship. All of the following laws apply to a company with *only one employee*:

- the **Michigan Elliott-Larsen Civil Rights Act** (prohibiting various forms of employment discrimination)

- the **Michigan Social Security Number Privacy Act** (regulating and restricting how employers use and display employee Social Security Numbers)

- the **Michigan Persons With Disabilities Civil Rights Act** (prohibiting job discrimination against, and requiring reasonable accommodations for, persons with disabilities unrelated to their jobs)

- the **Michigan Wages and Fringe Benefits Act** (setting forth various requirements, procedures, and deadlines in the payment of wages and fringe benefits)

- the **Michigan Occupational Safety and Health Act** (requiring workplace safety, similar to the federal Occupational Safety and Health Act)

- the **Michigan Employment Security Act** (requiring an account with the Michigan Unemployment Agency for unemployment compensation purposes)

- the **Michigan Workers Disability Compensation Act** (requiring workers' compensation insurance as long as one person is employed at least 35 hours per week for 13 or more weeks)

- the **Michigan Polygraph Protection Act** (prohibiting employment decisions premised on requiring individuals to submit to polygraph tests)

- the **Michigan Youth Employment Standards Act** (setting work restrictions for the employment of minors, provided at least one minor is employed)

- the **Michigan Whistle-Blowers' Protection Act** (prohibiting job discrimination against employees who report violations of law to public authorities)

- the federal **Uniformed Services Employment and Reemployment Rights Act** (prohibiting job discrimination based on military service and extending reemployment rights to veterans returning from military service)

- the federal **Fair Credit Reporting Act** (requiring various disclosures and procedures if an employer uses a third party to conduct reference checks for employment purposes)

Michigan's **Minimum Wage Law** applies to companies with *two or more employees* even if the federal **Fair Labor Standards Act** does not apply. Michigan's law regarding minimum wage sets forth many of the same protections as the federal law, which applies only to certain industries unless the employer has annual revenues of $500,000 or higher.

Michigan's **Bullard Plawecki Employee Right to Know Act**, which regulates the maintenance of employee personnel records, applies to Michigan employers with *four or more employees*.

More familiar federal laws come into play as a company's employee threshold increases:

- At 15 employees, the **Americans With Disabilities Act** (prohibiting job discrimination and requiring reasonable workplace accommodations for qualified individuals with disabilities) and **Title VII of the federal Civil Rights Act of 1964** (prohibiting job discrimination based on race, gender, religion and national origin) apply.

- With 20 employees, employers are required to provide **COBRA** continuation coverage (for employees who experience "qualifying events"), and the age discrimination prohibitions in the federal **Age Discrimination in Employment Act** apply as well.

- At the 50-employee threshold, companies are required to provide **Family and Medical Leave Act** job-protected leave for eligible employees.

- With 100 or more employees, an employer has a variety of notice obligations prior to a mass lay-off or plant closing under the federal **Worker Adjustment and Retraining Notification** Act.

The above, of course, is not meant to be an exhaustive list of the laws that apply to the workplace. Furthermore, each named law above (as well as many unnamed laws) typically has its own more detailed set of regulations—rules issued by the federal or state agency charged with enforcing the law—that fill in any gaps left unaddressed by the law.

Most of the above-mentioned laws have more detailed threshold requirements, and in most cases the legal protections or requirements go far beyond the parenthetical description offered. The above employee thresholds are not described in complete detail here—see the chapters that follow for a more detailed discussion—but merely to illustrate a company's compliance burden based on the number of individuals employed.

As this publication goes to press in mid December 2008, employers can anticipate still more change on the legal compliance horizon. With larger Democratic majorities in Congress for 2009-2010, as well as a new Democratic presidential administration about to take office, many expect new and perhaps significant legislation in the labor and employment areas.

What's New for 2009

Rarely does a year go by without at least some new legal compliance burdens or modifications to existing laws, but 2008 has been particularly significant.

At the federal level, the U.S. Congress amended both the Americans with Disabilities Act (ADA) and the Family and Medical Leave Act (FMLA). Congress also passed a new law that will prohibit employment discrimination based on genetic information; known as "GINA," or the Genetic Information Non-Discrimination Act, the law will become effective in November 2009. As the 2008 calendar year drew to a close, the U.S. Department of Labor issued final revised regulations for the FMLA that had been promised for years.

Michigan employers will need to take all of these changes into account.

In Michigan, perhaps the most significant legal change in 2008 came when the Michigan Legislature passed a law extending the time in which employees returning from military duty must report back to work to enforce their legal right to reemployment. On the horizon in Michigan too could be a workplace smoking ban, although as of mid-December no action had been taken.

These, as well as other noteworthy additions or revisions in this year's publication, include:

- discussion of amendments to the ADA (in Chapter 5) and the new forms of military-related leave and new regulations for the FMLA (in Chapter 11).

- inclusion of new discussion of the new federal GINA law (in Chapter 4).

- updates to Chapter 14 (on leaves of absence from employment for military duty) to reflect Michigan's new law extending the deadline by which employees must return to work following a leave of absence for military duty.

- updates in Chapter 8 to reflect Michigan's higher $7.40 minimum wage, $4.25 training wage, and 85-percent "sub-minimum" wage, as well as the current federal minimum wage of $6.55, which increases to $7.25 on July 24, 2009.

- updated forms, including the 2009 tax withholding tables (for Michigan only; the 2009 federal tax withholding table was not yet available from the IRS as this edition went to publication—see www.irs.gov for more information), and, more significantly, several new DOL forms related to the revised FMLA regulations that go into effect in mid-January 2009 (all of these forms will be available on the HR Michigan web site www.hrmichigan.com)

Some Basic General Liability Avoidance Advice

The purpose of this book, of course, is to help Michigan employers understand their legal obligations in the context of the employment relationship with the goal of reducing the occurrence of unlawful employment practices, which generally lead to liability and wasteful financial outlays. Proactive Michigan employers may consider some basic advice and proactive steps to reduce the potential for such liability, including outplacement services, releases, alternative dispute resolution, insurance for employment claims, and preventive audits.

Outplacement

Whether for economic or performance reasons, the decision to lay off or terminate a long-term employee is the most painful of all personnel decisions. Many companies consider hiring an outplacement firm, and paying the firm's fees (which in the case of executive employees can be substantial) to humanely facilitate the employee's transition to another job. The advantages are obvious: in addition to being fair to someone who has invested a great deal in your company, an employee who promptly finds another job will be less interested in pursuing a lawsuit.

If you decide to consider outplacement, carefully interview the firms available. One very important factor to consider is what the firm's track record is on placing the kind of employee you are terminating. Some companies advertise very good track records, such as a placement rate of 80% within six months following the termination at issue.

Releases

Whenever an employee is separated and given any consideration to which the employee is not otherwise entitled, including severance pay, paid continuation of benefits, outplacement assistance, a retirement incentive, or some other benefit, the employer should insist on obtaining a comprehensive release and waiver agreement from the employee in exchange for the benefits offered. With such an agreement, the employee contractually obligates herself to not to sue the company for all legal claims that might have arisen from the employment relationship.

Releases are technical legal documents, and the law of releases (as with all employment laws) changes rapidly. Among other things, a federal law known as the Older Workers' Benefit Protection Act (OWBPA) includes many technical requirements for releases in order to waive age claims (including that it be in writing and that the releaser be advised to consult counsel). Therefore, consulting legal counsel to draft or at least review your release is a relatively cheap way to reduce your employment liability. The costly alternative to not doing so could be a lawsuit you thought you could avoid, along with the possibility of not even getting back the benefits or compensation you paid the employee for the release in the first place!

Alternative Dispute Resolution

Given the relative explosion of wrongful discharge litigation over the last two decades, many employers have considered arbitration systems, including binding arbitration, even for non-union employees, as better alternatives to courtroom lawsuits before judges and juries that can frequently extend out for years after an employee's termination and cost tens of thousands of dollars in attorneys' fees to defend. The advantages of arbitration are self-evident: it is quicker and cheaper than court.

Experienced labor counsel can assist you in setting up a comprehensive system for arbitrating employment claims, which will in many cases reduce your general exposure to employment liability as well.

The Michigan Supreme Court struck down an employer's right to mandate arbitration of non-union employee civil rights claims where the provision requiring the arbitration is merely a non-contractual employee handbook provision. The Sixth Circuit Court of Appeals, the federal appeals court with jurisdiction for Michigan, clarified that an employee cannot be required to arbitrate employment disputes unless the employee has voluntarily signed an arbitration agreement to do so. Employers who actually contract in a separate writing with their employees for the arbitration of such claims must also be aware of other procedural and substantive requirements for the contract to be enforceable. Employers are therefore encouraged to seek the advice of labor counsel in setting up arbitration procedures for employee disputes, and Chapter 4 of this book addresses some of the key considerations that must be made regarding ADR policies and procedures.

Insurance Covering Employment Claims

Whenever your company is faced with the threat or fact of an employment lawsuit, you should review your current insurance policies to see whether the claim is covered.

If your present insurance policies do not cover insurance for employment claims, consult with your insurance agent. Many companies offer comprehensive insurance regarding claims for employment liability with a range of deductibles and premiums that may be attractive for your company in light of the alternative (expensive, uncovered litigation and attorneys' fees).

Preventive Audits

A comprehensive audit of your employment policies—including your employment application, employee handbook, individual employment contract, benefit policies, and any other written employment policies—by experienced labor and employment counsel also can be a relatively cheap way to reduce your employment liability exposure. Reviewing your current policies in light of the observations contained in this handbook can be a first step in that preventive direction.

A sample audit is discussed at the end of Chapter 3, while one possible template to follow for a comprehensive audit is included on the HR Michigan web site (www.hrmichigan.com).

CHAPTER 2: Pre-Hire Employment Policies

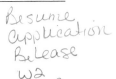

It can be very difficult for employers to locate and hire quality applicants for a variety of positions. The focus of this chapter is on how to maximize the chances of hiring quality applicants while operating within the legal criteria established by state and federal laws and court decisions that address the hiring process.

Means of Properly Screening Job Applicants

A number of employment screening devices are available to employers to help them in thoroughly reviewing the backgrounds of job applicants.

Job Application Forms

Even if an individual has prepared a resume, the employer should require the applicant to fill out an application form. Inconsistencies between the application form and the resume may indicate that false information is contained in one of the documents. The other potential legal danger of a resume is that the employer cannot control what information is conveyed in that document. Often, a job applicant will include on a resume statements identifying his or her age, race, religion, marital status, etc. Further, the use of a resume allows the applicant to avoid answering hard questions that can be included on a properly drafted application form.

It is both legal and prudent to ask, in writing, whether the applicant has ever been convicted (including plea bargains) of a crime. An employer may also ask whether the applicant has any criminal charges currently pending against him or her. It is not lawful, however, to inquire as to the individual's arrest record, unless the employer is a law enforcement agency.

The EEOC has taken the position that employers may not apply blanket rules that automatically disqualify applicants with convictions from employment. A legitimate reason for not hiring a person with a conviction must be shown.

The job application should also require the applicant to list all prior employment and state the reason for leaving each listed job, as well as the dates of employment at each job. Unreasonably long gaps in employment may suggest that an individual was unemployed for a period of time because of having been discharged (since he probably would not have voluntarily quit without having other employment secured), or even that he had been incarcerated.

The application should also contain language directly above the applicant's signature stating:

> I verify that the information given by me in this application is true, accurate, and complete. I understand that if I have given any false information on this application or if I have omitted any material facts, I may be disqualified from employment with the company, or if hired, I may be discharged immediately upon discovery of such false statements or omissions.

If the employer is an at-will employer, another statement should be included:

> I understand that, if hired, my employment is at-will, meaning that either the employer or I may terminate the employment relationship at any time with or without notice and with or without cause. This provision supersedes any oral or written representations to the contrary, unless the written statement is signed by the [designated officer, such as president] of the Company.

An authorization form may also be attached to the job application and should be signed by the applicant to assist the employer in fully discovering employment information from current and/or prior employers. This form should state:

> I hereby authorize my current and former employers to release any information contained in my personnel file or otherwise known by them to [name of prospective employer] in connection with my application for employment with [name of prospective employer]. I specifically release from liability any current or former employers, their agents, representatives, employees, officers or directors, for giving such information to [name of prospective employer].

Employers may limit their exposure to lawsuits by including a provision in job application forms by which the applicant agrees to shortened periods within which that person may bring a lawsuit against the employer. Language approved by the Sixth Circuit Court of Appeals and the Michigan Court of Appeals for this purpose reads:

> I agree that any claim or lawsuit relating to my service with the company must be filed no more than six (6) months after the date of the employment action that is the subject of the claim or lawsuit. I waive any statute of limitations to the contrary.

While such language may provide some protection against claims raised under state law, they are ineffective in shortening the limitations periods that apply to federal discrimination claims.

Job Interviews

During the selection process, it is essential to interview the job applicant. During the interview, the applicant should be specifically asked his or her reasons for leaving each job. These questions should be asked when the applicant does not have the filled out application form in front of him, so that it cannot be reviewed prior to answering the question.

The candidate may also be asked whether he has a criminal record or if any criminal charges are currently pending against him. As noted above, it is not lawful for any employer other than a law enforcement agency to inquire as to an applicant's arrest record.

A broad range of job-related questions can and should be asked of the applicant. These include questions about the applicant's work experience, work habits, attendance, managerial style, compatibility with managers with different styles, etc. Questions that seek job-related information are legal as long as they do not relate to the applicant's age, race, sex, marital status, religion, national origin, disability, height, weight, veteran status or union affiliation.

Inquiries that may cause an applicant to indicate his/her age, race, sex, etc., are generally prohibited. The Michigan Department of Civil Rights' Pre-employment Inquiry Guide lists a number of questions that can and cannot be asked. A portion of that guide follows:

Lawful and Unlawful Inquiries

Subject	Lawful Pre-employment Inquiries	Unlawful Pre-employment Inquiries
Name	Applicant's full name.	Original name of an applicant whose name has been changed by court order or otherwise.
	Have you ever worked for this company under a different name?	Applicant's maiden name.
	Is any additional information relative to a different name necessary to check work record? If yes, explain.	
Address or duration of residence	How long a resident of this state or city?	
Birthplace		Birthplace of applicant.
		Birthplace of applicant's parents, spouse, or other close relatives.
		Requirement that applicant submit birth certificate, naturalization or baptismal record.
Age	Are you 18 years old or older? This question may be asked only for the purposes of determining whether applicants are of legal age for employment.	How old are you? What is your date of birth?
Religion or creed		Inquiry into an applicant's religious denomination, religious affiliations, church, parish, pastor, or religious holidays observed.
Race or color		Complexion or color of skin.

Subject	Lawful Pre-employment Inquiries	Unlawful Pre-employment Inquiries
Photograph		Any requirement for a photograph prior to HIRE.
Height		Inquiry regarding applicant's height.
Weight		Inquiry regarding applicant's weight.
Marital status	Is your spouse employed by this employer?	Requirement that an applicant provide any information regarding marital status or children. Are you single or married? Do you have any children? Is your spouse employed? What is your spouse's name?
Sex		Mr., Miss, or Mrs., or an inquiry regarding sex. Inquiry as to the ability to reproduce or advocacy of any form of birth control.
		Requirement that women be given pelvic examinations.
Handicap/disability	Can you perform the essential duties of the job in which you wish to be employed, with or without accommodation?	Inquiries regarding an individual's physical or mental condition which are not directly related to the requirements of a specific job and which are used as a factor in making employment decisions in a way which is contrary to the provisions or purposes of the Michigan Persons With Disabilities Civil Rights Act.
Citizenship	Are you a citizen of the United States?	(Questions below are unlawful unless asked as part of the federal I-9 process.)
	If not a citizen of the United States, does applicant intend to become a citizen of the United States?	Of what country are you a citizen?
	If you are not a United States citizen, have you the legal right to remain permanently in the United States? Do you intend to remain permanently in the United States?	Whether an applicant is naturalized or a native-born citizen; the date when the applicant acquired citizenship. Requirement that an applicant produce naturalization papers or first papers.
	(To avoid discrimination based on national origin, the question above should be asked after the individual has been hired, even if it is related to the federal I-9 process.)	Whether applicant's parents or spouse are naturalized or native-born citizens of the United States; the date when such parent or spouse acquired citizenship.

Subject	Lawful Pre-employment Inquiries	Unlawful Pre-employment Inquiries
Native origin	Inquiry into languages applicant speaks and writes fluently.	Inquiry into applicant's (a) lineage; (b) ancestry; (c) national origin; (d) descent; (e) parentage, or nationality, unless pursuant to the federal I-9 process.
Education	Inquiry into the academic, vocational or professional education of an applicant and the public and private schools attended.	
Experience	Inquiry into work experience.	
	Inquiry into countries applicant has visited.	
Arrests	Have you ever been convicted of a crime?	Inquiry regarding arrests that did not result in conviction. (Except for law enforcement agencies.)
	Are there any felony charges pending against you?	
Relatives	Names of applicant's relatives already employed by this company?	Address of any relative of applicant, other than address (within the United States) of applicant's father and mother, husband or wife, and minor dependent children.
Notice in case of emergency	Name and address of person to be notified in case of accident or emergency.	Name and address of nearest relative to be notified in case of accident or emergency.
Organizations	Inquiry into the organizations of which an applicant is a member, excluding names or characters which indicate the race, color, religion, national origin, or ancestry of its members.	List all clubs, societies, and lodges to which you belong.

Reference Checks

To the extent possible, it is important to discover the prior work record of job applicants. An employer may find out through this process that an applicant has previously been fired for dishonesty, theft, physical assaults, substandard job performance, poor attendance, or the sale or possession of controlled substances. A prospective employer that does not seek this information will likely not discover it until it is too late.

A great number of wrongful discharge lawsuits could have been avoided if the employer had screened out an individual in the hiring process. In one informal survey, it was concluded that a majority of the people who sued their former employers had falsified information of some kind on the application form or on their resume. Had the falsifications been discovered during the hiring process, many employers could have avoided not only later lawsuits, but also the unpleasantness of having to discharge an employee.

Many employers have taken the position that they will not supply much, if any, information to prospective employers on a reference check. For this reason, it is particularly important to have an applicant sign the release authorization form included on the HR Michigan web site (www.hrmichigan.com). A former or current employer that has received a written authorization to release information may be more inclined to share reference information than is one that simply receives a phone call from a stranger claiming to be the human resources director of a potential employer.

Michigan has two laws relating directly to employment reference checking. The first (MCL 423.452) provides employers a qualified immunity from defamation liability where they receive a request for information about a former or current employee, and they disclose, in good faith, "information relating to the individual's job performance that is documented in the individual's personnel file...." Employers providing reference information should thus be careful to only communicate information that they believe to be true and that is documented in the employee's or former employee's personnel file.

The second law (MCL 380.1230b) goes even further. It requires schools to request applicants for employment to sign a statement that (1) authorizes the applicant's current or former employer(s) to disclose to the school any "unprofessional conduct" by the applicant, as well as any documents in the applicant's personnel file relating to that conduct, and (2) releases the current and/or former employer(s) from civil liability for making such disclosures. The law directs that a school may not hire any applicant who refuses to sign such a statement.

This law also requires any employer that receives a request for such information from any school to provide the information about the applicant's "unprofessional conduct," if any exists, as well as any documentation regarding the conduct that is in the applicant's personnel file, to the school within 20 days of receiving the request.

This law defines unprofessional conduct as "one or more acts of misconduct; one or more acts of immorality, moral turpitude, or inappropriate behavior involving a minor; or commission of a crime involving a minor." Whether the applicant was actually convicted of a crime is not a deciding factor in the determination of whether an individual engaged in "unprofessional conduct."

Criminal Record Checks

Employers may obtain information through a variety of sources relative to convictions of job applicants in all states. To do a criminal record check, one needs the applicant's name and social security number or date of birth. It is important to use only actual convictions rather than mere arrest records in making hiring decisions, because it is illegal to disqualify an applicant for an arrest where there has been no conviction. As discussed earlier, blanket rules automatically disqualifying applicants from employment because of any conviction are likely illegal. There must be a rational reason for the disqualification.

Fair Credit Reporting Act

Employers that obtain information on job applicants or employees from third parties to whom they pay a fee for such information need to be aware of the provisions of the federal Fair Credit Reporting Act ("FCRA"). These provisions were intended by Congress to assure that individuals who are subject to such investigations are made aware of them in advance and are notified when denied employment opportunities because of the information contained in the reports.

Employers that conduct their own background checks are not covered by this statute. The statute applies only if an employer pays a third party to obtain information about applicants or employees relating to that person's "credit worthiness, credit standing, credit capacity, character, general reputation, personal characteristics, or mode of living." This includes general reference checks, employment reference checks, and criminal records checks. If an employer obtains any of this information from a third party to whom it makes any payments, it is subject to a number of requirements.

Specifically, the Act requires such employers to do the following:

1. Make a written "clear and conspicuous" disclosure to the applicant before the report is procured, stating that a credit report may be obtained for purposes of making an employment decision. **This disclosure must be in a separate document** and not be merely a statement included as part of a larger document.

2. Obtain written permission from the applicant to procure such a report.

3. Provide the individual with a copy of the report and a description of his or her right to contest the content of the report with the agency before taking an adverse action against an applicant or employee because of the content of the report.

4. Provide "oral, written, or electronic notice" of the adverse action to the individual at or after the time the adverse action is taken, together with the name, address and phone number of the credit reporting agency; a statement that the adverse action was not decided upon by that agency; and a statement of the individual's right to contest the content of the report.

5. Certify to the credit reporting agency that the requirements of 2 and 3 above have been met.

6. Do not collect background information more than seven years old if the applicant/employee is expected to earn less than $75,000 per year.

Special rules apply to the situations in which the inquiries are made by an employment agency that is making a report to a prospective employer for the purpose of procuring an employee for that employer.

Credit information should not be used with respect to all categories of job applicants, but only for those jobs where there is a business necessity for hiring people with good credit backgrounds (law enforcement personnel, those handling cash, etc.). If there is no such business necessity, the employer could unwittingly incur liability under Title VII and Elliott-Larsen for race discrimination under a disparate impact theory.

Drug and Alcohol Testing

Generally, the testing of job applicants for controlled substances is legal. A number of steps must be taken before the implementation of such testing:

- The employer must determine whether its concerns about drug use in its work force or community justify the cost of a testing program.

- A clearly written testing policy must be formulated and communicated to applicants, and the application form should contain a specific statement indicating the applicant's acknowledgement that a drug test may be part of the application process.

- Particular testing methods that are reliable and match the employer's individual needs should be adopted.

- The testing procedure should include a confirmation test when the initial test is a positive one.

- The testing should be done on a consistent, non-discriminatory basis. If any applicants are to be tested, all applicants should be tested, or at least all applicants for certain classes of jobs (safety sensitive, drivers, those working with cash, etc.) should be tested. This will help to avoid a claim that the test is administered primarily to persons in protected classifications.

- The testing procedure must be one that protects the individual's privacy. The results of the test should not be revealed to anyone other than those who have an immediate need to know the test results.

- For unionized private sector employers, the National Labor Relations Board has held that the implementation of a drug testing program for employees is a mandatory subject of bargaining which must be negotiated with the union prior to implementation. However, it has also ruled that the testing of *applicants* is not a mandatory subject of bargaining because applicants are not union-represented. As to public sector employers, the Michigan Employment Relations Commission has made a similar ruling.

Aptitude, Personality, and Honesty Testing

Many employers use a variety of written tests to determine the suitability of applicants for specific positions. There have been numerous legal challenges to such tests on the basis that they tend to discriminate against certain protected groups on one of two bases. The first type of allegation is that they are used to intentionally discriminate against minority groups by being used as an excuse to fail to hire minority applicants. The more common legal challenge, however, is that these tests inadvertently result in a disproportionate percentage of minority applicants being disqualified on the basis of the tests.

A plaintiff or group of plaintiffs can establish a *prima facie* case of disparate impact discrimination if it can be shown that a disproportionate percentage of minority applicants are rejected on the basis of test scores. This can be proven by one of two means. The first is by the use of a "standard deviation test," which statistically demonstrates whether the disproportionate effect of the test can be statistically explained by randomness, or whether some impermissible factor (race, sex, etc.) is a more likely explanation for the impact of the test. The second means of proving an adverse impact of the screening device is the so-called "four-fifths" rule. Under this approach, if a selection device results in a selection rate for minority applicants which is less than four-fifths of the selection rate for non-minority applicants, an adverse impact may be demonstrated.

An employer can rebut this *prima facie* case by presenting evidence that the test is "job related." The classic statement of this is that "tests must measure the person for the job, not the person in the abstract." Job relatedness can be established through any of three types of "validation." The validation method most preferred by the EEOC is Criterion Validation. This type of validation compares test scores of employees with their subsequent performance ratings to determine if the test accurately predicted their ability to properly do the job.

The second type of validation is Content Validation, by which it is determined whether a skill or ability test is directly related to the applicant's ability to perform the job in question. An example is a word processing test for a secretary.

The third validation method, which is the least favored by courts, is Construct Validation. Under this type of analysis, a test is valid if it accurately measures traits that are believed to be necessary for the job (leadership, honesty, judgment, etc.). This type of validation is difficult because of the inevitable disagreements over what traits are necessary for the job and how to measure them with a written or oral examination.

Plaintiffs will prevail if they can prove that the stated job-related business purpose of the test is merely a pretext for discrimination. This may be established by a showing that other available tests or selection procedures serving the same end have a less adverse impact upon members of the protected group.

The main lesson for employers on this issue is that they should never use a personality/aptitude test as an employee selection tool unless the test to be used has been statistically validated for the specific position for which it is to be used.

At least one federal court has ruled that the MMPI test may constitute a "medical inquiry" under the Americans with Disabilities Act because, particularly where an applicant's test is reviewed by a psychologist, it may be used to identify certain psychiatric conditions. The significance of this decision derives from the fact that medical inquiries may not be made prior to the making of a job offer.

Pitfalls to Avoid in the Hiring Process

A great deal of work is obviously required to adequately screen job applicants. In the course of conducting these investigations, it is important for employers to avoid additional problems by asking the wrong questions or giving out improper or inaccurate information to the applicant.

Impermissible Questions

As discussed earlier, the Michigan Department of Civil Rights' Pre-employment Inquiry Guide is a good, general guide as to the types of questions that can and cannot be asked of job applicants, either in writing or orally. In asking interview questions, a general rule for employers is if the answer to the question is not likely to shed light upon an individual's qualifications or ability to perform the job, the question should not be asked. Clearly, any questions related to an applicant's age, race, national origin, sex, marital status, height, weight, protected handicap, religion, union affiliation, or prior workers' compensation filings should be avoided.

Some employers mistakenly believe that they must inquire as to an applicant's national origin in order to comply with the Immigration Reform and Control Act. National origin questions should not be asked of an applicant. The information used to fill out the I-9 forms should only be sought after the applicant has been *hired*. The I-9 form is to be filled out by both the new employee and the employer within 72 hours of the beginning of employment.

A particularly touchy area is that of the applicant's physical and/or mental condition at the time of hire. The Michigan Persons with Disabilities Civil Rights Act (MPDCRA) defines a protected disability as "a determinable physical or mental characteristic . . . which is unrelated to the individual's ability to perform the duties of a particular job or position, or is unrelated to the individual's qualifications for employment or promotion." For this reason, it is permissible for a prospective employer to ask an applicant whether he or she is presently able to perform the job for which he or she is applying, but it is illegal to ask an applicant to "list all injuries you have ever had." It is also unlawful to refuse to hire an individual because of a physical condition that does not presently disable him from performing the job, but which may at some future time result in a debilitating injury. This is true under both the Americans with Disabilities Act (ADA) and the MPDCRA.

Under the MPDCRA, if there is a "substantial probability of immediate injury" because of a present physical condition, however, the applicant may be disqualified from consideration for that position. Similarly, under the ADA, an individual may be disqualified from a position if his health condition constitutes a direct and immediate threat to the health or safety of himself or others.

In addition to prohibiting employers from discriminating against job applicants on the basis of an existing disability, the ADA also prohibits hiring decisions being made on the basis of a perceived disability or because of the applicant's health history. Thus, no questions should be asked about an applicant's health background, either in the interview or in the application form. Interviewers should avoid making any comments about apparent physical conditions of the applicant as such comments, even if meant innocently, can be used later against the employer.

The ADA also protects individuals who are not themselves disabled, but who are "associated with a person with a disability." Thus, a job applicant who has a disabled spouse or child is protected by the ADA, and an employer may not base its hiring decision on a concern that it may incur higher health care costs because a member of the prospective employee's family is disabled. Questions about the physical or mental condition of an applicant's family members should be avoided.

The EEOC's Technical Assistance Manual on the ADA lists a number of questions that can and cannot be asked on application forms and in job interviews. Among the questions that **cannot be asked** are the following:

- Have you ever had or been treated for any of the following conditions or diseases?
- Please list any conditions or diseases for which you have been treated in the past three years.

- Have you ever been hospitalized? If so, for what condition?

- Have you ever been treated by a psychiatrist or psychologist? If so, for what condition?

- Have you ever been treated for any mental condition?

- Is there any health-related reason you may not be able to perform the job for which you are applying?

- Have you had a major illness in the last five years?

- How many days were you absent from work because of illness last year? (Pre-employment questions about illness may not be asked, because they may reveal the existence of a disability. However, an employer may provide information on its attendance requirements and ask if an applicant will be able to meet these requirements.)

- Do you have any physical defects that preclude you from performing certain kinds of work? If yes, describe such defects and specific work limitations.

- Do you have any disabilities or impairments which may affect your performance in the position for which you are applying? (This question should not be asked even if the applicant is requested in a follow-up question to identify accommodations that would enable job performance. Inquiries should not focus on an applicant's *disabilities*. The applicant may be asked about her *ability* to perform specific job functions, with or without a reasonable accommodation.)

- Are you taking any prescribed drugs? (Questions about use of prescription drugs are not permitted before a conditional job offer, because the answers to such questions might reveal the existence of certain disabilities that require prescribed medication.)

- Have you ever been treated for drug addiction or alcoholism? (Information may not be requested regarding treatment for drug or alcohol addiction, because the ADA protects people addicted to drugs who have been successfully rehabilitated or who are undergoing rehabilitation, from discrimination based on drug addiction.)

- Have you ever filed a claim for workers' compensation benefits? (An employer may not ask about an applicant's workers' compensation history. Such questions are prohibited because they are likely to reveal the existence of a disability. In addition, it is discriminatory under the ADA to not hire an individual with a disability because of speculation that the individual will cause increased workers' compensation costs.)

Information about an applicant's ability to perform job tasks, with or without accommodation, can be obtained through the application form and job interview, as explained below. Other needed information may be obtained through medical inquiries or examinations conducted after a conditional offer of employment has been made.

It is also unlawful under the Workers Disability Compensation Act to ask an applicant if he or she has ever filed a workers' compensation claim or received workers' compensation benefits. The reason for this prohibition is that it is illegal to retaliate against an individual because he or she has filed a prior workers' compensation claim against an employer. Similarly, an applicant may not be asked questions that could solicit a response that he or she exercised rights under the federal Family and Medical Leave Act.

> A shorter list of **permissible questions** is also listed by the EEOC: An employer may ask questions to determine whether an applicant can perform specific job functions. The questions should focus on the applicant's *ability* to perform the job, not on a disability.

For example, an employer could attach a job description to the application form with information about specific job functions, or the employer may describe the functions or show the applicant a DVD of the job functions. This will make it possible to ask whether the applicant can perform these functions. It also will give an applicant with a disability needed information to request any accommodation required to perform a task. The applicant could be asked:

- Are you able to perform these tasks with or without an accommodation?

If the applicant indicates that he or she can perform the tasks with an accommodation, he or she may be asked:

- How would you perform the tasks, and with what accommodation(s)?

An employer may also ask the following questions of an applicant according to the EEOC:

- The applicant may be asked to describe or demonstrate how he or she will perform specific job functions, if this is required of everyone applying for a job in this job category, regardless of disability.

- If an applicant has a known disability that would appear to interfere with or prevent performance of a job-related function, he or she may be asked to describe or demonstrate how this function would be performed, even if other applicants do not have to do so.

- However, if an applicant has a known disability that would **not** interfere with or prevent performance of a job related function, the employer can only ask the applicant to demonstrate how he or she would perform the function if *all* applicants in the job category are required to do so, regardless of disability.

The interviewer is permitted to ask questions about the applicant's attendance record with other employers, and about the individual's ability to comply with the prospective employer's attendance rules. Caution must be exercised, however, in how such questions are asked. The EEOC, in its ADA Technical Assistance Manual, has provided the following guidance on inquiries about attendance:

- An interviewer may not ask whether an applicant will need or request leave for medical treatment or for other reasons related to a disability.

- The interviewer may provide information on the employer's regular work hours, leave policies, and any special attendance needs of the job, and ask if the applicant can meet these requirements (provided that the requirements actually are applied to employees in a particular job).

- Information about previous work attendance records may be obtained on the application form, in the interview or in reference checks, but the questions should not refer to illness or disability.

- If an applicant had a poor attendance record on a previous job, he or she may wish to provide an explanation that includes information related to a disability, but the employer should not ask whether a poor attendance record was due to illness, accident, or disability.

The ADA imposes three significant constraints on the use of pre-employment physical examinations. It states that an employer may not require a physical examination of an applicant unless:

1. the applicant is not compelled to submit to the examination until after the employer has made a job offer, which may be contingent upon the applicant passing the physical examination;

2. the employer requires all applicants for similar positions to submit to such an examination; and

3. the medical records, like all other employee medical records, are maintained in a separate, confidential file.

The medical information obtained in the post-offer medical exam may be used to disqualify the applicant from employment **only** if the reasons for the decision are "job related and consistent with business necessity" or if the applicant is rejected to avoid a direct threat to the health or safety of himself or others, **and** if no reasonable accommodation is available to enable the person to perform the essential functions of the job. A conclusion that the applicant poses a direct threat to health or safety must not be based on mere speculation that such a threat exists.

Physical Access to the Application Process

Under both the ADA and the MPDCRA, employers must assure that the means of applying for work are readily available to persons protected by those Acts. Employers must be sure that applicants have access to the place to which they must apply and be interviewed. Necessary accommodations may include an accessible location for applicants with mobility impairments, a sign interpreter for a hearing-impaired person, and a reader for a sight-impaired applicant. The EEOC suggests that "the employer may find it helpful to state in an initial job notice, and/or on the job application form, that applicants who need an accommodation for an interview should request this in advance."

Affirmative Action Plan Obligations

Not every employer is required to have and abide by an affirmative actions plan (AAP). In fact, most employers do not have to have such plans. Generally, only employers that are government contractors or subcontractors are required to have AAPs. A number of employers have also adopted voluntary AAPs.

Employers that are subject to AAPs should be sure to annually review and update their plans, and abide by the terms of those plans. With respect to recruitment and hiring, most AAPs set forth specific places in which the employer will advertise job openings. They also generally require employers to annually analyze their hiring and retention statistics. Whatever the requirements of a particular employer's AAP are, they must be followed.

The Michigan Constitution which bars public entities at the state and local levels from applying preferences based on gender, ethnicity, race, color or national origin relative to public employment. Such preferences may be used in two circumstances: (1) where the state or local public entity is receiving federal funds that require an affirmative action plan as a condition of receiving the funds; and (2) where a court order or consent decree in effect as of December 22, 2006 requires such a plan. None of this should affect voluntary affirmative actions plans in the private sector.

Job Security or Discharge Standard Representations

If an employer desires to maintain an employment-at-will discharge standard, all persons involved in the interviewing process must be trained to not make representations to applicants that are contrary to this standard. For example, the following types of comments to an applicant could possibly be contrary to the maintenance of an at-will standard:

- "Your job will continue until you reach retirement age."
- "We only fire people if we have a good reason."

- "About the only way you can get fired here is to get caught stealing."
- "No one is discharged unless they have previously been suspended."

An employer's documentation can also help to avoid an employee's claim that when she went through the application process a legitimate expectation of a just-cause standard was created. To do this, the application form should contain at-will language, as described above, including a statement that the at-will standard cannot be modified by any oral or written representations, except a written statement signed by a specific person within the company.

Misrepresentations of Fact

Employer representatives must take care to only give accurate information to applicants. If a question regarding pay, employment status, or benefits is asked and the interviewer is not sure of the answer, it is safer to admit not knowing the answer than to supply false information. An employer's misstatements about a prospective employee's job content and pay rate gave rise to claims for negligent and fraudulent misrepresentation in *Weisman v. Connors*. Another example of such a case involved a bank offering a three-year employment contract to an applicant even though a federal statute prohibited such arrangements (*Rohde v. First Deposit National Bank*).

A claim for negligent misrepresentation will exist where an employer negligently supplies false information to a job applicant, the employer intends that the applicant will rely on such information, the job applicant does rely upon that false information in accepting employment, and he or she is ultimately damaged as a result of that reliance.

If an employer determines that a job applicant has been given false information, it should act to immediately correct that misinformation.

Theories of Negligent Hiring and Negligent Retention

Courts in at least thirty states, including Michigan, have recognized a tort claim of negligent hiring or negligent retention of an unsafe employee. Such a claim is established where:

- the employer knew, or through a reasonable investigation should have known, that the employee or applicant was unfit for the job;
- a person to whom the employer owes a duty of protection is injured; and
- there exists a causal connection between the injury and the employment of the unfit person.

Basically, an employer must use reasonable care to hire safe and competent employees.

Legal Standard

In order for a plaintiff to establish liability because of an employer's negligent hiring or retention of an employee, the plaintiff must demonstrate (1) that the employer owed a duty to the victim; (2) that it breached that duty; and (3) that the breach of duty was the proximate cause of the plaintiff's injuries.

Duty to the Victim

Most courts that recognize the tort of negligent hire or retention state that a duty of reasonable care in hiring or retaining employees is owed only to those persons as to whom it is foreseeable that the employee will come in contact as a result of his or her employment. There is, unfortunately, no consensus about which groups of people this covers.

It is fairly clear, however, that an employer does have a duty of reasonable care in hiring individuals where those individuals will be placed in one-on-one contact with customers or other members of the public. An even higher standard of care will generally apply to employers whose business involves the safekeeping of others, such as security agencies, apartment complex management services, and the like. For such employers, it is especially important to perform criminal records checks on applicants and thoroughly investigate any gaps in their employment history or any other suspicious entries on their applications.

In a 2006 decision, the Michigan Supreme Court held that a hotel employer was not deemed to have imputed knowledge of an applicant's name being on the Sex Offender Registry and that it did not have a legal duty to perform a criminal records check and review the Sex Offender Registry before hiring an applicant. Had the employer in that case taken these actions before hiring the individual at issue, however, it could have avoided a sexual assault on a customer and the need to defend the resulting lawsuit.

Breach of the Duty to Third Parties

If an employer is found to have a duty of care to protect third parties coming in contact with its employees, it will be found to have breached this duty if it knew or should have known of the employee's incompetence, dishonesty, or bad character, but nonetheless hired or retained that employee. It is thus important for an employer to thoroughly investigate the background of its prospective employees in order to determine their fitness for the job. Certainly, an employer may be found to have breached this duty by hiring an individual with a criminal record for violent conduct, where that employer then places the employee in a job where he may come into isolated, personal contact with others. Similarly, liability may be incurred where an employee who was fired from a prior job for theft steals goods or money from a third party in the course of his employment.

Proximate Cause

In order for an employer to be found liable for the tort of negligent hire or retention, the plaintiff must prove that he was injured by an employee who was placed in a position to inflict injury upon him because of his job. For example, where a janitorial employee with a pass key enters a tenant's apartment and rapes, assaults, or robs the tenant, it is clear that there is a direct relationship between the employment and the third party's injury.

Liability Concerns in Providing References

Every employer is asked periodically to give references on current or former employees. Two questions are generally asked by employer representatives who receive such requests. The first is, "Can I be sued if I give out information about a former employee and he doesn't get the job because of what I said?" The other is, "If I know something really bad about the former employee, am I obligated to reveal it to the caller?"

The answer to the first question is that a person cannot be successfully sued by a former employee for defamation if the information conveyed was documented in his personnel file and the employer representative disseminating the information believed in good faith that it was true, accurate information.

As to the second question, Michigan's courts have ruled on several occasions that an employer does not have a duty to reveal bad information about an applicant to a prospective employer. It cannot, however, knowingly misrepresent information about the applicant, such as by saying that he was a model employee, when the truth is that he was fired for assaulting coworkers.

The lead case in this area is *Moore v. St. Joseph Nursing Home.* An employee worked for a nursing home, during which time he received 24 disciplinary actions, including a warning for physical violence. He was finally fired. He then applied for a job as a security guard. The information about his employment record was not revealed to the prospective employer, who hired the man. While working as a security guard for this new employer, he beat and killed a maintenance employee of the company. The estate of the deceased person filed suit against the nursing home for not conveying its knowledge of the employee's prior misconduct to the prospective employer. The court dismissed the case, holding that a former employer has no legal duty to disclose a former employee's acts of malfeasance to a prospective employer.

The key exception to this rule is the obligation of an employer or former employer to report "unprofessional conduct" to a school considering the employment of an individual, as discussed earlier in this Chapter on page 12.

New Hire Reporting Requirements

Employers must report new-hire information to the Michigan Department of Treasury for all new employees, regardless of the employer's size or type of business. Reports must be submitted no later than 20 days after the employee is hired or returns to work after a separation of employment. This includes all part-time, seasonal, and temporary employees.

The employer must supply its federal employer identification number, company name and company address, as well as the employee's name, address, and social security number. Employers may comply by submitting a hard copy of the Michigan W-4 or the Michigan Form 3281—the New Hire Reporting Form. Reports can be mailed to the Michigan New Hire Operations Center, P.O. Box 85010, Lansing, MI 48908-5010, or faxed to (817) 318-1659. Employers may also report electronically. Technical assistance may be obtained by calling (800) 524-9846.

Multi-state employers may select one state in which to report. These employers must notify the federal government of the selected state. Notification can be sent to the Department of Health and Human Services, Office of Child Support Enforcement, Multi-State Employer Registration, P.O. Box 509, Randallstown, MD 21133.

Summary

The hiring process is one by which an employer needs to do all that it can to assure that it is securing good, productive, and safe employees in a manner that is legal. In summarizing the contents of the above materials, these suggestions are made:

1. On employment application forms:

    a) Ask, "Have you ever been convicted of a crime? Explain fully."

    b) Ask, "Do you currently have any criminal charges pending against you? Explain fully."

    c) For law enforcement agencies only, ask "Have you ever been arrested?"

    d) Ask for the names of prior and current employers, together with positions held, name of supervisor, dates of employment, and reasons for leaving.

    e) Include a statement that the applicant understands that if false or incomplete information is supplied, the applicant will not be hired or retained.

    f) Employers desiring to establish or maintain an employment-at-will relationship should include a clear employment-at-will statement, and disclaim any contrary representations.

g) Attach a release form, allowing you to obtain information from prior and current employers.

h) Include a statement acknowledging a shortened period in which claims or lawsuits may be filed against the employer.

2. During the interview, ask about the applicant's prior work record when he or she cannot look at the application, and pay attention to any inconsistencies between the information obtained in the interview and that contained in the application.

3. Ask about unexplained gaps in the applicant's employment history. They could be due to legitimate situations, such as taking time off to raise children, or they could be caused by negative factors, such as incarceration.

4. In most cases, require the application form to be filled out, instead of merely accepting a resume. If both are obtained, observe any inconsistencies.

5. Questions relating to the applicant's race, color, national origin, age, religion, sex, protected handicap, marital status, height, weight, citizenship, or arrest record should not be asked either orally or in writing. Notations about such factors should not be made.

6. In the interview ask, "Are you able to perform the tasks of this job with or without an accommodation?" If the applicant indicates that he or she can perform the tasks with an accommodation, the employer may ask, "How would you perform the tasks, and with what accommodation(s)?"

7. Check the applicant's employment and personal references.

8. For certain positions, verify that the applicant does not have a criminal record.

9. After following the steps described earlier in these materials, conduct applicant drug tests.

10. Do not make representations that are contrary to the employer's personnel policies (i.e., employment-at-will, pay, or benefits).

11. Immediately correct any inaccurate information given to an applicant.

12. Make all employment decisions on the basis of job-related factors, unrelated to applicants' race, sex, age, etc.

13. Comply with all obligations contained in the employer's affirmative action plan, where one exists.

14. Include a statement in all application forms and advertisements that you are an equal opportunity employer and, if applicable, an affirmative action employer.

CHAPTER 3: Employment Status

Many lawsuits are grounded upon an individual's legal employment. For example, you, as the employer, may think that all of your employees are employed at-will and therefore can be terminated at any time, for any reason. One, some, or all of your employees, however, may have been led to believe (by an over-promising recruiter, for example) that he, she, or they will have a job as long as they do their job, and that, therefore, they can be terminated only for a good reason, or "just cause." This situation is ripe for litigation.

The first step for an employer to reduce liability in this regard is to carefully consider in what legal status it wants various categories of employees to be employed. Once the employer makes that determination, the employer should carefully and consistently make that status clear to all of its employees. In employment practices audits, a common flaw in employment systems is the failure to consistently define and maintain the legal status of employees. If you choose to make all of your employees at-will, then such choice should consistently be reflected and maintained in your employment application; personnel handbook; any other written policies, procedures, contracts, guidelines, or work rules; and in any oral statements made by interviewers or supervisors.

At-Will Employees

The legal status of employees that maximizes reduction of employment liability is at-will. At-will employees are hired for indefinite terms (that is, they have no fixed term or set time period of employment), and can be terminated at any time for any reason not prohibited by law. A classic formulation of at-will employment, which has been quoted in several Michigan court decisions as creating employment at-will, is one historically used by Sears, Roebuck and Co.:

> In consideration of my employment, I agree to conform to the rules and regulations of Sears, Roebuck and Co., and my employment can be terminated, with or without cause, and with or without notice, at any time, at the option of either the Company or myself. I understand that no store manager or representative of Sears, Roebuck and Co., other than the president or vice-president of the Company, has any authority to enter into any agreement for employment for any specified period of time, or to make any agreement contrary to the foregoing. (As referenced in, for example, *Batchelor v. Sears*; *Summers v. Sears*.)

Even if you create and consistently maintain this at-will status for all your employees, all regulatory employment laws still apply. You cannot terminate employees because of their sex, race, or other protected status, or in retaliation for filing a civil rights, workers' compensation, or similar claim, etc.

Although employment at-will status reduces your exposure to a wrongful discharge lawsuit, it may—if you are a non-union employer—increase your exposure to a union organization campaign. Union organizers hold out the promise of employment security under a just-cause clause as a strong reason to consider voting for a union. If you find it difficult to recruit certain classes of employees (i.e., executives or professionals), telling them they can be terminated at any time for any reason may not be what you need for effective recruitment and retention of qualified employees.

The moral is that although any legal consultant will tell you that employment at-will is best for reducing your wrongful discharge liability, you should consider employee morale, and the potential impact regarding union organization and recruitment before you adopt this legal status.

Just-Cause Employees

If you have any unionized employees, you probably are familiar with the legal status of a just-cause employee. It is typified by a provision to the effect that "X employee shall not be disciplined or discharged without just cause." In contracts with unions, whether just cause exists usually is determined by an external arbitrator. However, any employee can have "just cause" legal status protection by policy, and the method by which cause is determined can include internal dispute resolution panels, internal decision makers, external arbitrators, or other methods of dispute resolution.

Advantages of adopting just-cause legal status for your employees include the potential for union avoidance, enhanced ability to recruit and retain employees, and improvement of employee morale. Disadvantages include restriction of traditional management rights, including your traditional right to determine why and when an employee should be disciplined or discharged, and the relinquishment of ultimate decision-making power to an external arbitrator or some internal dispute resolution process.

Satisfaction Employees

If at-will language is too strong for your corporate culture from a personnel, recruitment, or retention standpoint, or if you are concerned with union avoidance, but you do not wish to go as far as creating just-cause protection for your employees, you may consider a legal status for your employees created by the following satisfaction language:

> The employment relationship will exist only so long as the employee's performance is fully satisfactory to the Employer. Any discharge must be approved by

the President. No official, officer, employee, or agent of the Company, with the exception of the President, has an authority to modify this satisfaction provision orally or otherwise, or to enter into any employment agreement for a specified period of time or to make any agreement contrary to the terms of this paragraph. The employee may not rely upon any verbal representations from anyone that in any manner modify or contradict the terms of this paragraph. Only the President may modify the terms of this paragraph, provided the change is in writing.

Satisfaction language such as that quoted above offers the employee some protection against arbitrary or capricious termination without the stricter requirement that there be just cause for termination. In the event of litigation, a jury's role in interpreting such language generally has been limited to a determination of whether the employer was in good faith dissatisfied with the employee's performance.

Term Contract Employees

At-will, just-cause, or satisfaction employees can be hired for indefinite terms or periods. If one of these statuses is created, and no term is specified, then employment is considered to be for an indefinite term.

You, as the employer, may wish to consider another legal status for your employees—that of the term contract. For example, you might want to hire an employee or group of employees for a specified period, such as six months, or one year, or two years, etc., as set forth in individual employment contracts. The general legal advantage of such a contract is that your commitment to the employee expires at the end of the term, and you can choose not to renew the contract for any reason not prohibited by law.

If you choose to hire employees under term contracts, any written employment agreement should include at least the following terms:

- The names of the parties.
- The duties to be performed by the employee.
- The compensation to be paid to the employee.
- The fringe benefits to which the employee will be entitled.
- The conditions under which either of the parties may terminate the agreement.
- A statement of how employment disputes will be resolved.
- Non-compete and trade secret agreements, where applicable.
- Disclaimer of other representations.
- A mechanism for amending the agreement.

In addition to specifying that the agreement may be terminated at the end of the term (non-renewal), you should specify the circumstances under which the agreement can be terminated prior to the end of the term (i.e., for cause, for satisfaction, or at-will – with or without notice).

In cases where term contracts apply only to upper-level management personnel, or to professional employees, you should consider entering into individual employment agreements covering the above terms. Where such status and terms apply to larger groups of employees, the same status and terms can be created in an employee handbook. Employers entering into such contracts should remember that Michigan provides a six-year statute of limitations for actions under breach of contract.

Independent Contractors

An employer may choose to engage in an independent contractor relationship with outside individuals (i.e., consultants, accountants, lawyers, doctors, etc.). Whether an individual is an independent contractor or an employee is determined by state and federal law (especially for tax purposes). Although there are numerous tests under state and federal law regulating the legal status of independent contractor vs. employee, they typically boil down to a basic control test. If individuals can come and go on their own time; generally direct their own work product; use their own facilities and supplies; and are free to work for other companies, they are probably independent contractors. If, on the other hand, you retain absolute control over how individuals' work products will be generated and when, where, and how they will work; provide facilities and supplies; and demand full-time attention to your work to the exclusion of all other projects, then they are probably employees.

It is not enough to simply call a worker an independent contractor to avoid the legally-imposed burden of being an employer. The legal distinction between "independent contractor" and "employee" is loosely defined because there is so much variety in working arrangements. If you wish to lawfully maintain independent contractor status, then the relationship terms should be structured in a manner that satisfies state and federal tests as generally discussed in the previous paragraph, including the specific IRS "twenty factor" test, listed below. Your accountant or labor lawyer can assist you in structuring and maintaining legally defensible independent contractor relationships. The items are loosely ranked in descending order by relative significance. Although rarely is a single factor controlling, there should be few, if any, factors indicating a worker is an employee for the worker to truly be an independent contractor.

This is important because if a worker is improperly treated as an "independent contractor," when in reality the worker should be treated as an employee, the employer may be later charged with paying the worker's (i.e. employee's) past, present, and future labor costs (e.g. wages, benefits, workers' comp, FICA, unemployment comp, all other withholdings, etc.).

In a legitimate "independent contractor" relationship the employer should take care only about the **result** to be achieved. The **means** of achieving that result should be left to the "independent contractor's" discretion. The **right to direct** or **right to control** indicates an employer/employee relationship, whereas the absence of such rights indicates an "independent contractor" relationship.

IRS Revenue Ruling 87-41

As a general rule, the IRS has refused to find independent contractor status in situations where the person for whom services are performed has the right to control and direct the individual who performs the services. The critical inquiry in these cases is the right to control the manner in which work is performed, not merely whether the work is done. Further, whether or not the employer actually exercises this right is irrelevant.

IRS Revenue Ruling 87-41 lists 20 factors used to determine whether a sufficient degree of control is present to establish an employer-employee relationship. These factors and a brief analysis of each follow:

1. Instructions

A worker who is required to comply with another person's instructions about when, where, and how he or she is to work is ordinarily an employee. This control factor is present if the person or persons for whom the services are performed have the right to require compliance with the instructions. For example, if you specify that an individual is expected to report to work at a specified site and to perform the contracted services strictly between the hours of 8:00 AM and 5:00 PM, Monday through Friday, that individual would likely be considered an employee. However, if you hire an individual to perform a specific service and that individual claims sole responsibility for determining his or her own hours of work, then that individual would likely be an independent contractor, provided all of the other factors are met as well.

- **Rule:** Do not regulate the hours of the independent contractor. Someone in his or her own business sets his or her own hours.

2. Training

Training a worker by requiring an experienced employee to work with the worker, by corresponding with the worker, by requiring the worker to attend meetings, or by using other methods, indicates that the person for whom the services are performed wants the services performed in a particular method or manner, thereby resulting in an employer-employee relationship.

- **Rule:** If the work requires independent or professional training or experience, then the chances of making the independent contractor label stick are much greater.

3. *Integration*

Integration of the worker's services into the business operations generally shows that the worker is subject to direction and control and that an employer-employee relationship has been established. When the success or continuation of a business depends to an appreciable degree upon the performance of certain services, the workers who perform those services must necessarily be subject to a certain amount of control by the owner of the business, and thus, they would likely be classified as employees.

4. *Services Rendered Personally*

If the services must be rendered personally (i.e. by a particular person), presumably the party for whom the services are performed is interested in the methods used to accomplish the work as well as in the results (employee status), as opposed to merely being interested in the contracted services being accomplished – no matter the individual(s) who perform the services (independent contractor status).

5. *Hiring, Supervising, and Paying Assistants*

If the person for whom the services are performed hires, supervises, and pays assistants for the worker, control over the worker(s) is generally demonstrated (and thus, employee status may exist). However, if the worker hires, supervises, and pays his own assistants pursuant to a contract under which the worker agrees to provide materials and labor and under which the worker is responsible (to the person for whom he is performing the services) only for the attainment of a result, this factor typically demonstrates an independent contractor status.

- **Rule:** It would be ideal if the independent contractor has his or her own employees. This is not practical in most real world situations and is not mandatory, however.

6. *Continuing Relationship*

A continuing relationship between the worker and the person for whom the services are performed indicates that an employer-employee relationship exists. A continuing relationship may even exist where the work is performed at frequently recurring although irregular intervals.

7. Set Hours of Work

The establishment of set hours of work by the person for whom the services are performed is a factor indicating control and thus likely establishes an employer-employee relationship.

8. Full-time Required

If the worker must devote substantially full time to the business of the person(s) for whom the services are performed, such persons have control over the amount of time the worker spends working and can consequently impliedly restrict the worker from doing other gainful work. An independent contractor, on the other hand, is free to work when and for whom he or she chooses.

9. Performing Work on Employer's Premises

If the work is performed on the premises of the person for whom the services are performed, that factor suggests control over the worker, especially if the work could be done elsewhere. The importance of this factor depends on the nature of the service involved and the extent to which you, as an employer, generally would require employees to perform such services on your company's premises.

10. Order of Sequence Set

If the worker must perform services in the order or sequence set by the person for whom the services are performed, the worker is therefore not free to follow his or her own pattern of work but must follow the established routines and schedules of the person for whom the services are performed – thereby likely demonstrating an employer-employee relationship.

- **Rule:** You may control the ends but not the details/means of the work.

11. Oral or Written Reports

A requirement that the worker submit regular written reports to the person for whom the services are performed indicates a degree of control, thus likely establishing an employer-employee relationship.

- **Rule:** Do not have independent contractors supply you with weekly or monthly reports. It suggests too much control.

12. Payment by the Hour, Week, Month

Payment by the hour, week, or month generally points to an employer-employee relationship, provided that this method of payment is not just a convenient way of paying a lump sum agreed upon as a job's cost. Payment made by the job or on a straight commission generally indicates that the worker is an independent contractor.

- **Rule:** Payment should be by the job rather than by unit of time (i.e., an hourly wage).

13. Payment of Business and/or Traveling Expenses

If the person for whom the services are performed ordinarily pays the worker's business and/or traveling expenses, the worker is ordinarily an employee.

- **Rule:** Do not pay the expenses of independent contractors. If someone owns/operates his own business, he should pay his own business expenses.

14. Furnishing Tools and Materials

The fact that the person for whom the services are performed furnishes significant tools, materials, and other equipment for the worker's use tends to show the existence of an employer-employee relationship.

- **Rule:** Independent contractors should supply their own work implements. If you have the equipment, consider leasing the equipment to the independent contractor.

15. Significant Investment

If the worker invests in facilities that he or she uses to perform services and those facilities are not typically maintained by employees (such as the maintenance of an office rented at fair value from an unrelated party), the worker typically is an independent contractor. Special scrutiny is given to certain types of facilities, such as home offices.

16. Realization of Profit or Loss

A worker who can realize profit or suffer a loss as a result of his or her services (in addition to the profit or loss ordinarily realized by employees) is generally an independent contractor, but the worker who cannot is an employee. The risk that a worker will not receive payment for his or her services, however, is common to both independent contractors and employees.

17. Working for More Than One Firm at a Time

If a worker performs more than minimal services for multiple unrelated persons or firms at the same time, the worker is typically an independent contractor. However, a worker who performs services for more than one person may still be an employee of each of the persons (i.e. the persons could be deemed "joint employers"), especially where such persons are part of the same service arrangement.

18. Making Service Available to General Public

The fact that a worker makes his or her services available to the general public on a regular and consistent basis indicates an independent contractor relationship.

- **Rule:** This gets right to the core of the matter. True independent contractors are in their own business. One would expect them, therefore, to make their services available to the public.

19. Right to Discharge

The right to discharge a worker is a factor indicating that the worker is an employee and the person possessing the right is an employer. An independent contractor generally cannot be fired so long as he or she produces results that meet the contract specifications.

- **Rule:** If you have the right to fire at-will, you have an employee.

20. Right to Terminate

If the worker has the right to end his or her relationship with the person for whom the services are performed at any time he or she wishes without incurring liability, that factor indicates an employer-employee relationship.

- **Rule**: The worker should incur liability for ceasing to provide services without providing notice and reason.

Leased or Temporary Employees

Given the trends toward "right-sizing" and the pressures to flexibly compete in a global economy, many employers are using more temporary or leased employees. Whether through the use of traditional temporary service agencies or more sophisticated employee-leasing arrangements, this legal status of employment is one that is created by the terms of your contract with a temporary service agency, or the terms of an employee-leasing arrangement. The terms of such arrangements should clearly specify how the parties share the risks of any potential employment liability, including workers' compensation and unemployment compensation. Any employment status for such employees (at-will, term, etc.), how the arrangement may be terminated, who is liable for fringe benefits and other employment costs and exposures, and all other items generally covered in an employment contract should be spelled out in the temporary employment contract or lease arrangement. Generally, such contracts and lease arrangements state that the temporary service agency is the employee's employer, and not the company at which the employee is assigned to work. In some circumstances, however, and despite the contractual language, both the temporary service agency and the company at which the employee is assigned to work could be deemed the employee's employer (that is, a joint employer status may exist). Employers seeking the services of temporary service agencies may wish to seek counsel and take measures in order to avoid a joint employer status with the temporary service agency.

Mixing Employment Statuses

The complexity of larger employers almost dictates that they will have different employment statuses for different categories of employees or kinds of work to be performed. Employers of any size should carefully consider the appropriateness of the various legal categories (at-will, just-cause, satisfaction, term contract, independent contractors, leased or temporary) for its particular workforce.

For example, the President of a company may serve at will to a Board of Directors, or high-level executives may serve at will to the President. On the other hand, the President and high-level executives may be hired under one- or two-year term contracts. This way, their performance may be evaluated for specific periods, and if things are not working out, the relationship can be ended by non-renewal without the stigma of abrupt termination at any time (as in an at-will relationship) or without the need for a determination that the termination was for cause (as in a just-cause relationship), which generally causes animosity.

A company reasonably could decide to have its highest- and lowest-level employees be employees at will, while maximizing the recruitment, retention, and union avoidance security for its other employees by creating a just-cause standard for them.

From a legal standpoint, there are no magic rules that apply to all corporate cultures that would dictate what legal statuses are appropriate for your company. The overriding rule from the standpoint of reducing employment liability is that once you decide what legal status is appropriate for employees, that status should be carefully created and consistently maintained in your application, contracts, handbook, policies, procedures, work rules, and any other writings or oral statements by your supervisors. Suggestions for preserving this consistency are included throughout this handbook.

Implied Employment Liability—the *Toussaint* Doctrine

In 1980, the Michigan Supreme Court raised the stakes for Michigan employers with regard to liability and exposure for employment decisions, especially those involving discharge. In a decision known as *Toussaint v. Blue Cross*, the Court eroded the traditional employment-at-will doctrine. The Court held that anything an employer puts in writing that expresses or implies a promise not to discharge except for cause, or certain representations an employer's agent makes orally, can give rise to a jury question about whether such written or oral expressions create a contract not to discharge but for just cause. The

Court also held that if such a contract is created, a jury can decide whether the employer breached the contract by not having just cause to discharge its employee.

Letting juries decide such questions gave rise to full employment for plaintiffs' lawyers. Jury verdicts in excess of one million dollars for single-plaintiff wrongful-discharge actions have become commonplace. As one plaintiff's lawyer remarks, in Michigan an employer does not receive a jury of its peers in wrongful discharge cases. Unlike criminal cases where a jury often is not terribly sympathetic to a charge of first-degree murder, in employment cases juries tend to sympathize with the long-term employee who has given his or her life to the company and is now on the street. Juries remember how other employers may have unfairly treated them or a relative. Various studies have shown that once a plaintiff gets to a jury in a wrongful discharge lawsuit, the odds of the plaintiff prevailing are 70–80%, and average jury verdicts amount to several hundred thousand dollars.

The concept of "front pay" comes into play where a judge or jury finds that the employer has made life so miserable for the plaintiff that reinstatement is not practical. Under such circumstances, the employer is required to pay the present value of everything the employee would have earned in salary and benefits from the date of discharge until the projected future date of retirement, less what he or she has earned, or should have earned, in other employment.

Reducing Your Risks

The above is the bad news. The good news is that the Michigan Supreme Court has cut back somewhat on the wrongful discharge risks facing Michigan employers. For example, the Court has recognized that an employer can, as long as it notifies employees in a reasonable manner, change their employment status from just-cause to at-will, even if they have been just-cause employees for many years.

There are many other steps that employers can consider to reduce the risk of employment liability. Contrary to some consultants' promises, there are no guaranteed methods of eliminating employment liability in Michigan. The purpose of this handbook is to outline a series of practical suggestions that can reduce your liability risks. Many of these suggestions also will make your workplace a fairer and more humane place to work from your employees' standpoint, who can and should be your most valuable assets. This can be a mutual gains goal, since the best defense to any legal challenge of your employment decisions is your ability to articulate a legitimate business reason, fairly and reasonably arrived at, and to explain and justify the action you took to all outside triers of fact (including a judge, jury, unemployment or workers' compensation referee, or civil rights investigator).

Human Resources Audits

The number of lawsuits challenging employment decisions and actions has risen dramatically in recent years, and jury verdicts in employment-related actions now average in the hundreds of thousands of dollars. Employers can reduce the risk of potential liability by taking the initiative in advance of litigation to review existing personnel policies and procedures and make the appropriate changes where potential problems are identified.

A Human Resources audit such as the sample audit guideline contained on the HR Michigan web site (www.hrmichigan.com) has been developed to assist employers in reviewing personnel policies and procedures and liability exposure at their companies and increasing awareness of areas within the human resources arena that may require "risk management." The following discussion highlights the factors you should consider in determining whether an audit is necessary and/or appropriate for your company.

Preventive Legal Audits

Preventive legal audits promote numerous goals such as (1) an awareness of legal issues and risks; (2) creation of a corporate culture which is aware of similar issues; (3) encouraging adoption of safer courses of action by using alternatives with lower risk factors; (4) avoiding lawsuits; (5) correcting actual or perceived legal or ethical problems (or the appearance of problems); (6) discouraging improper conduct and promoting compliance; and (7) promoting a positive business image.

Preventive audit results can be used to achieve many parallel objectives including: (1) uncovering problems early on before they evolve into bigger problems or lawsuits; (2) incorporating changes in the law into existing structures; (3) promoting a better work relationship between corporate client and counsel; (4) establishing a work environment which enables management and counsel to react faster to problems, investigations and lawsuits; (5) protecting directors and top management against legal liability; (6) encouraging appropriate corrective action to deal with problems discovered in the audit and thus limiting legal exposure; and (7) improving the corporate organization and related business practices.

Basic Considerations

The most important choice in planning an audit is deciding whether or not it will cover only specific issues or will, instead, be a broad assessment of overall human resource/EEO compliance. Sometimes, an employer with a number of facilities may have had a lot of EEO complaints and personnel problems at one facility. This may justify a "one issue" audit at that location. On the other hand, a company may be confronted with many EEO and wrongful discharge claims. This would warrant perhaps a broader audit which also examines company employee handbooks and applications, written policies, oral representations, etc.

Multi-facility employers also have to decide whether the audit will cover all of the facilities and all topics. Neither time nor money usually permits this approach and in such circumstances, it is better to limit the audit to one project rather than over-extend it. The same considerations apply with respect to the scope of the audit. Financial resources and time constraints are other considerations. By necessity, they will have an important effect on the nature of an audit. The more financial resources available, the more intensive the audit can be. Using company personnel can save money and have numerous collateral beneficial effects. On the other hand, it is sometimes necessary to use outside experts such as statisticians, computer experts, or outside counsel. When financial resources are limited, it is probably better to be cautious and focus on specific problems rather than conduct a broad and general audit.

No audit can be successful if top management is not committed to it. Without this commitment, access to crucial information may be limited and employees may be reluctant to support the project. To avoid these problems, the audit team must overcome suspicion, disinterest, and even hostility by first obtaining top management's support. This signals to the rest of the employees that top management is committed to the idea and that they had better cooperate.

There is no ideal size for an audit team. Basically, the group should be comprised of people knowledgeable in EEO law as well as the company's operations. The team should also be as small as possible. This enhances coordination and confidentiality. Ideally, most of the audit team should be staffed in-house. They, in turn, will avail themselves of the expertise of outside counsel in planning the study, evaluating the results, and making recommendations. This approach has obvious benefits including enhancing the prestige of those involved and the audit process. Outside expertise is necessary where recommendations are going to be made which might result in significant corporate reorganizations or criticisms. Candor is important but for obvious reasons, employees may not want to point fingers at either their co-workers or supervisors. Outside counsel can act where they cannot. Counsel must know the fair employment area. The attorney, who can either be in-house or from the outside, will be a tremendous resource in both designing the audit and evaluating its results. Moreover, and of extreme importance, participation of an attorney is essential if the results of the audit are to have any chance of being confidential, which they should be if they are to be candid, self-critical, and effective.

Audit Process

The audit should be comprehensive. It should encompass all aspects of the employment relationship from recruitment to termination. However, it is impossible in an audit of this type to address all state and local laws and regulations, all conceivable factual situations or all issues that may arise. To be effective, policies and procedures must be tailored to the company's needs. Thus, the audit presents questions designed to suggest "ideal" practices that may or may not be appropriate for every employer.

The audit will necessitate a review of the company's written personnel policies and procedures. The documents reviewed should include: 1) all written personnel policies and procedures; 2) any employee handbooks; 3) all recruitment materials; 4) all employment application forms; 5) all labor agreements; 6) all benefit plans and summary plan descriptions; 7) all EEO-1 reports for the last 6 years; 8) all affirmative action plans for the last 6 years; 9) all memoranda, internal and otherwise, pertaining to affirmative action and equal employment opportunity; 10) all employment-related charges (internal or external) and lawsuits; and 11) all consent decrees, conciliation agreements, etc. Analysis of these materials will provide a broad picture of the company's human resources/EEO compliance. To respond to all of the questions posed in the audit, it will likely also be necessary to conduct interviews with administrative and supervisory staff and decision-makers.

Once the audit has been completed, it will be incumbent on the company to develop and implement an action plan to address any potential problem areas identified. To be most effective, the audit should be viewed not as a one shot project but rather as part of an ongoing monitoring of the company's personnel policies and procedures.

Audit Confidentiality

Audits will contain statistical and self-evaluative materials which are extremely sensitive, candid, and often self-critical. If those materials were disclosed to the wrong parties, they could prove liability, create a discovery road map, or encourage new litigation and be Exhibit One in a lawsuit. For this reason, it is essential to preserve the audit's confidentiality. Several theories have arisen which can be used to successfully protect an audit from disclosure; however, the law in this area is still developing and there are not absolute guarantees. Therefore, there is always a risk that the report and, at the very least, the background materials collected, may be disclosed. For these reasons, it is crucial to structure the audit so as to maintain the best possibility of ensuring its confidentiality.

Failure to do so could result in a document turning out to be a major source of new liability.

Overview

As a general rule, an audit report is discoverable under the Federal Rules of Civil Procedure or the Michigan Court Rules. There are, however, three general privileges which might apply. The first is the "self-evaluative" privilege. This privilege is not based on any Federal Rule. It was created by the courts because they recognized that audits, to be effective, must be frank, candid, and self-critical. The self-evaluative privilege only extends to subjective evaluative information, not statistical and other objective information contained in an audit, affirmative action plan, etc. For this reason, in drafting the audit report one must decide whether to try and connect the self-evaluative sections with the factual or statistical information so as to increase the possibility that they will be protected under the self-evaluative privilege.

Another possible way to protect this type of information is through the attorney-client privilege. Unlike the self-evaluative privilege, this privilege is normally regarded as an "absolute" privilege insofar as materials protected by this privilege cannot be disclosed. It offers the best possible protection for an audit and every step should be taken to ensure that the audit falls within the privilege's scope. To come within the scope of the privilege, four general requirements must be met: (1) the lawyer to whom the communication is made must be acting as counsel; (2) there must be a communication between the lawyer and client; (3) the communication must be kept confidential by both client and counsel; and (4) the privilege must not have been waived by disclosures to non-privileged parties.

The last possible generally recognized privilege is that of attorney-work product. This privilege applies to materials prepared for or by a party or his lawyers "in anticipation of litigation or for trial." Usually, such information is not ordinarily subject to discovery. On the other hand, the materials must be disclosed if the party seeking it has "substantial need" of them in preparing his case and cannot obtain their equivalent without "undue hardship." In order for this limited privilege to apply, all of the prerequisites must be observed, the key being the information was prepared for or in anticipation of litigation. For all of these reasons, outside employment counsel should be actively and intensely involved in conducting the human resource audit and, if possible, should prepare the questionnaire, perform the interviews directly, supervise the investigation as closely as possible, and write the various reports.

Creating the Attorney/Client Privilege

It is clear that in order to protect the results of the audit as well as the work product of the audit it must be done either by in-house counsel or outside employment counsel in conjunction with the employer's Human Resources department. Access to all information obtained during the internal audit procedure should be limited to the H.R. department, counsel, and top level management. Great care must be taken in order to establish an attorney/client privilege and to avoid discovery of the work product of an internal audit. In support of these goals, the following steps should be considered and taken:

1. If litigation is pending or anticipated, all documents should indicate they are being prepared in anticipation or in connection with such litigation.

2. Employees will, by necessity, become aware that an internal audit is being conducted. Therefore, consider an initial communication to all employees involved informing them of the internal audit and that the results of the audit and any changes in policies will be communicated upon the conclusion of the audit.

3. Responsive documents should be addressed to the attention of in-house or outside counsel.

4. Responsive documents should be marked as "privileged" and "confidential" and treated as such.

5. All materials related to the audit should be disseminated to as few people as possible.

6. The chief operating officer should communicate to all appropriate parties authorizing a confidential internal audit. This notification should specify that information will be forwarded to counsel for review and for legal advice to ensure the organization is in compliance with existing employment laws. This communication should also indicate that all information must be kept confidential with access only to individuals who "have a legitimate right to know."

7. All communications and analyses of the internal audit should be done by counsel and marked "attorney/client privileged communications."

8. All documentation and work product should be kept in a separate restricted file and entitled "attorney/client confidential information."

9. There should be no public dissemination of any of the information with regard to an internal audit.

The Danger of Audits

Before one conducts an audit of either general workplace policies or an investigation into a particular decision or practice, it is crucial to recognize that while commendable, a majority of court decisions have not afforded employers the opportunity to shield such efforts from disclosure in the event of a discrimination lawsuit by a disgruntled employee. As noted earlier, a number of legal theories have been used by employers in an attempt to shield this information. They are (1) the self-evaluative privilege, (2) the attorney-client privilege, (3) the work product privilege, and (4) the ombudsman privilege. Generally speaking, courts have interpreted these doctrines narrowly and typically have permitted broad discovery, including access to sensitive personnel information and conclusions concerning an employer's equal employment efforts. The cases go both ways but, as noted above, one can never guarantee the documents will be treated as confidential.

The majority of the cases indicate that any voluntary audit-type activities are very likely to be discovered in future employment discrimination litigation and that the primary means to exclude the results of the audit from being admitted into evidence would be to demonstrate that its marginal probative value is outweighed by its prejudicial effect, an argument that has not received much judicial support. The bottom line is that employers are in a "catch-22" situation. While such audits may be desired and helpful, they are also potential "smoking guns" and must be viewed as liability documents. Therefore, even if one takes the appropriate precautions in an effort to preserve the privileged nature of the communications, study, audit, etc., there is no guarantee. Accordingly, before a company undertakes any investigation, audit, or study of its work force, for whatever reason, it must carefully evaluate the downside potential and, perhaps, step back and see if one is really necessary.

Conclusion

Human resource audits have become more commonplace. They offer preventive alternatives to the confrontational approach. Audits are not for all employers, however. Nevertheless, for the right employer under the right circumstances, they present a reasonable option for evaluating and correcting workplace problems before those problems turn into costly and disruptive litigation.

CHAPTER 4: Discrimination & Harassment

Several times a year, the media will report something to the effect that "XYZ Company has reached a multi-million dollar settlement with the EEOC (or a group of plaintiffs) to settle class-action employment discrimination and/or harassment claims." Compliance with state and federal EEO laws not only enhances a diverse workplace run on principles of fairness, it also protects a company and its supervisors from liability.

Michigan employers must be aware of a number of state and federal laws prohibiting discrimination and harassment in the workplace:

- Title VII of the Civil Rights Act of 1964 is a federal law which prohibits discrimination and harassment on the basis of sex, race, color, national origin and religion.

- The Age Discrimination in Employment Act prohibits discrimination against employees 40 years of age or older.

- The Americans with Disabilities Act prohibits discrimination against employees who are "qualified individuals with a disability."

- The Pregnancy Discrimination Act (PDA) prohibits discrimination on the basis of pregnancy.

- The Equal Pay Act which makes it unlawful to pay different compensation amounts based on one's gender for equal work on jobs of equal skill, effort, responsibility, and working conditions in the same establishment.

- In addition to the groups protected by federal law, the Michigan Elliott-Larsen Civil Rights Act (Elliott-Larsen), also prohibits discrimination on the basis of marital status, familial status, height, weight, and age (including employees under the age of 40). Elliott-Larsen also provides that "discrimination because of sex" specifically includes a prohibition on "sexual harassment."

- The Michigan Persons with Disabilities Civil Rights Act prohibits discrimination on the basis of an individual's disability.

Employers should also note that certain cities and counties within the State of Michigan have passed local ordinances banning sexual orientation discrimination, such as the Cities of Ann Arbor, Detroit, Flint, Lansing, Grand Rapids, and Kent County.

In 2006, Michigan voters approved Proposal 2's amendment to the state constitution. Effective December 23, 2006, this amendment prohibits public institutions, such as state government, public colleges and K-12 schools, from using affirmative action programs that give preferential treatment to groups or individuals based on their race, gender, color, ethnicity or national origin for public employment and contracting. For more information on Michigan's ban on affirmative action, please see the Affirmative Action chapter.

DISCRIMINATION

State and federal law prohibit discrimination which can take one of the following forms:

1. **Disparate treatment**—treating similarly situated employees differently based upon an unlawful consideration.

2. **Intentional discrimination**—having a predisposition to discriminate against a legally protected class of employees and acting on that predisposition.

3. **Disparate impact**—using a neutral criterion or test data that has an adverse impact on a legally protected class of employees.

In 1990, both the federal and state legislatures passed laws—the Americans with Disabilities Act (ADA) and the Michigan Persons With Disabilities Civil Rights Act (PWDCRA)—prohibiting discrimination on the basis of handicap or disability. In addition to protecting individuals from discrimination based on their disability, these statutes limit the types of inquiries that an employer can make about an employee's physical or mental condition and place an affirmative obligation on employers to provide a reasonable accommodation to employees with covered disabilities. The ADA and PWDCRA are discussed in more detail in Chapter 5.

Elliott-Larsen Civil Rights Act – State Law

The Elliott-Larsen Civil Rights Act prohibits discrimination against employees in any term or condition of their employment on the basis of sex, familial status, race, national origin, color, religion, marital status, height, weight or age. Unlike federal law, state law protects all individuals from age discrimination, not just those individuals over the age of 40. Although Michigan does not have separate pregnancy discrimination act, discrimination on the basis of sex under the ELCRA includes pregnancy discrimination.

In May 2006, the Michigan Court of Appeals ruled that an employer may owe a duty to third-parties to protect them from the uninvited sexual advances of its employees under a common law negligence theory. Employers are advised to heed all complaints of harassment or discrimination, even if those complaints are generated by a third party. Although employers are generally not liable for the torts committed by its employees outside the scope of their employment, an employer will be liable if the employer knew or should have known of the employee's propensity for impropriety, violence or disorder. Third party complaints to employers regarding employees' sexual comments, without any additional evidence of an employee's prior impropriety, violence or disorder may provide adequate notice and, thus, create a duty on the part of an employer to protect third parties against its employee's uninvited sexual advances.

The ELCRA provides for individual liability for an employer's agent. Unfortunately, it is unclear whether an agent is only a supervisor or whether it can also mean a non-supervisory employee. At the very least, individual supervisors can be held liable for discrimination and harassment.

Employers seeking to avoid discrimination claims under this statute must be aware of three separate legal theories for establishing the existence of unlawful discrimination (i.e., disparate treatment; intentional discrimination; disparate impact). Understanding how discrimination actions are proven will help an employer to ensure it is complying with anti-discrimination laws.

Disparate Treatment Discrimination

An individual makes a claim of disparate treatment discrimination where similarly situated individuals are treated differently. The presumption is that where all other factors are equal, the different treatment results from an unlawful consideration such as sex, race, age, or the like.

In order to prevail on a theory of disparate treatment discrimination, the individual must first show that he or she is a member of a protected class and was treated differently from individuals not in the protected class for the same or similar conduct. For example, if a man and a woman each have four consecutive absences, and the man receives a verbal warning while the woman is discharged, the woman may have met this first burden.

In the case of an applicant, as opposed to an existing employee, this first requirement can be met by showing that the individual belongs to a protected class, applied for a job that he or she is qualified for and was rejected, and the employer continued to seek applications from individuals with similar qualifications.

Once this initial burden, called the *prima facie* case, is met, the employer must then articulate a legitimate nondiscriminatory business reason for its decision. For example, the woman may have a prior record of absenteeism, while the man's absences are a first offense.

After the employer has articulated a legitimate nondiscriminatory business reason, the employee must then prove that this reason is a "pretext for unlawful discrimination." For example, the woman could show that her prior record of absenteeism was falsified by a supervisor who did not like women, or that men with a prior record of absenteeism were not discharged. The plaintiff must prove both that the employer's stated reason was false and that discrimination was the real reason for the action.

In 2006, the Michigan Civil Rights Commission made its first declaratory ruling in 40 years, holding that an employer's exclusion of prescriptive contraceptives from a health plan which covers other prescription drugs violates Michigan's Elliott-Larsen Civil Rights Act's sex discrimination provisions. Although the Commission rulings are not law, employers are advised to provide full coverage for all contraceptive drugs and services, if the employer's comprehensive health plan covers other drugs and services. If an employee filed a charge with the Michigan Department of Civil Rights (MDCR) alleging sex discrimination because his or her employer did not provide contraceptive coverage, the Commission's ruling is a strong indicator of how the MDCR would respond. The employer would then be left with the option of appealing the MDCR's decision to a state court.

Intentional Discrimination

Under a theory of intentional discrimination, the employee must first show that the decision-maker was predisposed to discriminate against a protected group and acted on that predisposition in making the employment decision. For example, an African-American employee who was terminated might claim that the supervisor making the termination decision had made offensive racial comments to the individual and had indicated that he would do whatever was necessary to get rid of all the African-American employees.

As with claims of disparate treatment, the employer will then have to articulate a legitimate, nondiscriminatory reason for its actions. For example, the employer may be able to show that the African-American employee had been stealing from the cash register.

Again, the employee will have an opportunity to show that the employer's articulated reason was a pretext for discrimination, so the African-American employee could show that he was innocent of theft and had been falsely accused by the supervisor who did not like African-Americans. As with disparate treatment discrimination, the plaintiff must prove both that the employer's stated reason was false and that discrimination was the real reason for the employment decision.

Adverse Impact Discrimination

Even where an employer does not intend to discriminate and applies its policies equally to all employees, the employer may be held liable if the policies have an adverse impact on a protected group. For example, if an employer requires that all employees be at least 5'8" tall, fewer women will qualify than men. Similarly, if an employer requires that its employees pass a physical examination that includes an eye examination, blind individuals will be adversely affected.

If an individual can show that a neutral employment practice has an adverse impact on a protected group, the burden then shifts to the employer to show that the employment practice is job related and justified by business necessity. For example, an airline may be able to show that pilots need to be a certain height in order to see over the instrument panel, and a delivery service would be able to show that its drivers need to be able to see.

Even if the employer can show that its practices are job related, an individual may still recover if an alternative test exists that would satisfy the same business necessity but would have less of an adverse impact. For example, a city wanting to hire strong police officers might require that all police officers be at least 5'10" tall and weigh 180 pounds. Clearly, this would have an adverse impact on women. Although the city could show that strength is an important requirement for police officers, the city could conduct strength tests, rather than using height and weight requirements. Such tests would be more job related and would have less of an adverse impact on women, since some women not meeting the height and weight requirements could pass the strength tests, and some tall and heavy men would fail.

Bona Fide Occupational Qualification

Generally, the courts treat claims based on sex, race, national origin, and the like in the same manner. However, one of the defenses to a claim of discrimination applies in practice only to certain classes.

Discrimination on the basis of a protected class is lawful where the discrimination is necessitated by a bona fide occupational qualification (BFOQ). However, courts have held that race is never a BFOQ (i.e., there is never a legitimate reason to determine that a position can only be held by a white employee), and sex will be a BFOQ only in very rare situations (i.e., the monitor for the female locker room may have to be female).

Weight and height are the categories most likely to meet the BFOQ exception. For example, a minimum or maximum height may be necessary where the employee is working in a closed area with a low ceiling or where an employee below a minimum height will not be able to reach the necessary equipment. However, because such requirements have an obvious adverse impact against a protected group, an employer must make sure that the requirements are absolutely necessary.

The statute also allows churches to require that an employee belong to a certain religion, so being a member of that religion can be a BFOQ for a church. However, being a member of a certain religion would not be a BFOQ for a secular employer.

Marital Status Discrimination

Discrimination on the basis of marital status is prohibited under Elliott-Larsen. Courts have held that this provision prohibits discrimination based on the fact that a person is married or single, but does not prohibit discrimination based upon the fact that a person is married to a particular individual.

In other words, an employer cannot choose to favor married applicants over single applicants or choose to insure only single employees but not married employees. On the other hand, an employer can establish an anti-nepotism policy even though this could cause an employer to discriminate against a man because his wife already has a job with the company.

Retaliation Prohibitions

In addition to prohibiting discrimination on the basis of protected categories, Title VII and Elliott-Larsen prohibit retaliation against persons who have made complaints of discrimination or otherwise opposed unlawful activity by the employer. For example, if an employee makes a good faith complaint of racial discrimination to the employer, or to a government agency such as the Michigan Department of Civil Rights, the employer may not retaliate against that employee. The employer can be held liable for retaliation even if the employee's original complaint was without merit. To establish a claim for retaliation, the employee need only show that (1) she engaged in protected activity (i.e. complained about discrimination or otherwise opposed unlawful activity); (2) that her complaint and or opposition was known by the employer; (3) that the employer took an employment action that was adverse to her; and (4) that her protected activity was a significant factor in the adverse employment action. Finally, as noted above, supervisors who are accused of retaliating against employees may be held individually liable under Michigan law.

In 2006, the US Supreme Court expanded the type of conduct that may be considered retaliatory, holding that an employee alleging retaliation must only show that the employer's actions were harmful to the point that they could dissuade a reasonable worker from making or supporting a charge of discrimination. Under this standard, employers must carefully consider any personnel actions that will affect an employee who previously complained of discrimination, even if the decision does not affect the employee's wages or benefits.

During that same year, the Sixth Circuit Court of Appeals held that an employee or former employee seeking to prove that she suffered an adverse employment action in the form of a lateral job transfer may no longer need to show the transfer was accompanied by a decrease in title, salary, responsibilities or benefits. Although the court did not offer a bright-line rule for determining when a transfer is retaliatory and when a job transfer is merely a business decision, employers must take a close look at the actions it takes to respond to complaints of workplace harassment. If the only reasonable solution to alleged sexual harassment is to transfer an employee, an employer should inquire whether she can transfer the alleged harasser instead of transferring the victim.

Avoiding Discrimination Liability—Elliott-Larsen

While it is true that employers can take action against at-will employees for no reason at all, the key to defending against a disparate treatment or intentional discrimination case is the employer's ability to explain its legitimate, nondiscriminatory business reason for an employment action. If different employees are treated differently for the same conduct, the employer must be able to prove, and hopefully document, the legitimate reason for the different treatment.

Title VII and the Age Discrimination in Employment Act

Generally, the federal laws prohibit the same conduct and apply the same standards as Elliott-Larsen. In addition to Title VII and the ADEA, federal law prohibits discrimination on the basis of pregnancy and requires that men and women with the same qualifications who are performing the same job be paid equally. Since such provisions are similar to those in Elliott-Larsen, they are not discussed separately in this handbook. However, there are several differences between Elliott-Larsen and the federal statutes, which are noted below.

Title VII

The remedy provisions of the two laws are different. Specifically, under Elliott-Larsen, an individual who believes that his or her rights have been violated may file a claim with the Michigan Department of Civil Rights. However, the employee is not required to do so. Instead, the employee may file a civil action and proceed directly to court. In the event that the employee prevails, he or she may recover lost wages, both past and future, and may recover for emotional distress caused by the discrimination.

In contrast, an employee who believes that his or her rights under Title VII have been violated must file a claim with the EEOC prior to proceeding to court. The EEOC then conducts an investigation and determines whether the claim has any validity. If the EEOC believes that unlawful discrimination may have occurred, it will attempt to resolve the matter prior to filing a court action. This requirement gives an employer an opportunity to take corrective action prior to being faced with the possibility of a large verdict.

Title VII also limits the damages that an employee may recover. As with Elliott-Larsen, an employee will be able to recover lost back pay. In some cases the employee also will be able to recover future damages, but the courts are more likely to consider reinstatement as an option under Title VII than they are under Elliott-Larsen. Most importantly, compensatory damages for emotional distress currently are limited in Title VII claims based on the number of employees employed by the company (the current maximum for these damages under federal law is $300,000.00). There is no such limit under the state law.

As noted under the Elliott-Larsen Civil Rights Act – State Law section of this chapter, there is no continuing violations doctrine under ELCRA, however, the continuing violations doctrine is still followed under federal law.

Finally, there is no individual liability for supervisors under federal law for discrimination, harassment *or* retaliation, which is contrary to Michigan law.

Age Discrimination in Employment Act

The Federal Age Discrimination in Employment Act (ADEA) protects only individuals who are 40 years old or over. The ADEA does not prohibit an employer from favoring older employees over younger employees who are also over 40. In contrast, Elliott-Larsen applies to discrimination against employees of all ages.

In a recent ruling by the U.S. Supreme Court, the Court found that plaintiffs could bring disparate impact claims under the ADEA, however the Court also ruled that the disparate impact liability is more narrow under the ADEA than under Title VII. Moreover, in May 2008 the Supreme Court held that a federal employee could bring a retaliation claim under the federal-sector provisions of ADEA, even through there is no express statutory basis for such a claim.

Under the ADEA, unlike Title VII, the employer may take any action otherwise prohibited where the differentiation is based on reasonable factors other than age. Perhaps the most significant difference between the ADEA and Elliott-Larsen is the fact that settlements of any claims under the ADEA are governed by the Older Workers Benefit Protection Act (OWBPA), which places restrictions upon an individual's ability to waive ADEA claims.

Any waiver of ADEA claims must meet the following requirements:

- The waiver must be part of a written agreement in terms understandable by the average individual.

- The waiver must specifically refer to the individual's rights under the ADEA.

- The individual may not be asked to waive rights or claims that may arise after the date the waiver is executed.

- The employer must offer consideration for the waiver in addition to what the employee is otherwise entitled.

- The individual must be advised in writing to consult with an attorney.

- If the waiver is part of an individual settlement or separation agreement, the individual must be given 21 days to consider the agreement. If the waiver is requested as part of an exit incentive or other employment termination program offered to a group or class of employees (i.e., an early retirement program), the individual must be given 45 days to consider the agreement.

- Following execution of the waiver, the individual must be given seven days within which he or she may revoke the agreement.

- If the waiver is sought as part of an exit incentive or other termination program offered to a group of employees, at the beginning of the 45-day period the employer must provide the involved employees with specific information regarding the group of employees covered by the program, the program's eligibility factors, any time limits for participating in the program, the job titles and ages of all individuals selected or eligible for the program, and the ages of all individuals in the same job classification who were not eligible or selected for the program.

Because of the requirements of the OWBPA, any settlement or similar waiver agreement with an employee over 40 years old should be carefully reviewed to make sure that the requirements of the Act are met and should be reviewed by counsel. This review should include the EEOC regulations that interpret those requirements and that provide, in part, that the 21 days may be shortened by consent from the individual, but the seven-day period may never be waived.

Pregnancy Issues

The Federal Pregnancy Discrimination Act (PDA) prohibits discrimination against an employee on the basis of her pregnancy. Elliott-Larsen states that discrimination on the basis of pregnancy shall be treated the same as discrimination on the basis of sex.

Pregnancy, in and of itself, is not defined as a disability under the ADA or the PWDCRA. However, a pregnant employee may suffer from complications that render her disabled or handicapped within the meaning of those statutes.

Once a pregnant employee receives an indication from her physician that she is disabled from working, the fact that the employee may not be protected under disability laws is irrelevant. Every court addressing the issue has held that an employer must provide a disabled pregnant employee with at least the same benefits that the employer provides other disabled employees. This means that a pregnant employee must have the same right to take a disability leave, must be granted the same length of leave, must be provided the same benefits while on that leave, and must be given the same rights to reinstatement as other disabled employees.

Furthermore, the Family and Medical Leave Act (FMLA) specifically states that an employee may take an FMLA leave not only for the birth of a new child, but also for prenatal care. Therefore, even though a pregnant employee may not be entitled to an accommodation under the ADA or the PWDCRA, the employee may be entitled to intermittent leave for doctor visits or to part-time status under the FMLA. The employer may require the same, but not more, documentary support for such leaves as the employer is allowed to require for other leaves under the FMLA. (For more information on FMLA, see Chapter 11.)

Genetic Information Non-Discrimination Act (GINA)

Signed into law on May 21, 2008, the Genetic Information Non-Discrimination Act, known as "GINA," does not actually go into effect until November 21, 2009.
GINA is designed to prohibit the improper use of genetic information in health insurance and employment. The law will prohibit group health plans and health insurers from denying coverage to a healthy individual or charging that person higher premiums based solely on a genetic predisposition to developing a disease in the future. The law also bars employers with 15 or more employees from using individuals' genetic information when making hiring, firing, job placement, or promotion decisions
Specifically, GINA:
- Prohibits discrimination based on "genetic information"

- Prohibits acquisition of "genetic information"
  - Purchasing
  - Requesting
  - Requiring employee to provide
- Contains an "inadvertent acquisition" exception (e.g., including acquiring medical information for FMLA certification purposes)
- Prohibits disclosure of "genetic information"
- Requires separate forms, medical files, and confidentiality for any "genetic information" in employer's possession (tracking ADA requirements)

GINA defines "genetic information" as information about "genetic tests" (DNA testing of genotypes, mutations, or chromosomal changes) for applicants, employees, and their family members or the manifestation of a disease or disorder in family members of an applicant or employee.

GINA's remedial structure tracks Title VII remedies, complaint procedures, etc.

In Michigan, genetic information discrimination is already prohibited by Michigan's Persons with Disabilities Civil Rights Act.

Avoiding Discrimination Liability

Obviously, the most important task in avoiding intentional discrimination claims is to make sure that individuals with a known predisposition to discriminate are not placed in supervisory positions. It also helps to have more than one person review and approve employment decisions, so that actions by someone who may later be shown to have a predisposition to discriminate are not final.

One key to avoiding disparate treatment and intentional discrimination claims is to treat all applicants and employees consistently. A standardized interview and other decision-making processes will assist an employer in making sure that all applicants and employees are treated equally.

A standardized interview process also will ensure that supervisors do not ask inappropriate questions that might reflect a predisposition to discriminate against a particular group. Employers should not ask questions that are unrelated to the job. Courts have held that questions about a person's accent may reflect a predisposition to discriminate on the basis of national origin, questions about a person's family may reflect a predisposition to discriminate on the basis of marital status, and questions about when a person graduated from high school or college may reflect a predisposition to discriminate on the basis of age.

The key to prevailing on adverse impact claims is to make sure that any employment policy having an adverse impact on a protected class is job related and justified by business necessity. The employer should be prepared to show that it is necessary for employees to meet a particular standard and that the test being used is the least restrictive method of measuring that standard.

As with intentional discrimination claims, the application and interview process is of primary importance in seeking to avoid adverse-impact claims. Questions that are unrelated to the job but screen out members of certain protected groups may give rise to such claims. Because of this, courts have held that questions about an applicant's financial condition may have an unlawful adverse impact on minorities.

As a general rule, an employer should not ask any question that would elicit information about a person's race, national origin, sex, age, marital status, handicap, or the like. In addition, an employer should not ask any question that may disqualify a member of a protected group, such as questions about height and weight, timing of educational degrees, or criminal convictions, unless the employer is prepared to show that the requirement is job related and justified by business necessity.

The following are some basic rules for helping you to avoid liability for unlawful employment discrimination:

- Adopt and promulgate an EEO policy statement:

    Company X is an Equal Opportunity Employer. Company X will not discriminate against any employee on the basis of sex, race, religion, national origin, age, height, weight, marital status, familial status, veteran status, or handicap or disability unrelated to an employee's ability to perform his or her job.

- Train anyone who interviews regarding lawful and unlawful pre-employment inquiries.

- Audit your employment application for unlawful pre-employment inquiries.

- Audit any testing for job-relatedness and disparate impact.

- Invest in training your supervisors on EEO matters.

- Make your employment decisions without regard to prohibited personal characteristics.

- Monitor your employment decisions to ensure that similarly situated employees are similarly treated.

- Monitor your hiring decisions for disparate impact.

- Post all notices from the EEOC and from the Michigan Department of Civil Rights.

- Remember that your best defense to any discrimination charge is your ability to truthfully articulate and document fair, legitimate business reasons for every personnel decision you make, including but not limited to hiring, evaluating, transferring, promoting, and discharging your employees.

HARASSMENT

State and federal courts have held that employers are prohibited from engaging in unlawful harassment and are likewise responsible for preventing unlawful harassment by others in the workplace, including coworkers and customers. The law requires employers to take prompt remedial action not only when it becomes aware of unlawful harassment ("actual notice"), but also when it reasonably should have become aware of it ("constructive notice").

In order to protect employees from any form of harassment, an employer must have a policy specifically prohibiting sexual and other unlawful harassment and allowing for a complaint procedure. Employers must also promptly investigate all claims of harassment, and where the employer concludes that harassment has occurred, must take prompt action to correct the situation. Several recent United States and Michigan Supreme Court cases emphasize the importance of communicating sexual harassment policies and complaint procedures to all employees and training supervisors on those policies and procedures.

Sexual Harassment

A great deal of law has evolved defining sexual harassment and an employer's obligation to prevent such harassment in the workplace. A summary of an employer's obligations with regard to sexual harassment is set forth below.

The Michigan Supreme Court has made it clear that the standards for liability under Michigan and federal law are somewhat different, therefore, it is important to note what preventive measures should be taken to avoid liability under both federal and state law.

Michigan's state law, Elliott-Larsen, defines discrimination because of sex to include sexual harassment. The law specifically defines sexual harassment as unwelcome sexual advances, requests for sexual favors, and other verbal or physical conduct or communication of a sexual nature when:

- submission to such conduct or communication is made a term or condition either explicitly or implicitly to obtain employment;
- submission to or rejection of such conduct or communication by an individual is used as a factor in decisions affecting such individual's employment;

- such conduct or communication has the purpose or effect of substantially interfering with an individual's employment.

Quid Pro Quo

The United States Supreme Court has stated that "quid pro quo" sexual harassment is not so much a basis for liability as it is a term to describe harassment that occurs when submission to unwelcome sexual advances and/or requests for sexual favors and/or other verbal or physical conduct or communication of a sexual nature is explicitly or implicitly made a condition of employment, or is used as a factor in decisions affecting an employee's employment. In other words, a supervisor engages in quid pro quo harassment when he or she conditions a benefit of employment, such as a promotion or a raise in pay (which only a supervisory-level employee or higher can approve), on the employee's willingness to go along with the supervisor's sexual advances.

In quid pro quo harassment cases, the supervisor relies upon his or her apparent or actual authority to extort sexual consideration from an employee. The employer that gives such authority to the supervisor, therefore, is strictly liable for the supervisor's actions. That is, the employer is liable even if it did not know what the supervisor was doing and had no opportunity to correct the situation. Because of this, it is imperative that employers train their supervisors regarding unlawful sexual harassment and carefully monitor their supervisors for any unlawful activity.

In Michigan, because Elliott-Larsen expressly defines quid pro quo harassment as one of the forms of prohibited gender discrimination, employers must be cognizant of the standards for quid pro quo harassment. When such harassment takes place by a supervisor or other employee who has the actual power to grant or deny the job benefit or condition of employment in question, then liability for the employer is automatic.

Hostile Environment

Hostile environment sexual harassment occurs where subjecting an employee to unwelcome sexual advances or requests for sexual favors and/or other verbal or physical conduct or communication of a sexual nature is sufficient to create an intimidating, hostile, or offensive working environment. Such an environment can be created where supervisors or coworkers make frequent sexual references in the workplace or otherwise expose an employee to offensive sexual conduct.

The United States Supreme Court has ruled that if the hostile environment is created by a supervisor with immediate or successively higher authority over the employee who is the subject of the sexual harassment, and there is tangible employment action taken against that employee (such as a denial of a promotion, transfer, failure to give a deserved raise, etc.), then the employer will be **vicariously** liable (i.e., regardless of whether it was aware of the harassment or took steps to prevent it). If no tangible employment action is taken, then the employer has the opportunity to reduce or avoid damages by proving, as an affirmative defense, that (a) the employer exercised reasonable care to prevent and promptly correct any sexual harassing behavior, and (b) the plaintiff employee unreasonably failed to take advantage of any preventive or corrective opportunities provided by the employer or to avoid harm.

The U.S. Supreme Court also ruled that "constructive discharge" which is a result of supervisor harassment can be considered a tangible employment action, thereby making the employer vicariously liable and precluding the affirmative defense described above. The Court explained that a "constructive discharge" will be treated as a formal discharge where the employee's working conditions were so objectively intolerable that a reasonable person in the employee's position would have felt compelled to resign. The employee will still need to demonstrate a tangible employment action in addition to the objectively hostile environment in order to render the employer vicariously liable.

In Michigan, the focus on hostile environment claims is not on whether tangible employment action was taken; that much is assumed if the hostile nature of the environment is severe enough. Nor is the focus on whether the person creating the hostile environment is a supervisor or not. Regardless of who creates the hostile environment, under Michigan law an employer will be liable for hostile environment harassment unless it adequately investigates and takes prompt and appropriate remedial action upon notice of the alleged hostile environment. Although an employer will not be liable if it does not have notice of the alleged hostile environment, if the employer (or its agents, i.e., a supervisor) unreasonably fails to take notice of possible harassment, this defense would not be available.

Further, the Michigan Supreme Court has ruled that gender based conduct or communication that is not specifically sexual in nature is not sexual harassment under Elliott-Larsen. This ruling, however, in no way diminishes the importance of having an effective sexual harassment policy and complaint procedure, promptly investigating complaints, and taking appropriate action in response to complaints of harassment. As a result of the changes in the law and the technical complexity of the differences between state and federal law, you should consult your employment counsel to review your policies and practices in this area.

Favoritism

Generally, sexual harassment requires that the sexual advances or conduct be unwelcome. Courts, however, have started to accept employee claims that welcomed sexual conduct can create a hostile working environment due to the effect it has not on the employee(s) involved directly in the welcomed conduct, but on the employees who are "left out".

For example, if a supervisor has a single paramour and favors that employee, all other employees, male or female, are equally disadvantaged because they do not have a relationship with that supervisor. If a supervisor has a series of paramours in the workplace, however, other members of the paramour's sex may feel that they need to develop a relationship with the supervisor in order to succeed in the workplace. This can lead to claims of quid pro quo harassment. It can also lead to claims of sex discrimination by individuals who are not of the paramour's sex, and therefore, cannot develop a relationship with the supervisor.

In addition, welcome sexual relationships in the workplace can lead to claims of hostile environment sexual harassment if other workers are exposed to sexual comments and conduct, even though the direct object of those comments and conduct is not offended due to his or her relationship with the offender.

Same Sex Harassment

The courts were previously divided as to whether male-to-male or female-to-female harassment is against the law. In 1998, the U.S. Supreme Court held that same-sex harassment is actionable where the harasser has targeted the victim on the basis of the victim's sex. This includes, for example, a homosexual male employee who makes unwanted sexual advances towards another male employee, or men on a work crew who harass other men who are not "masculine enough."

In 1993, Michigan recognized an action for same-sex sexual harassment by holding that an employee subjected to homosexual advances by a co-worker or supervisor may sue his or her employer for sexual harassment under Elliott-Larsen. The court also held, however, that sexual orientation is not specifically protected under Michigan law. Therefore, workplace harassment or discrimination based upon a person's actual or perceived sexual orientation would not be prohibited under Michigan law. Employers should note, however, that certain cities and counties in Michigan have passed local ordinances banning sexual orientation discrimination. It is recommended that employers check with their local government to determine if such an ordinance has passed in their city or county.

Designing a Sexual Harassment Policy

A sexual harassment policy should be designed to solicit complaints of sexual harassment so that an employer has an opportunity to investigate such claims and take prompt remedial action. A company's sexual harassment policy should contain the following elements:

- A statement that sexual harassment is unlawful and prohibited.
- A definition of sexual harassment in understandable terms, including examples.
- A statement that the policy applies to all employees.
- A directive to employees to report any problems involving perceived sexual harassment.
- A procedure for reporting the complaint, allowing at least two complaint routes (necessary so that the employee has an option where the harasser is also the person to whom he or she is supposed to complain).
- A statement that complaints will be promptly investigated, will be as confidential as possible, and will not result in retaliation for filing or taking part in the investigation of the complaint.
- An indication that appropriate disciplinary action will be taken, stating the range of possible disciplinary actions (i.e., "… up to and including discharge").
- An endorsement by top management.

The policy must be disseminated to all employees and supervisors, and discussed as a very important matter. Most importantly, the policy must be enforced. The following is a sample sexual harassment policy.

SAMPLE SEXUAL HARASSMENT POLICY

Sexual harassment is an infringement of an employee's right to work in an environment free from unlawful sexual pressure. [Company Name] prohibits unlawful sexual harassment of its employees.

In Michigan, the legal definition for sexual harassment includes:

> Unwelcome sexual advances, requests for sexual favors, and other verbal or physical conduct or communication of a sexual nature under the following conditions:
>
> (i) submission to the conduct or communication is made a term or condition either explicitly or implicitly to obtain employment.
>
> (ii) submission to or rejection of the conduct or communication by an individual is used as a factor in decisions affecting the individual's employment; or
>
> (iii) the conduct or communication has the purpose or effect of substantially interfering with an individual's employment, or creating an intimidating, hostile, or sexually offensive work environment.

Sexual harassment consists of overt verbal, written or physical conduct of a sexual nature, when that conduct has a substantial adverse effect on a person in the workplace. Unlawful sexual harassment includes, but is not limited to, the following:

- Demands for sexual favors accompanied by threats concerning an individual's employment status.
- Demands for sexual favors accompanied by promises of preferential treatment concerning an individual's employment status.
- Verbal, written or graphic communication of a sexual nature.
- Patting, pinching, touching or unnecessary contact with another employee's body

Any employee who believes he or she has been subjected to sexual harassment should immediately report, preferably in writing, any and all incidents. Complaints should be directed, at the employee's option, to either his/her supervisor, or to the Human Resources Director. Any complaint will be promptly investigated, and to the extent feasible, confidentiality will be retained in the investigation process. Employees will not suffer adverse employment consequences as a result of reporting a complaint or participating in the investigation of a complaint. Violations of the policy, however, will subject the offending employee to appropriate disciplinary action up to and including discharge from employment.

This policy is a sample only. You should not adopt this policy for your company without first consulting with legal counsel.

Racial Harassment

The development of the law in the area of racial harassment has, in large part, paralleled the developing law of hostile environment sexual harassment. Just as with hostile environment sexual harassment, an employer is liable for acts committed by supervisors on general agency principles, and for acts by coworkers or invitees where it is shown that the employer knew or should have known of the alleged harassing acts and failed to take prompt and effective remedial action.

Generally, courts have said that to be actionable, racial harassment must be so egregious, numerous, and concentrated as to add up to a campaign of harassment, or involve incidents sufficient to create a discriminatory and offensive work environment so heavily polluted with discrimination as to destroy completely the emotional and psychological stability of minority group workers.

Your company should have a separate anti-discrimination and harassment policy which includes prohibitions against racial harassment. This policy should be used in addition to a separate sex harassment policy. The following is a sample Anti-Discrimination and Harassment Policy:

SAMPLE ANTI-DISCRIMINATION AND HARASSMENT POLICY

[Company Name] prohibits unlawful discrimination and harassment based on race, color, religion, sex, national origin, age, disability, height, weight, familial status, marital status or veteran status. Discrimination or harassment of any employee is strictly prohibited and will result in discipline up to and including discharge.

Harassment is generally defined as verbal, written or physical conduct that denigrates or shows hostility or aversion toward an individual because of his or her race, color, religion, sex, national origin, age, disability, height, weight, familial status, marital status or veteran status. Unlawful harassment may occur when:

a. Submission to such conduct is either explicitly or implicitly made a term or condition of employment;

b. Submission to or rejection of such conduct by an employee is used as a basis for employment decisions such as promotion, assignment, demotion, discipline or discharge;

c. Such conduct has the purpose or effect of creating an intimidating, hostile or offensive working environment by:

   1. unreasonably interfering with an employee's work performance; or

   2. otherwise adversely affecting an individual's employment opportunities.

Depending on the circumstances, harassment may include, but is not limited to:

a. **Verbal harassment** (e.g., certain epithets, slurs, negative stereotyping, jokes, pranks or other threatening, intimidating or hostile acts that relate to race, color, religion, sex, national origin, age, disability, weight, height, familial status, marital status or veteran status which are disseminated in the workplace);

b. **Written harassment** (e.g., certain poems, letters, emails, cartoons, or other visual or physical renderings that denigrate or show hostility or aversion toward an individual or group because of race, color, religion, sex, national origin, age, disability, weight, height, familial status, marital status or veteran status which are disseminated in the workplace);

c. **Physical harassment** (e.g. unwelcome gestures, impeding movement or other threatening, intimidating, hostile or offensive conduct that is directed toward an individual because of his or her race, color, religion, sex, national origin, age, disability, weight, height, familial status or veteran status).

Any employee who believes he or she has been subjected to discrimination or harassment should immediately report, preferably in writing, any and all incidents. Complaints should be directed, at the employee's option, to either his/her supervisor, or to the Human Resources Director. Any complaint will be promptly investigated, and to the extent feasible, confidentiality will be retained in the investigation process. Employees will not suffer adverse employment consequences as a result of reporting a complaint or participating in the investigation of a complaint. Violations of the policy, however, will subject the offending employee to appropriate disciplinary action up to and including discharge from employment.

This policy is a sample only. You should not adopt this policy for your company without first consulting with legal counsel.

Harassment Investigations

A prompt investigation of a harassment claim, followed by appropriate remedial action, can help insulate an employer from harassment claims. An effective investigation of a harassment complaint has many of the same elements that comprise any other effective investigation into employee misconduct. Some of them include:

- The investigation must be promptly undertaken upon the employer's receipt of the complaint.

- A goal of the investigation into harassment complaints, as with other employee complaints or allegations of employee misconduct, must be to fully develop the necessary facts upon which to recommend action. This may necessitate meeting with the complaining person, alleged offender, and other persons suggested by either of the above.

- Disciplinary action should fit the misdeed. A verbal reprimand with written file confirmation regarding the conduct reported and stopped may be appropriate in one circumstance (i.e., hugging a coworker, uttering a racial epithet). Termination may be the order of the day in the case of a manager who was fully aware of the prohibited conduct but told a female subordinate she would only get a promotion if she provided sexual favors (in a case of sexual harassment).

- Confidentiality should remain a concern, to the extent possible, throughout the investigation and resolution of the complaint.

- Report back to the complainant and the alleged harasser as to the outcome of the investigation.

An employer establishing a procedure for investigating harassment claims should consider the following:

- Does the procedure require the complainant to write out his/her complaint?

- Who investigates the complaint? Male? Female? African-American? Caucasian? A team? Peer-level employee? Supervisor?

- Does the procedure caution that the employer has a duty to investigate complaints even where the alleged harasser is reluctant to pursue the matter?
- In what form will written witness statements be taken from those consulted during the investigation, and what notice (if any) should the witnesses be given of the conclusion of the investigation (not the result), so that they are not always waiting to be tapped for further proceedings?
- How can the employer guard against complaints from the alleged harasser?

The following are sample questions that an employer should ask an individual complaining of harassment:

- What happened and how did you react? The complainant needs to be more specific than, for example, "he made advances" or "she uttered racial slurs."
- When did the incident(s) happen? Where?
- Who knows that the incident(s) happened? Who witnessed or overheard the incident(s) in the workplace? Who witnessed or overheard the incident(s), if outside the workplace? To whom did you confide about the incident(s)?
- Did the incident affect your work? How?
- Do you know of anyone else in the workplace who has suffered the same kind of behavior?
- Have you notified anyone in management about the situation?
- What did that person do about it?
- How did you respond to the conduct?
- What do you want done about the situation?

Once the alleged harasser is identified and the complainant has been fully interviewed, the employer should set up a meeting with the alleged harasser as soon as possible. In this meeting, the employer should do the following:

- Describe the facts as given by complainant and ask whether they are true.
- If the alleged harasser agrees that the behavior occurred, and if indeed it rises to sexual or racial harassment, label it as such and tell him/her it is not acceptable.
- Tell the person your organization views the complaint seriously.
- Review the relevant harassment policy with the alleged harasser.
- Ask the alleged harasser for people to whom you should speak as part of the investigation.

Avoiding Harassment Lawsuits

In short, the way to minimize the potential filing of a lawsuit based on harassment is to:

- Adopt and enforce a strong anti-harassment policy. Enforcement in this setting MUST include training for supervisory and higher level employees whose responsibility it is to both administer the policy and be on the look-out for situations where harassment is pervasive but the victims are afraid to complain.

- Take all claims of harassment seriously, including claims from third parties.

- Take any remedial or disciplinary action that is warranted by the situation.

Apply that action equally to all persons, regardless of their gender or race, so that future harassment is prevented.

RECORDKEEPING REQUIREMENTS OF ANTI-DISCRIMINATION LAWS

In order to monitor compliance with anti-discrimination laws, both the state and federal statutes require that employers maintain records regarding their applicants and employees. An entire book could be devoted to specific federal statutes of many kinds that require some sort of recordkeeping. However, it is important that all employers are aware of their duty to preserve documents. Notably, it has been determined by some Federal courts that this duty can be triggered even before litigation is commenced or before a discovery order has been entered. Thus, an employer's failure to preserve documents can result in the imposition of sanctions including fines, dismissal of the plaintiff's case or a default judgment against an offending employer.

With the passage of the Sarbanes-Oxley Act of 2002, the failure to retain certain documents can also result in criminal sanctions. Among other things, the Sarbanes-Oxley Act of 2002 added two sections to the federal criminal code dealings with destruction, alteration, or falsification of records in Federal investigations. First, 18 U.S.C. § 1519 provides that:

> Whoever knowingly alters, destroys, mutilates, conceals, covers up, falsifies, or makes a false entry in any record, document, or tangible object with the intent to impede, obstruct, or influence the investigation or proper administration of any matter within the jurisdiction of any department or agency of the United States or any case filed under title 11, or in relation to or contemplation of any such matter or case, shall be fined under this title, imprisoned not more than 20 years, or both.

Second, 18 U.S.C. § 1512 provides that:

> (c) whoever corruptly – (1) alters, destroys, mutilates, or conceals a record, document, or other object, or attempts to do so, with the intent to impair the object's integrity or availability for use in an official proceeding; or (2) otherwise obstructs, influences, or impedes any official proceeding or attempts to do so, shall be fined under this title or imprisoned not more than 20 years, or both.

In addition to records that must be maintained, employers should maintain records that may be helpful in defending an employment discrimination lawsuit. The following topics include general nonexclusive lists of the types of records an employer should maintain, along with an indication of how long to preserve the records. Employers must be aware of the different requirements of the various anti-discrimination statutes. For example, while under Title VII an employer need only preserve compensation related documents for one year, the Equal Pay Act mandates that an employer retains these for two years.

Records to be Kept by All Employers

- Background information regarding each employee, such as name, address, occupation, date of birth, and compensation earned (three years).

- General personnel documents, such as:
    a. Employment applications (including online job applications), results of employment tests and resumes;
    b. Records of promotion, demotion, transfer, layoff, or termination;
    c. Rates of pay (one year from the date of making the record or taking the personnel action, unless a charge of discrimination has been filed with a governmental agency, in which case the record must be maintained until the charge is finally resolved).

- Job evaluations and job descriptions (two years).

- Adverse impact determinations, such as evaluations of the impact of testing (two years after the elimination of the testing at issue).

- Payroll records, records regarding fringe benefits (three years).

- Documents describing or explaining the basis for the payment of any wage differential (two years).

- Wage rate tables, records of additions or deductions from wages for nonexempt employees (two years).

- Tax information, including deductions for withholding (four years after the tax is due or paid, whichever is later).

- Records regarding unemployment compensation (six years after the calendar year in which the compensation is paid).

- Records regarding claims for workers' disability compensation (for the length of the employment; recommended that such records be maintained an additional six years after the end of employment).

- Records regarding all claims for accommodation under the ADA or the PWDCRA, including all documents supporting a claim of undue hardship (recommended three years after last date of employment).

- Job advertisements and internal postings (one year).

- Records regarding written seniority systems, merit plans, or employee benefit plans (two years).

Records to be Kept by Employers Subject to OSHA

- Information regarding work-related illnesses and injuries (five years following the end of the year in which the illness or injury last occurred).

- Records regarding exposure to hazardous materials in the workplace (duration of employment plus 30 years).

- Records regarding occupational noise exposure (two years for measurement records; duration of affected employee's employment for individual employee records).

Personnel Files and the Bullard-Plawecki Right-to- Know Act

The Bullard-Plawecki Employee Right to Know Act defines which records must be included in an employee's personnel file. The following records, if they exist, should be included in a personnel file:

- Any record that identifies the employee and that is, has, or may be used for that employee's employment qualifications, promotion, transfer, additional compensation, or disciplinary action.

- Any record within six months of its making, "concerning an occurrence or fact about an employee" kept by an executive, administrative, or professional employee, even if kept in that person's sole possession and not intended for access by others, if you want to preserve the employer's right to use such a record in a judicial (i.e., court) or quasi-judicial (i.e., MDCR or MUA) proceeding.

- Any written statement by an employee expressing disagreement with information in the record.

The following records should **not** be maintained in an employee's personnel file:

- Employee references, if the identity of the person making the reference would be disclosed.

- Staff planning materials relating to more than one employee, such as salary increases, bonus plans, promotion plans, and job assignments.

- Medical reports and records made or obtained by the employer.

- Personal information about an individual other than the employee, disclosure of which would constitute a clearly unwarranted invasion of that other individual's privacy.

- Separate records relating to criminal investigation of the employee.

- Separate records of grievance investigations not used for the purposes of obtaining background information.

- Education records covered by the federal Family Educational Rights and Privacy Act of 1974.

- Records kept by an executive, administrative, or professional employee, in their sole possession, and that are not accessible or shared with others, for reasons other than those listed above as general personnel documents.

All personnel records should be kept highly confidential. Medical records should be kept separate from general personnel records, and access should be limited to those with a need to know an employee's medical condition.

An employer should not maintain records regarding an employee's associations, political activities, publications or other communications regarding nonemployment activities unless the employee authorizes the employer to do so in writing, or the activities occurred on the employer's premises or during the employee's working hours.

Employers must provide employees an opportunity to periodically review their personnel records, if the employees request the review in writing. The review must take place at a location reasonably near the employees' place of employment and during normal office hours. After reviewing their personnel records, employees may obtain a copy of the information or part of the information at their own expense.

Alternative Dispute Resolution of Employment Discrimination Claims

Alternative Dispute Resolution (ADR) is a means of resolving disputes outside of the public court system. ADR techniques allow parties to resolve controversies without the time, expense, and acrimony involved in litigation.

ADR methods include, but are not limited to, settlement conferences, contractual arbitration, and mediation. While any of these techniques might be applied to employer-employee disputes, the issue of whether an employment contract may mandate the arbitration of civil rights claims has been the subject of much attention.

In contractual arbitration, the parties to a contract agree in advance that any disputes arising under that contract will be resolved through arbitration. If a dispute does arise, the parties submit the dispute to a neutral third party (the arbitrator) in lieu of bringing a judicial action in a court of law. The arbitrator conducts a hearing in which all parties have the opportunity to present evidence. The hearing is less formal than a judicial trial. After the hearing, the arbitrator renders a decision (sometimes called an "award") that is usually binding on the parties. A party who is dissatisfied with the arbitrator's award can ask the court to set the award aside. However, a court generally will set aside the award only if the arbitrator exceeded his contractual authority in making the decision. In other words, the court will not review whether the arbitrator's decision was right or wrong, but only whether the contract gave the arbitrator authority to decide the dispute.

Mandatory contractual arbitration provisions have long been a staple of collective bargaining agreements between employers and unions. In exchange for the job security and other advantages offered by the collective bargaining agreement, employees agree to resolve contract disputes through arbitration. Employees may not sue their employers in court for breach of the collective bargaining agreement; they must first bring the claim to arbitration.

Historically, courts have held that a mandatory arbitration provision in a collective bargaining agreement does not apply to statutory civil rights claims. In *Alexander v. Gardner-Denver Company*, the United States Supreme Court held that an employee's statutory right to a trial under Title VII could not be foreclosed by arbitration under the nondiscrimination clause of a collective bargaining agreement. In other words, an employee charging an employer with violation of a civil rights statute, such as Title VII, Elliott-Larsen, the ADA, PWDCRA, or ADEA does not have to arbitrate the claim prior to bringing a judicial action against the employer. This is true even if the collective bargaining agreement provides that the employer will not discriminate on the basis of race, sex, ethnicity, age, religion, handicap or disability, and so forth.

> ### EXAMPLE: MANDATORY ARBITRATION PROVISION
> The XYZ Company and its employees' union have entered into a collective bargaining agreement. The agreement provides that the XYZ Company will not discriminate in the terms, conditions, and privileges of employment on the basis of race, sex, ethnicity, religion, height, weight, age, handicap, or disability. The agreement also includes a mandatory arbitration provision that requires employees to arbitrate any claim that the XYZ Company breached the agreement. Jane believes that she was denied a promotion on the basis of her sex. Although sex discrimination is a breach of the collective bargaining agreement, and although employees are required to arbitrate claims of breach, Jane may sue the XYZ Company in court for the alleged civil rights violation.

In a related issue, the Michigan Supreme Court held in *Betty v. Brooks & Perkins* that a plaintiff claiming race and sex discrimination in violation of Elliott-Larsen would be permitted to sue her employer for the violation in state court, even though the collective bargaining agreement prohibited discrimination. This decision recognized an exception to the rule that employees' claims of collective bargaining breaches are federal claims, not to be heard by state courts. This case could be interpreted to mean that a compulsory arbitration provision in a collective bargaining agreement will not apply to civil rights claims, even when the civil rights violation is also a breach of the agreement.

By the early 1990s, the U.S. Supreme Court had relaxed its stance somewhat against compulsory arbitration of civil rights claims. In *Gilmer v. Interstate/Johnson Lane Corporation*, the Court enforced a provision in the plaintiff's employment contract (which was not a union collective bargaining agreement) that required the plaintiff to resolve disputes with the employer via New York Stock Exchange arbitration. The Court held that the circumstances in *Gardner-Denver* militating against arbitration were not present in *Gilmer*. The Court stressed that the union arbitration in *Gilmer* might involve a conflict of interest between the individual's rights and collective representation, whereas no such potential conflict was involved in the Stock Exchange arbitration.

After the decision in *Gilmer*, the question arose as to whether a mandatory arbitration provision in a collective bargaining agreement would be enforceable as to civil rights claims. Until recently, most of the federal circuit courts of `appeal addressing this question held that *Gilmer* did not apply to union arbitration, and that the decision in *Gardner-Denver* precluded compulsory arbitration of civil rights claims. However, in 1996, the Fourth Circuit Court of Appeals held in *Austin v. Owens-Brockway Glass Container, Inc.* that a plaintiff's claims of sex and disability discrimination would have to be submitted to arbitration.

In the ensuing years, federal appellate courts considering the issue decided in *Austin* split on the issue. Finally, in 2001, the U.S. Supreme Court revisited the question about the scope of the Federal Arbitration Act's (FAA) applicability to the arbitration of disputes arising under employment contracts, in the *Circuit City Stores, Inc. v. Adams*.

The employee in the *Circuit City* case was subject to an employment application arbitration agreement requiring the arbitration of all employment disputes, including age discrimination claims. After his discharge, Adams (the employee) brought an age discrimination suit in state court. Circuit City responded with a motion in federal district court premised on the FAA to enjoin the state court action and compel arbitration.

Although the district court granted Circuit City's motion, the Ninth Circuit reversed the decision on appeal. It found that the FAA did not apply to employment agreements containing mandatory arbitration provisions.

The Supreme Court focused its review on Section 1 of the FAA, which contains the following exclusionary language: "… nothing herein contained shall apply to contracts of employment of seamen, railroad employees, or any other class of workers engaged in foreign or interstate commerce."

Prior to the Supreme Court's *Circuit City* decision, this exclusionary language had sometimes been the basis for lower court rulings that the FAA did not apply to contracts of employment. The Supreme Court, however, disagreed, stating that the phrase "other class of workers" should be "controlled and defined" by the terms "seamen" and "railroads," thereby requiring the conclusion that the FAA's exclusion only applies to contracts of employment for employees engaged in transportation. Finally, the Court suggested that the FAA would have preemptive effect over any conflicting state anti-arbitration law.

In early 2002, in the case *EEOC v. Waffle House, Inc.*, the U.S. Supreme Court ruled that the existence of a presumptively valid individual employment agreement requiring arbitration of employment disputes did not bar the EEOC from suing in court on behalf of the employee and seeking traditional victim-specific remedies (i.e., backpay, reinstatement, etc.) where it was not a party to that agreement. The ruling is somewhat narrow and therefore should be limited to its facts.

In recent years, a body of federal case law has developed that, taken together, provides guidance regarding the ways in which a compulsory alternative dispute resolution (generally mandatory arbitration) procedure should be structured to be enforceable. The final section of this chapter sets forth suggestions for such a structure and policy.

In Michigan, the progression toward acceptance of compulsory arbitration developed differently. In *Heurtebise v. Reliable Business Computers, Inc.*, the Michigan Supreme Court considered whether a compulsory arbitration provision in an employee handbook is binding on employees. In the case, the plaintiff sued her employer for sex discrimination under Elliott-Larsen. The employer argued that its employee handbook was a binding employment contract, and that the contract provided for the mandatory arbitration of claims, including civil rights claims. The Court held that the handbook involved in that case did not create an employment contract between the employer and employees. This decision made it unnecessary to decide whether the compulsory arbitration provision would have been binding if the handbook had constituted a contract. Nonetheless, three of the justices went on to decide that question. They concluded that public policy precluded the enforcement of compulsory arbitration agreements in employment contracts. Because only three justices (a minority of the Court) made this decision, however, it was not binding precedent on lower courts.

Subsequently, in *Rushton v. Meijer, Inc. (On Remand)*, the Michigan Court of Appeals considered this issue. The Court of Appeals decided that the handbook in *Rushton*, unlike the handbook in *Heurtebise*, did create a binding contract between the employee and employer. However, the Court refused to enforce the compulsory arbitration provision. The Court decided, as a matter of public policy, that an employer could not require its employees, as a condition of employment, to waive prospectively their right to bring a civil rights action in a judicial forum.

Rushton was short-lived, however. In 1999, in *Rembert v. Ryan's Family Steak Houses, Inc.*, the Michigan Court of Appeals threw out its decision in *Rushton* and recognized that a pre-dispute agreement to arbitrate statutory employment discrimination claims was valid as long as the employee was not required to waive any statutory rights or remedies and the process for the arbitration was fair. The Michigan Supreme Court denied leave to appeal the *Rembert* case any further later that year, leaving the Court of Appeals' decision as the current law in Michigan.

Drafting or Adopting an Enforceable ADR Procedure

As noted above, federal and state courts have developed a body of law as to what procedural aspects must be in place for a pre-dispute arbitration or other ADR procedure to be valid and enforceable.

At the outset, it is important to note that any ADR clause must include the "where, when, what, and how" of the process to be valid. For instance, a general statement that "all disputes arising under the agreement shall be settled by arbitration" will not suffice. If the specifics are not addressed in the policy, then a dispute about the process may leave the parties no choice but to go to court—exactly the forum that was to be avoided by the employer in the first place. This discussion about the drafting of effective ADR policies is focused on the creation of final and binding arbitration programs, as they are the most common form of ADR and the types of programs that are most effective at keeping employers out of court. An employer should keep the following elements in mind when drafting or adopting an arbitration procedure:

- The policy must identify the types of disputes that are subject to the procedure (e.g., discharges, layoffs, suspensions).

- The clause could specify that the arbitration proceeding is the sole and exclusive avenue available to the employee/former employee in order to pursue his/her claims against the employer, including all statutory claims.

- The arbitration policy should be signed by each employee subject to it. This can be done in a stand-alone document, an employment application, a handbook receipt, or otherwise.

- To be fully effective, "entry of judgment" language should be included.

- A method of selection of the arbitrator should be included. Using an unbiased third party, such as the American Arbitration Association (AAA) to select the arbitrator pool has been endorsed by the courts as a fair selection procedure. Indeed, the courts have consistently invalidated arbitration agreements where the employer unilaterally controls the selection process as inherently unfair to employees.

- A method for the payment of the arbitrator must be included. Increasingly, courts are reviewing requirements that individuals must pay a portion of the arbitrator's fee. In Michigan, for example, the Sixth Circuit federal Court of Appeals has held that "cost splitting" provisions—requiring the employee and employer to split the cost of the arbitration—are inherently suspect and unenforceable except in very limited circumstances. The court found that to arbitrate a typical employment discrimination claim, employees would incur cost many times greater than the basic cost of litigating in a judicial, rather than an arbitral, forum and determined that such costs would deter many employees from arbitrating their claims.

- A method for the selection of the location for the hearing should be included, or the agreement should specify a location for all hearings.

- The agreement should specify the state whose laws the arbitrator will apply.

- The policy should provide that the arbitrator may award to a prevailing individual all of the remedies that would be available to that person had the case been tried in court. This includes attorney fees.

- Considerations should be given to incorporating the AAA's Supplementary Procedures for Complex Disputes for potentially substantial or complicated cases.

- The drafter should keep in mind that the AAA has specialized rules for arbitration in the construction, textile, patent, securities, and certain other fields. If anticipated disputes fall in one of these areas, the specialized rules should be considered for incorporation in the arbitration clause. An experienced AAA administrative staff manages the processing of cases under the rules.

Additional material to rely on when drafting or adopting an ADR clause is the "Due Process Protocol for Mediation and Arbitration of Statutory Disputes Arising Out of the Employment Relationship." This protocol was drafted by members of the ADR Section of the American Bar Association's Labor and Employment Law Section and is endorsed by several other labor relations organizations. The protocol was drafted to provide a guide for safeguarding procedural due-process concerns in agreements to resolve statutory employment disputes. The protocol explains that regardless of whether agreements to mediate/arbitrate statutory disputes are pre- or post-dispute, all agreements should be informed and voluntary. The full protocol can be reviewed on the American Arbitration Association's website: *www.adr.org*.

Right of Representation

Employees should have a right to be represented by a spokesperson of their choice during arbitration and/or mediation. The clause should reference sources of such assistance, such as bar associations, legal service organizations, and trade unions.

The method and amount of payment for such representation should be up to the employee and the representative. The protocol, however, recommends a number of existing systems providing employer reimbursement for at least a portion of the attorney fees. This reimbursement may be available to the employee as a remedy by the arbitrator.

In fact, an arbitrator is bound to provide the same remedies, including costs and attorney fees, as an employee would be entitled to receive under the relevant statute. In a recent Seventh Circuit case, an arbitration clause that required each party to pay its own attorneys' fees regardless of the outcome of the litigation, was unenforceable in a suit under Title VII. The court stated that Title VII's provision for the award of attorneys' fees to the prevailing party "is essential to fulfill the remedial and deterrent functions" of the statute and that an arbitration clause cannot prevent a prevailing party from receiving that to which they may be legally entitled.

Mediator and Arbitrator Qualifications

The protocol provides a number of requirements to ensure the selection of fair and knowledgeable mediators and arbitrators. First, a roster of available neutral mediators with diverse gender, ethnicity, and background should be established. Those individuals with expertise in statutory requirements in the employment field should warrant top-priority eligibility.

Second, the protocol recommends that potential mediators and arbitrators successfully complete a training program to educate them in all statutory areas and in how to conduct mediation hearings and arbitration sessions. Government agencies, bar associations, and the AAA can provide training on statutory issues, while a mentoring program using individuals with experience in the process could provide training in the conduct of arbitration or mediation.

Third, upon a request of the parties, the designating agency should use a list procedure, such as those proposed by the AAA, or select a panel composed of an odd number of mediators/arbitrators from its roster pool. The panel cards, including the names of the individuals, should be submitted to the parties before they are required to alternately strike names off the list leaving the single name of the arbitrator/mediator. In addition, the designating agency should provide the names of the parties and their representatives in recent cases decided by the arbitrators listed on the panel card.

Fourth, the mediator and arbitrator should have a duty to disclose any relationship that may pose a conflict of interest. Moreover, the arbitrator/mediator should be required to sign an oath stating the absence of any conflict of interest.

Fifth, the arbitrator should be bound by applicable agreements and statutes, and should have the authority to determine the time and place of the hearing, decide arbitrability issues, permit reasonable discovery, and issue an award resolving the dispute. Among other things, the award should include a statement regarding the disposition of any statutory claim(s). The arbitrator should be empowered to issue whatever relief would be available in court under the law. Finally, the arbitrator's award should be final and binding and the scope of review should be limited.

CHAPTER 5: Disability Discrimination

Both the Americans with Disabilities Act (ADA) and the Michigan Persons With Disabilities Civil Rights Act (MPWDCRA—formerly known as the Michigan Handicappers' Civil Rights Act) prohibit discrimination on the basis of disability in employment. The ADA and MPWDCRA also prohibit discrimination in other areas, such as public accommodations. However, only the employment provisions are addressed within this handbook.

Although originally both statutes were interpreted in similar ways, with the adoption of the ADA Amendments Act of 2008, there are now significant differences in the two statutes. The ADA is not intended as an exclusive remedy and will not preempt state laws that are equally or more strict. Therefore, a Michigan company must comply with both the ADA and the MPWDCRA, and an individual may bring an action under both statutes.

Employers Subject to ADA and MPWDCRA

The ADA provides that any employer engaged in an industry affecting commerce with 15 or more workers is covered by the Act. Private employers that have the requisite number of employees are included in the coverage of the employment provisions of the ADA. Public employers are also covered by the ADA. Although the Supreme Court has held that the 11th Amendment bars suits brought by individuals against the State for money damages, the ruling specifically does not bar claims against the State for injunctive relief, claims for money damages brought by the Equal Employment Opportunity Commission, or claims brought against other public entities such as municipalities. Employment agencies, labor organizations, and joint labor-management committees also are covered. Specifically excluded from the coverage of the employment provisions are the United States of America, corporations owned by the United States of America, Indian tribes, and private membership clubs (except labor unions) that are exempt under the Internal Revenue Code.

Unlike the employment provisions of the ADA, the MPWDCRA applies to any employer with one or more employees. The definition of employer under the MPWDCRA includes the state and other governmental entities, and agencies and entities exempt from taxation under the Internal Revenue Code.

Individuals Protected by ADA and MPWDCRA

In order to qualify for the protection offered by the ADA or the MPWDCRA, an applicant or employee must meet three separate tests:

- The individual must be disabled as that term is defined under the Acts.
- The individual must be otherwise qualified for the position.
- The individual must be able to perform the essential functions of the job, with or without accommodation.

Disability Defined

An employee can be disabled such that he or she is entitled to protection in three different ways.

1. "An impairment which substantially limits a major life activity"

First, an applicant or employee is protected if he or she has a physical or mental impairment that substantially limits his or her major life activities. An impairment is defined as a physiological disorder or condition, cosmetic disfigurement, or anatomical loss affecting one or more of several body systems, or any mental or psychological disorder. Physical characteristics such as height, eye color, and left-handedness that are in the normal range, and thus are not the result of a physiological disorder, are not impairments. The definition of impairment does not include predisposition to illness or disease, although the MPWDCRA now includes a prohibition against discrimination on the basis of genetic information. Pregnancy, obesity and advanced age, in and of themselves, are not impairments, although complications related to those conditions may be. Current use of illegal drugs is also not an impairment, although alcoholism may be.

Even if an individual has an impairment, he or she is not disabled under the ADA or MPWDCRA unless that impairment substantially affects one or more major life activities. Major life activities are those basic activities that the average person in the general population can perform with little or no difficulty, such as walking, seeing, hearing, or working. Where the only major life activity at issue is working, an individual must show that he or she is precluded from a broad range of jobs, not just the particular type of job at issue.

Temporary, non-chronic impairments of short duration, with little or no long-term or permanent impact--such as broken bones, the flu, or appendicitis--are usually not disabilities. Under Michigan law, in determining whether an individual is substantially limited in a major life activity, the effect of medicines, assisting devices, or other mitigating measures is to be taken into account, so that a person whose condition is controlled by medication may have an impairment but may not be substantially limited in any major life activity. Following the enactment of the ADA Amendments Act of 2008, however, such mitigating measures cannot be considered under the ADA except in the case of eye glasses and contact lenses. The stated purpose of the new statute was to overrule a number of court decisions which had limited the number of individuals protected by the ADA. Language in the original statute indicating that "individuals with disabilities are a discrete and insular minority" and that the ADA would protect 43 million people was deleted and replaced with language stating that the statute should be interpreted broadly. While an individual will still have to meet his or her burden of proof in litigation, as a practical matter employers will now have to assume that a much larger group of employees could be considered "disabled," because employers will usually not have enough information to know what the effect of a medical condition would be if it were not mitigated by medication.

An individual's representations about his or her abilities in social security or disability insurance applications will not necessarily preclude an ADA claim. For example, an employee may indicate that he or she is totally disabled and thus eligible for social security, but argue that he or she could have continued to work had appropriate accommodation been given. However, the individual must explain why the claim of inability to work in one forum is not inconsistent with the ADA claim.

This first definition of disability may extend to conditions such as orthopedic, visual, speech, and hearing impairments, epilepsy, multiple sclerosis, alcoholism, cancer, heart disease, mental retardation, emotional illness, and learning disabilities, if those impairments substantially limit a major life activity. An individual with the HIV virus may be protected even if the disease is asymptomatic, because the ability to procreate is substantially limited. Because the ADA Amendments Act is a clear repudiation of previous court decisions interpreting the definition of disability and there are no cases under the new amendments yet, it is difficult to predict where courts will draw the line. The case law and regulations stating that the determination of the existence of a disability is to be made on a case by case basis, and that no particular condition will automatically be ruled in or out of the definition, has not been overruled. However, as a practical matter, many disabilities will now be considered generically, as opposed to specifically as to an individual, because of the need to consider the condition in an unmitigated state. Moreover, an employer which decides that a particular condition is not protected runs a great risk, because if the court or jury disagrees and the employer has made no effort to accommodate the condition, the employer will be left with no defenses.

2. "Record of such and impairment"

An applicant or employee also may be disabled within the meaning of the Acts if he or she has a record of an impairment that substantially limits a major life activity. This definition is intended to include persons who have had a disability in the past, such as cancer or alcoholism, but have now recovered. Although current use of illegal drugs is not protected, an individual with a history of drug addition is covered. However, the United States Supreme Court has held that an employer can have a policy against rehiring individuals who have been terminated for misconduct, even though such a policy might preclude rehiring an individual who was previously terminated for drug use. The definition also includes persons who may have been misdiagnosed in the past as having a disability, such as those who were once identified as having a learning disorder. The mere fact that an individual previously has been labeled as disabled, such as a disabled veteran or someone who has received disability income, is not sufficient to classify the person as disabled within this section of the Act. The record of disability must involve an impairment that substantially limits a major life activity.

3. "Regarded as having such an impairment"

Third, an applicant or employee may be disabled if he or she is regarded as having an impairment. Under the ADA Amendments Act, such an individual no longer has to show that he or she is regarded as having an impairment that substantially limits a major life activity. Because the definition of impairment is extremely broad, this means that almost any employee could be regarded as having an impairment. However, the amendments attempt to limit this slightly by specifically excluding any impairment with an actual or expected duration of six months or less. This part of the definition of disabled protects those who have an impairment that is not substantially limiting. This section also protects those who have no impairment but are erroneously perceived as being disabled, such as a person who is rumored to have AIDS. Employers often unwittingly give rise to "regarded as" claims by raising the possibility of a disability where the issue has not been raised by the employee. For example, if an employee violates conduct rules and the employer suggests that the employee's behavior may be caused by a mental impairment, the employer may be accused of regarding the employee as disabled, whereas the disability issue would never have been implicated had the employer simply addressed the behavior as a disciplinary issue.

Finally, although the person is not "disabled" within the meaning of the ADA, a person is protected from discrimination even if he or she is not disabled if that person has a relationship to a disabled person or an organization of disabled people. This portion of the definition was included to prohibit employers from making adverse decisions about otherwise qualified employees based on assumptions about possible conflicts between job and responsibilities to a disabled person or concerns regarding the cost of insurance benefits. The inclusion of this criterion in the definition of who is protected from discrimination under the ADA, however, does not create an obligation for the employer to accommodate an individual who does not personally meet the definition of a disability.

Otherwise Qualified for the Position

Even if an individual is disabled as defined by the ADA or MPWDCRA, he or she is entitled to protection only if the individual is otherwise qualified for the position. For example, the individual must have the education, experience, or expertise required for the job.

Able to Perform Essential Functions

An individual must be able to perform the essential functions of the job that the employee holds or is seeking, with or without accommodation. Although the MPWDCRA talks in terms of "the duties of a particular job or position," while the ADA focuses on the "essential functions of the position," Michigan employers should assume that employees who can perform the essential functions of a job with accommodation are protected. An individual will be protected if he or she is capable of performing the essential functions of the job at the time of the employment decision, even if the individual suffers from a condition that weakens, restricts, or otherwise damages his or her health such that the applicant might not be able to perform the job in the future.

A function will be considered essential if the reason the position exists is to perform that job function. A function also may be essential because of the limited number of available employees among whom the function can be distributed. In addition, a function may be essential if it is so highly specialized that an individual would be hired for his or her ability to perform that function. In determining what functions are essential, courts will look to the employer's judgment, job descriptions, the amount of time spent performing the function, the consequences of not requiring an individual to perform the function, the terms of a collective bargaining agreement, and the work experience of those performing the job.

Examples of functions which have been found to be essential are the ability to get along with subordinates and the ability to meet consistently applied attendance requirements. Whether job rotation, punctuality, or the ability to work overtime are essential functions is determined on a case by case basis.

Drug and Alcohol Use

Alcoholism and drug addiction are disabilities under both the ADA and the MPWDCRA. However, both Acts specifically exclude from coverage current users of illegal drugs. In addition, although alcoholism is considered a disability by both Acts, employers are not required to accommodate attendance or performance problems caused by the use of alcohol. However, an employer cannot discriminate against an employee simply because he or she is an alcoholic, and an employer may be required to accommodate requests for time off for treatment. The U.S. Supreme Court recently addressed the issue of whether an employer violates the ADA when it refuses to rehire someone who was terminated for testing positive for drugs. The former employee argued that he was being discriminated against on the basis of a history of drug addiction. The Court disagreed and held that the employee was treated the same as others who were terminated for violating policies.

Genetic Testing

The MPWDCRA also prohibits any discriminatory action on the basis of "genetic information" and prohibits employers from requiring individuals to submit to a "genetic test" or to provide "genetic information" as a condition of employment or promotion.

"Genetic information" is defined in the MPWDCRA as information about a gene, gene product, or inherited characteristic of an individual derived from the individual's family history or a genetic test. "Genetic test" is defined in other laws and generally means a test that analyzes the human DNA, RNA, chromosomes, proteins and metabolites used in detecting or predicting disease-related components; it would not include routine chemical analysis of body fluids unless the test was conducted specifically to determine the presence, absence, or mutation of a gene or chromosome.

An employee may voluntarily provide his or her employer with genetic information that is related to the employee's health or safety in the workplace, and the MPWDCRA does not prohibit an employer from using genetic information obtained in this fashion to protect the employee's health and safety. Otherwise, no employer may directly or indirectly acquire or have access to any genetic information concerning an employee or applicant for employment, or a member of the employee's or applicant's family.

Prohibited Discriminatory Acts

The ADA and the MPWDCRA prohibit discrimination against protected individuals in regard to application procedures, hiring, promotion, termination, compensation, job training, and other terms, conditions, and privileges of employment.

The following are specific acts of discrimination prohibited by the ADA and the MPWDCRA:

- Limiting, segregating, or classifying a job applicant or employee in a way that adversely affects the opportunities or status of such applicant or employee because of his or her disability or genetic information

- Participating in a contractual relationship that has the effect of subjecting the applicant or employee to prohibited discrimination (i.e., contract with a labor union, referral agency, fringe-benefit provider, or training organization)

- Utilizing discriminatory standards, criteria, or methods of administration, including those that perpetuate discrimination

- Excluding or otherwise denying equal jobs or benefits because of an individual's relationship with an individual with a disability

- Failing to make reasonable accommodation or denying employment opportunities on the basis of the need to make such accommodation

- Using qualification standards, employment tests, or other selection criteria that screen out or tend to screen out individuals with disabilities, unless the criteria are shown to be job related and consistent with business necessity

- Failing to select or administer tests concerning employment in a manner that ensures that the tests accurately reflect the skills, aptitude, or other factors that the tests purport to measure, rather than merely reflecting the disability

- Requiring an individual to submit to a genetic test or to provide genetic information as a condition of employment or promotion

Medical Inquiries and Exams

Under the ADA, unlawful discrimination includes certain historically common practices regarding medical inquiries and medical examinations. Whether or not medical inquiries or examinations will be allowed, depends in part upon when the inquiry or examination takes place.

An employer can never subject an applicant to a pre-employment physical, ask whether the applicant has a disability, or inquire regarding the nature or severity of a disability before making an offer of employment. In addition, an employer cannot make pre-offer inquiries regarding an applicant's workers' disability compensation history.

An employer may make pre-employment inquiries regarding the ability of an applicant to perform job-related functions. If an applicant has a known disability that might interfere with job performance, an employer can ask the applicant how he or she would perform a job function, with or without accommodation, and can ask the applicant to demonstrate.

After an offer of employment is made, but prior to the commencement of employment, an employer may require the prospective employee to take a physical examination, and may make the offer of employment conditional upon the results of that examination, if:

- all entering employees in the same job category are subjected to such an examination;

- information obtained from the examination is kept in separate medical files and is treated as confidential; and
- the results of the examination are used in accordance with the Act (i.e., only those employees who cannot perform the essential functions of the job with or without accommodation are rejected on the basis of the medical examination).

An employer may conduct voluntary medical examinations that are part of an employee health program. In addition, an employer may conduct periodic physicals to determine fitness for duty or other medical monitoring as required by law, so long as the examinations are job related and consistent with business necessity. The information obtained in these examinations is to be kept separately and treated confidentially. Generally, only those with a need to know for purposes of safety or making accommodation should have access to the information.

Tests for illegal drug use are not considered medical examinations under either Act. Therefore, an employer's ability to do drug testing is not affected by the ADA or the MPWDCRA. However, to the extent that a drug test reveals the use of legal drug use, such as an antihistamine that might be evidence of asthma, the drug test may be considered a medical examination. Therefore, if drug testing is performed prior to making an offer, employers should instruct the agencies performing their drug testing to only report the existence of illegal drugs.

Physical agility tests are not medical examinations. Therefore, they can be required at any stage of the application or employment process. However, because such tests often have an adverse impact on individuals with certain types of disabilities, the employer needs to be able to show that the test is job related and consistent with business necessity.

Personality tests which are used to determine an individual's strengths and weaknesses for purposes of job placement are not medical examinations if they do not diagnose medical conditions (e.g., depression) and are not scored or evaluated by a medical professional, such as a psychiatrist or psychologist.

Reasonable Accommodation: ADA and MPWDCRA

Under both the ADA and the MPWDCRA, it is unlawful discrimination to fail to provide reasonable accommodation that would enable an otherwise qualified disabled individual to perform the essential functions of the job, unless that accommodation poses an undue hardship. The ADA Amendments Act clarifies that there is no duty to accommodate an individual who is only regarded as having an impairment. However there may be a duty to accommodate an individual who has a record of an impairment which substantially limits a major life activity, such as an employee who had cancer, has recovered, but is still required to have follow-up medical appointments.

Employers are required to make reasonable accommodation only for known physical or mental limitations of an otherwise qualified individual with a disability. Thus, the duty to accommodate generally is triggered by a request from an employee or applicant for accommodation, or at least a notice by the employee to the employer that the employee suffers from a disability. However, where an employee suffers from a mental disability that makes it difficult for the employee to articulate the need for an accommodation, and the employer is aware of both the disability and the accommodation need, the employer may have the burden of initiating the discussion.

The Michigan Department of Civil Rights and the Equal Employment Opportunity Commission (EEOC) both have issued posters, which all employers should display, that invite employees to inform the employer of accommodation requirements. Where an employee with a known disability is having difficulty performing the job, it is permissible for the employer to inquire into the need for an accommodation. However, it is safe to address the job performance only, allowing the employee to raise the issue of the accommodation. Otherwise, the employer runs the risk of perceiving the employee as disabled. Under the MPWDCRA, an employee's failure to make a written request for accommodation may bar a failure to accommodate claim if the employer has the Michigan Department of Civil Rights poster prominently displayed.

Once the need for an accommodation is known, the employer must engage in an interactive process with the employee. The employee has the burden of identifying the need for accommodation and suggesting possible accommodations, but the employer must also work to determine the appropriate accommodation. Failure to engage in the interactive process is not, in and of itself, a violation of the ADA, but inaction in the face of a request for accommodation may be used to demonstrate bad faith.

Reasonable accommodation is defined under the ADA only by example:

- Reasonable accommodation may include making existing facilities used by employees readily accessible to and usable by individuals with disabilities. This could include making structural changes or removing architectural barriers.

- Reasonable accommodation may require job restructuring; that is, modifying the job so that a person with a disability can perform the essential functions of the job. It may also include eliminating nonessential elements of the job, delegating or exchanging assignments, and redesigning procedures for task assignments. The MPWDCRA says that an employer with fewer than 15 employees is not required to restructure a position. The cases are clear that while changing a job to eliminate marginal duties, an employer is never required to eliminate essential functions of a job as reasonable accommodation. The obligation applies only to minor or infrequent duties. Where an employer has eliminated essential job functions in the past, such as exempting an employee from mandatory rotation between positions, the employer will have a more difficult time arguing that the job function is essential.

- Part-time or modified work schedules may be required as reasonable accommodation. However, the MPWDCRA specifically says that an employer with fewer than 15 employees is not required to alter an employee's work schedule.

- Where an employee cannot be accommodated in his or her existing job, an employer may be required to reassign that employee to a vacant position. An employer is not required to consider a transfer if the employee can be accommodated in his or her current position. Cases have consistently held that a position is not vacant if it would normally be automatically filled pursuant to the seniority provisions of a collective bargaining agreement. The Supreme Court has held that an employer is not required to reassign an employee to a position that would normally be filled pursuant to a consistently enforced seniority policy, even if that policy does not involve a collective bargaining agreement. However, where exceptions to the policy have been made in the past, an exception may also have to be made as a reasonable accommodation. The courts have not yet clearly defined the scope of the reassignment obligation. While the EEOC takes the position that a company may have to look company-wide for vacancies and automatically place the disabled employee in a position for which he or she is qualified, even if other employees are more qualified, some courts have limited the obligation to a particular location, and still others have held that the duty is simply to allow the employee to apply for vacancies. Employers with fewer than 15 employees will not have to transfer an employee as an accommodation, as such an accommodation is not required by the MPWDCRA.

- Acquisition or modification of equipment or devices may be a reasonable accommodation. The following are examples of equipment or devices that may be required: electronic visual aids, Braille materials, talking calculators, magnifiers, audio recordings, telephone handset amplifiers, telecommunications devices for the deaf, mechanical page turners, or raised or lowered furniture. However, personal items such as hearing aids or eyeglasses would not be included.

- Reasonable accommodation may require adjustment or modifications of examinations, training materials, or policies. The EEOC takes the position that this requirement may include the modification of attendance and leave of absence policies.

- The provision of qualified readers or interpreters may be a reasonable accommodation.

The list is not exhaustive. This means that what constitutes reasonable accommodation will be decided case by case, depending upon the particular facts of each situation. However, the case law does give some indication of accommodations that generally will not be required:

- An employer will generally not be required to eliminate or modify essential functions of a job or change a fundamental requirement of a job, although if an employee cannot perform the essential functions there may be an obligation to reassign that employee. An employer will not be required to lower consistently-applied standards.

- An employer is never required to bump an employee from a job or create a new position. An employer can choose to create a light duty position as an accommodation, but the employer can define the position as a temporary one and is not required to make it permanent.

- Cases have consistently held that an employer is not required to transfer an employee to a different supervisor to alleviate stress. However, these cases are usually based on the fact that the mere inability to work for one supervisor is not a substantial limitation of a major life activity. Theoretically, an employee could have other limitations which could meet this test and a transfer could be a reasonable accommodation.

- An employer is not required to provide an accommodation that requires other employees to work harder in a significant way, although assumption of extra minor duties may be required.

- Most courts, including the Michigan Supreme Court, have held that an employer is not required to place an employee on an indefinite leave. However, the 6th Circuit, while adopting this general proposition, has found in certain cases that a medical leave could be a reasonable accommodation if it did not impose an undue hardship. This position is consistent with the EEOC guidance on accommodations but has not been followed by most courts.

- While the ADA may require an employer to allow an employee to work at home in certain circumstances, most courts examining this on a case-by-case basis have agreed with the employer that such an accommodation has not been reasonable because of the types of documents required to do the job (i.e., confidential documents which should not leave the work site) or the level of supervision needed.

- An employer is never required to promote an employee as an accommodation.

The MPWDCRA, on the other hand, specifically lists the accommodations that may be required, including making facilities accessible, removal of marginal duties, modified work schedule, provision of assisting aids or devices, and provision of readers or interpreters.

Undue Hardship

Both the ADA and the MPWDCRA provide that an employer is not required to make reasonable accommodation if doing so would cause undue hardship. However, the definition of undue hardship under the MPWDCRA is very specific, while under the ADA it would be determined on a case by case basis.

Definition of Undue Hardship: ADA

The ADA defines undue hardship as an action requiring significant difficulty or expense when considered in light of the following factors:

- The nature and cost of the accommodation needed under the Act
- The overall financial resources of the facility or facilities involved in the provision of the reasonable accommodation
- The number of persons employed at such facility
- The effect on expenses and resources, or the impact otherwise of such accommodation upon the operation of the facility
- The overall financial resources of the covered entity
- The overall size of the business of a covered entity with respect to the number of its employees
- The number, type and location of its facilities
- The type of operation or operations of the covered entity, including the composition, structure, and functions of the workforce of such entity, and the geographic separateness, administrative, or fiscal relationship of the facility or facilities in question to the covered entity

This list of factors is not exhaustive, and the weight that will be attributed to each of these factors will vary with the facts of a particular situation. Moreover, the weight of a given factor turns on both the nature and cost of the accommodation in relation to the employer's resources and operations.

The cost of an accommodation is clearly a factor that may indicate that making the accommodation would pose an undue hardship. If an accommodation would cause undue hardship, the employer must provide the applicant or the employee the opportunity to provide the accommodation for him- or herself. Moreover, the employer must pay for that portion of the accommodation that would not cause an undue hardship if, for example, the State Vocational Rehabilitation Agency or the employee or applicant pays for the remainder of the cost of the accommodation. Employers should be aware that claiming an economic undue hardship may open corporate financial records to scrutiny.

Cost is not the only basis for an undue hardship defense. Among the factors the courts have looked to in determining whether an accommodation will cause undue hardship is what the impact will be on the other employees in terms of workload. For example, exempting an employee from overtime may not be required as an accommodation in certain situations where there are not other employees willing to voluntarily work the overtime and the accommodation would place an inappropriate burden on another employee. However, the mere fact that other employees may not like that the disabled or handicapped employee is allowed to have modified duties, will not be sufficient to create an undue hardship. Employers are not required to violate seniority or productivity provisions of a collective bargaining agreement as a reasonable accommodation. Courts have also looked at administrative issues, such as the hardship caused by unpredictable attendance, the need to maintain flexibility in assigning employees, and the benefits of rotating employees among positions.

Definition of Undue Hardship: MPWDCRA

Unlike the ADA, the MPWDCRA sets forth some specific formulas for measuring when an accommodation becomes an undue hardship. Those formulas tie the calculation of what constitutes an undue hardship to both the number of employees employed by an employer and the state average weekly wage. The more employees employed by the employer, the more money the employer will have to spend for equipment, devices, readers, and/or interpreters.

For the purchase of equipment or devices, such as a TDD or a voice-synthesized computer, the amount that an employer will be required to pay is outlined in the table below.

Number of Employees	Cost
Fewer than 4	1 × state average weekly wage
5–14	1.5 × state average weekly wage
15–24	2.5 × state average weekly wage

For the employer with 25 or more employees, an employer will be required to pay *at least* 2.5 × the state average weekly wage. This amount is a floor, not a ceiling.

For the hiring of readers or interpreters, the amount is as follows:

Number of Employees		Cost
4 or fewer	year 1	7 × state average weekly wage
	year 2 and future	5 × state average weekly wage
5–14	year 1	10 × state average weekly wage
	year 2 and future	7 × state average weekly wage
15–24	year 1	15 × state average weekly wage
	year 2 and future	10 × state average weekly wage

Again, for the employer with 25 or more employees, the requirements of the employer with 15 to 24 employees are used as a minimum requirement.

If the accommodation requires both the purchase of equipment or devices and the hire of readers or interpreters, the employer must do both, subject to the cost limitations set forth in the tables above. If the accommodation can be made either by the purchase of equipment, devices **or** the hire of readers or interpreters, the handicapped individual must be given the choice so long as neither is an undue hardship.

The MPWDCRA specifically exempts public employers and tax-exempt organizations from the formulas governing undue hardship. The history of the amended Act suggests that the formulas that place a clearly defined cap on what an employer must do to reasonably accommodate, are in the statute at the request of, and to assist small businesses. Public employers and tax-exempt organizations are excluded from those formulas so that they can be held to greater accommodation duties before they can claim undue hardship.

Safety of Self or Others

An employer is not required to hire an individual or to provide an accommodation if that individual or accommodation will pose a direct threat to the health or safety of the employee or others. The standard for direct threat is whether the individual poses a significant risk, which is defined as a high probability of substantial harm. A speculative or remote risk is insufficient. While the ADA states that an employer has a defense if the employee poses a direct threat to "others," the Supreme Court has held that the risk may be to either the employee or others.

In determining whether an individual poses a direct threat, the employer should consider:

- The duration of the risk
- The nature and severity of the potential harm
- The likelihood that the potential harm will occur

- The imminence of the potential harm

No one factor is determinative. Thus, if the risk could result in death, it may constitute a direct threat even if the likelihood of the harm is remote. On the other hand, a risk that is almost certain to occur in the near future may constitute a direct threat even if the potential danger is not severe.

This determination must be made on an individualized basis based upon objective, factual evidence about the nature or effect of a particular disability. Because an individualized assessment is required, blanket exclusions of a particular condition are usually not allowed. While not controlling, experience with the particular employee at issue will be instructive. Thus, if the employee has historically presented problems, it is more likely that direct threat will be found, whereas an employee who has worked for a significant period of time without incident is less likely to pose a direct threat.

If a significant risk can be reduced to a remote risk through reasonable accommodation, the employer is required to provide that accommodation so long as it does not impose an undue hardship.

Food Handling and Communicable Diseases

An employer is not required to employ an individual in a food-handling position if that individual has an infectious or communicable disease that is transmitted to others through the handling of food, as defined by the Secretary of Health and Human Services. Currently, this list includes diseases such as hepatitis. It does not include AIDS or HIV infection. Therefore, an employer cannot refuse to employ an individual in a food-handling position simply because that individual has AIDS or has tested HIV positive. If there is an accommodation that would eliminate the threat of transmitting the disease through food handling, the employer must provide that accommodation.

AIDS Issues

Acquired Immune Deficiency Syndrome (AIDS) is a disability within the meaning of the ADA and MPWDCRA. The Michigan Supreme Court has held that not only is a person with AIDS disabled, a person erroneously perceived as having AIDS is also disabled within the meaning of the MPWDCRA. The United States Supreme Court has held that a person with asymptomatic AIDS, or a person infected by the Human Immunodeficiency Virus (HIV) who has not yet developed AIDS symptoms, is disabled because that person is substantially limited in the ability to procreate.

A controversial issue is whether AIDS constitutes a direct threat to others that cannot be eliminated or reduced by reasonable accommodation. Courts have held that attorneys, an entertainer on a cruise ship, a firefighter, and a classroom teacher, all of whom had AIDS or were HIV positive, posed no direct threat to others. These courts have relied on medical evidence that the risk of HIV transmission through casual contact is highly improbable. Courts consider whether the job involves possible blood-to-blood contact, but reject arguments that AIDS might be spread by casual contact, saliva, urine, tears, or perspiration. Courts have criticized these arguments as speculative, or based on stereotyping, prejudice, and unfounded fear. Another relevant factor is the availability of protective garb and equipment to further minimize the already small risk.

On the other hand, courts have held that a surgical technologist and a surgical technician did pose a direct threat to others. Although evidence established that the risk was small, it was sufficient to render the technologist unqualified. The surgical technologist's duties included placing his hand in patients' surgical incisions, and handling surgical instruments by the sharp end. The technologist admitted that he had accidentally punctured himself on occasion. The court rejected the surgical technician's argument that he could be reasonably accommodated by eliminating all job functions that involved contact with the patient's body.

Another controversial AIDS issue is whether an employer can require an employee with AIDS or HIV to submit to a medical exam to determine whether that person is likely to spread AIDS or other infectious diseases to others. The Sixth Circuit Court of Appeals held that a grocery store could require such an exam for a produce clerk who came in close contact with customers and food, and who worked with sharp knives.

Conflicts with Other Federal Laws: ADA and MPWDCRA

It is a defense to a claim of discrimination under the ADA that another federal law or regulation requires an employer to take certain action or prohibits an employer from taking certain action (such as providing a specific accommodation). Thus, courts have consistently held that employers may rely on Department of Transportation regulations regarding drivers who have diabetes, certain seizure disorders, or a history of use of illegal drug use. Because the ADA is a federal law, and employers are required to comply with that law regardless of state law, it is not a defense that a state law may require or prohibit certain action.

Notification of Need for Accommodation

Under both the ADA and the MPWDCRA, an employer has an obligation to notify applicants and employees of their rights under the law. Under the MPWDCRA, an employer may do so by prominently displaying the posters published by the Michigan Department of Civil Rights. Those posters inform individuals that they must request an accommodation in writing within 182 days after the need for an accommodation becomes known. If an employer has complied with the posting requirements and an individual fails to comply with the written request requirement, the individual cannot bring an action for failure to accommodate under the MPWDCRA. The ADA does not provide employers with a comparable defense, but courts considering the issue have agreed that under most circumstances it is incumbent on the employee to advise the employer of the need for accommodation and to identify the accommodation desired.

Once an employee requests an accommodation, the employer and the employee are to engage in an "interactive process" to discuss the accommodation need. The employer may require medical certification of the existence of a disability and the employee's limitations. If the employee fails to provide the requested medical documentation, the employee may be deemed to have voluntarily withdrawn from the interactive process and thus may not be entitled to accommodation. The employer is not required to provide the most expensive or technologically advanced accommodation. However, if the accommodation offered is ineffective, the employer must continue to look for alternatives.

Remedies Under ADA and MPWDCRA

The employment provisions of the ADA will be enforced by the same remedies and procedures provided for in Title VII of the Civil Rights Act of 1964. Therefore, an employee desiring to bring an action under the ADA must first file a charge with the EEOC.

A plaintiff alleging violation of the ADA's Title I may request a jury, and may receive not only back pay, but also compensatory and punitive damages. Punitive damages will not be allowed in a case involving an alleged failure to accommodate where the employer has acted in good faith in attempting to find a reasonable accommodation that does not pose an undue hardship. Furthermore, punitive damages, together with other compensatory damages, are capped as listed below, provided that the employer has the requisite number of employees in each of 20 or more calendar weeks in the current or preceding calendar year:

- $50,000 if the employer has 15–100 employees
- $100,000 if the employer has 101–200 employees
- $200,000 if the employer has 201–500 employees
- $300,000 if the employer has more than 500 employees

Although some courts have held that individuals may be held personally liable under the ADA, a recent Sixth Circuit case holding that there is no personal liability under Title VII may indicate that a similar result will be reached under the ADA.

A person alleging a violation of the MPWDCRA may bring a civil action in circuit court for injunctive relief or damages. Damages may include all compensatory damages, as well as attorney fees. An individual may bring an action with the Michigan Department of Civil Rights alone, or in addition to, a civil action.

CHAPTER 6: Affirmative Action

Equal opportunity, diversity, and affirmative action are intrinsic to the missions and value statements of many companies. Most people would admit, however, to the lack of even a basic understanding of the distinction between these concepts, or, more importantly, their inter-relationship. The following explanation is one way to consider how they fit together:

Equal opportunity directly benefits the individual because it offers him or her a fair chance of participating in the workplace. At the same time, providing equal opportunities for employment benefits an organization at least indirectly by the resulting increase in diversity.

Diversity is the end-result of an organization's successful effort to provide equal opportunity for candidates and members of its community. In addition, organizations have a strong interest in having diverse populations in both the workplace. Compelling reasons for diversity stem not only from legal mandates, but from social, moral, and business imperatives.

Affirmative action is one strategy among many to pursue equal opportunity for individuals and diversity for organizations. It is typically pursued through outreach in recruitment, development, and retention programs. Organizations employ affirmative action both to engage in fair employment practices and to redress past inequities, and most federal contractors and subcontractors are required to develop and annually update Affirmative Action Plans.

Considerations in Developing and Managing Diversity Initiatives

Corporate America has long recognized the need to create a diverse leadership and a diverse workforce as a key element to a successful enterprise—indeed, 68 major corporations filed "amicus" briefs on behalf of the University of Michigan's affirmative action programs when they were recently considered by the U.S. Supreme Court (the cases are discussed further later in this chapter).

Despite the wide assumption of the inherent relationship between diversity and affirmative action, the operational definitions and programmatic strategies for pursuing the two remain complicated, and frequently obscure. Organizations rarely articulate the basic concept of diversity or describe the vision of what it means for them to be diverse. It is important to understand the particular implications of these ideas, however, as well as to define these terms within the context of a particular company's unique working environment.

Some analysts attempt to use numerical representation (associated with affirmative action) to demonstrate the benefits of diversity. A much broader perspective for developing diversity initiatives, however, results in more effective and valuable results. As programs are crafted, it is important to develop an operational definition of diversity that can guide the purpose and final outcome of any diversity initiative. It is not sufficient to include a broad reference to diversity in a corporate mission statement; rather, diversity must be defined within the contexts of the legal environment, the organizational culture, and changing demographics.

Planning and Implementing Diversity Initiatives

The following points should be considered in the development of diversity initiatives:

1. Link the company's initiatives to its overall mission. Given its mission and unique working environment, each organization must consider and define for itself what it means by "diversity;"

2. Articulate the purpose of the initiatives in order to provide a measure for their success;

3. Develop reasonable and realistic goals for each phase of any program;

4. Build consensus around the program's purpose, process, and implementation strategies;

5. Consider consensus-building and collaboration as continuous processes during the life of the initiative, not a one-time effort undertaken during the initial implementation phase. Success over an extended period of time must be an essential element of diversity efforts;

6. Link diversity efforts such as recruitment, development, and retention strategies to organizational performance;

7. Build and sustain an accountability framework with clearly-defined outcomes and structures of individual and group responsibility. A successful effort incorporates accountability for diversity with the organization's strategic business objectives;

8. Produce quantitative and qualitative reports to measure and quantify the organization's progress, and develop a communication plan to engage relevant constituent groups and stakeholders systematically and deliberately in planning, implementation, and evaluation. Share information freely and frequently - not just at the beginning and end of the initiative, but throughout the process, reporting not just successes, but also challenges and lessons learned;

9. Carefully plan the operational process, i.e., the committee structure, timeframes, reporting format, etc;

10. Establish linkages, where possible, with existing programs - internal programs at your company, comparable efforts at peer companies, and collaborative enterprises;

11. Conduct regular environmental scanning to evaluate internal and external factors that may potentially impact the effectiveness of the initiative;

12. Consider and have a thorough awareness of the company's existing cultures, norms, values, and practices. Understanding and accounting for these factors is essential to the success of any initiative;

13. View diversity initiatives as investments, rather than "feel good programs." Companies will be more likely to take them seriously, participants will have a greater stake in their success, and higher expectations will result in more positive outcomes;

14. Recognize the value of timeliness in developing and implementing diversity initiatives, linking outcomes to hot issues at the workplace, or on the national scene;

15. Encourage the development of innovative programs that capture the interest of those within the workplace. Use research approaches such as longitudinal studies, and the establishment of reliability and validity measures;

16. Seek and convey commitment from executive leadership that goes beyond lip service. Practice what you preach: the commitment to diversity should be evident in company business practices, not only in speeches delivered by leaders;

17. Secure adequate resources to support diversity initiatives;

18. Focus on the fairness of procedures. For example, in order to enhance support for affirmative action programs, it may be necessary to repeatedly emphasize the goal and practice of hiring only qualified applicants, as opposed to providing special treatment based on particular characteristics; and

19. Study "best practices" at peer companies.

Evaluation and Assessment of Diversity Initiatives

Examining outcomes and developing appropriate assessment models is critical to sustaining an effective program, and assessing its impact. To demonstrate the value of diversity, develop a systematic approach to diversity measurement, with clearly-articulated goals and well-grounded accountability structures. An assessment process is useful in delineating desired outcomes: identifying target audiences, defining diversity within local and national contexts, achieving consensus on desired outcomes, defining the methodologies for examining impact, and communicating the findings. Because an Evaluation Plan must be an integral part of any initiative, it is crucial to develop and implement sound evaluation strategies.

Key Steps in a Program Evaluation Process

Develop an assessment model that lends itself to formative and summative evaluation. A formative evaluation focuses on providing information to program planners on how to improve and refine a developing or ongoing program. A summative evaluation assesses the overall quality and impact of mature programs for purposes of accountability and policy-making. The formative and summative approaches to evaluation reflect two ends of a continuum, and evaluation models generally contain varying elements of both.

Considerations in developing an effective evaluation process:

1.　Deliberation and clear definition of the purpose of evaluation – why should you evaluate? The evaluation process and outcomes will be determined by the intended purpose of the evaluation;

2.　Clarification of evaluation objectives in order to allow appropriate measurement;

3.　Selection of criteria and indicators in order to determine which elements should be evaluated;

4.　Selection of those measures that characterize the level of progress toward program objectives;

5.　Identification of the data sources: consider collection and analysis of information from primary and secondary data sources;

6.　Considering qualitative and/or quantitative data analysis;

　　(a)　Qualitative analysis – the non-numerical examination and interpretation of observations for the purposes of discovering underlying meaning and patterns of relationships. This is most typical of field research and historical research;

　　(b)　Quantitative analysis - the numerical representation and manipulation of observations for the purposes of describing and explaining those observations;

7.　Securing adequate financial and staff resources for the Evaluation Plan;

8.　Defining the evaluation time-frame:

　　(a)　Will this evaluation be a one-time effort, or will there be some follow-up?

(b) Is the evaluation intended to capture a snapshot view, or is it designed to study the impact or effectiveness over a certain time period?

(c) How often will the selected indicators be measured?

9. Monitoring and assessing progress of the evaluation process:

(a) Following an action plan for carrying out the various phases of the process;

(b) Encouraging review and revision of the Evaluation Plan;

10. Eventual communication of the evaluation results:

(a) Determine the primary audience for evaluation results;

(b) Identify the vehicles to be used for communicating results;

(c) Decide how the results of the evaluation will be used;

(d) Focus on using the results to improve project operations or interventions; and

11. Basing future decision-making on the information gained through the evaluation process.

Affirmative Action Plans

Affirmative action programs or plans are designed to:

- remedy the present effects of past discrimination against protected classes of

- individuals by promoting equal opportunity for all qualified employees and applicants for employment; and

- prohibit discrimination in hiring and employment because of race, creed, color, national origin, sex, disability, age, or marital or familial status.

In a sense, such plans go beyond equal employment opportunity by requiring an employer to make an extra effort to recruit, hire, and promote members of groups protected by discrimination laws. The primary emphasis of such plans, then, is not only to ensure that the employer does not discriminate, but also to ensure that the company is at least attempting to utilize minorities and women in its own workforce in proportion to the percentage of qualified minorities and women existing in the workforce as a whole. By adopting such a plan, an employer also works to ensure fair and equitable treatment of all employees and applicants in recruitment, employment, promotions, demotions, transfers, layoffs, and terminations.

In *Grutter v. Bollinger* and *Gratz v. Bollinger*, twenty-five years after it first ruled on the issue, the United States Supreme Court addressed the issue of affirmative action in the context of higher education. In two separate opinions regarding the constitutionality of the admissions policies at the University of Michigan, the Court held that the educational benefits that flow from a diverse student body present a compelling state interest that justifies the use of race as a "plus" factor, among many factors, in the admissions process. The use of race as a factor has to be "narrowly tailored" in order to meet constitutional muster. For example, the law school's admissions process, including an individualized review of each application, was sufficiently "narrowly tailored." The undergraduate school's admission process, however, was not "narrowly tailored" where minorities automatically received 20 points on a 150 point scale, with 100 points being the general admission threshold, and did not provide for individualized consideration of each application.

Along the same lines, given that the Court cited with approval (and without qualification) its prior classic decisions regarding affirmative action in employment, the Court's *Grutter/Gratz* decisions do not appear to have any significant potential impact on affirmative action in employment law.

Voluntary Affirmative Action Plans

A voluntary affirmative action plan is one that is developed by an employer on its own initiative, not under court order or required by a government agency. Affirmative action programs contained in settlement agreements and consent decrees are considered voluntary. Voluntary plans are intended to correct under-representation of minority groups in an employer's workforce, which may or may not have resulted from past discrimination, and to attain a balanced workforce (balanced, at least, in the same proportion as the overall national workforce).

A voluntary affirmative action program undertaken by an employer should be reduced to writing. The plan should detail the employer's self-analysis, the findings of the self-analysis (including the statistical comparison), the nature of the plan, how it will address the problem identified, and the duration of the plan. An unwritten plan will be far more difficult to defend if challenged pursuant to Title VII.

Under Michigan law, a company may adopt a plan to eliminate present effects of past discriminatory practices or assure equal opportunity with respect to religion, race, color, national origin, sex, or handicap if the plan is filed with and approved by the Michigan Civil Rights Commission. Although affirmative action plans that are not approved by the Commission will not necessarily be unlawful, the Michigan Supreme Court has held that such plans may give rise to a *prima facie* case of discrimination because it is clear that a protected factor, such as race or sex, has been considered in the employer's employment decision. An employer using an unapproved plan will still be allowed to argue that the plan is valid under state and federal civil rights laws, but the risk of litigation is significantly greater than it would be if the plan were pre-approved.

Mandatory Affirmative Action Plans

While the adoption of an affirmative action plan is not mandated for private employers, there are certain situations in which a private employer may nevertheless be required to formulate a plan. For example, the Michigan Civil Rights Commission and the State Administrative Board require all contractors, vendors, and suppliers who provide or seek to provide goods and services to the state, and who are not in compliance with minimum standards of minority group and female utilization, to write affirmative action plans. These written plans must include goals, timetables, outreach, and recruitment efforts to meet minimum levels of utilization for minority, religious, and ethnic groups and women equivalent to their rate of representation in the workforce where contracts are performed. Minority groups are defined as African-Americans, Native-Americans, Asians, and Hispanic-speaking or Hispanic-surnamed Americans. The Department of Civil Rights is responsible for reviewing affirmative action plans and programs. In addition, contractors are encouraged to actively solicit and assist minority subcontractors in bidding and performing work for the state.

An employer seeking to do business with the federal government also is subject to certain mandatory affirmative action requirements. Non-construction contractors are required to adopt a written affirmative action plan. Although construction contractors are not required to adopt a written plan, they must meet special requirements.

The Department of Labor's (DOL) Office of Federal Contract Compliance Programs (OFCCP) is generally responsible for administering the federal government's affirmative action mandates covering minorities and women, disabled veterans, and disabled workers. The OFCCP promotes affirmative action by preconditioning the award of a government contract on a potential contractor's ability both to comply with federal equal opportunity requirements and to take affirmative action with respect to these classifications of employees. The OFCCP can require a contractor to file a written affirmative action plan within 120 days after the contract begins. It also can cancel, terminate, or suspend a contract and bar a potential contractor from future awards, if the contractor fails to comply with affirmative action requirements.

Legal Standards for Affirmative Action Plans

1. Federal Standards

The U.S. Supreme Court has held that all *governmental* affirmative action programs—including those adopted by the federal government—will be subject to strict scrutiny if challenged. Such a standard requires the government (local, state, or federal) that has adopted the challenged plan or program to prove that any protected classification in the plan/program is narrowly tailored to advance a compelling governmental interest. Under this standard, it is not enough that the government plan was developed to remedy societal discrimination in general; rather, the plan or program must be sufficiently limited in scope and duration so as not to last longer than the discriminatory effects it was specially designed to eliminate.

Affirmative action programs initiated by private employers are expressly protected by section 116 of the federal Civil Rights Act of 1991 and are not prohibited by Title VII. However, because affirmative action plans permit employers to engage in limited preferences based on race or sex, they must meet certain criteria in order to be upheld as lawful.

Title VII requires both public and private employers to satisfy two criteria before a voluntary affirmative action program will be upheld as lawful. First, the employer must have a legitimate reason for its program. Second, the program itself should not unnecessarily impede the employment opportunities of non-minorities.

2. State Standards

On November 7, 2006, Michigan voters adopted Proposal 2, which amends the Michigan Constitution to prohibit all state and local government entities, including schools, from discriminating or granting preferential treatment based on race, sex, color, ethnicity or national origin in public employment, public education, or government contracting.

Proposal 2 amends the Michigan Constitution to provide as follows:

(1) The University of Michigan, Michigan State University, Wayne State University, and any other public college or university, community college, or school district shall not discriminate against, or grant preferential treatment to, any individual or group on the basis of race, sex, color, ethnicity, or national origin in the operation of public employment, public education or public contracting.

(2) The state shall not discriminate against, or grant preferential treatment to, any individual or group on the basis of race, sex, color, ethnicity or national origin the operation of public employment, public education, or public contracting.

(3) For the purposes of this section "state" includes, but is not necessarily limited to, the state itself, any city, county, any public college, university, or community college, school district, or other political subdivision or governmental instrumentality of or within the State of Michigan not included in sub-section 1.

(4) This section does not prohibit action that must be taken to establish or maintain eligibility for any federal program if ineligibility would result in a loss of federal funds to the state.

(5) Nothing in this section shall be interpreted as prohibiting bona fide qualifications based on sex that are reasonably necessary to the normal operation of public employment, public education, or public contracting.

(6) The remedies available for violation of this section shall be the same, regardless of the injured party's race, sex, color, ethnicity, or national origin, as are otherwise available for violations of Michigan's anti-discrimination law.

(7) This section shall be self-executing. If any part or parts of this section are found to be in conflict with the United States Constitution or federal law, the section shall be implemented to the maximum extent that the United States Constitution and federal law permit. Any provision held invalid shall be severable from the remaining portions of this section.

(8) This section applies only to action taken after the effective date of this section.

(9) This section does not invalidate any court order or consent decree that is in force as of the effective date of this section.

In accordance with Article XII, Section 2 of the Michigan Constitution, this amendment took effect "at the end of 45 days after the date of the election at which it was approved." Thus, the amendment became effective on December 23, 2006.

Since the passage of this amendment, public entities have been forced to review, amend, and in some instances, completely revamp their existing policies in an effort to comply with the new anti-affirmative action law. For example, on April 9, 2007, Attorney General Mike Cox rendered an opinion ("Opinion 7202") in which he stated that the City of Grand Rapids' policies were in violation of the newly enacted Constitutional amendment. Specifically, Opinion No. 7202 determined that the City's bid discount process "rants preferential treatment to persons or groups based on race, sex, ethnicity, or national origin." It is important to note however, that the Attorney General did not find that the City was prohibited from maintaining a bid discount process, but rather clearly stated that the City should consider amending the process to remove reliance on the unconstitutional factors of race, sex, color, ethnicity, or national origin.

In reaction to this decision, the City of Grand Rapids enlisted the help of legal counsel in an effort to determine how, if possible, their efforts to achieve diversity in the areas of contracting and employment could be maintained. The resulting policies now contain language that does not run afoul of the new anti-affirmative action amendment. For example, instead of the City providing bid discounts to Disadvantaged Business Enterprises ("DBEs") only, the scope was expanded to include any firm that demonstrates a commitment to diversity. In addition, criteria such as the geographical residency of a potential contractor's employees is also utilized as a means to attain the same sought after diversity results, without specifically stating that the incentives which may be given are for women and/or minorities.

Michigan universities and colleges are also employing some of the same creative measures utilized by Grand Rapids in an effort to maintain and improve the diversity of their student populations. For example, Wayne State amended its admission policies on December 6, 2006 by: 1) automatically accepting all students whose grades and test scores meet a certain level; and 2) by adding more than two dozen broad exceptions that can weigh in favor of students who do not reach that automatic level. For example, extra weight is now given to applicants who live in a geographical area including Detroit versus extra weight being given to Detroit residents only. Extra weight is also given to those who have lived abroad or on an

American Indian reservation versus extra weight being solely given to American Indians. Michigan universities and colleges are also maintaining their ability to provide scholarships to women and minorities by utilizing newly formed private foundations to administer scholarship monies earmarked for diverse students.

Employer's Self-Analysis

For those Michigan employers that are federal contractors and/or subcontractors, rest assure that the passage of Proposal 2 has done nothing to impact your responsibility to continue to comply with the affirmative action requirements of Executive Order 11246. In fact, the anti-affirmative action amendment specifically sates that entities receiving federal monies are exempted from the mandates of the new law. In pertinent part, art. 1, § 26(4) of the Michigan Constitution provides as follows: "This section does not prohibit action that must be taken to establish or maintain eligibility for any federal program if ineligibility would result in a loss of federal funds to the state."

Thus, it is imperative that federal contractors in Michigan continue to compile all of the data that experts recommend private employers collect in an effort to maintain and/or increase their diversity efforts. Executive Order 11246 requires all contractors to update their affirmative action plans annually. In so doing, these employers have a snapshot of what its workforce looks like, and more importantly, the trends and patterns that led to the results reflected in the diversity, or lack thereof, of their employees. For example, by collecting information about hires, promotions, transfers and terminations, a contractor can ascertain whether they are underrepresented by way of minorities or women in a particular job group. They can see, for example, whether there are more women being terminated or whether minorities are not being hired. This information is priceless with respect to a company's ability to focus on their specific diversity needs and goals e.g., retention, recruitment, training, or all of the above.

EEOC Suggestions for Employers

The EEOC has recognized that because of historic restrictions by employers, labor organizations, and others, there are circumstances in which the available pool of applicants or employees, particularly of qualified minorities and women, for employment or promotional opportunities is artificially limited. In such cases, the EEOC encourages private employers to engage in the following:

- Training plans and programs, including on-the-job training, that emphasize providing minorities and women with the opportunity, skill, and experience necessary to perform the functions of skilled trades, crafts, or professions

- Extensive and focused recruiting activity

- Elimination of the adverse impact caused by invalidated selection criteria

- Modification, through collective bargaining where a labor organization represents employees or unilaterally where one does not, of promotion and layoff procedures

These steps may be taken where there is evidence of historic barriers to entry into the trade or profession that has limited the pool of qualified African-American applicants, thereby distorting the statistical comparison.

Guidelines for Affirmative Action Plans

Once an employer's self-analysis indicates that a plan of affirmative action can be justified, there are a number of appropriate affirmative action plans that may be implemented, including:

- The establishment of a long-term goal and short-range interim goals and timetables for the specific job classifications

- A recruitment program designed to attract qualified members of the group in question

- A systematic effort to organize work and redesign jobs in ways that provide opportunities for persons lacking journeyman-level knowledge or skills to enter and, with appropriate training, to progress in a career field

- Revamping selection instruments or procedures that have not yet been validated in order to reduce or eliminate exclusionary effects on particular groups in particular job classifications

- The initiation of measures designed to assure that members of the affected group who are qualified to perform the job are included within the pool of persons from which the selecting official makes the selection

- A systematic effort to provide career advancement training, both classroom and on-the-job, to employees locked into dead-end jobs

- The establishment of a system for regularly monitoring the effectiveness of the particular affirmative action program, and procedures for making timely adjustments in this program where effectiveness is not demonstrated

Once an affirmative action program has been selected, the employer must ensure that it is reasonable in relation to the problems disclosed by the self-analysis. Two elements of a close-fitting remedy must be considered:

- The remedy should directly address and not exceed the problem disclosed.

- The affirmative action plan must have a set duration base.

Content Requirements for Federally-Required Affirmative Action Plans

Employers who are covered federal contractors or subcontractors are required by federal regulations to maintain an affirmative action plan that includes a detailed organizational profile or workforce analysis, a job group analysis, and an availability analysis, as well as statements of goals, progress, and future commitments.

Suggested Content:

1. **Title Page and Table of Contents**

    - Title page should list the contractor's name and address; EEO identification number; facility covered by the plan; and plan year

    - Title page may include the names; job titles of the individuals who prepared and approved the plan

    - Table of contents may be included to assist in organizing and locating material

2. **Confidentiality Statement**

    - AAPs and supporting documentation are subject to disclosure under the Freedom of Information Act ("FOIA") and through discovery in litigation

    - AAPs should be reviewed carefully for statements or admissions that could be used against the contractor in employment discrimination or OFCCP proceedings

    - Contractors should include a statement of confidentiality which specifies the grounds on which the plan is considered exempt from disclosure under FOIA

Required Content:

1. Organizational Profile or Workforce Analysis

An organizational display is a detailed graphical or tabular chart or similar presentation of the contractor's organizational structure. The display must identify each organizational unit in the establishment and show the relationship of each organizational unit to the other organizational units in the establishment. For each organizational unit, the organizational display must indicate the name of the unit; the job title, gender, race, and ethnicity of the unit supervisor; the total number of male and female incumbents; and the total number of male and female incumbents in each of the following groups: Blacks, Hispanics, Asians, and American Indians/Alaskan Natives.

An organizational display is used to determine whether there are any organizational units where women and minorities are underrepresented or concentrated. It is meant to be a depiction of the staffing pattern within the establishment

Contractors are permitted to use either an organizational display or a workforce analysis as their organizational profile. A workforce analysis is a listing of job titles ranked from the lowest paid to the highest paid within each department, including department supervision.

2. Job Group Analysis

A job group analysis is a method of combining job titles within a federal contractor's establishment. It is the first step taken to compare the representation of women and minorities in a contractor's workforce with the availability of women and minorities in the relevant labor market who are qualified to be employed.

Job groups are formed by combining jobs at the establishment with similar content, wage rates, and opportunities. The job group analysis must contain a list of the job titles that comprise each job group. All jobs located at an establishment must be reported in the job group analysis of the establishment.

Similarity of content refers to the duties and responsibilities of the job titles that make up the job group. Similarity of opportunities refers to training, transfers, promotions, pay, mobility, and other career enhancement opportunities offered by the jobs within the job group.

3. Report of Placement of incumbents in job groups

The contractor must separately state the percentage of minorities and the percentage of women it employs in each job group.

4. Availability determination

This is an estimate of the number of qualified minorities or women available for employment in a given job group. In determining availability, the contractor must consider an "external" factor and an "internal" factor. The "external" factor is the percentage of minorities or women with the requisite skills in the reasonable recruitment area. The "internal" factor is the percentage of minorities or women among those promotable, transferable, and trainable within the contractor's organization

The "reasonable recruitment area" is defined as the geographical area from which the contractor usually seeks or reasonably could seek workers to fill the position in question. The number of qualified minorities or women available within this area is generally determined based on data available from the U.S. Census Bureau in a compilation known as Census 2000 Special Equal Employment Opportunity data (see also http://www.census.gov/hhes/www/eeoindex.html). The contractor should be prepared to explain its rationale for selecting the particular geographic area as the "reasonable recruitment area."

The term "those trainable" refers to employees within the contractor's organization who, with appropriate training the contractor is reasonably able to provide, could become promotable or transferable during the current AAP year.

To determine the internal availability factor, a contractor must identify "feeder pools" for the job group at issue. Feeder pools are job groups from which individuals could be expected to be promoted to the job group under consideration. The contractor is required to provide an explanation for the selection of that pool (or pools) as a feeder pool for the job group and ascertain which employees could be promoted or transferred with appropriate training that the contractor is reasonably able to provide.

The availability analysis is to be done by job group. However, when a job group consists of job titles with different availability rates, the contractor must come up with a "composite availability" for the job group. A "composite availability" is to be calculated by weighting the job availability for each job title within the job group according to the proportion of employees working in each job title to the total number of employees in the job group.

5. Comparison of incumbency to availability

Once the contractor has determined an availability number (or composite number) for each job group, it must compare the percentage of minorities and women working in each job group ("incumbency") with the calculated availability for those job groups.

When the percentage of minorities or women employed in a particular job group is less than would reasonably be expected given their availability percentage in that particular job group, the contractor should establish a placement goal in its affirmative action plan.

6. Placement goals

Placement goals serve as objectives or targets reasonably attainable if the contract makes good-faith effort to implement all aspects of its affirmative action program.

When required, a contractor must establish a placement goal for a particular job group that is at least equal to the availability figure derived for women and minorities for that job group.

7. Designation of responsibility for implementation

Contractors must designate an official within the organization to be responsible for implementing the equal employment opportunity and affirmative action programs described in the affirmative action plan.

8. Identification of problem areas

Contractors must perform an in-depth analysis of their total employment process—recruitment, applications, hiring, promotions, and terminations—to determine whether and where impediments to equal employment opportunity exist.

In doing so, at a minimum, contractors should evaluate:

- The workforce by organizational unit and job group to determine whether there are problems of minority or female utilization;

- Personnel activity (applicant flow, new hires, terminations, promotions, and other personnel decisions) to determine whether there are selection disparities;

- Compensation system(s) to determine whether there are gender, race, or ethnicity based disparities;

- Selection, recruitment, referral, and other personnel procedures to determine whether they result in disparities in the employment or advancement of minorities or women; and

- Any other areas that might impact the success of the affirmative action program.

9. Action Oriented Programs

Contractors should develop and execute action oriented programs designed to correct any problem areas and meet established goals and objectives. To demonstrate a good-faith effort in this regard, a contract must generally do something more, or other than, following the same procedures that produced inadequate results in the first place. The contractor must be able to demonstrate that it made good-faith efforts to remove barriers, expand employment opportunities and produce measurable results.

10. Periodic Internal Audits

Contractors are required to develop and implement auditing procedures that periodically measures the effectiveness of their total affirmative action program. Key components include:

- Monitoring records of all personnel activity to ensure that the non-discrimination policy is carried out (this includes placements, promotions, and terminations);

- Requiring internal progress reports on a scheduled basis regarding the attainment of equal employment opportunity and organizational objectives;

- Reviewing report results with all levels of management; and

- Advising top management of program effectiveness and submitting recommendations to improve unsatisfactory performance.

Duration of Exemptions Granted by the OFCCP

Under certain circumstances, the OFCCP can exempt specific contracts or groups of contracts and facilities from the requirements of Executive Order 11246. Specifically, the director can exempt:

1. certain contracts, subcontracts, or purchase orders when special circumstances in the national interest so require;

2. a government contractor or subcontractor that is a religious corporation, association, educational institution, or society, with respect to employment of individuals of a particular religion, but not from other requirements of the order; or

3. facilities that are separate and distinct from the activities performed under a federal contract when the exemption would not "impede the effectuation of this Order."

The director of the OFCCP can withdraw an exemption, however, when in his judgment such action is necessary or appropriate to achieve the purposes of the order. Withdrawal of the exemption does not apply to contracts or subcontracts made prior to the withdrawal. In other words, any contract or subcontract that is in existence BEFORE the OFCCP withdraws its exemption, will not be affected (*i.e.*, submission of an AAP will not be required for those particular contracts and/or facilities).

Record Retention

A contractor or subcontractor must maintain their current AAP and the AAP submitted the previous year. There is no indication in the law or its regulations that suggests that an AAP must be kept in a particular location (such as a corporate headquarters). The AAP should likely be maintained at each particular facility since the purpose of compiling an AAP is to provide the contractor(s) with a self-evaluation tool.

As previously discussed, an AAP must be updated annually. However, there is no specific due date outlined in the statutes or implementing regulations. Thus, it is reasonable to assume that an AAP will be due on the day it was prepared the previous year.

CHAPTER 7: Immigration Reform and Control Act

The Immigration Reform and Control Act of 1986 ("**IRCA**") gave rise to several important issues and liabilities for employers. Two of the most important employer problems are:

- Employers are expected to verify employment authorization and to investigate an employee if the employer has actual or constructive knowledge that an employee is or has become unauthorized to work in the U.S.

- Employers may be investigated for unfair immigration-related employment practices if the employer's inquiry goes beyond the requirements of the Form I-9 instructions and IRCA regulations. Complaints by protected individuals may be filed with the Office of Special Counsel for Immigration Related Unfair Employment Practices ("**OSC**"), in the Department of Justice's Civil Rights Division. If a complaint is substantiated, the employer may be subject to extensive fines.

Verification and Form I–9 Requirements

Since November 6, 1986, all employers are required to have new employees complete Form I-9, Employment Eligibility Verification, within three (3) business days of hire. The employee must present the appropriate documentation as specified in the United States Citizenship and Immigration Services ("**USCIS**") regulations, and the documentation must demonstrate the individual's identity and authorization to work in the U.S. Employers are prohibited from specifying which specific documents on the list will be accepted to demonstrate identity and authorization to work in the U.S. Employers are also prohibited from discriminating against employees based on citizenship, intended citizenship, and national origin. IRCA has broadened employees' rights beyond those provided under Title VII of the Civil Rights Act of 1964.

All employers in the U.S. must examine documents presented by individuals at the time of hiring. The documents presented by the employee must appear to be genuine on their face and show that they relate to the employee. Employers must determine whether the documents presented by the employee are from List A or Lists B and C of Form I–9. After receiving the documents, the employer must review Section 1 of the Form I–9 to determine whether it is completed correctly and must complete and sign Section 2 of the form.

The completed Form I–9 must then be maintained by the employer for three years from the date of hire or for one year after the employer-employee relationship ends, whichever is later. As long as an employee remains employed, the employer should retain the Form I-9. The previous sentence refers to the retention of Form I-9 when the employer/employee relationship ends.

Additionally, an employer must re-verify the work authorization of an employee whose work authorization expires during the term of employment. Section 3 of Form I–9 should be used for this purpose. The reverification of Form I-9 should be completed prior to the expiration of the employee's work authorization. The employer should provide the employee with the List of Acceptable Documents for purposes of completing Form I-9, and the employee should, once again, choose which documents to provide for the reverification process.

If an employee is unable to provide sufficient documents to complete the Form I-9 within the required period of time, or if the employee's work authorization has expired (except in the case where a timely renewal has been sought), the employer must terminate the employment. The employer should note that in some cases, an employee's work authorization may continue for 240 days after the timely filing of a request for extension of status.

On April 28, 2005, a new I-9 law designed to assist employers with the processing and storage of I-9 Employment Verification forms became effective. The new law introduces two important changes to the I-9 verification process. In particular, the new law will allow attestations on the Form I-9 to be made by an electronic signature in lieu of a traditional original signature on the actual paper form. Secondly, it will also allow employers to now retain and store I-9 forms in electronic format, in addition to the normal paper, microfilm or microfiche storage methods.

The Department of Homeland Security's Bureau of Immigration and Customs Enforcement (ICE) issued an interim rule on June 15, 2006, which defines what types of electronic signatures will be deemed acceptable under the new law, as well as what methods of electronic storage will be considered compliant. The specific requirements are available from the Federal Register Vol. 71, No 115, Thursday, June 15, 2006 Pages 34510 – 34517.

New I-9 Forms

In November 2007, the Department of Homeland Security issued a new version of the I-9 form. The new form contains an updated List of Acceptable Documents. The current version (as of December 2008) is Rev. 06/05/07N. Additionally, in August 2008, the USCIS announced that it will accept the new passport card as an acceptable "List A" document to establish identity and employment eligibility.

The new I-9 form is included in the forms section of this publication (as well as on the HR Michigan web site www.hrmichigan.com). Form I–9 can also be obtained from the USCIS by calling 1-800-375-5283, or by computer download from www.uscis.gov under the "Immigration Forms" section. Employers should continually check the USCIS website to be sure they are using the proper version of Form I-9.

Penalties for Violating IRCA

An employer should know that IRCA provides for penalties for various I-9 violations. For instance, failure to inspect documents and to create and maintain Form I–9 for every employee hired after November 6, 1986 can result in fines.

If the employer knowingly hires or continues to employ an employee who has become unauthorized to work in the U.S., the employer may be fined (under a three-tiered system) from $375 to $16,000 for each unauthorized worker depending on whether it is the employer's first, second, or third violation.

Also, if an employer has engaged in a pattern or practice of knowingly employing unauthorized workers, the employer may be put in jail for up to six months and fined $3,000 for each unauthorized worker, in addition to the (remove $10,000) fine for each unauthorized worker.

Avoiding Employer Sanctions—IRCA

Employers should develop a standard written policy on I-9 compliance. The policy can be used as a guide for employees charged with completing and maintaining I-9s in accordance with the USCIS regulations. The policy should instruct the employees on best practices for I-9 completion, re verification and retention.

It is recommended that employers consult with qualified immigration legal counsel in matters related to I-9 compliance. It is also recommended that the employer complete (or have immigration legal counsel complete) an internal audit of their I-9 forms to be sure that the employer is in compliance.

Antidiscrimination Provisions of IRCA

Employers of four or more employees are prohibited from engaging in unfair immigration-related employment practices in the hiring process on the basis of citizenship, intended citizenship, or national origin. Those protected from citizenship discrimination include U.S. citizens as well as lawful permanent residents, legalized aliens, refugees, and those claiming asylum who declare an intention to become U.S. citizens.

Avoiding Discrimination Liability—IRCA

To avoid liability under the antidiscrimination provision of IRCA, employers should:

- never request or suggest that an employee present particular documents from Lists A, B, or C of Form I–9. The employee has a right to decide which documents to present to the employer (i.e., one document from List A, or a document from List B and a document from List C).

- limit prescreening of job applicants to written statements that inquire: Are you legally authorized to work in the U.S.? Will you now or in the future require sponsorship for employment visa status?

U.S. Bureau of Immigration and Customs Enforcement Audits

The most prominent procedure used by the U.S. Bureau of Immigration and Customs Enforcement ("**ICE**") in selecting employers for audits is to respond to actual information or tips. However, under IRCA, there is no need to establish probable cause to request inspection of I–9 forms. Inspections are sometimes scheduled at random using tax withholding records and by targeting industries designated by each ICE district (e.g., manufacturing, construction, hotel, restaurant, food processing, business and personal service, and apparel and textile).

Notice of ICE Inspection

- IRCA requires that employers be given three days notice of the ICE's intention to conduct an inspection. Employers may consent to inspection on less than three days notice, although this is generally not advisable. No notice is required, however, in a lead-driven investigation if ICE has probable-cause, evidence of a violation and a warrant to enter the premise to inspect the I–9 forms.

Preparing for an ICE Inspection

- Always review the Notice of Inspection (NOI). Some NOIs are accompanied by subpoenas requesting specific personnel and payroll documents. Determine whether the inspecting agency is ICE or the U.S. Department of Labor ("**DOL**"). Only ICE may commence enforcement proceedings.

- Be aware that a subpoena requires a court order for enforcement and an employer can insist upon a court order without incurring penalties, whereas a warrant is a court order for which an employer can be penalized for noncompliance.

- Instruct employees not to destroy documents covered by the scope of the investigation or to falsify or "backdate" any information on any documents.

- Review I–9 records to determine level of compliance. Determine the number of paperwork violations and the number of hiring, recruiting, and referral violations. An employer should make corrections to the forms to demonstrate its good-faith compliance. Any changes or additions must be initialed and dated as of the date of the amendment of the form to avoid an obstruction-of-justice charge. If there is no I–9 form for an employee, prepare one and date it as of the date of creation.

- Prepare a list of all employees, including the date of hire and termination, as attorney-client work product. The employer should determine who are employees, who may be grandfathered (those hired before November 7, 1986), who performs services outside the U.S., who worked for the employer less than three days, which individuals are not receiving wages or other remuneration in the U.S. (such as B–1 employees), and which are independent contractors. The list may later be given to ICE to possibly eliminate their requests for additional information.

- Determine whether there have been previous visits by ICE and whether any citations or warnings have been issued.

- Assess I–9 verification policies and practices.

- Determine whether the knowing hire of unauthorized aliens has occurred, and whether any of those aliens are currently working for the employer. Suspend or terminate employees if proper verification cannot be completed prior to inspection.

> **Caution**: Termination of employees may raise IRCA discrimination violation issues and/or violations of employment or union contracts issues.

- Separate verification records from other records. ICE should not be given full personnel files of employees, since these files contain private information that is not germane to their investigation.

- Assess whether records should be brought to ICE or whether the employer should select a location on the business premises for conducting the inspection.

- Tour the employer's business premises to assess whether the appearance of employer business operations might raise further questions.

- If ICE has requested additional documentation, decide on the employer's response. For example, should the employer completely comply with the ICE request for documents or should the employer decline to provide any records other than the I-9 forms.

During an ICE Inspection

- Accompany government inspectors at all times when on the employer's premises.

- If the government inspector does anything other than audit the I-9 records, state to the inspector that consent for anything else has not been given. Even casual acts might be considered as consent, thereby potentially eliminating the need of the inspector to obtain a warrant. Employers have the right to insist that the government bring a warrant before it may enter employer premises to conduct a workforce survey or a search for verification records.

- Make copies of all records the government inspector wants to take with him/her.

- Ask for a receipt of all documents the inspector takes with him/her.

CHAPTER 8: Wage and Hour Issues

Michigan Wage and Fringe Benefits Act

The Michigan Wages and Fringe Benefits Act (MWFBA), commonly referred to as the "Payment of Wages and Fringe Benefits Act," was enacted in 1978 to regulate the time and manner of the payment of wages and fringe benefits.

One of its goals was to prevent employers from resorting to self-help in order to collect money owed to them for any reason by their employees.

Employers Subject to MWFBA

The statute covers all public and private employers employing one or more individuals. "Employer" includes:

- an individual, sole proprietorship, partnership, association, or corporation;
- the state of Michigan or an agency of the state;
- a city, county, village, township, school district, intermediate school district, or institution of higher education; or
- an individual acting directly or indirectly in the interest of such an employer.

"Employ" means to engage or permit to work.

Purpose of the MWFBA

The MWFBA regulates the payment of wages and fringe benefits. It also prohibits certain actions by employers with respect to wages and fringe benefits. "Wages" include all earnings regardless of whether determined on the basis of time, task, piece, commission, etc., for labor or services except those earnings defined as fringe benefits. "Fringe benefits" include compensation due an employee for:

- Holidays
- Time off for sickness or injury
- Time off for personal reasons or vacation
- Bonuses
- Authorized expenses incurred during the course of employment
- Contributions made on behalf of an employee

The statute does not mandate the provision of any particular fringe benefit or set of fringe benefits, but requires an employer to provide those fringe benefits specified by written contract or written policy. Promises of fringe benefits not reduced to writing are outside of the MWFBA's coverage. In addition, where payment is specified to occur at termination, it cannot be withheld unless agreed upon in writing, obtained with the full and free consent of the employee without intimidation or fear of discharge for refusing to agree.

Payment of Wages

All employers (other than those who employ individuals who harvest crops by hand) are required to pay their employees:

- on or before the first day of each calendar month, all wages earned during the first 15 days of the preceding calendar month, and

- on or before the 15th day of each calendar month, all the wages earned during the preceding calendar month from the 16th day to the end of the month.

Unless:

- The employer has established a regularly scheduled weekly or biweekly payday where such payday occurs on or before the 14th day following the work period in which the wages were earned; or

- The employer has established a monthly payday where the employer pays to the employee on or before the first day of each calendar month all wages earned during the preceding calendar month.

Employers employing individuals who hand-harvest crops must pay all wages earned in a week on or before the second day following the workweek unless another method of payment is agreed upon by written contract.

Nothing in the statute precludes an employer from paying wages more often than required by the statute.

All wages are to be paid in United States currency or by a negotiable check or draft payable upon presentation at a bank or established business without discount. Effective January 1, 2005, the Michigan Legislature amended the MWFBA to expressly permit employers to pay wages to their employees by payroll debit card.

Wages may not be deposited, electronically or otherwise, in a bank, credit union or savings and loan association, or through payroll debit cards unless the employee consents. Such consent must be given "freely," meaning without intimidation, coercion or fear of discharge or reprisal for refusal to permit the deposit. This provision covers both current as well as prospective employees. The 2005 amendments permit employers to pay employees by payroll debit cards without obtaining their written consent if they were issuing payroll debit cards to at least one employee as of January 1, 2005.

Payment of Wages Upon Termination

When the employment relationship is terminated, the MWFBA requires an employer to pay the employee all wages earned and due as soon as the amount can, with due diligence, be determined. Fringe benefits due an employee at termination must also be paid on the regularly scheduled payday for the period in which the termination occurs, unless otherwise specified in the terms of a written contact or written policy. In the case of employees who hand-harvest crops, the statute requires payment no later than three days after termination.

Note, however, that regulations interpreting this section of the MWFBA are far more stringent. Under the 1998 amendments, employees who quit or are discharged must receive payment of all wages due on the regularly scheduled payday for the period in which the termination occurs. Employees engaged in hand-harvesting must receive payment within one working day of termination.

With respect to employees working under a contract who are terminated, voluntarily or involuntarily, and the amount due cannot be determined until termination of the contract, employers must pay all wages as nearly as they can be estimated, as soon as the amount can with due diligence be determined. Final payment must be made in full at the termination of the contract.

Deducting Wages

Various kinds of deductions, including required charitable contributions and kickbacks, are forbidden under the MWFBA.

The statute forbids any deductions from an employee's wages, both directly or indirectly, without the full, free and written consent of the employee, obtained without intimidation or fear of discharge for refusal to permit the deduction, except those:

- required or expressly permitted by law; or
- required or expressly permitted by a collective bargaining agreement.

Except with respect to the overpayment of wages and/or fringe benefits, a deduction made for the benefit of the employer must have written consent from the employee for each wage payment subject to deduction, and the cumulative amount of the deductions may not reduce the gross wages paid to less than the minimum wage.

Example: Deducting Wages

An employer who loans an employee money is prohibited from unilaterally deducting the repayment from the employee's pay check unless, for each occasion, the employee has freely signed a consent. Alternatively, the employer can sue the delinquent employee in court and then collect on any judgment it thereafter obtains.

A deduction made for the benefit of the employer—such as reimbursement for damage to employer's property—requires a separate written authorization for each payment subject to deduction. On the other hand, deductions made for the benefit of the employee—such as periodic health-insurance premium contributions—require a one time written authorization.

An employer or his or her agent may not require any fees, gifts, tips, gratuities, or other remuneration or consideration from an employee as a condition of employment or continuation of employment. This section has been interpreted to prohibit "tuition contracts" which an applicant was required to sign as a condition of being hired, under which employees must repay their employer for employer-provided training in the event that employees do not remain employed for a specified period of time. (On the other hand, an employer's offer to fund employees' education with the understanding that the employees will repay, unless they remain with the employer for a specific period do not violate this provision.) Similarly, in at least one unpublished Michigan Court of Appeals decision, a claim against a restaurant asserting that "tip pooling" violated the MWFBA was allowed to proceed.

An employer may not require any employee or person seeking employment to contribute directly or indirectly to a charitable, social or beneficial purpose as a condition of employment or continuation of employment unless required or expressly permitted by law or by a collective bargaining agreement.

Overpayment of Wages or Fringe Benefits

Employers have the legal right, under certain specified conditions, to deduct a direct overpayment of wages or fringe benefits directly from an employee's paycheck without the employee's written consent, if such deduction is made within six months of the overpayment.

The overpayment deduction can only take place if all of the following conditions are met:

1. The overpayment resulted from a mathematical miscalculation, typographical error, clerical error, or misprint in the processing of the employee's regularly scheduled wages or fringe benefits.

2. The miscalculation, error or misprint described above was made by the employer, the employee or a representative of the employer or employee.

3. The employer provides the employee with a written explanation of the deduction at least one pay period before the wage payment affected by the deduction is made.

4. The deduction is not greater than 15% of the gross wages earned in the pay period in which the deduction is made.

5. The deduction is made after the employer has made all deductions expressly permitted or required by law or a collective bargaining agreement, and after any employee-authorized deduction.

6. The deduction does not reduce the regularly scheduled gross wages otherwise due the employee to a rate that is less than the higher of the then-current state or federal minimum wage.

Any employee who feels that his or her employer has violated the conditions of this statute has 12 months from the date of the alleged violation to file a complaint with the Michigan Department of Labor and Economic Growth, Bureau of Workers' & Unemployment Compensation (BWUC), Wage and Hour Division.

Employee Contributions to Political Committees

An employer may not make any deduction, other than for overpayments, from an employee's paycheck without the full, free and written consent of the employee, obtained without intimidation or fear of discharge for refusal to permit the deduction. Deductions that represent employee contributions to political action committees established under section 55 of Michigan's Campaign Finance Act are specifically referenced in this provision of the law as requiring a written consent.

Section 55 of the Campaign Finance Act was itself amended by Public Act 117 of 1994, to require that any employees who are contributing to any candidate, ballot, or other political committee separately established by the employer pursuant to an automatic payroll deduction plan must be given the opportunity to affirmatively consent to the deduction at least once every calendar year.

Recordkeeping Requirements of MWFBA

In general, employers are required to maintain certain information regarding each of their employees that are subject to the MWFBA, as well as provide their employees with information regarding their wages and the deductions.

Employers must maintain a record for each employee of the following information:

- Name
- Address
- Birth date
- Occupation or work classification
- Basic rate of pay
- Total hours worked in each pay period
- Separate itemization of deductions
- Listing or itemization of fringe benefits (where there are ten or more employees receiving the same benefits, a centralized listing or itemization may be utilized)

Employers must furnish to each employee on each payday a statement containing:

- Hours worked
- Gross wages paid
- Identification of pay period
- Itemization of deductions (and for each hand harvester paid on a piece-work basis, the total number of units harvested by the employee)

Records must be maintained for three years and may be inspected by the Director of the Department of Labor and Economic Growth or an authorized representative at any reasonable time.

Employers need not keep records showing hours worked nor furnish statements of hours worked by employees employed in a bona fide executive, administrative, or professional capacity (including an employee employed in the capacity of academic administrative personnel or teacher in an elementary or secondary school).

Retaliation Prohibitions—MWFBA

Retaliation by the employer against an employee is prohibited by the MWFBA. An employer may not discharge or discriminate against an employee because the employee:

- filed a complaint
- instituted or caused to be instituted a proceeding under or regulated by the Act
- testified or is about to testify in a proceeding
- exercised a right under the Act on behalf of himself/herself or others

An employee who believes he or she has been discharged for one of these reasons or otherwise discriminated against by the employer may file a complaint with the BWUC. The complaint must be filed within 30 days of the alleged discrimination/retaliation.

Claims of retaliation will be investigated by the BWUC. Where discrimination or retaliation has occurred, the BWUC can order rehiring or reinstatement with back pay.

Disclosure of Wages

The MWFBA contains an unusual provision relating to the disclosure by any employee of the wages he or she has received. Employers may not discharge, discipline or otherwise discriminate against (for example, in promotion or job advancement) an employee who discloses his or her wages. Moreover, employers may not require as a condition of employment, nondisclosure by an employee of his or her wages or require an employee to sign a waiver or other document that claims to deny the right to disclose his or her wages.

Enforcement of MWFBA

Complaints must be filed with the Michigan Department of Labor and Economic Growth, Bureau of Workers' & Unemployment Compensation, Wage and Hour Division, within 12 months of the alleged violation, and within 30 days of any alleged retaliation.

The Wage and Hour Division will investigate and attempt to informally resolve the complaint. Where the Wage and Hour Division is unable to do this, it will issue a determination as to the merits of the complaint, including any violations of the MWFBA as well as specific penalties assessed, if any.

Where the Wage and Hour Division determines that the employer has violated the statute, it can order the employer to pay the following:

- Back wages due to the employee
- Fringe benefits due to or on behalf of an employee in accordance with the terms of written contract or policy
- A penalty of 10% annually on wages and fringe benefits owed
- Exemplary damages of up to twice the amount of wages and fringe benefits due where the violation is flagrant or repeated
- Attorney fees, hearing and transcript costs, and civil money penalty of not more than $1,000

Either party may appeal an adverse decision by the Wage and Hour Division to an Administrative Law Judge within 14 days. After a hearing, the Administrative Law Judge will issue his or her findings, which, unless appealed, constitute the final disposition of the case. Either party may appeal an adverse decision by the Administrative Law Judge to the circuit court.

While an employee generally is entitled to file an action in state court against the employer regarding alleged violations of this statute, he or she may be required to pursue his or her administrative remedies prior to initiating any legal action.

Penalties for Violating MWFBA

- Violation of the MWFBA is a misdemeanor.

- Failure to pay wages and fringe benefits with intent to defraud is a misdemeanor resulting in a fine of not more than $1,000, not more than one year in prison, or both.

- Issuance of a check or other order for payment of wages by an employer who knows or should know that a check will not be honored is a misdemeanor resulting in a fine of not more than $1,000, not more than one year in prison, or both.

- Either of the following is *prima facie* evidence that the person at the time of issuance of the check or other order knew or should have known it would not be paid:

  - There was no account with the drawee at the time of issuance.

  - There were insufficient funds or credit with the drawee at the time of the issuance, and the employer failed, within five days of receiving notice of nonpayment, to pay the check.

Debarment Penalties

In her first Executive Order ("EO 2003-1") after taking office in 2003, Governor Jennifer Granholm mandated that any company doing business with the State of Michigan could be "debarred" or prevented from further business if such company violated certain state laws, including the MWFBA. Implemented pursuant to EO 2003-1, the Michigan Department of Management and Budget's ("DMB") debarment policy permits the DMB to debar any company upon a finding that the company (or an officer or 25% owner), "repeated[ly] or flagrant[ly]" violates the MWFBA. DMB will provide notice of the proposed debarment to a company subject to debarment in writing. The company must reply to the notice and request a hearing within twenty (20) calendar days. Failure to respond within 20 days will automatically result in debarment. After a hearing on the merits, a company subject to debarment may file a written protest to the Director of the DMB within ten (10) days. The DMB policy permits debarment for a period of up to eight (8) years. In June 2005, the DMB issued its first debarment under the new policy, debarring a company from doing business with the State of Michigan until 2013.

Reciprocity with Other States and Canada

The director of the Michigan Department of Labor and Economic Growth, Bureau of Workers' & Unemployment Compensation, Wage and Hour Division, may enter into reciprocal agreements with other states, Canada, or a Canadian province or territory for the collection of claims for wages, fringe benefits and penalties assessed under the statute.

Fair Labor Standards Act

Enacted in 1938, the Fair Labor Standards Act (FLSA) is a federal statute that was part of the New Deal social legislation passed during the Depression. The Act was intended to eliminate those labor conditions found by Congress to be "detrimental to the maintenance of the minimum standard of living necessary for health, efficiency, and general well-being of workers" employed in those industries engaged in commerce or in the production of goods for commerce. Since its enactment, it has been amended on many different occasions, generally to raise the minimum wage or expand coverage of the Act or both.

On April 23, 2004 the U.S. Department of Labor ("DOL") completed the most comprehensive overhaul of the FLSA in over fifty years and issued new regulations regarding what are commonly called the "white collar" exemptions (e.g., executive, administrative, professional, outside sales and computer employees). These changes are significant for the simple fact that the new regulations redefine which employees need not receive overtime (i.e., exempt) and which employees may be entitled to overtime for any time worked over forty hours in a work week (i.e., non-exempt). The DOL has been following through on its pronouncement after the 2004 amendment that it would vigorously enforce the new regulations by conducting audits of various companies across the country, including in Michigan. In addition the DOL has streamlined the process for obtaining opinion letters from the Wage and Hour Administrator, resulting in an increase in the number of interpretive opinion letters issued by the Administrator.

Employers Subject to FLSA

The term "employer" as used in the statute is broad in scope and includes any person acting directly or indirectly in the interest of a covered employer in relation to any employee and also includes a public agency.

The requirements of the FLSA extend to employers who are engaged in commerce or the production of goods for commerce, or who are handling, selling, or otherwise working on goods or materials that have been moved in or produced for commerce; and that has an annual gross volume of sales made or business done that is not less than $500,000 (exclusive of excise taxes at the retail level that are separately stated).

As defined under the FLSA, an "enterprise" is not merely an individual facility or company, but can include any related activities that have a common business purpose regardless of the organizational arrangement.

In addition, hospitals; institutions primarily engaged in the care of the sick, the aged, or the mentally ill (who reside on the premises); a school for the mentally or physically disabled or gifted children; and a preschool, elementary school, secondary school, or an institution of higher learning also are covered automatically regardless of the amount of business done or their actual involvement with interstate commerce.

Employers that are not covered by the FLSA are generally covered by Michigan's Minimum Wage Law (MMWL) of 1964, which applies to any company or person who employs two or more employees at any one time in a calendar year. The MMWL has many of the same requirements as the federal FLSA (although not as many exemptions) and its provisions are generally interpreted in a manner consistent with the federal statute. Further, effective July 1, 2008, Michigan's minimum wage ($7.40 per hour) is higher than the current federal minimum of $6.55 per hour, meaning Michigan employers must pay the state's higher minimum wage. The Federal minimum wage is set to increase to $7.25 per hour effective July 24, 2009.

Employees or Independent Contractors?

While "employees" are covered by the FLSA, independent contractors are not. In determining who is an employee under the FLSA (and therefore entitled to its protection), it is important to consider the statute's definitions of employee and employ. An "employee" is any individual employed by an employer. To "employ" means to suffer or permit to work.

An employer would do well to remember Senator (and later Supreme Court Justice) Hugo Black's remark that the FLSA contains "the broadest definition [of employment] that has ever been included in any one Act."

Judicial Construction

The following key principles generally guide the courts in determining whether an employment relationship exists:

- The FLSA is remedial in nature and therefore is given a liberal construction by the courts.

- Calling someone an independent contractor is insufficient, by itself, to establish that no employment relationship exists.

- Neither contractual language nor the subjective intent of the parties in a labor agreement can override the economic realities of the situation as determined to exist by a Court.
- The employee cannot waive his or her rights under the FLSA.

In an early FLSA case, the U.S. Supreme Court held that in order to determine whether an employee-employer relationship exists, the economic realities of the relationship are paramount.

Currently, courts weigh several factors, in light of the facts of each case, to determine whether an individual is an employee or an independent contractor. These factors include:

- **Degrees of control:** Does the alleged employer exercise control over the manner of performance (employee) as opposed to merely setting objectives (independent contractor)?
- **Investment:** Does the individual have an investment in equipment, i.e., risk capital? (Risk capital is consistent with being an independent contractor.)
- **Opportunities for profit and loss:** Is the worker presented with the opportunity to make a profit and suffer a business loss (independent contractor), or merely collect wages (employee)?
- **Permanency of relationship:** Is the relationship indefinite or of long duration? (The longer in duration, the more likely it is to be viewed as supporting the conclusion that an employer-employee relationship exists.)
- **Skill:** Does the individual provide a skill not readily obtainable elsewhere, using independent judgment (independent contractor), or is the work routine and uncomplicated (employee)?
- **Integrated part of the normal operation of business:** Does the individual perform an indispensable part of the alleged employer's business operation on an ongoing basis? (This is consistent with an employment relationship.)

In addition, courts rely on the criteria used by the Internal Revenue Service to determine the existence of an employer-employee relationship (see page 31 for the IRS Revenue Ruling's 20 factors). The courts must consider the circumstances of the whole activity; no one factor is decisive.

Employees or Trainees?

Trainees may be employees under the FLSA, depending on the circumstances. Generally, trainees have been deemed employees where the employer primarily benefits from the trainee's work. The Wage and Hour Division Administrator of the U.S. Department of Labor relies upon the following six criteria to make this determination:

1. Whether the training is for the trainee's benefit;
2. Whether the trainee displaces regular employees and works under close observation;
3. Whether the training is similar to training that would be provided in a vocational school;
4. Whether the employer obtains an immediate advantage from the trainee's work;
5. Whether the trainee will be hired at the end of the training period; and
6. Whether the employer and the trainee understand that the trainee will not be paid for the hours spent in training.

The Wage and Hour Administrator reaffirmed these factors and advised an employer in a recent Opinion Letter that the employer's "job view" program did not establish an employment relationship under the FLSA. Under the employer's program, the potential employees would spend about 7.5 hours observing the job before being offered a position. The employer maintained that the job view program would reduce turnover and employees might refrain from quitting current jobs to take work that might not suit them well. According to the Administrator, the job view program did not establish an employment relationship so long as the applicants were clearly advised that they had not been hired prior to the proposed job view day. As a practical matter, however, employers should remain mindful that there are a small number of circumstances in which trainees will not be covered by the FLSA.

Recordkeeping Requirements of FLSA

The FLSA requires every employer to "make, keep, and preserve such records of the persons employed by him and of the wages, hours, and other conditions and practices of employment maintained by him ... as [the Secretary of Labor] shall prescribe ... ." The Secretary has published regulations requiring that certain information be kept for either two or three years. The key requirements are given below:

Three Years

The following information must be recorded and kept for three years for those employees to whom the employer must pay minimum wage or minimum wage and overtime:

- Employee's full name, as well as any identifying number or symbol
- Home address (including zip code)

- Date of birth (if under 19 years of age)
- Sex
- Occupation in which employed
- Time of day and day of week on which workweek begins
- Regular hourly rate (for weeks in which overtime is due), the basis on which wages are paid (if different from the already mentioned hourly rate), and all payments that are excluded from the regular rate
- Hours worked each workday and the total hours worked in each workweek
- Total daily or weekly straight time earnings or wages (excluding overtime)
- Total premium pay for overtime hours for the workweek (excluding all straight time earnings)
- Total additions to or deductions from wages paid in each pay period (i.e., wage assignments)
- Total wages paid in each pay period
- Date of payment and the pay period covered by the payment
- Any retroactive wage payment being made under government supervision

Two Years

Basic employment and earnings records (i.e., time and earnings cards or sheets that contain daily starting and stopping times or other data that determine in whole or in part the earnings or wages of the employees) must be kept for two years.

Posting Requirements of FLSA

An employer must post a notice regarding the requirements of the FLSA where the employees can readily see it. Such posters are available from the U.S. DOL or the Michigan Chamber of Commerce.

Hours Worked

The FLSA requires a record of and compensation for all hours actually worked by non-exempt employees (rather than the average number of hours or an arbitrary figure even where agreed to by an employee).

In determining the actual hours worked, it is important to keep in mind that the FLSA defines "employ" as permitting to work. This concept is broad in scope; it strongly implies, and the courts have held, that the employer need not affirmatively act in order for there to be compensable work. Under the statute, mere knowledge by an employer of work performed by an employee on the employer's behalf is sufficient.

> **EXAMPLE: DETERMINING HOURS WORKED**
> An employee who stays beyond his normal quitting time to complete an assigned project or task without being asked or authorized to do so but where the employer is aware of the situation has probably performed compensable work under the statute.

Activities that frequently prove troublesome to employers in determining actual hours worked are listed below.

Conferences

Time spent by the employee in training or attending training conferences need not be counted as work time where all the following criteria are met:

- Attendance is outside the employee's regular work hours.
- Attendance is voluntary.
- The course, lecture or meeting is not directly related to the employee's job.
- The employee does not perform any productive work during such attendance.

Attendance is not considered voluntary if the employee is given to understand or led to believe that his or her present employment would be adversely affected by his or her nonattendance.

Where the employee on his or her own initiative attends a course or seminar by an independent entity, the time is not generally considered work for his or her employer even if the course given is related to his or her job.

Employer Sponsored Volunteer Activities

Many employers sponsor or host activities that benefit a charitable cause. Typically employees are asked to volunteer their time outside their normal working hours, but there are no overt ramifications if an employee chooses not to participate. The issue that consequently arises is whether the time spent volunteering by employees at the charitable activity is compensable time under the Act. Under the FLSA, time spent voluntarily in such activities outside an employees' normal working hours is not counted as hours worked so long as the volunteer activities are not the same or similar to the activities the employee is employed to perform. The regulations are equally clear, however, that time spent in work for public or charitable purposes at the employer's request, or under his direction or control, or while the employee is required to be on the premises, is working time.

Travel Time

TO AND FROM WORK

Such time is not compensable unless there is an express provision of a written or unwritten contract or a custom or practice in effect at the time of the activity that makes travel to and from work compensable.

BETWEEN JOB SITES

Time spent by employees, as a part of their normal duties, traveling between various job sites is generally counted as work time.

TO AND FROM CONFERENCES

Travel by means of public conveyance (e.g. plane, train, bus, etc.) to and from work-related conferences or seminars that keeps an employee away from home overnight is considered to be work time when it cuts across the employee's workday.

If the employee travels on what normally is a nonworking day (i.e., Saturday or Sunday), this time also is compensable where the travel cuts across what is typically the employee's daily work schedule (i.e., where the employee's daily work schedule is from 8:00 AM to 5:00 PM, Monday through Friday, he or she must be compensated for travel on Saturday or Sunday between 8:00 AM and 5:00 PM). The DOL has taken the position that, as an enforcement policy, it will consider overnight travel that occurs outside of an employee's normal work schedule and by means of public conveyance as not compensable.

Because it is only a DOL enforcement policy, it does not preclude an employee from bringing suit under the FLSA in order to obtain payment for all such overnight travel regardless of when it occurs.

On-call Time

The time spent by an employee waiting to work may be compensable time depending on whether, based on all the circumstances, the employee can use the waiting time effectively for his or her own purposes. Some common examples are listed below:

- When the employee is required to remain on the employer's premises or so close to it that he or she cannot use the time effectively for his or her own purposes, such time is compensable.

- If the employee is merely required to let company officials know where or how he or she may be reached, he or she is not working while on call.

- If the employee is equipped with a beeper, this is generally not considered work time.

- In any case, all time actually spent responding to any such a call(s) is considered work time.

Doffing and Donning Work Clothes

In November 2005, the United States Supreme Court ruled in *IBP, Inc. v. Alvarez* that the time spent walking between a changing area and a production area should be compensated under the Fair Labor Standards Act ("FLSA") if the employees are required to don and doff protective and safety gear in that changing area. IBP had conceded that the changing time was compensable, but argued that the time employees thereafter spent walking to the production floor should be non-compensable.

The Supreme Court held that the whistle blows and the time clock starts when an employee begins his/her first principal activity, in this case, donning the already noted protective gear. Whereas, the time clock stops running when the employee finishes his/her last principal activity, namely doffing the protective gear. With the exception of non-compensable break times, such as meal periods, anything occurring after the employee's first principal activity and before his/her last principal activity, including walking from the changing area to his/her work station, is also compensable time.

Dealing with a few related issues, the Court also ruled that time spent waiting to don integral and indispensable gear prior to shift start (unless the employer is responsible for the employee being required to wait) is non-compensable time because it occurs before the work day begins. Conversely, if an employee must wait to doff his/her integral and indispensable gear at shift end, that waiting time is compensable because, in that instance, the waiting occurs during the workday.

Tours of Duty

The DOL has taken the position that an employee who is on duty for less than 24 hours is working for the entire tour of duty even though he or she is permitted to sleep or engage in other personal activities when not busy.

Where an employee is required to be on duty for 24 hours or more, the employer and the employee may agree to exclude from hours worked *bona fide* meal periods and a *bona fide* regularly scheduled sleeping period of not more than eight hours.

- There must be express or implied agreement excluding the meal and sleep time from hours worked.

- There must be adequate facilities for sleeping and the employee must be able to enjoy an uninterrupted night's sleep.

- If the employee's sleep is interrupted by a call to duty, the interruption must be counted as hours worked. Where sleep is interrupted to the extent that the employee cannot get a reasonable night's sleep (at least five hours), the entire period must be included as work time.

Working for Related Organizations

Non-exempt employees who work at two different offices or departments of the same company must total the hours for that workweek and, if over 40 hours, must be paid overtime for the excess hours.

Where employees work for two different subsidiaries of the same parent company or for the parent company and a subsidiary, it is probable that the two companies would be found to be joint employers and that, as a result, the hours worked in a single workweek must be combined in order to determine overtime.

Minimum Wage under FLSA and State Law

Section 6 of the FLSA requires that employees be paid not less than the greater of the state or federal minimum wage for all hours worked. The federal minimum wage is $6.55 per hour, and will increase to $7.25 on July 24, 2009. Effective July 1, 2008, the Michigan minimum wage increased to $7.40.

As long as Michigan's minimum wage is higher than the federal minimum wage, even if the federal minimum wage is increased again by a Democratic-controlled Congress and White House after January 20, 2009, Michigan employers will still be subject to the state's higher minimum wage.

The U.S. DOL's web page is a reliable source for current information regarding minimum wage (*www.dol.gov*), as is the State of Michigan web page for the Wage and Hour Division in the Department of Labor and Economic Growth.

Wage Deductions and Minimum Wage

Occasionally, an employer will inadvertently violate the minimum wage provisions of the FLSA by deducting from an employee's pay for articles used by the employee in the course of employment (i.e., tools or a particular uniform). Where that deduction results in an employee's pay being reduced to less than the minimum wage in a particular workweek, the employer has violated the statute. Similarly, if an employee is required by the employer to provide tools of the trade that will be used in or are specifically required for the performance of the employer's particular work, a violation would occur in any workweek where the cost of such tools purchased by the employee results in less than a minimum wage being paid.

Tips and Tip Credits

Employers may pay tipped employees $2.13 per hour under federal law, or $2.65 per hour under Michigan law (the greater amount to be paid when employee is subject to both laws), if: (a) that amount plus the tips received equals at least the higher state minimum wage; (b) the employee retains all tips; and (c) the employee customarily and regularly receives more than $30 a month in tips. If an employee's tips combined with the employer's wages of at least $2.13/$2.65 an hour do not equal the state minimum hourly wage, the employer must make up the difference.

Where an employee is employed in an occupation in which he or she customarily and regularly receives more than $30 in tips per month, the employer is entitled to a wage credit in determining whether the employee was paid the minimum wage. Where applicable, the amount paid to the employee by the employer is deemed to be increased by an amount determined by the employer to accurately reflect the tips received; but in any case the amount of increase may not be more than one-half the minimum wage.

- This provision applies to full-time and part-time employees.
- Any appropriate recurring monthly period beginning on the same day of the calendar month may be used.
- **Caution**: When the employer has claimed a tip credit in excess of the actual amount of tips received by an employee, the employer can be required to pay the balance.

Employers choosing to use the tip credit provision must:

1. Notify each tipped employee about the tip credit allowance before the credit is utilized.
2. Demonstrate that the employee receives at least the minimum wage when combining direct wages and the tip credit allowance.
3. Permit the employee to retain all tips, regardless of whether the employer takes a tip credit for tips received, unless the employee participates in a valid tip pool.

The tip credit is not available when an employee who works both tipped and non-tipped jobs is performing the non-tipped function. An employer, however, may take the tip credit for time an employee spends performing duties related to the tipped job, even if not directed toward producing tips, if such duties are incidental to the regular duties and are generally assigned to such jobs.

Although the law prohibits any arrangement under which the tip becomes the property of the employer, employees who customarily and regularly receive tips may split or pool their tips among themselves. The following applies to "tip pooling" under the FLSA:

- The tip pooling arrangement need not be voluntary where it includes only employees who customarily and regularly receive tips.

- On the other hand, employees participating in a tip pool may not be forced to share their tips with employees who do not customarily and regularly receive tips. For example, waitpersons cannot be forced to share their tips with dishwashers.

- Only those tips in excess of tips used for the tip credit may be taken for the tip pool.

- The amount one contributes must not be a greater percentage of one's tips than is "customary and reasonable."

- Caution: Based on a recent court decision, there is a question as to whether tip pooling violates the MWFBA.

Overtime under FLSA

Section 7 of the FLSA requires that, for all hours worked over 40 in a workweek, a non-exempt employee receive compensation at a rate not less than one and one-half times the regular rate at which he or she is employed.

The workweek is the basic unit for determining overtime regardless of how often an employee is paid. It is defined as a fixed and regularly recurring period of 168 hours—seven consecutive 24-hour periods. It may begin on any day and at any hour of the day. Whenever an employee works over 40 hours in the designated workweek, he or she is entitled to overtime regardless of how few hours he or she may have worked in other weeks.

Another statutory concept that is peculiar to the FLSA and is significant to an employer's overtime obligations is regular rate of pay.

Regular Rate of Pay under FLSA

The FLSA requires that an employee be paid overtime at one and one-half times his regular rate. This term should not be confused with the employee's stated hourly rate (where paid by the hour). As noted below, regular rate includes other forms of compensation besides the stated hourly rate. The key considerations with regard to this term are as follows:

- It is not based solely on the declarations of the parties; it will be drawn from what actually happens under the employment contract.

- The regular rate is an hourly rate. Although the FLSA does not require employers to compensate their non-exempt employees on an hourly basis, those employees who are paid in some other fashion (i.e., piece rate, commission, or salary) must nevertheless be paid overtime compensation based upon an hourly rate that is derived from the totality of the employee's compensation.

- An employee's regular rate includes all remuneration for employment paid to, or on behalf of, the employee except the following:

    1. Gifts (the amounts of which, are not measured by, or dependent on, hours worked, production, or efficiency).

    2. Payments made for occasional periods when no work is performed due to vacation, holiday, illness, etc., or reasonable payments for traveling expenses or other expenses incurred by an employee in the furtherance of his or her employer's interests.

    3. Sums paid in recognition of services performed during a given period where the:

        Payment and the amount of the payment are determined at the sole discretion of the employer;

        Payment is made at or near the end of the period; and

        Payment is not made pursuant to any prior contract, agreement or promise causing the employee to expect such payments regularly.

    4. Payments made pursuant to a bona fide profit-sharing plan or trust or bona fide thrift-savings plan.

    5. Payments irrevocably made by an employer to a trustee or third person pursuant to a bona fide plan providing old-age, retirement, life, accident, or health insurance, or similar benefits for employees.

    6. A premium rate paid for certain hours worked in excess of eight in a day, 40 in a workweek, or in excess of the employee's normal or regular working hours.

    7. A premium rate paid for work on Saturdays, Sundays, holidays, or regular days of rest or the sixth or seventh day of the workweek where the premium is at least one and one-half times the rate for non-overtime hours on other days.

    8. A premium rate paid pursuant to an applicable employment contract or collective bargaining agreement for work outside the hours established by the contract or agreement as the regular workday (not exceeding eight hours) or workweek (not exceeding 40 hours) where the premium rate is not less than one and one-half times the rate for like work performed on a non-overtime basis.

Two types of compensation that frequently cause overtime problems for employers are bonuses and per-visit or flat-rate payments.

Bonuses

Where the bonus has been agreed upon in advance or is paid pursuant to a specific formula, it is part of the remuneration paid to the employee and must be included as part of the employee's regular rate.

Where the bonus is paid as a percentage of the employee's total earnings (straight time plus overtime), the bonuses need not be included in the employee's regular rate of pay. Certain exempt employee stock options, stock appreciation rights, stock purchases and similar employer-provided grants or rights programs are also included in overtime pay calculations, under specified conditions.

Per-visit or Flat-rate Pay

Where the employee has worked over 40 hours in a single workweek, the per-visit pay or the payment of a flat rate must be reduced to an hourly rate by dividing the total amount paid for the workweek by all of the hours actually worked. For each hour over 40, the employee must be paid an additional amount of one-half the hourly rate so computed.

Exemptions under FLSA: Under the regulations there are a number of job categories that are exempt from the statute's minimum wage and overtime provisions. Among these exemptions are the following:

- Executive, administrative, professional, or outside sales employees (e.g., the "white collar" exemptions).
- Employees employed at amusement or recreational establishments that meet certain criteria
- Employees engaged in the catching, propagating or farming of fish, shellfish, etc.
- Certain employees engaged in agricultural pursuits
- Seamen
- Babysitters (on a casual basis) or any person employed to provide companionship services for individuals who (because of age or infirmity) are unable to care for themselves

In addition, the Act exempts certain job categories solely from its overtime requirements. Among these exempt job categories are:

- Outside buyers of raw poultry, eggs, cream, or milk in their raw or natural state

- Certain salespersons, parts persons, or mechanics primarily engaged in selling or servicing automobiles, trucks, or farm implements

- Certain salespersons primarily engaged in selling trailers, boats, or aircraft

- Any person employed in domestic service in a household and who resides in a household

- Any employee for whom the Secretary of Transportation is authorized to establish qualifications and maximum hours. This exemption is generally limited to drivers, haulers, and loaders who perform their duties with regard to vehicles that are engaged in interstate commerce.

Among the most significant of the Act's exemptions are those pertaining to executive, administrative, professional, and outside sales employees—the so-called "white collar" exemptions. These job categories are exempt from the Act's minimum wage and overtime provisions. The requirements for these exemptions are elaborately defined in the regulations and guidelines published by the U.S. DOL.

Executive Exemption

A person is employed in an executive capacity where he/she:

- Is compensated on a salary basis at a rate of not less than $455 per week;

- Has as his/her primary duty the management of an enterprise in which the employee is employed or of a customarily recognized department or subdivision thereof;

- Customarily and regularly directs the work of two or more full-time employees; and

- Has the authority to hire or fire employees or whose recommendations as to hiring, firing, advancement, promotion or any other change of status of the employees are given particular weight.

Business Owner Exception: an employee who owns at least a bona fide 20 percent equity interest in the business in which the employee is employed and who is actively engaged in its management is an exempt executive.

Highly Compensated Employee Rule: an employee who is guaranteed total annual compensation of at least $100,000 and who customarily and regularly performs one or more of the exempt duties or responsibilities of an executive employee is exempt.

Administrative Exemption

A person is employed in an administrative capacity where he/she:

- Is compensated on a salary or fee basis of not less than $455 per week;

- Has as his/her primary duty the performance of office or non-manual work directly related to the management or general business operations of the employer or the employer's customers; and

- Whose primary duty includes the exercise of discretion and independent judgment with respect to matters of significance.

Highly Compensated Employee Rule: an employee who is guaranteed a total annual compensation of at least $100,000 and who customarily and regularly performs one or more of the exempt duties or responsibilities of an administrative employee is exempt.

Professional Exemption

A person is employed in a professional capacity where he/she:

- Is compensated on a salary or fee basis of not less than $455 per week;
- Has as his/her primary duty the performance of office or non-manual work requiring:

    (1) knowledge of an advanced type in a field of science or learning customarily acquired by a prolonged course of specialized intellectual instruction and which includes work requiring the exercise of discretion and independent judgment (e.g., "learned professionals"); or

    (2) invention, imagination, originality, or talent in a recognized field of artistic or creative endeavor (e.g., "creative professionals").

Highly Compensated Employee Rule: an employee who is guaranteed a total annual compensation of at least $100,000 and who customarily and regularly performs one or more of the exempt duties or responsibilities of a professional employee is exempt.

Computer Software Employees

A person is employed as an exempt computer employee where he/she:

- Is compensated on a salary or fee basis at a rate not less than $455 per week or is compensated on an hourly basis at a rate not less than $27.63 an hour; and

- Performs as his/her primary duty:

- (1) the application of systems analysis techniques and procedures, including consulting with users, to determine hardware, software or system functional specifications; or

- (2) the design, development, analysis, creation, testing or modification of computer systems or programs, including prototypes, based on and related to user or system design specifications; or

- (3) the design, documentation, testing, creation or modification of computer programs related to machine operating systems; or

- (4) a combination of the aforementioned duties; the performance of which requires the same level of skills.

No Discretion and Judgment Rule: an exempt computer employee is not required to exercise discretion and independent judgment. No particular education, certification, or licensure is required to qualify for this exemption.

Wage and Hour Interpretive Guidance

On October 26, 2006, the U.S. Department of Labor Wage and Hour Administrator issued an Opinion Letter emphasizing that an employee whose primary duties consist of installing, configuring, testing, and troubleshooting computer applications, networks, and hardware does not qualify under the Computer Software Employee exemption. The employer in this case planned to have shifts of IT Support Specialists working or on-call 24 hours a day. The job description stated that the IT Support Specialist (renamed from Help Desk Support Specialist) is responsible for the diagnosis of computer-related problems as requested by employees, physicians, and contractors of the employer. The IT Support Specialist conducts problem analysis and research, troubleshoots, and resolves complex problems either in person or by using remote control software. He or she ensures timely closeout of trouble tickets. According to the Wage and Hour Administrator, these duties were insufficient to satisfy the tests described above.

Outside Salesperson Exemption

A person is employed as an exempt outside sales employee where he/she:

- Has as his/her primary duty making sales or obtaining orders or contracts for services or for the use of facilities for which a consideration will be paid by the client or customer; and

- Is customarily and regularly engaged away from the employer's place or places of business in performing such duty.

General Considerations for Exemptions

- Exemptions are restricted to white-collar employees—i.e., the work performed must be office work or non-manual work.

- Exemptions are narrowly construed and the burden generally is on the employer to establish their existence.

- The employee's title is irrelevant.

- Nonexempt work includes any work performed by nonexempt subordinate employees.

- Discretion and independent judgment have been interpreted to mean that the person has the authority or power to make an independent choice free from immediate direction or supervision and with respect to matters of significance.

- It is expected that an executive employee will have as his or her primary duty the performance of managerial and supervisory functions (i.e., interviewing, selecting, and training employees; directing their work; appraising productivity, disciplining; planning work; etc.).

- The work performed by an administrative employee must be of substantial importance to the management or operation of the business. For that reason, it has been generally held that the exemption does not apply to clerks, secretaries, bookkeepers, etc.

- For a professional employee, the best evidence of the requisite professional training is possession of an appropriate academic degree. An advanced degree is often standard. The person in question must be more than a highly skilled technician.

Salary and Pay Practices

The executive, administrative and professional employee exemptions require (except for the computer-related occupations) that the employee be paid a salary. Like many other terms under the FLSA "salary" has a specifically defined meaning that may not always conform to its commonly understood definition.

Under the regulations, an employee is considered to be paid on a salary basis if he or she regularly receives "a predetermined amount constituting all or part of his compensation that is not subject to reduction because of variations in the quality or quantity of the work performed." The DOL's regulations further state that as a general rule, deductions from an employee's salary for absences occasioned by the employer or by the operating requirements of the business where the employee is available and willing to work invalidate the employee's exemption.

Employers may issue unpaid disciplinary suspensions of one or more full days if such suspensions are imposed in good faith for infractions of workplace conduct rules. Such suspensions must be imposed pursuant to a written policy applied uniformly to all employees. Employers may, likewise, issue full day suspensions for infractions of safety rules of major significance.

The following deductions, among others, invalidate the exemption:

- Deductions for absences of less than one day because the employee is handling personal business or due to sickness
- A policy authorizing the deduction from an exempt employee's salary for absences of less than a day regardless of whether the policy actually was enforced as to the particular employee or any employee

Under the regulations, employers are, however, afforded a "safe harbor" in which they may correct improper deductions and retain an employees' exempt status. Under the "safe harbor" rule, an employer will not lose the exemption where improper deductions have occurred if the employer:

- has a clearly communicated policy that prohibits improper salary deductions;
- has a complaint mechanism by which an employee can notify the employer of the failure to receive his or her full salary or if he or she believes an improper deduction has occurred;
- promptly reimburses employees for any improper deductions; and

- makes a good faith commitment to comply in the future.

Employers who repeatedly or willfully violate the FLSA will not be protected under the "safe harbor" provision.

In view of this, an employer is well advised to carefully review its pay practices as well as pay policies and consult with legal counsel for possible impact.

Enforcement of FLSA

The U.S. DOL is authorized under the FLSA to bring suit in federal district court to enforce the Act's provisions. Court action generally is preceded by an investigation conducted by the Wage and Hour Division. Where the investigation results in a finding of liability that is not resolved administratively, the matter will be submitted to the Solicitor of Labor who may then institute litigation.

Civil Suit by the Department of Labor

The DOL can seek back wages and liquidated damages. The Court is entitled to award back wages for at least two years prior to the date of filing the complaint and three years for a "willful" violation. A willful violation is one where "the employer knew or showed reckless disregard for the matter of whether its conduct was prohibited by the FLSA." Where the employer is found liable under the FLSA, an amount equal to the amount of back wages found to be owed will be assessed as liquidated damages unless the employer shows that the act or omission giving rise to the liability was in good faith and that it had reasonable grounds for believing that the act or omission was not a violation of the FLSA.

- The burden is upon the employer to introduce some proof of good faith and reasonable grounds.
- Where the federal district court declines to award liquidated damages, the Sixth Circuit Court of Appeals requires those courts under its jurisdiction (including those in Michigan) to award interest on the back pay from the date the claims accrued.

The DOL may seek an injunction forbidding further violations and ordering the payment of back wages. This section of the Act does not allow the court to award liquidated damages.

Civil Suit by the Employee

An employee is entitled to bring suit under §16(b) of the FLSA in either federal or state court. Under this section, the employee is entitled to obtain back wages and liquidated damages identical to that which the DOL can obtain under §16(c). In addition, the employee, if successful, may obtain reasonable attorneys' fees.

Civil Money Penalties

The FLSA amendments of 1989 provided for the assessment of civil money penalties for willful or repeated violations of the FLSA's minimum wage or overtime provisions. The law now subjects employers to a civil money penalty not to exceed $1,100 for each such violation as explained in the following subsections.

WILLFUL VIOLATION

A willful violation will be found where the employer knew its conduct was prohibited by the FLSA or showed a reckless disregard for the requirements of the Act. In general, all of the facts and circumstances regarding the conduct will be taken into consideration. Violations will be willful whenever:

- the employer's conduct is at variance with previous advice by the Wage and Hour Administrator or other agency representative; or

- the employer was advised during the course of a DOL investigation that the conduct in question violated the statute; or

- the conduct in question is at variance with conduct that the employer was advised was required to comply with the Act.

REPEATED VIOLATIONS

A repeated violation will be found where there has been a prior decision or a finding by the DOL, a court, an administrative tribunal, or another tribunal authorized to make such a determination, that the employer has violated the minimum wage or overtime provisions of the Act.

AMOUNT OF PENALTY

In determining the amount of the penalties, the trier of fact will consider all relevant facts and circumstances including:

- Size of employer

- Gravity of the violation

- Employer's good-faith efforts to comply

- Previous history of violations including whether the employer is subject to an injunction against violations of the Act

- Employer's explanation for the violations, including whether the violations resulted from a bona fide legal dispute

- Employer's commitment to future compliance
- Interval between violations
- Number of employees involved
- Whether there is any pattern to the violations

PROCEDURE

The Wage and Hour Division of the U. S. DOL will make the initial determination as to the amount of the penalty, if any. Where the employer wishes to challenge this determination, it is entitled to a hearing on the matter before an administrative law judge who is authorized to determine the appropriateness of the penalty amount. Should the employer wish to challenge the administrative law judge's decision, it may seek a final decision from the Secretary of Labor.

Michigan Minimum Wage Law of 1964

The Michigan Minimum Wage Law (MMWL) sets the minimum wage for employers in the State of Michigan who are not covered by the federal Fair Labor Standards Act (FLSA). As subsequently amended, the statute also requires the payment of overtime for non-exempt employees who work over 40 hours in a workweek and prohibits wage discrimination based on sex.

Employers Subject to MMWL

The MMWL covers all employers who employ two or more employees, 16 years of age or older, at any one time within a calendar year. "Employer" means a person, firm or corporation, including the state and its political subdivisions, agencies, and instrumentalities, as well as a person acting in the interest of the employer. Thus, as in the FLSA, supervisors who have control over the wages and working conditions of an employee may be held liable for violations of this statute. An "employee" means anyone 16 years of age or older employed by an employer on the employer's premises or at a fixed site designated by the employer. At any point during the year on which an employer begins to employ at least two persons, the employer is covered for the remainder of the calendar year.

Like the FLSA, the MMWL defines "employment" broadly to mean "to engage, suffer or permit to work." Accordingly, it would cover many situations that typically would be viewed as something other than an employment relationship.

Independent Contractors

Individuals who purportedly act as independent contractors may nevertheless be found to be employees. In this regard, Michigan has adopted the factors identified above under the

FLSA (see page 129). Whether an employment relationship exists depends upon all the surrounding circumstances.

Leased Employees

Many companies now lease some or all of their employees from leasing companies who are responsible for all wages and benefits. Such an arrangement, however, may not relieve them of possible liability under the MMWL. As with the FLSA, a joint employment relationship may be found to exist under the MMWL, thus making both lessor and lessee jointly liable for violations of the Act, such as failure to pay proper overtime.

Special Requirements of MMWL

Minimum Wage under MMWL

As noted above, currently the minimum wage in Michigan is $7.40 an hour.

Training Wage and Sub-Minimum Wage

Michigan employers may pay a sub-minimum wage (a "training wage") of $4.25 per hour for employees under the age of 20 for the first 90 days of employment, and thereafter the above minimum wage would apply. A further exception applies for minors under the age of 18, who may be paid a sub-minimum wage of 85 percent of the current minimum wage (which is $6.55 per hour based on the $7.40 minimum wage).

Overtime under MMWL

An employee must be paid one and one-half times his or her regular rate for all hours worked over 40 in a workweek.

Compensatory Time Off

In lieu of monetary overtime compensation, an employee may receive compensatory time off at a rate of not less than 1½ hours for each hour of overtime worked. Any such compensatory time system is subject to all of the following:

- The employee must be permitted to accrue up to a total of 10 days of compensatory time per year without a loss of pay.

- The compensatory time must be provided pursuant to:

    (1) the applicable provisions of a collective bargaining agreement, memorandum of understanding, or any written agreement between the employer and the employees representative; or

    (2) (when the employees are unrepresented) a plan adopted by the employer and provided in writing to its employees which provides the employees with a voluntary option to receive compensatory time for overtime work.

- Employer shall not directly or indirectly intimidate, threaten or coerce or attempt to intimidate, threaten or coerce an employee with regard to his/her right to request or refuse compensatory time in lieu of payment of overtime compensation.

- An employee cannot accrue more than 240 hours of compensatory time.

- An employer must

    (1) maintain a record of compensatory time earned by the employee by pay period;

    (2) provide the employee with a record of compensatory time earned by or paid to the employee in a statement of earnings for the pay period in which the compensatory time is earned or paid.

- Upon request of the employee, the employer must provide monetary compensation for the compensatory time earned at a rate not less than the employee's regular rate at the time the compensatory time was earned.

- Upon termination of employment, the employee must be paid for unused compensatory time at a rate not less than the employee's regular rate at the time the compensatory time was earned.

- The employee is permitted to use the accrued compensatory time for any reason unless its use would unduly disrupt the employer's operation.

- Unless prohibited by a collective bargaining agreement, an employer may terminate a compensatory time plan upon not less than 60 days notice to the employees.

Regular Rate of Pay under MMWL

Unlike the FLSA, the MMWL does not specify what constitutes the "regular rate at which the employee is employed." The Michigan Department of Labor and Economic Growth's Wage and Hour Division, however, has issued a rule for the computation of regular rate of pay that is less extensive than that under its federal counterpart:

- Where an employee is paid at an hourly rate plus commission or salary plus commission, the regular rate is obtained by dividing the sum (wages plus commission) by the number of hours worked in that week.

- Where an employee is paid on a piece-rate basis, the regular rate is obtained by adding together the total earnings of the workweek "from piece rates and all other earnings" and dividing the sum by the number of hours worked in that week.

Exemptions under MMWL

There are a few exemptions from the overtime requirements that are applicable to private (rather than governmental) employees. The overtime provisions do not apply to:

- An employee employed in a bona fide executive, administrative or professional capacity. Although the statute fails to define "bona fide executive, administrative, or professional capacity," rules promulgated by the BWUC set forth criteria that are essentially identical to the requirements set forth for these positions under the FLSA.

- An employee employed by an amusement or recreational establishment where the establishment:
    - Does not operate for more than seven months in a calendar year;
    - Is open primarily to provide leisure activities for those who attend; and
    - Is open to the general public at a fixed site.

    This exemption is not applicable to employees at a central office, warehouse or office that services the establishment.

- An employee employed in agriculture (including farming in all of its branches, such as the cultivation and harvesting of crops; dairying; the raising of livestock, bees, fur bearing animals, or poultry; etc.).

- Any employee who is not subject to the minimum hourly wage provisions of this Act.

Wage Reductions Due to Gratuities

The minimum hourly rate of an employee is $2.65 an hour if all of the following occur: (1) the employee receives gratuities in the course of his or her employment; (2) the gratuities equal or exceed the difference between $2.65 per hour and the minimum hourly rate established under MMWL; (3) the employee declares the gratuities for purposes of the Federal Insurance Contribution Act (FICA); and (4) the employer informed the employee of the provisions of this section.

Statements to Employees Under MMWL

The employer must furnish each employee for each pay period a statement of:

- Hours worked by the employee
- All wages paid
- All deductions made

Recordkeeping Requirements of MMWL

Under the MMWL the employer must keep employment records for each employee showing the following:

- Name
- Home address
- Date of birth
- Occupation
- Total daily hours worked (computed to the nearest unit of 15 minutes)
- Total hours worked in each pay period
- Total hourly, daily, or weekly basic wage
- Total wages paid each pay period
- Itemization of all deductions made each pay period
- Separate itemization of all credits for meals, tips, and lodging against the minimum wage taken each pay period
- Where the employee is paid on a piece-rate basis, a record of the piece-rate paid and the total number of units made or harvested
- If a credit is taken for gratuities received by the employee, a statement signed and dated by the employee confirming the amount of gratuities received
- Where gratuity credits are taken after gratuities are pooled and redistributed, a consent statement signed by the employee in question
- If a credit is taken for meals and/or lodging provided to an employee, a statement signed by the employee acknowledging that the meals and/or lodging were received
- If employees of a hospital or institution agree to have their overtime computed on the basis of a 14-day work period, a written agreement or written employment policy arrived at between the employer and employees and dated prior to the effective date of the agreement

All of this information must be preserved for three years. Such records are subject to inspection by the BWUC's Wage and Hour Division at any reasonable time.

Enforcement and Sanctions under MMWL

The BWUC's Wage and Hour Division is authorized to investigate each employer subject to this statute to determine compliance or to investigate any complaints alleging violations of the MMWL. Enforcement is both civil and criminal in nature. Both the BWUC and the aggrieved employee may bring an enforcement action.

Where the BWUC determines that there is reasonable cause to believe that the employer violated the MMWL, it must seek voluntary compliance (including the payment of any back wages). Where voluntary compliance is not achieved within a reasonable period of time, the BWUC may bring a civil action to recover back wages, liquidated damages, costs and attorneys' fees and, in addition, the employer is subject to a civil fine of not more than $1,000.

An employee also is entitled to bring a civil action for violation of the statute at any time within three years of the alleged violation and can obtain:

- the difference between what the law required and what the employee actually received
- an equal additional amount as liquidated damages
- costs and reasonable attorneys' fees

Any person who violates any provision of this statute or any regulation or order is guilty of a misdemeanor.

Non-Application of MMWL

The MMWL does not apply to the following:

- Any employer subject to the FLSA minimum wage provisions unless such application results in a minimum wage lower than that provided by the MMWL
- Persons employed in summer camps for not more than four months
- Employees with disabilities covered by a deviation certificate or other special certificate pursuant to §14(c) of the FLSA
- Agricultural fruit growers, pickle growers, tomato growers, or other agricultural employers who traditionally contract for harvesting on a piece-work basis

Retaliation Prohibitions Under MMWL

Employers are prohibited from discharging or in any manner discriminating against any employee because the employee has testified or is about to testify in any investigation under the provisions of the MMWL. Such an employer may be found guilty of a misdemeanor.

Equal Pay

Under federal (Equal Pay Act of 1963) and Michigan (MMWL and Elliott-Larsen) law, employers are prohibited from paying wages to employees in an establishment at a rate less than the rate at which the employer pays wages to employees of the opposite sex in the establishment for equal work on jobs, the performance of which requires equal skill, equal effort, and equal responsibility; and which are performed under similar working conditions.

Differentials in pay are permitted where payment is made according to:

- A seniority system
- A merit system
- A system that measures earnings by quantity or quality of production
- Any factor other than sex

An employer in violation of the equal pay provisions is prohibited from reducing the wage rates of an employee in order to comply with the equal pay provisions of the EPA and MMWL.

The equal pay provisions are enforced in the same manner as the minimum wage and overtime provisions of the FLSA and MMWL.

Michigan Youth Employment Standards Act

The Michigan counterpart to federal child labor laws (which are discussed below) is the Michigan Youth Employment Standards Act (MYESA). MYESA is broader in some respects than its federal counterpart, yet less restrictive in others. Strict adherence to the statute's requirements is particularly important in view of the fact that the statute relies on criminal, rather than civil, penalties to enforce its provisions.

Employers Subject to MYESA

MYESA covers every employer that employs a minor. An "employer" is defined as a person, firm, corporation, the state or a political subdivision of the state, an agency of instrumentality of the state and an agent of the employer. MYESA defines a "minor" as a person under 18 years of age but does not include individuals who are:

- 16 years of age or older and have completed requirements for high school graduation;

- 17 years of age or older and have passed the general education (GED) test; or
- Emancipated (e.g., married minors).

In addition, MYESA specifically does not apply to minors engaged in the following occupations, which are exempted from coverage:

- Domestic work or chores at private residences
- Shoe shining
- Solicitation, distribution, or sale of publications or political or advertising matters
- Fundraising work performed as members of recognized youth-oriented organizations (such as Boy Scouts or Girl Scouts) as long as they do not replace employees in occupations for which workers are ordinarily paid
- Employment in a business owned and operated by the minor's parent or guardian
- Farm work performed in compliance with BWUC standards
- Employment by an educational institution where the minor (who must be at least 14 years old) is enrolled
- Work pursuant to a work-study contract between an employer and a school district that provides supervision, provided the student is at least 14 years old

Minimum Age Under MYESA

MYESA prohibits the employment of minors younger than 14 years of age, with the following exceptions:

- Youth athletic program referee or umpire (at least 11 years old)
- Golf caddie (at least 11 years old)
- Employment in farming operations (at least 13 years old)
- Bridge caddy at any event sanctioned by the American Contract Bridge League or other national bridge league association (at least 11 years old)
- Employed to perform services which entail the setting of traps for formal or informal trap, skeet, or sporting clays shooting events (at least 13 years old)

Hour Restrictions Under MYESA

MYESA prohibits minors from:

- being employed for more than six days in a week
- averaging more than eight hours per day in a single week

- working more than 48 hours in a week (or, where the minor is enrolled in school, from working and going to school more than 48 hours in a week)
- working more than 10 hours in a day

The Act further prohibits the employment of minors under the age of 16 during school hours (unless the minor is enrolled and employed under a work-related educational program) or between the hours of 9:00 PM and 7:00 AM.

On the other hand, 16- and 17-year-olds may not be employed between the hours of 10:30 PM and 6:00 AM, except that if the minor is a student in school, he or she may be employed until 11:30 PM on Fridays and Saturdays, during school vacation periods and during periods when the minor is not regularly enrolled in school.

An exception to some of these time periods exists for 16 and 17 year old minors employed in the cleaning, sorting or packaging of fruits or vegetables. With respect to such agricultural processing, and as long as the employer has on hand the minor's written parental consent, the minor may be permitted to work as follows:

- when school is not in session
- 11 hours in one day
- 62 hours in one week; however, a minor may not work more than 48 hours during any week without his/her consent
- may not be employed between 2:00 AM and 5:30 AM

Meals and Rest Periods

Under MYESA, minors may not work more than five continuous hours without a 30-minute meal or rest period.

Adult Supervision Required

MYESA prohibits any minor from being employed in an occupation that involves a cash transaction:

- After sunset or 8:00 PM, whichever is earlier
- At a fixed location, unless the employer or another employee at least 18 years of age is present

In addition, the BWUC has promulgated a rule under the Act that specifies that a minor may not be employed in any occupation unless the employer, or an employee who is 18 years of age or older, provides supervision. This administrative rule is not as stringent as the statutory prohibition because the MBSR has interpreted it to permit an adult supervisor to be occasionally absent for brief periods of time.

Restricted Occupations under MYESA

Occupations Involving Alcoholic Beverages

In general, all minors are prohibited from working in, about, or in connection with that part of an establishment where alcoholic beverages are prepared, distilled, brewed, manufactured, bottled, consumed, distributed or sold with the following exceptions:

- 16- and 17-year-old minors may work in such an establishment where the sale of food and other goods constitutes at least 50% of gross receipts.

- 14- and 15-year-old minors may work at establishments where alcoholic beverages are sold at retail and at least 50% of the total income is derived from the sale of food or other goods. They may not, however, work in those areas of the establishment where alcoholic beverages are consumed or sold for consumption on the premises (e.g., lounge, bar and dining areas). On the other hand, 14- and 15-year-old minors would be able to work in areas such as the kitchen, coat room or parking lot.

Hazardous Occupations

Aside from the explicit statutory prohibition involving alcoholic beverages, MYESA authorizes the BWUC to issue rules regarding appropriate working conditions for minors. Pursuant to that authorization, the BWUC has issued rules that prohibit some minors from working in occupations deemed to be hazardous. The list is very similar to the list of hazardous occupations issued by the DOL, with several notable additions, including:

- A minor may not be employed in any occupation involving the use of or exposure to hazardous substances that essentially are defined as a "substance or mixture of substances [that is capable of causing substantial personal injury, impairment or substantial illness through absorption, inhalation or personal contact]."

- A minor may not be employed in any occupation that requires the use of respiratory equipment.

- A minor under 16 years of age may not be employed in any occupation involving work in a confined space.

Work Permits

With some exceptions pertaining to farming, minors 14–18 years of age may not be employed in any occupation regulated by MYESA without a work permit from the school district in which he or she resides or in which the minor's place of employment is located.

Such a permit is conclusive evidence of the minor's age and must be:

- Obtained by the minor
- Kept on file at the place of employment
- Returned to the school district upon termination of the minor's employment

Permits can be revoked where there is evidence of poor school attendance that is adversely affecting the minor's academic performance or where the employment violates federal or state law.

Sample work permits regarding age (the CA-6 or CA-7 forms) are included on the HR Michigan web site (www.hrmichigan.com)

Deviations from Provisions

An employer may file an application with the BWUC's Wage and Hour Division for a deviation from the legal hours of employment as well as from the list of prohibited occupations. Such deviations are limited to minors who are 16 years or older. As to the legal hours of employment, however, no deviations are permitted regarding the total hours of work (when school is not in session) or the total hours of work and school (when school is in session).

A request for a deviation generally must include identifying information regarding the minor, the employer, the nature of work, and number of hours to be worked as well as the written permission of parent or guardian. In addition, an employer seeking a deviation from the prohibited occupation standard must explain how the deviation will be in the best interests of the minor and how his or her safety, health and personal well-being will be protected.

A denial of an application for a deviation may be appealed to the appropriate circuit court. If granted, the deviation must be kept on file at the minor's place of employment.

Recordkeeping Requirements of MYESA

Concerning any minors that are employees, an employer must keep the following on the premises:

- A record of the daily number of hours worked together with starting and ending times
- A copy of any work permits or deviations

In addition, an employer is required to post notices regarding MYESA's requirements. These may be obtained from the BWUC's Wage and Hour Division.

Enforcement and Sanctions under MYESA

The BWUC's Wage and Hour Division enforces MYESA through court actions. MYESA authorizes the BWUC to conduct inspections of any place where "a minor may be employed" and to review any records "which may aid in the enforcement of the Act."

Generally, violations of MYESA or the BWUC's rules constitute a misdemeanor punishable by imprisonment for not more than one year, or a fine of not more than $500, or both.

A significant exception pertains to employers (**e.g.**, restaurants or convenience stores) that allow a minor to perform cash transactions after sunset or 8:00 PM without the presence of the owner or an adult. In that situation, MYESA provides for a progression of criminal sanctions; the third offense constitutes a felony punishable by imprisonment of not more than 10 years, or a fine of not more than $10,000, or both.

In addition, Michigan's Worker's Disability Compensation Act also contains a special penalty for those employers that illegally employ a minor who is injured on the job. The minor is entitled to double compensation in the absence of fraudulent use of permits or certificates of age.

Federal Child Labor Laws

Employers Subject to Federal Child Labor Laws

Federal child labor laws are found in various provisions of the Fair Labor Standards Act (FLSA). Accordingly, they apply generally to employers covered by the FLSA, including employees who are employed in hospitals, schools (public or private), institutions providing care to the physically or mentally ill, disabled, or aged residing on the premises; employees who are involved in or manufacture goods for interstate commerce; and to all employees employed in businesses that handle, sell, or work on goods that have been moved in or produced for interstate commerce and do business annually of at least $500,000.

The federal law does not apply to minors:

- Under 16 years of age who are employed by their parents, except for mining and manufacturing occupations and those deemed hazardous by the DOL
- Who deliver newspapers

- Employed as actors or performers in motion pictures, theatrical, radio, or television productions

General Restrictions Under Federal Child Labor Laws

The child labor provisions of the FLSA restrict:

- The hours and type of work 14- and 15-year-olds may perform
- The type of work 16- and 17-year-olds may perform (but not their hours of work)

Note: Employers who are required to follow the federal requirements may also be subject to more stringent state requirements.

Minimum Age Under Federal Child Labor Laws

Under the federal statute, the minimum age for employment is 14 years. Employers can protect themselves from unintentional violations by keeping on file age certificates for each minor employee (i.e., work permits obtained by the minor from his or her school district).

Restricted Occupations Under Federal Child Labor Laws

For 14- and 15-Year-Old Minors

The various rules and regulations promulgated by the DOL severely restrict the jobs in which a 14- or 15-year-old minor may legally be employed. Unfortunately, the lines between prohibited job and permissible employment are frequently unclear because the DOL's pronouncements on the subject do not always mesh easily with one another. The employment of minors in particular occupations or industries has been banned entirely while their employment in certain retail, food service and gasoline service occupations generally is allowed. Employment in all other occupations is somewhat uncertain and should be carefully reviewed.

Among the many occupations from which 14- and 15-year-old minors are completely excluded are:

- Any manufacturing or mining occupations
- Processing occupations such as filleting of fish, dressing poultry, and commercial laundering
- Operation of any hoisting apparatus or power-driven machinery (other than office machines, vacuum cleaners, floor waxers, and the like)
- Occupations (except general office or sales work) connected with construction

- Work in connection with maintenance or repair of the establishment, machines or equipment

Furthermore, for any minor who is a student in school, working periods can only take place during a period when school is not in session.

For All Minors

Under federal law, all minors (including 16- and 17-year-olds) are prohibited from working in certain occupations that are deemed hazardous. Some of the more significant prohibited occupations involve:

- Motor vehicle driving on public roads except where incidental to the minor's employment and certain conditions are met
- Any power-driven hoisting apparatus such as a crane, derrick, high-lift truck, or elevator
- Power-driven woodworking machines
- Power-driven metal-forming, -punching, and -shearing machinery
- Power-driven bakery machinery
- Power-driven saws or shears
- Roofing, demolition, or excavation
- Power-driven paper-products machine operations

Apprentices/Student Learners

There are exemptions from some of the hazardous occupations (such as power-driven woodworking machines or metal-forming, -punching, and -shearing machines) solely for 16- and 17-year-old apprentices and student learners where they meet prescribed criteria. In general, the apprentice or student must be involved in an apprenticeship program or be enrolled in a course of study and training in a private school or a cooperative vocational training program under recognized state or local educational authority; his or her involvement in the hazardous occupation is incidental to his or her training; such work is intermittent and of short duration; etc.

Hour Restrictions under Federal Child Labor Laws

Even in those occupations in which 14- and 15-year-olds may be employed, there are nevertheless the following restrictions as to hours of work:

- No work during school hours

- No work before 7:00 AM or after 7:00 PM (or after 9:00 PM from June 1st through Labor Day)
- Not more than three hours of work per school day (or eight hours for non-school days)
- Not more than 18 hours of work per school week (or 40 hours for non-school weeks)

Special School Programs

Some of the restrictions for minors between 14 and 15 years of age are modified when they are employed as part of a school-supervised, school-administered program known as the Work Experience and Career Exploration Program (WECEP). The key points regarding the establishment of such a program are:

- The program must be approved by the state educational agency.
- The program must include special classroom time.
- The program must grant school credits for both in-school-related instruction and on-the-job experience.
- A written training agreement must be signed by the student, the employer, the school's representative, and the student's parent or guardian.
- Under such a program, minors can be employed in any occupation except mining, manufacturing, or those occupations declared to be hazardous or otherwise prohibited by the DOL.
- Students in the program may be employed during school hours, for as many as 23 hours in a school week and up to three hours in any day.

Penalties for Violating Federal Child Labor Laws

Alleged violations of the federal child labor provisions are investigated by the U.S. DOL. If the Department concludes that there were violations, it is authorized to assess a civil money penalty of $11,000 for each employee found to be the subject of such a violation. In determining the amount of the penalty, the Department will consider the size of the business and the gravity of the violation. In evaluating the size of the business, the Department will take into account, among other things, the following:

- The number of employees (and, if agricultural employment, the days of hired farm labor used)
- The dollar volume of sales or business done

- The amount of capital investment and financial resources

In evaluating the gravity of the violation, the Department will take into account, among other things, the following:

- Any history of prior violations
- Any evidence of willfulness or failure to take reasonable precautions to avoid violations
- The number of minors illegally employed
- The age of the minors so employed and the records of the required proof of age
- The occupations in which the minors were so employed
- Exposure of such minors to hazards and any resultant injury to such minors
- The duration of such illegal employment
- The hours of the day in which the minors were employed and whether such employment was during or outside school hours

Should the employer wish to contest the amount of civil money penalty assessed, the employer may file an exception to the determination. The matter will then be referred to an administrative law judge for a hearing and final determination of the penalty. An appeal from the administrative law judge's decision may be made to the Secretary of Labor.

Where the employer fails to remit the assessed civil money penalty, the DOL is authorized to institute legal action in federal court to collect the penalty amounts. In addition, the DOL is authorized to seek injunctive relief from the court to enjoin any further violations of the federal child labor laws.

CHAPTER 9: Employee Benefit Law

Employee benefits and benefit plans are subject to extensive federal regulation via the Employee Retirement Income Security Act (ERISA), the Internal Revenue Code (Code), the Consolidated Omnibus Budget Reconciliation Act (COBRA), the Health Insurance Portability and Accountability Act (HIPAA) and other federal and state laws and regulations. The complexity of this regulation, particularly ERISA and the Code, is so vast that any comprehensive treatment of the law is beyond the scope of this handbook. The following is intended to provide a basic introduction to ERISA, tax-qualified plans, COBRA and HIPAA, and offers some general principles that can serve to prevent or minimize employee benefit liability. Employers are urged to retain expert employee benefit counsel to address concerns regarding their own employee benefit plans.

Employee Retirement Income Security Act

In 1974, Congress enacted the Employee Retirement Income Security Act (ERISA) for the purpose of regulating both welfare benefit and retirement plans, and ERISA has been amended many times since. To accomplish this goal, Congress set forth various standards and requirements governing fiduciary responsibilities, disclosure, participation, eligibility and vesting and accrual of benefits. It also provides a civil enforcement mechanism to protect employees from employer violations of the statute.

Agency Responsibility under ERISA

Responsibility for implementing, interpreting and enforcing the various provisions of ERISA are divided among three federal agencies - Internal Revenue Service (IRS), Department of Labor (DOL) and Pension Benefit Guaranty Corporation (PBGC). The IRS has jurisdiction chiefly regarding participation, benefits accrual, vesting and funding. The DOL has responsibility for reporting and disclosure and fiduciary obligations as well as civil enforcement of the statute. The PBGC is authorized to administer, enforce and fund the plan termination insurance program through premiums imposed on all covered defined benefit retirement plans.

ERISA Key Definitions

Among the definitions that are critical to an employer's understanding of ERISA and its requirements are the following:

Plan

A "plan" is generally defined as any fund or program established or maintained by an employer and/or an employee organization that provides retirement income or results in a deferral of income to some time after the termination of employment. In general, there are two types of retirement plans: defined benefit plans and defined contribution plans. Defined benefit plans promise you a specified monthly benefit at retirement. A defined contribution plan permits a participant or employer (or both) to contribute a specified annual amount to an individual account under the plan.

Welfare Benefit Plan

"Welfare benefit plans" are employer or employee organization-sponsored benefit plans that provide medical, health, dental, surgical or hospital-care benefits; sickness, accident, disability, death, dependent care assistance, unemployment, pre-paid legal services, scholarship or vacation benefits; or apprenticeship or other training programs, whether through insurance or otherwise.

Participant

The definition of "participant" generally includes any employee or former employee who is or may become eligible to receive a benefit from an employee benefit plan or whose beneficiaries may be eligible to receive such a benefit.

Fiduciary

"Fiduciary" includes any person or entity to the extent they exercise any discretionary authority or control concerning the management of the plan or concerning the management or disposition of its assets; render investment advice for a fee or other compensation regarding any of the assets of the plan; or have any discretionary authority or responsibility in the administration of the plan.

Party in Interest

"Party in interest" includes:

- Any fiduciary, counsel or employer-sponsor of an employee benefit plan
- A person providing services to such a plan
- An employer, any of whose employees are covered by such plan
- An employee organization, any of whose members are covered by such plan
- A 50% (or more) owner of the employer or employee organization sponsoring such plan

- A corporation or partnership, 50% or more of which is owned by the employer or employee organization sponsoring the plan or by a fiduciary or by a service provider to the plan
- Certain family members of persons described above

Reporting and Disclosure Rules

Under ERISA and the Code, the plan administrator is required to submit various reports and documents to the DOL, the IRS and, for certain defined benefit plans, the PBGC, as well as make disclosure of information to plan participants and beneficiaries. Some of these reports and disclosures must be performed periodically; others are required to be done only upon the occurrence of a certain event. The more significant of these are listed below:

Annual Report

An annual report (Form 5500) is an extensive summary of financial, actuarial, participant, service provider and plan fiduciary information that:

- Must be filed on Form 5500 with the Employee Benefits Security Administration (EBSA), a division of the DOL, within seven months after the end of the plan year.

Civil penalties can be imposed upon those responsible for a failure to file the report of up to $1,100 per day. Criminal sanctions may be imposed for willful violations, including a fine of up to $100,000 (or $500,000 where the violator is not an individual) imprisonment for up to 10 years, or both. In addition, where an administrator fails to provide copies upon request, he or she may be subject to a penalty of $110 per day.

To encourage annual reporting, the DOL has implemented the Delinquent Filer Voluntary Compliance (DFVC) Program. The DFVC Program drastically reduces applicable penalties for plans that elect to correct eligible failures to file the annual report through the program.

Summary Annual Report

The summary annual report is required pursuant to regulations promulgated by the DOL. It is provided to plan participants and beneficiaries and summarizes the information contained in the annual report.

While there is no particular form, the format is prescribed by regulation. This report must be provided within nine months after the close of the plan year.

Criminal penalties (identical to those relative to the annual report) can be imposed for a willful failure to prepare and furnish a copy of the summary annual report.

Summary Plan Description

The summary plan description (SPD) summarizes information regarding an employee benefit plan and includes such information as the identity of the plan administrator and trustee or trustees (if different from the administrator); plan eligibility requirements; circumstances that may result in disqualification, ineligibility, or denial or loss of benefits; the procedures to be followed in presenting claims for benefits; and remedies available for redress of claims denied in whole or in part.

An SPD must be furnished to participants and plan beneficiaries and written in a manner that can be understood by the average plan participant. The SPD generally must be provided within 90 days after an employee becomes a participant or a beneficiary begins receiving benefits. Additionally, it must be furnished upon the request of any participant or beneficiary and also must be provided to the DOL if it requests a copy.

If an administrator fails to provide the SPD within 30 days of a request, the administrator may be found personally liable to such participant or beneficiary in the amount of up to $110 per day from the date of such failure. A willful violation is subject to the same criminal penalties as noted under the annual report.

Summary of Material Modification

A summary of any material changes in the terms of the plan or any of the information contained in the SPD must be written in a manner that can be understood by the average plan participant and furnished to plan participants in the same manner as the SPD. The summary of such modification or changes must be furnished within 210 days after the end of the plan year in which the change is adopted.

If an administrator fails to provide this summary upon request, a penalty may be imposed of up to $110 per day following such a request. A willful violation is subject to the same criminal penalties as noted under the annual report.

Participation, Vesting, and Accrual

Participation

As a condition of participating in a qualified retirement plan, a plan may require that an employee complete one year of service (i.e., 12-month period with 1,000 hours of service) and attain the age of 21. Such an employee must be admitted to the plan within six months after both conditions have been met. If a plan provides immediate 100% vesting, the plan may require two years of service.

Vesting

In general, for single employer qualified retirement plans there are two alternative methods of vesting permitted under the statutes:

- 100% vesting after three years but no vested right to a benefit before that time (i.e., a "cliff" vesting schedule); or
- 20% vesting after two years and 20% each year thereafter until the employee is 100% vested after six years (i.e., a "graded" vesting schedule).

More liberal vesting schedules will also satisfy ERISA and the Code.

When a retirement plan is terminated, each participant immediately fully vests in his or her account balance or accrued benefit. A "partial termination" occurs when a significant number of employees covered by a retirement plan are terminated. The IRS may require immediate vesting for the terminated participants.

Retirement plan provisions requiring employees to forfeit vested benefits because of employee misconduct are prohibited.

ERISA and tax law specifically prohibit the assignment or alienation of pension benefits. The garnishment or levy of pension benefits is therefore barred. However, ERISA does not prohibit the assignment or alienation of welfare benefits.

Accrual

ERISA does not specify the level of pension benefits an employee must receive upon retirement. However, the statute does define the degree to which benefits must accrue to the employee on an annual basis. For a defined benefit plan, these rules are intended to prevent postponing the earning of a pension until the employee's later years.

ERISA and tax law prohibit amendments to the pension plan that have the effect of reducing accrued benefits, known as the "anti-cutback" rules.

Minimum Funding

ERISA requires that defined benefit plans (and money purchase pension plans) receive certain minimum funding annually so as to ensure that there is sufficient money to pay the promised benefits. Each plan that is subject to the minimum funding rule is required to establish a funding standard account that determines the minimum contribution to be made each year. The actuarial assumptions used to determine the minimum amount of funding must be reasonable or result in a total contribution equivalent to that which would occur if each assumption were reasonable.

Generally, the minimum contributions must be made quarterly. Where the plan is not minimally funded, it will have an accumulated funding deficiency that will be subject to a 10% excise tax. If after a specified period of time the deficiency remains uncorrected, an additional tax of 100% of the deficiency will be imposed.

Under certain circumstances an employer may request a waiver of the minimum funding requirements from the IRS. The deadline to apply for such waiver is no later than the 15th day of the third month following the close of the plan year for which the waiver is requested.

Effective beginning in the 2008 plan year, the Pension Protection Act of 2006 implements new minimum funding rules that apply to all defined benefit plans. The new rules generally require amortization of unfunded current liabilities over a seven-year period.

Fiduciary Responsibilities

Each employee benefit plan must be established and maintained pursuant to a written document that names at least one or more fiduciaries which "shall have authority to control and manage the operation and administration of the plan."

Except for certain insured plans, retirement plan assets are to be held in trust and are subject to the exclusive authority and direction of the trustees (who are either named in the trust document or appointed by the fiduciary) except to the extent that:

- The plan specifically provides that the trustees are subject to the direction of the fiduciary; or
- The authority to manage, acquire, or dispose of assets is delegated to one or more investment managers.

In addition, 401(k) plans commonly permit participants to direct the investment of their accounts. ERISA §404(c) provides that if the participant exercises control over the assets in his or her account, the participant will not be considered to be a fiduciary because of such exercise, and no other fiduciary will be held liable for any loss or breach resulting from the participant's exercise of control over the account. This exception to the fiduciary rules applies only if the participant (i) has the opportunity to exercise control over the assets in his or her account and (ii) has the opportunity to choose the manner in which all or part of such assets are invested. The second condition is satisfied only if the participant has a broad range of investments from which to choose.

Named fiduciaries are permitted to designate other persons to handle fiduciary responsibilities and in such instances the named fiduciary will not be responsible for any act or omission on the part of the designated person unless the fiduciary breached its fiduciary obligations in designating the individual or continuing the delegation.

ERISA imposes two significant obligations on a fiduciary:

- The fiduciary must discharge its duties with respect to a plan solely in the interest of participants and beneficiaries for the purpose of providing benefits to participants and their beneficiaries and defraying the reasonable expenses of administering the plan.

- The fiduciary must carry out its duties with the skill, prudence and diligence that a prudent person acting in like capacity and familiar with such matters would use.

The fiduciary must diversify the investments of the plan so as to minimize the risk of large losses, and must act in accordance with the plan documents and consistent with ERISA. Also, the fiduciary can be held liable for the breach of fiduciary responsibility by another fiduciary where:

- It participates knowingly in, or knowingly undertakes to conceal, an act or omission by another fiduciary, knowing such act or omission is a breach;
- It has enabled the other fiduciary to commit a breach by failing to carry out its own fiduciary obligations; or
- It has knowledge of a breach by the other fiduciary and has failed to make reasonable efforts to remedy the breach.

A fiduciary also is prohibited from causing the plan to engage in various prohibited transactions.

Prohibited transactions mean certain transactions between the plan and a party in interest such as the sale, exchange or lease of any property; lending of money or extension of credit; furnishing of goods, services or facilities; and transfer to or use by or for the benefit of a party in interest of any assets of the plan. A fiduciary also is prohibited from engaging in various forms of self-dealing.

There are several statutory exemptions. ERISA also provides for administrative exemptions from the list of prohibited transactions where the DOL finds that it is:

- Administratively feasible;
- In the interests of the plan and its participants and beneficiaries; or
- Protective of the rights of participants and beneficiaries of such plan.

Scope of Liability

The DOL shall impose a civil penalty against a fiduciary breaching its fiduciary responsibility under ERISA or any other violation of the fiduciary provisions of ERISA, or against any other person knowingly participating in the breach or violation.

The fiduciary is personally liable for any losses to the plan resulting from such breach, must restore to such plan any profits obtained through the use of the assets; and shall be subject to such other equitable or remedial relief as the court may deem appropriate, including removal of such fiduciary.

Interference with Protected Rights

ERISA makes it unlawful for any person:

- To discharge, fine, suspend, expel, discipline, or discriminate against a participant or beneficiary for exercising any right to which he or she is entitled under ERISA or the provision of a welfare benefit plan; or

- To discharge, fine, suspend, expel, or discriminate against a participant or beneficiary because he or she has given information to or has testified in any inquiry or proceeding relating to ERISA.

Enforcement of ERISA

Participant and Beneficiary Actions

Under ERISA, a participant or beneficiary of an employee benefit plan may bring an action under ERISA in order to:

- Recover benefits due him or her under the terms of the plan, enforce his or her rights under the terms of the plan or clarify his or her rights to future benefits under the terms of the plan;

- Enjoin any act that violates any provision of Title I of ERISA or the terms of the plan, or to enforce any of the provisions of Title I or any term of the plan;

- Obtain appropriate equitable relief;

- Obtain relief against fiduciaries who breach their obligations under ERISA; or

- Obtain information from the plan administrator as required by ERISA and recover penalties for the administrator's failure to do so.

Department of Labor Actions

The DOL is authorized to file an action in order to:

- Obtain appropriate relief including equitable relief where a fiduciary breaches its obligations;

- Enjoin any act or practice that violates any provision of Title I; or

- Assess civil money penalties against the plan administrator for failure to provide an annual report; against a party in interest for engaging in a prohibited transaction; and against a fiduciary for any violation of its fiduciary responsibilities or its knowing participation in such a breach or violation by any other person.

The DOL also is authorized to conduct investigations to determine whether "any person has violated or is about to violate any provision of Title I or any regulation or order thereunder." Pursuant to that authority, the DOL can:

- Require the submission of reports, books and records and the filing of data in support of any information required by Title I to be filed with the DOL;
- Enter places of business, inspect books and records and question any person "as he may deem necessary to enable him to determine facts relative to such investigation"; or
- Subpoena such witnesses and records as are necessary to conduct such an investigation.

Fiduciary Actions

A fiduciary may bring an action to cure a breach by any other fiduciary; to enjoin any act or practice that violates any provision of Title I or the terms of the plan; to obtain other appropriate equitable relief; and to enforce any provision of Title I or the terms of the plan.

ERISA Jurisdiction

In general, ERISA grants exclusive jurisdiction for enforcement actions brought under Title I to the federal courts. In the case of those actions brought to recover benefits by a plan participant or fiduciary, the statute provides that the federal district courts have concurrent jurisdiction with state courts.

If brought in federal court, the action may be initiated in the district where the plan is administered, where the violation took place, or where a defendant resides.

Preemption under ERISA

In general, ERISA provides that the provisions of Titles I and IV of ERISA supersede "any and all state laws insofar as they may now or hereafter relate to any employee benefit plan." However, the statute also provides for a number of exceptions to ERISA's preemptive sweep, including state laws that regulate insurance, banking or securities.

Tax-Qualified Retirement Plans

Retirement plans come in many shapes and sizes. For example, profit sharing plans, pension plans, simplified employee pension plans (SEP), 401(k) plans, 401(k) plans with a "Roth" feature, savings incentive match plans for employees of small employers (SIMPLE) and employee stock ownership plans (ESOP) all are popular forms of retirement plans. However, all retirement plans can be classified into two types - defined contribution plans or defined benefit plans.

Profit sharing plans, 401(k) plans, SIMPLEs and ESOPs are defined contribution plans. The benefit under a defined contribution plan is always expressed as a single-sum amount similar to a savings account balance. This benefit is called the employee's account balance and it increases or decreases each year as the company makes additional contributions and as fund earnings and losses are allocated to the employee's account.

The classic pension plan is referred to as a defined benefit plan. The benefit under these plans generally is expressed as a monthly payment that will start being paid to the employee when he or she reaches normal retirement age (commonly age 65) and will continue to be paid until the employee dies. This payment form is known as an annuity. The amount of the monthly payment is determined by a formula - for example, 2% of final compensation times years of service. The benefit increases each year as the employee earns additional service credit and as his or her compensation increases.

Retirement plans, in most cases, are subject to the requirements of ERISA. A retirement plan may also elect to be tax qualified under the requirements of the Code. The Code rules governing tax-qualified retirement plans somewhat mirror ERISA's requirements; however, the Code rules are much more technical than the rules under ERISA. In fact, the Code rules governing tax-qualified retirement plans are some of the most complicated provisions of the Code. They are lengthy and subject to frequent change.

Why would anyone want to deal with these technical and ever-changing rules? Because tax-qualified retirement plans produce significant tax benefits for the sponsoring company and the participating employees. These benefits include:

- Tax deductions for contributions made to the plan by the company
- Tax exempt earnings on assets held in the plan's trust
- Deferral of income tax on vested plan benefits until those benefits are paid out
- The ability to roll over distributions to IRAs, a 403(b) plan, a 457 governmental plan or another tax-qualified plan

Governing Rules for Retirement Plans

Minimum Participation Rules

A defined benefit retirement plan must cover a minimum number of employees. Specifically, the plan must cover 50 employees, or the greater of 40% of all employees who would be eligible to participate, or two employees. If there is only one employee, then that employee must be covered. Different rules apply to multiemployer plans, union plans and "separate lines of business" of one employer. Participation in defined benefit plans and other plans are governed by the length of service and age rules discussed above.

Minimum Coverage Rules

A defined contribution plan must pass one of two alternate coverage tests described in the Code. The first test compares ratios and is passed if the plan benefits a percentage of non-highly compensated employees that is at least 70% of the percentage of highly compensated employees benefiting under the plan. Highly compensated employees are described below and non-highly compensated employees are employees who are not highly compensated.

This test involves two X÷Y computations. In the first computation, X represents the number of non-highly compensated employees who benefit under the plan and Y represents all non-highly compensated employees of the company. In the second computation X represents the number of highly compensated employees who benefit under the plan and Y represents all highly compensated employees. Employees who have not met minimum age and service requirements, nonresident aliens and employees covered by collective bargaining agreements, if retirement benefits have been bargained, may be excluded from Y.

The two ratios must then be compared. The non-highly compensated ratio always must be at least 70% of the highly compensated ratio. This means that, if 100% of the highly compensated employees benefit under the plan, then at least 70% of the non-highly compensated employees must benefit under the plan. Similarly, if 50% of the highly compensated employees benefit under the plan, then at least 35% of the non-highly compensated employees must benefit under the plan.

Clearly, any increase in the Y figure without a corresponding increase in the X figure would create difficulties in passing the test. For example, hiring a large number of new employees who are excluded from the plan would have this effect.

The second test is a two-part test that is briefly described as follows:

- The definition of the employee group covered by a plan (that is, hourly, salaried, or the employees of a specific plant or business location) must be reasonable and nondiscriminatory; for example, established for valid business reasons and representing a fair cross section of the total employee population; and

- Taking into account all company retirement plans, the average benefit percentage (that is, benefits or contributions as a percentage of compensation) for non-highly compensated employees must be at least 70% of the average benefit percentage for highly compensated employees.

The term "highly compensated employee" has a special meaning. Specifically, it includes any employee who is a five-percent owner, any employee who earned more than $110,000 in 2009 or, at the election of the employer, any employee who is in the top paid 20% of all employees and earned more than $110,000 in 2009. These pay figures are adjusted annually for cost-of-living increases.

For purposes of the participation and coverage tests, it may be necessary to take into account employees of related companies and certain contingent workers that the company may not be treating as employees. For example, if the company whose plan is being tested is the parent or subsidiary (wholly or partially owned) of another company or if there are other related businesses, then it may be necessary to treat the employees of those other companies as if they were employed by the company whose plan is being tested. In other words, those employees must be added to the Y figure. Leased employees also are consolidated with the company's own employees for purposes of testing participation and coverage. Adding individuals to the Y figure makes the tests harder to pass.

Vesting in Retirement Plans

Most plans contain the vesting provisions that are discussed above.

Qualified Joint and Survivor Annuity Requirements

Retirement plans that provide a life annuity payment option (annuity plans) are required to pay retirement benefits to a married employee in the qualified joint and survivor annuity form. This form provides a reduced benefit for the employee during his or her lifetime and at least 50% of that amount is paid to the spouse if he or she survives the employee. This payment form is automatic unless the employee elects a different form of payment and the employee's spouse consents to the waiver in writing.

Annuity plans also must provide a qualified pre-retirement survivor annuity automatically to the surviving spouse of any vested employee who dies before his or her pension benefits commence. The amount of the death benefit is equal to the 50% surviving spouse benefit as if the employee had retired under the qualified joint and survivor annuity. The cost of the benefit may be charged to the employee (by reducing his or her retirement benefit). Alternatively, the employer can subsidize this cost. This requirement applies even if the employee no longer works for the company.

Under a non-annuity plan - that is, a plan that does not provide an annuity payment option - the employee's designated beneficiary for the death benefit must always be the spouse unless the spouse consents in writing to an alternate beneficiary.

Top-Heavy Rules for Retirement Plans

In general, a plan is top heavy if the accrued benefits of all key employees exceed 60% of the accrued benefits of all employees. Key employees include certain officers and shareholders of the company.

If a plan should become top heavy a minimum contribution must be made or a minimum benefit must be accrued on behalf of each employee who is not a key employee.

Qualification of a Retirement Plan

If a company wishes to receive assurances from the IRS that its retirement plan is indeed qualified, it may request a ruling from the IRS, in the form of a determination letter, which confirms that the form and coverage of the plan comply with the qualification requirements as of a specific date. However, a plan can lose its qualified status in the course of its administration and operation or if the company does not have the form of the plan updated for changes in the law.

There are, of course, retirement plans that are not tax-qualified - for example, supplemental executive retirement plans (SERPs) and other forms of non-qualified deferred compensation arrangements. This chapter does not discuss these non-tax-qualified retirement plans.

Cafeteria Plans

A cafeteria plan allows an employer to offer a selection of non-cash employee welfare benefits as part of its total compensation package to its employees. Participants may choose among two or more benefits consisting of cash (i.e., taxable benefits) and qualified non-taxable benefits. If such a plan is offered, it must be in writing. Cafeteria plans are governed by Code §125.

Implementing a cafeteria plan allows an employer to adapt its compensation plan to its employees' needs and preferences, and to accommodate the special benefit needs of two-wage-earner families. This type of plan also develops employee appreciation for fringe-benefit costs as part of overall compensation, while providing employees with a means of paying for benefits on a pre-tax basis.

Cafeteria plans assist the employer in controlling future benefit cost increases and save FICA and FUTA tax payments on pay deferred by employees under such a plan.

All participants in the plan must be employees, including former employees. Partners and 2% or more shareholders of S corporations may not participate in a cafeteria plan.

Types of Cafeteria Plans

Cash Payment

The simplest form of cafeteria plan is a cash payment received in lieu of coverage. For example, in order to keep costs down, employers often offer to make cash payments to employees who have other healthcare coverage (often through a spouse) if the employee will waive coverage under the employer's plan.

Premium Conversion

Premium conversion or premium-only plans permit employees to pay for the contributory portion of healthcare and other coverage with before-tax pay reductions. Because of escalating healthcare costs, many employers in recent years have been forced to ask employees to contribute to the cost of their coverage. A cafeteria plan lessens the blow by permitting employees to pay on a before-tax basis. There is no employer money in this model; the only money or cash is the salary reduction.

Reimbursement Accounts and Flexible Spending Accounts

Reimbursement accounts or flexible spending accounts (FSAs) funded with before-tax pay reduction are another form of cafeteria plan. For example, a healthcare reimbursement account funded through pay reduction under a cafeteria plan permits employees to pay on a pre-tax basis healthcare expenses that are unreimbursed through the primary medical plan. This, in effect, permits employees to circumvent the 7.5% floor on deductible medical expenses.

Traditional Plans

Traditional plans, or full-flex, generally are what one thinks of in connection with cafeteria plans. Under these plans, the employer allocates so-called benefit dollars or credits to each employee. The amount allocated generally is based upon the employer's cost in providing a standard package of fringe benefits to the employee. The cafeteria plan usually offers a wide range of benefits, and each benefit is assigned a cost or price tag. The employee may purchase as many benefits as he or she can afford with the allocated benefit dollars. If the cost of the selected benefits exceeds the employee's benefit dollars, the employee can pay for the difference with pre-tax pay. If the cost of the selected benefits is less than the employee's allocated benefit dollars, the employee can receive the unused benefit dollars as additional cash compensation. In this model there is both employer money (benefit dollars) and pay reduction.

Employees may choose among taxable and nontaxable benefits with no cash payments. For example, employee choices among healthcare and life insurance (non-taxable benefits) and dependent life insurance and group auto insurance (taxable benefits) also would be a cafeteria plan. Generally, these arrangements are funded with employer money but salary reduction also can be used.

Cafeteria Plan Benefit Types

The types of benefits that may be offered under a cafeteria plan are discussed in the following subsections.

Taxable Benefits

- Cash
- Vacation days, provided that they cannot be used or cashed out in a subsequent plan year
- Group term life insurance in excess of $50,000
- Group term life insurance for spouses and dependents
- After-tax contributions to tax-qualified plans
- Any other taxable benefit that does not defer the receipt of compensation, provided that the employer treats the benefit as cash for income tax and withholding purposes

Qualified Benefits

- $50,000 of group term-life insurance
- Accident and health plans (including healthcare FSAs and disability plans)
- Dependent-care assistance up to $5,000 ($2,500 for married employees filing separately)
- Adoption assistance
- Group legal services
- Accidental death and dismemberment
- Deferrals under 401(k) plans
- Qualified tuition reduction
- Qualified employer-provided transportation

Certain fringe benefits such as education assistance and qualified transportation fringes, among others, may not be offered under a cafeteria plan under any circumstances, even as a taxable benefit.

Legal Operating Rules for Cafeteria Plans

Compensation may not be deferred, directly or indirectly, under a cafeteria plan. Consequently, a cafeteria plan may not offer a benefit that defers the receipt of compensation.

Participants generally may not carry over unused benefits or contributions to a subsequent plan year (subject to the 2½-month "grace period" which is discussed in the section below entitled "Use-It-or-Lose-It Rule for FSAs"). For example, vacation days cannot be carried over or cashed out in a subsequent plan year. However, they may be cashed out before the earlier of the last day of the cafeteria plan year or the last day of the employee's taxable year to which the elective contributions used to purchase the unused days relate. Participants also cannot:

- Purchase an insurance benefit that extends beyond the end of the cafeteria plan year end; or
- Purchase a benefit with a deferred compensation element - for example, long-term-care insurance and life insurance with a cash-surrender feature.

Benefit Elections

Benefit elections must be made before benefits become currently available - i.e., before the beginning of each plan year. These elections may not be revoked after benefits begin, except in the case of:

- Significant changes in the cost of a health plan
- Significant changes in the coverage under a health plan
- Changes in family status, including changes in the number of dependents
- Commencement or termination of adoption proceedings
- Change in residence
- Termination of employment or a change in work schedule
- Failure to make required contributions
- Any event that would call for a special enrollment period under HIPAA

Written Plan Document

Cafeteria plans must be contained in a written plan document. This document must specify:

- A description of each of the benefits provided under the period for which the coverage extends;
- The plan's eligibility rules;

- The procedures for making elections under the plan, including the period during which elections may be made, the extent to which elections are irrevocable and the periods with respect to which elections are effective;

- How employer contributions are made to the plan, such as by pay reduction agreements between the participant and the employer or by non-elective employer contributions to the plan;

- The maximum amount of employer contributions available to any employee under the plan;

- The maximum amount of pay reductions available to any employee under the plan, stated as a maximum dollar amount or a maximum percentage of compensation, or as a formula or method of determining the maximum amount or percentage; and

- The cafeteria plan year.

Salary Reductions

Pay or salary reduction agreements between participants and employers must be in writing, specify the period over which the agreement runs (for example, the plan year), authorize a specific amount of salary reduction and be signed by the employee.

Flexible Spending Accounts

Flexible Spending Accounts (FSAs) may be established to pay the following expenses:

- Uninsured medical, dental and vision-care expenses

- Dependent-care expenses incurred to enable an employee and his or her spouse to work

Separate FSAs must be established for each of the expenses; different kinds of expenses (i.e., medical and dependent care) cannot be paid out of a single FSA.

Employees must elect before the beginning of the plan year a specified dollar amount to be deposited into each FSA. This amount may be withheld from the employee's salary pro rata at each pay period during the plan year.

Use-It-or-Lose-It Rule for FSAs

A participant's FSA must be used up or spent for eligible expenses incurred during the plan year. Incurred means when the service (medical, child care, etc.) was rendered and not the date of billing or payment.

Amounts not spent at the end of the plan year must be forfeited unless the plan has been amended to allow reimbursement of eligible expenses incurred within a 2½-month "grace period" following the close of the plan year. Forfeitures and other experience gains (i) may be used to reduce the required premiums for the following year; (ii) may be returned to the participants as dividends or premium refunds; or (iii) may be used to reimburse claims incurred in the next plan year, if the reimbursements are made in a nondiscriminatory manner.

Expenses may be paid from the FSA after the close of the plan year provided the expenses were incurred during the plan year (or grace period, if so amended).

Coverage Period of FSAs

An FSA may not operate so as to cover only periods during which an expense is anticipated. For example:

- Month-by-month or expense-by-expense arrangements will not qualify.
- 12-month coverage period is a safe harbor (i.e., sufficient).
- Initial plan year or short plan year (on account of change in plan year) of less than 12 months is permitted.

Special Rules for Healthcare FSAs

- Insurance premiums may not be paid from a healthcare FSA.
- Healthcare FSAs must pay expenses up to the maximum level of coverage throughout the entire plan year. In effect, this makes the employer the insurer of the FSA. For example, assume that an employee elects to withhold salary at a rate of $100 a month to be deposited into a healthcare FSA. This means that his or her maximum level of coverage is $1,200 (12 × $100) for the year. The employee must be eligible to receive the maximum amount of coverage ($1,200) at all times throughout the plan year, reduced by prior payments. Therefore, if the employee submits a $1,200 healthcare expense to the plan in January when he or she has deposited only $100 into the FSA, the full $1,200 must be available for payment. If the employee terminates employment in February, the plan will be out $1,100 (the employer will have to make up the deficit in the FSA).
- Terminated employees may not submit eligible healthcare expenses incurred after termination of employment but before the end of the plan year unless they continue to make their required premium payments - their periodic deposits. For example, assume the employee in the above example terminates employment in June when he or she has deposited $600 into the FSA but before he or she has

submitted any healthcare expenses to the FSA. Assume also that the employee does not incur any eligible healthcare expenses until after he or she terminates employment. The previously deposited $600 will be available for payment on account of healthcare expenses incurred after termination of employment only if the employee continues to make his or her $100 monthly deposits into the plan. Of course, these periodic $100 deposits will have to be made by the employee on an after-tax basis since the employee no longer has pay from which to withhold the deposits.

- A healthcare FSA may pay eligible expenses only if the employee provides:
    1. a written statement from an independent third party provider stating that the expense has been incurred and the amount of the expense; and
    2. a written statement by the employee that the expense has not been paid or is not payable under any other coverage

    This rule eliminates any advance-payment arrangements.

- Healthcare FSAs are subject to COBRA.

Nondiscrimination Rules for Cafeteria Plans

Each benefit provided under a cafeteria plan is tested for discrimination based upon the Code rules applicable to that type of plan.

Highly compensated participants lose the tax benefit of Code §125 for the plan year if the plan discriminates in favor of highly compensated employees as to eligibility to participate, contributions or benefits. "Highly compensated participant" means a participant who is an officer, a 5% shareholder, highly compensated or a spouse or dependent of such an individual. A plan will not discriminate as to eligibility to participate if:

- The plan benefits a group of employees who qualify under a classification set up by the employer and found by the IRS not to be discriminatory in favor of employees who are highly compensated; and
- An employee may participate in the plan no later than the first day of the plan year following completion of three years of employment.

A cafeteria plan will not be considered to discriminate if the employer contribution to the plan is sufficient for every participant to buy 75% of the best medical benefit or the average medical benefit selected by highly compensated employees, and any additional employer contribution or benefits are proportionate to pay.

Key employees lose the tax benefit of Code §125 for the plan year if nontaxable benefits for key employees in a given year exceed 25% of all such benefits provided under the plan. "Key employee" is defined as an officer having compensation above $160,000 for 2009; a 5% owner; or a 1% owner with compensation above $150,000 for 2009.

A plan maintained under a collective bargaining agreement generally will not be treated as discriminatory.

Consolidated Omnibus Budget Reconciliation Act (COBRA)

In April 1986, President Ronald Reagan signed the Consolidated Omnibus Budget Reconciliation Act of 1985 (COBRA). This Act amended the Code, ERISA and the Public Health Service Act (PHSA) to require private employers and most public employers with 20 or more employees to offer the option of continued healthcare coverage to employees and their dependents under certain circumstances where they would otherwise lose such coverage. The topics in this chapter related to COBRA discuss the most important aspects of this statute and the most common questions asked about it.

The requirements of COBRA apply to all private employers with 20 or more employees on more than 50% of its typical business days during the preceding year. They also apply, through amendments to the PHSA, to all states that receive funds under that Act and to the political subdivisions, agencies or instrumentalities of such states, provided that such entities had at least 20 employees on a typical business day during the preceding year. Because Michigan **does** receive funds under the PHSA, COBRA requirements **do** apply to all Michigan political subdivisions, agencies and instrumentalities with 20 or more employees.

Small employer plans are those healthcare plans whose members each have fewer than 20 employees, and they are exempt from COBRA. However, if one or more members of the plan reach the 20-employee level, all members of the plan may be subject to COBRA unless certain actions are taken promptly. Employers that are parties to a Multiple Employer Welfare Arrangement (MEWA), however, will be viewed individually relative to reaching the 20-employee threshold.

COBRA requires, when certain qualifying events occur, that employees and dependents who are covered under the employer's healthcare plan be offered the option of continuing such coverage at their own cost for a maximum of either 18, 36 or (under limited circumstances) 29 months, depending upon the qualifying event that applies to such persons.

An employer is required to offer continued coverage to an employee's spouse or dependent for up to 36 months in the event of:

- The death of the employee;

- The divorce or legal separation of the spouse from the employee;
- A dependent child ceasing to be a dependent child under the terms of the healthcare plan; or
- The covered employee becoming entitled to Medicare coverage.

An employer is further required to offer continued healthcare coverage to an employee and/or spouse or dependent for up to 18 months when:

- The employment relationship terminates, either voluntarily or involuntarily, unless the employee is discharged for gross misconduct. Neither COBRA nor the proposed regulations pertaining to COBRA define what constitutes gross misconduct. According to the proposed regulations, a layoff, strike, walkout or lockout will constitute a qualifying event if it results in a loss of coverage.
- An employee's hours are reduced such that he or she is no longer covered under the healthcare plan.

If an employee meets the Social Security definition of "disabled" at any time during the first 60 days of COBRA continuation coverage, coverage for the employee and his or her eligible family members may be extended for an additional 11 months, for a total of 29 months. To be eligible for the extension, the employee must notify the plan administrator of his or her disabled status before the end of the initial 18-month coverage period and within 60 days of the Social Security disability decision. Within 30 days of a Social Security determination that the employee is no longer disabled, the employee must report this fact to the plan administrator.

Notification Obligations under COBRA

There are a number of notification obligations under COBRA, several of which are discussed below.

Upon the Effective Date of the Act and to New Employees

When an employer becomes subject to COBRA, it must send a notification to all employees who are covered by the plan and their spouses explaining their rights under COBRA. This notification also must be given to all new employees when their coverage commences under the plan. A sample notification is included on the HR Michigan web site (www.hrmichigan.com).

Upon the Occurrence of a Qualifying Event

Within 30 days of an employee's death, termination, reduction in hours or eligibility for Medicare coverage, the employer must notify the plan administrator of the occurrence of the qualifying event.

If the qualifying event consists of divorce, separation or the cessation of dependent child status, the affected employee or dependent must notify the plan administrator of this qualifying event within 60 days. The employer does not have a notification obligation with respect to these qualifying events.

Also, a proceeding in bankruptcy under Title 11 of the United States Code with respect to any employer from whose employment a covered employee retired at any time is a qualifying event.

Within 14 days of being notified of the occurrence of a qualifying event, the plan administrator must notify the affected persons of their options under COBRA. A sample notice for employees and beneficiaries, including spouses and dependents, is included on the HR Michigan web site (www.hrmichigan.com).

Extended Coverage Option

Within 60 days of the later of the loss of coverage or the date of notification by the plan administrator of his or her rights, the affected person may elect to continue his or her healthcare coverage. Notification of the individual's election must be made to the plan administrator and must have retroactive effect to the date of the loss of coverage, unless the plan provides otherwise. An individual who signs a waiver of continuation rights may, during the election period, revoke the waiver and choose to continue coverage.

An individual electing continued coverage may be charged up to 102% of the applicable premium, which may be paid on a monthly basis if so desired by the individual. As to employees who are eligible for coverage for up to 29 months because of a Social Security disability, the employer may charge up to 150% of the applicable premium for months 19 through 29.

The applicable premium may be adjusted every 12 months; the individual is not guaranteed that the premium in effect on the date of his or her election will continue throughout the entire 18- or 36-month period. COBRA sets forth a detailed explanation of how self-insured employers may calculate their applicable premium. Because of the nature of this explanation, self-insured employers are advised to discuss this aspect with their plan administrator or legal counsel.

The first payment from the affected individual, for the period of coverage following the qualifying event, must be made within 45 days of the date of his or her election. COBRA provides a grace period for payments after the initial payment, equal to the longer of 30 days or the grace period allowed by the plan or insurance company.

Types of Benefits under COBRA

Basically, an employer must offer coverage identical to that provided under the plan to similarly situated active individuals. Thus, health insurance, dental insurance, optical insurance, HMO coverage and similar programs must be included in the option for continued coverage if they are offered to employees (or dependents as the case may be) on the date of the qualifying event. If the healthcare plan is modified during an individual's continuation period, those modifications, whether reductions or increases, must be made available to the individual receiving continued coverage.

An employee may pick and choose from among the group health programs (medical, dental or optical, for example) made available depending on whether the employer has aggregated the various benefit programs into a single group health plan or disaggregated the benefits into separate group health plans. This determination is made by reference to the instruments governing the benefit arrangements.

Continuation Coverage Length

Continued coverage must extend for a maximum of 18, 29 or 36 months, depending upon the nature of the qualifying event. Coverage may be terminated before the expiration of such period upon the occurrence of any one of the following:

- Termination of the healthcare plan. An employer must extend the same coverage to qualified individuals as it does to current employees and dependents, and if the current employees and dependents have no healthcare plan, individuals who have incurred a qualifying event have none either. However, if the employer terminates the qualified individual's plan, but continues to maintain another group health plan, the employer must permit the individual to elect to be covered under such a plan if it is maintained for similarly situated active employees.

- Nonpayment of premium by the affected individual, taking into account the applicable grace period.

- The affected individual becomes covered under another group healthcare plan. If that individual is merely eligible for coverage under another plan but does not actually become subject to it, the continued coverage must continue. However, when the individual is actually covered by a new group health plan, even if its benefit levels are lower than those of the first employer, the first employer's obligations under COBRA terminate. An employer, however, must continue COBRA coverage for former employees who are actually covered by a new group health plan if that plan excludes or limits coverage for pre-existing conditions.

- An ex-spouse receiving continued coverage remarries with actual coverage under another insurance policy.

- A dependent who has had a qualifying event becomes entitled to Medicare benefits.

- The plan terminates the individual's coverage for cause (other than nonpayment of the premium) on the same basis that it would terminate the coverage of a similarly situated active employee.

The end of the maximum coverage period is measured from the date of the qualifying event, even if coverage does not cease on that date. For example, where the employer agrees to extend the employee's coverage, at its own cost, for six months after the date of termination, the 18-month continuation period generally will begin on the date of the termination, not upon the expiration of the extended coverage.

The original 18-month continuation period may be extended if, during the original 18-month period, another qualifying event occurs which would give rise to a 36-month continuation period. In this case, the persons to whom the second qualifying event occurs may elect to continue their coverage for up to 36 months, but only from the date of the original qualifying event. For example:

> An employee's employment terminates on December 31, 2006, so that his and his family's coverage may be continued until June 30, 2008. They elect coverage. After this election and before the expiration of the 18-month period, the employee and spouse are divorced. The spouse and dependent children may then elect COBRA continuation coverage through December 31, 2009.

During the final 180 days of the continued coverage, the plan must provide the individual the option of enrolling in a conversion health plan, but only if such an option is otherwise available to similarly situated active employees. If the plan does not otherwise allow for conversion coverage, such coverage need not be offered to individuals at the end of the COBRA period.

Penalties for Violating COBRA

Private employers, which are taxable under the Code, could lose their income tax deductions for the cost of their healthcare plans if they violate COBRA. Further, highly compensated employees may have the cost of the employer-provided coverage included in their gross income for federal income tax purposes. Both private- and public-sector employers who violate the Act may be sued by affected individuals for equitable relief, to force the employer to abide by the law and reimburse the affected individuals for any healthcare costs they incurred during the violation of the Act. Public employers could probably also be sued under 42 USC 1983 for damages and under 42 USC 1988 for attorney fees for violations of this Act.

Congress modified the original penalties for noncompliance with COBRA to reflect differences in treatment between major and minor violations of the Act. An excise tax of $100 per day for each individual violation may be assessed. If it is determined that noncompliance was due to reasonable cause and not willful neglect and the noncompliance is corrected within 30 days, the excise tax generally will not apply. A special audit rule also is included to encourage employers to monitor their own compliance. Also, ERISA imposes a penalty of $110 per day for failure to provide the required COBRA notices.

Avoiding Benefit Liability

The following practical suggestions are designed to limit liability for or prevent lawsuits based upon promises employers make regarding benefits they provide.

1. Take a more realistic approach to commitments made when seeking to solicit, reward and retain quality employees. Do not promise or agree to more than you are willing or able to afford now or in the future.

2. To avoid the retiree health insurance problem, consider simply not providing life and health insurance benefits to retirees other than COBRA-required continued health insurance.

3. If benefits are provided, clearly and unambiguously limit their duration through plain and explicit language in the applicable benefit section itself and also spell out the circumstances under which the benefits will cease; can be modified, reduced or eliminated; and who, if anyone, has the authority to modify express company policy. Consider a wrongful discharge disclaimer allowing only the company president to modify, in writing, these benefits.

4. Do not avoid potential benefit problems. Ignorance is not bliss. Review past and present labor contracts, negotiation notes and proposals; correspondence with the union, employees, retirees and their spouses; unilaterally established plans; SPDs; insurance booklets; and past practice. Undertake a similar analysis with regard to salaried employees and retirees. See if they accurately and clearly state the nature and duration of a benefit and any limiting features.

5. Avoid ambiguous or conflicting communications. Establish a specific benefit level as opposed to an open-ended commitment. Never give the impression, directly or indirectly, that retiree welfare benefits are tied to or viewed as pension benefits.

6. All company forms and communications should clearly reflect the limited duration and nature of the benefits. In describing retiree insurance benefits, do not use unlimited duration language such as "until death" or "for life." Also, avoid neutral language such as "will pay" unless accompanied by limiting language.

7. Do not use limiting duration language to describe certain non-benefit terms and conditions and then fail to do so when describing benefits.

8. Use great care in administering your benefit programs, especially retiree orientation programs. Company representatives always should clearly distinguish welfare benefits from pension benefits. Establish a standard format and always follow it. Educate company representatives, provide periodic training, monitor their performance and discourage ad hoc oral discussions with retirees, spouses, employees and the union.

9. Consider putting all relevant information associated with retiree orientation programs in writing and spell out in unambiguous, plain language that retiree welfare benefits are transitory and can be reduced, terminated or modified by the company upon plant sale or closure or at the end of the labor contract, whichever occurs first. Non-union retirees and spouses should receive similar memos reflecting appropriate modifications to deal with their situation.

10. Remember, ERISA contemplates welfare plans, and SPDs should expressly state the circumstances under which those benefits can be reduced or terminated. In addition, the DOL issued a policy to the effect that an SPD does not comply with ERISA unless it spells out the circumstances under which the plan may be terminated and other relevant rights, obligations and contingencies.

11. The Financial Accounting Standards Board now requires public corporations to provide data on post-retirement welfare benefits, including a description of the benefits, their costs and the company's funding and accounting policies for these benefits. Many employers are either unaware of or not following this rule. The Governmental Accounting Standards Board has imposed similar requirements on governmental employers.

12. All welfare benefits for union employees should be limited to the term of the contract and the limiting language should be included in the exact sentence describing that particular welfare benefit; for example, "During the term of this agreement, the Company will reimburse retirees from Medicare Part B." Any companion welfare plan, insurance contract and SPD should be coordinated with the labor contract and have the same expiration date. Make sure benefit language is clear, consistent and unambiguous.

13. Do not create any benefit obligations that, to avoid being illusory, must continue beyond the expiration of the labor agreement or a salaried employee's separation.

14. Do not provide retiree welfare benefits when there is no contract, i.e., a strike. Many employers discontinue active but not retiree health insurance benefits. If the company, for collective bargaining purposes, does not want to stop retiree insurance benefits, then it should prepare a notice informing the retirees of the decision and, at the same time, make it clear that these benefits have expired but that the company is simply continuing them for humane reasons unrelated to any legal obligation it might have.

15. Do not implement or agree to early retirement programs without careful consideration. They only increase the retiree health insurance problem. They also may drastically increase defined benefit pension plan liabilities.

16. Develop a paper trail that supports the position that retiree insurance benefits are not permanent and can be changed by the company. Do the same with respect to verbal statements and related company practices. This extends to your dealings with all benefits.

17. Present and future retirees can be treated differently. It may be inappropriate or too late to attach limiting conditions on post-retirement welfare benefits for present retirees. This consideration does not, however, apply to those who have not yet retired.

18. Develop policies and prepare written statements that assure maximum flexibility for the future, allowing unilateral modification or termination for employee and retiree welfare benefits. Policies and provisions that are blatantly unfair should, however, be avoided.

19. Consider instituting a pre-funded, post-retirement welfare program. If so, decide how and how much.

20. Consider establishing, for both active and retired employees, a percentage cost-sharing arrangement for welfare benefits. This approach has the advantage of meeting increased benefit costs without any change in the welfare plan or the employer's policy. Also consider conditioning both increases and continuation of welfare benefits on the financial condition of the employer.

21. When buying a new company or plant, obtain assurances in the purchase and transfer documents that you also are not assuming a huge, unfunded pension or welfare benefit liability due the seller's employees or retirees. Documents should include an indemnification clause to cover damage claims and legal fees associated with such disputes.

22. Know your state wage and insurance laws; they vary and can have a significant impact on your welfare benefit program.

23. Know the tax and equal employment opportunity implications of your benefit package; often they will have a significant bearing on whether to provide a benefit and, if so, how, when, how much and in what form. Be familiar with ERISA requirements and the DOL implementing regulations.

24. Review all written materials that say anything about pension and welfare benefits, including past and present employee handbooks, personnel policies and procedures, manuals, bulletin board postings and all internal documents. Look at them from the retiree's and/or "just discharged and going to get even" perspective. Read every word from their point of view and assume that every word in these policies creates an enforceable right to certain employee benefits. Then eliminate words and phrases that can be used against you as an employer. If you did not find any ambiguities or over-commitments you did not look hard enough. The bottom line: delete every single word and phrase that can be used against you as a basis for creating a benefit commitment to which you did not agree.

25. Define your own benefit program and its terms. Prepare an SPD, written in clear language, that states exactly what the benefit is, how long it lasts, etc. Make sure it is in plain language and readily understood. Run it by others to see if they understand it; if not, revise it.

26. As a part of your paper trail, generate favorable documents at key transactions (i.e., time of hire, change in employment benefit policies, time of retirement, transfer, discharge, strikes, etc.). Consider using a disclaimer to the effect "I understand and agree the Company has the right to alter or terminate these benefits at any time or for any reason."

27. ERISA requires plan participants to exhaust internal claims dispute procedures found in the governing welfare benefit plan. Make sure you establish one. Failure to exhaust those administrative remedies can bar subsequent ERISA claims.

28. Comply with ERISA reporting, disclosure and fiduciary obligations. If you do, then judicial review is deferential and limited to an arbitrary and capricious standard.

29. Do not get involved in multiemployer pension plans. You could end up with a tremendous amount of unfunded liability and increase the union's bargaining power at the negotiating table.

30. Coordinate benefit programs with workers' compensation benefits, Social Security disability pay, etc., so as to avoid duplicative, overlapping payments.

31. Address in advance eligibility requirements for severance pay benefits when there is a change in control of the employer. Many companies have not and, in the event of sale, could be stuck with those obligations even though employees do not lose one day of work.

32. Create a benefit-record retention program. Retain all employee benefit plans permanently. Set up retention programs for related documents.

33. Consider going to self-insurance for reasons discussed in this topic.

34. Include a provision in your pension plan allowing for the reversion to the company of any surplus in the plan in the event the plan is terminated and there is a surplus of assets. Failure to do so could result in the employer not being able to recoup its excess contributions.

35. Remember there is no age limit for an employer's health insurance obligations for older workers. An employer cannot force an employee to use Medicare's health insurance after age 65.

36. The Retirement Equity Act of 1984 (REA) requires plan administrators to:
    - Obtain written spousal consent when plan participant elects an alternate beneficiary, or desires payments be made by a means other than qualified joint and survivor annuities; and
    - Notify participants receiving lump-sum distributions of the tax consequences of that distribution.

37. Observe COBRA continued health coverage and its notice requirements.

38. Remember that the Multiemployer Pension Plan Amendments Act (MPPAA) requires that an employer initiate arbitration within certain specified limitations periods in order to challenge the plan's assessment of withdrawal liability and, with certain limited exceptions, an employer's failure to do so may constitute a waiver of defenses to the plan's determination of liability.

39. If sued, check to see if your insurance policy covers these claims. Probably not, but better safe than sorry.

40. Consider leasing employees if possible. Remember, however, that leased employees may be treated as your own employees for purposes of the tax treatment of benefit plans under Code §414(n). If leased employees constitute less than 20% of your non-highly compensated workforce and these employees are covered by a safe-harbor money-purchase pension plan providing contributions of 10% of compensation and 100% vesting, leased employees need not be covered by your

tax-qualified retirement plans. However, they may still be counted as employees for discrimination testing under the Code for some welfare benefit plans.

On August 17, 2006, the Pension Protection Act of 2006 (PPA) was signed into law. The PPA makes sweeping changes to funding, investment, qualification and other retirement plan rules. Some of the PPA's provisions are effective immediately, while others do not require changes until the 2007 or 2008 plan year, or later. Be aware that these changes are on the horizon and consult your attorney or other qualified benefit adviser regarding what you need to do.

Chapter 10: Health Insurance Portability and Accountability Act

The Health Insurance Portability and Accountability Act of 1996 (HIPAA) established new requirements for self-funded and insured group health plans, with varying effective dates. Group health plans will need to change their plan documents and administrative procedures in order to comply with the various requirements of the Act.

The most important and most publicized provisions of HIPAA relate to individuals who want to leave one job for another and the impact of that job change on their insurance coverage. A primary focus of the Act was to address the perceived problem of "job lock," in which a person is unable to leave one job for another because of a fear of losing insurance coverage for a period of time because of a pre-existing health condition of that employee or one of his/her dependents.

Pre-existing Condition Limits

The maximum pre-existing condition exclusion allowed for group health plans is 12 months (18 months in the case of a late enrollment). This maximum exclusion applies to private sector plans, as well as government and church plans. A "pre-existing condition" is defined as a medical or mental condition for which medical advice, diagnosis, care or treatment was recommended or received preceding the effective date of coverage under a group health plan or health insurance coverage. The only pre-existing conditions for which an exclusion might apply are those for which medical advice, diagnosis, care or treatment was recommended or received within the six-month period preceding the enrollment date. The enrollment date is the day coverage begins, or, of there is a waiting period, the first day of the waiting period.

The regulations contain several examples of how these standards are to be applied:

Example 1. (i) Facts. Individual A is diagnosed with a medical condition 8 months before A's enrollment date in Employer R's group health plan. A's doctor recommends that A take a prescription drug for 3 months, and A follows their commendation.

In this Example 1, Employer R's plan may impose a preexisting condition exclusion with respect to A's condition because A received treatment during the 6-month period ending on A's enrollment date in Employer R's plan by taking the prescription medication during that period. However, if A did not take the prescription drug during the 6-month period, Employer R's plan would not be able to impose a preexisting condition exclusion with respect to that condition.

Example 2. (i) Facts. Individual B is treated for a medical condition 7 months before the enrollment date in Employer S's group health plan. As part of such treatment, B's physician recommends that a follow-up examination be given 2 months later. Despite this recommendation, B does not receive a follow-up examination, and no other medical advice, diagnosis, care, or treatment for that condition is recommended to B or received by B during the 6-month period ending on B's enrollment date in Employer S's plan.

In this Example 2, Employer S's plan may not impose a preexisting condition exclusion with respect to the condition for which B received treatment 7 months prior to the enrollment date.

Example 3. (i) Facts. Same facts as Example 2, except that Employer S's plan learns of the condition and attaches a rider to B's certificate of coverage excluding coverage for the condition. Three months after enrollment, B's condition recurs, and Employer S's plan denies payment under the rider.

In this Example 3, the rider is a preexisting condition exclusion and Employer S's plan may not impose a preexisting condition exclusion with respect to the condition for which B received treatment 7 months prior to the enrollment date. (In addition, such a rider would violate the provisions of § 54.9802–1, even if B had received treatment for the condition within the 6-month period ending on the enrollment date.)

Example 4. (i) Facts. Individual C has asthma and is treated for that condition several times during the 6-month period before C's enrollment date in Employer T's plan. Three months after the enrollment date, C begins coverage under Employer T's plan. Two months later, C is hospitalized for asthma.

In this Example 4, Employer T's plan may impose a preexisting condition exclusion with respect to C's asthma because care relating to C's asthma was received during the 6-month period ending on C's enrollment date (which, under the guidelines stated above, is the first day of the waiting period).

Example 5. (i) Facts. Individual D, who is subject to a preexisting condition exclusion imposed by Employer U's plan, has diabetes, as well as retinal degeneration, a foot condition, and poor circulation (all of which are conditions that may be directly attributed to diabetes). D receives treatment for these conditions during the 6-month period ending on D's enrollment date in Employer U's plan. After enrolling in the plan, D stumbles and breaks a leg.

In this Example 5, the leg fracture is not a condition related to D's diabetes, retinal degeneration, foot condition, or poor circulation, even though they may have contributed to the accident. Therefore, benefits to treat the leg fracture cannot be subject to a preexisting condition exclusion. However, any additional medical services that may be needed because of D's preexisting diabetes, poor circulation, or retinal degeneration that would not be needed by another patient with a broken leg who does not have these conditions may be subject to the preexisting condition exclusion imposed under Employer U's plan.

HIPAA prohibits the use of pre-existing condition exclusions to two groups of persons. First, no such exclusions may be applied to an individual for the medical condition of pregnancy. Second, pre-existing condition exclusions may not be applied to newborn children or to adopted children who are covered under creditable coverage within 30 days of the birth or adoption, and do not have a significant break in coverage.

Example 6: Seven months after enrollment in Employer W's group health plan, Individual C has a child born with a birth defect. Because the child is enrolled in Employer W's plan within 30 days of birth, no pre-existing exclusion may be imposed with respect to the child under Employer W's plan. Three months after the child's birth, C commences employment with Employer X and enrolls with the child in Employer X's plan 45 days after leaving Employer W's plan. Employer X's plan imposes a 12-month exclusion for any pre-existing conditions.

In this example, Employer X's plan may not impose any pre-existing condition exclusion with respect to C's child because the child was covered within 30 days of birth and had no significant break in coverage.

A plan may not impose a pre-existing condition exclusion on any participant or dependent without first giving written notification to the participant of that fact. This notice must include the following information:

- The existence and terms of any such exclusion
- The individual's right to demonstrate creditable coverage

- The individual's right to request a certificate from a prior plan
- A statement that the plan will assist the individual in obtaining a certificate from a prior plan

Credited Periods of Prior Coverage

Group health plans are required to credit periods of previous coverage toward a pre-existing condition period. Portability of health coverage is obtained through the crediting of prior coverage. To avoid a pre-existing condition exclusion, an individual must not experience a break in coverage for 63 consecutive days or more, and must have enough prior coverage credits to offset the new employer's pre-existing condition period. Waiting periods are not considered a break in coverage. These principles can be better explained through examples.

Example 1: Credited Periods of Prior Coverage. Jamie is covered under a group health plan for one year. She terminates employment, takes COBRA coverage and becomes covered under a new employer's plan with a 12-month pre-existing condition provision. She does not experience any break in coverage. No pre-existing condition may be applied to her because she did not experience a break in coverage and her prior coverage of 12 months can be applied to the new employer's 12-month pre-existing condition provision. If she failed to take COBRA coverage and had a lapse in coverage of 63 days or more, she would be subject to the new employer's 12-month pre-existing condition provision.

Example 2: Credited Periods of Prior Coverage. Mary worked for Employer A and was covered under Employer A's group health plan for four months. She leaves Employer A and becomes covered under Employer B's health plan 50 days after leaving Employer A. Employer B's health plan has a 12-month pre-existing condition provision. Employer B's pre-existing provision can apply, but must be reduced by the four months of coverage Mary had with her prior employer. The maximum pre-existing condition period for Mary is thus eight months.

Example 3: Credited Periods of Prior Coverage. Jim worked for Employer A and was covered under Employer A's group health plan for one year. He leaves Employer A and does not elect COBRA coverage. He starts working for Employer B 40 days after leaving Employer A. Employer B's health plan has a 60-day waiting period and a 12-month pre-existing condition provision. Jim has a total lapse in coverage for 100 days. The pre-existing condition provision cannot apply to Jim because the waiting period does not count toward the number of days in his break in coverage. Under HIPAA, Jim is considered to have a break in coverage for only 40 days, and the pre-existing condition exclusion does not affect his coverage.

The requirement that an individual not have a break in coverage of 63 days or more in order to be able to credit prior coverage to his new plan is explained by two examples in the Regulations:

Example 4: Credited Periods of Prior Coverage. Individual A works for Employer P and has creditable coverage under Employer P's plan for 18 months before A's employment terminates. A is hired by Employer Q, and enrolls in Employer Q's health plan, 64 days after the last day of coverage under Employer P's plan. Employer Q's plan has a 12-month pre-existing condition period.

In this example, because A had a break in coverage of 63 days, Employer Q's plan may disregard A's prior coverage and A may be subject to a 12-month pre-existing condition exclusion period.

Example 5: Credited Periods of Prior Coverage

Same facts as in the previous example, except that A is hired by Employer Q and enrolls in Employer Q's plan on the 63rd day after the last date of coverage under Employer P's plan.

In this example, A has a break in coverage of 62 days. Because A's break in coverage is not a significant break in coverage, Employer Q's plan must count A's prior creditable coverage for purposes of reducing the plan's pre-existing condition exclusion period as it applies to A.

Types of Creditable Coverage

Creditable coverage includes coverage of an individual under a group health plan (including a governmental or church plan), individual health insurance coverage, Medicare, Medicaid, military sponsored health care, a program of the Indian health service, a state health benefits risk pool, the Federal Employees Health Benefit Program, a public health plan as defined in regulations and any health benefit plan of the Peace Corps Act. It does not include, however, individual short-term, limited-duration (less than 12 months) policies.

Administrative Demands of Crediting Coverage

There are two administrative sides to crediting prior coverage:

- Issuing certifications of coverage as plan participants leave the former plan
- Crediting prior plan coverage by accepting the certification and applying it to the plan's pre-existing condition provision of the participant's new plan

Employers will need to implement careful procedures to ensure that they are in compliance.

Who Must Issue Certifications of Coverage?

Any provider of healthcare coverage as described in "Types of Creditable Coverage" must provide these notices under certain circumstances. In the case of an employer's group health plan, the plan itself has the obligation to provide these certificates. However, this responsibility may be delegated to the issuer of the insurance policy as part of a written agreement between the plan and the issuer. Even if the issuer fails to provide these notices as it agreed to do, the plan will be deemed to have met its certificate obligations by having agreed with the issuer that it will be responsible for this administrative act.

Under What Circumstances Must a Certification Be Issued?

A certificate must be issued to an individual any time that he or she loses coverage under the plan (including at the expiration of COBRA benefits) or at such times as the individual would have lost coverage but for COBRA. The plan must also issue a certificate whenever an individual or an entity at the request of the individual, requests a certificate within 24 months after the coverage ceases.

What Must the Certification Include?

The certification from the plan or other healthcare payer must be a written statement showing:

- The date the certificate was issued
- The name of the plan
- The name of the participant or dependent to whom the certificate applies
- The name, address, and phone number of the plan administrator or issuer providing the certificate
- The phone number to call for further information
- Either:

a. a statement that the individual had at least 18 months of creditable coverage, or

   b. the date any waiting period (or affiliation period) began

   c. the date creditable coverage ended

The certificate may be sent by first class mail; registered mail is not required.

When Must Plans Begin Providing Certifications?

HIPAA requires that certifications must be issued starting on June 1, 1997 to all individuals who have left the plan since October 1, 1996. The certifications must cover periods starting from July 1, 1996.

When Must Plans Begin Accepting Certifications?

Many plans will have to provide certifications before they are required to accept certifications because the effective dates differ for accepting and providing certifications. Plans must start accepting certifications and crediting prior coverage to their pre-existing condition exclusions for the first plan year beginning after June 30, 1997.

What are the Implications of HIPAA Effective Dates?

As of January 1, 1998, virtually all employers with group health plans are required to both provide certifications and to accept and apply certifications from new employees.

What Happens if the Individual is Unable to Obtain a Certificate?

There may be circumstances in which a new hire is unable to procure a certificate from the plan under which he was previously covered. In such a case, the plan or insurance issuer must take into account all the information that it does obtain or that is produced by the individual in order to determine if the individual has creditable coverage and whether he is entitled to an offset as to the pre-existing condition exclusion period.

According to the regulations,

> A plan or issuer shall treat the individual as having furnished a certificate under paragraph (a) of this section if— (*1*) The individual attests to the period of creditable coverage; (*2*) The individual also presents relevant corroborating evidence of some creditable coverage during the period; and (*3*) The individual cooperates with the plan's or issuer's efforts to verify the individual's coverage. (B) For purposes of this paragraph (c)(3)(i), cooperation includes providing (upon the plan's or issuer's request) a written authorization for the plan or issuer to request a certificate on behalf of the individual, and cooperating in efforts to determine the validity of the corroborating evidence and the dates of creditable coverage. While a plan or issuer may refuse to credit coverage where the individual fails to cooperate with the plan's or issuer's efforts to verify coverage, the plan or issuer may not consider an individual's inability to obtain a certificate to be evidence of the absence of creditable coverage.

Documents that may be used to establish creditable coverage, in the absence of a certificate, include explanations of benefit claims, correspondence from a plan or issuer indicating coverage, pay stubs showing payroll deductions for healthcare coverage, a health insurance identification card, a certificate of coverage, and third-party statements verifying coverage. Creditable coverage verification may also be obtained through phone conversations with the prior plan's representatives.

Within a reasonable period of time of receiving a certificate or other information regarding creditable coverage, the plan or issuer must make a determination as to the individual's period of creditable coverage and notify that person of the determination. It must also submit to the individual, in writing, its determination as to the period of pre-existing condition exclusion. This notice must include the basis for that determination and the source and substance of the information upon which it relied in reaching the determination. A written explanation of the appeal process must also be supplied and the individual is to be given a reasonable period of time in which to submit additional evidence of creditable coverage.

Special Enrollment Periods

Group plans are required to provide special enrollment periods for individuals who do not enroll in the plan at the first opportunity and subsequently lose other sources of coverage. An individual must be allowed to enroll under at least one health benefit plan if:

- The employee (or dependent) had been covered under another group health plan or had an individual health policy at the time coverage was initially offered;

- The employee stated in writing at the time initial enrollment was offered that other coverage was the reason for declining enrollment in the plan, if the plan sponsor requires this;

- The individual lost their coverage as a result of a certain event, such as the loss of eligibility for coverage, expiration of COBRA continuation coverage, termination of employment, reduction in the number of hours of employment, or employer contributions towards such coverage were terminated; and

- The employee requested such enrollment within 30 days of termination of the coverage.

Dependent Special Enrollment Periods

"Dependent" is not defined as any individual who is or may become eligible for coverage under a group health plan because of a relationship to a participant. If a plan provides dependent coverage and a person becomes a dependent through marriage, birth or adoption, the plan must provide a dependent special enrollment period of not fewer than 30 days. If an individual seeks to enroll a dependent during the first 30 days, coverage must become effective:

- In the case of marriage, no later than the first day of the first month beginning after the date the request was received
- In the case of a dependent's birth, the date of such birth
- In the case of adoption or placement for adoption, the date of such adoption or placement for adoption

HMO Special Enrollment Periods

For a group health plan that offers medical care through an HMO, the group plan may provide for an affiliation period if:

- There is no pre-existing condition exclusion imposed.
- No premium is charged to the participant or beneficiary during the affiliation period.
- The affiliation period is applied uniformly without regard to any health-status-related factors.
- It does not exceed two months (or three months in the case of a late enrollee).

Limits on Evidence of Insurability

Group health plans may not establish eligibility rules based on any of the following health-status-related factors:

- Medical condition (including both physical and mental illness)
- Claims experience
- Receipt of health care
- Medical history
- Genetic information
- Evidence of insurability
- Disability

This provision should not be construed to prevent a group plan from establishing limitations or restrictions on the amount, level, extent, or nature of the benefits offered. A rider to HIPAA that was defeated would have required that health plans contain lifetime maximum benefits of no less than $10,000,000.

Premium contributions for individuals with health-status-related factors may not be higher than premiums for individuals who do not have such health-status-related factors. This provision should not be construed to prevent a group health plan from establishing premium discounts, rebates, or modifying co-payments or deductibles in return for adherence to nondiscriminatory wellness programs. For example, if a wellness program bases a reward on the satisfaction of a standard related to a health factor, the program must make the reward available to all similarly situated individuals (and allow a reasonable alternative standard for obtaining the reward in certain cases and properly disclose that reasonable alternative standard), the program must be reasonably designed to promote health and prevent disease and it must give eligible participants the opportunity to qualify for the reward at least once per year, and the total reward must be limited to 20 percent of the cost of employee-only coverage under the plan.

Long-term Care

Employer contributions to an employer group plan providing qualified long-term care coverage that do not exceed certain limitations are excludable from an employee's income. The benefit limits are equal to $270 per day for flat-rate payments, or actual expenses. The per-day rates will be indexed to inflation. Long-term care insurance is not permitted under a cafeteria plan or an FSA, and is not subject to COBRA.

In order for an individual to be eligible for benefits under this insurance, he or she must be unable to perform at least two of the specified activities of daily living for at least 90 days, have a similar level of disability as determined by regulations to be promulgated, or require substantial supervision to protect his or her health and safety due to a cognitive impairment.

Medical Savings Accounts

Beginning in 1997, federal tax-favored medical spending accounts (MSAs) are available to employees of employers having no more than 50 employees and self-employed individuals. MSAs are available to these people provided they are covered under a high-deductible plan. A "high-deductible plan" is a plan with an annual deductible of between $1,950 and $2,900 for an individual, and between $3,850 and $5,800 for a family. The maximum out-of-pocket expenses (including the deductible) must be no more than $3,850 for an individual and no more than $7,050 for a family. This MSA provision is a limited four-year pilot program; however, those individuals who set up MSAs during the pilot period may continue their MSAs beyond the pilot period.

For an employee to be eligible for an MSA, the employee must be covered under an employer-sponsored high-deductible health plan and must not be covered under any other health plan (with some exceptions). Contributions can be made to an MSA either by the individual or by his or her employer. Contributions cannot be made by both the employer and the employee in the same year. The maximum annual contribution that can be made to an MSA for a year is 65% of the deductible under the high-deductible plan for individual coverage and 75% of the deductible for family coverage.

Accelerated Life Insurance Payments

Life insurance proceeds will not be subject to federal income tax where they are paid to a terminally ill or chronically ill individual. A "terminally ill" person is an individual whose physician certifies that the patient can be expected to die within 24 months.

In order for the payments to a chronically ill person to be nontaxable, they must meet several other requirements. They must be for "long-term care services" that are not covered by other insurance, the insurance contract must meet certain consumer protection requirements and the per diem payments may not exceed a per diem limit.

This provision does not apply to all life insurance policies. A policy issued because of the individual's relationship as a director, officer or employee or because of that person's interest in a trade or business is not subject to this non-taxability provision.

Disclosure Requirements of HIPAA

Group health plans are required to provide a summary description of any reduction in covered services or benefits to participants no later than 60 days after the date of the adoption of the change.

Additional information can be obtained through the DOL's website at: *www.dol.gov/dol/topic/health-plans/portability.htm*.

HIPAA Privacy and Security Requirements

HIPAA focused to a large extent on making it easier for employees to transfer health care coverage from one employer to another. HIPAA also contains a subchapter entitled "Administrative Simplification," provisions requiring the Department of Health and Human Services to promulgate standards governing a number of areas, including the electronic data interchange of health information, security standards for health care transactions, and privacy standards for use and disclosure of protected health information. The focus of the remainder of this chapter is the latter sets of regulations, the "Privacy Rule" and the "Security Rule."

The authority granted to HHS to issue the Privacy and Security Rules applies only to covered entities (as explained below) and employers, as such, are not covered entities. Health plans, however, are covered entities—and this is how most employers will be affected by the new rules. Moreover, employers' ability to obtain health information for legitimate purposes (such as determining leave eligibility and disability accommodation issues) will be affected by the constraints imposed by the Privacy Rules on the employees' health care providers.

The Secretary of HHS has delegated responsibility for civil enforcement of the Privacy Rule and the Security Rule to two different divisions, the Office of Civil Rights (OCR) for the Privacy Rule and the Centers for Medicare and Medicaid Services (CMS) for the Security Rule. What are the risks of non-compliance? There is no private right of action for violation of the privacy rules promulgated by HHS. There are, however, civil monetary penalties for such violations, and, in cases of certain violations, criminal penalties as well. Civil penalties may not exceed more than $100 per person, per violation and not more than $25,000 per person per year. "Knowing" violations of the Rules subjects a person to a $50,000 fine and imprisonment of not more than a year. If the offense is committed under false pretenses, a fine of $100,000 and prison term of up to five years is authorized. If the offense is committed with intent to sell, transfer or use protected health information for commercial advantage, personal gain or malicious harm, a fine of $250,000 and a prison term of up to ten years is authorized.

On April 20, 2007, to coincide with the fourth anniversary of the Privacy Rule, the OCR launched an enhanced website on HIPAA compliance and enforcement. *See* http://www.hhs.gov/ocr/privacy/enforcement/ The purpose of the new website was to make it easier for consumers, health care providers and others to get information about how the Department enforces health information privacy rights and standards. The cite contains valuable information on how the OCR processes complaints, what it considers during the investigation process, numbers of complaints received, and examples of complaints and resolutions by the type of issue presented and the type of covered entity involved. This website and the OCR's "Frequently Asked Questions" on the HIPAA Privacy Rule are very useful resources in resolving HIPAA issues.

Overview of Privacy Regulations: Purpose and Scope

The Privacy Rules have three major purposes:

1. To protect and enhance the rights of consumers by providing them access to their health information and controlling inappropriate use of that information;

2. To improve the quality of health care by restoring trust in the health care system among consumers, health care professionals, and those involved in the delivery of care;

3. To improve the efficiency and effectiveness of health care delivery by creating a national framework for health privacy protection that builds on state and local efforts, whether public or private.

PREEMPTION

The third objective of the Rules is achieved through a very broad preemption provision. In a nutshell, the Privacy Rules preempt contrary state law provisions, unless state law is more stringent. "State law" means a constitution, statute, regulation, rule, common law, or other state action having the force and effect of law. There are limited exceptions, and a procedure whereby a state can officially request the Secretary of HHS to except certain laws.

PROTECTED HEALTH INFORMATION

The Rules protect "protected health information" (PHI), defined to mean health information transmitted or maintained in any form or medium that either identifies the individual or can reasonably be used to identify the individual and that (1) is created or received by a health care provider, health plan, employer and other designated entities; **and** (2) relates to the past, present or future physical or mental health or condition of an individual, the provision of health care to an individual, or to the past, present or future payment for the provision of health care to an individual.

"Health information" is broadly defined to include any information (oral or recorded in any medium) that is created or received by a health care provider, health plan, public health authority, employer, life insurer, school or university, or health care clearinghouse and relates to the past, present or future physical or mental health or condition of an individual, the provision of health care to an individual or the past, present or future payment for the provision of health care information to an individual.

Protected health information *excludes*:

- Education records covered by the Family Educational Rights and Privacy Act (FERPA);
- Specific information in records excepted by FERPA as set forth in 20 USC § 1232g(a)(4)(B)(iv) (i.e., treatment records on a student over 18 years old);
- Employment records held by a covered entity in its role as employer.

The latter provision was added by the August 2002 amendments. It is simply a clarifying amendment, as the original final Rules did not intend to reach employment records held by a covered entity in its capacity as employer. However, as the Rules did not clearly spell this out, they were amended to so provide. (See discussion later in this chapter on the effect on employers as sponsors of health plans.)

COVERED ENTITIES DIRECTLY RESPONSIBLE FOR COMPLIANCE

The privacy provisions apply to *covered entities*. A "covered entity" is (1) a health plan; (2) a health care clearinghouse; (3) a health care provider who transmits health information in electronic form; and (4) Medicare prescription drug card sponsors).

What are *health plans*? The regulations list numerous examples including:

- A group health plan, defined to mean a plan that is either insured or self-insured, to the extent the plan provides medical care, that either:
    a. has 50 or more participants; or
    b. is administered by a third party.
- Any other individual or group plan or combination of individual or group plans, that provides or pays for the cost of medical care.

Life, disability and workers' compensation insurers are not "health plans," nor are employers or plan sponsors. Regarding workers' compensation, the Rules provide that a health plan may disclose PHI as authorized by and to the extent necessary to comply with workers' compensation or other similar programs that provide benefits for work-related injuries or illness without regard to fault.

Essential Definitions and Concepts

Disclosure means the release, transfer, provision of access to, or divulging in any other manner of information outside the entity holding the information. *Use* means the sharing, employment, application, utilization, examination, or analysis of such information within an entity that maintains such information.

Treatment, Payment, Health Care Operations (TPO): A broad category of permissible uses and disclosures by covered entities for protected health information.

- *Treatment* means providing health care, including referrals and consultation.
- *Payment* is broadly defined to include activities taken by a health plan to obtain premiums or fulfill responsibility to provide benefits, obtain reimbursement for benefits, and other activities, such as determination of eligibility or coverage (including coordination of benefits), risk adjustments, collections, medical necessity reviews and utilization review.

- *Health Care Operations* again is broadly defined to include services and activities necessary to carry out the covered functions of the covered entity with respect to treatment or payment (e.g., auditing claims and claims appeals).

Consent vs. Authorization: In common usage, we might think of a patient's "consent" or "authorization" to use or disclose health information as meaning the same thing. In the world of the HIPAA Privacy Rules, these words have very different meanings.

- *Consent* refers to the use or disclosure of protected health information for treatment, payment or healthcare operations. The original "final" Rules required that certain health care providers obtain a Consent from each patient prior to using protected health information for certain purposes. This requirement has been eliminated in the August 2002 amendments, and Consents are now optional.

- *Authorization* is required for uses other than treatment, payment or health care operations. As the OCR guidance states, an authorization is a more customized document that gives covered entities permission to use specified PHI for specified purposes. The Rules provide the requirements for a valid authorization. (Discussed in Part V below.)

Minimum Necessary: This standard operates to limit the content of a permissible use or disclosure in certain situations. If a covered entity uses or discloses PHI for TPO, the covered entity must make reasonable efforts to limit the PHI to the minimum amount necessary to accomplish the intended purpose of the disclosure.

- The information that is the "minimum necessary" need not be determined on a case-by-case basis, but can be established in advance by general criteria or protocols suited to the particular issue.

- The "minimum necessary" standard does not apply to uses and disclosures pursuant to an authorization that meets the requirements of the Privacy Rules.

General Privacy Rules

ONLY "PERMITTED" OR "REQUIRED" USES AND DISCLOSURES ARE ALLOWED

A covered entity may not use or disclose protected health information unless "permitted" or "required."

PERMITTED USES AND DISCLOSURES

The general rule is that PHI may be used and disclosed without the individual's consent or authorization for the following enumerated purposes:

1. to the individual;

2. for treatment, payment, or health care operations; typical allowable uses and disclosures include:

a. enrollment,

b. eligibility,

c. claims adjudication and payment,

d. pre-certification and referral,

e. coordination of benefits,

f. utilization review,

g. to review status of claims payment, and

h. audit and quality control.

The August 2002, amendments clarify that a covered entity may disclose PHI for the payment activities of another covered entity and for certain health care operations of another covered entity.

Special rules pertain to psychotherapy notes, defined to mean notes recorded in any medium by a mental health professional documenting or analyzing conversations during private, group, or family counseling that are separated from the rest of an individual's medical record. Psychotherapy notes may not be used or disclosed for most treatment, payment or health care operations without an authorization. Moreover, an authorization for psychotherapy notes may not be combined with an authorization for disclosure of other PHI.

"incident" to a use or disclosure otherwise permitted or required;

This provision was added with the August 2002 amendments, and is designed to provide flexibility to covered entities. An incidental use or disclosure is a "secondary" use or disclosure that cannot reasonably be prevented, is limited in nature, and that occurs as a by-product of an otherwise permitted use or disclosure. The comments to the amendments are given as examples of incidental disclosure sign-in sheets in doctors' waiting rooms, x-ray lightboards in hospitals, and patient information that might be visible in a hospital room. Incidental use and disclosure is permitted only so long as the covered entity has implemented the minimum necessary standard, and has reasonably safeguarded protected health care information to limit incidental uses or disclosures.

1. pursuant to and in compliance with an "authorization" that complies with the form required by the regulations;

2. with respect to health care providers, for facility directories and uses and disclosure for involvement in an individual's care and notification purposes;

3. as permitted by § 164.512 (See Part V regarding use of PHI in litigation and for workplace safety obligations).

4. as permitted by § 164.514 (to the extent relevant here, subsection (g) allows uses and disclosures for underwriting and related purposes).

If a health plan receives PHI for underwriting, premium rating, or other activities relating to the creation, renewal, or replacement of a contract of health insurance or health benefits, and if the insurance or benefits are not placed with the health plan, the PHI received by the health plan may not be used or disclosed for any other purpose, except as may be required by law.

REQUIRED DISCLOSURES

Individual right of access. In general, an individual has a right of access to inspect and obtain a copy of protected health information about the individual except for psychotherapy notes; information compiled in reasonable anticipation of or for use in a civil, criminal or administrative action or proceeding; and PHI that is covered by the Clinical Laboratory Improvements Amendments of 1988 (CLIA).

There are special rules regarding: when denial of access is reviewable and when it is not; the method of requesting access; time limits for response by the covered entity; manner of providing access; manner of communicating denial of access.

Individual right to an accounting. An individual also has a right to receive a written accounting of disclosures of protected health information going back six years (assuming that the covered entity had a duty to comply with the regulations during this time). There are special rules regarding what an accounting of disclosure must contain.

Disclosures to HHS for compliance review.

Effect on Employers *as* Employers

Employers regularly deal with leave requests and disability accommodation issues arising out of their employees' medical conditions. The Family and Medical Leave Act requires employers with more than 50 employees to grant unpaid leave for "serious health conditions." Both the federal Americans with Disabilities Act and Michigan's Persons with Disabilities Civil Rights Act obligate employers to accommodate their employees' disabilities. Medical records are regularly subpoenaed for use in litigation, administrative hearings and arbitrations. The Privacy Rules will govern the method of obtaining such records and how much is disclosed, but do *not* govern the employer's use and disclosure of the information.

The Rules are structured so that their application is dependent upon the entity that uses or discloses protected health information, and the purpose for which the PHI is used or disclosed. Employers *as* employers are not covered entities, and the Rules clarify that medical information held by an employer in its role as employer is not protected health information. The Department of Health and Human Services stresses, however, that a covered entity must remain vigilant that records maintained in its role as a covered entity be protected. "Individually identifiable health information created, received, or maintained by a covered entity in its capacity as a health care provider or health plan remains protected health information. It does not matter if the individual is a member of the covered entity's work force or not."

DISABILITY AND LEAVE DETERMINATIONS: INFORMATION TO BE USED FOR PURPOSES OTHER THAN "TREATMENT, PAYMENT OR HEALTH CARE OPERATIONS"

An employer seeking information to determine an employee's eligibility for leave, disability benefits, accommodation, to justify absences, etc., is not a covered entity seeking information for "treatment, payment or health care operations" as those terms are defined in the Rules. Thus, protected information will be disclosed by a health care provider only if "authorized" by the individual.

AUTHORIZATIONS

As noted, an authorization is the vehicle pursuant to which protected health information may be disclosed or used for purposes other than treatment, payment or health care operations. Sample authorizations for the disclosure of PHI by a health care provider to an employer are included on the HR Michigan web site (www.hrmichigan.com). One authorization permits disclosure of PHI generally pertains exclusively to psychotherapy notes.

When individual is entitled to copy. If a covered entity seeks an authorization from an individual, the covered entity must provide the individual with a copy of the signed authorization.

When an authorization can be required. A health plan may condition enrollment in the plan or eligibility for benefits on an employee's signing of an authorization if the authorization is sought before the individual is enrolled in the plan and is sought for the health plan's eligibility or enrollment determinations or for its underwriting or risk rating determinations. The authorization may not extend to use or disclosure of psychotherapy notes, and may not be combined with any other authorization.

"Authorization" generally required for use and disclosure for purposes other than treatment, payment or health care operations. Subject to limited exceptions, a covered entity generally may not use or disclose protected health information for purposes other than treatment, payment or health care operations without a valid authorization. This means that the doctor, clinic or hospital from which the employer requests treatment or status information will insist that it be provided an authorization that complies with the Privacy Rules.

The Rule governing authorizations was significantly revamped by the August 2002 amendments, to both clarify and simplify the requirements. The following apply to all authorizations.

Core elements of a valid authorization. An authorization must be written in plain language and contain:

- a description of the information to be used or disclosed that identifies the information in a specific and meaningful fashion;
- the name or other specific identification of the person(s) or class of persons authorized to make the requested use or disclosure;
- the name or other specific identification of the person(s) or class of persons to whom the disclosure can be made;
- a description of each purpose of the requested use or disclosure. The statement "at the request of the individual" is a sufficient description if the person about whom the medical information relates asks for the authorization and does not want to provide a statement of the purpose;
- an expiration date or expiration event that relates to the individual or purpose of the use or disclosure;
- signature of the individual and date, and if the authorization is signed by a personal representative, a statement of the representative's authority.

Additional requirements of an authorization. In addition to the above core elements, the authorization must also contain statements sufficient to notify the individual of:

- the individual's right to revoke the authorization in writing and a description of how he may do so;
- the ability or inability of a covered entity to condition treatment, payment, enrollment or eligibility for benefits on the authorization by stating either:
    a. that the covered entity may not require an authorization; or
    b. where an authorization may be required pursuant to § 164.508(b)(4), the consequences to the individual of a refusal to sign the authorization;
- a statement that the information is subject to re-disclosure by the recipient, and no longer be subject to the protections of the Rules.

"Minimum necessary" provisions do not apply in this situation. As noted above, the Privacy Rules generally require covered entities to take reasonable steps to limit the use, disclosure, and requests for protected health information to the "minimum necessary to accomplish the intended purpose."

The "minimum necessary" provisions do not apply to uses or disclosures made pursuant to an authorization. Thus, when an employee signs an authorization for disclosure of PHI by his doctor for his employer's leave determinations, the minimum necessary rules do not apply. Health care providers should not limit the disclosure based upon this concern, although in at least the initial months of compliance, lack of familiarity with the Rules may cause some problems.

LITIGATION

Consent or authorization not required, but other requirements may apply. Employers in litigation with an employee or former employee frequently seek medical records to investigate claims affecting liability or damages. Attorneys will need to recognize that there will be added hoops to jump through to obtain records from health care providers.

Again, the request for records will be by the employer as employer or its counsel—neither of which is a covered entity. The request will be made *to* a covered entity, the hospital, doctor or clinic. The Rules govern how the health care provider will respond. Briefly, the Rules permit disclosure without an authorization or consent:

- in response to an order of a court or an administrative tribunal, to the extent expressly authorized by the order; the "minimum necessary" standard does not apply to the release of information pursuant to this section. However, the information provided must be limited to that required to comply with the order or directive in question.

- in response to a subpoena or discovery request, the records may be produced without a consent or authorization, only if the covered entity receives satisfactory assurances that either the individual has been given notice or a protective order has been requested:

    a. **Notice to the individual**. The covered entity must receive satisfactory assurances from the party seeking the individual's protected health information that the individual has received notice of the request. Satisfactory assurances exist when the party seeking the information informs the covered entity, in writing, and provides appropriate documentation, that it has written to the individual and described the reason for seeking the individual's protected health information, and the individual has either not objected or the individual's objections have been resolved.

        i. The party requesting the protected health information must make a good faith attempt to provide written notice to the individual (or, if the individual's location is unknown, to mail a notice to the individual's last known address);

ii. The notice must include sufficient information about the litigation or proceeding in which the protected health information is requested to permit the individual to raise an objection to the court or administrative tribunal.

b. **Qualified protective order.** The covered entity must receive satisfactory assurances from the party requesting the individual's protected health information that the party seeking the information has requested a qualified protective order to prevent the protected health information from being disclosed outside of the lawsuit or proceeding in question. Satisfactory assurances exist when the party seeking the protected health information informs the covered entity in writing, and provides appropriate documentation, that a request for a protective order has been presented to the court or administrative tribunal with jurisdiction over the dispute, or has been agreed to by the parties. A qualified protective order must:

i. Prohibit the parties from using or disclosing the protected health information for any purpose other than the litigation or proceeding for which such information was requested; and

ii. Require the return to the covered entity or destruction of the protected health information (including all copies made) at the end of the litigation or proceeding.

c. The minimum necessary standard does not apply to disclosures made pursuant to a HIPAA-compliant subpoena or discovery request.

Added Complication—Limited preemption of state law. State law is preempted by the Privacy Rules only if it is more lenient than the Rules. In a state such as Michigan that imposes additional requirements to obtain medical records, those requirements must be met as well.

If, for example, state law requires a written release or waiver of the doctor-patient privilege, the health care provider will insist that the requester of the records provide that document in addition to satisfying the Privacy Rules procedures.

Strategies for obtaining records. Given the cumbersome nature of all the HIPAA subpoena requirements, litigants may opt for simply providing the individual's signed authorization (HIPAA compliant) to the health care provider, along with a state-form subpoena. Note, however, that if this approach is followed, a separate authorization must be supplied for psychotherapy notes.

"Public Health" Activities—OSHA and MIOSHA Compliance

Employer's statutory obligations. Under OSHA, MIOSHA, and other statutes, employers have record-keeping and reporting obligations regarding workplace accidents and safety. For example, OSHA rules require employers to monitor employees' exposure to certain substances and to remove employees from exposure when toxic thresholds have been met. To obtain the relevant health information necessary to determine whether an injury or illness should be recorded or whether an employee must be medically removed from exposure at work, employers must refer employees to health care providers for examination and testing.

Employers' ability to obtain PHI—health care providers need not obtain authorizations in this setting. When employers perform this function, they will not be "covered entities," and may disclose medical information without HIPAA compliance concerns. But how do they *get* the information from health care providers?

The Privacy Rules, allow health care providers to disclose employees' PHI to employers without an authorization from the employees to allow for the effective functioning of these statutes. To be exempt from the authorization requirement, the following limitations apply:

- The health care provider must be a member of the employer's workforce or provide health care to an employee at the request of the employer.

- The health care and disclosure must be in connection with medical surveillance of the workplace or to evaluate whether the employee has a work-related illness or injury.

- The employer must need the disclosed information for purposes of complying with OSHA, the federal Mine Safety Act or state law serving a similar purpose.

- The health care provider must give notice to the employee that the PHI is being disclosed to the employer. If the health care is provided on the work site of the employer, this notice may be given by posting the notice in a prominent place at that location.

Workers' Compensation

Workers' compensation carriers are not covered entities. Workers' compensation insurance is specifically excluded from HIPAA. Carriers and entities that self-insure workers' comp coverage are not covered by the Rules even though they provide coverage for health care services and they use and disclose PHI. Generally, these entities can disclose PHI to any entity without having to comply with HIPAA.

Disclosures to workers' compensation carriers. Workers' compensation carriers must obtain PHI from covered entities such as doctors, hospitals, health plans, HMOs, and other insurers to administer benefits. The Privacy Rule permits disclosure of PHI without individual authorization to workers' compensation insurers, state administrators, employers and other persons or entities involved in workers' compensation systems as authorized by and to the extent necessary to comply with laws relating to workers' compensation or other similar programs, established by law, that provide benefits for work-related injuries or illness without regard to fault. This includes programs established by the Black Lung Benefits Act, the federal Employees' Compensation Act, the Longshore and Harbor Workers' Compensation Act, and the Energy Employees' Occupational Illness Compensation Program Act.

The covered entity is required to reasonably limit the amount of PHI disclosed under §164.512(l) to the "minimum necessary" to accomplish the workers' compensation purpose (unless the disclosure is required by law or pursuant to the individual's authorization). The "minimum necessary" limitation includes disclosure of PHI to obtain payment for healthcare provided to an injured or ill worker.

Effect on Employers as Sponsors of Health Plans

REGULATIONS APPLY DIRECTLY ONLY TO "COVERED ENTITIES" AND EMPLOYERS, AS SUCH, ARE NOT COVERED ENTITIES

HIPAA Privacy Regulations will affect employers who offer health plans to their employees because the Rules govern the flow of PHI from a covered entity to an employer that is the plan sponsor.

HEALTH PLANS' USE AND DISCLOSURE FOR TREATMENT, PAYMENT AND HEALTH CARE OPERATIONS

Health plans are covered entities, and may use or disclose protected health information for treatment, payment, health care operations, but the minimum necessary rules apply.

Health plans' *use* of PHI. For uses of protected health information, the health plan must identify those persons or classes of persons in its work force who need access to the PHI to carry out their duties, and, for each person or class of persons, identify the PHI to which access is needed and conditions appropriate to this access. In addition, the health plan must make reasonable efforts to limit the access of these persons to only "needed" PHI.

Health plans' *disclosure* of PHI. For disclosures of PHI, the minimum necessary Rules require that a health plan implement policies and procedures (which may be standard protocols) that limit the PHI disclosed to the amount reasonably necessary to achieve the purpose of the disclosure. This Rule applies to disclosures that the health plan makes on a routine and recurring basis. For other disclosures, the health plan must develop criteria designed to limit the PHI disclosed to the information reasonably necessary to accomplish the purpose for which the disclosure is sought and review requests for disclosure on an individual basis in accordance with these criteria.

Requests *to* the health plan for PHI. A request for PHI to a health plan can be relied upon as meeting the minimum necessary requirements if the request comes from another covered entity, or a professional employee or a business associate of the health plan for the purposes of providing professional services to the health plan if the professional represents that the information requested is the minimum necessary.

Requests *by* the health plan for PHI. When requesting information from other covered entities, the health plan must limit any request for PHI to information that is reasonably necessary to accomplish the purpose for which the request is made. If a request for PHI to other covered entities is made on a routine and recurring basis, the health plan must implement policies and procedures (which may be standard protocols) that limit the PHI requested to the amount reasonably necessary to accomplish the purpose for which the request is made.

GENERAL RULE FOR GROUP HEALTH PLANS—NO DISCLOSURE OF PHI TO EMPLOYER/SPONSOR WITHOUT PLAN AMENDMENTS

A group health plan may not disclose protected health information to the plan sponsor (employer) and may not allow its insurer or HMO to disclose protected health information to the plan sponsor unless the plan documents restrict the use and disclosure of such information by the plan sponsor as set forth below. *Exceptions*:

- "Summary" health information can be disclosed to the plan sponsor for obtaining premium bids or modifying or terminating the plan. Summary health information is information that may be individually identifiable:

    a. that summarizes the claims history, claims expenses, or types of claims experienced by individuals for whom a plan sponsor has provided health benefits under a group health plan; and

    b. from which information detailed in the "de-identified" health information provision has been deleted, except that 5-digit zip codes may be used.

- Information on whether an individual is participating in a group health plan, or is enrolled in or disenrolled from a health insurance issuer or HMO offered by the plan can also be disclosed.

PERMITTED DISCLOSURES OF PHI TO EMPLOYER/SPONSOR

The Privacy Rule is crafted so as to require the "plan" to require that its "sponsor" agree to be bound by the Rules if the sponsor is going to receive PHI from the plan, even though the sponsor is not itself a covered entity.

Subject to the provisions below, a group health plan may:

- disclose PHI to the plan sponsor to carry out administrative functions, consistent with the provisions below;

- not permit a health insurer or HMO to disclose PHI to the plan sponsor except as authorized in rule;

- not disclose or permit an insurer or HMO to disclose PHI to the plan sponsor unless the Notice of Privacy Practices so states;

- **not disclose PHI to the plan sponsor for the purpose of employment-related actions or decision or in connection with any other benefit or employee benefit plan of the plan sponsor** (§ 164.504(f)(3), emphasis added).

AMENDMENT OF PLAN DOCUMENTS

The plan documents must be amended to incorporate safeguards to achieve the provisions set forth above with the following provisions:

- Establish the permitted and required uses and disclosures of protected health information by the plan sponsor consistent with uses and disclosures authorized by the Privacy Rules, specifically that the plan will use and disclose protected health information for purposes related to health care treatment, payment for health care and health care operations;

    - *Payment* includes activities undertaken by a plan to obtain premiums or determine or fulfill its responsibility for coverage and provision of plan benefits that relate to an individual to whom health care is provided. These activities include, but are not limited to, the following:

        i. determination of eligibility, coverage and cost sharing amounts

        ii. coordination of benefits

        iii. adjudication of health benefit claims

        iv. subrogation of health benefit claims

        v. risk adjusting amounts due based on enrollee health status and demographic characteristics

        vi. billing and collection activities and related health care data processing

        vii. claims management and related health care data processing

viii. obtaining payment under a contract for reinsurance

ix. medical necessity reviews or reviews of appropriateness of care or justification of charges

x. utilization reviews

xi. reimbursement to the plan

- *Health Care Operations* include, but are not limited to, the following activities:

    i. quality assessment

    ii. population-based activities relating to improving health or reducing health care costs, protocol development, case management and care coordination, contacting health care providers and individuals with information about treatment alternatives and related functions;

    iii. rating provider and plan performance, including accreditation, certification, licensing or credentialing activities;

    iv. underwriting, premium rating and other activities relating to the creation, renewal or replacement of a contract of health insurance or health benefits, and ceding, securing or placing a contract for reinsurance of risk relating to health care claims;

    v. conducting or arranging for medial review, legal services, and auditing functions, including fraud and abuse detection and compliance programs;

    vi. business planning and development;

    vii. business management and general administrative activities of the plan;

    viii. resolution of internal grievances; and

    ix. due diligence in connection with the sale, transfer, merger or consolidation of all or part of the covered entity with another covered entity or, following completion of the sale, transfer, merger, or consolidation, will become a covered entity.

- Provide that the group health plan will disclose protected health information to the plan sponsor only upon receipt of a certification by the plan sponsor that the plan documents have been amended and the plan sponsor agrees to:

    a. not use or disclose the information other than as permitted or required by law;

    b. ensure that any agents, including a subcontractor, to whom it provides protected health information agree to the same restrictions;

    - **not use or disclose the information for employment-related actions and decisions or in connection with any other benefit or employee benefit plan of the plan sponsor unless authorized by the individual** (emphasis added);

    - report any inconsistent uses or disclosures to the group health plan;

    - make available protected health information in accordance with the right of access provision, § 164.524;

    - make available protected health information for amendment and incorporate amendments as required by the Rules, § 164.526;

    - make available protected health information required to provide an accounting of disclosures as required by the Rules, § 164.528;

    - make its internal practices, books and records available to the Secretary of HHS for compliance review;

    - if feasible, return or destroy protected health information, and retain no copies of such protected health information when no longer needed, or if return or destruction is not feasible, limit further uses and disclosures to those purposes that make the return or destruction infeasible;

    - ensure that "adequate separation" is established.

RETENTION OF PLAN AMENDMENTS

Plan amendments must be maintained in written or electronic form for six years from the later of the date of its creation or the date it was last in effect.

ADEQUATE SEPARATION: FIREWALLS

Pursuant to § 164.504(f)(2)(iii), the plan documents must:

- describe those employees or classes of employees or other persons under the control of the plan sponsor to be given access to protected health information; all employees who receive information in the ordinary course of business must be included in the description;

- restrict the access to and use by such employees to plan administration functions that the plan sponsor performs; and

- provide an effective mechanism for resolving any issues of noncompliance by such employees, including disciplinary sanctions.

- Note the difficulties if an employee or class of employees has multiple responsibilities, such as plan administrator and HR manager. The employer will have to establish protocols to ensure that the employee not use PHI for impermissible purposes.

NOTICE OF PRIVACY PRACTICES

As a covered entity, a group health plan must provide "adequate notice" of its uses and disclosures of PHI, an individual's rights under the Rules and the plan's duties. The obligation varies depending on whether the plan in question is insured or self-insured. The contents of the required Notice are set forth in detail in the Rules.

- Variations in the obligation to maintain and disseminate based on insured status and amount of PHI that a plan has.

    a. **Insured plan that has no PHI other than summary PHI and enrollment/disenrollment information.** This type of plan need not itself maintain or provide a Notice of Privacy Practices. Rather, the insurer or HMO will provide the Notice of Privacy Practices.

    b. **Insured plan that has PHI in addition to summary PHI and enrollment/disenrollment information.** This type of plan must maintain a Notice of Privacy Practices, and provide it upon request.

    c. **Self-insured plan.** This type of plan must maintain and disseminate the Notice of Privacy Practices. The Notice must have been provided on or before the plan's compliance deadline to individuals then covered by the plan—meaning the named insureds, not the dependents. The Notice must be posted on a covered entity's web site if the site is used to provide information about benefits. The Notice may be disseminated by e-mail under certain circumstances, but the individual retains the right to request a hard copy. New enrollees are entitled to Notice, and material changes to the Notice must be re-disseminated. At least every three years, the plan must notify individuals then covered by the plan of the availability of the notice and how to obtain it.

- The following language is required, prominently displayed:

  THIS NOTICE DESCRIBES HOW MEDICAL INFORMATION ABOUT YOU MAY BE USED AND DISCLOSED AND HOW YOU CAN GET ACCESS TO THIS INFORMATION. PLEASE REVIEW IT CAREFULLY.

- Description of uses and disclosures for treatment, payment, health care operations and at least one example of each.

- Description of other purposes for uses and disclosures for which written authorization is not required.

- If uses and disclosures are limited by more stringent law, a description of those limitations.

- Statement that other uses and disclosures will be made only with authorization.

- Statement that individual has the right to revoke authorizations.

- Statement of the five individual rights under the Rules.

- Statement of the right to receive a paper copy of the Notice.

- Statement of the covered entity's legal duties, including the duty to maintain privacy of PHI, provide and abide by the Notice of Privacy Practices (NPP), and provide notice of changes in the NPP.

- Statement that the individual has a right to complain to the plan or to HHS.

- Identification of the contact person.

- Effective date.

Distinction Between Certain Insured and Self-Insured Group Health Plans—Duties Under the Rules' "Administrative Requirements"

In addition to imposing affirmative privacy obligations, the Privacy Rules also require covered entities to take extensive action to ensure that compliance with the privacy obligations will not be left to chance. These obligations are set forth in the administrative requirements of § 164.530 and are detailed below.

EXEMPTION FOR INSURED GROUP HEALTH PLANS

Some group health plans are exempted from these requirements. Section 164.530(k) exempts group health plans that provide benefits solely through an insurance contract or an HMO and that do not create or receive protected health information other than summary health information or information on whether the individual is participating in the plan.

Such insured plans are subject to only a few of the administrative requirements set forth in § 154.530. They must not retaliate against anyone for exercising rights afforded by the Rules, and cannot require anyone to waive the right to file a complaint with the Secretary of HHS as a condition of enrolling in a health plan.

SELF-INSURED GROUP HEALTH PLANS AND PLANS THAT CREATE OR RECEIVE PROTECTED HEALTH INFORMATION

The exemption from the administrative requirements is limited. It does not apply if:

- the plan is not wholly insured;

- the plan is insured, but nonetheless receives or creates PHI other than summary PHI and enrollment/disenrollment information.

If the group health plan is not exempt, it is subject to the following requirements.

ADMINISTRATIVE REQUIREMENTS

A non-exempt covered entity must appoint a privacy officer who is responsible for the development of policies and procedures. This position must be documented. Implementation of this requirement is left to the discretion of the covered entity. While HHS recognized that there may be some advantages to establishing formal qualifications, it concluded the disadvantages outweigh the advantages. Implementation will vary widely depending on the size and nature of the covered entity, with small offices assigning this as an additional duty to an existing staff person, and large organizations creating a full-time privacy official.

The privacy officer should:

- Know the rules (EDI, privacy, security)

- Develop overall privacy policies

- Develop Notice of Privacy Practices

- Track use and disclosure of PHI

- Make sure legal drafting is complete (e.g., plan amendments, Business Associate contracts and authorizations)

- Establish structures to ensure individual rights

- Develop and implement appropriate firewalls

- Implement and enforce Individual Rights

- Develop Employee Training Program

- Develop complaint process and sanctions

- Establish programs to audit and monitor Business Associates and internal compliance
- Coordinate with other laws

A non-exempt covered entity must develop policies and procedures to comply with the Privacy Rules. They must be reasonable, take into account the size and type of activities that relate to PHI undertaken by the health plan and be changed as necessary and appropriate to comply with the law. Necessary policies:

- Policies regarding use and disclosure of PHI
- Minimum necessary policies
- Authorization policies
- De-identification policies
- Employee training and sanction policies
- Record retention policies
- Individual Rights policies
- Security policies

Necessary procedures:

- Procedures to obtain authorizations
- Procedures to enforce individual rights and prevent retaliation
- Complaint procedures
- Procedures for handling inquiries
- Procedures for developing, maintaining and distributing the Privacy Notice
- Procedures for protecting PHI

A non-exempt covered entity must appoint a contact person who is responsible for receiving complaints and providing information about Notices of Privacy Practices, and document the designation.

A non-exempt covered entity must provide a process for individuals to make complaints regarding policies and procedures; complaints and dispositions must be documented.

A non-exempt covered entity must train all members of its workforce on its policies and procedures regarding protected health information, including updated training as policies and procedures change. *Note:* Current employees must be trained as of the compliance date. New employees must be trained within a reasonable time. Training must be documented and maintained.

A non-exempt covered entity must have in place administrative, technical and physical safeguards to protect the privacy of protected health information. *Note*: The health plan must reasonably safeguard PHI from any intentional or unintentional use or disclosure that would violate the Rules. Examples include shredding documents prior to disposal, locking doors to medical records departments or file cabinets, limiting personnel with access to keys, passwords, and encrypting information transmitted over open networks.

A non-exempt covered entity must apply sanctions against members of its workforce who fail to comply with the privacy policies and procedures; sanctions must be documented when applied.

A non-exempt covered entity must mitigate to the extent practicable any known harmful effect of a use or disclosure of protected health information in violation of the Rules.

A non-exempt covered entity must maintain copies of policies, procedures and notices in written or electronic form, and retain the copies for six years from the later of creation or last date in effect.

Health plans in this category are prohibited from retaliating against individuals for exercising rights under the Rules, and from conditioning any benefit on the individual's waiver of the right to file a complaint with the Secretary of HHS.

Additional Requirements: Disclosures of Protected Health Information to Parties Other Than the Plan Sponsor

THE BUSINESS ASSOCIATE RULES

Apart from disclosures to the plan sponsor, the health plan may have contracts with third party administrators, managed care providers, insurers, etc. These entities are "business associates," defined by the Rules to mean a person (other than an employee of the covered entity) who performs a function for the covered entity that involves the use or disclosure of individually identifiable health information, such as claims processing or administration, data analysis, utilization review and billing.

HHS has no authority to directly regulate the practices of these third party entities, at least to the extent that they are not covered entities themselves. HHS devised a clever way to effectively regulate them, however, by imposing limitations on the disclosures that can be made to them by covered entities. Thus, a health plan may disclose protected health information to a business associate only if it receives "satisfactory assurances" that the business associate will appropriately safeguard the information. These assurances must be documented in a written contract that meets the requirements of the Privacy

Rules. This means that the business associate must agree to safeguard the confidentiality of protected health information in a manner consistent with the obligations imposed by the Rules on the covered entity/health plan itself.

WHEN NON-COMPLIANCE OF THE BUSINESS ASSOCIATE MAY BE ATTRIBUTED TO THE COVERED ENTITY

A covered entity "is not in compliance" with the general privacy obligations set forth in the Rules if it knows of a pattern or activity or practice of the business associate that constituted a material breach or violation of the business associate's obligation under the contract, unless the covered entity takes reasonable steps to cure the breach or end the violation, and, if such steps are not successful, to either terminate the contract or report the violation to the Secretary of HHS.

DEADLINE EXTENSION FOR BUSINESS ASSOCIATE CONTRACTS

Covered entities (except for small health plans that had until 2004 to comply) are given an extra year to change existing business associate contracts. This extension applies only to "evergreen" or automatically renewing contacts in existence as of October 15, 2002. The extension will last a full year only if the contract is not affirmatively renewed or modified during that year.

MODEL BUSINESS ASSOCIATE CONTRACT

The August 2002 amendments to the Privacy Rules provided sample business associate contract provisions. These provisions appear on the HR Michigan web site (www.hrmichigan.com).

Individual Rights

Individuals are granted a number of rights, including:

Notice and a full description of the covered entity's disclosure and use practices, and the individual's rights and the covered entity's legal duties. For group health plans, this notice may be provided by the insurer or HMO if the benefits are provided solely by the insurer or HMO and the plan does not receive any PHI other than summary information. The Notice must describe:

- the Plan's uses and disclosures of PHI
- privacy rights with respect to PHI
- the Plan's duties with respect to PHI
- rights to file a complaint with the Plan and HHS
- who to contact for further information about the Plan's privacy practices

The notice must be provided no later than the compliance date for the individuals covered by the plan, at the time of enrollment for new enrollees, and within 60 days of a material change. Every three years, the plan must remind currently covered individuals about the availability or and how to obtain the notice.

The right to inspect and copy protected health information about the individual in the Plan's "Designated Record Set," which does not include psychotherapy notes, information compiled in reasonable anticipation of or for use in a civil, criminal or administrative action or proceeding, or PHI that is covered by the Clinical Laboratory Improvements Amendments of 1988 (CLIA).

- An individual can be required to request access to PHI in writing as long as the individual is informed of such a requirement;

- A covered entity must respond to a request for access no later than 30 days after receipt of the request.

- An individual's request to access PHI can be denied for the following reasons:

    - If PHI is created during research, the access to PHI may be temporarily suspended if the individual is notified in advance.

    - If the records where PHI is held are subject to the federal Privacy Act of 1974, if applicable.

    - If the PHI was obtained from someone other than a health care provider under a promise of confidentiality and the access requested would reveal the source of the information.

    - Access is reasonably likely to endanger the life or physical safety of the individual or another person.

    - The PHI refers to another person (except for a health care provider) and access is reasonably likely to cause substantial harm to that person.

    - The request is made by the individual's personal representative and access is reasonably likely to endanger the life or physical safety of the individual or another person.

- An individual has the right to review a denial based on the last three reasons, endangering the life or the individual or another person.

- The regulations explicitly set out the manner of providing access and of communicating denial of access.

An individual has the right to have covered entity amend or correct PHI in a Designated Record Set for as long as the PHI is maintained in the designated record set. A request to amend can be denied only for the following reasons:

- The information is accurate and complete as it is.
- The covered entity to whom the request was made did not create the information (unless the individual has a reasonable basis to believe that the originator of the PHI is no longer available to make an amendment).
- The information is not in a Designated Record Set.
- The individual would not be able to inspect or copy the information.

An individual can be required to request an amendment in writing as long as the individual is informed of such a requirement. A covered entity must act on an individual's request for amendment no later than 60 days after receipt of the request. The manner in which a request is granted or denied is set forth in the regulations.

Under § 164.528, **an individual has a right to receive a written accounting** of uses and disclosures of protected health information going back six years (assuming that the covered entity had a duty to comply with the regulations during this time). Exceptions:

- to carry out treatment, payment and health care operations;
- to the individuals themselves;
- "incident" to a permitted or required use or disclosure;
- pursuant to a valid authorization;
- to family or friends involved in an individual's care;
- for national security or intelligence purposes; or
- to correctional institutions or law enforcement officials.

Any accounting of disclosures to an individual pursuant to this rule must include:

- The date of the disclosure.
- The name and address (if known) of the person or organization that received the PHI.
- A description of the PHI that was disclosed.
- A statement for the purpose or basis for the disclosure, or a copy of any request for the PHI that prompted the disclosure.

The covered entity must act on the individual's request for an accounting of disclosures within 60 days of the individual's request. The covered entity is allowed one 30-day extension. One accounting in any 12 month period must be provided free of charge.

An individual has a right to request restrictions on certain uses and disclosures beyond the basic protections granted by the Rules. However, a covered entity is not required to agree to the restriction. If a covered entity does agree to a restriction, the restriction would not apply to the following:

- An individual accessing his or her own PHI
- An individual requesting an accounting of his or her own PHI
- Instances for which an authorization or opportunity to agree or object is not required

If a restriction is agreed to, it will be honored until one of the following occurs:

- The individual agrees or requests a termination in writing or orally and such a request is documented.
- The covered entity terminates its agreement. Such a termination is only effective with respect to PHI created or received after the covered entity has informed the individual of the termination.

Under §164.522(b), **an individual has the right to request to receive communications** of PHI from the health plan by alternative means or alternative locations and the health plan must accommodate such reasonable requests as long as:

- the individual states that disclosure of all or part of the information to which the request pertains could endanger the individual;
- the individual specifies how payment will be made if there is a cost of accommodating the request;
- the individual specifies the alternative address or method of contact; and

the individual can be required to put in writing a request to receive confidential communication of PHI.

Upcoming Amendment to the Privacy Rule

The Genetic Information Nondiscrimination Act of 2008 not only amends the portability rules and prohibits discrimination in the workplace based on genetic information, but also requires amendments to the Privacy Rule to provide that genetic information is treated as "health information" and to prohibit group health plans and insurance issuers from using or disclosing PHI that is genetic information for underwriting purposes. HHS is expected to formulate new regulations in 2009.

Overview of Security Rule: Purpose and Scope

The Security Rule specifically focuses on protecting the **confidentiality, integrity, and availability of electronic protected health information ("EPHI")** as defined in the Security Rule. The EPHI that a covered entity creates, receives, maintains, or transmits must be protected against reasonably anticipated threats, hazards, and impermissible uses and/or disclosures. The requirements, standards, and implementation specifications of the Security Rule apply to the same "covered entities" that are reached by the HIPAA Privacy Rules. Many employers that are not direct health care providers are nonetheless subject to the HIPAA Security Rule by two mechanisms. First, companies that maintain health plans for their employees will have personnel who perform health plan functions (among other functions, typically). As a result, some protected health information ("PHI") of beneficiaries of the plan will reside on, be transmitted over, and be accessible by a company's computer and other electronic systems, rendering the PHI into EPHI. In this way, the Security Rule reaches the company in its health plan functions directly, as a covered entity.

Second, the company as health plan sponsor becomes obligated through amendments to the plan documents. Security Rule Standard "Requirements for Group Health Plans" requires that the plan document be amended to provide that the plan sponsor will "reasonably and appropriately safeguard electronic protected health information created, received, maintained, or transmitted to or by the plan sponsor on behalf of the group health plan." Specifications under this Standard effectively incorporate all of the other standards and specifications of the Security Rule. In this manner the Security Rule binds plan sponsors indirectly. The approach is analogous to the way both the Privacy and Security Rules reach other non-covered entities through contractual business associate agreements.

The "Security Rule" regulations became effective on April 21, 2003. The initial compliance date for covered entities other than small health plans was April 20, 2005; small health plans (those with revenues of $5 million or less) had until April 20, 2006 to comply.

Fundamental Obligations of a Covered Entity

The Security Rule requires that each covered entity must:

Ensure the confidentiality, integrity, and availability of EPHI that it creates, receives, maintains, or transmits;

Protect against any reasonably anticipated threats and hazards to the security or integrity of EPHI; and

Protect against reasonably anticipated uses or disclosures of EPHI that are not permitted by the HIPAA Privacy Rule.

Electronic Protected Health Information

The Rule protects "electronic protected health information" ("EPHI"). PHI is, as employers know from their Privacy Rules compliance, health information transmitted or maintained (in any form or medium) that identifies an individual or can reasonably be used to identify an individual and that (1) is created or received by a health care provider, health plan, employer and other designated entities; and (2) relates to the past, present or future physical or mental health or condition of an individual, the provision of health care to an individual, or to the past, present or future payment for the provision of health care to an individual. Electronic PHI – EPHI - is PHI that is transmitted by or maintained in an electronic medium.

ESSENTIAL DEFINITIONS AND CONCEPTS

In complying with the Security Rule, covered entities must be aware of the definitions provided for confidentiality, integrity, and availability as given by 45 C.F.R. § 164.304.

- **Confidentiality** means "the property that data or information is not made available or disclosed to unauthorized persons or processes."

- **Integrity** means "the property that data or information have not been altered or destroyed in an unauthorized manner."

- **Availability** means "the property that data or information is accessible and useable upon demand by an authorized person."

In addition, to understand the requirements of the HIPAA Security Rule, it is helpful to be familiar with the security terminology the Rule uses. The Security Rule is separated into six main sections. Each includes several mandatory standards, and a larger number of implementation specifications with which a covered entity must comply or which it must otherwise address.

Security Standards: General Rules. The general requirements all covered entities must meet. These establish flexibility of approach. They identify standards and implementation specifications, both *required* and *addressable* (described in more detail below). They identify decisions a covered entity must make regarding addressable implementation specifications. And they require the maintenance of security measures to continue reasonable and appropriate protection of electronic protected health information.

Administrative Safeguards. Administrative actions, policies, and procedures to manage the selection, development, implementation, and maintenance of security measures to protect EPHI and to manage the conduct of the covered entity's workforce in relations to EPHI.

Physical Safeguards. Physical measures, policies, and procedures to protect a covered entity's EPHI and to control access to it.

Technical Safeguards. The technology and the policy and procedures for its use that protect EPHI and control access to it.

Organizational Requirements. Standards for business associate contracts and other arrangements; and requirements for group health plans.

Policies and Procedures and Documentation Requirements. Requirements to implement reasonable and appropriate policies and procedures to comply with the standards, implementation specifications and other requirements of the Security Rule.

Many of the standards contain implementation specifications, which are more detailed descriptions of the method or approach that can be used to meet a particular standard. Some are required; others are addressable. All standards are required, however, and covered entities therefore must comply with each.

- A *required* specification, like a standard, must be complied with according to its terms.
- An *addressable* specification must be assessed by the covered entity to determine whether it is a reasonable and appropriate safeguard for implementation in light of the covered entity's environment. In deciding what security measures to use, the covered entity may take into account its **size, its complexity, and its capabilities; its technical infrastructure including hardware and software capabilities; the probability and criticality of potential risks to EPHI; and the costs of particular security measures**. After assessment, the covered entity must decide if it will implement the specification according to its terms, implement an equivalent alternative measure that allows the entity to comply with the standard, or not implement the specification or any alternative because such measures are not rea-

sonable and appropriate for the environment. **These assessments must be documented.**

For example, the Security Rule specification for "Contingency Operations" is addressable. A small county health plan with a workforce of one person may reasonably determine that an appropriate back-up plan is to maintain a copy of EPHI on a portable disk which is stored off-site in a locked and fireproof safe. Obviously, a large employer with a health plan covering hundreds of employees and an information technology system supporting multiple users and applications will be obliged to have, or to develop, a much more sophisticated contingency plan.

SUMMARY OF ADMINISTRATIVE, PHYSICAL AND TECHNICAL SAFEGUARDS

Standards – Required **Implementation Specifications**

(R)=Required
(A)=Addressable

Administrative Safeguards

Standards – Required	Implementation Specifications
Security Management Process	Risk Analysis (R)
	Risk Management (R)
	Sanction Policy (R)
	Information System Activity Review (R)
Assigned Security Responsibility	
Workforce Security	Authorization and/or Supervision (A)
	Workforce Clearance Procedure Termination Procedures (A)
Information Access Management	Isolating Health care Clearinghouse Function (R)
	Access Authorization (A)
	Access Establishment and Modification (A)
Security Awareness and Training	Security Reminders (A)
	Protection from Malicious Software (A)
	Log-in Monitoring (A)
	Password Management (A)
Security Incident Procedures	Response and Reporting (R)
Contingency Plan	Data Backup Plan (R)
	Disaster Recovery Plan (R)
	Emergency Mode Operation Plan

	(R)
	Testing and Revision Procedure (A)
	Applications and Data Criticality Analysis (A)
Evaluation	
Business Associate Contracts and Other Arrangement	Written Contract or Other Arrangement (R)

Physical Safeguards

Facility Access Controls	Contingency Operations (A)
	Facility Security Plan (A)
	Access Control and Validation Procedures (A)
	Maintenance Records (A)
Workstation Use	
Workstation Security	
Device and Media Controls	Disposal (R)
	Media Re-use (R)
	Accountability (A)
	Data Backup and Storage (A)

Technical Safeguards

Access Control	Unique User Identification (R)
	Emergency Access Procedure (R)
	Automatic Logoff (A)
	Encryption and Decryption (A)
Audit Controls	
Integrity	Mechanism to Authenticate Electronic Protected Health Information (A)

Person or Entity Authentication

Transmission Security Integrity Controls (A)

Encryption (A)

PROCEDURAL APPROACH TO COMPLIANCE

The HIPAA Security Rule may be characterized as highly procedural in nature, and as requiring significant documentation. This is true both with respect to the substantive requirements of the Rule – it imposes on covered entities obligations to implement, maintain, and assess a large number of procedures the intended effect of which is to protect the availability, the confidentiality, and the integrity of EPHI. The Rule also imposes requirements with respect to how the covered entity brings itself into compliance. Risk assessment is required. Documentation of the risk assessment process is required. Implementation of policies and procedures is required. Documentation of final policies and procedures is required. Training is required. Documentation of training is required. Monitoring of security incidents is required. Documenting and maintaining the documentation of security incidents is required. And so on.

Complying with the HIPAA Security Rule may seem daunting as a result. It can be done by moving through key compliance activities, remembering that they are to be performed with a keen sensitivity to the realities of the EPHI environment, the risks to EPHI, the capacities and resources of the covered entity, and the obligation for good documentation. Also, companies that have already complied with the HIPAA Privacy Rules will find that some of those policies are applicable and helpful in Security Rule compliance and may be adopted for that purpose. Similarly, companies that are subject to other security regulations, such as Sarbanes-Oxley, often find that they already have policies and procedures in place that meet some of the Security Rule specifications. In such instances, the reliance on existing policies may be formally adopted as a policy and documented in order to comply with particular Security Rule specifications.

Here are key compliance activities. In performing each, the assessment and activity must be documented.

1. *Designate a Security Officer.*

2. *Assemble a Security Team.* This group will do much of the compliance work, in consultation with other members of the organization as needed. The Team should reflect the appropriate needs and resources of the covered entity. It will typically include an in-

dividual responsible for human resources, an individual responsible for information technology, and an individual with overall business responsibility. In larger organizations, it will include representatives from across the organization and others, such as those responsible for contracting, benefit plan administration, and risk management.

3. *Conduct a Risk Analysis.* The Security Team must

  (a) Inventory all EPHI and the electronic devices (personal computers, laptops, handheld devices, portable disks and drives, and the like) by which EPHI is stored, transmitted, or made available, and the software applications and other tools that apply to it.

  (b) Identify existing policies, procedures, and security measures already in place that might be responsive to Security Rule standards and implementation specifications.

  (c) Conduct a risk analysis, identifying the potential risks of improper disclosure, potential risks to confidentiality, and the vulnerability of EPHI to internal and external risks (natural or man-made) should be considered.

4. *Implement Risk Management Measures.* Document findings from the risk analysis and develop a plan of solutions to reasonably and appropriately address all security risks.

5. *Conclude a Review and Assessment of Each Standard and Specification, and Assure that an Appropriate Policy, Procedure, and/or Assessment Exists and Is Documented.*

Note that one important set of activities that will be required (but not the only one) is to establish information access controls. Covered entities must either identify existing policies, or must draft written polices and procedures for EPHI access and controls.

Here as elsewhere it is important to determine the appropriate people to assume documentation responsibilities.

6. *Amend Business Associate Agreements.* Make appropriate changes so that agreements include language protecting EPHI.

7. *Amend Plan Documents and Summary Plan Descriptions.* Such amendments are required by the standard imposing Requirements for Group Health Plans. This means incorporating provisions requiring the plan sponsor to:

(a) Implement administrative, physical, and technical safeguards that reasonably and appropriately protect the confidentiality, integrity, and availability of the EPHI that it creates, receives, maintains, or transmits on behalf of the group health plan

(b) Ensure that the adequate separation of employees and information required by the privacy rule is supported by reasonable and appropriate security measures

(c) Ensure that any agent (including a subcontractor) to whom the plan sponsor provides EPHI agrees to implement reasonable and appropriate security measures to protect the EPHI

(d) Report to the group health plan any security incident of which the plan sponsor becomes aware.

8. *Conduct Security Awareness Training.* All personnel who have responsibility for or access to EPHI must be trained on the requirements of the Security Rule and on the covered entity's compliance policies and procedures. Sometimes training sessions may be taped or placed on dvd's for circulation through large organizations. Training and awareness include among other things periodic security reminders, user education regarding virus protections, confidentiality practices, the importance of login success and failure and the use of passwords.

CHAPTER 11: Family and Medical Leave Act

The Family and Medical Leave Act (FMLA) provides eligible employees of covered employers the right to take up to 12 work-weeks of unpaid leave in a 12-month period for the birth of a child, for placement of a child for adoption or foster care, to care for a close family member (spouse, parent, son, or daughter) with a serious health condition, or when the employee's own serious health condition makes the employee unable to perform his or her job.

The FMLA does not preempt state family or medical leave laws. Also, FMLA benefits must be provided to an individual in addition to and separately from any other rights or benefits that the individual may have under federal and state anti-discrimination laws, including the Americans With Disabilities Act. Employers are free to agree to leave policies which are more generous than those mandated by statute.

Rights granted by the FMLA may be enforced by employees in court, individually or as a class action, or by the Department of Labor ("DOL"). Available remedies include actual damages, interest, double damages, attorney fees, and reinstatement.

The DOL has recently issued revised FMLA regulations, which become effective January 16, 2009. In addition, the FMLA was amended in early 2008 to provide additional leave rights for otherwise eligible employees who (1) have family members called up for or serving on active military duty or (2) are "next of kin" or a family member of someone with a serious injury or illness attributable to military duty. Because the new leave rights and DOL's new regulations have not yet been interpreted by any courts, and because the DOL will have new leadership under a new presidential administration, the information set forth below should be confirmed with qualified employment counsel after this edition's publication.

Employers Covered By The FMLA

A "covered employer" is defined as a private employer with 50 or more employees during 20 or more weeks in the current or previous calendar year, and any public employer, regardless of the number of persons employed. In determining whether the 50-employee threshold has been met, leased, temporary, and part-time employees are all to be counted. Under certain circumstances, employees of companies that are closely related may be counted together if the companies have common management, the labor relations functions are centralized, or there is common ownership or financial control.

The United States Supreme Court has held that, unlike the Americans With Disabilities Act and certain other discrimination statutes, the 11th Amendment does not bar all individual FMLA claims against a state for money damages. Those claims which are based on the serious health condition of a parent, spouse, or child, and those based on the birth or adoption of a child, are not barred. However, courts considering the issue since the Supreme Court's ruling have held that individual claims for money damages based on an individual's serious health condition are precluded by the 11th Amendment.

Joint Employers

The regulations contain special rules for joint employment arrangements, including individuals engaged through temporary help or leasing agencies. The placement agency generally is considered the primary employer and thus is responsible for giving required notices, providing leave, maintaining health benefits, and restoring employment. The entity using the services of the employee is treated as the secondary employer and is responsible for compliance with the prohibited acts provisions with respect to its leased employees, including prohibitions against interfering with an individual's attempt to exercise FMLA rights. The secondary employer also is responsible for accepting an employee returning from leave in place of any replacement employee.

A joint employment relationship generally will be considered to exist when there is an arrangement between employers to share an employee's services or to interchange employees; where one employer acts directly or indirectly in the interest of the other employer in relation to the employee; or where the employers share control over the employee, because one employer controls the other, or both are under common control. The existence of a joint employment relationship is not determined by any single criterion. Instead, the entire relationship is viewed in its totality. The new regulations make clear that where an employer his hired an outside organization to provide a certain service, such as payroll, and the employer is paying for the services as opposed to paying for the provision of employees, the two entities are not joint employers are responsible only for their respective employees.

Successor Employers

An eligible employee of a covered employer who commences FMLA leave before the business is sold to a successor in interest is entitled to be restored to employment by the successor employer. If the successor employer employs fewer than 50 persons, it is only obligated to complete the cycle of any FMLA leave requests initiated by employees of the predecessor employer, where the requesting employees met the eligibility criteria at the time the leave was requested.

Employees Eligible For FMLA Leave

To be an "eligible employee," an individual must meet all three of the following qualifications. He or she must:

- have worked for the employer for at least 12 months,
- have worked at least 1,250 hours during the year preceding the start of the leave, and
- be employed at a worksite where the employer employs at least 50 employees within a 75 mile radius.

Although the DOL regulations suggest that an employer can expand eligibility by having more generous policies, the United States Supreme Court has made it clear that only individuals meeting all of the above requirements will be considered eligible under the FMLA. The DOL has not significantly changed its regulations in light of the Supreme Court decision. However, the DOL has agreed that if an individual is basing a claim on an employer's representations but would not otherwise qualify for FMLA leave, the employee will have to show that he or she was harmed by relying on those representations.

For purposes of determining eligibility, the 12 months of service is cumulative and need not be consecutive. Therefore, if an employee worked for the employer in the past and that employment added to the current tenure exceeds 12 months, the employee will generally meet the first requirement. However, under the new regulations, if there has been a break in service of seven years or more between the first employment and the current tenure, then the previous service will not count toward the 12 months unless the break was caused by military service, the employee has contractual rights to recall following a layoff, or the employer has a policy agreeing to count the prior service. If an employee is maintained on the payroll for any part of a week, then the week counts as a week of employment. An employee who has worked any part of 52 weeks is deemed to have worked for 12 months.

Whether an employee has worked the minimum 1,250 hours of service is to be determined according to the principles established under the Fair Labor Standards Act for determining compensable hours of work. In other words, only actual hours of work will count toward this requirement. Paid time off for vacations, holidays, and sickness will not be counted. However, if an employee is reinstated with back pay as the result of an arbitration or litigation, the employee must also be given credit for FMLA purposes. Where an employer maintains no records of actual hours worked for exempt employees (i.e., bona fide executive, administrative, and professional workers), any such employee who has worked for the employer for at least 12 months will be presumed to have worked 1,250 hours during the previous 12 months unless the employer can clearly demonstrate otherwise.

The requirement that the employee be employed at a worksite where the employer employs at least 50 employees within 75 miles is a bit confusing. The DOL rejected the method of measuring this distance "as the crow flies" in favor of a more difficult system of measuring this distance based on surface miles of public roads, using the most direct routes between worksites. The DOL also dictated that for employees who work on the road, such as sales representatives, the "worksite" would be the home office, even if that was thousands of miles away. Some courts have rejected this regulation, holding that the "worksite" is the place where the work is actually performed, such as the sales territory, but the DOL has not revised this regulation. However, it has agreed that if an individual remains on an assignment from an employee leasing agency for more than one year, then the place of the assignment will become the worksite.

The determination of whether an employee has worked for the employer for at least 1,250 hours in the past 12 months and has been employed by the employer for a total of at least 12 months must be made as of the date leave commences. The 50-employee/75-mile component of the eligibility test, however, is to be determined at the point in time the employee requests the leave. If there are not 50 employees within 75 miles of the worksite at that time, the employee may renew the request at a later date.

Conditions For Which FMLA Can Be Taken

Serious Health Condition

The FMLA is not intended to cover short-term conditions for which treatment and recovery are very brief, since such conditions, according to the Congressional reports, would generally be covered by sick leave policies. However, the definition of "serious health condition" in the regulations to the FMLA is extremely broad and covers:

- Any period of incapacity or treatment in connection with or consequent to inpatient care (i.e., an overnight stay) in a hospital, hospice, or residential medical care facility.

- Any period of incapacity involving an inability to attend work, school, or other regular daily activities of more than three consecutive calendar days, that also involved continuing treatment by (or under the supervision of) a healthcare provider. "Continuing treatment" can be two or more in-person visits with the healthcare provider in a 30 day period (absent extenuating circumstances delaying the second treatment) or a single visit to the healthcare provider that results in a regimen of continuing treatment under the supervision of the healthcare provider, such as medication or therapy. Over-the-counter medications, bed rest, drinking fluids, exercise, and other similar activity that can be initiated without a visit to a healthcare provider are not, by themselves, sufficient to constitute a regimen of continuing treatment.

- Continuing treatment (two ore more visits a year) by (or under the supervision of) a healthcare provider for a chronic or long-term health condition that is incurable or so serious that, if not treated, would likely result in a period of incapacity of more than three consecutive calendar days. The definition of chronic conditions includes conditions such as asthma, epilepsy, and diabetes, as to which there may only be rare episodic periods of incapacity of less than three days, and the individual may rely on self-treatment or rest at home to deal with the episode. Pregnancy also is dealt with as a chronic condition, such that episodes of severe morning sickness, for example, which may not require an absence from work for more than three days, may entitle the employee to intermittent FMLA leave.

- Continuing treatment by a healthcare provider for prenatal care.

A "healthcare provider" is defined by the regulations to include not only MDs and DOs but also podiatrists, dentists, clinical psychologists, optometrists, chiropractors (for limited purposes), nurse practitioners, clinical social workers, nurse-midwives (provided that they are performing services within the scope of their practice as defined under state law) and Christian Science Practitioners. The recent regulations also add physician's assistants to this list if they are acting under the direction of the doctor. This list includes "any healthcare provider from whom the employer or the employer's group health plan... will accept certification of existence of a serious health condition to substantiate a claim for benefits."

Voluntary or cosmetic treatments that are not medically necessary are not serious health conditions unless inpatient hospital care is required. Treatments for allergies, stress, or substance abuse may constitute serious health conditions. Absence from work because of the employee's use of a controlled substance, however, does not qualify as a reason for FMLA leave. The new regulations make it clear that a request for leave for substance abuse treatment, which is covered by the FMLA, does not immunize an employee from discipline for violations of a substance abuse policy, such as a positive drug test or absences caused by substance abuse. Among the conditions that will not generally qualify as serious health conditions are the common cold, the flu, earaches, an upset stomach, minor ulcers, headaches (other than migraine), and routine dental problems. However, if complications result from these conditions, they may qualify. In addition, several minor ailments added together may be found to reach the level of a serious health condition. Generally, courts are finding that a serious health condition exists if one of the tests outlined in the regulations is met, even if the condition otherwise might not be considered serious.

An employer is entitled to obtain appropriate certification of an employee's need for FMLA leave. The DOL has developed optional forms for an employee's use in obtaining a medical certification from a healthcare provider. Copies of all referenced forms are provided on the HR Michigan Web Site (www.hrmichigan.com). Different forms are used depending on whether the medical leave is for the employee's own serious health condition, the serious health condition of a family member, the serious illness or injury of a covered service member, or a "qualifying exigency" of a service member. These forms are all new and should be used in place of the previous single DOL form. An employer may develop its own form, but no additional information can be required. Whether an employer uses the government's form or its own, the only information that may be sought from the healthcare provider regarding a serious health condition is as follows:

- Information sufficient to determine whether the employee has had medical care which qualifies as in-patient treatment or continuing care of a healthcare provider under one of the definitions set forth in the regulations

- Whether the employee is able to perform the essential functions of his job and, if not, which job functions the employee is unable to perform

- Symptoms and diagnosis of the condition

- The length of anticipated incapacity

- An estimated treatment schedule for follow-up appointments

Unless an employer wishes to rely on the employee's identification of the essential functions of the employee's own job for purposes of the healthcare provider's certification, the employer will be required to provide the healthcare provider with a description of the employee's essential job functions. If the medical certification is incomplete, the employer must advise the employee in writing of the additional information that is necessary and must give the employee seven calendar days to return the completed form. An employee who fails to provide the necessary certification is not considered to be on an FMLA leave, and he or she is not considered to have the protection of the Act.

Although this is the only information allowed under the FMLA, if the employee is seeking additional benefits, such as worker's disability compensation or disability pay, the employee can require additional information in order to approve the paid time off, but not to approve the FMLA. The employee must be advised that he or she can still take FMLA leave even if he or she does not provide the necessary information for the paid leave.

If an employer questions the adequacy of a medical certification, it may not request additional information from the healthcare provider who gave that certification. The employer may, without the employee's consent, contact the healthcare provider to confirm that the medical certification is authentic (i.e., that it was issued by the healthcare provider). The employer may, with the employee's consent, contact the healthcare provider for clarification, such as interpreting handwriting or asking the meaning of a term used. The employer is now allowed to have these communications directly and no longer needs to work through its own healthcare provider. If the employer has concerns about the medical certification, it may require the employee to obtain a second medical opinion at the employer's expense, from a healthcare provider designated by the employer, provided that he or she is not employed by or utilized on a regular basis by the employer. If there is a disagreement between the two healthcare providers, a third opinion, from a healthcare provider agreed upon by the employer and the employee, will be final and binding, and must be paid for by the employer. An employer must reimburse the employee for all out of pocket expenses incurred in connection with the second and third opinions and the employee cannot be compelled to travel outside normal commuting distances for such opinions.

An employer also may request re-certification for the need of the continuation of leave at reasonable intervals. Generally, the employer cannot request re-certification more often than every 30 days, unless the employer has reason to believe that the employee's condition has changed. The 30-day limitation does not apply under certain circumstances, such as where the original medical certification indicates an anticipated absence of more than 30 days. The DOL has recently agreed that an employer can have a policy stating that all certifications expire after one year and must be renewed. This allows an employer to start the process, including the option of obtaining second and third medical opinions, from scratch after one year. In addition, the employer can now always request a re-certification every six months, even if the original certification makes it clear that the leave may need to extend beyond that period.

Serious Health Condition Of A Parent, Spouse, Or Child

In order to confirm that there is a family relationship between the employee requesting leave and the person regarding whom the leave is being requested, the employer may require the employee to provide "reasonable documentation or statement of family relationship." This documentation may take the form of a simple statement from the employee, or a child's birth certificate, a court document, or the like.

The definition of "child" is very broad and includes not only naturally born and adopted children, but also foster children, stepchildren, and other legally recognized relationships. A son or daughter includes a child 18 years or older who is incapable of self-care because of a mental or physical disability. For this provision only, the FMLA refers to the ADA definition of "disability." Employers should note that the ADA definition changed effective January 1, 2009 due to the Americans With Disabilities Amendments Act, which is discussed in a separate chapter.

"Parent" is defined as any individual who was responsible for the employee when the employee was a child. This responsibility can include providing financial support. The new regulations clarify that "parent" does not include a parent-in-law.

"Spouse" is defined by state law. Therefore, while generally a spouse will be the person to whom the employee is legally married, in some states a spouse may include a relationship recognized by common law.

Birth Or Adoption Of A Child

The FMLA allows an employee to take leave for the birth or adoption of a child. In such a situation, the employee need not have any disability whatsoever, and the child may be perfectly healthy. Generally, an employee will be eligible for adoption leave only where the child being adopted is under 18 years of age, unless the child is incapable of self-care because of a physical or mental disability. Any birth or adoption leave must be concluded within a 12 month period beginning on the date of the birth or placement, unless either state law or the employer's polices provide leave to be taken during a longer period.

Both men and women are eligible for this type of leave. However, if both parents work for the same employer, they are entitled to only a total of 12 weeks of leave for each child, not 12 weeks per parent. Note that this is not true for the serious health condition of a child, where each parent is entitled to 12 weeks of leave.

The regulations do not permit an employer to require a medical certification to be provided for birth, adoption, or foster care.

Leaves Regarding Covered Service Members

On January 28, 2008, President Bush signed the National Defense Authorization Act, which included an amendment to the FMLA to provide leave for service members and their families under certain circumstances. Portions of these amendments went into effect immediately. However, because the amendments allowed for FMLA leave for certain "qualified exigencies" but did not provide any definition of that phrase, that portion of the amendments did not go into effect until interpreting regulations were issued. Therefore, the "qualified exigency" provisions discussed below go into effect on January 16, 2009.

Leaves involving covered service members vary from other FMLA leaves in four ways.

First, an employee who takes a leave of absence in order to serve on active duty is given full credit for the time off as if the employee had continued working for purposes of determining whether the employee has worked for 12 months and has worked for 1,250 hours in the previous year.

Second, in addition to normal FMLA leave for the serious health condition of a parent, spouse, or child, a person who is "next of kin" to a covered service member can take FMLA leave for the serious health condition of that individual. "Next of kin" is defined as the nearest blood relative other than the parent, spouse or child of the covered service member. In many cases, the covered service member will designate this individual in writing as part of the military protocol. Where no such designation has been made, it is possible that more than one person qualifies as the next of kin. It is important to note that the covered service member could include an adult child with a serious health condition, even if that individual does not meet the "incapable of self-care and disabled as defined by the ADA" definition of "child" for other provisions of the FMLA.

Third, the amendments to the FMLA introduce a new type of leave which has nothing to do with anybody's serious health condition or the birth or adoption of a child, but instead is for "qualifying exigencies" arising out of the military service of a covered family member. As with other forms of FMLA leave, this leave is limited to 12 weeks in the normal FMLA 12 month period. "Qualified exigencies" are defined to include the following:

- Issues that arise from the fact that a covered service member is called to active duty within seven days of deployment. *This leave is limited to the period of time of no more than seven days leading up to the deployment.*

- Leave to attend official military events related to active duty or to attend family support or assistance programs and informational briefings related to the call to active duty.

- Leave to arrange for alternative child care for a child (as defined by the FMLA) of a covered service member, to provide childcare on an emergency basis (but not a routine, regular, or every day basis), to enroll a child of a covered service member in school, or to attend school meetings for the child of a covered service member where the leave is necessitated by the active duty or call to active duty of the covered service member.

- Leave to make financial or legal arrangements to address the covered service member's absence for military duty, or to act as the covered service member's representative for purposes of obtaining military service benefits. Leave can only be taken to obtain military service benefits while the service member is away on active duty or within 90 days of termination of that active duty.

- Leave to attend counseling by someone other than a health care provider for the employee, the covered service member, or a child of the covered service member, provided that the need for counseling arises from the military service.

- Leave to spend time with a covered service member who is on a short-term, temporary, rest and recuperation leave during the period of deployment. *This leave is limited to five days for each military rest and recuperation visit.*

- Leave to attend post-deployment functions, such as arrival ceremonies or reintegration briefings, that occur within 90 days following the termination of active duty status, or to address issues that arise from the death of the covered service member, such as making funeral arrangements.

- Leave for "additional activities." These are not defined by either the FMLA or the regulations. The regulations state that such leave is allowed "to address other events which arise out of the covered military member's active duty or call to active duty status *provided that the employer and employee agree that such leave shall qualify as an exigency, and agree to both the timing and duration of such leave.*"

Fourth, an employee may take FMLA leave for the "serious injury or illness" of a covered service member. This is different from leave for a "serious health condition." "Serious injury or illness" is defined as an injury or illness that is incurred in the line of duty on active duty that may render the service member medically unfit to perform the duties of her office, grade, rank or rating. Leave can be taken for a covered service member (a) who is on the temporary disability retired list, (b) who is undergoing medical treatment, recuperation, or therapy for the serious illness or injury; or (c) who is assigned to a military medical treatment facility as an outpatient or is otherwise receiving outpatient care at a unit established for members of the armed forces. This FMLA leave does not apply to care for former members of the armed forces who are on the permanent disability retired list. This leave is not limited to 12 weeks in a 12 month period defined by the employer. An employee caring for a covered service member with a serious illness or injury is eligible for up to 26 weeks of FMLA leave within a 12 month period. The 12 month period is defined as a rolling year beginning on the first day of leave. If the individual needs to care for more than one service member or the original service member has a subsequent injury, the individual may be entitled to take more than one period of 26 weeks of leave, but the individual cannot take more than 26 weeks for the same illness or injury for a single service member.

Duration and Conditions of FMLA Leave

Duration Of Leave

Except for employees taking leave for the serious injury or illness of a covered service member as discussed above, a covered employee is entitled to take 12 weeks of FMLA leave in a 12 month period. Employers are permitted to utilize any one of the following methods for determining the 12-month period in which the 12 weeks of leave entitlement may occur, provided that the chosen method is uniformly applied:

- The calendar year;
- Any fixed 12-month leave year, such as a fiscal year, a year required by state law, or a year starting on an employee's anniversary date;
- The 12-month period measured forward from the date an employee's first FMLA leave begins; or
- A rolling 12-month period measured backward from the date an employee uses any FMLA leave.

An employee's entitlement to FMLA leave is measured in weeks, not days or hours. When the employee is off on such a leave for a week, he or she is to be charged for one of his or her twelve available weeks. A holiday occurring during the week does not affect this calculation; the week is still counted as a week of FMLA leave. However, in situations where the employer's operations temporarily cease for one or more weeks and employees generally are not expected to report for work during that period, this time will not be counted against the employee's FMLA entitlement.

For eligible part-time employees and those qualifying individuals who work variable hours, the FMLA leave entitlement is calculated on a pro rata or proportional basis. If an employee who normally works a schedule of 30 hours per week needs to change to 20 hours per week on a reduced leave schedule, then the 10 hours of FMLA leave equals one-third of a week of FMLA leave each week. If an employee's work schedule varies from week to week, the average weekly hours worked during the 12 months prior to the start of FMLA leave will be used to calculate the employee's normal work schedule for this purpose.

Where FMLA leave is requested for the purpose of caring for a family member with a serious health condition or for the employee's own serious medical condition, leave may be taken intermittently or on a reduced leave schedule when medically necessary. In the case of leave for the birth or placement of a child for adoption, the employer has the option of whether or not to allow intermittent leave. An employee may not take off more time than is necessary to address the circumstance causing the need for the leave, meaning that the leave time should be limited to the time necessary for treatment or recovery from illness. An exception to this rule is made where returning to work at the end of a short leave period is impossible, such as when a pilot needs only two hours of leave for a doctor's appointment but then cannot rejoin a flight in mid-air. In such cases, the employee can be charged for the full amount of work missed.

The regulations address the issue of the calculation of FMLA leave time where the leave is taken intermittently or on a reduced leave schedule. If an employee takes leave on such a basis, only the amount of leave actually taken may be counted toward the 12 weeks of leave to which the employee is entitled. For example, if an employee who normally works five days a week takes off one day, the employee would use 1/5 of a week of FMLA leave. Similarly, if a full-time employee who normally works eight-hour days works four-hour days under a reduced leave schedule, the employee would use 1/2 week of FMLA leave each week. Employers must allow employees to take FMLA leave for periods as brief as the shortest period of the time that the employer's payroll system uses to account for absences or leave.

The regulations provide that an employee does not begin using his or her 12 weeks of leave unless the employer specifically informs the employee that the leave is being treated as FMLA at the beginning of the leave. However, in *Ragsdale v. Wolverine Worldwide, Inc.*, the United States Supreme Court threw out this provision of the regulations, holding that an employee does not become eligible for additional leave simply because the leave was not designated as FMLA at the beginning. Cases since *Ragsdale* have held that if the employee had no choice (e.g., the employee had a condition which would require her to be on leave whether or not he or she received the proper FMLA notices), then the FMLA is not violated simply because the employer delayed in designating it as an FMLA leave. On the other hand, where the employee could have modified the timing of the leave, some courts have held that the employer is estopped from changing its position on whether the leave is covered by the FMLA after it is too late for the employee to change his or her behavior. The new regulations retain the provision previously ruled invalid by the Supreme Court but require the employee to establish harm caused by the employer's failure to properly designate leave. Whether courts will continue to find the regulation invalid remains to be seen.

Pay During Leave

Accrued paid vacation or paid personal leave may be substituted for any FMLA qualifying purpose so long as the employer's policies would generally allow paid leave for such a purpose. For example, accrued paid medical or sick leave may be substituted to care for a seriously ill close family member, but only where the employer normally would allow such paid leave to be used for another's serious health condition. Likewise, an employee does not have the right to use paid sick days to care for a seriously ill spouse if the employer's leave plan does not allow paid sick leave to be used for that purpose. Ultimately, it is the employer's responsibility to designate whether the time off will be applied to the FMLA leave.

The new regulations allow a public employer to require that their employees' compensatory time banks be used as a form of accrued paid leave for purposes of substitution of paid leave for unpaid leave. (replace old paragraph with this one).

Continuation Of Benefits During Leave

An employer must maintain the employee's coverage under any group health plan on the same conditions as coverage would have been provided if the employee had been continuously employed during the leave. An employer is not required to continue non-health-insurance benefits during the period of the FMLA leave. However, FMLA leave cannot constitute a "break in service" such that an employee loses accrued pension, retirement, and other benefits.

An employer must continue to provide group health benefits to an employee on FMLA leave on the same basis as if the employee were an active employee. In the case of paid FMLA leave, the employee's share of premiums must be paid by the method normally used during any paid leave, such as payroll deduction. If FMLA leave is unpaid, the employer may require that payment be made to the employer or to the insurance carrier in any of the following ways:

- Payment would be due at the same time as it would be if made by payroll deduction.

- Payment would be due on the same schedule as payments are made under COBRA.

- Payment would be prepaid pursuant to a cafeteria plan at the employee's option (however, the IRS still needs to approve this).

- The employer's existing rules for payment by employees on leave without pay may be followed, except that prepayment of the premiums prior to the commencement of the leave would not be allowed unless the employee voluntarily agreed to prepayment.

- Under another system voluntarily agreed to between the employer and the employee. Any such arrangement must be clearly specified in advance and in writing.

In any event, the employer cannot require more of an employee using unpaid FMLA leave than the employer requires of other employees on other unpaid leave.

The obligation to continue benefits ends, subject to COBRA, when:

- the employee informs the employer of his of her intent not to return to work at the conclusion of the leave;
- the employee fails to return from the leave;
- the employee exhausts his or her FMLA leave; or
- if and when the employee's employment would have terminated in the absence of the leave, such as in the case of a layoff where the employee would not have had bumping rights.

Before an employer may terminate health insurance coverage of an employee on FMLA leave due to the failure of the employee to timely make a required premium payment, the employer must give written notice of the possible loss of coverage. This notice must be given 15 days before the coverage will cease because of the nonpayment. Normally, coverage may only end at the end of the 30-day grace period allowed for premium payments, provided that the required 15 days notice is given. However, if the employer has a written policy that employees on other unpaid leaves may have their coverage ended retroactively to the first date of the period to which the missed premium relates, that policy may be applied to an FMLA employee. The new regulations emphasize an employer's responsibility to reinstate an employee to previous coverage following the conclusion of a leave and note the difficulty in doing this if an employee's benefits have been terminated during the leave.

Under certain circumstances, an employer may recover its share of premiums paid while an employee is on unpaid FMLA leave if the employee fails to return to work after termination of the leave. The regulations prohibit an employer from recovering its share of health insurance premiums for any period of paid FMLA leave. An employer may recover premiums it paid for maintaining group health plan coverage during any period of unpaid FMLA leave if the employee fails to return to work after the employee's FMLA leave entitlement has expired, unless the employee does not return to work due to:

- continuation, recurrence, or onset of a serious health condition that would entitle the employee to FMLA leave; or
- other circumstances beyond the control of the employee.

The regulations give the following examples of circumstances beyond the employee's control:

- An employee's spouse is unexpectedly transferred to a job location more than 75 miles from the employee's worksite.
- A relative or individual other than an immediate family member has a serious health condition and the employee is needed to provide care.
- The employee is laid off while on leave.
- The employee is a key employee who decides not to return to work upon being notified of the employer's intention to deny restoration.

The regulations state that a mother's decision not to return to work in order to stay home with a newborn child is not a circumstance beyond the employee's control. It is deemed to be beyond the parent-employee's control, however, if the parent wishes to stay home with the child because the child has a serious health condition.

An employee who does not return to work for at least 30 calendar days after expiration of leave is considered to have failed to return to work.

Return-to-Work Rights Under FMLA

Upon return from a FMLA leave, an employee is entitled to be returned to the same position he or she held at the beginning of the leave, or to "an equivalent position with equivalent benefits, pay, and other terms and conditions of employment." These obligations exist even if there are no vacant positions at the time the employee's leave ends. An employer is expected to be able to return the employee immediately and is not allowed to make the employee wait until a suitable position can be found.

The employee's right to reinstatement is limited to whatever it would have been had he or she not been on the leave. If an employer can prove that the employee would have been laid off during the FMLA leave period, then that employee is not entitled to reinstatement. If an employee was hired for a specific term or only to perform work on a discrete project, the employer has no obligation to restore the employee if the employment term or project is over and the employer would not otherwise have continued to employ the employee.

An employer may have a uniformly applied policy requiring all employees who take a leave under the FMLA to present medical evidence that they are able to return to work relative to the condition for which the employee took the leave. A broader medical clearance is not permitted. The new regulations allow an employer to provide the employee's physician with a list of essential job functions and to obtain a certification that the employee can perform those functions. An employer is also allowed to use the authentication and clarification procedures discussed in connection with the initial medical certification procedure at the time of an employee's return to work.

Generally, an employee will lose the FMLA reinstatement protection if the employee cannot return to his or her original position at the conclusion of FMLA. However, if an employee can return to the job but has a 40 hour work restriction, the question will be whether working more than 40 hours a week is an essential function of the position. If it is an essential function, then the employer has no obligation to restore the employee to the position held prior to the leave until the employee can fully perform the job. If it is not an essential function, the employee may be required to return the employee and accommodate the restriction. Of course, even where an essential function is involved, if the employee has not used all 12 weeks of leave, the employer may be required to allow the employee to work a reduced schedule and use intermittent leave until the full 12 weeks is used.

Equivalent Position

An "equivalent position" must have the same pay, benefits, and working conditions, including privileges, perquisites, and status. It must involve the same or substantially similar duties and responsibilities, which must entail substantially equivalent skill, effort, responsibility, and authority.

An employee is entitled to any unconditional pay increases that may have occurred during the FMLA leave period, such as cost-of-living increases. Pay increases conditioned upon seniority, length of service, or work performed must be granted if it is the employer's practice or policy to do so with respect to other employees on leave without pay. An employer is not required to grant additional paid vacation, sick, or personal days to an employee on FMLA leave.

An employee must be reinstated to the same or geographically proximate worksite where the employee had been previously employed. He or she is ordinarily entitled to return to the same shift or the same or an equivalent work schedule. The same or an equivalent opportunity of bonuses, profit-sharing, and other similar discretionary and non-discretionary payments must exist in the new position.

Restoration of Benefits

Benefits must be resumed upon the employee's return to work at the same level as they were provided when leave began, without any new qualification period or physical exam. Some employers may find it necessary to modify life insurance or other benefit programs in order to be able to restore employees to equivalent benefits upon return from FMLA leave, make arrangements for continued payment of costs to maintain such benefits during unpaid FMLA leave, or pay these costs subject to recovery from the employee following return from leave.

The new regulations state that while an employer cannot penalize an employee for taking FMLA leave, such as counting the absence as a point or occurrence under an attendance policy, the employer does not need to give the employee attendance incentives for which the employee has not qualified unless the same incentives are given to other employees on comparable non-FMLA leaves. Therefore, an employer can deny a perfect attendance bonus if the employee missed the bonus due to unpaid FMLA leave, but cannot deny the bonus if the employee used paid vacation time for the leave and others on vacation receive the bonus. (replace old paragraph with this one)

As to pay increases, a couple of scenarios could apply to a particular circumstance. Because restored employees are not entitled to accrue seniority during the FMLA leave, pay increases based on performance reviews given after 12 months of completed service may be delayed by the period of time the employee spent on FMLA leave. Pay increases geared to the employee's anniversary date may not be delayed.

Key Employees

A "key employee" is defined as "a salaried FMLA-eligible employee who is among the highest paid 10% of all the employees employed by the employer within 75 miles of the employee's worksite."

An employer may deny reinstatement rights to a key employee only when the key employee's restoration will cause "substantial and grievous economic injury" to the operations of the employer. This section must be read closely, as it specifies that the pertinent question is whether such an injury will not result from the key employee's absence, but from "the restoration of the employee to employment."

In order to deny a key employee restoration rights, the employer must meet a number of notice requirements.

Posting and Notice Requirements of FMLA: Common Questions

Employer Requirements

Every employer subject to the FMLA is required to post and keep posted on its premises, in conspicuous places where employees are employed, a notice explaining the Act's provisions and providing information concerning the procedures for filing complaints of violations of the Act with the DOL. If the employer routinely posts its notices electronically, FMLA notices may be posted in the same fashion. FMLA notices may be obtained from the DOL's website at *www.dol.gov/esa/regs/compliance/posters/fmla.htm*, or by writing to the following address:

> U.S. Department of Labor
> Employment Standards Administration
> Wage and Hour Division
> Washington, DC 20210

When an employer's workforce is comprised of a significant portion of workers who are not literate in English, the employer may be required to provide a translated notice.

If an employer has any written guidance for employees concerning employee benefits or leave rights, such as in an employee handbook, then information concerning FMLA entitlement and employees' obligations under the FMLA must be included in the handbook or other document. For example, if an employer provides an employee handbook to all employees that describes the employer's policies regarding leave, wages, attendance, and similar matters, the handbook must incorporate information on the Act.

If the employer does not have any written policies, manuals, or handbooks describing employee benefits and leave provisions, then the employer must provide written guidance to all existing employees and to all new employees when they are hired. This is a change from the original regulations, which required only that such notice be given at the time an employee requested leave. Employers may duplicate and provide the employee with a copy of the FMLA notice that is available from the DOL Wage and Hour Division. Again, these notices can be provided electronically and may have to be translated from English.

The new regulations anticipate a two stage process when an employee requests FMLA leave. The first phase occurs when an employee indicates that a leave is needed. At that point, the employer has five business days to determine whether the employee is eligible (i.e., whether the employee has worked for one year, has 1,250 hours, and has 50 employees within 75 miles). If eligibility is denied, the employer must provide the employee information regarding the basis for the denial. In the same seven day period, the employer must provide the employee information regarding what he or she must do to complete her request for FMLA leave and the ramifications of failing to take the necessary steps. The DOL has developed a form which includes all of the necessary information for this first notice. While the form is optional, an employer must give the employee all of the notices set forth in the form, including:

- The employee's obligation to submit a completed medical certification form within 15 days and the fact that leave can be delayed or denied if the employee fails to do so

- The employee's right to maintain health care benefits, the steps the employee must take to continue health care benefits, and the circumstances under which the employee would be required to repay the employer for those benefits

- The effect of the leave on an employee's sick days, vacation , or other paid time off

- Whether the employee is considered a "key employee"

- Communications the employee must have with the employer regarding her status and intent to return to work

- The amount of leave the employee is eligible to take and the 12 months period that is used for calculating that leave

- The employee's reinstatement rights

Once the employee turns in the medical certification, the employer has five business days to designate the time off as FMLA leave. There is another form for this purpose. If the leave is being denied, the employee must be so advised in writing.

Employee Requirements

An employee must give 30 days advance notice to the employer of the need to take FMLA leave when the need for the leave is foreseeable for the birth or placement of a child for adoption or foster care, or for planned medical treatment for a serious health condition of the employee or a close family member. An employee is not required to use any magic language in requesting FMLA leave. It is enough that the employee has provided the employer with sufficient information to determine that the leave is protected by the FMLA. Simply calling in "sick" is not sufficient to alert an employer to FMLA coverage. The safest course is for an employer to make it very clear to employees what they must do if they are invoking their FMLA rights and what forms of notice will not be presumed to refer to the FMLA absent additional information.

When it is not practicable to provide such advance notice, or when the need for the leave is not foreseeable, notice must be given "as soon as practicable." The original regulations stated that this would ordinarily be within one or two business days of when the employee learns of the need for the leave. However, many employees were abusing this provision by waiting two days. The employer should make it clear to employees that failure to give notice as soon as possible may result in a delay or denial of the leave request. Where notice of less than 30 days is given the employer may ask the employee why additional notice was not possible and may delay the leave if appropriate (e.g., the leave is for a doctor's appointment which can be rescheduled) or deny the leave altogether (e.g., the employee has already taken the day off). Verbal notice is sufficient to inform the employer that the employee will need leave. An employer also may require an employee to comply with its usual rules when requesting leave as long as those rules do not require more notice than can be required by the FMLA. (replace old with this new info)

Remedies

An employer which violates the FMLA may be liable for lost compensation resulting from the violation. This includes lost wages, which may include front pay, as well as attorney fees. Where the violation is deemed to be willful, the employee may recover double damages. Following a split in the courts, the new regulations clarify that FMLA claims can be released under the normal provisions allowed for release of employment claims. (replace last two sentences with this one)

FMLA Interplay with Other Laws

The United States Constitution

As is discussed above, the United States Supreme Court has held that the 11th Amendment does not bar individual FMLA lawsuits against states for money damages. The basis for this ruling was the legislative history regarding the need for primary care givers, who are often women, to be able to take care of babies and family members. However, because the provision of FMLA leave for the serious health condition of an individual employee is gender-neutral, such claims are barred by the 11th Amendment.

State Workers' Compensation and Family and Medical Leave Laws

Nothing in the FMLA supersedes any provision of state or local law that provides greater family or medical leave rights than those provided by the Act. Employees are not required to designate whether the leave they are taking is FMLA leave or leave under state law, and an employer must comply with the appropriate provisions of both. Without identifying particular states, the regulations provide a few examples of how to integrate leave under FMLA and state law. The preamble to the regulations indicates that even the procedural aspects of state law that are inconsistent with the Act are not preempted.

Several provisions in the FMLA regulations relate to workers' compensation laws. Comments to the regulations state that the FMLA does not protect an employee who refuses light-duty work from being disqualified from workers' compensation benefits. Additionally, where an employee is receiving workers' compensation benefits due to a work-related injury or illness, such an absence may be counted against the employee's FMLA entitlement if the employer properly designates it as such at the beginning of the leave.

Where an employee is receiving pay under some provision other than the FMLA, such as worker's compensation, an employer can require more documentation than the FMLA would normally allow so long as the employer is applying a consistently enforced policy that is otherwise lawful.

The Americans with Disabilities Act

The regulations provide some general guidance regarding the interrelationship between the FMLA and the ADA, principally by way of examples. The comments to the regulations clearly provide that where one of these statutes offers a superior right to an employee on a particular issue, the employer must provide the superior right to the employee.

Essentially, an employer must afford a qualified individual with a disability, within the meaning of the ADA, the employee's FMLA rights at the same time that the employer makes any reasonable accommodations and takes other steps in accordance with the ADA. For example, if an employee became disabled, a reasonable accommodation under the ADA might be accomplished by providing the employee with a part-time job with no health benefits. However, the FMLA would permit an employee to work a reduced leave schedule until 12 weeks of leave were used, with health benefits maintained during this period. At the end of the FMLA leave entitlement, an employer is required to reinstate the employee in the same or an equivalent position, with equivalent pay and benefits, to that which the employee held when the leave commenced. The employer's FMLA obligations would be satisfied if the employer offered the employee an equivalent full-time position. If the employee were unable to perform the equivalent position because of disability, and the employee had exhausted his or her FMLA entitlement, the ADA may permit or require the employer to make a reasonable accommodation at that time by placing the employee in a part-time job, with only those benefits provided to part-time employees.

If the FMLA entitles an employee to leave, an employer may not, in lieu of FMLA leave entitlement, require the employee to take a job with a reasonable accommodation, or require the employee to return to a light-duty position prior to the expiration of the employee's job-protected leave entitlement. However, the ADA may require that an employer offer the employee the opportunity to take such a position.

The EEOC has indicated that having one confidential medical file to try to comply with the confidentiality requirements of the ADA and the FMLA may not always satisfy the confidentiality requirements of the ADA. For this reason, the regulations require that medical records created for purposes of the ADA and FMLA must be maintained in accordance with ADA confidentiality rules.

It is important to note that an employee may be protected by the FMLA even where the ADA does not require accommodation. For example, while a number of ADA cases hold that an employer is not required to modify its consistently enforced attendance policies, the FMLA makes clear that an employee cannot be penalized under those policies for absences protected by the FMLA.

Collective Bargaining Agreements

The regulations state that the rights granted by the FMLA may not be diminished by any employee benefit program or plan. The regulations then continue: "… provisions of a [collective bargaining agreement] which, because of seniority or otherwise, provide for reinstatement to a position that is not equivalent (i.e., provides lesser pay) are superseded by FMLA." Employee labor organizations alike are therefore encouraged to be aware of their employees' FMLA rights where new collective bargaining agreements are negotiated.

The Uniformed Services Employment and Reemployment Rights Act of 1994

As discussed in more detail in Chapter 14, the USERRA requires that all returning veterans receive all benefits of employment that they would have received if they had been continuously employed. This includes FMLA leave. Therefore, an employer must add the number of hours the employee would have worked but for military service to the hours actually worked to determine whether the re-employed service person has sufficient hours for FMLA eligibility.

CHAPTER 12: Workers' Disability Compensation

The Michigan Worker's Disability Compensation Act ("MWDCA" or the "Act"), MCL § 418.101, et seq, is a statutory scheme that requires employers to provide wage and medical benefits to certain injured employees without regard to fault. The Act requires all employers to arrange for payment of workers compensation benefits by procuring insurance from a carrier or obtaining approved self-insured status.

An injured employee seeking to recover workers' disability compensation benefits must prove the following three elements by a preponderance of the evidence:

1) A physical or psychiatric injury or occupational disease,

2) Arising out of and in the course of employment, that

3) Results in a disability.

An employee meeting this burden will be entitled to recover lost wage benefits (for 2008, up to $739.00 per week) for the duration of the disability, as well as medical expenses related to the injury and vocational rehabilitation.

The final outcome of each worker's disability compensation case depends upon the unique factual situation and medical data of the employee involved. The topics in this chapter provide a general overview of the MWDCA's application, as well as procedural guidelines for handling a workers' disability compensation claim.

Employers and Employees Covered by the MWDCA

The MWDCA applies to virtually all employers in Michigan. In general, the act covers public employers, private employers with more than 3 employees at one time, and private employers with less than three employees, if at least one employee was regularly employed for at least 35 hours a week for 13 weeks in the last year. Additionally, all employees of covered employers are generally "covered" under the Act. If an employer purchases worker's disability compensation insurance for an employee, the employer will have assumed liability for any injuries covered by the MWDCA, even if the employer would not otherwise be covered under the act.

1. Independent Contractors

Although independent contractors are generally not covered under the Act, merely labeling a worker an "independent contractor" will not automatically exclude him or her from coverage under the Act. Courts and the Workers Compensation Bureau will most likely disregard this designation if the economic realities demonstrate that the worker is in fact an employee.

2. Farm workers

An agricultural employer will be covered only if it has at pays at least three employees hourly wages or salaries or if it employed at least one employee 35 or more hours per week for five or more consecutive weeks. Only those specific employees of the agricultural employer will be covered. In addition, an agricultural employer may still voluntarily cover his employees.

3. Partnerships and Small Businesses

Employees of partnerships and small business are covered so long as they meet the general requirements outlined above. Section 161, however, provides that under certain circumstance partners and officers who are shareholders may exempt themselves from the Act.

4. Family Employees

Household, or family, employees are not protected if (1) they are the wife, child or other member of the employer's family living in the home, or (2) they work less than 35 hours per week for 13 weeks or longer during the year. Further, those who own and operate a sole proprietorship, with no employees, are not covered under the Act.

5. Real Estate

A real estate salesperson or broker will not be protected by the MWDCA if (1) at least 75% of the person's compensation is directly related to volume of sales, and not number of hours worked, and (2) the person has a written agreement with a real estate broker stating that the person is not considered an employee for tax purposes.

6. Subcontractors and General Contractors

Contractors are responsible for the payment of compensation benefits to employees of its uninsured subcontractors. This responsibility is automatically insured by the Standard Policy issued to the contractor and the contractor must supply evidence that the subcontractor had workers' compensation insurance in force covering work performed by the subcontractor. For each subcontractor with employees for which such evidenced is not furnished, the contractor will pay an additional premium.

7. List of Employers Who Must Carry Workers' Compensation Coverage.[*]

- All private employers regularly employing 1 or more employees 35 hours or more per week for 13 weeks or long during the preceding 52 weeks.

- All private employers regularly employing 3 or more employees at one time, including part-time employees

- Agricultural employers if they employ 3 or more employees 35 hours or more per week for 13 or more consecutive weeks.

- Householders employing domestic servants if they employ anyone 35 hours or more per week for 13 weeks or longer during the preceding 52 weeks.

- All public employers.

Injuries and Illnesses Covered

The MWDCA covers any personal injury due to causes and conditions that are characteristic of the employer's business and which arise out of and in the course of the employment. Covered injuries include physical injuries such as lost limbs, back strains, heart attacks, hernias, and the like, as well as psychological disabilities such as schizophrenia, depression and anxiety, so long as the disability arises out of actual events of employment rather than unfounded perceptions. A compensable injury need not be the result of a single workplace accident or occurrence. In some instances, injuries caused by day-to-day employment activities, such as frequent bending or lifting, are actionable under the Act.

The MWDCA also covers occupational diseases that are due to causes and conditions characteristic of and peculiar to the employer's business, such as silicosis and emphysema caused by frequent exposure to air pollutants, even though there is no particular accident or injury triggering the disability.

The MWDCA does not cover ordinary diseases of life to which the public is generally exposed outside of the employment, such as ordinary stress. However, the employment does not have to be the proximate cause or the sole cause of the employee's disability in order to be compensable. Rather, the disability will be compensable if the employment contributed to a disability, aggravated a pre-existing condition, or caused the disability.

---

[*] The following list is taken directly from the Michigan Department of Labor & Economic Growth Workers' Compensation Agency's publication "General Information Regarding Rights and Responsibilities Under the Act," (May 2007).

Thus, conditions of the aging process, such as arthritis, degenerative disc disease and arteriosclerosis, are considered compensable injuries if contributed to, aggravated, or accelerated by the employment in a significant manner.

For example, while arteriosclerosis is generally not work-related, if an employee with arteriosclerosis suffers a heart attack while performing heavy lifting on the job, the employer will be liable for workers' disability compensation benefits if the heavy lifting triggered the heart attack. Similarly, if an employee suffers from a pre-existing back condition that was not work-related, but aggravates that condition to the point of disability while working, the employee will be entitled to benefits. Interestingly, the MWDCA has a specific provision for hernias, stating that in order to be covered a hernia must be clearly recent in origin and result from a strain arising out of and in the course of employment, and be promptly reported to the employer.

Arising Out of and In the Course of Employment

The MWDCA is a "no fault" statute. Therefore, unless some exception to the Act is met, the employer will be liable under the Act for all work-related injuries, without regard to cause. In order to recover benefits, the employee must demonstrate a causal connection between the employment and the disability. Thus, the employer is liable for the negligence of its employees. An employee will be covered even if the injury was caused by his or her own negligence, unless such negligence was willful. The employer also cannot argue that the employee assumed the risks inherent in the employment. One of the few exceptions to this provision is that an employee cannot recover if he or she is injured by reason of his or her intentional and willful misconduct.

In order to be covered, the disability must be caused by something that happened at work and must be caused by something work-related. Courts look to the following factors to determine whether the disability is covered:

1) Where and when did the accident happen (i.e., did it occur while working)?

2) How did the accident happen (i.e., did it occur as a result of the employee's performance of his or her job duties)?

On-premise Injuries

Section 301(3) of the MWDCA states: "An employee going to or from his or her work, while on the premises where the employee's work is to be performed, and within a reasonable time before and after his or her working hours, is presumed to be in the course of his or her employment."

Generally, an employee injured on the employer's premises, such as a parking lot or the employee's work area, will be covered by the MWDCA. As is stated in Section 301(3), this will be true even if the employee is not actually working at the time of the injury. The Act presumes that employees, in the normal course of their duties, spend downtime beginning and finishing the day's work. Thus, an employee attacked in the parking lot after work is considered in the course of his or her employment and entitled to compensatory benefits.

Off-premise Injuries

An injury arises out of and during the course of employment where the risk of the injury suffered by the employee is a direct result of his or her employment, even if the employee is not on the employer's premises. It is enough that the employer required the employee to be in the location where the injury occurred. Therefore, an employee who is injured while traveling for the employer will be entitled to benefits even when the injury occurs outside the State of Michigan.

Non-compensable Injuries

Certain injuries will not be compensable even if they occur on the employer's premises or during working hours. For example, an employee who is injured while traveling for his employer will not be protected if the injury occurred as a result of a deviation from the employment travel plan.

Similarly, an employee who sustains an injury while engaged in a primarily recreational or social activity is not covered by the MWDCA. Therefore, an injury that occurs during the employee's lunch hour, away from the employer's premises, is not compensable if the lunch was personal rather than business in nature.

An injury that occurs during horseplay or a serious deviation from the employee's job duties also is not compensable. Thus, an employee was denied coverage when he climbed on a filing cabinet and was killed after touching an electrically charged rail. Less serious types of horseplay may, however, be compensable if it is determined that they are a normal part of the employment under the circumstances.

Intentional and willful employee misconduct that results in a personal workplace injury is not compensable because it is not deemed to arise out of or during the course of employment. For example, an injury that results from an employee's violation of an established, announced, and consistently enforced work rule is considered willful misconduct and not compensable.

Despite the limitations discussed above and the fact that the employee bears the burden of proof, employers should be aware that there is a strong likelihood that the Bureau of

Workers' Disability Compensation will find that a disability is work related, if there is any evidence linking the injury or disease to the workplace.

Disability Under MWDCA

To be considered disabled, an employee must demonstrate an injury that results in a limitation or reduction of his or her maximum reasonable wage-earning capacity in work suitable to his or her qualifications and training, resulting from a personal injury or related disease covered under the MWDCA.

An employee will be considered disabled for purposes of the MWDCA, if he or she can no longer work full time or can work only with restrictions that lessen the employee's wage-earning capacity. In other words, an employee who is able to take light-duty assignments, but can no longer perform his or her prior job duties will be considered disabled if the light-duty work pays less than the prior job.

Worker's Disability Compensation Benefits

An employee is entitled to continue receiving benefits as long as he or she remains disabled, even if the employee would have lost his or her job for reasons unrelated to the disability, such as a layoff, so long as the employee has not been able to establish a new wage earning capacity. An employee, however, is not entitled to receive benefits if he or she would be unable to work for other reasons, such as incarceration.

If the employee receives and rejects a bona fide offer of employment for which he or she is qualified, whether from the existing employer or another potential employer, the employee will be considered to have voluntarily removed himself from the work force and will no longer be entitled to benefits. Reasonable employment opportunities are those within the employee's capacity to perform that pose no clear and proximate threat to the employee's health and safety and, are a reasonable distance from the employee's residence.

Special Benefits

An employee is not entitled to worker's compensation benefits for the first week of a work-related disability because the Act provides that no compensation is available for an injury that does not last at least one week. After that waiting period, an employer must pay a disabled employee weekly wage-loss benefits beginning on the eighth day of disability for the duration of the disability and must retroactively pay the first week if the disability lasts longer than two weeks.

Wage-Loss Benefits

Wage-loss benefits generally will equal 80% of the employee's previous after-tax income, so long as this amount does not exceed the state average weekly wage, which is adjusted regularly. For 2008, the state average weekly wage is $820.04. A partially disabled worker is paid the difference between his or her after-tax average weekly wage before the injury, and his or her after-tax average weekly wage after the injury. Generally, an employee's entitlement to wage recovery will be based on the length of the disability. Benefits continue as long as the worker is disabled. Beginning at age 65 benefits are reduced by 5% each year until age 75, when benefits will have been reduced to 50%. Section 361 of the MWDCA provides for specific lengths of recovery for certain injuries.

Medical Benefits

Where necessary, an employer must pay for the injured employee's medical expenses resulting from the work-related injury, which may include reasonable medical, surgical, and hospital services and medicines, or other attendance or treatment. Under the Act, a worker is entitled to "all reasonable and necessary medical care." These benefits continue so long as the need for care is related to the work-related injury. The employer may be required to pay continuing medical expenses even after the employee is able to return to work and is no longer receiving wage-loss benefits. In other words, even if the employee is able to return to work without restrictions and therefore is no longer suffering any wage loss, the employee may continue to require medical treatment at the employer's expense.

Vocational-Rehabilitation Benefits

If the employee suffers a permanent disability that will preclude him or her from returning to the same line of work in the future, the employer may be required to provide vocational rehabilitation.

Death Benefits

If an employee dies as a result of the injury, benefits must be paid to surviving dependents for 500 weeks from the date of the death. In some cases, benefits may have to be paid even beyond the 500 weeks for minor children. Despite any independent earning capacity, however, a child under the age of 16 is presumed to be totally dependent. A surviving spouse must prove that he or she was factually dependent on the deceased worker. An employer must also pay funeral and burial benefits for an employee who dies as a result of the injury.

The Exclusive Remedy Provision of the MWDCA

The MWDCA is deliberately broad in its scope and covers virtually all employment in Michigan. With few exceptions, the right to benefits provided by the Act is an employee's exclusive remedy against the employer for all tort claims. Therefore, an employee suffering a work-related injury is limited to certain benefits and cannot bring a personal injury tort action against the employer for emotional distress, damages, and the like.

Claims allowed by statute

There are several exceptions to the exclusive remedy provision of the MWDCA. First, the Act does not bar other claims that are allowed by statute. Specifically, the Act does not bar lawsuits for discrimination or harassment under the Elliott-Larsen Civil Rights Act and other employment-related statutes. Any recovery under one Act, however, would be set off against recovery under the other so that the employee does not recover the same damages (i.e., lost wages) twice.

Intentional torts

The exclusive-remedy provision also does not bar lawsuits for intentional torts. A tort by an employer is intentional only if the employer acted deliberately and specifically intended an injury. The employer is deemed to have intended the injury if the employer had actual knowledge that an injury was certain to occur and willfully disregarded that knowledge. The plaintiff must show that the employer made a conscious choice to injure the employee and that the employer deliberately acted or failed to act in furtherance of that intent. The mere fact that an accident was likely to occur does not render the tort intentional; the employee must show that the injury was sure and inevitable. It is not easy to predict, however, when a court will find that an injury was "sure and inevitable" rather than merely probable.

Third-party claims

The MWDCA does not bar third-party claims. Therefore, while an employer cannot be held liable as the employer in an independent tort action, the employer may be held liable in a products liability action if the employer also designed or manufactured the machine that led to the injury.

Public-policy tort claims

Finally, the MWDCA does not bar public policy tort claims for retaliation in violation of the Act itself. Therefore, if an employer retaliates against an employee for making a claim for worker's disability compensation, the employer may be liable for tort damages above and beyond those provided by the Act.

MWDCA Procedure

The MWDCA is enforced by the Workers' Compensation Agency, which is part of the Michigan Department of Labor & Economic Growth.

When an employee suffers a work-related injury, an employee is required to complete a Report of Claim. Assuming the injury is disabling, the employer must then pay workers' compensation benefits, unless it disputes the claim. If the claim results in either (1) disability for more than seven consecutive days (not including the injury date), (2) death, or (3) specific loss, the employer must file a Basic Report of Injury with the Bureau.

If the employer decides to dispute the claim, it must file a Notice of Dispute and provide the basis for it, such as an argument that the injury is not work-related or is not disabling. The employer is entitled to have the employee submit to an independent medical examination at the employer's expense. The employee's failure or refusal to appear for such an examination is a basis for suspending benefits.

Once a Notice of Dispute is filed, an employee wishing to pursue his or her rights must file an Application for Mediation or Hearing. This document identifies the date and nature of the injury, the date of the disability, health care providers treating the employee for the condition, and the like. The Bureau of Worker's and Unemployment Compensation will forward this Application to the employer and the employer's insurance carrier. A response is due within 30 days. Both the employer and the employee are required to immediately produce all pertinent medical records in their possession.

Although the MWDCA does not have a statute of limitations as such, an employee cannot recover benefits going back more than two years prior to the filing of the Application for Mediation or Hearing. However, where an occupational disease, as opposed to an injury, is at issue, the clock does not start running until the employee knew or should have known of the disease, which means that in certain circumstances an employee may be able to recover for diseases incurred many years ago. If the employer initially voluntarily pays wage loss benefits and then terminates them, the employee must file the Application within one year.

Discovery

The MWDCA does not provide for formal discovery, such as interrogatories, requests for production of documents, or discovery depositions. However, the Act does mandate certain disclosures of information. For example, each side must provide all medical evidence that it has in its possession upon request. This includes any medical reports resulting from an independent medical examination. Parties also may subpoena documents for trial. In addition, parties may conduct informal discovery, such as interviewing witnesses, hiring a private investigator to determine the claimant's ability to perform certain functions, and the like.

Trial

At trial in a workers' compensation case, all medical testimony is presented by way of *de bene esse* deposition. Typically, each party will depose an expert medical witness who has conducted an independent medical examination. In addition, treating physicians may be deposed. Therefore, only lay witnesses will testify at trial. These witnesses generally will include the claimant, any witnesses to the alleged accident, a representative from the employer who can discuss the claimant's job duties and any other witnesses to the claimant's ability to work or the cause of the claimant's disability.

Settlement

Worker's compensation matters may be resolved in three ways. First, a magistrate may make a ruling following a trial and order that benefits be paid or not paid. If the employer is liable, the employer will be ordered to pay benefits for the time period at issue, including a lump sum for any past benefits in addition to the weekly benefits going forward. Second, the employer may voluntarily pay benefits. Finally, the parties may choose to formally settle their case.

Any settlement of a workers' disability compensation claim must be approved by a magistrate from the Bureau of Workers' and Unemployment Compensation through a procedure known as redemption. The redemption takes the form of a lump sum paid to the employee in return for the employee's agreement to give up his or her rights to benefits under the MWDCA. Redemption relieves an employer of all further liability arising out of the workplace injury. No matter can be redeemed until at least six months after the injury that created the claim. This time limitation allows the parties to adequately consider the consequences of their agreement.

Under redemption, an employee may, but is not required to, agree to a resignation and waiver of seniority. This resignation has been held to preclude a subsequent lawsuit against an employer under a breach-of-contract theory.

A redemption agreement must be submitted to a magistrate and placed on the record at a hearing. This redemption hearing is important in that it allows an employer to make a record of the employee's injury redeemed in the workers' compensation proceeding. An employee will be prohibited from recovering injuries for damages referenced in a workers' compensation redemption. Generally, the defense attorney will elicit testimony indicating that the employee understands that the redemption covers all injuries to date arising out of the employment, whether or not those injuries were the specific subject of the workers' disability compensation claim and whether or not the employee knows of those injuries at the time of the redemption. Such a procedure precludes an employee from making a claim, at a later date, that the injury was more serious than he or she thought, or that other injuries also were suffered.

MWDCA Insurance Requirements

The MWDCA requires that all employers either maintain worker's disability compensation insurance or be "self-insured." An employer cannot be self-insured simply by failing to purchase insurance and determining to self-insure. Rather, the employer must apply for self-insured status and must meet certain defined requirements, such as proof of solvency. Self-insurance can only be maintained after the employer demonstrates to the MWDCA a sound financial condition and after receiving permission from the MWDCA. Employers may also receive "group self insurance" in which several small employers join together to obtain approval for self-insurance as a group. As with the general self-insurance requirements, employers in a group-self insurance plan must get permission and prove their financial viability.

An employer is not required to maintain worker's disability compensation insurance for independent contractors. However, if the independent contractor does not maintain his or her own insurance, the employer may nonetheless have to provide worker's compensation benefits, and then go after the independent contractor for reimbursement.

While there are various funds designed to protect employees of employers who fail to maintain insurance or become insolvent, an employer should not rely on those funds. The MWDCA provides that an employer who fails to maintain proper insurance as required by the Act may be liable for criminal penalties of $1,000 or six months in jail. Each day without insurance is viewed as a new offense, which means an employer could be fined $1,000 per day. Both the company and its officers and directors may also be civilly liable for failure to maintain insurance.

Requirements for Workers' Compensation Coverage[†]

[†] The following list is taken directly from the Michigan Department of Labor & Economic Growth Workers' Compensation Agency's publication "General Information Regarding Rights and Responsibilities Under the Act," (May 2007).

- Purchase a policy from a licensed and approved insurance carrier. Contact your insurance agent for further information.
- Purchase a policy through the assigned risk pool. Your insurance agent will be able to assist you.
- Secure coverage through a self-insured group fund. Contact the Bureau of Workers' Disability Compensation for a list of the self-insured group funds.
- Receive authorization from the bureau director to be an individual self-insurer. Contact the bureau for further information.
- File an exclusion form with the bureau director. Contact the bureau to request an exclusion form.

CHAPTER 13: National Labor Relations Act

The National Labor Relations Act (NLRA) regulates the relationship between private-sector employers, unions, and employees. The Act established the National Labor Relations Board (NLRB) to administer the NLRA by (1) conducting representation elections to determine if employees will be represented by a union; (2) deciding whether the composition of bargaining units needs to be clarified; and (3) investigating and prosecuting unfair labor practice charges. The topics in this chapter describe how the NLRB processes election and unfair labor practice cases; defines what are unfair labor practices; describes the process of collective bargaining; and discusses the Employee Free Choice Act, which if enacted, will substantially change the law relating to the law of collective bargaining and how unions can be selected to represent groups of employees.

The law governing labor relations is complex and requires a thorough knowledge of NLRB practices and procedures. Although this chapter helps employers to understand basic principles, and provides a road map of how typical election and unfair labor practice cases are handled, it is recommended that counsel experienced in NLRB matters be retained immediately after an organizational effort commences or an unfair labor practice charge is filed.

By 2007, the percentage of private sector employees belonging to unions had shrunk to 7.5%. For this reason, unions are increasingly interested in convincing more workers to join their ranks.

Election Cases

Election Petitions

The NLRA gives employees the right to a secret ballot election to decide whether or not they will be represented by a union for purposes of collective bargaining. The process of a representation election starts with the filing of a Representation Petition by the interested union with the NLRB. For the NLRB to order an election, the Petition must be supported by at least 30% of the employees in the proposed bargaining unit. Unions will generally not file petitions and undertake the time and expense of a campaign until they have at least 50-60% of the affected employees' signatures. Thus, in most cases in which a Petition has been filed, the employer can be assured that at least half of its employees in the proposed unit have signed authorization cards for the union.

The Petition, which is on a pre-printed form, identifies the union that is attempting to organize the employer's employees; indicates that the union has submitted to the NLRB, with the Petition, authorization cards signed by at least 30% of the employees the union seeks to represent; specifies the number of employees involved; and describes the bargaining unit the union seeks to represent.

Authorization cards state that the employees who signed the cards want the union to represent them for purposes of collective bargaining. The purpose of the cards is to assure that there is sufficient interest in representation by the employees to justify the NLRB expending the time and effort necessary to arrange an election. Employers are not permitted to see the authorization cards submitted to the NLRB.

The bargaining unit description in the Petition lists the job classifications of the employees that the union seeks to represent. For example, if the union seeks to represent employees employed at a production facility, the petition might describe the bargaining unit as "All full-time and regular part-time production and maintenance employees employed by the employer at its facility located at A Street, Detroit, Michigan; but excluding office clerical employees, guards, and supervisors as defined in the Act."

The union may seek to represent a bargaining unit limited to a single department, comprised of various job classifications of employees grouped together, or encompassing all employees in a single job classification at multiple locations of the same employer. Relative to employers with multiple facilities, a rebuttable presumption exists that employees at a single site of employment constitute an appropriate bargaining unit, rather than employees at multiple facilities.

The NLRB has determined how elections are to be conducted where a union seeks to represent both the regular employees of an employer as well as the "temporary" workers assigned to that employer by a staffing services company. Under these circumstances, in *Oaklawn Care Center*, the NLRB held that these two separate groups of workers cannot be joined together in a single bargaining unit without the consent of both the primary employer and the staffing services firm.

A Petition for Election also may be filed by a group of employees, in limited circumstances, to obtain a decertification election to determine whether employees no longer want to be represented by the incumbent union. This issue will be discussed later.

Pre-election Hearings

Immediately after the Petition is filed, the NLRB will issue a Notice of Hearing that specifies a date, time, and place for the parties to present evidence concerning unresolved pre-election issues. The hearing is generally scheduled on a date within two weeks after the union files the Petition. In the vast majority of cases, the hearing never takes place because the parties reach a voluntary agreement as to the composition of the group of eligible voters. The process of reaching an agreement as to the eligible voters is generally one that involves the employer and the union explaining their positions to an NLRB Agent, who often engages in "shuttle diplomacy" to get the parties to agree.

The primary purpose of the pre-election hearing is to determine which job classifications will be included in or excluded from the unit. The NLRB generally determines whether a bargaining unit is appropriate based on a "community-of-interest" analysis. The NLRB's primary concern is that employees who have substantial mutual interests in wages, hours, and other terms and conditions of employment be grouped together. Special rules have been established for healthcare institutions pursuant to which eight bargaining units have been identified as being automatically appropriate.

The employer may seek to exclude from the unit certain job classifications that the union included in the Petition. It may also seek to add positions that the union did not include in the Petition. This stage of the process is a critical strategic point in the campaign. For example, the employer may seek to include in the unit a group of workers who it believes will vote against the union. The upside to this decision is that this inclusion may dilute or counter union support in the group proposed by the union. On the other hand, if the employer loses the election, the union will be representing a larger group of employees than it initially sought to represent.

At the hearing, both the employer and the union have the right to present evidence as to why certain positions should be in or out of the unit. Such evidence will normally relate to the job duties, pay, benefits, and interactions of the job classifications in question, as well as any prior bargaining history that may exist. The hearing is a formal proceeding, at which witnesses are sworn in and a transcript is made of the proceedings. Each side may present its own witnesses, cross-examine the other party's witnesses and enter relevant documents into evidence.

A hearing also may be held if the NLRB's jurisdiction over the employer is disputed. Jurisdictional standards are based on minimum annual dollar volumes. For example, the NLRB asserts jurisdiction over any non-retail employer that has interstate sales or purchases of at least $50,000. The $50,000 standard may be satisfied either directly or indirectly. The indirect standard is satisfied if an employer sells $50,000 of goods to a customer located in the state in which the employer is located, and the customer, in turn, sells the goods to a customer located outside the state. The NLRB's jurisdictional standard for retail establishments is $500,000 in annual sales. The NLRB also has adopted annual revenue standards for various other private entities, including educational and healthcare institutions, hotels, motels, and apartments and condominiums. The NLRB will assert jurisdiction over all but the smallest employers. Jurisdictional issues are rarely litigated.

After the hearing, the parties may obtain a transcript of the proceedings and submit post-hearing briefs in support of their respective positions. The NLRB usually issues a decision within 30 days of the hearing and, immediately thereafter, either schedules the election or dismisses the Petition for lack of jurisdiction.

Voluntary Election Agreements

It is not necessary that a hearing be held if the employer and union are able to agree on a bargaining unit description and other pre-election matters. There are two types of voluntary election agreements:

- Agreement for Consent Election
- Stipulation for Certification upon Consent Election

The primary difference between the two is that, under the Agreement for Consent Election, the parties have no right to appeal the local NLRB office's decision on unresolved pre-election issues to the five-member NLRB located in Washington, DC. Accordingly, most attorneys recommend that employers opt for the Stipulation for Certification Upon Consent Election, preserving the right to appeal to the Board.

Both voluntary election agreement forms set forth the agreed-upon bargaining unit description, the payroll eligibility date, the date and time of the election, where the election will be held, and the basis of the NLRB's jurisdiction over the employer. The payroll eligibility date is always the weekly or biweekly payroll period immediately preceding the date the NLRB approves the parties' agreement to proceed to an election.

Although the date of the election is subject to agreement between the employer and union, the NLRB typically requires that the election be held within 42 days after the date the Election Petition is filed. The time of the election also is subject to agreement of the parties. However, the NLRB requires that the election be held during working hours and when all employees are scheduled to work. The place of the election must be an enclosed area on the employer's premises, located away from offices occupied by supervisors. Before the election, the NLRB provides the employer a Notice of Election that must be posted in the workplace at least three full days before the election. The NLRB may set aside the election results if the Notice is not posted in a timely manner.

On extremely rare occasions, elections may be conducted by mail. The ballots in this type of election are mailed to eligible voters, who mark their ballots and mail them back to the NLRB. Most employers oppose mail ballot elections because voter turnout tends to be lower than in an on-site election, and the chances of fraud are higher.

Campaigns

Employers are required to provide the NLRB an alphabetical list of eligible voters, called the *Excelsior* list, which sets forth employee names and addresses. Each employee's first and last name must be included; entries such as "J.Smith" may cause the Board to find that the list is deficient. The list must be provided within 7 days of the direction of the election or the Board's approval of a consent-election agreement. The NLRB will set aside election results favorable to the employer if the complete and accurate list is not provided to the union in a timely manner.

Once the Petition is filed, the employer is prohibited from making any changes in wages, benefits or other terms and conditions of employment, unless the decision to make the change was made prior to the Petition filing date. The timing of such decisions should be well-documented by the employer.

Automatic pay increases, such as annual cost of living adjustments, should continue to be made, even after the petition is filed. Discretionary pay raises, however, are prohibited in the absence of union approval. Improved wages, benefits or terms or conditions of employment are viewed by the NLRB as being inducements to employees to vote against the union, and reductions are viewed as retaliation against employees for signing authorization cards and pursuing unionization. An illegal post-petition change by the employer in terms and conditions of employment may cause a successful election to be voided, resulting in a new election. In egregious situations, the election result may even be reversed, resulting in a union victory.

The rules that apply to unions and employers during organizing campaigns are not the same. The biggest difference is that while employers are barred from making any promises to employees about future pay, benefits or working conditions, unions are free to make whatever promises they want to make, no matter how outlandish they may be. The theory behind this is that an employer's promise carries greater weight, as it is able to unilaterally change wages and other conditions of employment, but a union does not have that power or authority.

At the outset of the campaign period, employers should establish campaign themes designed to persuade employees to vote in favor of maintaining a union-free environment. An employer should identify its strong points in terms of existing wages, benefits, and other terms and conditions of employment, as well as its weak points. Information about the union should be gathered and used appropriately during the campaign. Employers often hire outside consultants to assist them during the pre-election campaign and to train supervisors on how to conduct themselves during the campaign.

Unions conduct their campaigns by mail, e-mail, telephone and fliers, and through meetings with individuals and groups of employees. They also use web sites to communicate information to employees. Employers do have the advantage of having access to voters whenever they are at work. One-on-one discussions as well as well-organized group meetings can be very effective campaign tools for employers.

The NLRB requires there be no interference with employee freedom of choice in terms of voting. Accordingly, the NLRB will set aside the election results if either the employer or union engages in unfair labor practices or other objectionable conduct that could affect the outcome of the election. During the pre-election period, for example, employers cannot:

- Discipline or discharge employees because of their union activity or sympathies, or threaten to do so.
- Increase or decrease wages, benefits or other terms and conditions of employment, as discussed above.
- Promise or threaten to make such changes.
- Solicit grievances from employees or promise to remedy grievances.
- Interrogate employees as to their union activities or sympathies.
- Conduct surveillance of employee union activity.
- Give speeches to a captive audience of employees during the 24 hours before the election.

There are also limits on what unions can do in the course of a campaign. They may not threaten or attempt to intimidate voters; give money or gifts to voters in an effort to persuade them; appeal to racial or other prejudices; or engage in a range of other misconduct.

There are two basic approaches to educating employees about the options they face in the election. One is to convince them that the employer has been fair with them in the past and will continue to be a fair, caring employer in the future. Alternatively, the message can be sent that even though management mistakes have been made, the employer has now heard the employees' concerns and wants a fair chance to show its good faith over the next year without a union's involvement.

The second approach is one by which the employer educates the voters about the union seeking to represent it. Most campaigns tend to be a combination of the two approaches. In the vast majority of elections, it is in the employer's long term interest to run a positive campaign, keeping in mind that, regardless of the outcome of the election, management and eligible voters will have to work together to meet production or service needs in an efficient manner.

Among the types of facts the employer should explain to voters, if they apply, are the following:

- A history of fairness in dealing with employment issues.
- A history of caring about the personal problems and accomplishments of workers.
- Opportunities for advancement given to workers.
- The fairness of the pay and benefits provided by the employer.

In order to fairly educate employees about the union that is seeking to represent them and obtain their dues payments, the employer must itself obtain information about the labor organization. There are many sources of such information:

- LM-2s (labor organization financial statements) are available from the U.S. Department of Labor.
- Copies of unfair labor practice charges and decertification petitions (together with the outcomes of the elections) filed against the labor organization can be obtained from the NLRB through Freedom of Information Act requests.
- Copies of representation petitions filed by the labor organization and the election tallies can also be obtained from the NLRB through FOIA.
- Press reports about the labor organization can be located on-line.
- Records of duty of fair representation cases filed against the union may be located through the appropriate federal district court or the NLRB.

These documents may be obtained directly by the employer or through a variety of consulting groups that specialize in locating and supplying this type of information.

A critical factor in virtually every election is the credibility of management. For this reason it is absolutely essential for the employer to convey its message to the voters in an honest, sincere and convincing manner. Emotional diatribes against unionism are usually counter-productive, and may well lead to unfair labor practice charges.

It helps to have documentation to support statements that are made to employees. Often, an employee will not believe information imparted by a management official until a government document, union newsletter, or newspaper article containing the same information is provided to the individual. If management gives inaccurate information to employees and the union is able to prove the falsity of the statement, the employer's credibility is going to be damaged. It is thus of paramount importance to be able to provide support for key statements made in oral presentations, letters or memos to employees.

There are three basic ways for the employer to communicate its message to voters: 1) written communications, given to the employee at work or sent to his/her home; 2) formal group meetings, in which a variety of issues related to the election may be discussed; and 3) one-on-one personal contacts between supervisors or managers and individual employees. With respect to the group meetings, it is important to remember that no such meetings may be conducted in the 24-hour period preceding the beginning of the election.

It is also important to know that neither an employer nor its agents can make any threats or promises, interrogate employees about union activities or leanings of themselves or others, engage in surveillance of union activities, solicit grievances, or attempt to intimidate voters. Further, they may not discriminate or retaliate against an employee or group of employees because of their union sympathies. An employer engaging in such actions runs the risk of having a winning election voided, or even worse, having the NLRB enter a bargaining order, requiring the employer to recognize the union as the representative of its employees. The latter remedy will only be implemented where the Board determines that the employer's conduct was so egregious that a fair election cannot later be conducted.

An employer can, however, relate factual information about itself and the union to employees. Supervisors and managers can share experiences they have had working in other unionized facilities. They may express their opinions that a union would not be a positive thing for the employees and they may predict, in a non-threatening manner, what they think the future of the company will be with or without a union. They may relate the company's position in its competitive market and indicate that the granting of pay or benefit increases may make the company less competitive in the market, resulting in a loss of jobs. Thus, although there are substantial restrictions on what supervisors and managers may say and do, there are a great many things they can and should do during an organizing campaign.

A major strategic issue facing employers is one of timing. In any campaign, a party wants to peak on election day. For this reason, it makes sense to develop at a very early stage of the campaign a campaign calendar, in which the employer identifies the dates on which fliers with specific themes will be distributed and when group meetings on specific subjects will be held. Most employers facing a campaign for the first time want to fire all their ammunition as soon as possible after receipt of the Petition. This is generally not the best strategy, however, as all of the employer's efforts should build support among employees to the point where it is at its peak on election day.

Shortly before the election, both the employer and the union are to designate an election observer; someone who will identify eligible voters as they arrive at the polling place and mark them off the voter list. The observers must be non-supervisory employees. If there is only one polling time, each side will designate one observer. If there are multiple voting times, each side may designate a different observer or the same observer for each polling time.

In the 24-hour period preceding the opening of the polls, the employer may not conduct group meetings, or "captive audience" meetings, with employees. It may still talk with individuals, but may not pull groups of employees together during this period.

Elections

On the date of the election, an NLRB agent arrives at the employer's facility sufficiently in advance of the starting time of the election to conduct a brief pre-election conference. This conference is held between the employer and union representatives, their attorneys, and the election observers.

During the pre-election conference, the NLRB agent describes the election procedure and cautions the employer and the union that no campaigning may take place and no supervisory personnel may be in or near the voting area. The observers are advised of their function during the election; that is, to check off the names of eligible voters on the list of eligible voters as each voter casts his or her ballot. The observers also may challenge voters. For example, if the union believes a voter is a supervisor and, therefore, is not eligible to vote in the election, the union observer advises the NLRB agent of the challenge. The NLRB agent then places the challenged ballot in an envelope and writes on the envelope the name of the voter, the reason for the challenge and the parties' respective positions as to the eligibility of the voter. Additionally, the NLRB agent will challenge all voters whose names do not appear on the eligible voter list.

The NLRB agent provides the voting booth and a ballot box that the parties are entitled to examine during the pre-election meeting.

Immediately after the election, the NLRB agent counts the ballots. The employer and union representatives, their attorneys, and eligible voters who are not supposed to be working may be present when the ballots are counted. The NLRB agent examines the ballots before they are counted and may determine that any improperly marked or defaced ballots are invalid. After the ballots are counted, the NLRB agent issues a Tally of Ballots. The Tally indicates the number of votes for and against the petitioning union and the number of challenged ballots. If the number of challenged ballots could affect the results of the election and, therefore, be determinative, the NLRB attempts to obtain the parties' agreement as to which of the challenged ballots may be counted. Absent the parties' agreement, the NLRB conducts an investigation, or a hearing, to determine eligibility issues. After the eligibility ballot issues are resolved, either by agreement of the parties or a decision of the NLRB, a revised Tally of Ballots is issued that sets forth the final election results.

For the union to become the elected representative of the employees, it must win a majority of the votes cast. If there is a tie, the union loses the election.

In order to promote stable labor-management relations, the Act provides that, following the certification of an election, there cannot be another representation or decertification election within 12 months.

Objections to Elections

Both the union and the employer have seven days after the NLRB issues the Tally of Ballots in which to file objections to the conduct of the election. Post-election challenges are claims by the losing party that the winning party engaged in unfair labor practices or other objectionable conduct that affected the outcome of the election. The NLRB conducts an investigation and/or a hearing to determine whether the objections are valid. The parties are entitled to obtain a transcript of the hearing, if one is held, and to submit written briefs in support of their positions. The NLRB then issues a decision, usually within 30 to 60 days of the hearing, concluding either that a new election must be held or upholding the results of the election. In rare cases involving egregious employer misconduct that would render a fair re-run election impossible, the Board can issue a bargaining order. This order would require the employer to recognize and bargain with the union without the need for a new election.

Voluntary Recognition and Neutrality Agreements

In some circumstances, an employer may choose to voluntarily recognize a union as a representative of its employees. Voluntary recognition is usually the result of pressure from a major customer of the employer.

Some employers, again usually due to pressure from major customers, sign neutrality agreements, by which they commit to not actively contest a union's efforts to gain recognition through an election. In such situations, an election is held, but the employer does little to oppose the union's campaign.

Decertification and Deauthorization Elections

There are two types of elections that the Board can conduct in unionized workplaces. A Decertification election is an election process by which employees seek to free themselves of the union. A Deauthorization election is the process by which employees seek to eliminate from their collective bargaining agreement the provision by which the employer is authorized to deduct union dues from their pay checks and forward them to the union. For either election to occur, a Petition supported by 30% or more of the bargaining unit employees must be submitted to the NLRB.

A Petition for a Decertification election can only be filed during two time periods: (1) when there is no collective bargaining agreement in effect and at least 12 months have passed since the initial certification of the union; or (2) within a window period of between 60 and 90 days prior to the expiration date of the collective bargaining agreement. This type of petition may only be filed by employees; if the employer participates in any way in the processing the petition, the NLRB will reject it.

When a union has been voluntarily recognized by an employer, without employees having the opportunity to vote for or against it, a different rule applies. In such circumstances, employees need not wait 12 months before filing a Decertification Petition. Instead, they may file it within a "reasonable time" after the voluntary recognition.

A Decertification election is a contest between employees and the union. Thus, the employer is not to campaign or assert any pressure on either side. As in the case of a representation election, the union must win a majority of the votes cast to remain as the representative of the employees. If there is a tie vote or a majority of voters choose "no union," the union ceases to be the representative of the employees.

A Petition for a Deauthorization election can be filed at any time that a collective bargaining agreement is in effect. The purpose of this election is to remove from the collective bargaining agreement the provision that authorizes the employer to deduct union dues from employees' paychecks and forward the money to the union. In order for this to happen, a majority of the employees in the entire bargaining unit must vote for deauthorization; the outcome of the election is not necessarily decided by the majority of the votes that are actually cast.

In most instances in which a bargaining unit votes for deauthorization, the union that is no longer receiving dues will file a disclaimer of interest with the NLRB, effectively ending its representation of the bargaining unit.

Unfair Labor Practice Cases

The NLRA prohibits employers and unions from engaging in conduct defined as unfair labor practices. It is an unfair labor practice for an employer to:

- interfere with, restrain, or coerce employees in the exercise of their right to organize or engage in other protected concerted activity, defined as group activity, the purpose of which is to improve or protest wages, hours, or working conditions.

- dominate or interfere with the formation or administration of a labor organization or contribute financial support to it.

- discriminate against employees in regard to their hire or tenure of employment or any term or condition of employment, to encourage or discourage membership in any labor organization.

- discharge or otherwise discriminate against an employee because the employee files an unfair labor practice charge with the NLRB or gives testimony in a NLRB proceeding.

- refuse to bargain in good faith with a union certified by the NLRB.

It is an unfair labor practice for a union to:

- restrain or coerce employees in the exercise of their right to organize or to engage in protected concerted activity, or an employer in the selection of its representatives for purposes of collective bargaining or the adjustment of grievances.

- cause or attempt to cause an employer to discriminate against an employee, or to discriminate against an employee with respect to whom membership in a labor organization has been denied or terminated on some ground other than the employee's failure to pay the periodic dues and initiation fees uniformly required as a condition of membership.

- refuse to bargain in good faith with an employer.

- engage in or encourage employees to engage in a strike whose purpose is to force the employer to cease doing business with another employer; to force or require another employer to recognize or bargain with a labor organization; to force an employer to recognize or bargain with a particular union if another union has been certified; to force an employer to assign particular work to employees represented by another labor union or force an employer or self-employed person to join a labor organization; or to use only vendors or suppliers whose employees are represented by a labor union.

- require employees, as a condition to becoming a member of a labor organization, to pay a fee the NLRB finds excessive or discriminatory.

- cause an employer to pay or deliver any money in the nature of an exaction for services that are not performed or not to be performed.

- picket or threaten to picket where the purpose is to force the employer to recognize the union as the collective bargaining representative of employees where the employer has recognized a different labor union, a certified board election has been conducted in the preceding 12 months concerning the employees, or the picketing has been conducted for 30 days without a petition for an election being filed with the Board.

Unfair labor practice charges must be filed within six months after the alleged unlawful conduct on which the charge is based.

NLRB Procedures in Unfair Labor Practice Cases

Immediately after an unfair labor practice charge is filed, the NLRB sends a copy to the Charged Party, either the employer or union.

The NLRB conducts an investigation that may involve obtaining affidavits (sworn written statements) from witnesses. For example, if an employee files a charge against an employer claiming he or she was discharged because of his or her union activities, the NLRB first obtains an affidavit from the employee and other employee witnesses who have knowledge concerning the discharge. The NLRB then asks the employer to arrange meetings with supervisors involved in the discharge decision. An alternative to allowing supervisors to give affidavits is for the employer to simply file a position statement with the Board. The Board, however, tends to give more weight to affidavits, where it can actually meet with and question witnesses, than to a position statement drafted by legal counsel. In most cases, it is thus more persuasive to the Board to provide witnesses. There may be situations in which this is not the case, so the strategy decision on this issue will vary case-by-case.

The NLRB generally conducts investigations of unfair labor practice charges expeditiously. Within 30 to 45 days after a charge is filed, the NLRB will issue either a written notice advising that the Charge has been dismissed or issue a Complaint and a notice setting a trial date. If the charge is dismissed, the Charging Party may appeal the decision to the NLRB Office of Appeals. If a Complaint is issued, there is no right to appeal. The Charged Party, or Respondent, must file an Answer to the Complaint within 14 days and must either agree to settle the case or defend itself at trial.

The trial usually is scheduled for a date three to four months after the Complaint is issued. Postponements of the initial trial date are granted for good cause. An Administrative Law Judge employed by the NLRB conducts the trial. An NLRB attorney presents evidence on behalf of the Charging Party, which may also be represented by its own counsel. The Respondent, either the employer or union, is virtually always represented by an attorney. Post-trial briefs may be submitted by each party. A decision is usually issued within three to six months. The losing party may appeal the decision to the five-member NLRB in Washington, DC. Unfavorable decisions of the Board may be appealed to a federal Circuit Court of Appeals. Although decisions of the federal appellate courts may be appealed to the United States Supreme Court, the high court very rarely grants requests for review.

Remedies Against Unfair Labor Practices

The remedy ordered by the NLRB when an employer or union is found to have committed an unfair labor practice depends on the nature of the violation.

For example, if the NLRB determines that an employee was discharged by an employer because of his or her union activities, a make-whole order may be issued, requiring the employer to pay the employee for all lost wages and benefits, plus interest, and to reinstate the employee.

If the NLRB determines that an employer or union has refused to bargain in good faith, a bargaining order is issued requiring good faith negotiations.

If an employer engages in widespread unfair labor practices prior to an election, the NLRB has the discretion to seek a bargaining order, even if the union loses the election, and also may seek an injunction in federal court requiring that the employer cease and desist engaging in unfair labor practices. Injunctions may also be sought in other extremely limited situations.

The NLRB requires, as a remedy in all cases, posting of a written Notice to Employees at the employer's facility, or a Notice to Union Members at the union's facility, specifying the nature of the unfair labor practice committed and assuring that the guilty employer or union will not engage in similar conduct in the future.

Collective Bargaining

Employers and unions are required to bargain in good faith. This means that, after a union is certified by the NLRB as the collective bargaining representative of employees, or is voluntarily recognized by the employer, the parties must meet on mutually agreeable dates and negotiate over terms and conditions of a collective bargaining agreement. If agreement is reached, the parties are required to reduce the agreed-upon terms and conditions to writing and sign it.

Collective bargaining agreements need not conform to any particular format, but typically they specify management's rights; wage rates in each job classification; hours, breaks, meal times, and fringe benefits; that union dues will be deducted from employee paychecks; the employer's right to discharge employees only for just cause; a grievance procedure that leads to final and binding arbitration; and other terms and conditions of employment.

If the parties are unable to agree to contract terms after good faith negotiations, and an impasse is reached, the employer is entitled to unilaterally implement the terms set forth in its final offer to the union during negotiations.

Each party possesses a significant economic weapon to force the other to accede to its demands and break an impasse. Employers have the right to lock out employees; they may refuse to allow employees to work until the union agrees to the employer's demands. On the other hand, the union may persuade employees to exercise their right to strike. If the employees go out on an economic strike (one relating to a dispute over mandatory subjects of bargaining), the employer has the right to temporarily or permanently replace them. When the strike ends and the striking employees return to work, the employer need not reinstate them if permanent replacements remain employed. If permanent replacements have been hired, strikers have the right to be placed on a preferential hiring list. They may only be brought back to work as job openings occur.

However, if the employer commits an unfair labor practice that either leads to, or causes the continuation of the strike, the NLRB may conclude that the walkout is an unfair labor practice strike. The significance of such a finding is that an employer cannot permanently replace unfair labor practice strikers. When an unfair labor practice strike ends and the striking employees return to work, the employer must reinstate them, even if it means terminating replacement workers.

Employee Participation Committees

Many employers have created employee participation committees to address various work-related issues. In 1992, the NLRB issued its *Electromation* decision that raised serious questions as to the continued viability of these types of committees for non-union employers.

In *Electromation*, the NLRB decided that five employee action committees created by a non-union employer to address no-smoking rules, absenteeism, and attendance bonus programs were labor organizations and that they were unlawfully dominated by the employer. The Board ordered that the committees be disbanded. The basis for this decision was that by "dealing with" the committees on mandatory subjects of bargaining, the employer was treating the committees like unions. The NLRA prohibits employers from "dominating or assisting" unions, and the Board held that the employer in that case was dominating and assisting these committees by selecting their members, setting their agendas and allowing employees to participate in them on paid time.

So long as an employer does not "deal with" such committees over terms and conditions of employment, they will not be considered to be labor organizations, and even if the employer dominates them, the NLRB would probably not find the arrangement to be illegal.

Employee Representation in Discipline Situations

When the U.S. Supreme Court issued its *Weingarten* decision in 1975, it held that an employee at a unionized company has a legal right under the NLRA to insist on union representation during an investigatory interview, if the employee reasonably believes that the interview could lead to his or her discipline. These employee "rights" have come to be known as "Weingarten rights."

Twenty-five years later, in *Epilepsy Foundation of Northeast Ohio*, the NLRB extended Weingarten rights to non-union employees. In this case, an employee in a non-union setting was discharged for refusing to meet, without a requested coworker present, with his superiors to discuss a possible disciplinary situation. The NLRB ordered that the employee be reinstated with back pay.

In 2004, in a case titled *IBM, Inc.*, the Board returned to the original Weingarten ruling, by holding that the right to have a co-worker present at an investigatory interview only applies to unionized employees.

Thus, when an employer requests a disciplinary interview with a unionized employee to discuss even the smallest infraction that could possibly lead to the discipline of that employee, the employee can choose to have a union representative present.

No-Solicitation Rules

To provide themselves with maximum protections in the event of a unionization effort, employers should put into effect policies that prohibit employees from engaging in acts of solicitation of co-workers during working time and in work areas. To be legally effective, these policies may only prohibit employees from engaging in solicitations of co-workers whenever either of those employees is on paid working time and in areas of the facility where work is performed. They cannot limit solicitation discussions in non-working areas such as break rooms or parking lots.

In a 2007 decision, the NLRB decided the issue of the extent to which employers can bar on-site e-mail solicitations of employees by other employees. It concluded that employers may implement and apply non-solicitation rules that bar certain types of solicitations, including union solicitations, while permitting others. These rules may not however, single out union solicitations. An example of a permissible non-solicitation rule, the Board stated, is one that allows solicitations for charitable organizations such as the United Way and Red Cross, but bars non-charitable solicitations, such as those for Avon or a labor union.

Beck Rights

Unionized federal contractors (except those in right to work states) are required to post notices informing employees of their rights under the U.S. Supreme Court decision in *Communications Workers v. Beck*. That decision allowed employees paying union dues to opt out of dues allocated for political contributions or other activities not related to administration of their collective bargaining agreements.

A Word of Caution about Relying on NLRB Decisions

The National Labor Relations Board is a highly politicized body, and its decisions tend to be more pro-union or pro-employer depending upon whether a Democratic or Republican President has appointed a majority of the Board. For this reason, Board cases on which one might reasonably rely in taking a given course of action may be overruled when a new case dealing with the same issue is presented to a differently composed Board.

Employee Free Choice Act

As of the writing of this Chapter, Congress is considering passage of the Employee Free Choice Act. If enacted, this law will dramatically affect the process of how unions are selected by employees and how initial labor agreements are formed.

The main feature of the Act, as currently drafted, is that it essentially will do away with secret ballot elections where unions are trying to organize employees of a private sector employer. Under the current National Labor Relations Act, in order for a union to be selected by employees, it must present authorization cards to the NLRB showing that at least 30% of the relevant employee group is interested in having the union represent them. After verifying the signatures, the NLRB then conducts a secret ballot election, generally within 45 days, to determine if the union will represent the employees.

Under the proposed amendments to the Act, if a union can present the NLRB with authorization cards signed by a majority of the employees in the relevant employee group, there will not be an election: the union will be certified as the representative of the employees. This would be a huge change in the law that would dramatically change the landscape of labor-management relations.

Once the union is certified, if a collective bargaining agreement is not agreed upon within 90 days, either party can ask for mediation, through the services of the Federal Mediation and Conciliation Service (FMCS). If, after 30 days of mediation, there is no agreement reached, the FMCS may refer the matter to compulsory, binding arbitration by which the terms of the new contract will be resolved. The term of any new contract must be two years.

The FMCS and the NLRB will have to develop regulations in order to implement this law. In particular, the NLRB will have to develop a new authorization form. The FMCS will have to determine how arbitrators will be selected and how the arbitration process will work.

Despite the fact that the Act would eliminate secret ballot elections for initial representation elections, it would not change the process by which unions can be decertified. The current process for decertification, which does involve a secret ballot election, would not be altered.

CHAPTER 14: Military Duty and Employment Rights

Introduction

This chapter summarizes, in question and answer format, the key aspects of federal and state law that provide re-employment rights and protections from discrimination for employees who serve in the military.

The federal law known as "USERRA"—the Uniformed Services Employment and Re-employment Rights Act of 1994—covers all employers (who employ at least 1 person) and prohibits job discrimination and offers a variety of protections, including a variety of return-to-work rights for up to 5 years, to employees who have voluntarily left or been called away from work to serve in the military. The United States Department of Labor (DOL) issued regulations that became effective in January 2006 that further define an employee's rights and an employer's obligations and responsibilities under the USERRA law. Where significant, the DOL's USERRA regulations are explained throughout this chapter at various relevant points. Finally, more information is available on USERRA at the DOL's website at http://www.dol.gov/vets/programs/userra/main.htm.

In Michigan, a 1950s-era law was amended in April 2008 to provide a longer period than USERRA requires for employees to seek reemployment when they are returning from military service of up to 180 days in length. This difference is noted in the discussion below. In all other basic respects, Michigan law tracks USERRA's requirements.

Is your company covered by USERRA?

USERRA applies to any employer that either pays an individual a salary or wages to perform work or controls an individual's employment opportunities. This broad definition includes an individual or organization to which an employer delegates the performance of any employment-related responsibilities. However an entity that performs only "ministerial functions," such as personnel file maintenance or, presumably, paycheck processing, is not considered an employer.

Consider the example of a security guard hired by a security company and assigned to a work site of another company. Both the security company and the site owner have

USERRA obligations to the security guard employee. Even though the site owner is not the security guard's employer per se, it would be subject to USERRA liability if it caused the security guard's removal from the job because of the individual's service obligations.

A hiring hall, whether operated by a union or an employer association, also is an employer under this definition. A hiring hall may be delegated the performance of employment-related responsibilities such as hiring or job assignments and thus would be a USERRA-covered employer.

Other covered employers include:

- states and their political subdivisions, such as counties, parishes, cities, towns and townships, villages, and school districts.

- successors in interest, provided there is substantial continuity between their operations (including products or services produced), facilities, workforce, and working conditions and those of the former employer, a determination that is made on a case-by-case basis. A company can be covered as a successor in interest even without notice of any potential reemployment claims by employees of the predecessor company at the time of the merger, acquisition, or other form of succession.

- foreign employers with a physical location and employees in the United States.

- American employers with employees in foreign countries, as long as compliance with USERRA does not violate the law of the country in which the workplace is located.

- employers with only one employee.

What legal rights do employees have under USERRA?

USERRA offers two types of rights to employees – (1) protection against discrimination based on military affiliation or retaliation for pursuing rights available under USERRA and (2) job protection and return-to-work rights in the situation where an employee takes a leave of absence from employment to perform voluntary or involuntary (e.g., draft) military duty.

All non-temporary employees, regardless of whether they are employed on a full-time or part-time basis, and regardless of the type of job performed, are covered by USERRA's return-to-work provisions. If an individual is employed for a temporary period of time (temporary being determined on a case-by-case basis), however, no return-to-work rights apply. An employee on a fixed-term contract (e.g., one year or seasonal) is entitled to return-to-work rights only within the time frame of the contract, unless it is customary for the contract to be renewed at the expiration of its term. In such case, the employee's job restoration rights would be extended.

By contrast, all employees and applicants for employment, whether temporary or not, are protected from discrimination based on their military status, affiliation, or service and retaliation for making complaints or pursuing rights under USERRA.

Independent contractors are not eligible for USERRA's protection and therefore do not enjoy return-to-work rights.

How long do employees have rights under USERRA?

USERRA provides return-to-work rights for any employee absent from his or her job for military service for up to five (5) years. The 5-year protection period may be comprised of one single 5-year military deployment, or it may be counted cumulatively from several shorter periods of leave.

DOL's USERRA regulations clarify that the 5-year period of protection relates only to the employer for which the employee worked at the time a period of service began. In other words, the 5-year period of protection begins anew when the employee begins employment with a new employer, even if the employee had previous protected service time with another employer.

There are limited exceptions in which USERRA's leave protections would apply for more than five (5) years, which are not relevant in most situations. Employers may refer to the DOL "Resource Guide" or contact employment counsel if they have questions as to whether an employee's leave period may be protected beyond 5 years.

Employees (and applicants for employment) never lose their protection against discrimination based on their military affiliation or duty. The DOL has taken the position, which is set forth in its regulations and supported by the text of the USERRA law, that there is no statute of limitations after which an individual loses his or her protection against military discrimination.

Is there any type of military service that is not protected by USERRA?

In short, no.

USERRA covers any "service in the uniformed services," and includes both voluntary and involuntary service. Voluntary service includes the action of an employee to enlist while employed; involuntary service includes employee reservists called to active duty while employed.

The types of covered leaves for "service" include active duty, active duty training, initial active duty for training, full-time National Guard duty, and examinations to determine a person's fitness for duty. Covered "uniformed services" include the Army, Navy, Marine Corps, Air Force, Coast Guard, all of their reserves, the Army National Guard or Air National Guard, commissioned corps of the Public Health Service, and, notably, *any other category of persons designated by the President in a time or war or emergency*. (Note that, under similar state law in Michigan, which is described briefly in the next section, the Michigan governor may also designate any category of service, such as public health service in the time of a local disaster, as qualifying for protection under a state law similar to USERRA.)

The Katrina and related hurricane disasters in the Gulf Coast region in the fall of 2005 illustrate this point. Employees who are part of a National Disaster Medical System (known as "NDMS") team under the authority of the Federal Emergency Management Agency are entitled to USERRA protections and return-to-work rights if they are deployed by the federal government to a disaster area to provide medical assistance or support.

Is an employee's state National Guard service subject to USERRA?

No, but a Michigan law that provides parallel protection to USERRA would cover any employee's national guard service that was the result of orders from state civilian authorities.

While USERRA covers any *federal* "service in the uniformed services," that does not technically include an employee's National Guard service under orders from *state* government officials. It is a 1950s-era Michigan law that extends essentially the same protections as employees have under USERRA for those employees who perform military or reserve duties based on orders from Michigan's governor or other appropriate state authorities. That law—Public Act 133 of 1955—was updated in 2002 to bring its legal protections for employees in line with those established in USERRA (and it was amended again in 2008 to provide an even longer period than USERRA requires for employees to seek reemployment in certain circumstances, as noted in the further discussion below).

Are there any circumstances under which an employee on military leave would lose his or her USERRA return-to-work rights?

Yes – but only in limited situations.

An employee on military leave for service would lose his or her USERRA return-to-work rights if he or she was separated from the service with a dishonorable or bad conduct discharge or on any condition other than honorable (as each military branch may define).

Employees on leave who are absent from service without authority for more than three months or who are imprisoned in a civilian court may also be denied their USERRA rights.

Finally, a commissioned officer who is dismissed in the context of a court martial or by order of the President in time of war may be denied USERRA rights.

Employees and applicants for employment never lose their USERRA protection against military discrimination.

What notice must the employee give of the need for military leave?

USERRA requires any employee who is to go on a military service leave to give advance notice to his or her employer of the need for leave.

Unless military necessity prevents it, or it is otherwise impossible or unreasonable, employees must give the employer notice of their need for leave as far in advance as is reasonable under the circumstances.

For example, if the military directs the employee to report in an extremely short period of time to respond to an emergency situation, the employee may not have time to provide notice personally to the employer, or the employer's representative may not be available at that time.

Department of Defense guidelines recommend that employees give notice to their employers at least 30 days before departing for service "when it is feasible to do so."

The DOL regulations require no particular form for the notice. It may be oral or in writing, it may be informal, and it need not follow any particular format. This means employers may not deny employees USERRA leave or protections simply because of their failure to give notice in the format or by the method the employer requests or expects. Further, the employer must accept the notice as long as it comes from the employee or an appropriate officer of the branch of uniformed service in which the employee's service will be performed.

An important point to remember is that the notice requirement is not a permission requirement. An employee does not need the employer's permission or approval to be USERRA-protected or to depart for service. Moreover, the notice is simply notice of the need to depart. An employee has no obligation to give notice of intent to return to employment (or not) after military service. Whether or not the employee states intentions about returning to work has no effect on the USERRA right to reemployment.

A final cautionary note regarding the content of the employee's notice: Even if an employee tells the employer at her departure that she is not planning to return to work, she still would have the right to be reemployed, provided she otherwise met USERRA's eligibility requirements.

How is the employer to treat the employee's time on leave?

i. **Compensation.** USERRA does not require an employer to pay an employee on military leave. In recent surveys, however, it has been found that as many as 1 in 2 employers provide some sort of wage differential benefit for employees on military duty leave to help close the pay gap between military wages and the employer's wages. A survey of Fortune 500 companies found this number to be as high as two-thirds.

ii. **Use of vacation or other paid leave benefits.** An employer cannot *require* an employee on military leave to use any paid vacation, annual, or similar available accrued leave. The employer must *allow* any paid accrued leave to be used for this purpose, however, if the employee requests to do so.

An employee is not entitled to use any paid accrued sick leave, however, even upon his or her request, although the employer may allow the use of such leave if it does so for other kinds of leave not related to the employee's sickness.

iii. **FMLA eligibility.** Under normal circumstances, and assuming the employer is otherwise covered by the FMLA, an employee must have worked for the employer for at least 12 months and 1,250 hours in the 12 months preceding the requested FMLA leave in order to be eligible for the leave.

When an employee who has been on military leave for an extended period returns to work and shortly thereafter needs FMLA leave, he or she may not have actually worked 1,250 hours in the 12 months preceding the leave. However, USERRA requires that the employer count all time and hours the employee *would have worked but for the military leave* toward the employee's FMLA eligibility. This requirement applies to both aspects of the employee's eligibility – 12 months of work with the employer and 1,250 hours worked in the 12 months preceding the requested leave.

iv. **Group health benefits.** Employers must offer employees on a covered military leave the opportunity to continue their group health insurance coverage, if any exists, for up to 24 months.

USERRA does not require employers to establish or maintain group health plans for their employees. Nor does it require employers who do provide coverage to make it available to employees who take military leave for service if they did not already participate in the group coverage when the leave began.

In all other situations, however, USERRA provides that employees must have the opportunity to elect continuation coverage for the shorter of up to 24 months or the length of their leave. The DOL regulations provide both guidance and flexibility regarding how employees may elect and pay for the continuation of their coverage.

The opportunity for employees to elect health plan continuation coverage under USERRA is similar to that under the Consolidated Omnibus Budget Reconciliation Act of 1985 (COBRA). There are important differences, however. COBRA applies only to employers with 20 or more employees. USERRA applies to all employers. And, while the duration of COBRA coverage varies depending on the nature of the qualifying event, USERRA's continuation period is set at 24 months.

More importantly, the USERRA regulations leave employers and health plan administrators with a great deal more flexibility than COBRA permits regarding the manner in which employees are to elect and pay for their continuation coverage. Indeed, the regulations leave such matters completely up to employers and health plan administrators, provided they develop reasonable rules for each that are consistent with both the terms of the group health plan and USERRA itself. The regulations make it optional even whether to develop such rules at all, but the failure to do so exposes employers and plan administrators to more significant coverage obligations in certain circumstances.

The DOL regulations closely follow USERRA's requirements for how much employees on leave may be required to pay for their coverage. The employer may not require employees on leave for 30 days or less to pay any more than their regular share of the premium. If employees normally pay no portion of the premium they cannot be required to make a premium contribution while on leave.

Employees on leave for 31 or more days may be charged no more than 102 percent of the full premium for the plan.

Employers and plan administrators have a number of options for dealing with employees departing for a covered leave who either fail to elect or to pay for continuing coverage. The options are dependent on whether the employee was able to provide advance notice of the need for leave and whether the plan has reasonable rules for how employees are to elect and pay for coverage continuation. The options are as follows:

Employee neither gives advance notice nor elects coverage: The plan administrator may cancel the employee's coverage upon the employee's departure. If it is later determined that the employee was unable to provide advance notice of leave because of military necessity, or that it was impossible or unreasonable to do so, the plan administrator must reinstate coverage on the employee's election and payment of all unpaid premium amounts due.

Employee gives notice but fails to elect coverage: The plan administrator may cancel the employee's coverage on departure, but must reinstate coverage retroactive to that date if the employee elects coverage within the time established by the plan's reasonable rules for doing so. If the plan has not developed such rules, the employee may elect retroactive coverage continuation at any time during the 24-month coverage period or during the leave, whichever is shorter.

Employee elects coverage but does not pay: Plan administrators may develop and enforce reasonable rules for cancellation of coverage if an employee who elected continuation coverage fails to make timely payments.

The DOL regulations provide additional rules and clarification for multiemployer health plans that are beyond the scope of this book.

v. **Seniority rights.** Employees returning from military leave are entitled to have their seniority set as if they had been continuously employed during the period of leave. They are also entitled to all rights and benefits based on seniority that they would have attained with reasonable certainty had they been employed during the leave.

vi. **Non-seniority rights.** Employees who are on a military leave must be treated as if they are on a leave of absence regarding any non-seniority-related rights and benefits. In other words, while away on military leave, employees are entitled to participate in any rights or benefits that are not based on seniority that are available to employees on non-military leaves of absence, whether such leaves are paid or unpaid. If there is a variation in terms of benefits and rights among the various types of leaves of absence available from the employer, the employer must afford the employee the most favorable treatment available.

The employee would also be entitled to any non-seniority-related rights or benefits that became effective or available while he or she was on leave.

vii. **Pension benefits.** Employers must offer employees returning from leave pension plan benefits as if no break in employment during the time of military service has occurred. Further, an employer may not cause an employee to forfeit any benefits that may have already accrued to the individual under the plan and may not require a returning employee to re-qualify for participation in the plan.

In pension plans that require or allow employee contributions (whether matched by the employer or not), employees are permitted—but cannot be required—to make up any missed contributions from their leave period. The time for making up such contributions begins with the employee's re-employment and continues for a period up to three times the length of the employee's military leave period (but not to exceed 5 years). If an employee cannot or does not make up any missed contributions, the employer is not required to contribute any matching contribution associated with the employee's missed contributions that are not made up, and the employee's resulting pension may be less.

Any pension plan contributions, whether from the employee or employer, that are calculated based on the employee's compensation must be calculated on the rate of compensation the employee would have earned or attained had she remained continuously employed.

A final note—if the employee was on a leave greater than 90 days, the employer may require the employee to submit documentation showing entitlement to re-employment before treating the employee as not having had a break in service for pension purposes.

When do employees have to return to work?

The legal deadline under USERRA by which an employee on military leave must return to work depends on the length of the employee's military leave, and, to a lesser degree, on any changed circumstances at the employer during the employee's leave, as explained further below.

As noted above, however, as of April 2008, Michigan law (Public Act 106 of 2008) provides employees returning from military service a longer time to seek reemployment than USERRA requires. Thus, Michigan employers must permit reemployment to their employees in Michigan for a longer time following the employee's completion of leaves.

Specifically, Michigan law provides that employees absent for a period of service (including leave for fitness exams) that was up to 180 days in length may return to work or seek reemployment at any time **up to 45 days following their release or discharge from service**. This is significantly longer than USERRA's return-to-work deadlines, which are only 8 hours after the employee's return to his or her residence from service for leaves of 30 days or less (or for any leaves for fitness exams) or 14 days after service of 31-180 days, respectively.

USERRA's reemployment periods for service leaves of up to 180 days do contain an exception for employees who cannot return by USERRA's deadlines through no fault of their own. It is conceivable, therefore, that an employee could seek and have a USERRA right to reemployment even beyond Michigan law's 45-day deadline if circumstances legitimately beyond the employee's control prevented the employee from returning within those time periods.

If the employee's length of service was **more than 180 days**, both USERRA and Michigan law provide that the employee must submit an application for re-employment (written or verbal) no more than 90 days after completing service.

These deadlines may be extended for up to two years or more if the employee is unable to return to work within the required time period because the employee is hospitalized or convalescing from a disability incurred or aggravated during her military service.

A returning employee may not be entitled to prompt re-employment, however, if the employer's circumstances have changed during the employee's leave. For example, an employee who would have been laid off during the period of leave if she had not gone on leave need not be re-employed unless (or until) she would have recall rights to return to work in accordance with the employer's normal policies (or any applicable collective bargaining agreement).

Can the employer require documentation upon the employee's return?

Yes, as long as the employee's period of service was **more than 30 days**.

If the employee was on military leave for a period of service of **31 days or more**, the employer can require documentation that shows that the employee's application for re-employment is timely, that the employee was not on leave for more than 5 years, and that the employee was separated from the military service under honorable (non-disqualifying) circumstances.

If the employee cannot immediately obtain the requested documentation, the employer must still return him or her to work within the appropriate time periods. The employer may take action (i.e., discipline or termination) against the employee at a later time if it finds out that the employee did not meet the requirements above for reemployment rights.

In its regulations, the DOL has identified the following types of documentation that may be used by an employee to demonstrate his or her eligibility for USERRA return-to-work rights:

- DD (Department of Defense) 214 Certificate of Release or Discharge from Active Duty;
- Copy of duty orders prepared by the facility where the orders were fulfilled carrying an endorsement indicating completion of the described service;
- Letter from the commanding officer of a Personnel Support Activity or someone of comparable authority;
- Certificate of completion from military training school;
- Letter from National Disaster Medical System (NDMS) Team Leader or Administrative Officer verifying dates and times of NDMS training or Federal activation;
- Discharge certificate showing character of service; or
- Copy of extracts from payroll documents showing periods of service.

The DOL regulations note that not all of these documents will be available and/or necessary in every instance for an employee to establish his or her eligibility to return to work under the protection of USERRA.

What position is an employee entitled to upon his or her return from leave?

In sum, an employer is obligated to consider the "escalator" principle when deciding the position or job into which a returning employee must be placed. The same holds true for determining the employee's pay rate upon return. Both take on particular relevance if the employee's leave of absence was lengthy, as is not uncommon with military deployments in today's geopolitical environment.

The "escalator principle" requires employers to return employees to work in the job position and with the pay and benefits rate that they would have attained if they had not taken the military leave. In other words, the employer must try to imagine the position and pay the employee would be in if he or she had kept working instead of taking the military leave.

One possible application of the "escalator" principle, for example, involves determining whether an employee on leave would have been promoted to a new position if the employee remained continuously employed. If promotion would have been based on a skills test or examination the employee missed while on service leave, the regulations clarify that the employee should be placed in an appropriate reemployment position, allowed time to adjust, then given an opportunity to make up the test. If the employee passes the test and it can be determined that the employee consequently would have been promoted, the employee then should be promoted. Benefits of the promotion—for example, the pay rate—are to be retroactive to the date (to the extent it can be ascertained with reasonable certainty) the employee would have received the promotion but for the service leave.

All applications of the "escalator" principle presume that the employer can determine with "reasonable certainty" the position, pay rate, or seniority-based benefits that the returning employee would have attained but for taking a protected leave. In such situations, "reasonable certainty" is defined as a high probability that the employee would have received the seniority or seniority-based right or benefit if continuously employed. "Reasonable" certainty does not mean "absolute" certainty. Employees need not show that there is no doubt that they would have attained the job position or benefits at issue but for the leave.

One way employees can show with reasonable certainty that they would have received a benefit is to show that other employees with similar seniority have received the right or benefit.

In actual practice, the implementation of the "escalator principle" may not be very easy, and an employer's obligations regarding the position to which an employee should be returned following a military leave are quite specific. Specific guidelines for choosing the position into which a returning employee should be employed are discussed in detail below. First, however, are some more general factors to consider.

If two or more employees are entitled to re-employment in the same position, the position shall be offered to the employee who left the position first. The employee not offered the position shall be entitled to any other position that provides similar status, seniority and pay to the original position, consistent with the circumstances of the individual employee's case. In the event that the employee not offered the position sustained or aggravated a disability in or during his or her service, and such disability would have required the employer to make reasonable efforts to accommodate the employee in the original position he or she left, then the employer shall offer the employee a position in accord with USERRA's normal provision for accommodating such an employee, provided the position offers similar status, seniority, and pay to the original position, in light of the circumstances of the individual employee.

If the employee is not qualified to return to either the position that he or she would have had if the employee had remained continuously employed, or the position that the employee left at the commencement of the service period, for any reason other than disability, illness, or injury sustained during or aggravated by the service, and the employee cannot become qualified in spite of reasonable efforts by the employer to qualify the employee, then the employee can be re-employed in any other position of lesser status and pay that the employee is qualified to perform, with full seniority.

As with an employee's notice obligations, the position in which an employee shall be re-employed varies depending on the length of the employee's service.

Service of 90 Days or Less

If the employee's service was for 90 days or less, the employee must be re-employed in one of the following specific position(s) in the following order of priority:

- **in the position that he or she would have held had the employee been continuously employed throughout the period served**, provided the employee is qualified to perform the duties such a position requires (or can become qualified after reasonable efforts by the employer to qualify the person); or

- if the employee is not qualified to perform the duties of the above position after reasonable efforts by the employer to qualify the employee to perform those duties, then **in the position that he or she held when the period of service commenced**; or

- if the employee cannot become qualified to perform either of the above positions, then in a position that is the nearest approximation to the positions described above that the employee is able to perform.

Note that with respect to the first two positions described above, employers do not have the option of offering other jobs, even if they are equivalent in terms of seniority, status and pay.

Service of More than 90 Days

If the employee's service was for 91 or more days, the employee must be re-employed in one of the following specific position(s) in the following order of priority:

- in the position that he or she would have held had the employee been continuously employed throughout the period served, or a position of equivalent seniority, status, and pay, provided the employee is qualified to perform the duties such

- a position requires (or can become qualified after reasonable efforts by the employer to qualify the person); or

- if the employee is not qualified to perform the duties of the above position after reasonable efforts by the employer to qualify the employee to perform those duties, then **in the position that he or she held when the period of service commenced, or a position of equivalent seniority, status, and pay**; or

- if the employee cannot become qualified to perform either of the above positions, then in a position that is the nearest approximation to the positions described above that the employee is able to perform, including other positions of lesser status and pay that the employee is qualified to perform, but with full seniority.

Note here that, for employees returning from a service leave of more than 90 days, the employer is not bound to re-employ the employee in the exact position he or she would have attained or left. Rather, the employer has more flexibility to consider other positions of equivalent seniority, status and pay.

No matter the length of an employee's service, employers are required to make reasonable efforts to qualify returning employees who are not qualified for the position they would have held or left for reasons other than a disability incurred or aggravated by their military service. To meet this obligation, employers must provide refresher training, and any other training necessary to update a returning employee's skills in situations where the employee is no longer qualified due to, for example, changes in technology in the workplace. Training is not required, however, if it would be an undue hardship for the employer to provide it.

Accommodations for Disabilities Incurred in, or Aggravated by, Military Service

USERRA requires employers to apply a three-step analysis to determine where to re-employ an employee returning from military service with a disability incurred in, or aggravated by, his or her service. As in a normal situation (outside of USERRA), employers have an undue hardship defense to providing accommodations.

First, the employer must make reasonable efforts to accommodate the employee's disability so that the employee can perform the job he or she would have attained if they had remained employed. Note that this may not be the position held by the employee when he or she left. Further, employers must make this first-step accommodation analysis for any employee returning from leave with a disability incurred in or aggravated by his or her service, regardless of the length of the employee's leave. Employers in this situation continue to be obligated to provide reasonable training or other qualification assistance if doing so would qualify the employee for the position notwithstanding any disability or accommodation issues.

Second (if the employee is not qualified for or unable to perform the job he or she would have attained despite reasonable accommodation efforts), the employer should place the employee in a job with equivalent seniority, status, and pay to the position described in the first paragraph above (again provided the employee is qualified for such a position or can become qualified through reasonable efforts by the employer).

Third, if, despite the employer's accommodation and retraining/requalification efforts, the employee is not able to perform either of the positions described above, the employer may place the employee in a position that most closely approximates the position described in paragraph (2) above in terms of seniority, status, and pay.

Is an employee returning from military leave protected against discharge?

Yes, depending on the length of the employee's military service.

Any employee whose period of military service was **181 days or more** may only be discharged for cause for one year after the employee's return to work.

For employees whose service was **31-180 days**, protection from a discharge without cause only extends for six (6) months from the employee's return to work, while employees who served **30 days or less** do not have protection from discharge.

This job protection applies even if the employer otherwise maintains an "at-will" employment relationship with its employees.

All employees, regardless of the length of their military service, are protected from discrimination in employment because of their military service.

Can the employer use temporary workers to fill in for employees on military leave?

Yes. While the reservists are gone on active duty, it is likely that most employers will need to have their job duties performed by other individuals. Any substitute or temporary employees hired for this purpose should be clearly informed that the reservists have a right to reemployment. Employers should document this notice to temporary employees and require them to sign a document indicating their understanding that they are working in their positions on a temporary basis and that they can be removed at the will of the employer, including specifically upon the return of an employee from military leave. Employers that take this action will help to defeat claims by temporary substitute employees that they were wrongfully demoted, discharged, or laid off by the employer upon the reservists' return.

Are there any posting or other notice requirements that employers must provide to employees?

Yes. As part of the Veterans Benefits Improvement Act passed by Congress in December 2004, employers are required to give notice to "all persons entitled to rights and benefits under USERRA." The easiest way for employers to meet this obligation is to post a DOL-approved poster describing USERRA rights in a prominent place where employees customarily check for such information. In other words, if you have a general area where you post legally-required postings of employment information and legal rights, the new USERRA poster should be posted there as well.

A copy of the DOL-approved USERRA poster is included on the HR Michigan web site (www.hrmichigan.com). It can also be accessed and printed from the DOL's internet site at the following address: www.dol.gov/vets/programs/userra/poster.pdf.

While posting the DOL's model USERRA poster is the suggested way for employers to meet the USERRA's notice requirements, it is not mandatory that the DOL's model poster be put up on the employer's bulletin boards as long as the employer provides the required notice content to its employees in some other form. DOL regulations published with the model poster state that employers can also meet the notice requirements, for example, by handing out or mailing copies of the model poster to all employees, or—in workplaces in which all employees utilize email—by sending out the required content of the notice or the poster itself via email.

How are legal complaints handled under USERRA or Michigan law?

The DOL regulations outline two options for employees who believe their USERRA rights have been violated:

- Aggrieved employees may file a complaint (in writing or online) with DOL's Veterans' Employment and Training Services (VETS)

- File a private lawsuit in an appropriate federal or state court.

VETS is charged with investigating any complaints by employees who claim USERRA violations. In conducting an investigation, VETS has subpoena power, but, ultimately, has no further legal power or authority to order an employer to comply with USERRA or to issue any relief—such as back pay or damages—to the employee.

If VETS determines that the employee's complaint has merit, it will make reasonable efforts to ensure future USERRA compliance and to address the employee's concerns. If unsuccessful, VETS must notify the employee of the results of its investigation and of the employee's right to pursue private legal action.

Upon receipt of the VETS notice described above, the employee may either pursue private legal action or ask VETS to refer the complaint to the U.S. Attorney General. In the latter instance, the Attorney General reviews the complaint for merit and, in its discretion, may initiate legal action on the employee's behalf to attempt to obtain legal relief.

In a legal action, whether brought by the Attorney General or by the employee privately, a court is authorized to order compliance with USERRA and to award damages for any lost back pay or benefits, liquidated damages in an amount equal to any lost back pay or benefits (for willful violations), attorneys' fees and litigation costs, and any other equitable relief that seems appropriate to vindicate the employee's rights and/or losses.

There is no statute of limitations for bringing a USERRA complaint. The regulations specifically recognize, however, that one federal court has applied a four-year statute of limitations, and further recognize that equitable defenses may be available to the employer if the employee delays in bringing a complaint for an unreasonably long period of time so as to prejudice the employer's ability to defend against the claim.

Finally, of some note, the DOL regulations also specifically recognize that employers may not bring legal actions under USERRA.

An employee who is denied reemployment is also entitled to bring a civil lawsuit against his employer in a Michigan circuit court based on Michigan law, which limits the employee's remedy in such a case to reinstatement to employment and recovery of his attorneys' fees. Technically speaking, employees do not have the same right to sue their employers for military-based discrimination under Michigan law, which is treated separately than a denial of reemployment rights. Michigan law between employers who discriminate against employees on the basis of the employee's military status or service are guilty of a misdemeanor, which carries criminal penalties, whereas employers who deny employees reinstatement to employment may be sued by their employees in civil court.

CHAPTER 15: Miscellaneous Employment Laws

The subject of an employee's privacy rights is currently the focus of more media attention than ever before. Given the increase in the sheer number of plaintiff attorneys specializing in employment cases, this public awareness of privacy concerns has generated a growing amount of litigation, making this area another hot topic of concern for employers.

An employer can be held liable under a common-law invasion-of-privacy theory if the employer conducts acts that intrude into the private affairs of an employee or applicant in an objectionable or offensive manner. Privacy is guaranteed by the U.S. Constitution and also by many state constitutions. Sometimes in the work environment, balancing employees' rights to privacy with other needs of the employer can be difficult. Issues such as AIDS and the detection of alcohol and drug abuse have added even more privacy considerations and controversies.

Privacy rights of employees may be protected by federal, state, or by medical or general privacy laws. For example, under the ADA, medical records are not allowed to be part of the personnel file. Medical records must be kept separate and confidential.

In the work environment, claims of invasion of privacy usually are based either on accusations of intrusion into an individual's affairs or on the disclosure of embarrassing facts. In a 1987 case, the U.S. Supreme Court determined that employees are not entitled to an absolute expectation of privacy in the workplace, however the Court still allows for reasonable expectations of privacy.

Michigan law recognizes four types of invasion of privacy.

Intrusion

This action arises where someone obtains private or secret information through the use of highly intrusive means. For example, where a newspaper reporter poses as a cleaning woman and sneaks into a person's private office to obtain private or secret information, then publishes that information, the individual may have an action for intrusion. In the employment context, such an action most often arises when the employer hires a private investigator to uncover private or secret information about the employee.

False Light

Even if true, statements that place another in a false light are actionable if the false light in which the individual was placed would be highly offensive to a reasonable person and the speaker acted recklessly. This action puts an employer in danger of being held liable for true statements if a false implication can be drawn from them.

Public Disclosure of Private Facts

An individual may bring an action for invasion of privacy where confidential or private information about the individual is disclosed to the public. Employers are vulnerable to actions for public disclosure of private facts whenever personnel information about an individual is disclosed to a third party without the individual's consent.

Appropriation

Unlike the others, this action for invasion of privacy does not necessarily involve negative publicity, but rather the use of someone's likeness without permission. Employers should be aware of this when preparing promotional literature featuring employees.

Defenses to Invasion of Privacy Claims

Employers have several defenses and strategies available to them when faced with invasion of privacy lawsuits.

Conditional Privilege

One defense is the conditional privilege that covers communications made in the course of business to those with a need to know. Of course, employers need to be careful not to exceed the scope of this privilege.

Lack of Publicity

A second defense is lack of publicity, which differs from publication. Even if a plaintiff could prove that the employer relayed some personal information to a person without a need to know, the court may rule that the small degree to which the information became known would not constitute the publicity required to maintain a claim for invasion of privacy. This small degree of publicity would prevent the plaintiff from asserting an invasion-of-privacy claim. Employers, however, are safest by taking all possible precautions to be sure that those without a need to know the information do not know it. Exactly what degree of publicity is a small degree, is undefined.

Consent

A third defense is consent. An individual who consents in writing in advance to acts or publicity that would otherwise invade his or her privacy has no cause of action. Again, the employer should not exceed the scope of his or her consent.

Guidelines for Personnel Record Contents

The following six directives are intended to present a practical overview of issues to which employers should pay attention in order to avoid litigation that, particularly in this area, can often be prevented.

1. Include the following in anyone's personnel record:

   - Any record that identifies the employee and that is, has, or may be used for that employee's employment qualifications, promotion, transfer, additional compensation, or disciplinary action.

   - Any record within six months of its making, "concerning an occurrence or fact about an employee" kept by an executive, administrative, or professional employee, even if kept in that person's sole possession and not intended for access by others, if you want to preserve the employer's right to use such a record in a judicial (i.e., court) or quasi-judicial (i.e., MDCR or MUIA) proceedings.

   - Any written statement by an employee expressing disagreement with information in the record.

2. Do **not** include the following in a personnel record:

   - Employee references, if the identity of the person making the reference would be disclosed.

   - Staff planning materials relating to more than one employee, such as salary increases, bonus plans, promotion plans, and job assignments.

   - Medical reports and records made or obtained by the employer, if available to the employee from the doctor or medical facility.

   - Personal information about an individual other than the employee, disclosure of which would constitute a clearly unwarranted invasion of that other individual's privacy.

   - Separate records relating to a criminal investigation of the employee.

   - Separate records of grievance investigations not used for the purposes of obtaining an employee reference.

- Education records covered by the federal Family Educational Rights and Privacy Act of 1974.

- Records kept by an executive, administrative, or professional employee, in their sole possession, and that are not accessible or shared with others, unless to be used for the purposes specified in number one above.

3. Do not gather or keep any record of an employee's associations, activities, publications, communications, or non-employment activities. There are only **two exceptions** to this rule:

    - Where such information is submitted in writing by the employee to the employer or is authorized, in writing, by the employee to the employer to be kept or gathered.

    - Where such a record applies to activities that occur on the employer's premises or during the employee's working hours with that employer and the activities interfere with the performance of the employee's duties or the duties of other employees.

    - If one of these two exceptions applies, the record must be included in the employee's personnel record.

4. Do not divulge a disciplinary report, letter of reprimand, or other disciplinary action to a third party, to a party not a part of the employer's organization, or to a party who is not a labor organization representing that employee, without providing statutory notice.

Before disciplinary records are disclosed to any of these third parties, you must first send written notice by first class mail to the employee's last known address (mailed on or before the day the information is divulged from the personnel record). However, be careful. Even if you comply with the written-notice provision, you may still be sued for invasion of privacy or defamation if you disseminate the information to somebody who does not have an absolute need to know it. Obtaining the employee's written consent in a release is the safest way to disseminate such information.

There are only **three occasions** when you can disclose the information without written notice:

- Where the employee specifically has waived written notice as part of a written, signed employment application with another employer.

- Where the disclosure is ordered in a legal action or arbitration (including in response to a valid subpoena issued by an attorney).

- Where information is requested by a government agency as a result of a claim or complaint by an employee.

5. Before the disclosure of personnel record information to a third party, delete any disciplinary records more than four years old, and be sure to include any statement of disagreement submitted by the employee. There is only one exception to this rule, and that is where release of the information is ordered in a legal action or arbitration to a party.

6. If you engage in a criminal investigation of an employee, upon completion of the investigation or after two years, whichever comes first, notify the employee that such an investigation was conducted. If disciplinary action is not taken, destroy the separate investigative file and all copies of the material in it.

The only exception to this rule is when the employer is a criminal justice agency involved in the investigation of alleged criminal activity for violation of an agency rule. This exception would apply, for example, to a municipal police department or any prosecutor's office.

When a criminal-justice-agency employer completes a criminal investigation, it must still notify the employee, but need not destroy the records. If no disciplinary action is taken, however, it must make a notation in the file of the final disposition of the investigation. In addition, the file cannot be used in any future consideration for promotion, transfer, additional compensation, or disciplinary action.

7. Upon written request, you must provide your employees with an opportunity to periodically review their personnel records. Generally, an employee can exercise this right two times per year. The review must take place during normal business hours at a location near the place of employment. If the requesting employee would need to take time off from work to review the personnel record during normal business hours, you must provide another reasonable time and location for review.

8. If an employee disputes information contained within the employee's personnel record, you can remove or correct that information upon mutual agreement. If no resolution can be reached, the employee can write a statement explaining the employee's position and have it placed in the same location as the disputed information. This statement is to be produced to third parties, along with the personnel record, as long as the disputed information is also part of the employee's personnel record.

Protecting Employee Privacy

Employers often gather applicant and employee information such as resumes, interview reports, pre-employment investigations, pension information, medical records, results from psychological tests, conviction records, credit reports, drug test results, performance appraisals, and salary data. In fact, over half of the nation's largest companies use investigative firms to obtain information about applicants and employees from previous employers and other sources. Employers should have employees sign a written release allowing a background check before conducting such an investigation. Some employers use a separate release form. Other employers include release language on their applications. (See *Sample Authorization to Release Information* at www.hrmichigan.com Forms and Checklists section)

Employers need to be aware of the dangers involved in having access to employee records. Not only could disclosing this information be detrimental to the employee, but it could also lead to lawsuits against the employer.

Be sure to determine who has access to company records such as personnel files. The company should limit access on the basis of a need-to-know rule. For example, an employee's supervisor would rarely have a basis for reviewing an employee's medical records. In addition, supervisors with access to personnel files should be trained in record-keeping practices and procedures.

The Company should develop procedures for review of personnel records by union representatives, supervisors, wage-and-hour investigators, and anyone else that might have a right to review certain records. Employee medical, psychological, and disciplinary records are extremely sensitive and extra precautions must be taken to prevent their disclosure where not absolutely necessary.

Employers are allowed, under the ADA, to disseminate information about an employee's disability or need for an accommodation to only three sources:

- An employee's supervisor if the supervisor has a need to know (for example, if an employee needs a particular device or piece of equipment to perform certain job duties, a supervisor can be advised of the need for an accommodation and the means for making the accommodation).

- First-aid people who need to know about an employee's condition so that they can take appropriate steps in case of a medical emergency (for example, notice to first-aid workers about an employee's epileptic condition or diabetes).

- The government if there is an inquiry, authorized by federal law, asking for data on the workforce (for example, the government can obtain drug and medical information on drivers).

Employer Searches

Many private employers mistakenly believe that the United States Constitution's Fourth Amendment prohibition against unreasonable searches and seizures applies to them, and that an employer, therefore, cannot search an employee's desk, locker, or storage area without violating the Constitution. Absent a specific state or local statute, the Constitution does not apply to searches or seizures undertaken by an employer when there is no government involvement. Therefore, if a private employer conducts a search on its own facilities, or of its own property, the Constitutional prohibition is not applicable. Given the reported high usage of drugs, threats of violence, or use of weapons at the workplace, such searches may be increasingly necessary to enforce employment rules, prevent serious injury and prevent the commission of crimes on the job.

In most cases, the court will find that an employee has little expectation of privacy in a locker. An employer has the right to conduct a general search of lockers, particularly if there is a belief that drugs are being used by employees at work. Nevertheless, employers should still be careful about the manner in which searches are conducted.

Private employers can minimize employees' claims of abuse by establishing the right to search such areas through an express written Company policy. There are obvious personnel relations consequences to such a policy that should be considered before implementation. But if drug usage, sale, or other such abuses are occurring in the workplace, such a policy could end any confusion and should be considered a necessary precaution because of the many cases being brought to court on this issue.

Employers who conduct drug tests also should be aware of the privacy concerns associated with this type of testing. Moreover, in the union context, drug testing standards, procedures, and requirements are mandatory subjects of bargaining.

Defamation

Never disseminate reasons for an employee's discharge (or any other sensitive personnel information) to anyone who does not have an absolute need to know.

The safest practice with regard to requests for reasons for discharge by other employers is to adopt a written policy stating that unless the former employee gives his written consent, the only information disseminated will be name, starting and ending dates of employment, and job title.

Types of Defamation

DEFAMATION:

A statement that tends to lower an individual's reputation in the community, exposing him or her to public hatred, contempt, or ridicule, or causing him or her to be shunned or avoided, or injuring him or her in business or occupation.

LIBEL:

Defamation in writing or other permanent form such as a television broadcast or videotape.

SLANDER:

Oral defamation in a nonpermanent form.

Elements of a Defamation Claim

- A false and defamatory statement of fact that is communicated to a second person about a third person. The publication may be written or verbal.

- The publication must be unprotected by a legal privilege.

- Fault amounting to at least negligence on the part of the publisher (i.e., writer or speaker).

- Damages to an employee's reputation are presumed when an employer disparages an employee's work performance or the employee's lack of integrity in performing the job or otherwise disparages the employee's trade or profession. Damages also are presumed when the employer accuses the employee of a crime involving moral turpitude or of having a contagious disease such as herpes or AIDS. In such cases, while damages may still be contested, the necessary element of damages will be presumed.

Defenses to Defamation Claims

Truth is an absolute defense.

Caution: No matter how firm your conviction that truth is on your side, remember that truth is very difficult to prove at trial. The burden of proving that the statement is true is often on the employer; i.e., the employee does not need to prove that the statement is false. Also, truth is generally a jury question. This means that even if you win, it will cost you a great deal of money in legal fees, as the case will not be dismissed prior to trial.

Make sure you have a written, signed release that has been reviewed by an attorney before you disseminate information to prospective employers about a former employee. If feasible, have the employee resign rather than be terminated. Some courts outside Michigan have held the employer liable for statements made by the employee himself if the employer knew or should have known that the employee would be required to make such statements. For example, the employer may be held liable when the employee tells prospective employers the reason for his discharge. If the employee resigned, such statements are not necessary.

An absolute privilege means the publisher cannot be held liable for the statement under any circumstances (i.e., a witness' testimony under oath at trial). The Michigan Supreme Court has held that statements made by an employer to the Michigan Unemployment Insurance Agency ("MUIA") about an employee seeking unemployment benefits are absolutely privileged.

Absolute privileges are rare. For example, while statements made to the MUIA are absolutely privileged, statements made to other employees in the course of preparing the MUIA statements, or copies of the MUIA statement sent to supervisors or management personnel, are not absolutely privileged. Be careful about who has access to sensitive or defamatory information. Do not depend on an absolute privilege unless so advised by an attorney.

The publisher is protected from liability for defamatory statements so long as they are made in good faith to persons with an absolute need to know. This qualified privilege most commonly is invoked by employers and can be lost if the statements are not made in good faith or if the statements are published beyond the scope of those with a need to know.

A statement made by an employee's supervisor to a department head performing an evaluation would be protected by a qualified privilege if the department head needed the supervisor's input regarding the employee prior to the evaluation. However, a statement made by the supervisor to one employee regarding the evaluation of another employee would not be protected by a qualified privilege, since the employee has no need to know.

Michigan has a one-year statute of limitations for defamation claims. The statute begins running on the date the statement is made.

Defamation when Investigating an Employee

If you believe an employee is guilty of some sort of wrongdoing and decide to conduct an investigation, be very careful about what you say to other employees and to whom you say it. Remember that only those with an absolute need to know should be informed of your suspicions.

For example, when interviewing another employee, don't name the suspect unless it is absolutely necessary to disclose the name to that particular employee. If you need to reveal details, make sure that the party understands the need for confidentiality. It is no defense to say "some employee in the reservations department who always wears a black jacket and lives in Waterford who shall remain nameless." Make sure the employee cannot be identified unless it is essential to identify the employee to a particular person. Don't interview the employee or witnesses in a public area where you might be overheard. Don't discuss the particulars of the matter with supervisors or employees unless you need their input. Again, when in doubt, don't name or otherwise identify the employee or the specific circumstances.

Defamation when Terminating an Employee

Once again, be careful who is involved in this process and what they are told. Don't have other employees present at the time of the termination. Limit the supervisors present at the time of the termination to those who were involved in the termination decision. Use as few supervisors as possible. Don't put the reasons for the termination in a letter to the employee and then copy the entire department. Don't tell record keepers in personnel why the employee was terminated when all they need to know is to stop sending the employee a paycheck.

In *Tumbarella v. The Kroger Co.*, the employee was fired for theft after being stopped by security guards and accused of stealing. Kroger sent a letter to all other Kroger store managers stating that the employee had been terminated for theft and should not be hired at a different Kroger location. The Michigan Court of Appeals held that the employee's supervisor had a need to hear the allegations of the security guards so that he could investigate the incident. The Court also held that the Kroger store managers had a need to know who had been terminated so that they would not hire the same person at a different Kroger location.

However, the Court would not dismiss the case on summary judgment because the employer made some mistakes that raised a jury question on whether Kroger had abused its qualified privilege. For example, Kroger made no effort to keep the letter to other managers confidential. Some managers may have informed the terminated worker's coworkers about the reason for the discharge. The coworkers had no need to know. Some stores posted the letter on a bulletin board in the management office so that it could be viewed by anyone who walked by. The envelope in which the letter was mailed did not indicate that the material was confidential, so the letter was opened by secretaries and other people who did not have a need to know the contents of the letter. Similarly, the security guards did not keep their allegations confidential. They stopped the employee in an open area and accused her of theft. Because of these mistakes, Kroger was forced to go through a full jury trial.

Defamation when Communicating to Outside Parties

When giving references, it is prudent to give only the employee's name, dates of employment, and job title, unless you have a written, signed release from the employee that has been reviewed by an attorney, or unless you are comfortable in disclosing any information that may now be disclosed pursuant to Michigan's disclosure of personnel files law (see *Reference Checks*).

Caution: Don't even say good things about the employee without a release. Don't lie and say the employee was a great worker when, in fact, he was terminated. If the employee has the same problem at the next job, the next employer might sue you for giving a false reference. Furthermore, you could be vulnerable to a future suit by unknown third parties. For example, if ABC Company fires an employee for embezzlement and gives XYZ Brokerage Company a good recommendation, ABC could be sued later by XYZ's clients after the employee absconds with their money.

If you believe there is particular information that the prospective employer ought to know (i.e., the employee was fired for embezzling funds and is now applying for a job at a bank; the employee teacher resigned after allegations that he had been sexually involved with one of his 14-year-old students and is now applying for a job as a high-school teacher), don't give out the information without a written, signed release. However, you can tell a prospective employer, "I would be happy to talk to you about Mr. Smith, but I can't do so without a written release." If the former employee refuses to sign a written release, the prospective employer is on notice that there may be problems or that the employee has something to hide. Alternatively, you may choose to disclose any documented information relating to the employee's on-the-job performance (see Chapter 2).

Care also must be taken when making statements to third parties other than prospective employers. For example, in *Shannon v. Taylor AMC/Jeep Inc.*, the employer informed several customers that the employee had been terminated for his involvement with stolen parts. The Court refused to dismiss the case on summary judgment. The defendant claimed that the customers needed to be informed so that business relations would not be harmed if a customer later found out that they were in possession of stolen parts. The Michigan Court of Appeals held that the customers had no interest in knowing why the employee was terminated unless a particular customer was in possession of the stolen parts. As the issue of whether the employee had actually stolen the parts was a fact question for the jury, the case could not be dismissed prior to trial.

Defamation in Written Information

Be especially careful when putting anything in writing. Do not put the reasons for an employee's termination in a written letter and send it to the employee or others unless absolutely necessary. A written statement is often the catalyst for a lawsuit.

For example, if an employee is terminated for wrongdoing for which there are no witnesses (such as an employee who is terminated for cheating on an exam when nobody saw him cheat but the circumstantial evidence points to cheating), a letter stating "this is to confirm that we have terminated you for cheating on the exam," which is copied to several supervisors, may cause the employee to file suit. If you want to confirm a termination in writing, the letter can state "this is to confirm that you were terminated on October 17, 2004, for the reasons discussed in my meeting with you on that date."

If sensitive information must go in an employee's personnel file, place it in a sealed envelope marked "Confidential: To Be Opened by John Smith, Supervisor, Only." That way, other employees with access to personnel files will not see the information. If you feel that you must write a letter to a prospective employer or to the employee concerning a termination, have it reviewed by an attorney before you mail it.

Remember: Think before you speak, and when in doubt, say as little as possible!

Michigan's Social Security Number Privacy Act

Policy Requirement

As employers, you most likely obtain the social security numbers of every current, retired and past employee of your Company. Social security numbers are a valued commodity. Under Michigan's Social Security Number Privacy Act, it is your responsibility to take all reasonable steps to protect your employees' social security numbers.

The first step in protecting the social security numbers in your possession is to implement a Social Security Number Privacy Policy, which you must place in your Employee Manual. This policy must:

1. Ensure the confidentiality of social security numbers.
2. Prohibit the unlawful disclosure of social security numbers.
3. Limit who has access to social security numbers.
4. Describe how to properly dispose of documents that contain social security numbers.

5. Establish penalties for violating the privacy policy.

Since January 1, 2006, the law has required employers who use or obtain social security numbers to have such a policy in place. A sample Social Security Number Privacy Policy is included on the HR Michigan web site (www.hrmichigan.com).

General Prohibitions

You can no longer publicly display more than four sequential digits of a social security number, including any public display or posting over a computer network, website, or any electronic medium or device. For example, more than four digits of a social security number cannot be:

- Used as the primary account number for an individual.
- Placed on an identification badge or card, membership card, permit or license.
- Required in electronic transmissions unless the connection is secure or the transmission is encrypted.
- Mailed with the number visible from outside the envelope.
- Enclosed in a mailing unless:
    - required under state or federal law;
    - sent as part of an application or enrollment process initiated by the individual;
    - sent to confirm the accuracy of an individual's social security number for an account, contract, policy or insurance benefit, or to establish, service, amend, confirm the status of, or terminate the account, contract, policy or benefit;
    - mailed by or at the request of an individual whose social security number appears in the document or that individual's parent or legal guardian; or
    - mailed in a manner consistent with specific federal regulations.

Public Employers

Public employers must also redact social security numbers from documents that must be released under the Freedom of Information Act.

In addition, public employers must inform the individual at the time of collecting their social security numbers:

- The purpose for the collection.

- The intended use of the social security number.
- Whether the law requires the number to be provided.
- The consequences of not providing the number.

Financial Institutions

Federal law requires financial institutions to protect and secure customers' nonpublic personal information, including social security numbers. Financial institutions must:

- Ensure the security and confidentiality of customer records and information;
- Protect against any anticipated threats or hazards to the security or integrity of these records; and
- Protect against unauthorized access to or use of these records or information that could result in substantial harm or inconvenience to any customer.

These requirements should be kept in mind as you draft and implement your social security number privacy policy.

Limited Exceptions

If you were using social security numbers before March 1, 2005 in the ongoing, ordinary course of business for primary account numbers or employee or customer identification, you are permitted to continue your practice. If you stop this practice for any reason, you cannot restart it. Social security number usage is also permitted if:

- Authorized by state/federal statute, court order, or pursuant to legal discovery.
- Used as part of a criminal investigation or prosecution.
- Used administratively in the ordinary course of business to:
    - verify a person's identity in regards to a current or proposed issue (transaction, account, etc.);
    - lawfully investigate an individual;
    - prevent identity theft or other crime;
    - lawfully pursue or enforce a person's legal rights;
    - lawfully investigate or enforce a child or spousal support obligation or tax liability; or
    - administer employee benefits or retirement programs.

Penalties for Violations

A knowing and intentional violation of the act involves criminal liability for a misdemeanor, punishable by imprisonment for not more than 93 days or a fine of not more than $1,000, or both.

Remedies

The Act permits a person alleging a violation of its terms to sue for money damages. If the person proves the employer knowingly violated the statute, the person is entitled to receive at least $1000 per violation, as well as attorney fees.

Even so, there is a safe harbor. Employers are not liable if they take reasonable measures to enforce their policies in compliance with the Act, the federal fair credit reporting act, or the federal financial-institution privacy statutes.

In addition, at least 60 days before bringing a suit, the person must give the employer a written demand, stating the accusations about an improper disclosure and the amount of the damages. The person must also provide reasonable documentation of the asserted violation and damages.

Workplace Smoking Bans

Campaigns to ban smoking in the workplace, and more generally in most public places, have picked up steam in recent years.

In Michigan, the following localities have enacted smoke-free workplace regulations:

- The City of Detroit
- The City of Grand Rapids
- The City of Marquette
- Traverse City
- Alger County
- Antrim County
- Berrien County
- Calhoun County
- Charlevoix County
- Chippewa County
- Emmett County
- Genesee County
- Ingham County
- Lenawee County
- Mackinac County

Marquette County
Midland County
Otsego County
Ottawa County
Saginaw County
Schoolcraft County
St. Clair County
Washtenaw County
Wayne County

In addition, the District of Columbia, Puerto Rico, and twenty-nine states (Arizona, California, Colorado, Connecticut, Delaware, Florida, Hawaii, Idaho, Illinois, Iowa, Louisiana, Maine, Maryland, Massachusetts, Minnesota, Montana, Nevada, New Hampshire, New Jersey, New Mexico, New York, North Dakota, Ohio, Pennsylvania, Rhode Island, South Dakota, Utah, Vermont, and Washington) have enacted smoke-free workplace laws, suggesting that Michigan might not be far behind. In fact, a 2007 Michigan bill proposing to ban smoking in 100% of all workplaces, including restaurants and bars, garnered much support in both the State House of Representative and the State Senate. Although it failed by a small margin in the House of Representatives, do not expect the issue to go away any time soon.

Ingham County's workplace smoking ban is typical. It prohibits smoking in all work sites within Ingham County (excluding restaurants, tobacco specialty stores, and other limited areas), including the following work places: restrooms, lobbies, reception areas, hallways, common work areas, auditoriums, classrooms, conference and meeting rooms, private offices, elevators, cafeterias, employee lounges, stairwells, employer-owned vehicles, and all other enclosed facilities. Employers are permitted to designate a smoking room for employees, provided it is an enclosed area that does not share ventilation systems with other non-smoking areas of the workplace and also provided the employer simultaneously designates an equivalent non-smoking room for employees. Finally, employers are required to adopt and post a no-smoking policy (and post no-smoking signs as well) and communicate the policy to all employees. The smoking ban also prohibits any form of retaliation against employees, applicants, or customers who exercise their rights to a smoke-free environment based on the regulation.

The regulation provides for citations and monetary fines for violations.

If your company employs people in any of the above-listed counties, or you are not sure whether your county regulates smoking in the workplace, visit your county's Internet site or contact the county's public health officer for more information.

Privacy Protection Act

Both federal and state laws exist to protect employee privacy in particular situations. In 1974, Congress passed the Privacy Protection Act, which requires federal government agencies to give public notice of the information contained in personnel records. The Act also established the Privacy Protection Study Commission for private employers in order to investigate private organizations' recordkeeping policies and individual privacy-related issues. In 1976, the Commission made the following recommendations for employers:

- Employers should regularly review employee records. Outdated or inaccurate information should be discarded or corrected. Retaining inaccurate information could cause liability for employers. In the mid-1990s, in a follow-up study on the effectiveness of the Commission's recommendations, the University of Illinois conducted a survey of 275 Fortune 500 corporations. Forty-five percent of the survey respondents did not have a policy for periodic personnel file review.

- Regular reviews should examine how the company communicates what it discloses to others. The University of Illinois' study showed that 80% of the companies disclose information to credit grantors, 58% give information to landlords, and a high percentage also disclose information to charitable organizations. Yet, less than half of the companies inform employees and applicants of company disclosure policy.

Monitoring Telephones and Computers

Many employers believe they have compelling business reasons for monitoring employees' telephone calls and computer use. For example, a company may want to be sure that its customers are being treated in a professional manner and given correct information. To avoid invading the employees' privacy or violating wiretapping laws, the company should let the employees know in writing that their calls will be monitored. Eavesdropping on personal phone calls, however, may constitute an invasion of privacy.

In an effort to keep tabs on employees in the workplace, employers are increasingly turning to sophisticated surveillance and monitoring devices. Employers are using traditional monitoring techniques such as electronic bugging devices, wiretaps, voice-activated tape recorders, and hidden pinhole cameras; as well as newer advances in technology like computer monitoring, telephone accounting, and infrared cameras capable of taking photographs in the dark or through solid walls, to be sure their employees are doing a satisfactory job.

Employers are taking such steps for a variety of reasons. They are attempting to combat employee theft, to uncover drug and alcohol use (and abuse), and, increasingly, to monitor employee job performance in an effort to increase productivity. It is surveillance and monitoring in this latter area that has aroused the greatest concern.

A report issued by the Office of Technology Assessment in Washington, DC, found that the manufacturing of equipment and software for telephone monitoring is the fastest growing segment of the telecommunications industry. This technology allows employers to monitor both the pattern and content of employee telephone calls. Similar technology allows employers to monitor employees working on computers by recording the number of customers served, mistakes made, and even the number of keystrokes per minute. The report estimates that at least six million U.S. office workers currently are monitored by such computer surveillance techniques.

Both unions and employee activist groups have expressed concern that such surveillance and monitoring techniques intrude upon employees' rights of privacy in the workplace. And while such concerns have found little legal support in the private sector, which is not covered by the protections of the Fourth Amendment to the U.S. Constitution, the situation could change dramatically in the near future.

Video Surveillance

Although there is no clear rule prohibiting employers to videotape employees in the workplace, some courts have held that employees may have a reasonable expectation of privacy in some circumstances. Whether an employer may legally videotape its employees depends on the particular facts of the cases, who is conducting the taping and the nature of the setting in which the taping is done. In the union context, employers are generally required to bargain over the use and placement of security cameras.

Surveillance of employees off the job may be permissible in some circumstances where the employer can prove there is a business-related reason for the investigation. The investigation must be conducted in a reasonable manner. Unwarranted investigation into an employee's private life would probably constitute an invasion of privacy.

E-Mail Monitoring

In 2000, an estimated 130 million U.S. workers sent 2.8 billion e-mail messages. In an effort to evaluate worker productivity and prevent inappropriate or illegal use, many employers engage in some type of e-mail monitoring. According to a report issued by the American Management Association in May 2003, 40% of employers report using software to control e-mail content through key word or phrase searches. Nineteen percent of these employers also monitored internal e-mail messages. Only 10 percent of employers did not engage in any monitoring.

According to the 2007 Electronic Monitoring & Surveillance Survey conducted by the American Management Association and The ePolicy Institute, more than one-fourth of the employers surveyed have fired workers for misusing company e-mail systems, while nearly one-third of the employers surveyed have fired workers for misusing the Internet at work.

Employers enjoy relative freedom in monitoring their employees' e-mail and internet usage. Although there have been several recent attempts to enact legislation to regulate an employer's ability to monitor e-mail and internet use, none of these bills have survived. Thus, employers may continue to monitor these activities provided that they remain in compliance with: (1) the Electronic Communications Privacy Act of 1986; (2) the United States Constitution; (3) state constitutions; and (4) common-law rights to privacy.

Subpoena of Employee Records

The right of privacy is cited in a growing number of court decisions involving the use or disclosure of personnel records. This issue arises in a variety of contexts, but most frequently it is seen in disputes arising from disclosure of documents from an employee's personnel file to a third party. Most employers are aware of the dangers of disclosing personnel documents without the employee's permission. However, most employers assume that disclosure to a third party pursuant to a subpoena is not only permissible, it is required.

An increasing number of courts are allowing employees to assert claims of invasion of privacy, defamation, or intentional infliction of emotional distress against current or former employers who release personnel records even where the employer has merely produced the records in response to a subpoena.

The problem typically arises where an employer is subpoenaed to produce documents to an attorney or in a deposition rather than to the court or administrative body. In many states, including Michigan, an attorney can issue a subpoena without any prior court review of relevancy. If the documents are subpoenaed for production to the court at a trial or hearing, the opportunity usually is available for court review of the subpoena, whether on the motion of the affected employee or upon inquiry from the employer at the time of the hearing. In the discovery phase, however, where documents are to be produced to an attorney or at a deposition, this opportunity for court review is not so readily available. The employer, therefore, is particularly vulnerable if it decides to simply turn over the documents. The following steps may help to reduce potential liability:

- The employer should have a rule that all subpoenas of employee records should be directed to a single designated individual, often the personnel director.

- If necessary, the employer should contact the attorney who issued the subpoena and request more time to respond. Discovery dates are rarely cast in stone and the attorney who issued the subpoena should be willing to give the employer more time to respond.

- The employer should notify the employee, preferably in writing, that the personnel records are being subpoenaed and provide the date by which the employer has been asked to produce the records.

- If the employee expresses an objection to production of the records, the employer should so notify the person issuing the subpoena and consult legal counsel for further guidance.

- Even if the employee does not object to production of the documents, the employer still should contact the attorney who issued the subpoena and ask for identification of the issues in litigation that require the disclosure of the records.

- If the attorney will not agree to modification of the subpoena, the employer should consult legal counsel before producing the records. It is possible that the risks in disclosing the documents will justify the expense of obtaining a decision from the court.

Regulation of Polygraphs

In 1981, the Michigan legislature enacted a Polygraph Protection Act (PPA) to regulate the use of polygraph tests in employment. The primary aims of the PPA are to protect employee privacy, to discourage compelled testing of employees, and to provide remedies for violations of the Act.

Prohibited Employment Practices

Under the PPA, employers and employment agencies cannot take any of the following actions as a condition of employment-related decisions or the provision of employment benefits or privileges:

- Request or require that an employee or applicant for employment submit to a polygraph examination.

- Administer, cause to be administered, threaten to administer, or attempt to administer, a polygraph examination to an employee or applicant for employment.

- Require an employee or applicant for employment to expressly or impliedly waive any practice prohibited under the Act.

The employment-related decisions contemplated by the PPA include promotions and other changes in employment status. Furthermore, an employer shall not refuse to hire an applicant for employment because the applicant refuses to take a polygraph examination.

The PPA does not prohibit the employee or applicant for employment from voluntarily requesting a polygraph examination, nor does the Act prohibit an employer from fulfilling such a request, provided that the testing complies with the procedures stated in the Act.

The PPA prohibits the employer or employment agency from disclosing to any other persons the results of a polygraph examination or the refusal of an employee to take a polygraph examination. The Act states that the information obtained during a polygraph examination is not admissible in a criminal proceeding.

Testing Requirements of PPA

The employer or employment agency must provide the employee or applicant with a copy of section 3 of the PPA and section 19 of the Polygraph Examiners Act (PEA) before the examination is conducted.

The employer must employ a test examiner or intern who is licensed by the State of Michigan for the detection of deception, verification of truthfulness, or measuring or recording the presence or absence of stress in the vocal response of the employee or applicant.

The examiner must inform the employee or applicant of the specific question areas to be explored before the examination and may not ask questions prohibited under section 19(j) of the PEA pertaining to the individual's sexual practices; labor union, political, or religious affiliations; or marital relationship, except where such questions have a bearing on the areas or issues under examination.

The examiner must inform the employee or applicant that he or she has the right to accept or refuse to take the examination, the right to halt an examination in progress at any time, and the right to refuse to answer any questions or to give any information. The examiner also must advise the individual that any information provided could be used against the employee or applicant or made available to the employer unless otherwise specified or agreed to in writing by the employee or applicant for employment. The examiner also shall provide the employee or applicant with a copy of the exam results and all reports or analysis done by the examiner that are provided to the employer.

Penalties for Violating PPA

A violation of the PPA involves criminal liability for a misdemeanor, punishable by imprisonment for not more than 90 days, or a fine of not more than $1,000, or both.

Remedies under PPA

The PPA permits a private cause of action for a person alleging a violation of its terms. The available remedies include both injunctive relief and money damages. If an employee is discharged in violation of the Act, the individual is entitled to double damages for all lost wages. The court also may award as damages the individual's reasonable attorney fees.

Federal Employee Polygraph Protection Act

The Federal Employee Polygraph Protection Act (FEPPA) was enacted in 1988. The Act makes it unlawful for any employer engaged in interstate commerce to:

- directly or indirectly require, request, suggest, or cause an employee or prospective employee to take or submit to a lie-detector test.

- use, accept, refer to, or inquire about the results of any lie-detector test of any employee or prospective employee.

- discharge, discipline, discriminate against in any manner, or deny employment or promotion to, or threaten to take any such action against any employee or prospective employee who:

    1. refuses, declines, or fails to take or submit to any lie-detector test;
    2. has taken a lie-detector test and the decision is based on the results of the test;
    3. has filed a complaint for a violation of the Act;
    4. has testified or is about to testify in any such proceeding; or
    5. exercises rights afforded him or her or others under the Act.

Under FEPPA, a "lie-detector test" includes a polygraph, deceptograph, voice-stress analyzer, psychological-stress evaluator, or other similar device, whether mechanical or electrical that is used to render a diagnostic opinion regarding the honesty or dishonesty of an individual.

FEPPA does not preempt any provisions that are contained in state or local laws or negotiated in collective bargaining agreements that adopt more restrictive application on the use of lie-detector tests than are required by the Act.

Posting Requirements of FEPPA

The Secretary of Labor is required to print and distribute notice of the pertinent provisions of FEPPA. Employers must post and maintain the notices in conspicuous places on the premises where such notices are customarily posted.

Enforcement of FEPPA

FEPPA gives the Secretary of Labor authority to:

- issue rules and regulations as required to effectuate the Act and to cooperate with regional, state, and other agencies.
- furnish technical assistance to employers, labor organizations, and employment agencies to help effectuate the purposes of the Act.
- investigate and inspect as required, the keeping of records necessary or appropriate for the Act.

Employers violating FEPPA may be assessed a civil fine of not more $10,000, based on the Labor Secretary's consideration of the person's previous record in complying with the Act and the gravity of the violation.

The Secretary is authorized to petition U.S. District Courts and request temporary or permanent restraining orders and injunctions to require compliance with FEPPA. In addition, the request may include any available legal or equitable relief incident to enforcement of the Act, including employment reinstatement, promotion, and the payment of lost wages and benefits.

FEPPA also authorizes employees or applicants to bring a private action against an employer for violations of the Act. The statute of limitations is three years from the date of the alleged violation. The private action, which could also include a class action, must be brought in a court of competent jurisdiction. As in actions brought by the Secretary of Labor, an employer may be liable for legal and equitable remedies including, but not limited to, employment, reinstatement or promotion; payment of lost wages and benefits; and costs including attorneys' fees.

The rights and procedures provided by FEPPA may not be waived by contract or otherwise unless the waiver is part of a written settlement agreement (signed by the parties) to the pending action or complaint under the Act. The no-waiver clause is not violated by arbitrating a claim brought under this Act if arbitration is required by a collective bargaining agreement. Liability also may extend to the polygraph examiner where the examiner can be viewed as an employer because:

- the examiner is providing expertise to the employer, or

- the examiner represented to the employer that he/she would:
- inform the employer which employees could be examined lawfully, and
- conduct examinations in compliance with the Act.

Non-application of FEPPA

FEPPA does not apply to the United States Government or state or local governments. It does not prohibit administration of a lie-detector test to:

- experts or consultants in the Department of Defense.
- employees of any contractor of the Department of Defense.
- an expert or consultant under contract with the Department of Energy regarding atomic-energy defense activities or any employee of any contractor doing the same work.
- NASA, Defense Intelligence Agency, FBI, Justice Department, or CIA employees.
- experts or consultants under contracts to the above agencies where sensitive cryptologic information is produced, processed, or stored for any of the agencies.

Exemptions under FEPPA

In an exemption for ongoing investigations, the FEPPA does not prohibit an employer from requesting an employee to submit to a polygraph test if:

- the test is in connection with an ongoing investigation of economic loss or injury to the business by theft, embezzlement, or misappropriation.
- the employee had access to the property that is the subject of the investigation.
- the employer has a reasonable suspicion that the employee was involved in the incident.
- the employer executes a statement provided to the examinee before the test that:
    1. sets forth with particularity the specific incident being investigated and the basis for testing particular employees;
    2. is signed by a person (other than a polygraph examiner) who is authorized to legally bind the employer;
    3. is received by the employee at least 48 hours, excluding weekend days and holidays, prior to the time of the examination;
    4. is retained by the employer for at least three years; and contains at a minimum:

- an identification of the specific economic loss or injury;
- a statement that the employee had access to the property; and
- a statement describing the basis of the employer's reasonable suspicion that the employee was involved.

This exemption for ongoing investigations also does not apply to an employee who is discharged, disciplined, denied employment or promotion, or discriminated against based on the results or refusal to take the polygraph test without additional supporting evidence. The evidence required by such subsection may serve as additional supporting evidence.

Another exemption exists under the FEPPA for employers engaged in manufacturing, distributing, and dispensing of controlled substance. The exemption allows them to use polygraph tests only for applicants whose work would involve direct access to the manufacture, storage, distribution, or sale of any such controlled substance; or for a current employee if there is an ongoing investigation of criminal or other misconduct involving drug theft and if the employee had access to the person or property under investigation.

FEPPA also does not prohibit polygraphs on applicants by a private employer whose primary business purpose is to provide armored car personnel or to design, install, and maintain security alarm systems; or applicants for other uniformed or plainclothes security positions whose function includes protecting:

- facilities, materials, or operations with a significant impact on the health or safety of a state or political subdivision or the United States, including facilities producing, transmitting, or distributing electric or nuclear power, public-water-supply facilities, shipments or storage of radioactive or other toxic wastes, and public transportation; or
- currency, negotiable securities, precious commodities or instruments, or proprietary information.

This exemption does not apply to other applicants for security positions who would not be employed to protect the facilities, materials, operations, or assets described above. The exemption also would not apply in case of a discharge, discipline, or other adverse employment action taken against the employee based on the results, or failure to take the test, or refusal to take the test, and is the sole basis for such decision.

The exemptions for ongoing investigations, security services, and drug security will not apply unless, throughout all phases of the test:

- the examinee is permitted to end the test at any time;
- the examinee is not asked questions in a manner designed to degrade or intrude on the person;
- the examinee is not asked questions about:
    1. religious beliefs or affiliations,
    2. beliefs or opinions on racial matters,
    3. political beliefs or affiliations,
    4. any matter relating to sexual behavior and beliefs, or
    5. opinions on or lawful activities regarding unions or labor organizations;
- the examiner does not conduct the test if there is sufficient written evidence by a physician that the examinee suffers from medical or psychological condition or is undergoing treatment that might cause abnormal responses during the actual testing.

Pretest Conditions

During the pretest period:

- the examinee must be provided with reasonable written notice of the time, date, and location of the test and the examinee's right to obtain and consult legal counsel or an employee representative before each phase;
- the examinee must be informed of the nature and characteristics of the tests and instruments involved;
- the examinee must be informed in writing if a two-way mirror, camera, or other device for observation will be used; whether any other device for recording or monitoring the test will be used; and whether the employer or examinee may (with mutual knowledge) make a recording of the test;

the examinee must read and sign a written notice informing him or her:

1. that he or she cannot be required to take the test as a condition of employment,
2. that any statements may constitute additional supporting evidence for an adverse employment action (see *Exemptions under FEPPA*, page 334),
3. of the limitations prescribed in FEPPA,
4. of the legal rights and remedies available to the examinee if the test is not conducted in accordance with the Act, and

5. of the legal rights and remedies of the employer under this Act;

- the examinee must be provided an opportunity to review all questions to be asked during the test and be informed of the right to terminate the test at any time.

During a Polygraph Test

During the test, the examiner must not ask any relevant questions that were not presented in writing for review to the examinee before the test.

Before any adverse employment action, the employer shall conduct a further interview of the examinee on the basis of the test results and provide the examinee with a written copy of the test results and a copy of the questions asked during the test along with the corresponding charted responses.

The examiner shall not conduct and complete more than five polygraph tests on a calendar day on which the test is given and shall not conduct any such test for less than the 90-minute duration.

Polygraph Examiner Qualifications

Exemptions to FEPPA will not apply unless the polygraph examiner:

- has a valid and current license from state licensing authorities for the state in which the test is conducted, if required by the state; and
- maintains a minimum of a $50,000 bond or equivalent amount of professional liability coverage.

For the exemptions to apply, moreover, the examiner's opinions about the test must be in writing and must be based only on an analysis of polygraph test charts. The opinion cannot contain information other than admissions information, case facts, and interpretation of the charts relevant to the purpose and stated objectives of the test. It also cannot include any recommendation concerning the employment of the examinee. The examiner must maintain all opinions, reports, charts, written question lists, and other records relating to the test for a minimum of three years after administration of the test.

Disclosure of Information Obtained by Polygraph

The information obtained during a polygraph test may not be disclosed to anyone other than the examinee except:

- any other person specifically designated in writing by the examinee,

- the employer that requested the test, or
- any court, governmental agency, arbitrator, or mediator in accordance with due process of law pursuant to an order from a court of competent jurisdiction.

Whistleblowers' Protection Act

The long-standing doctrine of employment at-will, by which an employer or employee may terminate an employment relationship at any time, for any reason or for no reason, has been the subject of spirited debate over the years.

Perhaps the most vigorous criticism of the doctrine has occurred on those occasions when employees were discharged after reporting alleged workplace misconduct to governmental bodies empowered to investigate the allegations. Critics argued that permitting the termination of employees in retaliation for blowing the whistle on their employers' misconduct was an injustice that undermined the public policy of encouraging individuals to report known or suspected violations of federal, state, or local laws.

The legislative response resulted in a statutory exception to the employment-at-will doctrine. In 1981, the Michigan legislature enacted the Whistleblowers' Protection Act (WPA) to protect employees who report a violation or suspected violation of any local, state, or federal law. The protection also is extended to employees who are about to, but have not completed, reports of infractions. The protection also extends to those employees who participate in hearings, investigations, legislative inquiries, or court cases.

Protected Activities

In particular, the WPA states that an employer shall not discharge, threaten, or otherwise discriminate against an employee regarding his or her wages, terms, conditions, location, or privileges of employment because the employee, or a person acting on his or her behalf, reports or is about to report, verbally or in writing, a violation or suspected violation of a law, regulation, or rule of the United States, the State of Michigan, or political subdivision of the state.

The question of whether a person is an "employee" under the WPA is determined by the economic reality test. This inquiry focuses on who controls the worker's duties; the payment of wages; the right to hire, fire, and discipline; and whether the performance of the duties is an integral part of the employer's business and contributes toward the accomplishment of a common goal. For example, the Act does not apply to an attorney, who claims he is an employee because he provides occasional advice to a client, but does not have an office at that client's place of business and is not otherwise controlled by the client. On the other hand, a foster-care worker who reports an abuse to a social worker also is covered by the Act.

The protection extends not only to employees who initiate a report, but also to employees who are requested by a public body or court to participate in the investigation, hearing, or inquiry. Discharging an employee for filing an assault complaint with the prosecuting attorney's office against a coworker would be a violation of the WPA.

The WPA's protection applies only to reports and investigations involving a "public body," which is defined under the Act to include state officers, employees, agencies, and other bodies of the executive branch of state government; agencies, boards, commissions, councils, and members or employees of the legislative branch; county, city, township, village, inter-county, inter-city, or regional governing bodies; school districts, special districts, or municipal corporations or boards, or any department, commission, council, agency or any members or employees thereof; any other body created by state or local authority; police or other law enforcement agencies; and judicial employees.

Because the Act's definition of a "public body" only includes state and municipal authorities, a Michigan court concluded in an unpublished opinion that a report to a federal authority (i.e., the Nuclear Regulatory Commission) was not protected by the statute. This is true even though reports to state agencies are covered when they involve federal violations. Based on the same definition of a "public body," another Michigan court found that a Hospital's peer review committee was not a "public body" within the meaning of the Act. Although Michigan requires all hospitals, public and private, to establish peer review committees, the hospital's committee was created by the hospital through its own internal bylaws and procedures and not by any state or local authority.

Courts have refused to expand the Act's coverage beyond the scope stated by the legislature. The protection does not apply, therefore, to any employee who knowingly makes a false report to an agency. It also does not apply where an employer erroneously believes that an employee has made a report, when in fact, that employee has not engaged in protected activity. Similarly, complaints about a company's internal auditing practices do not invoke coverage under the WPA. Such matters involve a corporate management dispute, not the state's public policy. A complaint regarding internal institutional problems, such as a police officer's allegation that he was fired by a university for reporting student misconduct, would not be covered, since it does not allege any misconduct rising to the level of lawbreaking by the employer.

Proving Violations of the WPA

In order to prove a violation of the WPA, an employee must show by clear and convincing evidence that the adverse employment action taken by the employer was caused by the employee's participation in reporting the lawbreaking. The employee's subjective good-faith belief that he or she was reporting a violation of the law entitles him or her to protection.

However, the circumstances surrounding whether a particular report caused a person's discharge is one of the most hotly contested questions litigated under the WPA. In addressing the question, courts often look at the proximity of time between an employee's report of the misconduct and the subsequent termination or other adverse employment decision. In some cases, the courts have determined that a close proximity leads to only one conclusion—that the discharge was in retaliation for reporting misconduct and so was prohibited by the WPA.

More recently, courts have held that an employer's knowledge that a person has made a report is only one factor in determining whether the report actually caused the termination decision. For example, in the case of employees slated for layoffs who reported safety violations shortly before the layoffs were enacted, the court decided that the WPA did not protect the workers since evidence showed that their fate was decided long before the reports were made about safety violations. The key to this kind of outcome in a WPA lawsuit is that an employee's report does not immunize him or her from an otherwise legitimate and/or unrelated adverse job action by the employer.

Enforcement of WPA

The WPA provides an employee with a private right of action for money damages or injunctive relief. A suit under the Act must be filed within 90 days of the alleged violation of the Act.

A suit under the WPA, like other private state lawsuits, may be brought in the circuit court for the county where the violation occurred or in the county where the person against whom the complaint is filed either resides or has its principal place of business. In addition, the WPA has an added provision that permits the action to be brought in the county where the complainant resides, as an added protection to shield the employee from further risk of retaliatory consequences.

Remedies under WPA

Available remedies under the WPA permit reinstatement of an employee, with or without fringe benefits and with or without seniority rights. The plaintiff may also receive the payment of all back wages, payment of all actual damages, or any combination of these. The court, at its discretion, may order the company to pay the employee all or a portion of the costs of the lawsuit including reasonable attorney and witness fees.

The WPA is the exclusive remedy for an employee who is wrongfully discharged for reporting the violation of the law. It bars any common-law cause of action for retaliatory discharge, breach of an implied covenant of fair dealing, or other claims that are covered in the Act. The Michigan Supreme Court has determined that a plaintiff who brings an action under the WPA is entitled to a jury trial.

Garnishments and the Consumer Credit Protection Act

Employers frequently are presented with court orders requiring employers to garnish money from the earnings of employees. Such an order generally directs that the funds withheld from the employee's paycheck be forwarded to a prescribed destination to satisfy a debt the employee owes to a creditor who has enlisted the assistance of the court in collecting the debt.

The relative certainty of payment by wage garnishment led to excessive credit extension and reliance on the garnishment process by some creditors. As a result, federal and state laws were adopted to oversee the process and insure that employees were protected from excessive garnishments and unscrupulous credit practices.

In 1970, as part of the Consumer Credit Protection Act (CCPA), Congress enacted laws governing the procedures and limits to which an employee's wages may be subjected to garnishment. The policy and restrictions reflected in the Act follow from the express congressional findings that:

- restrictions are necessary to discourage predatory extensions of credit.
- the application of garnishment remedies was resulting in disruptive work performance, including discharge of employees.
- wide disparities regarding garnishment practices existed between different states, and in order to address those problems, it was necessary for Congress to enact federal regulations that would:
    1. benefit interstate commerce,
    2. protect wage earners from burdensome garnishments, and
    3. decrease the need for individual bankruptcy petitions.

Definition of Earnings

The "garnishment" is a legal or equitable procedure through which the "earnings" of an individual are required to be withheld for payment of any debt. The CCPA includes in the definition of "earnings" any compensation paid or payable for personal services whether called "wages," "salary," "commission," "bonus," or otherwise and includes periodic payments pursuant to pension or retirement programs. It defines the term "disposable earnings" to include that part of a person's earnings that remain after the deduction from those earnings of any amounts required by law to be withheld.

Restrictions on Garnishments

The CCPA prohibits an employer from discharging an employee because his or her earnings have been subjected to garnishment for more than one indebtedness. Furthermore, the garnishment may not exceed the lesser of:

- 25% of the disposable earnings of an individual for any workweek; or
- the amount by which the disposable earnings for that week exceed 30 times the federal minimum hourly wage when the earnings are payable.

The garnishment ceiling is less restrictive, however, when an order for support of any person is issued by a court or by virtue of an administrative procedure established by state law that affords substantial due process and that is subject to certain judicial review.

Federal law prohibits any federal or state court, or any federal or state agency, from making or executing any orders or processes that violate the federal CCPA. The Secretary of Labor, however, may exempt garnishments issued under state law if the Secretary determines the state laws provide restrictions on garnishment that are substantially similar to the federal laws.

States can enact even stiffer protections from garnishment. The CCPA does not exempt any employer from complying with state laws that prohibit garnishments; that provide more limited garnishments than are permitted under the federal law; or that prohibit the discharge of an individual because his or her earnings have been garnished for more than one indebtedness.

Garnishments for Family Support

In the case of an individual paying court-ordered support for another person, the maximum percentage of disposable earnings subject to garnishment shall be 50% of the individual's disposable earnings for that week, if the individual is supporting another spouse or dependent child. The maximum is 60% of the individual's disposable earnings for that week, if the individual is not supporting another spouse or dependent child. The percentages may be increased by five percent respectively if the garnishment order includes payment of support that is more than 12 weeks old prior to the beginning of the workweek.

Michigan Provisions for Garnishments

Under Michigan law, both circuit courts and district courts may authorize the garnishment of property to satisfy judgments. State law permits pre-judgment garnishments when an individual is not subject to the state's jurisdiction or cannot be located within the state, and the obligation or property garnished is applied to the satisfaction of the judgment after judgment is rendered. Unlike property or other obligations, however, wages owing to an individual for work performed cannot be subjected to pre-judgment garnishment. Such a claim is only effective after it has been reduced to judgment. In the early 1990s, Michigan enacted legislation providing that an order to garnish periodic payments owed to a person will remain in effect, and is not dissolved, until one or more of the following events occur:

- The amount garnished equals or exceeds the amount of the judgment, interest, and costs.
- The expiration of 91 days from the date the Writ of Garnishment is issued.
- As otherwise ordered by the court.

In some cases a garnishment may be dissolved by posting a bond in accordance with the rules of the Supreme Court.

Multiple Garnishments

The employer is not liable for a second garnishment against an employee if the employer is required to satisfy another garnishment against the same employee and the other garnishment has a higher priority or has the same priority but was received at an earlier date.

The priority of Writs of Garnishment under state law is:

1. Garnishments for court-ordered child and family support.
2. State or governmental garnishments for tax liabilities.
3. Any other garnishment.

The employer is entitled to a $6.00 fee when the garnishment for periodic payments is served upon it. Michigan's Act further states that periodic payments include wages, earnings, land-contract payments, rent, and other periodic debt or contract payments.

Enforcement of Garnishment Laws

The federal CCPA is enforced by the Secretary of Labor through the Wage and Hour Division. It does not create an individual private right of action. Therefore, an individual who contends an employer has violated the Act must report the alleged offense to the

U.S. DOL, which is authorized to act on the individual's behalf. The Act does not permit an individual to bring a suit against the employer for the alleged violation.

Michigan law, like the federal law, also forbids the discipline or discharge of an employee because of one or more garnishments. An employer violating the state law will be required to reinstate the employee and reimburse all lost compensation. Michigan law provides a private right of action for the employee to bring suit for reinstatement. Venue for the lawsuit is proper in the county where venue would be proper against the employee or where venue would be proper against the employer and employee or personal jurisdiction cannot be obtained over the employee.

Penalties for Violating Garnishment Laws

A violation of the federal CCPA is punishable by criminal and monetary sanctions. A responsible company or individuals may be subjected to a $1,000 fine or imprisonment for not more than one year or both.

Any person summoned as a garnishee or its officer, agent, or other person who appears and answers for a corporation summoned as a garnishee who knowingly and willfully answers falsely on its disclosure or examination under oath, violates the law. Such a person is liable to the person garnishing wages and must pay out of his or her own goods and estate the full amount due on the judgment recovered with interest to be recovered, in a civil action.

Noncompete Covenants in Michigan

Some of the most important assets a company owns are its intellectual property—patents, trademarks, copyrights, and trade secrets. How does a company protect these valuable assets that are placed in the hands of its employees? Many companies have responded to the need to protect their secrets by requiring employees to sign noncompete agreements. How will the employees react? Are they enforceable? What else can be done to protect a company's valuable secrets?

Frequently Asked Questions

Should a Company Require its Employees to Sign Noncompete Agreements?

Perhaps the most important consideration in determining whether the use of noncompete agreements is appropriate is the company's corporate "culture." An employer must balance its need to protect its proprietary information against the "message" an employer sends to its employees when it requires employees to enter into agreements which restrict their ability to seek new employment.

Are Noncompete Agreements Enforceable Under Michigan Law?

In 1985, Michigan repealed its long-standing prohibition against the use of noncompete agreements in an employment setting. Instead, the Michigan legislature allowed employers to obtain an agreement which protects an employer's "reasonable competitive business interests" and which "expressly prohibits an employee from engaging in employment or a line of business after termination of employment if the agreement or covenant is reasonable as to its duration, geographical area, and the type of employment or line of business." Thus, Michigan came into line with most states which allowed the use of reasonable noncompete agreements to protect a company's legitimate business interests such as trade secrets or goodwill. As discussed below, however, the reasonableness of differing restrictions varies widely by industry and by your particular circumstances.

Are Job Applicants and Independent Contractors Considered "Employees" for Purposes of Noncompete Agreements?

Traditionally, noncompete agreements have been considered within the scope of an employer-employee relationship only, and the Michigan statute covers agreements between "employers" and "employees."

Recent Michigan case law, however, has found that a noncompetition agreement between an employer and its independent contractors was enforceable.

Job applicants can also be covered. Interpreting the Michigan statute, one federal appellate court in concluded that under the Act – and consistent with other Michigan statutes barring the exchange of "consideration" (i.e., something of some value) to obtain employment – a hiring offer to an applicant could be conditioned upon the signing of a noncompete agreement.

What Type of Activities Can be Restricted After an Employee Leaves a Company?

The typical noncompete agreement attempts to limit an employee's ability to work for a competitor for a set period of time after leaving employment with a company. In addition, agreements often require that an employee refrain from calling on or soliciting business from the customers of the former employer or seeking to hire away employees of the former employer.

To be enforceable against the employee, the departing employee does not need to be using or threatening to use confidential information or skills specially acquired from the employer. Moreover, as discussed below, the standards for reasonableness as to the scope and duration of the agreement depend upon the circumstances. For example, this year a federal court in Michigan enforced a noncompete agreement against popular radio personality John Mason when he left Radio One. Mason said he only wanted to use the knowledge and skills he gained before starting with Radio One, but the radio objected that it had invested a lot of time and money building a customer and advertising base relating to Mason. The court found it reasonable to broadly prevent Mason from appearing on any radio station within 75 miles of Radio One's transmitters for six months.

How Specific Should a Noncompete Agreement be Regarding the Restricted Activity?

While broad-reaching provision can be upheld, they present greater risk of non-enforcement. It is crucial that an employer specifies in the noncompete agreement that an employee is prohibited from physically operating a business in a specific area as well as servicing that area. Under Michigan law, for example, a covenant not to compete does not bar a former employee from physically operating a business, which was outside a contractually specified "target" area, even though the former employee serviced customers who were within the target area. According to the court that considered this case, the term "operate" in the contract referred to the physical location of the business as opposed to where its business activities were conducted.

How Long Should a Noncompete Agreement be in Force?

There is no rule of thumb that governs the length of a noncompete agreement. An employer should consider the time period it would take to replace an employee and re-establish contacts with its customer base. Courts often look to the industry to gauge the length of a reasonable noncompete agreement. For example, in the employment recruitment business, at least one court has held that a six-month covenant was reasonable in that the "life" of a job opening could last up to six months. Other courts have enforced noncompete agreements for longer periods of time up to one year.

Although it is rare that a court will enforce a noncompete agreement beyond one year absent extraordinary circumstances or the payment to the former employee of compensation for that time period, one Michigan court recently upheld a two-year agreement. In an unpublished decision in *Virchow Krause & Co. v. Schmidt*, an accountant left her employer to practice at another accounting firm. She signed a 24-month noncompete agreement. Soon, the old firm was bought out by another accounting business. In holding that the agreement had been properly assigned to the new firm, which could seek to enforce it, the court did not find any reason to question the validity of the contract's duration (although it expressed a doubt whether the contract was unenforceable for other fact-specific reasons about how it was entered).

In another unpublished case this past year, *Neocare Health Systems, Inc. v. Teodoro*, the court specifically found a five-year noncompete clause was reasonable in preventing a home health care worker from providing the very same services to the employer's patients. It is worth seeking guidance from counsel in crafting a durational clause that makes the most sense for your business and in your industry.

Do the Covenants Need to be Limited to a Specific Geographical Area?

Strictly speaking, the answer is no. While the statute speaks of a geographical area, the *Teodoro* court (above) upheld an agreement against a home health care worker, which did not contain a geographical limitation and only specifically banned providing the same home health care services to the employer's patients and customers. Arguably, however, the home-based nature of the business created an unspoken geographical limitation.

Courts will evaluate the territorial scope of the company's and former employee's activities in determining the reasonable geographic scope of the agreement. Salespersons that have a limited territory will likely be restricted from working in that territory if a noncompete agreement is enforced. On the other hand, companies which have a nationwide scope of business and whose employees may work throughout the United States could prohibit a former employee from working anywhere in the United States for a competitor.

Aren't Courts Reluctant to Enforce an Agreement Which Bars a Person from Seeking Employment with a New Company?

While there is no discernible trend and, in fact, most courts deal with noncompete agreements on a case-by-case basis, courts more frequently view a company's intellectual property and trade secrets as being valuable assets which merit protection. Thus, courts need to balance a company's need to protect its business against an employee's desire to seek new employment.

How do Courts go About Balancing Those Interests?

Courts will look to the nature of the interest seeking protection; that is, does the company possess a trade secret or a substantial relationship with its customers that merit protection against an employee's desire to move to another company? Courts will often look at whether the employee was treated fairly, the compensation received, the length of the covenant, and whether the employee can be placed in a different position with a new company so as to avoid treading upon the former employee's proprietary information.

Should a Company Offer to Compensate the Employee During the Period of the Noncompete Agreement?

While there is no requirement under the Michigan statute that the employee be compensated, it is a powerful argument to tell a court that the employer will be compensating the former employee for the length of the noncompete agreement so that the former employee has a source of income. Under Michigan law, there need be no special compensation, and the promise of continued employment is sufficient to support a noncompete agreement. Nonetheless, companies that wish to prevent an employee from bolting to a competitor (or at least delay the time when the former employee can begin work) should consider compensating the employee during the period of the noncompete agreement.

Can an Employer Enforce a Noncompete Agreement if the Employee is Terminated as Opposed to the Employee Voluntarily Leaving?

If a company terminates an employee for poor performance, it is difficult to convince a court that the former employee represents such a threat to the employer that a noncompete agreement should be enforced. In fact, many noncompete agreements provide that the agreement is enforceable only if the employee voluntarily leaves the company for a new job.

Which Employees Should be Required to Sign Noncompete Agreements?

A company should not make wholesale use of noncompete agreements with all employees. Rather, it should evaluate its business activities and determine which employees have access to confidential information or will be put in the position of developing substantial contacts and goodwill with customers where the company makes a significant investment in their activities. Typically, engineers, research and development personnel, salespersons, and executives would be the targets of such agreements. In fact, companies which require all employees to sign noncompete agreements regardless of their position in the company sometimes face the argument in court that the employer's policies are harsh and overreaching such that noncompete agreements should not be enforced.

Should the Noncompete Agreement be Discussed in an Exit Interview with a Departing Employee?

Not only should employees be reminded of their obligations to the company but it is advisable to inform the new employer of the existence of noncompete agreements. It is surprising how many times a new employer does not know that the person it is hiring has signed such an agreement with a former employer.

Should Companies Discuss Noncompete Agreements During the Hiring Process?

When interviewing prospective employees, one should ask whether the prospective employee has entered into any noncompete agreements. Likewise, if a company plans to ask a new employee to enter into a noncompete agreement, that subject should be discussed during the interview process. It is advisable to give the prospective employee a copy of the proposed noncompete agreement and make reference to it in any job offer letter. This heads off an argument in litigation that the employee was given the noncompete agreement to sign on the first day on the job after terminating employment elsewhere such that the employee had no choice but to sign the agreement. While Michigan law does not prohibit a company from asking its existing employees to sign noncompete agreements, courts, in balancing the needs of the employer and employee, often look to whether or not the agreement was foisted upon the employee without warning.

Should Employers Require Existing Employees to Sign Noncompete Agreements?

Again, corporate culture plays a large role in this decision. There is nothing which prohibits a company from asking its current employees to sign agreements. Michigan law does not require any special compensation to the existing employees as the promise of continued employment, even in an at-will situation, is sufficient consideration for the agreement. Nonetheless, if an employer is considering asking its existing employees to sign noncompete agreements, it is advisable to time the execution of such agreements with the granting of a promotion, bonus, or salary increase. This at least creates an argument that employees were offered something in addition to their current employment in exchange for the agreement.

Can Employers Require Union Employees To Sign Noncompete Agreements For Continued Employment?

Where there is a union contract, employers cannot terminate employees for "cause" for refusing to sign noncompete agreements. The employees' refusal to contract with their employer on an individual basis apart from the union contract and without the participation of the union, does not provide a basis for "just cause" termination.

If an Employee who has Signed a Noncompete Agreement Leaves, Should the Employer Run to Court?

The decision whether or not to sue a former employee for breaching a noncompete agreement is complicated. Not only must a company evaluate whether the former employee poses a threat to the company but it also must consider whether an adverse decision from a court will render its agreements with other employees unenforceable. Further, a company must consider what resources will need to be expended in litigation and whether the former employee's new employer will learn some competitive intelligence during the course of the lawsuit. If the departing employee is carrying off proprietary information or was a key player in the company, the decision becomes easier. The more difficult situation is with mid-level employees who have access to proprietary information or have established customer relationships. In these types of cases, courts look to the level and stature of the employee in the company and the compensation paid to the employee as critical factors in deciding whether or not to enforce a noncompete agreement.

What Else Can be Done to Protect a Company's Proprietary Information?

Companies should consider requiring all employees who have access to proprietary information to enter into confidentiality agreements preventing departing employees from using the company's trade secrets in a new job. In fact, during the interviewing process for prospective employees, the company should ask if the prospective employee has entered into such agreements with another company.

As companies and courts come to realize that propriety information and long-standing customer relationships are two of the most valuable assets of any entity, they have focused more and more on preventing departing employees from walking off with those valuable assets. It seems as if almost every week the Wall Street Journal reports on a new high profile trade secret lawsuit (the *Dow Chemical/General Electric* litigation, the Silicon Valley wars). The almost 20-year-old statute repealing Michigan's long-standing prohibition on the use of noncompete agreements has proven to be a blessing and a curse. It provides employers with added ammunition to protect its valuable assets and yet on the other hand noncompete agreements are an impediment to hiring new employees. The only things that are predictable are that there will be more use of noncompete agreements with more litigation and that the outcome of such lawsuits is highly unpredictable.

Michigan's Concealed Weapons Law

Since July 1, 2001, it has been easier for Michigan residents to obtain a permit allowing them to carry a concealed weapon (known as "CCW permits"). A concealed weapon, as defined by Michigan law, is a (1) loaded or unloaded firearm that is 30 inches or shorter or (2) a firearm that looks like something other than what it is (e.g., a pen or camera). Under the law, county gun boards are required to issue CCW permits to any citizen at least 21 years old who has no felony convictions and no history of mental illness. Applicants with misdemeanor convictions must wait, depending on the seriousness of the misdemeanor, between three to eight years before receiving a CCW permit. All applicants must complete an eight-hour pistol safety-training course and submit to a comprehensive background check.

The law has dramatically increased the number of Michigan residents who seek CCW permits. **Employers should be aware that the law expressly permits employers to enact a policy prohibiting their employees from carrying a concealed weapon while on company property or on company business. Such policies should be included in employee handbooks and/or collective bargaining agreements.**

Furthermore, the policy should be part of a larger, comprehensive program to prevent workplace violence in general. Such a program may reduce the possibility of serious workplace violence, and help an employer avoid expensive litigation. The company's workplace violence program and CCW policy should be reviewed by legal counsel before implementation. Chapter 19 of this book addresses workplace violence issues in some more detail.

Employment Laws Influenced by World Events

Since September 11, 2001, there has been increased focus on workplace safety and security, particularly with respect to companies' ability to conduct extensive background checks on current and prospective employees, vendors, and other third parties. Obviously, these concerns did not emerge on September 11. In the years leading up to September 11, federal and state governments already required background checks for workers in nuclear, financial services, airport and childcare industries. In the wake of September 11, however, Congress sought to prevent future terror acts by expanding the breadth of individuals subject to mandatory background checks. Congress rushed to pass the USA Patriot Act of 2001 ('Patriot Act") and soon after, the Public Health Security and Bioterrorism Preparedness and Response Act of 2002 ("Bioterrorism Response Act"), which largely expanded mandatory background checks to port workers, those transporting hazardous materials and a greater number of airport workers.

Several additional legislative initiatives have been introduced in order to increase security in "at-risk" areas, including, background checks on applicants for private security officer employment, tighter security for the transportation of all cargo entering the United States, and background checks on employees working in the chemical industry. Perhaps the most comprehensive national security bill yet, the "Justice Enhancement and Domestic Security Act of 2003, includes, in part, stronger protection against identify theft. The Bush Administration is also considering a variety of additional background checks and security clearance measures, including plans to expand the number of transportation workers subject to background checks beyond those who transport hazardous materials.

Employers have responded both reactively (to the initial federal mandates) and proactively (to those bills likely to pass) by implementing a wide variety of safeguards that are designed to reduce potential liability and increase workplace security. Depending on the exact nature of a company's business, certain provisions in the recent terror legislation may also impose additional affirmative duties on companies to register with federal agencies or submit annual reports. Employers are now also conducting more extensive background checks of existing employees, new hires, vendors, independent contractors and third-party guests, in addition to increasing the physical security in and around facilities. Although much of the recent terror legislation is only applicable to companies utilizing any chemicals or toxins that are strictly regulated by the Centers for Disease Control and Prevention ("CDC"), employers must still ensure that any additional proactive security measures are implemented in compliance with current federal regulations and any state laws. Failure to successfully navigate the myriad of federal and state regulations and enacting the proper policies could result in future liability or other loss.

Patriot Act of 2001

The USA Patriot Act, which was passed by Congress in direct response to the events of September 11, 2001, contains various provisions peripherally related to the workplace. The Act gives the FBI and other federal agencies greater rights to access business records, including access to and surveillance of computer records and Internet use. Other provisions relate to enhancing information sharing among federal agencies regarding immigration data and related matters. However, in September 2004, a federal district court judge declared that section 505 of the Patriot Act was a violation of free speech and unreasonable search-and-seizure protections guaranteed by the First and Fourth Amendments respectively. Section 505 made it legal for the FBI, through a National Security Letter (NSL), to obtain customer records from communication firms, such as internet service providers or telephone companies. The firm was then barred from ever disclosing it had received the letter.

If the FBI or a national security agency comes knocking at your workplace door, employers should be generally aware of the USA Patriot Act's provisions that authorize greater federal access to your business records than previously existed, and should consult counsel as to specific applicability.

In the interest of national security, the Patriot Act was signed into law in part, to establish certain specific requirements for control of and use of biohazardous materials referred to as "Select Agents." Among the requirements is that facilities must identify select agents in its possession and eliminate access to these select agents (the ability of an individual to gain entry into a space where a select agent is used or stored) for a population of individuals who have been defined by the Act as "Restricted Persons." The Act also provides criminal penalties for possession of select agents that cannot be justified for specified peaceful purposes and requires annual reporting.

Bioterrorism Response Act of 2002 – "Select Agents"

The Bioterrorism Response Act of 2002 expanded the reach of the Patriot Act in regulating the possession and transfer of select agents. The Act required the Department of Health and Human Services ("HHS") to be more aggressive in the establishment and maintenance of the select agent list. Under the Act, HHS must also establish and enforce safety and training procedures governing the possession of select agents. The Act further requires that the agencies must ensure that all facilities limit access of select agents to "only those individuals the registered facility determines have a legitimate need to handle or use" them. Finally, the Act requires that each facility provide identifying information of the personnel with access to select agents, which is then forwarded to the Attorney General for review.

Bioterrorism Response Act of 2002 – "Food Facilities"

Title III of the Bioterrorism Response Act also requires domestic and foreign facilities that manufacture, process, pack or hold food for human or animal consumption in the United States to register with the FDA. According to the FDA, registration will assist the agency to determine the location and cause of a potential threat and permit the agency to quickly notify facilities that might be affected.

Fair Credit Reporting Act Considerations

Companies seeking to increase security at their facilities while meeting the new federal mandates must do so while still working within the confines of the Fair Credit Reporting Act and other state laws that may limit the types of information that companies may obtain and use when making employment or contracting decisions. Traditionally, companies needed to comply with FCRA in connection with conducting background checks on new hires because these types of background checks clearly qualified as a "consumer report," triggering FCRA compliance (see further discussion on this topic in Chapter 2). FCRA investigative consumer reports regarding current employees which are ordered for employment purposes also trigger the protections of the Act. When an employer orders a report in connection with a promotion, reassignment or retention, it is considered for employment purposes. However, disclosure requirements are not triggered for employment purposes unless the employee specifically applied for the new position.

More generally, because of the broad scope of FCRA, companies would be wise to ensure compliance with FCRA when meeting the new federal mandates and conducting any type of connected "security clearances" on vendors, independent contractors and other third-party guests.

Employers should also review various other terrorism-related issues, including emergency evacuation plans (consider your employees with disabilities), ADA and FMLA requests which might be relevant to a terrorist attack (such as post-traumatic stress disorder, acute stress disorder, fear of travel, etc.), and general workplace safety issues (e.g. response to violence or threats of violence, mail handling procedures).

In 2003, President Bush signed into law the Fair and Accurate Credit Transaction Act (FACTA). FACTA amends the FCRA in several areas. Now, if an employer uses a consumer reporting agency for an investigation, it excuses the employer from complying with the FCRA if the investigation involves a violation of law or regulations, suspected misconduct or a violation of any pre-existing written policies.

Additionally, for employers that obtain "consumer reports" from third-party reporting agencies for credit or employment purposes, FACTA is relevant because it now sets standards for how a company should dispose of any information in a consumer report, as well as any information in other documents that are created based on the information in any consumer reports.

The Federal Trade Commission (FTC) adopted what is known as "the Disposal Rule" to define those standards.

The Disposal Rule requires disposal practices that are reasonable and appropriate to prevent the unauthorized access to—or use of—information in a consumer report. For example, reasonable measures for disposing of consumer report information could include establishing and complying with policies to:

- burn, pulverize, or shred papers containing consumer report information so that the information cannot be read or reconstructed;

- destroy or erase electronic files or media containing consumer report information so that the information cannot be read or reconstructed; or

- conduct due diligence and hire a document destruction contractor to dispose of material specifically identified as consumer report information consistent with the Disposal Rule.

Considering that Michigan now enforces the Social Security Number Privacy Act (discussed above), it is obvious that state and federal lawmakers want employers to be very careful about protecting the privacy of employee data that is personal and confidential in nature.

CHAPTER 16: Employee Layoffs

Companies large and small have had to face the difficult decision to downsize or "right-size," which cannot always be done by attrition. Whenever long-term employees lose their jobs and new jobs are difficult to find, the situation is ripe for wrongful discharge litigation. Such litigation, in the specific context of layoffs, has been based upon theories including breach of express or implied contract, employment discrimination (especially age discrimination), deprivation of promised or vested employee benefits, and tacked-on tort claims to increase the damage potential. Employee layoffs are often fertile ground for class action lawsuits, and such actions frequently join individual defendants. Other potential actions include claims of tortious interference with contract, fraud, intentional/negligent/or innocent misrepresentation, retaliation and/or defamation.

Although there are no guaranteed methods available to prevent lawsuits, the topics in this chapter provide information to consider that will maximize the chances that a reduction in force will be defensible from a legal perspective.

Avoiding Liability for Reductions-in-Force

The right to lay off is such a significant management right, especially in difficult times, that it should be clearly and strongly expressed and reserved in any of your employment contracts and handbooks. Otherwise, the Company takes the risk that the nature and the boundaries of such right, as a matter of contract, will be implied by a court, jury, or other trier of fact.

Even if employees are at-will, and their employment can be terminated at any time for any lawful reason, it still does not hurt to include express notice and reservation of your right to layoff in a policy manual or handbook.

Particularly with just-cause employees, the reservation of the right to layoff should be made clear and distinguished from termination for cause. Accordingly, a policy might spell out that the judgment of the employer that layoffs for economic reasons are necessary automatically constitutes cause for termination.

The right to layoff is one management right that, even in collective bargaining agreements, should be, and almost always is, broadly and clearly defined. For example:

> In the event the Employer determines, in its sole judgment, that it is necessary to reduce the number of employees, or to discontinue a position to which an employee is assigned, or to eliminate a program or department in whole or in part, or to reorganize a program or department in whole or in part, whether due to lack of work, reallocation of resources, change in company priorities, efficiency or

economy of operations, budgetary reductions, or similar reasons, the Employer agrees to provide the laid-off employee with the following period of notice: [insert three days or two weeks or a period increasing with years of service, etc.; depending upon your corporate culture and the category of employee]. The Employer's decision and judgment as to the number of employees to be laid off, and the necessity for the layoff, shall not be grievable or subject to any other appeal.

You also should consider reserving the right in your employment contracts and writings to effect temporary layoffs (one day, two weeks, etc.), as compared with indefinite layoffs.

If you have adopted a corporate resolution to the effect that no one but the President has the right to make oral promises about employment, that also will reduce your exposure to lawsuits based upon allegations to the effect that "X promised me a job as long as I did my job," or based upon other oral promises.

A company forced to layoff employees should, with the advice of experienced labor counsel, consider the following steps to reduce its exposure to wrongful-discharge litigation arising out of the layoff, particularly when the layoff involves several employees:

1. Before announcing the reduction-in-force, you should do two things: (i) prepare an internal memo describing the business/financial reason for the reduction; and (ii) prepare an internal memo describing the process and objective selection criteria by which you will conduct the reduction.

2. Develop a theme: layoff decisions must be fair and job-related. An unfair process is often viewed as discriminatory. Particularly with mass layoffs, you want to project the perception that the company had to cut jobs in order to save jobs.

3. Establish and document possible alternative expense-reduction measures, and provide an explanation where considered measures are not practical. Include comparisons with other companies in the industry where possible. List possible alternatives to layoff, including elimination of unprofitable operations, cutting non-labor related expenses, restrictions on travel, eliminating contract positions, or consolidation or regionalization of functions, etc. Consider personnel alternatives, including early retirement programs, a hiring freeze, promotion freezes, pay cuts, reduced workweeks, and attrition (not filling positions left empty through resignations, retirement, or terminations for cause). You want to avoid one-for-one replacements. Consider allowing voluntary layoffs before mandating involuntary separations.

4. Throughout the layoff process, designate a team that includes legal counsel with the role of monitoring public statements and comments, with an eye to developing good documents and avoiding bad documents.

5. If the affected workforce is non-union, allow for controlled input by employees or groups of employees, and comply with any applicable written policies on layoffs, appeal procedures, etc. Specify in your policies what, if any, recall rights are available, and monitor hiring, promotions, and salary increases for at least one year after the layoff (so as not to give the appearance that the economic justification for the layoff was not valid). For example, if you layoff an employee in December, and in January you hire a different replacement who is in a different protected group from a discrimination standpoint, that decision will be hard to defend.

6. If the affected workforce is unionized, comply with any applicable duty to bargain over the impact and effects of the layoff on the bargaining unit, and comply with any applicable collective bargaining provisions on notice, consultation, layoff, recall, severance pay, etc.

7. When special considerations such as early retirement or one-time severance payment programs are implemented, comply with the Older Workers Benefit Protection Act (OWBPA) amendments to the ADEA, and obtain releases that comply with the detailed requirements of the OWBPA.

8. Before selecting any particular individual employee for a layoff, establish and document a selection plan that sets forth job-related factors for the layoff that do not have a disparate impact on any protected group (age, sex, race, etc.). Include procedures as to how those factors will be consistently applied to choose individual employees for the layoff. Consider establishing an EEO oversight committee (include a management executive, a human-resources person, and an attorney) to monitor the layoff for discriminatory impact on any protected group. Each decision-maker's layoff decisions should be reviewed for job-relatedness. If the employees in your layoff include all the women and minorities in your workforce, and you do not have a documented selection plan for job-related reasons, your decision will be hard to defend if a civil rights lawsuit is filed.

9. Consider the possible application of the federal WARN Act, which governs plant closings and mass layoffs, as well as the impact of other employment laws relating to termination, including the Michigan Payment of Wages and Fringe Benefits Act, COBRA, and ERISA.

10. Consider the adoption of alternative dispute resolution procedures applicable to claims brought over the layoff, especially in light of the United States Supreme Court's decision in *Gilmer v. Interstate/Johnson Lane Corporation* (1991), which enforced an agreement to arbitrate an age discrimination claim. A discussion of limitations on the use of alternative dispute resolution in civil rights cases appears elsewhere in this publication.

11. Take pains to not give laid-off employees claims that they would not otherwise have, such as a claim for defamation. For example, make it clear in documents and exit interviews that the decision was based upon economic reasons, not performance deficiency or misconduct.

Documenting Layoff Decisions

All planning documents should contain an affirmation of the company's commitment to its EEO policy, and any documents evaluating which employees should be laid off must only be based on job-related factors. The following lists of good and bad documents are based upon experiences with actual class-action layoff litigation, often based upon civil rights challenges:

Good Documents

Good documents are made in accordance with the decision-making process, and include the following information:

- Why the layoff was necessary (the business reasons for decision)
- Alternatives considered
    1. Nonpersonnel alternatives—limited duty to consider
    2. Personnel alternatives:
        a. Open Window
        b. Hiring Freeze
        c. Promotion Freeze
        d. Pay Cuts
        e. Reduced Workweeks
        f. Attrition
        g. Eliminating Contract Positions
- How to implement the layoff
- Prohibited selection criteria ("what not to do")
- The Company's anti-discrimination policy
- Advance communications with employees concerning the need for action
- Specific instructions on selection procedures, including "do's" and "don'ts"
- "Objective" job-related standards used for selecting employees to be laid off

- Candid performance evaluations
- Detailed job-related statements of reasons for individual decisions
- Candid, consistent communications of reasons for the selection to the employee
- Acknowledgments from volunteers for early retirement
- Releases or waivers of claims
- Efforts made to secure other jobs for laid-off employees
- Special severance benefits and compensation counseling
- Audit of actions taken by decision makers
- Outplacement services offered to laid-off employees

Bad Documents

- Unexplained references to age (i.e., in lists of employees to be laid off)
- A list of employees eligible for early retirement
- Memoranda using terms such as "younger," "older," "junior," "senior," "potential," "deadwood," "peaked," "vitality," "lean," "flabby," "overqualified," etc.
- Non-objective, non-job-related evaluations
- Outdated evaluations
- Disproportionate impact evaluations (i.e. – statistical analyses)
- Handbooks guaranteeing lifetime employment
- Glowing reference letters (or letters that the employees to be terminated were permitted to draft)
- Advertisements for jobs in newspaper during layoff
- Offer letters, etc., during or when contemplating layoffs
- Speeches or annual reports that state layoffs are a good opportunity for young people to move ahead in the company

Worker Adjustment and Retraining Notification Act (WARN)

The Worker Adjustment and Retraining Notification Act of 1988 (WARN) took effect on February 4, 1989. Although WARN is more commonly known as the Plant Closing Act, it applies not only to plant closings but also to mass layoffs, including reductions in force. In addition to the statutory provisions, the U.S. Department of Labor has issued regulations establishing basic definitions and rules for giving notice. The Department of Labor has also published a non-authoritative employer's guide to WARN in July 2003. *See* http://www.doleta.gov/layoff/pdf/EmployerWARN09_2003.pdf.

WARN prohibits a covered employer from ordering a plant closing or a mass layoff without giving 60 days prior notice to the employees or their representatives and to designated state and local government officials. Failure to comply with the statute may result in substantial monetary liabilities.

Employers Subject to WARN

WARN applies to any employer who:

- employs 100 or more full-time employees (excluding part-time employees who work fewer than 20 hours per week or who have been employed for fewer than six of the preceding 12 months); or

- employs 100 or more employees, whether full-time or part-time, who in the aggregate work at least 4,000 hours per week exclusive of overtime.

A creditor can also become liable for providing notice under WARN when it becomes so entangled with its borrower that it has assumed responsibility for the overall management of the borrower's business. In addition, affiliated companies may be considered a single "employer" for purposes of WARN. Likewise, independent contractors and subsidiaries that are wholly or partially owned by a parent company may be considered part of the parent or contracting company depending on their degree of independence from the parent.

WARN is triggered whenever an employer permanently or temporarily shuts down either an entire site of employment, or one or more facilities or operating units within a single site, if the shutdown results in an "employment loss" for at least 50 or more full-time employees during any 30-day period.

Additionally, an employer must give requisite WARN notice prior to instituting a mass layoff, which is defined as a reduction in force (not the result of a plant closing) that results in an "employment loss" during any 30-day period and affects:

- at least 33% of the employees and at least 50 employees; or
- at least 500 employees.

WARN defines "employment loss" as:

- a termination other than for cause, voluntary departure, or retirement;
- a layoff exceeding six months; or
- a greater than 50% reduction in hours worked for any individual employee for six consecutive months.

A layoff or a termination does not count as an "employment loss" if an employee is transferred or reassigned, so long as the transfer does not constitute a constructive discharge or an involuntary termination.

Rolling Layoffs – Aggregation

An employer cannot implement rolling layoffs with the purpose of evading WARN. While employers must consider whether a plant closing or a mass layoff results in the minimum number of employment losses during a 30-day period, WARN also contains provisions for aggregating separate actions during a 90-day window. Aggregation does not occur, however, if the employer is able to demonstrate that the employment losses resulted from separate and distinct actions that were not an attempt to avoid providing notice.

Employer Notification Obligations under WARN

When WARN is triggered, an employer must give 60 days written notice to the following parties:

- Each representative of the affected employees or if there is no representative, to each affected employee, including part-time employees;
- The state dislocated worker unit (created under Title II of the Job Training Act); and
- The chief elected official of the unit of local government where the closing or layoff will occur (if there are two units of local government, i.e., county and city, the notice must be given to the entity to which the employer paid the most taxes in the prior year).

The term "affected employees" includes certain employees who are not included in determining whether a plant closing or a mass layoff triggers the act. Rather, an employer must provide notice to any employee who may reasonably be expected to experience a job loss. Consequently, circumstances may require an employer to provide notice to part-time employees.

If the employer notifies the employees individually, a notice in their paycheck or a letter sent to their last known address is sufficient. If the employer is notifying the representative of the affected employees (e.g., a union official), a written notice to the representative suffices. The regulations provide detailed guidance on the content of the notice provided to each of the identified parties.

Exceptions to and Limitations of WARN Notification Requirements

WARN provides for a number of exceptions and limitations to the notification requirement. In light of the Act's purpose, these exceptions and limitations are strictly construed and narrowly interpreted. Accordingly, employers should be cautious about relying upon them.

- An employee does not suffer an employment loss and WARN, therefore, does not apply if the layoff or closing is a result of the relocation or consolidation of all or part of the employer's business provided that:

    The employer offers to transfer the employee within six months to a different site of employment; and

    The transfer is within a reasonable commuting distance or the employer offers and the employee accepts within 30 days an offer to transfer the employee within six months to another location regardless of commuting distance.

- The Act does not apply to closings or layoffs affecting a temporary facility or to closings or layoffs as a result of the completion of a particular project or undertaking if the employees were hired with the understanding that their employment was limited to the duration of the project or undertaking.

- The Act does not apply to closings or layoffs that constitute a strike or lockout and are not intended to evade the WARN Act requirements. The Act does not require the employer to give the WARN Act notice to economic strikers when hiring permanent replacements.

- The 60-day notification period may be reduced in certain circumstances. However, the employer still must notify the employees of an impending layoff or closing as soon as is practicable under the circumstances and, at that time, must give a brief statement of the reasons for reducing the notification period. The Act provides for this reduction in notice in the following situations:

The "faltering company" exception. A faltering company may order a shutdown before giving its employees 60 days notice if at the time notice would have been required, the employer was actively seeking capital or business with a realistic opportunity of obtaining the financing, provided that:

- If obtained, the capital or business would have prevented or postponed the closing; and

- The employer reasonably and in good faith believed that giving the required notice would have precluded the employer from obtaining the necessary capital or business.

The "unforeseeable business circumstances" exception. An employer may order a plant closing or layoff before the conclusion of the 60-day period if the closing or layoff is caused by business circumstances (for example, loss of a major customer) not reasonably foreseeable at the time notice would have been required.

The "natural disaster" exception. If the plant closing or mass layoff is caused by a natural disaster, such as a hurricane, no notice is required.

Purchase and Sale of Business

In the event of a purchase or sale of all or part of a business, the seller is responsible for providing the required notice of any plant closing or mass layoff up to and including the effective date of the sale. After the effective date of the sale, the purchaser is responsible for providing the notice. Any employee who is employed by the seller on the date of the sale is considered an employee of the purchaser immediately after the sale.

Enforcement and Penalties Under WARN

Any employer who fails to give notice pursuant to WARN will be liable to each affected employee for full back pay and benefits for each day that notice was not given up to 60 days. This penalty is not reduced by unemployment insurance or by any contractually required severance pay, nor will the employer's liability be reduced by an employee's interim earnings from other employment. Simply stated, the employer must pay to each aggrieved employee a full day's pay plus certain benefits (including reimbursement for covered medical expenses incurred during the employment loss) for each day, up to 60 days, that the required notice was not given.

Moreover, an employer also is subject to civil penalties up to $500 per day for failure to give notice to the local government officials. This penalty, however, is relieved if each employee is paid the required amount of back pay and benefits within three weeks from the date of the closing or layoffs.

Employers should note that the payments and remedies provided by WARN are in addition to any payments, rights, or remedies provided the employees by contract or other statute. However, if a contract requires notice, the notice period required by the Act will run concurrently with the period required by the contract. Additionally, WARN does not permit a court to enjoin an employer from a plant closing or mass layoff for failure to give the required notice.

Lastly, WARN can be enforced by a lawsuit in federal court by any employee or the representative of the employees, individually or as a class action, or by a unit of local government. Attorneys' fees may be awarded to the prevailing party.

CHAPTER 17: Making Good Discipline and Discharge Decisions

A company is not in business primarily to provide employment, but its business could not be accomplished without employees. Having employees, therefore, is clearly and obviously a benefit to the company.

How a company treats its employees, and how consistently it makes and administers decisions affecting their employment, can also affect the company's "bottom line." Employees who are treated consistently and made to feel appreciated are likely to be among the most productive and efficient assets of the company, leading to a direct *positive* impact on your company's financial success.

On the other hand, employees who are treated poorly and inconsistently, *or who simply perceive that they are treated poorly or inconsistently*, are most likely to be adversaries in a civil lawsuit, arbitration, or administrative action when they are negatively affected by employment decisions. Significant financial liability is often at stake when an employee challenges your company's employment decisions, and that liability can have a direct *negative* impact on your company's bottom line. Even if your company ultimately prevails, defense costs – economic and non-economic – can be prohibitively high.

For all of these reasons, your company can enhance its output and productivity and avoid (or at least reduce) preventable costs and liability by making reasonable and consistent discipline and discharge decisions regarding your employees.

THE (WRITTEN) FOUNDATION FOR DISCIPLINE AND DISCHARGE

Avoiding or reducing liability for your company's employment decisions regarding discipline and discharge begins long before any such employment decisions are actually made. Whether you can justify and/or defend employment decisions typically depends on what is set forth in the written "foundational" materials regarding employment with your company.

Documents such as employment applications, employee handbooks, individual employee contracts, a listing of workplace conduct rules, and written employment evaluations will often be key evidence in any legal challenge to discipline or discharge decisions. In a more positive, proactive vein, these documents can also be used to shape an employment environment that leaves employees feeling that they are treated justly, even when disciplined or discharged. Conversely, when poorly crafted or not followed in practice, they can be the distorted basis for employee perceptions of uneven or discriminatory treatment and, at worst, they will be evidence used against you in a lawsuit, arbitration, or administrative action.

Start by reviewing all of your company's written materials that say anything about discipline, discharge or layoff, including your employment application, written contracts, employee handbooks, supervisory manuals, personnel manuals, and all other written policies. Try to put yourself in the shoes of an employee who was just subjected to an adverse employment action and consider that that employee may consult with a lawyer who will "fly speck" all of these documents to see if you really followed your policies precisely as written. If you have not, you can be sure the lawyer will use these materials against you and point out your failings to a third party, such as a judge, jury, arbitrator, or government employee.

Undertaking this review will give you an opportunity to modify or eliminate all words, phrases, and policies that do not apply to your employees and that could be used against your company. Some examples of words or phrases that you may not actually want if you are an "at will" employer include "lifetime employment," "permanent employment," "employment for as long as you do a good job," or "just cause." You should also watch for all-inclusive or overly generalized policies that are intended to apply only to hourly employees. You should make clear which policies apply to various groups of employees.

With respect to discipline specifically, and particularly if you intend to maintain or preserve an "at will" employment environment, you should review workplace conduct rules and any description of the discipline that will follow for one or more violations of the rules. Be sure you have reserved the flexibility to deal with disciplinary situations on a case-by-case basis that allows you to factor in any aggravating or mitigating circumstances, the employee's past record and, if appropriate, seniority. The best way to preserve such flexibility is to include a written disclaimer in any type of progressive discipline policy that clearly states that the company reserves the right to impose any level of discipline, up to and including discharge – even for a first offense of any given workplace conduct rule – based on the facts of each situation. At the same time, be sure that your employees will have enough guidance, even if only generally, to know and expect what the actual consequence will be for violating any particular workplace standard.

If, in this review, you do not find any "over" commitments or standards that would actually be hard to meet in practice, *you probably have not looked hard enough*. If your employment decisions are challenged, you must be prepared to stand by and be bound by your written policies as if they were enforceable contract obligations. Indeed, by some legal theories, your company may actually be bound by what its written policies say – or, in some situations, even by what management-level employees say – even though your company employee handbook may disclaim any contractual relationship between the company and its employees.

The bottom line for your review is that you should delete every single "over" commitment that could be used against the company as a basis for a limitation on your right to discipline, discharge, or lay off.

While employee handbooks, employment contracts, or workplace conduct rules help to establish the foundation of the employment environment, a written performance evaluation will often be at the heart of your company's employment decision-making. When created, administered and relied upon properly, this document will often be the best evidence that your company has acted appropriately, reasonably, and without discrimination. Done tactfully, it can also be a motivational and instructional tool for employees.

On the other hand, when a company fails to properly and accurately record its assessment of an employee's performance, whether due to an evaluator's queasiness about criticizing a subordinate in writing or the company's failure to train supervisors how to evaluate their subordinates properly, it leaves itself without any objective evidence to back up its claim of poor performance, for example, when it finally gets fed up with an employee and wants to discharge him or her.

To be sure, performance evaluations take a lot of time and effort to do correctly. The payoff for doing so, however, is generally worth it.

Consider the following tips when preparing performance evaluations:

- Maintain an ongoing file of the employee's job performance throughout the year. Doing so will give the evaluator objective evidence from the entire evaluation period from which to make conclusions, while failing to do so will leave the evaluator scrambling to try to remember specific examples of good or poor performance. In addition, before preparing the evaluation, review all disciplinary notices, commendations, and other relevant documents from the evaluation period.

- Do not consider or refer to the employee's race, color, national origin, religion, sex, age, marital or family status, height, weight, disability, genetic information, or union or veteran status or affiliation.

- Evaluate employees at approximately the same time each year. An employer can evaluate all employees within the same month or evaluate each employee on his or her anniversary date. While the latter allows for more focused attention on each employee – especially where the evaluator is responsible for a large number of evaluations – it also may require more

- administrative attention and may be impractical depending on the needs of the company.

- Perhaps most importantly, *be forthright and candid*. For the written evaluation to be effective, the evaluator must be candid about the employee's strengths *and* weaknesses. An evaluator's failure to list shortcomings can create significant problems when the employee is later demoted, disciplined, or discharged for poor performance that existed at the time of the evaluation but was not brought to the employee's attention in the evaluation. The problem in this situation is two-fold. First, the company's action may be seen as unfair if the written evaluation did not put the employee on notice of the company's performance concerns and give the employee a chance to correct any deficiency. Second, it may be difficult for a judge, jury or arbitrator to believe that the company's true motivation for the adverse employment action was poor performance when the only document that is supposed to be an objective record of the company's assessment of performance does not reflect any performance concerns. In this latter situation, it may be easier to conclude that the company's true motivation was unjust or some form of unlawful discrimination.

- Each evaluator should be consistent in evaluating the employees for whom the evaluator is responsible. One employee should not be praised or criticized for conduct that is ignored or discounted from other employees. This is an invitation for an employment discrimination claim. When a company has multiple evaluators, a centralized, objective person should be assigned the task of reviewing all evaluations to assure consistency.

- Train your evaluators how to properly perform and administer evaluations.

- Be sure that specific factual statements in the written evaluation can be supported. Remember that Michigan law gives employees the right to review and copy evaluation forms and other contents of their personnel records.

- When practical, both the supervisor/evaluator and an objective human resources representative should attend the evaluation meeting with the employee.

- At the evaluation meeting, ask the employee to acknowledge in writing that he or she received and understands the evaluation.

- Under Michigan law, an employee may submit a written statement to the employer to disagree with any portion of the evaluation. The employer is required to include such a statement in the employee's personnel record.

The law sets a 5-page limit on the employee's statement (on sheets of 8½" x 11" paper).

- Be sure that the factors upon which an employee is evaluated are relevant to his or her job.

- Evaluations utilizing point systems should be used with great care. While an unweighted point system may not accurately reflect the employee's overall job performance, an *improperly weighted system* may be even worse. The weighting should bear some relationship to the relative importance of the criteria and to the overall value of the employee to the employer.

IMPOSING DISCIPLINE PROPERLY

As noted above, if you want to maintain the "at will" employment status for your employees, but also want to follow a progressive discipline system, you should describe and preface that system in your company's employee handbook, workplace conduct rules, or written policy with a disclaimer that expressly states that the system sets forth discretionary guidelines and that it does not alter the "at will" status of employment.

You should also be generally aware of a union employee's right, under state and/or federal labor laws, to have a representative present during a disciplinary interview if the employee reasonably believes that the interview may lead to discipline. Under a United States Supreme Court decision known as the *Weingarten* case, and under a similar provision in Michigan's public employment labor relations law (known as "PERA"), represented employees have the right to refuse to submit to an interview that they reasonably fear may result in discipline unless they are accompanied by a representative of their choice If you were to continue a disciplinary interview after denying an employee's request for representation, or if you were to discipline an employee for refusing to participate in the interview without representative, your company would be committing an unfair labor practice. Over the years, The National Labor Relations Board has gone back and forth on whether "Weingarten" rights apply to non-union employees. Currently, the Board's position is that these rights do not exist for non-union employees.

The following additional considerations should be taken into account.

Would Imposing the Discipline Violate Any State or Federal Law?

Michigan and federal law prohibit discipline based on unlawful discrimination or imposed in retaliation for the employee's exercise of any rights granted by state or federal law. These include laws relating to civil rights (such as protection from discrimination based on an employee's gender or race), occupational safety and health, wage and hour practices, and employee "whistle-blowing." A variety of other laws protect employees against mandatory polygraph exams, certain types of consumer credit practices, and adverse employment actions for jury or military service.

Has Discipline Been Consistently Imposed for the Infraction at Issue?

Probably the most important consideration is whether all similarly situated employees are subjected to the same level of penalty for the same type of infraction unless there is a real, objective and supportable basis for imposing more or less severe discipline.

Among the first questions you can expect to be asked by employment law counsel prior to imposing discipline are, "What level of discipline have you imposed on other employees in the last year or two who have committed this same offense?" and "If you are imposing different discipline than you have previously for other employees, what is your rationale?"

These are very important questions from a legal standpoint because you may be risking significant liability if, for example, you impose a 3-day suspension on an African American employee for starting a fight in the workplace and your disciplinary records show that you only gave written warnings to 2 Caucasian employees who started fights on other occasions – assuming all other factors are equal. In a valid progressive discipline system, this differentiation would be valid only so long as objective factors *other than* the employees' respective races exist to justify the differing level of discipline between the employees. In other words, you will have to prove, for example, that the African American employee had been warned and disciplined for earlier occasions of starting fights, while the Caucasian employees were first-time offenders.

Is the Discipline Consistent with Public Policy?

Many courts have ruled that an employer who imposes some adverse employment action on an employee can be sued if the employer took the action for some reason that runs afoul of generally accepted public policy.

Examples of adverse employment actions that could violate public policy include discipline imposed for an employee's refusal to violate a law or insistence that the company comply with a law. Other specific circumstances include (but are not necessarily limited to) discipline or discharge for an employee's refusal to give false testimony to a legislative committee, for refusal to participate in an illegal price-fixing scheme, or for refusal to tamper with pollution control reports.

Is the Discipline Reasonable?

At the end of the day, when you find yourself defending an adverse employment decision, possibly the strongest defense is that the action was reasonable under the circumstances and that the employee was warned of the consequences and given an opportunity to improve before action was taken. Arbitrators and juries will be much more inclined to uphold the company's discipline decision(s) if the company gave consideration to these concepts, as well as all of the "just cause" considerations described more fully below.

MAKING DEFENSIBLE DISCHARGE DECISIONS

There is no magic to deciding on and carrying out an employee's discharge that will prevent an employee from challenging the discharge in court, before an arbitrator, or with an administrative body. Nevertheless, if you consider the following points prior to making the decision and carrying out the discharge, you can very likely reduce the risk of financial liability for the decision.

Often, wrongful discharge cases are not decided on a legal basis – that is, whether an "at will" employment relationship existed from a legal standpoint, or whether there was "just cause" for discharge. Rather, as noted above, the outcome of these cases generally depends on whether the decision-maker felt that the discharge was fair, reasonable, and consistent. To maximize the chances of such an outcome consider the following guidelines, which all relate to the framework and practices that should be in place outside of the actual discharge decision.

- Adopt and abide by a written employee evaluation system that is honest, realistic and accurate. Be rigorous in your administration of the evaluation system by ensuring that the employee's performance problems, as well as warnings to the employee about them, are documented and acknowledged by the employee.

- Personally meet with the employee to discuss problems when they occur. Document these meetings and make sure the employee receives an acknowledged copy that is also included in the employee's personnel records. This documentation should serve as constructive criticism through which the employee is given a chance to improve and also warned of the consequences of failing to do so. Complying with this step will go a long way toward meeting a "reasonable" objective if/when you get to a point of making a discharge decision.

- Adopt a formal progressive discipline system. Employees should be given, where appropriate, advance warnings of their deficiencies and opportunities to improve prior to being discharged. If you want to maintain "at will" employment status for your employees, however, be sure to include a disclaimer that the system is merely a guideline that does not alter the employee's "at will" status, and that the company reserves the right to discharge an employee even for a first offense.

- Consider putting the employee on a written performance improvement plan. Clearly state the objective goals and areas of improvement you desire and provide a reasonable period of time (e.g. 30 or 60 days) for the employee to demonstrate improvement. If no appreciable changes are made after the period of time in the plan, discipline or discharge may be the next step.

- Give a "last chance" warning, particularly with long-term employees. The warning should clearly specify that the employee will be discharged if the actions are repeated – and then you must be prepared to actually make and carry out the discharge if the employee unjustifiably repeats the behavior or action at issue. Ideally, obtain the employee's signature to acknowledge his or her receipt and understanding of the last warning.

Sometimes, even if you have carefully and consistently followed the above framework, an employee's discharge will be necessary or inevitable. Following the steps below before and when you actually carry out the discharge will help to reduce any legal risk or exposure from the discharge.

- Before an employee is discharged, have the factual basis for the discharge reviewed by someone else in the company *other than* the person recommending the discharge (or by legal counsel). Several questions should be answered before a final decision is made to discharge the employee:

    - *What is the reason(s) for discharge that will be given by the company if a dispute arises?*

    - *How does the reason given for the discharge square with company handbooks, policies and procedures, and/or representations concerning reasons, causes, standards, and procedures for termination?*

    - *How strong and objective is the evidence of the event that is the basis for the discharge?*

- *If you follow a progressive discipline system, is evidence of progressive or prior discipline documented? Were any steps in the system missed (or not documented)? If so, why? Was the employee warned with the most recent prior discipline that discharge was the next step?*

- *What do the employee's evaluations say? Do they support or lend credence to the reason for the discharge? Do they contradict it (example: glowing written evaluations leading up to a performance-based discharge are suspect)?*

- *Has the decision-maker looked at the employee's entire personnel record? If not, has a human resources representative conducted such a review?*

- *How have similar situations been handled in the past? Is there any evidence of a pattern of discharging employees in any certain protected classification (i.e., gender, race, ethnicity, etc.) more frequently than employees outside that classification for the same conduct?*

- *Has the employee been given an opportunity to explain his or her actions prior to making the discharge decision?*

- *Are there compelling explanations or sympathies in favor of the employee? On the other hand, are there aggravating circumstances that warrant discharge even for a relatively minor infraction?*

- *Should there be a "last chance" warning (keeping in mind that this must be considered for consistency as well, with the company prepared to explain why a Caucasian employee, for example, was given a "last chance" warning when an African American employee was not)?*

- *Would a transfer to a different job or shift (or, perhaps, a leave of absence) solve the employee's problem, such that an otherwise productive and/or positive employee can be rehabilitated and maintained?*

- Discharge forms must be completely, accurately and truthfully completed. They should be consistent with company policies concerning reasons for discharge and should be broad enough to include all of the reasons relied upon for the discharge.

- Have another person (or two) present when the employee is told of the impending discharge, and have someone other than the person issuing the discharge take notes of what is said by all parties present. When you state the reasons for termination, make sure they are factual and accurate. Avoid defamatory words.

- Ask yourself this question: Will your decision-maker be a good witness? Is he or she believable, genuine, sincere, and convincing? A judge, jury, or arbitrator will need to think so.

Boundaries of Just Cause

In a union environment, a company will generally have to meet a "just cause" standard to justify discipline and, more importantly, discharge decisions. Even in wrongful discharge litigation, whether your company maintains an "at will" environment or not, the best defense to any wrongful discharge lawsuit is often a well-documented "just cause" for dismissal. Therefore, employers should pay careful attention to whether their discharge decisions stand up to the following 7-factor test of "just cause," which was developed by a well-known arbitrator in the late 1960s and continues to be cited even today.

Generally speaking, a "no" answer to any one or more of the questions below could signify that "just cause" does not exist for the employment decision at issue. All of the factors, however, are very fact-specific and whether "just cause" exists for a particular decision cannot be pigeon-holed quite that easily. Nevertheless, employers would be wise to measure their actions against this test.

1. *Notice*

    Did the employee have notice or a warning of the possible or probable disciplinary consequences of employee's conduct?

    - The notice may be given verbally or in writing – regardless of which, you should be able to establish with some form of competent evidence that notice was, in fact, given.

    - Failure to provide actual notice, however, does not always require a "no" answer to this question. Certain offenses, such as insubordination, coming to work intoxicated, drinking intoxicating beverages on the job, assaulting a coworker, or theft of the property of the company or of fellow employees, are so serious that any employee is deemed to know already that engaging in such conduct would lead to discharge.

2. *Reasonable Rule or Order*

Is the company's rule or managerial order reasonably related to the orderly, efficient and safe operation of the company's business?

- If an employee believes that the rule or order is unreasonable, he or she is nevertheless expected to obey it unless he or she sincerely feels that to obey the rule or order would seriously and immediately jeopardize his or her personal safety and/or integrity.

3. Investigation

Did the company, before administering discipline to the employee, make an effort to discover whether the employee did, in fact, violate or disobey a rule or order of management?

- This is the employee's "day-in-court" principle. An employee has the right to know with reasonable certainty the offense for which he or she is being charged and to have an opportunity to defend or explain his or her behavior.

- The company's investigation should normally be completed before its disciplinary decision is made. Of course, there may be circumstances in which management must act immediately in response to the employee's behavior. In such cases, the best course of action is to suspend the employee pending investigation, with the understanding that:

    - The final disciplinary decision will be made *after* the investigation.

    - If the employee is found innocent after the investigation, he or she will be restored to his or her job with full pay for time lost.

4. Fair Investigation

Was the company's investigation conducted objectively?

- While a management official may be both prosecutor and judge, he or she should not also be a witness against the employee. In other words, the company official who conducted the investigation and/or made the decision to discharge will likely not be the best witness to testify to a jury or arbitrator as to what the employee did to cause the employer's discharge decision. Rather, the company should find witnesses who are actually, well, witnesses – the coworkers who were eye-witnesses to the employee's violation of the work rule, for example.

- Is there any evidence that the company rushed to judgment? Will the employee be able to demonstrate that the company ignored so-called "exculpatory" evidence or trumped up weak evidence of misconduct?

5. *Proof*

At the investigation, did the decision-maker have before him or her substantial evidence or proof that the employee actually committed the alleged misconduct at issue?

- The employer is not required to meet a criminal burden of proof ("beyond a reasonable doubt") to justify its discharge decision. The evidence, however, should be substantial and objective and, if possible, subject to corroboration.

6. *Equal Treatment*

Has the company applied its rules, orders and penalties evenhandedly and without discrimination to all employees?

- A "no" answer to this question will almost always defeat any notion of "just cause," and will generally be good proof of discrimination of some kind as well. In the arbitration setting, a "no" answer here will almost certainly result in the discipline being revoked. If there is to be a "no" answer to this question, the company *must* establish a legitimate reason for the difference in treatment among employees.

- If the company has been lax in enforcing its rules and orders consistently in the past, but decides to apply them consistently in the future, the company may avoid a finding of discrimination by giving notice to all employees of its intention to begin consistently enforcing all rules as written. The company must thereafter be fully prepared to consistently enforce its rules – and actually do it.

7. *Penalty*

Was the degree of discipline administered by the company in a particular case reasonably related to the seriousness of the employee's proven offense and the record of the employee in his or her service with the company?

- A trivial, proven offense does not merit harsh discipline unless the employee properly has been found guilty of the same or other offenses a number of times in the past. (There is no rule as to what number of previous offenses constitutes a good, a fair or a bad record. Therefore, reasonable judgment must be used.)

- An employee's record of previous offenses may never be used to prove whether he or she is guilty of the immediate or latest one. The only proper use of his or her record is to help determine the severity of discipline once he or she has properly been found guilty of the immediate offense.

- Given the same proven offense for two or more employees, their respective records provide the only proper basis for discriminating among them in the administration of discipline for an offense. Thus, if employee A's record is significantly better than those of employees B, C, and D, the company may properly give a lighter punishment than it gives the others for the same offense, and this would not constitute true discrimination.

* * * * * * * * *

Unless the employee at issue has signed a valid, legally enforceable agreement to release your company from liability for a discharge, there can be no guarantee that the employee will not challenge the decision in court, arbitration, or an administrative action. By following the steps outlined in this chapter, however, you will have acted as proactively as possible toward reducing the likelihood that a decision-maker will find that your company acted improperly.

CHAPTER 18: Unemployment Benefit Issues

Many Michigan employers must observe the requirements of the Michigan Employment Security Act (MESA), which provides for the contribution of unemployment taxes, reimbursement of benefits, and ultimate payment of unemployment benefits to eligible claimants. A basic understanding of the issues surrounding the MESA, and employers' rights under the Act, is crucial.

The MESA was enacted to combat the threat that unemployment poses to the health, morals, and welfare of the state. MESA created a mechanism to provide for the systematic accumulation of funds, during periods of employment, to be used for the benefit of individuals who become unemployed through no fault of their own.

The Michigan Unemployment Insurance Agency (UIA) is the state agency within the state Department of Labor and Economic Growth that administers the MESA. UIA is a current moniker that succeeds many other names with which employers may be more familiar, such as the Michigan Unemployment Agency, the Bureau of Workers and Unemployment Compensation, etc.

For a comprehensive and inexpensive guide to UIA coverage, liability, records, reports, penalties, taxes, payment of benefits, etc., the UIA Employer Handbook is recommended. Employers can receive a copy of the $15.00 handbook – which describes all topics discussed under this section – by completing and mailing the order form included in the back of this book. The listed price includes shipping and handling.

This Chapter discusses the basic issues facing employers covered by the MESA, highlights the practical concerns associated with contesting a claim for benefits, and describes the most recent amendments to the MESA. The Michigan Unemployment Insurance Agency is generally referred to as either the "UIA" or the unemployment agency.

Basic Provisions

Coverage Under MESA

An "employing unit" becomes liable under the MESA when it: (1) pays $1,000.00 or more in wages for covered employees in a single calendar year; or (2) employs at least one employee in covered employment in 20 or more calendar weeks in a calendar year; or (3) purchases or otherwise acquires an employer already covered under the Act; or (4) pays at least $1,000 in cash for nursing care, housekeeping, or a similar service, in any quarter; or (5) pays $20,000 in cash in any quarter for agricultural services, or employs 10 or more agricultural workers in each of 20 different calendar weeks; or (6) elects to be covered under the MESA.

Covered Employment

Employers are required to contribute only for workers engaged in covered employment, or employment that takes place in Michigan, is controlled from Michigan, or when no other state collects unemployment taxes for the worker. Employment is also covered if the worker's residence is in Michigan. Services performed in the employ of the United States government or an instrumentality of the United States government, exempt under the constitution of the United States from the contributions imposed by this Act, are not covered by the Act. True independent contractors – who work under the direction and control of another and provide their own equipment – are not entitled to benefits from the contracting employer. Merely labeling an employee an independent contractor, however, does not permit an employer to escape coverage under the MESA.

Definition of "Unemployed"

Under the MESA, claimants are considered "unemployed" for any week that they perform no services *and* receive no remuneration, or for any week of less than full-time work where the remuneration is less than the claimant's weekly benefit rate. All amounts paid to a claimant by an employer for a vacation or holiday, and amounts paid in the form of retroactive pay, pay in lieu of notice, severance payments, salary continuation, or other remuneration intended by the employer as continuing wages, excluding a supplemental unemployment benefit plan, shall be considered remuneration in determining whether an individual is unemployed.

The Difference Between Reimbursing and Contributing Employers

All covered employers must pay state unemployment taxes. Some employers are allowed to simply reimburse the UIA for dollars paid to their employees under the Act, while others must contribute taxes. Contributing employers pay state unemployment taxes on the first $9,000.00 of wages paid to each worker performing covered services in a calendar year. Under state law, all for-profit employers are contributing employers. The actual amount of the unemployment tax is computed using the employer's state unemployment tax rate.

The Unemployment Insurance Tax

Both contributing and reimbursing employers must pay an unemployment insurance tax. For contributing employers, the tax is determined by multiplying the first $9,000 of a covered employee's annual wages by the employer's unemployment tax rates. The tax rate begins at 2.7%, but changes after the first two years of coverage based upon a number of factors, including the employer's history of benefit claims. Reimbursing employers pay taxes equal to the benefits paid to their employees plus the amount of extended benefits and training benefits paid during any calendar quarter that is attributable to service in the employ of such organization and which is not reimbursable by the federal government. Each calendar quarter, contributing employers receive a Quarterly Tax Report that requests information about an employer's payroll for that quarter. The Report shows the employer's tax rate for that year.

Determination of Tax Rates

The UIA uses three separate components to determine an employer's tax rate. These are:

(1) The Chargeable Benefit Component (CBC) – determined by dividing the total unemployment charges against the employer by the amount of wages, subject to contributions, paid by the employer for the most recent 5 years (ranging from 0% to 6.3%);

(2) The Account Building Component (ABC) – based upon the employer's payroll for the current year (ranging from 0% to 3%); and

(3) The Non-Chargeable Benefits Component – used to pay benefits that cannot be charged to a specific employer's account (will not exceed 1%).

Note that the minimum tax rate is .06%. Employers that violate unemployment tax and compensation laws may also incur additional percentage increases, up to a total tax rate of 13%. Presently, however, an across the board tax rate reduction lowers the maximum tax rate.

In addition to the state unemployment tax, contributing employers must also pay a federal unemployment insurance tax. If an employer pays the state tax on time, it will receive a credit toward the federal tax. The net federal tax, after full credit, is .8% multiplied by the first $7,000.00 of wages of each employee covered under federal law.

The Charging of Benefits Against Employer Accounts

Benefits paid to employees are charged against an employer's account for the quarter in which they are made. If the UIA discovers that any of those benefits were improperly paid, it will credit the employer's account, as well as make a corresponding credit to the employer's non-chargeable benefits account. No credit will be allowed to employers for benefits paid to a claimant as a result of an employer's failure to provide the UIA with separation, employment and wage data.

Record-Keeping and Filing Requirements for Covered Employers

Under the MESA, covered employers must maintain accurate payroll records for each covered employee for *at least* 6 years after the time period in which wages were paid. Further, covered employers must file a Registration for Michigan Business Taxes Form, as well as quarterly tax reports. A full description of the payroll records, filings, and appropriate forms for each filing is contained within the UIA's Employer Handbook. Failure to file the appropriate forms on time will result in penalties. Willful violations of the Act can result in both civil and criminal penalties.

Employment of Seasonal Workers

Employers of seasonal workers may request the ability to deny benefits to workers between seasons if the employer has given workers a "reasonable assurance" of returning to work the following season. This rule also applies to schoolteachers, some other school employees and professional athletes claiming unemployment benefits.

Pregnant Workers on Leave of Absence

Pregnant workers placed on mandatory leaves of absence are entitled to unemployment compensation, as long as they are able to work during the leave. Pregnant workers who take voluntary leaves of absence, however, will not be considered "unemployed" and may not receive benefits during the voluntary leave period.

Claims for Benefits and Qualifying Requirements

Claimants may file their claim in-person, by mail, telephone, or the Internet. The claim must be filed on or before Friday of the week following the week containing the last day of work. However, the unemployment agency will not usually deny claims solely because they are filed outside of this time period. Claimants qualify for benefits by having wages of at least $2,774.00 in one quarter of employment, and having total wages in the other three quarters of one and one half times the highest amount of wages in any quarter of the "base period" ($4,161.00). Claimants may also qualify by having wages in at least two quarters and total wages for all four quarters of at least 20 times the state average weekly wage, which in 2008 was $16,400.80.

The UIA awards benefits to eligible claimants for a specified number of weeks. Under the MESA, an eligible claimant may be awarded benefits for not more than 26 weeks, but not less than 14 weeks, in a given benefit year. If a claimant dies or is declared mentally incompetent during this period, benefits for weeks of unemployment before death become immediately due and payable to that person's legal heir or guardian.

Claimants' Eligibility Requirements

To be eligible for benefits, claimants must be unemployed and available to accept suitable full-time work. Claimants must also show that they are actively seeking work. Finally, claimants must register with the unemployment agency for work within 5 days of applying for benefits. Eligible claimants receive up to $362.00 per week. Claimants must periodically re-certify their eligibility if they wish to continue receiving benefits. Also note that employers are only charged for benefits that jobless workers actually collect. If a claimant collects less than the total amount for which they receive an award, the balance of the award is not charged against the employer's account. A claimant who limits his availability to jobs that do not require work on his or her Sabbath is not deemed ineligible for benefits.

If a claimant cannot demonstrate that he or she is expected to return to his or her previous work within 120 days, that claimant must register for work at the unemployment agency and seek assistance in finding a job. Also, claimants must demonstrate that they possess the ability to work. Claimants are required to present evidence that they can return to the same type of work they did in the past. If they cannot, benefits will be denied.

The Formula for Determining Benefits

The weekly benefit rate for a claimant is determined by calculating 4.1% of the claimant's wages paid in the calendar quarter of the base period in which the claimant was paid the highest total wages, plus $6.00 for each dependent, up to a maximum of 5 dependents.

Re-Qualifying After Receiving Benefits

A worker can re-qualify for benefits by going back to work and earning wages. The amount of wages a worker must earn to re-qualify is the lesser of: (a) the worker's weekly benefit amount times seven, or (b) 40 times the state minimum hourly wage times seven.

The Determination of Benefits

Following a claim for benefits, the UIA issues a written determination to both the employer and the claimant. The document contains the decision of the UIA, as well as the reasons for that decision. Following the initial determination, the claimant or employer may protest the decision. Any protest must be received in writing by the 30th day after the date the determination was issued. Following the protest, the UIA issues a re-determination of the initial determination. This second document affirms or reverses the initial determination, and either grants or denies benefits to the claimant. The UIA's decisions rest upon existing facts of the particular matter and the applicable law.

Coordination of Unemployment and Workers' Compensation Benefits

Occasionally, an employee simultaneously files both worker's compensation and unemployment benefits claims for overlapping periods of time. Fortunately, the Legislature provided for this contingency. The Workers Disability Compensation Act provides that net weekly benefits under the Act shall be reduced by 100% of the amount of benefits paid or payable under the Michigan Employment Security Act. Thus, there is a dollar for dollar set-off between the two acts. Also, the Michigan Supreme Court has held that lump-sum pension payments under employer-funded plans should be coordinated with unemployment benefits.

Appeal to the Unemployment Insurance Agency ALJ

If an employer does not prevail upon the determination or re-determination, the next available avenue is an appeal to the Unemployment Insurance Agency ALJ, sometimes referred to as an Administrative Law Judge or ALJ. Appeals must be received within 30 days of the mailing of the last determination/re-determination. Upon receipt, the unemployment agency ALJ schedules and sends out notices for a hearing. Both the employer and claimant may be represented by an attorney at the hearing. In order to make the hearings accessible to claimants, every claimant can request and receive the assistance of an agent – an advocate appointed by the UIA – at the hearing. The materials below discuss how to prepare for and prevail at an UIAN ALJ hearing.

Preparing a Case for the ALJ

The ALJ's decision is one that can be of great significance to an employer, so it is important to know how to best prepare and present one's case.

The employer must be prepared to marshal all of its facts, make sure that its witnesses will be available for the hearing, prepare them for their testimony, and present the most effective case possible. ALJs may allow the employer to present its case through oral argument and documents. The most common practice, however, is for the ALJ to permit only witness testimony without giving parties the opportunity to make opening or closing arguments. For this reason, it is essential to make sure that witnesses are thoroughly familiar with the facts underlying the claimant's allegations, and the employer's decision. Because ALJ dockets are invariably crowded, ALJs prefer to conduct hearings as efficiently as possible. Preparation is essential to reduce unnecessary delay.

ALJs are not constrained to follow the determinations and/or re-determinations issued below. An ALJ possesses the discretion to look at all of the evidence anew. Presenting a case to the ALJ is crucial because the hearing is the employer's final opportunity to present factual evidence. Although an ALJ decision can be appealed, the employer is no longer freely permitted to introduce new evidence. Appeals usually involve questions of law, rather than fact. The steps necessary to prepare for a hearing are outlined below.

1. Identify and Collect the Relevant Documents

Prior to the hearing, the employer must gather all relevant documents. The following documents should be made available to counsel or the employer's representative as far in advance of the hearing as possible:

a. The collective bargaining agreement, work rules, handbook, personnel policies, etc., which govern the employee's conduct;

b. Signed acknowledgments (if any) demonstrating that the claimant received and understood the applicable policies and work rules;

c. The employee's entire personnel file and the personnel files of all similarly situated employees and former employees;

d. Written statements or notes from any witnesses;

e. Summaries of information prepared by management employees relative to the case;

f. Copies of prior unemployment agency decisions on similar or identical issues;

g. Any documents tending to show the applicability of disqualifying provisions.

2. Identify and Prepare Witnesses

Employers must identify all persons who have first-hand knowledge of the facts relevant to a case. Hearsay evidence is generally not admissible, and where it is admitted, it generally is not given very much weight. All of the employer's witnesses should be interviewed in advance of the hearing to obtain their knowledge of the case. They must also be prepared for their testimony so that they can most effectively present management's case at the hearing through straightforward questions and answers. Employer witnesses will be cross-examined by the claimant or claimant's representative, so it is essential that they be prepared for this occurrence. They must understand the procedures to be utilized, the questions that they will be asked, and how to conduct themselves at the hearing. Finally, witnesses must be prepared to present the employer's case without using technical language or confusing, industry-specific terms. If the ALJ cannot easily grasp concepts used by an employer's witnesses, the employer is not likely to prevail.

3. Identify the Documents to be Used at the Hearing

Discretion should be utilized in determining which documents will be used as exhibits. Some documents may contain information that can be submitted equally well through oral testimony. This should certainly be done where the document also contains damaging information. Employers should obtain the best documents for the hearing – documents that are vague or difficult to understand will not be persuasive unless explained by a well-prepared witness.

4. Remember that Credibility is Everything

An ALJ probably will not render a decision in favor of a party who he or she believes has lied. Management must make sure that its witnesses testify in a credible and consistent manner, and that they do not contradict themselves or each other. To ensure this, employers should conduct a preparation session that includes all employer witnesses. Equally important is the ability to successfully attack a claimant's credibility. Management can assist counsel in preparing this attack by providing him or her with the employee's personnel record and information regarding statements made by the opposing party or his or her witnesses relative to the facts of the case.

5. Focus on the Pertinent Issues

Where a claimant's case is weak, he or she will usually assert peripheral and irrelevant matters in an effort to confuse the issue. In such cases, management must set aside the smoke screen and focus the ALJ on the facts that are truly relevant. If management must utilize peripheral issues in order to win, however, it should probably reevaluate its position on the case.

6. Proceed with Proper Decorum

Emotional outbursts or attacks on the other party are not persuasive and may damage an employer's case. Attempts to browbeat or humiliate any opponent are usually counterproductive. Aggressive cross-examination of adverse witnesses is often a potent weapon to be used, but the degree to which an opponent is to be attacked must be carefully measured. Conversely, the aggressiveness of an opponent's cross-examination of an employer witness may be moderated by the use of well-timed objections. Prior to the hearing, the employer should remind its witnesses to answer any questions from the ALJ directly. Failure to do so will most likely decrease the credibility of the witness in the ALJ's eyes.

Recommendations for ALJ Hearings

In addition to the general suggestions provided, the following specific recommendations should be observed.

1. Examine the "UIA Media" Prior to the Hearing

An employer has the right to examine the unemployment agency's file on a case prior to the hearing. In most cases, the file is available for review prior to the hearing date. The most significant document is the claimant's handwritten statement of his case. This is usually a good indication of the version of the facts that the claimant will submit to the ALJ. It is important to know the content of this statement so that when the claimant testifies in a manner inconsistent with the written statement, his or her credibility can be effectively attacked.

These documents should be examined prior to the day of the hearing for two reasons. First, it will give the employer time in which to gather documents to rebut any claims set forth in this statement, and to locate and prepare witnesses who may have evidence contrary to the statements made by the claimant. Second, some ALJs prefer that the parties review unemployment agency media prior to the hearing so that their time is not taken up waiting for the employer to finish reading the documents.

2. Identify the Disqualifying Provision That Applies to the Case

It is critical, in both the employer's written responses to the unemployment agency and in the hearing, to understand the provision(s) of the Act under which the employer is trying to disqualify the claimant. The reason for the disqualification must be contained in the employer's written responses to the unemployment agency, because the reasons listed in the notice of hearing are the only issues that may be raised at the hearing. Thus, if the employer's best argument is that an employee voluntarily quit without good cause attributable to the employer, it should not state that the employee's separation was due to intentional misconduct.

A claimant may be disqualified for various periods of time where he or she:

a. Left work voluntarily without good cause attributable to the employer or employing unit. Note that a claimant who leaves work is presumed to have left work voluntarily without good cause. If the individual has an established benefit year in effect and, during that benefit year, has left unsuitable work within 60 days after the beginning of that work, such leaving shall not be disqualifying.

b. Was discharged for misconduct connected with the individual's work, or for intoxication while at work unless the discharge was subsequently reduced to a disciplinary layoff or suspension.

c. Failed without good cause to apply for available suitable work of which the individual was notified by the employment office or the unemployment agency.

d. Being unemployed, failed without good cause to report to the individual's former employer or employing unit within a reasonable time after notice from that employer or employing unit for an interview concerning available suitable work with the former employer or employing unit.

e. Failed without good cause to accept suitable work when offered, or to return to the individual's customary self-employment, if any, when directed by the employment office or the unemployment agency.

f. Lost his or her job by reason of being absent from work as a result of a violation of law for which the individual was convicted **and** sentenced to jail or prison. This provision does not apply if conviction of a person results in a sentence to county jail under conditions of day parole or when the conviction was for a traffic violation that resulted in an absence of less than ten consecutive workdays from the individual's place of employment.

g. Is discharged, whether or not the discharge is subsequently reduced to a disciplinary layoff or suspension for participation in a strike or other concerted action resulting in curtailment of work or restriction of or interference with production, contrary to the provisions of an applicable collective bargaining agreement; or participation in a wildcat strike or other concerted action not authorized by the individual's recognized bargaining representative.

h. Was discharged for an act of assault and battery connected with the individual's work.

i. Was discharged for theft connected with the individual's work.

j. Was discharged for willful destruction of property connected with the individual's work

k. Committed a theft which occurred subsequent to a notice of layoff or discharge, but prior to the effective date of layoff or discharge, resulting in loss or damage to the employer who would otherwise be chargeable for the benefits, notwithstanding that the original layoff or discharge was under non-disqualifying circumstances.

l. Was employed by a temporary help firm, where the temporary help firm provided the employee with a written notice before the employee began performing services for the client stating in substance both (A) that within 7 days after completing services for a client of the temporary help firm, the employee is under a duty to notify the temporary help firm of the completion of those services, and (B) that a failure to provide the temporary help firm with notice of the employee's completion of services pursuant to sub-subparagraph (A) constitutes a voluntary quit that will affect the employee's eligibility for unemployment compensation should the employee seek unemployment compensation following completion of those services; and where the employee did not provide the temporary help firm with notice that the employee had completed his or her services for the client within 7 days after completion of his or her services for the client.

m. Was discharged for illegally ingesting, injecting, inhaling, or possessing a controlled substance on the premises of the employer, refusing to submit to a drug test that was required to be administered in a nondiscriminatory manner, or testing positive on a drug test, if the test was administered in a nondiscriminatory manner.

3. Be Organized

Many cases are scheduled for a one-hour time slot and most ALJs are very protective of this limitation. An employer who is fumbling around to find documents and doesn't seem to have its questions and witnesses organized will not make a friend of the ALJ. Management's presentation at the hearing should be as concise as possible. A focused presentation of a few strong arguments is more effective than a presentation of a few strong arguments and numerous weak ones. Similarly, it is important to be on time for the hearing. It can be especially embarrassing to be late for a hearing where the employer is trying to disqualify a claimant who was discharged for repeated tardiness. Note that the proceedings before the ALJ are recorded. Following the hearing, the ALJ creates a transcript summarizing all the testimony and exhibits. The employer should always request and retain a copy of the transcript, whether it intends to appeal the decision or not. Such information may become useful in future lawsuits or unemployment proceedings.

4. In Intentional Misconduct Cases, Be Sure to Prove that the Claimant Knew That His Conduct Was Proper Before He Engaged in It

"Misconduct" has been defined by the Michigan Supreme Court to mean conduct evidencing a willful or wanton disregard of an employer's interests. A critical element of disqualifying an employee for intentional misconduct is to establish that he or she had knowledge of the rule that was violated or had previously been warned not to engage in the type of conduct that led to the discharge. Without such proof, it may be difficult to establish that the claimant's misconduct was "intentional." Proof of this element may be established through introduction of a specific provision contained in the employer's handbook, along with the employee's signed acknowledgment of receipt. Some examples of behavior constituting misconduct include:

1. Failure of a municipal employee to reside within the city where employed, where such residence was required by the employer;
2. Sleeping on the job;
3. Intoxication on the job, if such intoxication can be substantiated;
4. An employee's refusal to carry out a foreman's order, coupled with a threat to punch the foreman;
5. An employee's failure to pay union dues;
6. A series of acts that, taken together, evidence a willful disregard of an employer's interests; and
7. Leaving work early after eight reprimands, concurrent with unsatisfactory work performance

Examples of acts found not to constitute misconduct are:

1. Violation of a collective bargaining agreement provision;
2. Mere inefficiency;
3. Failure in the result of good performance as the result of inability or incapacity;
4. Good-faith errors in judgment;
5. Ordinary negligence in isolated instances;
6. An employee's use of vulgar language, if that type of language is condoned by the employer, or regularly tolerated in the workplace, and is not friendly badgering; and
7. Where an employee whose wages were garnished twice within nine months (in violation of an employer rule) was discharged.

5. In "Voluntary Quit" Cases, Prove That the Employer Did Not Engage in Conduct Which Would Cause a Reasonable Person to Quit

An employee who quits and then seeks unemployment benefits must establish that the resignation was due to conduct attributable to the employer. For instance, an employee who quits after being given the choice of resigning or being fired will be considered to have been discharged rather than having resigned. Similarly, an individual who quits her job because her payroll checks have been bouncing will not be deemed to have voluntarily quit and will receive benefits. Also, an employee who is prevented from returning to work by a physical condition or illness will not be deemed to have quit if the employer cannot offer the employee a job he or she is capable of performing. Many similar examples exist. Any witness with knowledge of the reasons for the claimant's resignation must be brought to the hearing. Employers must also bring written resignation notices or exit interview notes, if they exist.

Appealing an ALJ Decision

There are three different ways to appeal adverse ALJ decisions. The first is to request a re-hearing from the ALJ. This avenue may be pursued only if the employer acquires newly-discovered relevant evidence after the date of the hearing.

The second way to seek review of a decision is to appeal to the Michigan Employment Security Board of Review. Under Michigan law, all parties may appeal to the Board of Review. The Board will supply a copy of the transcript to each party. Subsequently, the Board will review the transcript of the ALJ hearing in an attempt to decide whether the ALJ made correct findings of fact based upon the evidence presented.

After reviewing the transcript, the Board will affirm, modify, or reverse the ALJ's decision. The Board may also remand the case to the ALJ for a further hearing in order to obtain more facts necessary to decide the case.

Although the Board of Review may entertain additional oral argument, such argument is usually not allowed. If oral argument is desired, the employer must so state in its appeal. The Board of Review will accept additional written argument if all parties agree that written argument may be considered, or if all parties are represented by an attorney or agent, or if the Board requests written argument.

The third and final avenue is a direct appeal to a circuit court. Employers may only utilize this method if both parties agree, or if an appeal has already been heard and decided by the Board of Review.

Notable Recent Statutory Amendments

As a result of pressure on lawmakers to increase unemployment benefits as plant closings and layoffs become commonplace, the Michigan Employment Security Act was amended in 2002. The Act raised the maximum weekly benefit from $300 to $362 dollars and allowed unemployed individuals to receive such benefits immediately. The amendments took effect on April 29, 2002.

The amendments provided for the reduction of taxes for employers who do not lay off any workers for five years or more. Additionally, the law provided tax savings to employers by reducing the taxable wage base from the first $9,500 of an employee's wages to the first $9,000 of such wages. Also, the amendments shifted the burden of proof to the claimant in cases involving an individual who voluntarily quits his or her job or who is fired for misconduct. Prior to the amendments, employers were required to demonstrate that a claimant left work voluntarily without good cause. Now, claimants are presumed to have left work voluntarily without good cause and must submit evidence to rebut this presumption.

The law also requires an Indian tribe or tribal unit to pay reimbursements instead of contributions to the Unemployment Compensation Fund, unless it elects otherwise. Indian tribes do so under the same terms and conditions as all other reimbursing employers. This newly-added provision also requires that Indian tribes or tribal units that elect to make contributions shall file a written request for that election prior to January 1 of the calendar year in which the election will be effective. If the Indian tribe fails to make reimbursement payments in lieu of contributions, within 90 days after the mailing of a notice of delinquency, the tribe will lose the ability to make payments in lieu of contributions immediately, unless the delinquent amount is paid in full.

The amended law also created the Unemployment Insurance Agency (UIA) within the Department of Labor & Economic Growth (formerly known as the Department of Consumer and Industry Services). The UIA received all of the authority, powers, functions, duties, and responsibilities of the unemployment agency. The UIA is headed by a director, who is appointed by the Governor.

Section 3 of the amendments states the goals of the UIA as follows: (1) to reduce and prevent unemployment; (2) to promote the reemployment of unemployed workers; (3) to carry on and publish the results of investigations and research studies; and (4) to investigate, recommend, advise and assist in the establishment of reserves for public works to be used in times of business depression and unemployment.

Other notable 2002 amendments to the Act included:

a. An increase in the number of weeks a person must work (from 13 to 26 weeks, depending on the reason for disqualification), or alternatively, the amount a person must earn (again, depending on the reason for disqualification), to qualify for benefits after a disqualifying act or discharge.

b. The classification of severance pay as "wages" for purposes of unemployment status and amount of benefits determinations.

c. A decrease in the maximum "nonchargeable benefits component" of the formula that determines an employer's contribution, depending on the number of weeks in which there were no benefit charges against the employer's account (from 1.0% for 60 months with no charges and decreased by 0.1% for every additional 12 months with no charges, with reductions in 0.01% increments after calendar year 2002 for 60 months, and 12-month increments thereafter).

d. A requirement that an Indian tribe or tribal unit pay reimbursements instead of contributions to the Unemployment Compensation Fund, unless it elects otherwise.

e. The creation of an Internet site to track receipt of correspondence from the employer to the unemployment agency.

f. A reduction in the amount one must unlawfully convert before becoming subject to a damages provision. Under the amended Act, if an employer, officer of an employer, or benefits claimant knowingly or willfully appropriates or converts money to be used for the payment of benefits under the Act, that person shall repay that amount plus damages equal to four times that amount (if the amount is over $500.00). The Amended Act also lowers the threshold for imprisonment for 1 year or less.

g. An increase in the penalties for those who willingly or intentionally fail to comply with any of the provisions of the Act.

h. As noted above, a decrease in the "taxable wage limit" to $9,000 (from $9,500) for 2002 and for all calendar years following 2002. The taxable wage limit is used to determine the amount of contributions due from an employer under the Act. This amendment also stated that tips, that are actually reported to the employer by an employee who receives tip income, will now be used to determine the amount of an employer's contribution.

i. Renaming the "commission" the "unemployment agency."

SUTA "Dumping" Prevention

In 2004, President Bush signed into law the State Unemployment Tax Act ("SUTA") Dumping Prevention Act of 2004. Under the Act, unemployment tax "dumping" occurs when a covered employer forms a new company and transfers some employees to the new company, which is assigned a lower, "new company" unemployment tax rate, with the intent of reducing overall unemployment taxes. Dumping can also be accomplished by transferring employees to a subsidiary with a lower tax rate, or by arranging to transfer employees to another employer with a lower tax rate. Under the Act, employers found to have engaged in this practice face a monetary penalty up four times the amount of the employer's savings through dumping.

In response to the federal law, Michigan enacted four laws that went into effect on July 1, 2005 to prohibit "state unemployment tax act dumping." Employers commit SUTA dumping when they transfer portions of their payroll (i.e., employees) to subsidiaries, shell companies, or other employers with lower unemployment tax rates.

The Michigan Department of Labor and Economic Growth previously estimated that dumping creates losses to Michigan's unemployment trust fund at an estimated $62 to $95 million per year. To combat this practice, the UIA assembled a team of investigators to build cases against companies currently engaged in dumping practices, with an eye toward bringing civil and criminal penalties against those companies.

Michigan is taking an aggressive approach to enforcing the new SUTA dumping laws. In just its first month of enforcement in 2005, a SUTA dumping team announced the recovery of approximately $55,000 in unpaid taxes, penalties and interest from three Michigan employers. The Michigan Unemployment Insurance Agency alleged that all three employers engaged in SUTA dumping by failing to pay their full share of unemployment taxes. The first employer, which agreed to repay approximately $10,000, set up two unemployment insurance accounts with the Unemployment Insurance Agency and transferred employees from one account to another, depending on which account had the lower tax rate at the time. The second employer, which agreed to pay over $28,500, established a new unemployment account and transferred its employees to that account. The third employer agreed to repay approximately $17,000 after it created a new account with a lower tax rate and transferred some of its employees to the new account.

The Director of Michigan's Unemployment Insurance Agency indicated that the Agency identified these three employers with the help of tips. The Agency employs field auditors and fraud investigators trained to identify possible cases of SUTA dumping. In the near future, the Agency will also begin using specially designed computer software to identify patterns of employer behavior that demonstrate unemployment tax avoidance. More recently, the Unemployment Insurance Agency announced that it received a $112,035 grant from the U.S. Department of Labor to help Michigan detect and prevent SUTA dumping. The Agency announced that the funds will be used to implement the software referenced above and to train agency staff who enforce anti-dumping laws.

As it is clear that Michigan will continue to aggressively enforce its SUTA dumping laws in these tight budget times, employers are encouraged to consult either with their employment counsel or the UIA to make sure that its actions do not run afoul of these laws.

CHAPTER 19: Safety and Health Issues

One of the most significant issues affecting Michigan employers today is the question of what steps an employer must take to provide employees with safe workplaces and equipment. Science and technology play increasingly significant roles by introducing new equipment, materials and applications to the workplace that change the physical makeup of the worksite. Through studies and research, scientists have uncovered many previously unseen dangers, such as the effects that protracted or even occasional exposure to various chemicals may have on workers.

The United States Congress passed the Occupational Safety and Health Act (OSH Act) to see that these types of issues would be addressed. The OSH Act also encouraged individual states to adopt their own conforming plans, which the states could administer. Michigan responded with the adoption of the Michigan Occupational Safety and Health Act (MIOSHA), which is now primarily responsible for workplace safety and health enforcement. However, the Occupational Safety and Health Administration (OSHA) oversees state programs to assure their conformity with safety requirements, and retains authority to resume enforcement from nonconforming states. Further, many plans adopt by reference OSHA standards as their own, and enforce the rules locally.

These issues are considerable and are generating an increasing amount of attention and significance. In recent years, bills have been introduced in both houses of Congress to dramatically increase enforcement efforts, employee training programs, and penalties for violations, including larger fines and greater imposition of criminal liability.

Employers should be familiar with the structures of the OSH Act and MIOSHA and the relationship between the federal and state agencies. Obviously, it is not feasible in this handbook to detail all of the standards affecting Michigan employers. Employers must know the requirements with the Hazard Communication Standard, community Right-To-Know laws, emergency planning regulations, and other environment-based standards that affect employees and the workplace.

The Michigan Occupational Safety & Health Administration (MIOSHA), previously known as the Bureau of Safety Regulation, is the proper name for the Michigan agency regulating workplace safety and health.

MIOSHA is organized into the General Industry Safety & Health Division and the Construction Safety & Health Division. In the past Occupational Health responsibilities were performed in a separate Division. MIOSHA's integration of occupational health responsibilities into the General Industry and Construction Safety Divisions is intended to provide more coordinated inspections of safety and health conditions at employers' workplaces. The Management and Technical Services Division performs standards development, data collection and analysis, Freedom of Information Act request processing, laboratory services, equipment maintenance, information technology, and financial services. MIOSHA's Consultation, Education & Training Division assists employers in addressing workplace safety and health issues. The Appeals & Contested Division handles all formally contested citations resulting from MIOSHA enforcement action.

The basic MIOSHA organization chart, as of December 2008, looked like this:

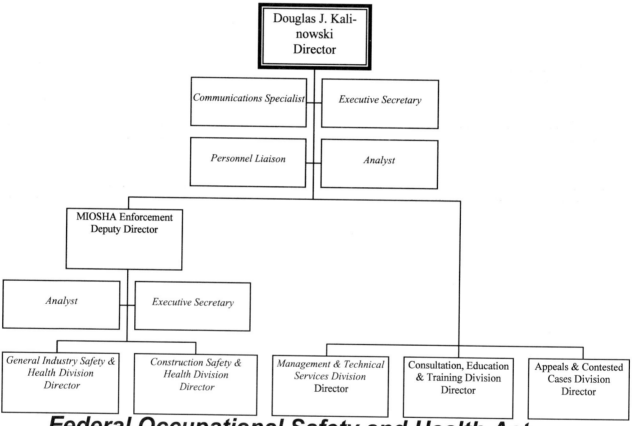

Federal Occupational Safety and Health Act

The Occupational Safety and Health Act (OSH Act) of 1970 marked the first comprehensive federal law governing safety and health conditions. Prior to enactment of the OSH Act, federal job safety and health efforts were limited to individual laws covering federal contractors. The OSH Act does not govern the working conditions of employees in industries where another federal agency exercises statutory authority to prescribe or enforce occupational safety and health standards.

Federal Agencies Created by the OSH Act

Three agencies were created to implement the OSH Act's objective of providing safe and healthful working conditions for all workers.

The best-known agency, the Occupational Safety and Health Administration (OSHA), is part of the United States DOL and is responsible for the promulgation of safety and health standards through the rule-making proceedings as well as through the OSH Act's general duty clause.

The Occupational Safety and Health Review Commission (OSHRC) is the adjudicative agency that determines the propriety of contested citations.

The National Institute for Occupational Safety and Health (NIOSH), in the Department of Health and Human Services, is the agency that researches and recommends workplace health standards.

Enforcement of the OSH Act

General responsibility for enforcement of the OSH Act is vested in the Secretary of Labor, who may issue citations carrying monetary penalties for violations. An Assistant Secretary of Labor for Occupational Safety and Health has been delegated this general responsibility and functions as the chief administrator of the OSH Act.

OSHA Inspections

Enforcement of OSHA safety and health standards takes place by on-site inspections of work sites. Inspections may be initiated by a specific complaint about an unsafe working condition or in accordance with a routine schedule designed by patterns of illnesses and injuries. In either case, if an employer refuses to permit the inspection, OSHA can pursue a search warrant in federal district court requiring the employer to allow access to the facility for OSHA inspectors to determine if any safety or health violations exist.

OSHA Citations

Citations should specify the safety and health violations found by OSHA after conducting a workplace inspection. In addition to specific standards, the OSH Act requires employers to provide safe and healthful working conditions for employees under its general duty clause. Citations will specify the amount of any fine assessed, which is determined primarily by the severity of the violations.

OSHA Violations, Standards, and General Safety

Violation types include other-than-serious (often referred to as non-serious), serious, willful, and repeat. OSHA must consider the employer's good faith, the gravity of the violation, the employer's history of compliance and the size of the company when it assesses a penalty. Criminal sanctions also exist for willful violations involving the death of an employee but enforcement of these is vested in Department of Justice rather than in OSHA.

When an employer can demonstrate that an alternative proposed method will be at least as effective as the OSHA standard in providing safe and healthful working conditions to employees, OSHA is authorized to grant a variance from its standard to the employer.

Occupational Safety and Health Review Commission

The desire for a separate forum to resolve disputes involving citations led to the creation of a second agency under the OSH Act. The Occupational Safety and Health Review Commission (OSHRC) is an independent body responsible for adjudicating cases involving challenges to OSHA citations. The Commission has three members, appointed by the President, by and with the advice and consent of the Senate, for staggered six-year terms.

An employer challenges a citation by filing a Notice of Contest with the OSHA office that issued the citation. That office sends the citation and Notice of Contest to the Review Commission of Adjudication, which assigns an administrative law judge to conduct a hearing and to recommend a decision embodying findings of fact and conclusions of law. If there is no appeal of the administrative law judge's decision, it becomes a final order of OSHRC. Challenges to the recommended decision may be filed with the OSHRC, in the form of a petition for review.

A decision by the OSHRC on the petition for review may be further challenged in the federal courts of appeals. As with other cases decided by the federal courts of appeals, review may then be sought in the Supreme Court.

National Institute for Occupational Safety and Health

The third agency established under the OSH Act is the National Institute for Occupational Safety and Health (NIOSH). Part of the Public Health Service in the Department of Health and Human Services, the agency conducts research activities concerning safety and health in the workplace.

Either employers or employees may request NIOSH to conduct health hazard evaluations in addition to the research data the agency collects in its routine research investigations. NIOSH retains jurisdiction over research and its study of industrial problems is not preempted even when a state enforces its own safety and health requirements under a state plan. NIOSH cannot issue citations for violations observed during an employee-initiated health hazard evaluation or research investigation.

The agency's major purpose is to recommend new safety and health standards to OSHA. A form called a criteria document details the safety or health risk addressed by NIOSH and recommends a standard with provisions that will alleviate the identified risk. Data in the criteria documents frequently motivate OSHA to initiate rule-making proceedings to set a new safety or health standard.

Employers Subject to the OSH Act

The coverage of the OSH Act provisions must be understood in the context of other programs involving federal oversight of local matters. There must be a basis for federal involvement, in this case the promotion of interstate commerce by promoting safe workplaces and a uniformity of minimum work safety regulations coordinated between various governmental entities. There are two areas of consideration:

- The general coverage of the Act in terms of jurisdictional bases.
- The Act's exemption relating to industries and employers with respect to workplaces in the United States and its territories.

The term "employer" is defined as a person engaged in a business affecting commerce who has employees. The term "person" is defined as one or more individuals, partnerships, associations, corporations, business trust, legal representatives, or any organized group of person. Thus, in order for an employer to be covered by the Act, it must:

- be in a business affecting commerce, and
- have employees.

Employers in OSHA litigation have addressed each of those qualifications. It should be noted that OSHA has generally determined that most Indian Tribal enterprises are subject to OSHA inspections.

Business Affecting Commerce

Congress' use of the "affecting commerce" language to define the term "employer" indicates Congress intended the scope of coverage under the OSH Act to be as broad as is permissible under the commerce clause of the Constitution. Thus, virtually any effect of an employer's business on interstate commerce, no matter how indirect or minimal, will likely be sufficient to bring it within the affecting commerce language. Furthermore, the degree of involvement or particular impact on interstate commerce by an individual entity may not be the determinative factor as to whether jurisdiction exists under the "affecting commerce" test. At least one court has held that where a statute such as the OSH Act requires only that a particular business affect commerce, then jurisdiction is confirmed if the business is in a class of activity that as a whole affects commerce.

The Court's view is consistent with the Act's legislative history, which indicated an intention to make coverage of the Act as broad, generally speaking, as the authority vested in the federal Government by the commerce clause of the Constitution. Applying that test, very few businesses can escape coverage of the Act because they do not affect interstate commerce.

However, courts have held that the Act does not apply to an employer if there is an insufficient showing that the business is by its nature, engaged in interstate commerce or that it is within a class of activity engaged in interstate commerce.

Employing Other Persons

For a business to come within the scope of the OSH Act, it must have employees. Like the "affecting commerce" term, the term "employee" is construed broadly in light of the remedial purpose of the Act. If any other person is deemed to be an employee for purposes of the Act, even if the person would not be an employee for other purposes, the employer is within the coverage of the Act.

Therefore, even if the employees worked on a very informal basis or are paid at least partly in kind rather than in cash, the determination that there is one employee is sufficient for OSH Act coverage.

Regulations Affecting OSH Act Coverage

OSHA regulations state that professionals, agricultural employers, Indians, and nonprofit charitable organizations are not excluded from coverage. Churches and religious organizations are also covered by the OSH Act when they employ persons in secular activities. Employers of domestic household employees, however, are not subject to the Act.

Employers Subject to Other Regulations

Employers covered by the OSH Act may be excluded from its requirements as to the working conditions of their employees if the working conditions are regulated by another federal agency. The OSH Act provides that "Nothing in this Act shall apply to working conditions of employees with respect to which other federal agencies … exercise statutory authority to prescribe or enforce standards or regulations affecting occupational safety or health."

This exemption requires that the other federal agency possesses that statutory authority to adopt regulations affecting job safety or health and that it actually exercises that authority.

Actual Regulation Required

This partial residual authority to regulate job safety, resulting from an agency's regulations of other aspects of the employer's activities, is not enough to provide this exemption. Therefore, when a federal agency or department has authority to regulate safety and health working conditions but does not exercise that authority, then those working conditions are subject to OSHA regulations.

That is, OSHA coverage is displaced by an exercise of another agency's authority only for the working condition embraced by that exercise. If the agency has not acted to regulate the activities for which the employer was cited, OSHA jurisdiction will be helpful.

Courts holding the OSH Act is not preempted until another agency exercises its authority over job safety or health, have generally exempted railroad workers protected by the federal Railroad Administration's job safety rules and aircraft maintenance workers covered by the Federal Aviation Administration's manuals on safety instructions for maintenance personnel during airline ground operations.

Once an exercise of authority by another agency has taken place, it will preempt OSHA jurisdiction even though the other agency's standards or enforcement procedures are not as rigorous.

Agency Authorized to Protect Worker Safety

In addition to the exercise of authority over job safety or health by another agency, another requirement is, that the other agency must be vested with statutory authority to adopt or enforce regulations affecting employee safety or health.

The statutory authority of an agency to promulgate safety regulations may be rejected when relied on by an employer who is only affected by the agency through a construction contract. Such a peripheral contract does not vest the agency with exclusive authority over the employer as to job safety because it has no statutory authority to regulate occupational safety or health in those circumstances.

Once an employer has demonstrated that:

- Its activities are regulated by a federal agency other than the OSHA,
- Such agency has statutory authority to prescribe and enforce regulations affecting the safety or health of employees' working conditions,
- The agency has exercised its authority.

The final issue remaining is the breadth of the exemption from OSHA coverage to which the employer is entitled.

Some employers contend that once another federal agency exercises its job safety authority with respect to some working conditions of their employees, those employees are entirely exempt from OSHA coverage even with regard to working conditions that the other agency has chosen not to regulate. This view has been rejected by the courts who have refused to apply the exemption broadly when the other agency does not purport to regulate the occupational safety and health aspects of the affected facilities. Furthermore, the courts are reluctant to read the exemptive statute in a manner that would leave thousands of workers in particular areas of an industry exposed to unregulated industrial hazards that would utterly frustrate the legislative purpose of the OSH Act.

The burden is on the employer to plead and prove that particular working conditions are excluded from OSHA coverage. If the employer fails to raise this defense or to introduce evidence to prove it, he will lose on this issue and the OSH Act will be applicable.

OSHA's Four Pronged Comprehensive Ergonomics Plan

In March 2001 Congress repealed the Ergonomics Program Standard developed and promulgated by the Occupational Safety and Health Administration (OSHA) under the Clinton Administration. The repealed Ergonomics Program Standard contained wage replacement provisions, extensive job analysis, employee training and other provisions that were criticized by business and industry as overly burdensome and excessively costly. OSHA's new Four Pronged Comprehensive Ergonomics Plan is not a mandatory standard. It does not contain specific workplace ergonomic program requirements to which employers must comply.

It is expected that all states that administer and enforce safety and health programs ("state plan states," such as Michigan), will implement the new OSHA Four Pronged Comprehensive Ergonomics Plan. The new OSHA Ergonomics Plan is composed of the following:

1. VOLUNTARY GUIDELINES

OSHA will develop industry and task-specific guidelines to reduce and prevent ergonomic injuries, often called musculoskeletal disorders (MSD). OSHA has previously provided guidance on ergonomic issues in the meat packing industry and has recently released ergonomic guidelines for nursing home providers. OSHA expects to issue additional industry guidelines in the future.

2. ENFORCEMENT

While there is no specific ergonomics program standard, OSHA and MIOSHA can and have cited employers for ergonomic hazards in the workplace under the General Duty Clause. The General Duty Clause requires employers to provide employees a safe and healthful workplace free from recognized hazards. OSHA has indicated that it will have special ergonomic inspection teams that will place an emphasis on industries/employers who are deemed to be not addressing ergonomic hazards in their workplaces. OSHA has also indicated that it will work closely with Department of Labor attorneys to develop and implement an enforcement plan and legal strategy to maximize successful prosecutions of employers that do not address ergonomic hazards in their workplaces. Again, it is expected that state plan states like MIOSHA, will follow OSHA's enforcement strategy and work with the state Attorney General to prosecute employers relating to ergonomic hazards.

3. COMPLIANCE ASSISTANCE

Under its new ergonomics plan, OSHA has stated that it will provide compliance assistance tools to employers proactively addressing ergonomic issues. The compliance assistance tools will include internet-based training, information on how to implement ergonomic programs, specific job guidelines, grant programs, and employer recognition for successful ergonomic programs.

4. ERGONOMICS RESEARCH

OSHA will create a national advisory committee to advise OSHA on gaps in ergonomics research. Throughout the debate on ergonomics issues there has been a consistent assertion that not enough is known about how MSDs develop. OSHA has indicated that the newly formed national advisory committee will work together with the National Institute for Occupational Safety and Health (NIOSH) to stimulate and encourage needed ergonomic/MSD research.

It appears, at this time, that while there is significant Congressional and labor union support for the promulgation of a mandatory ergonomics program standard, there will be no mandatory ergonomic program standard containing specific enforceable requirements in the near future.

It is clear however that ergonomic hazards/MSDs are now generally considered a "recognized hazard" in the workplace and that employers will face potential OSHA/MIOSHA enforcement relating to ergonomic hazards under the General Duty Clause. OSHA's new Four Pronged Comprehensive Ergonomics Plan could be a good opportunity for employers, who have not already done so, to voluntarily address ergonomic issues in their workplaces before a mandatory ergonomics program standard is imposed.

State Plans for Occupational Safety and Health

Administration of the OSH Act is not vested exclusively in the federal government, but contemplates participation by the states to assure every working man and woman works under safe and healthful working conditions. The policy expressed in the OSH Act is to encourage state participation in the administration and enforcement of occupational safety and health laws. The encouragement includes providing grants to states to help them in identifying their needs and responsibilities in occupational safety and health, to develop plans consistent with the OSH Act, to improve the administration and enforcement of state occupational safety and health laws, and to conduct their own experimental and demonstration projects.

In order to assure the adequacy of state safety and health laws and regulations, Congress explicitly preempted states from asserting jurisdiction over safety and health issues covered by OSHA standards without formal approval.

Establishment of State Plans

Under the OSH Act, a state may operate its own job safety and health program if it meets certain minimum requirements. If these requirements are met, enforcement activities are performed by the state and the federal operations are curtailed. States wishing to conduct their own job safety and health programs covering the same "issues" as the federal program must submit their plans to OSHA. The agency defines the term "issues" as "any ... industrial, occupational, or hazard grouping that is found to be administratively practicable and ... not in conflict with the purposes of the Act."

OSHA must approve a state plan if it meets the OSH Act's requirements of:

- providing for the development and enforcement of state safety and health standards that are as protective as the federal standards;
- assuring that the designated state agency possesses the necessary legal authority and qualified personnel to enforce its standards;
- assuring that the state will adequately fund the administration and enforcement of its standards;
- providing right of entry and inspection of covered workplaces that is as effective as the access provided in the federal Act; and
- covering employees of the state and its political subdivisions in the state program.

OSHA may continue to carry out inspections and enforce standards after a state safety plan has been approved until OSHA determines its plan approval requirements are satisfied. The determination, based on the actual operation of the state plan, cannot be made until three years after the plan is approved.

Thereafter, federal OSHA standards are no longer applicable in the state. However, if a state omits from its coverage of any hazards, industries, or occupational groupings covered by the federal statute, then federal Standards and authority to conduct inspections continues within the state as to such hazards, industries, or occupational groupings. That is, if a state covers health hazards but not safety hazards, federal occupational safety standards remain in force in the state, and federal authority to inspect for violation of those standards continues.

Evaluation and Approval of State Plans

The OSH Act requires OSHA to continue evaluating the operation of approved state plans. If it finds, after notice and an opportunity for hearing, that a state is failing to comply substantially with any provision of its plan, it must withdraw approval of the plan and the state again becomes subject to federal OSHA authority. States may appeal OSHA's decision to withdraw approval of or rejection of a plan to the United States Court of Appeals.

If a state declines to submit a plan or has been rejected, that state lacks authority to enforce state job safety or health standards covering issues addressed by federal OSHA standards. Approval of a state plan qualifies it for a grant of up to 50% of the cost of it operation.

The approval process for a state plan begins with its submission to the Assistant Secretary of Labor for Occupational Safety and Health. A notice in the Federal Register summarizes the plan, invites public comment, and states where the public may view the plan. If a hearing is requested, the Assistant Secretary may hold a formal or informal hearing concerning plan approval, but none is required. If the Assistant Secretary proposes to reject a plan, however, the state must be provided an opportunity for a formal hearing. After the plan, the public comments, and the hearing request have been evaluated, the Assistant Secretary publishes the decision on the plan's approval in the Federal Register.

Developmental Status of State Plans

The OSH Act requires that a state plan provide for the development and enforcement of safety and health standards that are or will be as effective as the federal standards. OSHA may approve a state plan, even if it does not meet all of the requirements under the Act, if it includes satisfactory assurances by the state that it will take the necessary steps to bring its program into conformity with these criteria within the initial three-year review period.

Developmental plans must include a timetable for full compliance. During this development period, as the state adopts standards and increases enforcement activities, federal involvement decreases. State employers, however, are subject to inspection by federal or state compliance officers, or both, although federal and state inspectors should attempt to coordinate their activities.

OSHA regulations also provide that federal enforcement proceedings will not be initiated against an employer for violating a federal standard while complying with an approved state standard or with a variance granted by the designated state agency in accordance with the state plan, as long as the employer has not filed with OSHA for the same variance.

Operational Status of State Plans

An approved state plan achieves operational status when the enabling legislation has been enacted in the state, approved standards have been adopted, a sufficient number of qualified personnel are enforcing the standards, and provisions for appealing citations and penalties are in effect.

A state plan may become operational as to all affected employers and employees, or only as to certain issues such as particular industrial, occupational, or hazard groupings. Once a state plan is deemed operational, the state will conduct all enforcement activity for those issues and the federal role is limited to monitoring the state activity.

When a state plan is operational, the state and federal governments enter an operation agreement detailing enforcement activities and reporting procedures for accidents and complaints, and the process for returning to federal enforcement if the state fails to comply with the agreement.

Certification Procedure for State Plans

A state plan is eligible for certification by completion of the developmental steps. OSHA monitors the certified plan for one to two years, at which time the Assistant Secretary determines whether the criteria for state plan approval in OSHA regulations are being followed. A positive determination makes the final approval for a state plan and the federal standards will no longer apply in the state. OSHA will no longer have authority to enforce standards in the state, except for any issues covered by the OSH Act that are not part of the state plan.

The plan must remain at least as effective as the federal program and remains subject to federal monitoring. A substantial failure to continue compliance with the requirements may lead to revocation of certification, resumption of federal enforcement authority, or withdrawal of plan approval.

Complaints Against State Plans

The complainant will be informed if there is no investigation or, if an investigation results from the complaint, the findings and any remedial activity. OSH Act regulations require states to inform employers, employees, and the public of their right to complain to OSHA about state program administration.

Approved State Plans

Since passage of the OSH Act, twenty six state plans have been approved. In six states, including Michigan, some or all of the standards differ from federal OSHA standards.

States that do not have approved plans are precluded from enforcing job safety and health standards covering "issues;" that is, industrial, occupational, or hazard groupings which are covered by the federal OSHA program.

Coverage of State Employees Only

OSH Act regulations allow states to submit plans to cover only state and local government employees. Since the federal Act does not cover state and local government employees, a state lacking a state plan is not preempted from enforcing job safety and health standards covering such employees. The regulations for such plans apply requirements similar to those covering private employees.

Michigan Occupational Safety and Health Act

The two statutes which regulate occupational safety and health in Michigan are the federal OSH Act and the Michigan Occupational Safety and Health Act (MIOSH Act), MCLA 408.1001 et seq. The MIOSH Act is an approved state plan under OSH Act regulations, and so has primary enforcement responsibilities for workplace safety and health.

Generally, when federal and state legislation cover the same subject matter, federal enforcement will prevail. However, the OSH Act authorizes approved state plans to enforce safety issues if the state standard covers an area where:

- no federal standard exists,
- the employer is not subject to federal rules, or
- a more restrictive state standard is required by compelling local conditions and will not unduly burden interstate commerce.

MIOSHA enforces workplace safety and health regulations for all Michigan employers except in maritime employment, mine employment, and domestic employment. The Coast Guard is charged with enforcing maritime safety, and mine safety is regulated by the federal Mine Safety and Health Act.

General Rights and Duties under MIOSHA

Employers have both general and specific duties under MIOSH Act as they do under the OSH Act. Each Act has a "General Duty" clause obligating employers to provide a workplace and equipment to employees which are free from recognized hazards that are causing, or are likely to cause, death or serious physical harm to employees.

General Duty Clause in MIOSHA

This "catch-all" provision is included because it is impossible for governmental bodies to enact regulations or laws that cover every conceivable safety or health condition. The General Duty clause is only implicated when no specific safety or health standard directly relates to the alleged violation.

Certain conditions must be present for a violation of the General Duty clause to be established. First, the alleged violation must be recognized by the employer or the employer's industry as a hazard, or must be such that an ordinary, reasonable person familiar with the employer's industry would recognize the condition as presenting a hazard. Second, the hazard must be one which is likely to cause death or serious physical injury. There must also be a feasible method of abatement. Feasibility includes both technological and economic feasibility.

Employer Obligations under MIOSHA

Section 11 of MIOSHA also imposes a number of specific obligations upon covered employers. They must:

- comply with the Act and all rules and standards promulgated under the Act,
- post notices and use other appropriate means to keep their employees informed of their protections and obligations under the Act, including applicable rules and standards, and
- provide personal protective equipment at their expense when it is specifically required to be provided at the employer's expense in a rule or standard.

MIOSHA also imposes general obligations upon employers. Among these are requirements that employers:

- pay for any medical examinations or tests required by a MIOSHA standard;
- make available for employee inspection or copying, any general health surveys of workplace conditions which could adversely affect the employee's health or physical well-being;
- upon request, make available to an employee for inspection or copying, any medical records or health data relating to that employee;
- not require or permit an employee to operate equipment or engage in any process determined by MIOSHA to be imminently dangerous, unless the employee's presence is necessary to correct a hazardous situation;

- promptly notify MIOSHA (within 8 hours) of a fatality or the hospitalization of three or more employees resulting from the same incident;
- promptly notify employees who were or are being exposed to certain harmful or toxic substances at levels that exceed MIOSHA standards; and
- not discharge or in any way retaliate against an employee who has filed a complaint, instituted a MIOSHA proceeding, testified in such a proceeding, or who has exercised any right afforded by MIOSHA.

Employee Obligations under MIOSHA

Employees also have certain obligations imposed upon them by MIOSHA. They are required to:

- act and comply with all rules and standards promulgated under, and with all orders issued pursuant to the Act; and
- not remove, displace, damage, destroy or carry off a safeguard furnished or provided for use in a place of employment, or interfere in any way in the use of such devices by any other person.

Safety Standards

Safety standards are defined as guidelines that indicate conditions; or the adoption or use of one specifically prescribed practices, means, methods, operations, or processes necessary to provide safe and healthful employment in places of employment for workplace activities.

These standards are promulgated by three state commissions:

- The Occupational Safety Standards Commission (standards for occupational safety)
- The Construction Safety Standards Commission (standards for construction safety)
- The Occupational Health Standards Commission (standards for occupational health)

These Commissions are operated under the Michigan Occupational Safety and Health Administration (MIOSHA).

Initiation of Safety Standards

Employers, unions, and individuals all are allowed to participate in the process by which standards are promulgated. The process begins with a written request by any person, or it can be initiated by the appropriate Commission. If a proposed standard is initiated by the Commission, it must conduct a public hearing before implementing the standard.

PUBLIC HEARING NOTICES

A notice of the public hearing must generally be placed in at least three newspapers throughout the state (including one in the Upper Peninsula), if the proposed standard is to apply to a broad range of employers. The MIOSHA must also give written notice to all parties who have asked to be notified of such public hearings. This notice must be given between 30 and 90 days prior to the public hearing. After the public hearing and compliance with a number of procedural requirements, a proposed standard will become final.

Emergency Safety Standards

The procedures for initiating safety standards do not apply to adoption of emergency standards that may be put in place without public notice or hearings. Emergency safety standards may be implemented "when necessary to protect employees," and emergency health standards may be implemented when "employees are exposed to substances or agents determined to be toxic or physically harmful, and the emergency standard is necessary to protect employees from the danger."

An employer may challenge the application of a standard to its specific setting before a citation is issued. It must first petition the appropriate director (of General Industry Safety and Health Division, or Construction Safety and Health Division) for a declaratory ruling. His or her ruling is binding upon all parties. The ruling may, however, be appealed, or may be contested in the administrative proceedings following the assessment of a citation against the employer.

Variances to Safety Standards

A "variance" is an order authorizing an employer to deviate from an established standard. There are three types of variances: experimental, temporary, and permanent.

For either permanent or temporary variances, public hearings may be conducted at the request of any interested party, including the employer. The burden of proof is always on the employer requesting a deviation from the established standards.

After applying for a variance, an employer may seek an interim order, authorizing it to continue operating the equipment or carrying on the practices or procedures which do not comply with the standard until the variance request is decided.

EXPERIMENTAL VARIANCES

This type of variance may be granted when necessary to permit an employer to test different techniques for safeguarding the safety and health of employees. The employer must obtain MIOSHA approval before conducting the test.

TEMPORARY VARIANCES

Temporary variances are available when a new standard is enacted and an employer cannot comply by its effective date because of the unavailability of professional or technical personnel, materials, or equipment, or because the necessary construction or alterations cannot be completed by that date. The employer must also show it is taking all available steps to safeguard its employees from the covered hazard, and that it has an effective program for complying with the standard as soon as possible.

A temporary variance may also be granted where a standard is in the process of being amended, and the employer is in compliance with the amended standard, but not the existing standard.

PERMANENT VARIANCES

A permanent variance may be given if an employer can establish that it already provides at least as much protection for employee safety as that set forth in the standard.

Occupational Injury and Illness Recordkeeping Rule

On January 2, 2002, a federal OSHA Occupational Injury and Illness Recordkeeping rule went into effect. OSHA developed and adopted the new recordkeeping rule. MIOSHA adopted recording and reporting requirements that are substantially identical to the federal revision. The revised OSHA standard is 29 CFR 1904; the MIOSHA occupational injury and illness rule is Part 11 of MIOSHA rules.

The OSHA revised Occupational Injury and Illness Recordkeeping Standard in 2002 maintains the basic structure and recordkeeping practices of the old system. The revised rule however employs new forms and somewhat different requirements for recording, maintaining, posting, retaining and reporting occupational injury and illness information.

Employers Subject to Rule

Most employers are subject to the revised injury and illness recordkeeping standard. Partially exempt employers must still report to OSHA or MIOSHA, within eight hours, any occupational fatalities or catastrophes (incidents involving the hospitalization of three or more employees). The following employers are exempt from most requirements of the new rule:

- Smaller employers with 10 or fewer employees;
- Low hazard industry such as:
    - Retail

- Service
- Finance
- Insurance
- Real estate

[The low hazard exemption generally applies to employers with Standard Industrial Classification (SIC) codes within SIC 52–89. Appendix "A" to the new rule has a more complete list of partially exempt industries.]

There are certain industries or businesses that were not previously covered under the old injury and illness recordkeeping rule that are covered under the new rule. These newly covered industries include:

d. Auto & Home Supply Stores (SIC 553);

e. Boat Dealers (SIC 555);

f. Recreational Vehicle Dealers (SIC 556);

g. Automotive Dealer, Not Elsewhere Classified (SIC 559);

h. Other industries in SIC codes, 571, 572, 593, 596, 598, 651, 655, 721, 734, 735, 736, 833, 836, and 842.

If an employer has any question about whether they are subject to the new injury and illness recordkeeping standard, the employer should carefully ascertain its SIC code number. Employers can refer to the SIC code numbers they use in other government filings such as environmental and tax filings. An employer may also inquire to OSHA or MIOSHA as well as seek the assistance of legal counsel who practices health and safety law to determine if the employer is subject to the new rule.

Highlights of the Rule

Each employer required to keep records of fatalities, injuries and illnesses must record each fatality, injury, and illness that involves all of the following:

- Is work-related;
- Is a new case; and
- Meets one or more of the general recording criteria.

Work-Relationship

An employer must consider an injury or illness to be work-related if an event or exposure in the work environment either caused or contributed to the resulting condition. According to OSHA guidance documents, a case is presumed work-related if, and only if, an event or exposure in the work environment is a *discernable cause* of the injury or illness or of a *significant* aggravation of a pre-existing condition. The work event or exposure need only be one of the discernable causes; it need not be the sole or predominant cause.

It should be specifically noted that under the pre-2002 injury or illness recordkeeping rule **any** aggravation of a pre-existing condition by a workplace event or exposure makes the case work-related. Under the current rule, only a *significant* aggravation of a pre-existing condition by a workplace event or exposure makes the case work-related.

The rule states that if it is not obvious whether the precipitating event or exposure occurred in the work environment or elsewhere, the employer "must evaluate the employee's work duties and environment to decide whether or not one or more events or exposures in the work environment caused or contributed to the resulting condition or significantly aggravated a pre-existing condition."

This means that the employer must make a determination whether it is *more likely than not* that work events or exposures were a cause of the injury or illness, or of a significant aggravation to a pre-existing condition. If the employer decides the case is not work-related, and OSHA or MIOSHA subsequently issues a citation for failure to record, OSHA or MIOSHA would have the burden of proving that the injury or illness was work-related. While the OSHA or MIOSHA will have the burden of proving that the injury or illness is work-related, in the event of a citation an employer should document its rationale for all non work-related injury and illness determinations.

New Case

Only new cases are recordable. Work-related injuries and illnesses are considered to be new cases when the employee has never reported similar signs or symptoms before, or when the employee has recovered completely from a previous injury or illness and workplace events or exposures have caused the signs or symptoms to reappear.

General Recording Criteria

A significant change from the old rule is the elimination of different criteria for recording work-related injuries and work-related illnesses. The old rule required employers to record all work-related illnesses, regardless of severity. The new rule has one set of criteria for work-related injuries and illnesses.

Employers must record new work-related injuries and illnesses that meet one or more of the general recording criteria or meet the recording criteria for specific types of conditions. Specific conditions include hearing shifts meeting the applicable criteria, needlesticks and sharps injuries involving potential exposure to contaminated blood, medical removal required under other health and safety standards, as well as a positive TB skin test when there is a known workplace exposure. Recordable work-related injuries and illnesses are those that result in one or more of the following:

- Death, (all work place heart attacks must be reported whether believed to be work-related or not)
- Days away from work,
- Restricted work,
- Transfer to another job,
- Medical treatment beyond first aid,
- Loss of consciousness, or
- Diagnosis of a significant injury or illness.

The revised occupational injury and illness recordkeeping rule specifically addresses each of the above recording criteria. For instance, Lost Workday Injury (LWDI) and the Lost Workday Injury and Illness (LWDII) terms have been eliminated. The new rule uses the terms Days Away from work, Restricted work, or Transferred to another job (DART). The method for calculating DART has been changed. Instead of "work days" counted under the old rule, the new rule uses "calendar" days. Additionally, under the new rule, employers do not count days away or days of restriction beyond 180 days.

Another helpful change made by the 2002 rule is definitions *for medical treatment* and *first aid*. First aid is defined by a specific list of treatments. For instance, first aid includes:

- Using nonprescription drugs at nonprescription strengths;
- Using wound coverings such as band-aids, gauze pads, or using butterfly bandages or steri-strip or other wound closing devices;
- Using hot and cold therapy;
- [See specific list contained in the rule for complete list]

All treatment not specifically listed as first aid is considered medical treatment.

Specific provisions in the rule provide guidance with regard to the general recording criteria. An employer should carefully review the new rule in the process of making recording determinations. The following flow chart provides the basic decision-making process for determining recordability of injuries and illnesses.

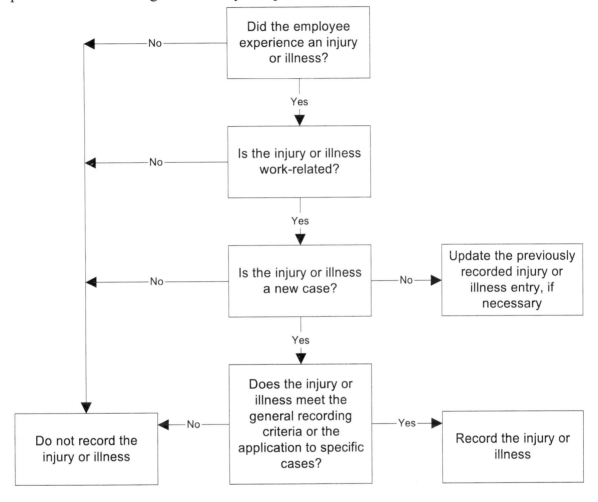

Forms

One very obvious change made by the 2002 occupational injury and illness recordkeeping rule is the use of a series of forms for tracking injuries and illnesses. Employers who operate establishments that are required by the rule to keep injury and illness records are required to complete three forms: the OSHA 300 Log of Work-Related Injuries and Illnesses, the annual OSHA 300A Summary of Work-Related Injuries and Illnesses, and the OSHA 301 Injury and Illness Incident Report.

Employers are required to keep separate 300 Logs for each establishment that they operate if the establishment is expected to be in operation for one year or longer. The 300 Log must include injuries and illnesses to employees on the employer's payroll as well as injuries and illnesses of other employees the employer supervises on a day-to-day basis, such as temporary workers or contractor employees who are subject to daily supervision by the employer. Within seven calendar days of the time the fatality, injury, or illness occurred, the employer must enter any case that is work-related, is a new case, and meets one or more of the recording criteria in the rule on the Log and Form 301. Current versions of the MIOSHA 300, 300A, and 301 forms are included on the HR Michigan Web Site (www.hrmichigan.com).

Certification

High-level company executives face potential liability under the requirements that the 300A Log/Summary be "certified" by a "company executive." A company executive must certify that they have examined the MIOSHA 300 log and that they reasonably believe, based on their knowledge of the process by which the information was recorded, that the annual summary is correct and complete. The company executive who certifies the log must be any of the following persons:

- An owner of the company, only if the company is a sole proprietorship or partnership.
- An officer of the corporation.
- The highest ranking company official working at the establishment.
- The immediate supervisor of the highest ranking company official working at the establishment.

The rule states that whoever knowingly makes a false statement, representation, or certification in an application, record, report, plan or other document filed or required to be maintained pursuant to the act, or fails to maintain or transmit records or reports as required under the act, shall be subjected to the provisions of section 35(7) of the MIOSHA act. Section 35(7) of the MIOSHA act provides for a criminal misdemeanor with penalties of $10,000 or 6 months in jail, or both.

Other Provisions Of The Revised Recordkeeping Rule

There are several other changes to the occupational injury and illness recordkeeping rule of which employers should be aware. For instance, the form 300A Summary is required to be posted for three months instead of one as under the old rule. Form 300A Summaries must be posted on February 1 and remain posted until April 30. Employers must also establish a procedure for employees to report injuries and illnesses and must educate/train employees in the procedure. Certain injuries and illnesses (e.g., sexual assaults, HIV infections, mental illnesses) are subject to employee privacy concerns and an employer must record such injuries and illnesses in a manner to protect the employee's confidentiality. There are also additional provisions relating to access to employee injury and illness records.

Conclusion

The revised occupational injury and illness recordkeeping rule seeks to provide clearer regulatory requirements and simplify the overall recordkeeping system for employers. While many of the changes have the potential to provide the sought after benefits, some of the changes (i.e., company executive certification) have the potential to create greater employer liability for occupational injury and illness recordkeeping.

OSHA and MIOSHA have attempted to write the new occupational injury and illness recordkeeping rule/standard in "plain language." The new rule uses a question and answer format that is an improvement over prior rules and standards. The plain language and question and answer format do not however eliminate all gray areas. Both OSHA and MIOSHA have performed extensive outreach and education efforts, including teleconferences and live seminars. Additionally, many very good resources are available on the OSHA and MIOSHA websites (*www.osha.gov* and *www.michigan.gov/miosha*).

Employers should take advantage of all of these resources in learning the new occupational injury and illness recordkeeping requirements. After OSHA and MIOSHA provide what they believe is an appropriate period for employers to learn the new system, employers should expect that OSHA and MIOSHA to actively enforce the new rule.

Consultation Education and Training

The Consultation, Education and Training Division (CET) of MIOSHA helps employers with safety and health matters. It has no enforcement powers but may provide safety brochures, films, video cassettes, or speakers.

A particularly significant service of CET is an on-site consultation program. At the employer's invitation, a CET inspector will conduct a safety or health inspection of a facility, similar to an enforcement inspection, but no citations or penalties will be issued. However, the employer must have first agreed to correct all discovered serious violations and CET will verify the corrections. The report of the CET inspector cannot be used by MIOSHA if the employer corrects the discovered violations in a timely manner. Employers may contact the CET Division by writing to P.O. Box 30643, Lansing MI 48909, or calling (517) 322-1809.

Workplace Enforcement Inspections

Workplace enforcement inspections by MIOSHA may be conducted for a variety of reasons, including:

- Accidents and/or fatalities.

- A high incidence of injuries or illnesses in the workplace.
- The employer may be in a targeted industry.
- To check on the abatement of prior violations.
- The request of an employee or employee representative.

Notice of Workplace Enforcement Inspection

The employer generally will not receive advance notice of the inspection. Where advance notice is given, it will usually not exceed 24 hours. An employer will normally only receive advance notice when:

- such notice could enable the employer to abate an imminent danger as quickly as possible.
- the inspection could most effectively be conducted after working hours or where special precautions are necessary for the inspection.
- notice is necessary to assure the presence of employer and employee representatives or the appropriate personnel to assist in the inspection.
- MIOSHA determines that advance notice would enhance the probability of an effective inspection.

MIOSHA Enforcement Approach - "Focused Inspections" for General Industry/Manufacturing

In 2004, MIOSHA proposed an enforcement approach that appears to depart from the traditional planned wall-to-wall MIOSHA inspections. Rather than routinely conducting "wall-to-wall" inspections on targeted employers, MIOSHA will look at a Company's major work activity and the machines and processes associated with it. MIOSHA will then conduct an inspection that focuses on the Company's major work activity and will specifically evaluate employee exposure for that activity during:

- Regular operation of the machine
- Setup/threading/preparation for regular operation of the machine
- Clearing jams or upset condition
- Running adjustments while the machine is operation
- Cleaning of the machine
- Oiling or greasing of the machine
- Scheduled/unscheduled maintenance
- Lockout/tagout

If MIOSHA's evaluation of the above focus areas demonstrates adequate compliance MIOSHA indicates the inspection will be concluded. However, if a "significant" number of hazards are identified the inspection will be expanded to a full review (wall-to-wall inspection) of the Company.

Companies should look closely at their major work activity, specifically review the focus areas and make sure that the Company's guarding and operating procedures adequately limit employee exposure to potential hazards. By doing so a Company could avoid a more extensive wall-to-wall MIOSHA inspection and the disruption to the Company's operations caused by such an inspection.

Lockout/Tagout Standards

General Industry Safety Standard, Part 85, Control of Hazardous Energy Sources, requires that employers develop a program to prevent employee injury from unexpected/unintended motion, energization, start up, or the release of stored energy when equipment repair, servicing and/or maintenance work is being performed. It is mandatory that all workers understand that a potentially dangerous condition exists when a machine is being serviced or repaired and that the people who operate the equipment are aware of the servicing activity.

MIOSHA Part 85 – Control of Hazardous Energy is the comprehensive industry lockout/tagout standard. It requires that an employer plan for the control of energy during servicing and/or maintenance of machines and equipment by doing the following:

- Establishing an energy control program.
- Developing, documenting, and utilizing lockout/tagout procedures.
- Providing appropriate training to employees.
- Providing equipment required by the lockout/tagout procedures at no cost to the employees.
- Assuring continuing competency through inspection and training.

Part 85 Exclusions/Exceptions

Lockout/tagout standards do not apply to "Normal Production Operations." Servicing and/or maintenance during normal production operations *are* covered if:
- An employee is required to remove or bypass a guard or other safety device;
- An employee is required to place any part of his or her body into an area on a machine or piece of equipment where work is actually performed upon the material being processed;
- An employee is exposed to an associated danger zone during a machine operating cycle.

Minor Tool Changes & Servicing

Minor tool changes and adjustments, and other minor servicing activities, (lubrication, cleaning or un-jamming, servicing of machines or equipment, and making adjustments or tool changes) are not covered if:
- They take place during normal production operations
- Are routine, repetitive, and integral to the use of equipment for production; and
- Work is performed using alternative protective measures which provide effective employee protection

Cord and Plug Connected Equipment

Part 85 does not apply to work on cord and plug connected electrical equipment for which exposure to the hazards of unexpected energization or start up of the equipment is controlled by the unplugging of the equipment from the energy source. The unplugged cord must be under the exclusive control of the employees conducting the service or maintenance activities.

Hot Tap Operations

Part 85 also does not apply to hot tap operations involving transmission and distribution systems for substances such as gas, steam, water, or petroleum products when they are performed on pressurized pipelines, provided that the employer demonstrates the following: 1) continuity of service is essential; 2) shutdown of the system is impractical; and 3) documented procedures are followed, and special equipment is used which will provide proven effective protection for employees.

Part 85 Energy Control Program

A lockout/ tagout program is designed to address risks posed by hazardous energies. Before service/maintenance activities begin, the machine or equipment shall be isolated from the energy source and rendered inoperative. At a minimum, an employer's lockout/tagout program must include: A) documented energy control procedures, B) employee training, and C) periodic inspections.

Procedures for each type of machine or equipment must be developed, documented and utilized to address how potentially hazardous energy will be controlled during machine or equipment servicing and maintenance. Employers must also make sure that the established procedures are followed.

A. Application of Controls/Specific Machine/Equipment Procedure

When a machine specific documented procedure is required, it must include the following actions and elements which must be done in the order listed below when locking or tagging out equipment:

1. Preparation for shutdown

    All authorized employees must know the type and magnitude of the energy, the hazards of the energy to be controlled, and the method or means to control the energy before the employee turns off a machine or equipment.

2. Notify all affected employees

    The authorized employee turning off the power must warn the affected employees in the work area that power will be shut off, the reason for the shut-down, and that the equipment will be locked/tagged out.

3. Machine or equipment shutdown

    Procedures must be established for turning off or shutting down each piece of equipment. An orderly shutdown must be utilized to avoid additional or increased hazards to employees as a result of the equipment stoppage

4. Machine or equipment isolation

    Physically locate all energy isolating devices that are needed to control the energy of the machine or equipment. Isolate the machine or equipment from the energy sources.

5. Lockout or tagout device application

    The authorized employee places locks or tags in the appropriate energy isolating location. A lockout device is defined as a device, such as a key lock, that utilizes a positive means or holds an energy isolating device in a safe position and prevents the energizing of a machine or equipment.

    A tagout device is defined as a prominent warning device, such as a tag and means of attachment, that can be securely fastened to an energy isolating device, to indicate that the energy isolating device and the equipment being controlled may not be operated until the tagout device is removed.

    - Only authorized employees shall place the lockout or tagout device on each energy isolating device;
    - Lockout devices need to be affixed properly so that it will hold the energy isolating devices in a **SAFE** or **OFF** position;
    - Tagout devices, when used, must be placed to clearly indicate that operation or movement of the energy isolating device from the **SAFE** or **OFF** position is not allowed.

6. Release of stored energy
   - After lockout or tagout devices have been placed on the energy isolating devices, all potentially hazardous or residual energy must be relieved, disconnected, restrained and otherwise rendered safe. .

7. Verification of isolation

   Before starting work on a machine or equipment that has been locked out or tagged out, the authorized employee must verify that the machine or equipment has been isolated or de-energized. This is generally accomplished by first establishing that no personnel are exposed and then testing the effectiveness of the lockout/tagout by attempting to cycle the machine or start the equipment at the motor control center panel or start/stop switch (key/lock system). Verification of isolation must be continued if there is a chance of the re-accumulation of stored energy during the service/maintenance activity.

8. Use of Tagout Systems

   A tagout system may be utilized by an employer when an energy isolating device is not capable of being locked out. When the energy isolating device is capable of being locked out, the employer must use lockout unless it can be demonstrated that the utilization of a tagout system will provide full employee protection. After January 2, 1990, whenever replacement, major repair, renovation or modification of a machine or equipment is performed, and whenever new machines or equipment are installed, it must be capable of accepting a lockout device.

   Whenever tagout systems are used, all other procedures consistent with the lockout program must be followed. Additional control measures must also be taken to reinforce the tagout system. Lockout is a sure means of ensuring de-energization of equipment. Therefore, when a tagout program is used for equipment capable of being locked out, an employer must demonstrate the following:

   - The tagout program will provide a level of safety equivalent to that obtained by using a lockout program;
   - Full compliance with all tagout-related provisions of this standard together with such additional elements as are necessary to provide the equivalent safety available from the use of a lockout device;
   - Implementation of additional safety measures such as the removal of an isolating circuit element, blocking of a controlling switch, opening of an extra disconnecting device, or the removal of a valve handle to reduce the likelihood of inadvertent energization.
   - Tags must contain warnings against energizing the equipment, such as DO NOT START, DO NOT OPEN, DO NOT CLOSE, DO NOT ENERGIZE, or DO NOT OPERATE;

- o Tags must be able to indicate the identity of the employee applying the device.

Tags must be attached to energy isolating devices securely enough that they cannot be accidentally removed and must be in plain view and at the same location as the energy isolating device. When tagout systems are used, employees must also be trained in the following limitations of tags:

- o Tags are only warning devices placed on energy isolating devices, and do not provide physical restraint on those devices that is provided by a lock;
- o Once a tag is attached to an energy isolating means, it is not to be removed without the authorization of the authorized person responsible for it;
- o A tag should also never be bypassed, ignored, or otherwise defeated;
- o Tags must be legible and easily understood by all authorized employees, affected employees, and all other employees whose work operations are in or near the area;
- o Tags and their means of attachment must be made of materials which will withstand the environmental conditions encountered in the workplace;
- o Tags may evoke a false sense of security, and their meaning needs to be understood as part of the overall energy control program;
- o Tags must be securely attached to energy isolating devices so that they cannot be accidentally detached during use.

Exception to Machine/Equipment Specific LOTO Procedure Requirement

- Must meet all of the following requirements:
    - o Machine or equipment has a single energy source, that is identifiable and capable of isolation.
    - o Isolation and locking out of the single energy source will completely de-energize and deactivate the machine or equipment.
    - o Machine or equipment is isolated from that energy source and locked out during service or maintenance.
    - o Machine/equipment has no potential for stored or residual energy after shutdown which would endanger an employee
    - o Single lockout device will achieve a locked out condition
    - o Lockout device is under the exclusive control of the authorized employee performing the service or maintenance
    - o Servicing or maintenance does not create hazards for other employees
    - o Employer utilizing the exception, has had no accidents involving the unexpected activation or re-energization of the machine or equipment during service or maintenance

Locks v. Tags

- Locks hold an energy isolating device in a safe position & prevent equipment from being energized.
    - Must be applied properly & energy isolating device must be in good condition.
- Tags provide a warning that the energy isolation device and equipment may not be operated turned on.
- Tagging system must provide a level of protection equivalent to lock system
- Equipment installed after Jan. 2, 1990 must be capable of accepting locks.

Testing or Positioning of Equipment/Machines

- When lockout or tagout devices must be temporarily removed from the isolating device and the machine/equipment to test or position it for service/maintenance, and re-energization is required, the temporary removal of lockout/tagout devices and subsequent re-energization must follow this sequence:
    - Clear machine/equipment of tools and other miscellaneous materials;
    - Remove all employees from the machine/equipment area;
    - Remove lockout/tagout devices;
    - Energize and proceed with testing or positioning;
    - De-energize and reapply lockout/tagout devices.

B. Lockout/Tagout Employee Training

There are three (3) different levels of training requirements: 1) Authorized Employees, 2) Affected Employees and 3) Other Employees

Authorized Employee

An Authorized Employee is one who will be issued and apply lockout/tagout devices in order to perform service and/or maintenance. An Authorized Employee must be trained in:

- Recognition of locations, types and magnitudes of potential hazardous energy sources in the work area;
- Proper lockout/tagout procedures;
- Proper use of lockout/tagout devices (and any related equipment) used by the employer;
- Lockout or tagout device removal;
- Explanation of applicable MIOSHA standards.

Affected Employee

An Affected Employee is one whose job requires him/her to operate or use a machine or equipment on which servicing or maintenance is being performed under lockout/tagout or whose job requires him/her to work in an area in which servicing or maintenance is being performed.

An Affected Employees needs instruction in:

- Purpose of the energy control procedures;
- Use of the lockout/tagout procedures;
- Prohibition on tampering with lockout/tagout equipment.

Other Employee

An "Other Employee" is one whose work operations are or may be in an area where energy control procedures may be utilized.

Other employees must be instructed about:

- The employer's lockout/tagout procedures; and
- Attempts to restart or re-energize machines or equipment which are locked out or tagged out is prohibited

Employee Retraining

Authorized and affected employees must be retrained whenever the following occurs:
- New or revised energy control procedure is implemented;
- A change in their job assignments (regarding lockout/tagout);
- Change in machines, equipment or processes present a new hazard;
- Periodic inspections show, or the employer has reason to believe, that inadequacies in the employee's knowledge or use of the energy control procedures exists.
    - Employers must certify that employee retraining has been completed and is kept up to date. The certification must contain each employee's name, dates of training and items covered.

C. Periodic Inspection and Review

At least annually, a periodic inspection of the energy control procedures for equipment/machines involved in the Lockout/Tagout Program must be performed by departments to ensure that proper procedures and the requirements of Part 85 are being followed. The inspection must be performed by an employee other than the authorized employees utilizing the lockout/tagout procedure. The inspection should include a review between the inspector, authorized employees, and any other affected employees. Typical items covered in an inspection would include:

- Review of current energy control methods;
- Correct energy source identification;
- Proper lockout device usage;
- Methods used to release stored energies;
- Review of employee responsibilities and procedures they use under those responsibilities, including following proper lockout/tagout steps;
- Employee complaints regarding deficiencies in the Lockout/Tagout Program.

These inspections shall at least provide for a demonstration of the procedures and may be implemented through random audits and planned visual observations. These inspections are intended to ensure that the energy control procedures are being properly implemented and to provide an essential check on the continued utilization of the procedures.

- When lockout is used, the employer's inspection shall include a review of the responsibilities of each authorized employee implementing the procedure with that employee;
- Group meetings between the authorized employee who is performing the inspection and all authorized employees who implement the procedure would constitute compliance with this requirement;
- When tagout is used, the employer shall conduct this review with each affected and authorized employee.

If the review shows inadequacies in any lockout/tagout procedures, corrections must be made. The inspector should record on the inspection form any appropriate changes that have been made and that re-training is required.

D. Employer Certification

The employer must certify that the periodic inspections have been performed. Additionally, the certification must include the date of the inspection, the employees that were included in the inspection, the identity of the equipment/machinery on which the inspection procedure was utilized and the name of the person who performed the inspection.

E. Recordkeeping

All Lockout/Tagout Program records must be maintained by the employer. The records must include:

- Employee attendance sheets;
- Specific lockout/tagout procedures for equipment/machines covered by the pro-

gram;
- Completed Periodic Inspection of Lockout/Tagout Procedures forms for all equipment/machines in the program;
- Training summary including energy control program procedures and applicable requirements of Part 85.

F.   Outside Contractor Lockout/Tagout

When the work of an outside contractor involves equipment/machines covered under the Lockout/Tagout Program, the employer must: 1) Ensure that there is an appropriate exchange of information regarding lockout/tagout procedures to be used by both the employer and the outside contractor (Host employer and Contractor should exchange and each other's energy control programs and the machine/equipment specific energy control procedures for any equipment involved in the Contractor work) and 2) Specifically inform all employees involved of any differences (i.e., restrictions and prohibitions) between the two programs.

(A sample Lockout/Tagout procedure is provided at the end of this Chapter).

Requests for Workplace Inspections by Employees – Complaint Inspections

An employee or a representative of employees may request an inspection if they believe an existing condition "threatens physical harm to an employee" or presents an "imminent danger" to employees.

When an employee or employee representative believes that an imminent danger exists, no written request is required; he or she may contact MIOSHA in any manner. An "imminent danger" is defined as:

A condition or practice in a place of employment which is such that a danger exists which could reasonably be expected to cause death or serious physical harm either immediately or before the imminence of the danger can be eliminated under the enforcement procedures otherwise provided.

When notified of such a condition, MIOSHA should immediately inspect or take other action necessary to abate the dangerous condition.

An employee or employee representative who believes that a threat of physical harm exists due to a workplace condition must give written notice of this belief to MIOSHA. The complaining individual must sign the notice and describe his/her request in detail.

MIOSHA must determine whether there are reasonable grounds for the complaint. If it finds that reasonable grounds do exist, it will conduct an inspection. MIOSHA must supply the employer with a copy of the request no later than the time of the inspection. Upon request, the name of the complainant will be deleted before the complaint is given to the employer.

If MIOSHA decides there are no reasonable grounds for the complaint, it will notify the complainant of its determination. The complainant may then, in writing, request an informal review of the determination. MIOSHA may schedule a conference with the complainant and/or the employer, and either affirm the previous determination or conduct an inspection.

Workplace Enforcement Inspection

Inspections are to be conducted at "reasonable times" to avoid unreasonably interfering with the employer's operations. Safety Officers generally try to be cooperative about the scheduling of inspections in order to not unduly disrupt operations.

The Safety Officer conducts a pre-inspection, opening conference upon arrival to inform the employer why he/she is there, and to enlist the employer's assistance in conducting the inspection. An employer has the right to request identification from the Safety Officer and to ask why the inspection is being conducted. If it is the result of an employee complaint, the employer has the right to see a copy of the complaint, although the identity of the complainant may be protected.

An employer may refuse to permit an inspector to enter the premises, but the refusal carries considerable risk. MIOSHA may consider the refusal as evidence that the employer has something to hide, which may result in a more thorough inspection, if and when one is conducted.

MIOSHA may obtain a search warrant to enter the premises for an inspection if an employer refuses entry to the Safety Officer. MIOSHA may attempt to obtain a search warrant before its initial visit to the site if the employer has the reputation for resisting inspections.

Both the employer and employees may have a representative accompany the inspector on the walk-around inspection. The employer may decide who its representative(s) will be. An employee representative will also normally be selected for the inspection. The Safety Officer may speak with any other employees the Safety Officer selects either in front of the representatives or in private.

The employees who accompany the Safety Officer may not have their pay reduced for time away from work during the inspection, nor may the employer take any disciplinary action against an employee for his or her involvement in the inspection or the post-inspection, Closing Conference.

The Safety Officer is free to look at conditions, equipment, and materials, and may take photographs where it is desirable to do so. Safety Officers must protect trade secrets and may not divulge to others, the information received or photos taken during the inspection.

The employer's MIOSHA Forms 300 and 301 will generally be examined, as will the annual summary 300A form, if the inspection occurs between February 1 through April 30. The Safety Officer will also look at bulletin boards to see if the required MIOSHA posters are posted.

The Safety Officer will conclude with a Closing Conference and determine whether to meet with the employer and employee representatives separately or together. The findings of the inspection will be disclosed and the specific citations recommended for issuance will be identified. The final written citations will be reviewed by the inspectors supervisors and occasionally differ from the information given at the post-inspection Closing Conference.

Citations for Safety and Health Violations

Citations may be issued under specific standards, or under the general duty clause. When a violation is found, the Safety Officer may take several actions:

- Shut down the unsafe operation if there is an imminent danger.
- Recommend the issuance of a citation for a serious violation.
- Recommend the issuance of a citation for an other-than-serious violation.
- Give notice of a *de minimis* violation.

The Safety Officer will set a date for abatement of the violation, taking into consideration the seriousness of the hazard and the difficulty of achieving the abatement.

Citation Penalties

PENALTY AMOUNTS FOR BASIC CLASSIFICATIONS

Classification	Maximum
Serious	$7,000
Other than serious	$7,000
Willful or repeat	$70,000 (Minimum for willful = $5,000)
Failure to abate	$7,000 per calendar day beyond final abatement date

REPEATED VIOLATIONS

Penalty increase factors	Original $ value multiplied
First repeat	2×
Second repeat	4×
Third repeat	10×

OTHER THAN SERIOUS (NO INITIAL PENALTY)

First repeat	$200
Second repeat	$500
Third repeat	$1,000

REGULATORY VIOLATIONS

OTS Violation	Recommended penalty
MIOSHA poster	$1,000
Annual Summary	$1,000
Citation posting	$3,000
Reporting FAT/CAT	$5,000
Employee Records	$1,000
Failure to notify employee rep.	$2,000

RATES OF REDUCTION

The size of the employer reduction shall be based on the maximum number of employees at the inspected worksite at any one time during the previous 12 months.

Number of employees	Percentage
1 to 25	60%
26 to 100	40%
101 to 250	20%
251 or more	None

GOOD FAITH REDUCTION

Program status	Written	Unwritten
Fully implemented	30%	20%
Partially implemented	15%	10%
Not implemented	None	None

Shutting Down the Operation

Where MIOSHA determines that an "imminent danger" exists, it may shut down the operation creating the danger. Procedurally, the Safety Officer informs MIOSHA of the imminent danger, and MIOSHA then authorizes the inspector to tag the dangerous equipment and order the cessation of the use of the dangerous equipment or unsafe procedure. The Safety Officer is also authorized to remove all persons from the area of the danger, except for those persons necessary to correct the danger.

An employer may appeal an order to shut down an operation by requesting MIOSHA's regional supervisor to review the order. The supervisor must conduct his review within 24 hours of the employer's request.

If an employer refuses to abide by the order, MIOSHA may seek a restraining order in circuit court. An employee affected by the employer's actions or inaction may also seek an order compelling MIOSHA to act, if MIOSHA arbitrarily or capriciously fails to pursue an injunction.

It is unlawful for an employer to permit any employee to operate tagged equipment or work on a process that has been tagged as an imminent danger, unless the employee's presence is necessary to correct the problem. An employee who refuses to work on tagged equipment or on a tagged process may not be disciplined or otherwise adversely treated for such a refusal.

Serious and Other-Than-Serious Violations

A serious violation is issued when there is a substantial probability that death or serious physical harm could result and the employer knows or should know of the presence of the violation.

An "other than serious" violation is given where the violation is one that is not likely to lead to serious harm or death.

Citations for these violations must be issued within 90 days of the completion of the physical inspection or investigation of the establishment, describe in detail the nature of the violation, identify the standard or section of MIOSHA which is violated, and state a reason for the violation to be abated and indicate a specific penalty amount if warranted.

The citation will be mailed by registered mail to the employer, which must immediately post the citation at or near the place of the violation, until the abatement is made, or for three days, whichever is later. The employer must notify MIOSHA whether it intends to comply with the abatement and the abatement date. If it fails to abate or appeal in a timely manner, additional penalties may be assessed.

De Minimis *Violations*

A *de minimis* violation is one that bears no relationship to employee safety and health. The citation for such a violation must be posted by the employer for three days at or near the place of the violation, but there is no abatement requirement, and no requirement to notify MIOSHA of whether the violation has been abated.

Isolated Incident/Employee Misconduct

MIOSHA Section 33(6) generally provides that an employer may seek to have a citation dismissed if the employer can show that the violation is the result of unpreventable employee misconduct. In order to establish the unpreventable employee misconduct defense an employer must show:

- the employer established work rules designed to prevent the violation;
- the employer effectively communicated its work rules to its employees;
- the employer has taken steps to discover rule violations; and
- the employer has effectively enforced the rules once violations have been discovered.

If the employer can establish each of the above items, the citation should be dismissed/vacated.

Employer Appeals According to MIOSHA

Employers have the right to appeal citations, penalties, or the time required for abatement, within 15 working days of receipt of the citation. The appeal should be mailed to MIOSHA. A late appeal will only be considered if the employer demonstrates good cause for failing to meet the deadline, and that it has a meritorious defense. MIOSHA has 15 working days in which to act on the appeal. When an employer appeals a citation, it must send a copy of the appeal to the affected employees or to the employee representative. Upon the filing of the decision of MIOSHA, a copy of the appeal must also be sent to the employee representative and must be posted until a notice of hearing is received, at which time the notice of hearing must be posted until the hearing is concluded.

MIOSHA's decision may be appealed to the Board of Health and Safety Compliance and Appeals, within 15 working days, by filing a notice of appeal with MIOSHA. A prehearing conference will be held, which may be attended by an MIOSHA Appeals Officer and the Safety Officer. If the conference does not resolve the issue, a formal hearing will be scheduled. Witnesses, documents, and arguments may be presented at the hearing, and depositions may be used for witnesses who cannot appear. The hearing officer will issue a report which will be acted upon by the Board. The Board may affirm, modify, or vacate the proposed report of the Administrative Law Judge.

An appeal from the decision of the Board may be taken in one of two ways. First, the employer may request a rehearing within 60 days of the delivery of the Board's decision. Alternatively, it may appeal to a state Circuit Court. This appeal may be filed in the county in which the employer resides or has a principal place of business, or in Ingham County. It must be filed within 60 days after the mailing of the Board's decision, or within 60 days of the Board's denial of a request for a rehearing. The filing of this appeal does not automatically stay enforcement of the citation or order.

The judicial appeal is limited to the record made before the administrative agency; new evidence may not be submitted to the court. The Board's decision may be reversed by the court if it determines that the decision was:

- in violation of the Constitution or a statute;
- in excess of the agency's authority or jurisdiction;
- made under an unlawful procedure which prejudiced the employer;
- not supported by competent, material, and substantial evidence;
- arbitrary, capricious, or was clearly an abuse of discretion; or
- affected by other substantial and material errors of law.

The court may affirm or reverse the Board's decision, or it may remand the case back to the Board for further proceedings. The circuit court decision may be appealed to the Michigan Court of Appeals. The Court of Appeals has discretion as to whether to hear the appeal.

Handling Hazardous Materials

Employers are responsible for limiting many of the risks associated with employees' handling of hazardous chemicals and other materials, under both federal OSHA and state MIOSHA requirements.

In addition to the discussions of OSHA and MIOSHA operations generally, the topics in this section analyze the obligations of Michigan employers under a particular set of regulations, the Hazard Communication Standard (HCS).

History of Hazardous Substances Regulation

OSHA first published a notice of proposed rule making to regulate hazardous substances in the workplace in 1981. The initial rule placed the burden on employers to assess the potentially hazardous nature of workplace substances, but was withdrawn and replaced by a new proposed rule, published in early 1982. The new rule, titled Hazard Communication, placed the burden on chemical producers to evaluate and determine the hazards of their products, to label containers making note of those hazards, and to supply material safety data sheets (MSDSs) to the purchasers of their products. Employers, in turn, were required to develop a hazard communication program, label containers holding hazardous substances in the workplace, and to maintain and provide employees with access to MSDSs.

OSHA published the final Hazard Communication Standard (HCS) in November 1983. Many critics, including organized labor, argued the limitation to manufacturers was inadequate. Consequently, several states including Michigan in 1986, passed "right to know" acts applying the HCS to virtually all state employers. OSHA was persuaded that its regulations should be expanded to cover other than just manufacturing employers. In 1987, OSHA adopted a revised final regulation which basically extended the HCS to all employers.

In addition to communicating to end users, chemical manufacturers, importers, and employers are also required to disclose certain information to appropriate governmental entities. Title III, the Emergency Planning and Community Right-To-Know Act of 1986, requires covered companies to annually disclose to the state and local government the following:

- Substances stockpiled at each facility
- The substances sent for off-site disposal
- The substances disposed of on-site
- The substances released into the affected community

The governmental entity must in turn make the information available to the public. Title III has four subparts, consisting of:

- Emergency planning for accidents
- Notification of spills

- Annual reporting of chemical inventories
- Annual reporting of routine and accidental toxic chemical discharges into the environment

In 1986, the Michigan legislature passed our state's "right-to-know" laws as an amendment to the MIOSHA legislation. The laws expanded on the original OSHA hazard communication standards and incorporated the federal regulatory scheme. Chemical manufacturers and importers were therefore required to determine which substances were hazardous and to thereafter provide information to end users regarding the hazardous nature of those substances.

Hazard Communication

The HCS is intended to ensure that all chemicals produced and/or imported are initially evaluated for their potential hazardous properties, and that information about such hazards is provided to end users (employers and employees) through a comprehensive communications program. The program must include container labeling and other warnings, MSDSs, and employee training. The HCS also requires that the comprehensive program include the development and maintenance of a written hazard communications program for the workplace, and that this include the listing of hazardous chemicals present in the workplace, the labeling of workplace containers used to store hazardous chemicals, the preparation and distribution of MSDSs to employees and other downstream users, and the development and implementation of employee training programs and protective measures.

For a detailed advisory guideline for employer compliance with the HCS, see the Appendix E excerpt from the Code of Federal Regulations.

Application of HCS

The HCS generally applies to any chemical known to be present in the workplace to which employees may be exposed under normal working conditions or foreseeable emergency conditions. Therefore, employers whose employees would not be exposed to hazardous chemicals under normal conditions or in foreseeable emergencies are exempt (i.e., office and administrative personnel).

An employer that merely ships and/or stores sealed containers, which are not opened while in the workplace, need only do the following:

- Ensure that warning labels on the sealed containers of hazardous chemicals not be removed or defaced.
- Verify that MSDSs are received or obtained with any incoming containers, and that such MSDSs are maintained.

- Ensure that employees on each work shift have access to the MSDSs.
- Ensure that employees are provided with pertinent information and training.

The HCS does not require that the following chemicals be labeled:

- Any pesticide
- Any food, food additive, color additive, cosmetic, or medical or veterinary device
- Any beverage containing alcohol intended for nonindustrial use
- Any consumer produce

The HCS also does not apply to:

- Hazardous waste
- Tobacco or tobacco products
- Wood or wood products
- Articles that do not otherwise result in exposure to a hazardous chemical
- Food, drugs, cosmetics, or alcoholic beverages in a retail establishment
- Food, drugs, or cosmetics intended for personal consumption by employees while in the workplace
- Any consumer product or hazardous substance
- Any drugs when sold in final form for direct administration to the patient

Employers who engage in agricultural operations are covered by the Michigan Pesticide Act and the Insecticide, Fungicide and Rodenticide Act (federal), and are consequently exempt from the Right-To-Know Act.

Hazard Determination

Chemical manufacturers and importers must evaluate the chemicals which they produce or import, to determine if the substances are hazardous. The HCS does not require that employers make such determinations unless the employer chooses not to rely on the evaluation performed by the manufacturer or importer.

Although employers are not generally responsible for evaluating chemicals, an employer who creates a chemical either through mixing other chemicals or through processing, thereby becomes the chemical manufacturer responsible for hazard evaluation and identification.

Written Hazard Communication Program

Employers must develop, implement, and maintain a written hazard communications program at the workplace. At the very least, this program must describe the appropriate labeling, warning, MSDS, and must provide for training. The written program must:

- include a list of the hazardous chemicals known to be present in the workplace.
- identify those chemicals in a manner that allows location of the appropriate MSDS.
- provide for training.
- describe the methods which will be used to inform employees of the hazards of non-routine tasks and hazards due to chemicals contained in unlabeled pipes located in the workplace.

Labeling of Hazardous Materials

Hazardous chemical containers must be labeled, tagged, or marked by the manufacturer, importer, or distributor. The label must include:

- Identity of the hazardous chemical
- Appropriate hazard warnings
- The chemical manufacturer's name and address

Employers must ensure that all chemical containers are appropriately labeled, tagged or marked with the chemical's identity and the appropriate hazard warnings. Workplace pipe containers and transmission systems must also be appropriately labeled. The labels must provide a prominent warning that is legible and in English.

Material Safety Data Sheets

Chemical manufacturers, importers, and distributors are required to provide a Material Safety Data Sheet (MSDS) to chemical purchasers. The purchaser (usually an employer) must in turn make the MSDS available upon request by an employee. There must be an MSDS for every hazardous chemical used by the employer. The MSDS must be in English (it should also be in any appropriate foreign language), and must, at a minimum, contain the following information:

- The chemical identities used on the label. If a single substance, it must state its chemical and common names; if a mixture, the chemical and common names of its ingredients.
- The physical and chemical characteristics of the hazardous chemical (i.e. vapor pressure, flash point).

- The physical hazards of the hazardous chemical, including the potential for fire, explosion, and reactivity.

- The health hazards of the hazardous chemical, including signs and symptoms of exposure, and any medical conditions which are generally recognized as being aggravated by exposure to the chemical.

- The primary route(s) of entry into the body.

- The OSHA permissible exposure limit.

- Whether the hazardous chemical is listed in the National Toxicology Program (carcinogens) or has been found to be a potential carcinogen.

- Any generally applicable precautions for safe handling and use which are known to the chemical manufacturer, importer, or employer preparing the MSDS (including hygienic practices, protective measures during repair and maintenance of contaminated equipment, and procedures for clean-up of spills and leaks).

- Any generally applicable control measures such as appropriate engineering controls, work practices, or personal protective equipment.

- Emergency and first aid procedures.

- The date the MSDS was prepared or last revised.

- The name, address and telephone number of the chemical manufacturer, importer, employer, or other responsible party preparing or distributing the MSDS, who can provide additional information with regard to the chemical.

If the manufacturer, importer, distributor, or employer becomes aware of any significant information regarding a chemical's hazards, or ways to protect against the chemical's hazards, the new information must be incorporated into the MSDS within three months.

MSDSs must be organized in the workplace in a "systematic and consistent manner." The employer must maintain copies of the required MSDS for each hazardous chemical in the workplace. The MSDS must be available and accessible to employees during each work shift, and be available, upon request, to a designated employee representative (usually a union representative).

Employees must be trained to locate and interpret the MSDS forms. MIOSHA requires employers to permanently post the Michigan Right-To-Know poster, #2105, which provides information on the location of MSDS and informs employees that:

i. Employers must make MSDSs available.

j. Employees must be notified of new or revised MSDSs.

k. Employers cannot retaliate against employees (discipline, discrimination, discharge) for exercising their right under the Michigan Right-To-Know law.

Within five days after receipt of a new or revised MSDS, the employer must post notice of the new or revised MSDS for a period of ten working days.

Employee Information and Training

Employers must provide employees with information and training on hazardous chemicals in the employee's particular work area both at the time of the employee's initial job assignment and whenever a new hazard is introduced into the work area.

The information that must be provided includes:

- HCS requirements,
- any operations in the employee's work area where hazardous chemicals are present, and
- location and availability of the written hazard communication program, including the required list(s) of hazardous chemicals and MSDSs.

The following information must be posted throughout the workplace:

- Location of the MSDS.
- The person's name from whom the MSDS can be obtained.
- That the employer cannot retaliate against an employee who exercises his/her rights under the Right-To-Know Act.
- That the MSDS can also, or as an alternative, be obtained from the Department of Public Health (the address and telephone number shall be included).

Employers must also provide the following:

- Methods and observations that may be used to detect the presence or release of a hazardous chemical in the work area (e.g. monitoring devices, visual appearance, odor, etc.).
- The physical and health hazards of the chemicals in the work area.
- The measures employees can take to protect themselves from these hazards, including specific procedures the employer has implemented to protect employees from exposure (e.g. work practices, emergency procedures, and personal protective equipment to be used).

- The details of the hazard communication program developed by the employer, including an explanation of the labeling system and the MSDS, and how employees can obtain and use the appropriate hazard information.

Trade Secrets

A chemical manufacturer, importer, or employer may withhold from the MSDS a substance's specific chemical identity provided:

- The employer can demonstrate that the information is a "trade secret."
- The information in the MSDS nevertheless discloses the properties and effects of the hazardous chemical.
- The MSDS notes that the specific chemical identity is a trade secret.
- The chemical identity is disclosed in medical emergency and some non-emergency situations.

The chemical manufacturer, importer, or employer must disclose the specific chemical identity of a trade secret chemical if a treating physician or nurse determines that a medical emergency exists and disclosure is necessary for treatment.

In non-emergency situations, the chemical manufacturer, importer, or employer must disclose the specific chemical identity of a trade secret chemical if a health professional, employee, or designated employee representative makes such a request, provided:

- The request is in writing.
- One or more of the following health needs for the information is evident and described in detail:
    - To assess the hazards to which employees will be exposed.
    - To conduct workplace atmospheric samplings to determine exposure levels.
    - To conduct pre-assignment or periodic medical surveillance of exposed employees to provide medical treatment to exposed employees.
    - To select or assess appropriate personal protective equipment.
    - To design or assess engineering controls or other protective measures.
    - To conduct studies to determine the health effects of exposure.
    - The request explains in detail why disclosure of the specific chemical identity is essential and why the disclosure of other information would not be satisfactory.

- The request includes a description of the procedures to be used to maintain the confidentiality of the disclosed information.
- The requesting party agrees in a written confidentiality agreement that the information will not be used for any purpose other than the health needs asserted.

A chemical manufacturer, importer, or employer may deny a written request for disclosure. The denial must be in writing, must include evidence to support the employer's position, must state the specific reasons why the request is being denied, and must be provided within thirty days after the request is received.

If the denial is referred to OSHA, and OSHA determines that the information requested is not a bona fide "trade secret," or that the requesting party has a legitimate medical or occupational health need for the information, the chemical manufacturer, importer, or employer will be subject to citation by OSHA.

With respect to the Michigan Right-To-Know Act, an exposed employee, health professional, or authorized employee representative may petition the Director to review a denial of a written request for disclosure of a specific chemical identity. An employer who claims a "trade secret" must be prepared to defend its position upon request by the Director of the Department of Public Health. The Director will consider the following factors in determining whether a specific chemical identity may be withheld as a trade secret:

- The extent to which the information is known outside the employer's business.
- The extent to which it is known by employees and others involved in the employer's business.
- The extent of measures taken by the employer to guard the secrecy of the information.
- The value of the information to the employer and the employer's competitors.
- The amount of effort and money expended by the employer in developing the information.
- The ease or difficulty with which the information could be properly acquired or duplicated by others.

Specific chemical identities, even if arguably trade secrets, must be disclosed to the Director of Public Health upon request. The Director shall consider and require any prudent measures necessary to protect the health of employees or the public in general while maintaining the confidentiality of any trade secrets. Records and information obtained during the course of such review shall be exempt from disclosure under the Michigan Freedom of Information Act.

Violations of HCS

There are no *de minimis* violations of the Right-To-Know Act. All violations are considered either "serious" or "other-than-serious" violations. Under most circumstances, MIOSHA is likely to determine a violation should be considered "serious."

Guidelines for Employer Compliance with HCS

The following text is excerpted from the Code of Federal Regulations sections which set forth the Hazard Communication Standard (HCS).

APPENDIX E TO SEC. 1910.1200 (ADVISORY)—GUIDELINES FOR EMPLOYER COMPLIANCE

The Hazard Communication Standard (HCS) is based on a simple concept—that employees have both a need and a right to know the hazards and identities of the chemicals they are exposed to when working. They also need to know what protective measures are available to prevent adverse effects from occurring. The HCS is designed to provide employees with the information they need.

Knowledge acquired under the HCS will help employers provide safer workplaces for their employees. When employers have information about the chemicals being used, they can take steps to reduce exposures, substitute less hazardous materials, and establish proper work practices. These efforts will help prevent the occurrence of work-related illnesses and injuries caused by chemicals.

The HCS addresses the issues of evaluating and communicating hazards to workers. Evaluation of chemical hazards involves a number of technical concepts, and is a process that requires the professional judgment of experienced experts. That's why the HCS is designed so that employers who simply use chemicals, rather than produce or import them, are not required to evaluate the hazards of those chemicals. Hazard determination is the responsibility of the producers and importers of the materials. Producers and importers of chemicals are then required to provide the hazard information to employers that purchase their products.

Employers that don't produce or import chemicals need only focus on those parts of the rule that deal with establishing a workplace program and communicating information to their workers. This appendix is a general guide for such employers to help them determine what's required under the rule. It does not supplant or substitute for the regulatory provisions, but rather provides a simplified outline of the steps an average employer would follow to meet those requirements.

1. BECOMING FAMILIAR WITH THE RULE

OSHA has provided a simple summary of the HCS in a pamphlet entitled "Chemical Hazard Communication," OSHA Publication Number 3084. Some employers prefer to begin to become familiar with the rule's requirements by reading this pamphlet. A copy may be obtained from your local OSHA Area Office, or by contacting the OSHA Publications Office at (202) 523-9667.

The standard is long, and some parts of it are technical, but the basic concepts are simple. In fact, the requirements reflect what many employers have been doing for years. You may find that you are already largely in compliance with many of the provisions, and will simply have to modify your existing programs somewhat. If you are operating in an OSHA-approved State-Plan State, you must comply with the state's requirements, which may be different than those of the federal rule. Many of the State-Plan States had hazard communication or "right-to-know" laws prior to promulgation of the federal rule. Employers in state-Plan states, such as Michigan, should contact their state OSHA offices (MIOSHA) for more information regarding applicable requirements.

The HCS requires information to be prepared and transmitted regarding all hazardous chemicals. The HCS covers both physical hazards (such as flammability), and health hazards (such as irritation, lung damage, and cancer). Most chemicals used in the workplace have some hazard potential, and thus will be covered by the rule.

One difference between this rule and many others adopted by OSHA is that this one is performance-oriented. That means that you have the flexibility to adapt the rule to the needs of your workplace, rather than having to follow specific, rigid requirements. It also means that you have to exercise more judgment to implement an appropriate and effective program.

The standard's design is simple. Chemical manufacturers and importers must evaluate the hazards of the chemicals they produce or import. Using that information, they must then prepare labels for containers, and more detailed technical bulletins called material safety data sheets (MSDS).

Chemical manufacturers, importers, and distributors of hazardous chemicals are all required to provide the appropriate labels and material safety data sheets to the employers to which they ship the chemicals. The information is to be provided automatically. Every container of hazardous chemicals you receive must be labeled, tagged, or marked with the required information. Your suppliers must also send you a properly completed material safety data sheet (MSDS) at the time of the first shipment of the chemical, and with the next shipment after the MSDS is updated with new and significant information about the hazards.

You can rely on the information received from your suppliers. You have no independent duty to analyze the chemical or evaluate the hazards of it.

Employers that "use" hazardous chemicals must have a program to ensure the information is provided to exposed employees. "Use" means to package, handle, react, or transfer. This is an intentionally broad scope, and includes any situation where a chemical is present in such a way that employees may be exposed under normal conditions of use or in a foreseeable emergency.

The requirements of the rule that deal specifically with the hazard communication program are found in 29 CFR §2910.1200 in paragraphs (e), written hazard communication program; (f), labels and other forms of warning; (g), material safety data sheets; and (h), employee information and training. The requirements of these paragraphs should be the focus of your attention. Concentrate on becoming familiar with them, using paragraphs (b), scope and application, and (c), definitions, as references when needed to help explain the provisions.

There are two types of work operations where the coverage of the rule is limited. These are laboratories and operations where chemicals are only handled in sealed containers (i.e., a warehouse). The limited provisions for these workplaces can be found in paragraph (b) of this section, scope and application. Basically, employers having these types of work operations need only keep labels on containers as they are received; maintain material safety data sheets that are received, and give employees access to them; and provide information and training for employees. Employers do not have to have written hazard communication programs and lists of chemicals for these types of operations.

The limited coverage of laboratories and sealed container operations addresses the obligation of an employer to the workers in the operations involved, and does not affect the employer's duties as a distributor of chemicals. For example, a distributor may have warehouse operations where employees would be protected under the limited sealed container provisions. In this situation, requirements for obtaining and maintaining MSDSs are limited to providing access to those received with containers while the substance is in the workplace, and requesting MSDSs when employees request access for those not received with the containers. However, as a distributor of hazardous chemicals, that employer will still have responsibilities for providing MSDSs to downstream customers at the time of the first shipment and when the MSDS is updated. Therefore, although they may not be required for the employees in the work operation, the distributor may, nevertheless, have to have MSDSs to satisfy other requirements of the rule.

2. IDENTIFY RESPONSIBLE STAFF

Hazard communication is going to be a continuing program in your facility. Compliance with the HCS is not a "one shot deal." In order to have a successful program, it will be necessary to assign responsibility for both the initial and ongoing activities that have to be undertaken to comply with the rule. In some cases, these activities may already be part of current job assignments. For example, site supervisors are frequently responsible for on-the-job training sessions. Early identification of the responsible employees, and involvement of them in the development of your plan of action, will result in a more effective program design. Evaluation of the effectiveness of your program will also be enhanced by involvement of affected employees.

For any safety and health program, success depends on commitment at every level of the organization. This is particularly true for hazard communication, where success requires a change in behavior. This will only occur if employers understand the program, and are committed to its success, and if employees are motivated by the people presenting the information to them.

3. IDENTIFY HAZARDOUS CHEMICALS IN THE WORKPLACE

The standard requires a list of hazardous chemicals in the workplace as part of the written hazard communication program. The list will eventually serve as an inventory of everything for which an MSDS must be maintained. At this point, however, preparing the list will help you complete the rest of the program since it will give you some idea of the scope of the program required for compliance in your facility.

The best way to prepare a comprehensive list is to survey the workplace. Purchasing records may also help, and certainly employers should establish procedures to ensure that in the future purchasing procedures result in MSDSs being received before a material is used in the workplace.

The broadest possible perspective should be taken when doing the survey. Sometimes people think of "chemicals" as being only liquids in containers. The HCS covers chemicals in all physical forms—liquids, solids, gases, vapors, fumes, and mists—whether they are "contained" or not. The hazardous nature of the chemical and the potential for exposure are the factors that determine whether a chemical is covered. If it's not hazardous, it's not covered. If there is no potential for exposure (i.e., the chemical is inextricably bound and cannot be released), the rule does not cover the chemical.

Look around. Identify chemicals in containers, including pipes, but also think about chemicals generated in the work operations. For example, welding fumes, dusts, and exhaust fumes are all sources of chemical exposures. Read labels provided by suppliers for hazard information. Make a list of all chemicals in the workplace that are potentially hazardous. For your own information and planning, you may also want to note on the list the location(s) of the products within the workplace, and an indication of the hazards as found on the label. This will help you as you prepare the rest of your program.

Paragraph (b) of this section, scope and application, includes exemptions for various chemicals or workplace situations. After compiling the complete list of chemicals, you should review paragraph (b) of this section to determine if any of the items can be eliminated from the list because they are exempted materials. For example, food, drugs, and cosmetics brought into the workplace for employee consumption are exempt. So rubbing alcohol in the first aid kit would not be covered.

Once you have compiled as complete a list as possible of the potentially hazardous chemicals in the workplace, the next step is to determine if you have received material safety data sheets for all of them. Check your files against the inventory you have just compiled. If any are missing, contact your supplier and request one. It is a good idea to document these requests, either by copy of a letter or a note regarding telephone conversations. If you have MSDSs for chemicals that are not on your list, figure out why. Maybe you don't use the chemical anymore. Or maybe you missed it in your survey. Some suppliers do provide MSDSs for products that are not hazardous. These do not have to be maintained by you.

You should not allow employees to use any chemicals for which you have not received an MSDS. The MSDS provides information you need to ensure proper protective measures are implemented prior to exposure.

4. Preparing and Implementing a Hazard Communication Program

All workplaces where employees are exposed to hazardous chemicals must have a written plan which describes how the standard will be implemented in that facility. Preparation of a plan is not just a paper exercise—all of the elements must be implemented in the workplace in order to be in compliance with the rule. See paragraph (e) of this section for the specific requirements regarding written hazard communication programs. The only work operations which do not have to comply with the written plan requirements are laboratories and work operations where employees only handle chemicals in sealed containers. See paragraph (b) of this section, scope and application, for the specific requirements for these two types of workplaces.

The plan does not have to be lengthy or complicated. It is intended to be a blueprint for implementation of your program—an assurance that all aspects of the requirements have been addressed.

Many trade associations and other professional groups have provided sample programs and other assistance materials to affected employers. These have been very helpful to many employers since they tend to be tailored to the particular industry involved. You may wish to investigate whether your industry trade groups have developed such materials.

Although such general guidance may be helpful, you must remember that the written program has to reflect what you are doing in your workplace. Therefore, if you use a generic program it must be adapted to address the facility it covers. For example, the written plan must list the chemicals present at the site, indicate who is to be responsible for the various aspects of the program in your facility, and indicate where written materials will be made available to employees.

If OSHA/MIOSHA inspects your workplace for compliance with the HCS, the OSHA/MIOSHA safety officer will ask to see your written plan at the outset of the inspection. In general, the following items will be considered in evaluating your program.

The written program must describe how the requirements for labels and other forms of warning, material safety data sheets, and employee information and training, are going to be met in your facility. The following discussion provides the type of information compliance officers will be looking for to decide whether these elements of the hazard communication program have been properly addressed:

4-A. LABELS AND OTHER FORMS OF WARNING

In-plant containers of hazardous chemicals must be labeled, tagged, or marked with the identity of the material and appropriate hazard warnings. Chemical manufacturers, importers, and distributors are required to ensure that every container of hazardous chemicals they ship is appropriately labeled with such information and with the name and address of the producer or other responsible party. Employers purchasing chemicals can rely on the labels provided by their suppliers. If the material is subsequently transferred by the employer from a labeled container to another container, the employer will have to label that container unless it is subject to the portable container exemption. See paragraph (f) of this section for specific labeling requirements.

The primary information to be obtained from an OSHA-required label is an identity for the material, and appropriate hazard warnings. The identity is any term which appears on the label, the MSDS, and the list of chemicals, and thus links these three sources of information. The identity used by the supplier may be a common or trade name ("Black Magic Formula"), or a chemical name (1,1,1,-trichloroethane). The hazard warning is a brief statement of the hazardous effects of the chemical ("flammable," "causes lung damage"). Labels frequently contain other information, such as precautionary measures ("do not use near open flame"), but this information is provided voluntarily and is not required by the rule. Labels must be legible, and prominently displayed. There are no specific requirements for size or color, or any specified text.

With these requirements in mind, the compliance officer will be looking for the following types of information to ensure that labeling will be properly implemented in your facility:

1. Designation of person(s) responsible for ensuring labeling of in-plant containers;
2. Designation of person(s) responsible for ensuring labeling of any shipped containers;
3. Description of labeling system(s) used;

4. Description of written alternatives to labeling of in-plant containers (if used); and,

5. Procedures to review and update label information when necessary.

Employers that are purchasing and using hazardous chemicals—rather than producing or distributing them—will primarily be concerned with ensuring that every purchased container is labeled. If materials are transferred into other containers, the employer must ensure that these are labeled as well, unless they fall under the portable container exemption (paragraph (f)(7) of this section). In terms of labeling systems, you can simply choose to use the labels provided by your suppliers on the containers. These will generally be verbal text labels, and do not usually include numerical rating systems or symbols that require special training. The most important thing to remember is that this is a continuing duty—all in-plant containers of hazardous chemicals must always be labeled. Therefore, it is important to designate someone to be responsible for ensuring that the labels are maintained as required on the containers in your facility, and that newly purchased materials are checked for labels prior to use.

4-B. Material Safety Data Sheets

Chemical manufacturers and importers are required to obtain or develop a material safety data sheet for each hazardous chemical they produce or import. Distributors are responsible for ensuring that their customers are provided a copy of these MSDSs. Employers must have an MSDS for each hazardous chemical which they use. Employers may rely on the information received from their suppliers. The specific requirements for material safety data sheets are in paragraph (g) of this section.

There is no specified format for the MSDS under the rule, although there are specific information requirements. OSHA has developed a non-mandatory format, OSHA Form 174, which may be used by chemical manufacturers and importers to comply with the rule. The MSDS must be in English. You are entitled to receive from your supplier a data sheet which includes all of the information required under the rule. If you do not receive one automatically, you should request one. If you receive one that is obviously inadequate, with, for example, blank spaces that are not completed, you should request an appropriately completed one. If your request for a data sheet or for a corrected data sheet does not produce the information needed, you should contact your local OSHA Area Office for assistance in obtaining the MSDS.

The role of MSDSs under the rule is to provide detailed information on each hazardous chemical, including its potential hazardous effects, its physical and chemical characteristics, and recommendations for appropriate protective measures. This information should be useful to you as the employer responsible for designing protective programs, as well as to the workers. If you are not familiar with material safety data sheets and with chemical terminology, you may need to learn to use them yourself. A glossary of MSDS terms may be helpful in this regard. Generally speaking, most employers using hazardous chemicals will primarily be concerned with MSDS information regarding hazardous effects and recommended protective measures. Focus on the sections of the MSDS that are applicable to your situation.

MSDSs must be readily accessible to employees when they are in their work areas during their work shifts. This may be accomplished in many different ways. You must decide what is appropriate for your particular workplace. Some employers keep the MSDSs in a binder in a central location (i.e., in the pick-up truck on a construction site). Others, particularly in workplaces with large numbers of chemicals, computerize the information and provide access through terminals. As long as employees can get the information when they need it, any approach may be used. The employees must have access to the MSDSs themselves—simply having a system where the information can be read to them over the phone is only permitted under the mobile worksite provision, paragraph (g)(9) of this section, when employees must travel between workplaces during the shift. In this situation, they have access to the MSDSs prior to leaving the primary worksite, and when they return, so the telephone system is simply an emergency arrangement.

In order to ensure that you have a current MSDS for each chemical in the plant as required, and that employee access is provided, the compliance officers will be looking for the following types of information in your written program:

1. Designation of person(s) responsible for obtaining and maintaining the MSDSs;

2. How such sheets are to be maintained in the workplace (i.e., in notebooks in the work area(s) or in a computer with terminal access), and how employees can obtain access to them when they are in their work area during the work shift;

3. Procedures to follow when the MSDS is not received at the time of the first shipment;

4. For producers, procedures to update the MSDS when new and significant health information is found; and,

5. Description of alternatives to actual data sheets in the workplace, if used.

For employers using hazardous chemicals, the most important aspect of the written program in terms of MSDSs is to ensure that someone is responsible for obtaining and maintaining the MSDSs for every hazardous chemical in the workplace. The list of hazardous chemicals required to be maintained as part of the written program will serve as an inventory. As new chemicals are purchased, the list should be updated. Many companies have found it convenient to include on their purchase orders the name and address of the person designated in their company to receive MSDSs.

4-C. EMPLOYEE INFORMATION AND TRAINING

Each employee who may be "exposed" to hazardous chemicals when working must be provided information and trained prior to initial assignment to work with a hazardous chemical, and whenever the hazard changes. "Exposure" or "exposed" under the rule means that "an employee is subjected to a hazardous chemical in the course of employment through any route of entry (inhalation, ingestion, skin contact or absorption, etc.) and includes potential (i.e., accidental or possible) exposure." See paragraph (h) of this section for specific requirements. Information and training may be done either by individual chemical, or by categories of hazards (such as flammability or carcinogenicity). If there are only a few chemicals in the workplace, then you may want to discuss each one individually. Where there are large numbers of chemicals, or the chemicals change frequently, you will probably want to train generally based on the hazard categories (i.e., flammable liquids, corrosive materials, carcinogens). Employees will have access to the substance-specific information on the labels and MSDSs.

Information and training is a critical part of the hazard communication program. Information regarding hazards and protective measures are provided to workers through written labels and material safety data sheets. However, through effective information and training, workers will learn to read and understand such information, determine how it can be obtained and used in their own workplaces, and understand the risks of exposure to the chemicals in their workplaces as well as the ways to protect themselves. A properly conducted training program will ensure comprehension and understanding. It is not sufficient to either just read material to the workers, or simply hand them material to read. You want to create a climate where workers feel free to ask questions. This will help you to ensure that the information is understood. You must always remember that the underlying purpose of the HCS is to reduce the incidence of chemical source illnesses and injuries. This will be accomplished by modifying behavior through the provision of hazard information and information about protective measures. If your program works, you and your workers will better understand the chemical hazards within the workplace. The procedures you establish regarding, for example, purchasing, storage, and handling of these chemicals will improve, and thereby reduce the risks posed to employees exposed to the chemical hazards involved. Furthermore, your workers' comprehension will also be increased, and proper work practices will be followed in your workplace.

If you are going to do the training yourself, you will have to understand the material and be prepared to motivate the workers to learn. This is not always an easy task, but the benefits are worth the effort. More information regarding appropriate training can be found in OSHA Publication No. 2254 which contains voluntary training guidelines prepared by OSHA's Training Institute. A copy of this document is available from OSHA's Publications Office at (202) 219-4667.

In reviewing your written program with regard to information and training, the following items need to be considered:

1. Designation of person(s) responsible for conducting training;

2. Format of the program to be used (audiovisuals, classroom instruction, etc.);

3. Elements of the training program (should be consistent with the elements in paragraph (h) of this section); and,

4. Procedure to train new employees at the time of their initial assignment to work with a hazardous chemical, and to train employees when a new hazard is introduced into the workplace.

The written program should provide enough details about the employer's plans in this area to assess whether or not a good faith effort is being made to train employees. OSHA does not expect that every worker will be able to recite all of the information about each chemical in the workplace. In general, the most important aspects of training under the HCS are to ensure that employees are aware that they are exposed to hazardous chemicals, that they know how to read and use labels and material safety data sheets, and that, as a consequence of learning this information, they are following the appropriate protective measures established by the employer. OSHA compliance officers will be talking to employees to determine if they have received training, if they know they are exposed to hazardous chemicals, and if they know where to obtain substance-specific information on labels and MSDSs.

The rule does not require employers to maintain records of employee training, but many employers choose to do so. This may help you monitor your own program to ensure that all employees are appropriately trained. If you already have a training program, you may simply have to supplement it with whatever additional information is required under the HCS. For example, construction employers that are already in compliance with the construction training standard (29 CFR 1926.21) will have little extra training to do.

An employer can provide employees information and training through whatever means are found appropriate and protective. Although there would always have to be some training on-site (such as informing employees of the location and availability of the written program and MSDSs), employee training may be satisfied in part by general training about the requirements of the HCS and about chemical hazards on the job which is provided by, for example, trade associations, unions, colleges, and professional schools. In addition, previous training, education and experience of a worker may relieve the employer of some of the burdens of informing and training that worker. Regardless of the method relied upon, however, the employer is always ultimately responsible for ensuring that employees are adequately trained. If the compliance officer finds that the training is deficient, the employer will be cited for the deficiency regardless of who actually provided the training on behalf of the employer.

4-D. OTHER REQUIREMENTS

In addition to these specific items, safety officers will also be asking the following questions in assessing the adequacy of the program:

- Does a list of the hazardous chemicals exist in each work area or at a central location?
- Are methods the employer will use to inform employees of the hazards of non-routine tasks outlined?
- Are employees informed of the hazards associated with chemicals contained in unlabeled pipes in their work areas?
- On multi-employer worksites, has the employer provided other employers with information about labeling systems and precautionary measures where the other employers have employees exposed to the initial employer's chemicals?
- Is the written program made available to employees and their designated representatives?

If your program adequately addresses the means of communicating information to employees in your workplace, and provides answers to the basic questions outlined above, it will be found to be in compliance with the rule.

5. CHECKLIST FOR COMPLIANCE

The following checklist will help to ensure you are in compliance with the rule:

_____	Obtained a copy of the rule.
_____	Read and understood the requirements.
_____	Assigned responsibility for tasks.
_____	Prepared an inventory of chemicals.
_____	Ensured containers are labeled.
_____	Obtained MSDS for each chemical.
_____	Prepared written program.
_____	Made MSDSs available to workers.
_____	Conducted training of workers.
_____	Established procedures to maintain current program.

_____ Established procedures to evaluate effectiveness.

6. FURTHER ASSISTANCE

If you have a question regarding compliance with the HCS, you can contact MIOSHA Consultation Education and Training (CET) Division (517-322-1809) or Michigan's OSHA Area Office for assistance by calling (517) 377-1892. In addition, each OSHA Regional Office has a Hazard Communication Coordinator who can answer your questions. Free consultation services are also available to assist employers, and information regarding these services can be obtained through the Area and Regional offices as well. Michigan's OSHA Regional Office can be contacted by calling (312) 353-2220. Contact information may also be found by calling OSHA's Office of Information and Consumer Affairs at (202) 219-8151 for further assistance.

Chemical Contamination Plans and Title III

Emergency Planning

Title III's "emergency planning provisions" require state and local governments to develop emergency preparedness and response plans. An emergency response commission, designated by the governor of each state, oversees the planning process.

Each state emergency response commission designates local emergency planning districts and appoints local planning committees for the districts. The local committee develops an emergency response plan for its particular district and establishes procedures for receiving and processing public requests for information concerning chemicals and chemical spills within the district. To carry out this function, the local committee must identify locations at which hazardous chemicals are present.

The local emergency response plan must include the following:

- Notification procedures
- Methods for determining that a chemical spill has occurred
- The probable effects of a spill on an area and local population
- Identification of emergency facilities and those persons responsible for the facilities
- Evacuation plans
- Schedules of training programs for emergency response personnel
- Methods and schedules for exercising emergency response plans

Title III imposes various reporting requirements on business owners and operators in order to provide state and local governments with the information necessary to implement emergency response plans. Any facility which has an "extremely hazardous substance" present in an amount equal to or greater than the designated "threshold planning quantity," or which has otherwise been designated by the governor, must notify the state emergency response commission in writing that it is subject to Title III's emergency planning requirements.

A facility subject to Title III's emergency planning notification requirements must notify the state emergency response commission of the company's name and address, and must designate a facility representative to participate in the local planning process. Notification to the state and designation of the representative must be completed within 60 days after the facility first acquires any extremely hazardous substances which require reporting.

Failure to comply with Title III's emergency planning notification requirements is punishable by a civil penalty of up to $25,000 for every day that the failure to comply continues.

Emergency Releases

Title III's "emergency release" reporting provisions require that covered facilities (those that produce, store, or use hazardous chemicals) notify both the local committee and state commission in the event any designated chemical or hazardous substance is released in amounts equal to or greater than the "specified reportable quantities."

Although there is no definitive list of "hazardous chemicals," a substance is generally considered a hazardous chemical under the OSH Act and §304 if it is a carcinogen, toxic or highly toxic agent, reproductive toxin, irritant, corrosive, sensitizer, or an agent which damages the lungs, skin, eyes, or mucous membranes.

Section 304 facilities must report any "release" of covered chemicals in amounts exceeding reportable quantities. "Release" means any spilling, leaking, pumping, pouring, emitting, emptying, discharging, injecting, escaping, leaching, and/or dumping.

Section 304 exempts certain types of releases from its reporting requirements. Included are:

- Federally Permitted Releases—releases which occur pursuant to a federal or state discharge permit
- Continuous Releases—a release which is stable in quantity and rate is subject instead to annual reporting under the Comprehensive Environmental Response, Compensation, and Liability Act of 1980 (CERCLA)

- Waste Disposal Facilities—disposal which occurs in compliance with Environmental Protection Agency (EPA) regulations

- Releases from Facilities Not Handling "Hazardous Chemicals"—a very narrow exemption which applies only to those facilities which neither produce, use, nor store a "hazardous chemical" as defined in Title III

- Exempt Releases Under CERCLA Section 101(22)

Notice of any reportable release must be given to both the state emergency response commission and to the affected local emergency response committee, and in some cases, to the National Response Commission. An initial notification can be made by telephone and must include information regarding the identity and amount of the released chemical, the release's duration, and any health hazards posed by the release. A follow-up written notice must update the initial information and must specify the actions taken in response to the release.

Failing to comply with Title III's emergency release reporting requirements may result in civil penalties of up to $25,000 per violation, and up to $25,000 for each day during which the violation continues. The penalty can increase to $75,000 per day for subsequent violations. Criminal penalties of up to $25,000 and/or imprisonment for up to two years can also be imposed on those who knowingly and willingly violate § 304's reporting requirements. Imprisonment of up to five years and fines of up to $50,000 apply to subsequent convictions.

Chemical Inventories

To allow governmental dissemination of information to the public, §311 and 312 require businesses subject to HCS to annually submit a chemical inventory (either the MSDS, or a list of chemicals for which the facility maintains MSDSs) to the state emergency response commission, the local emergency planning committee, and the local fire department. Such reporting must be made within three months after the date when the covered chemical first becomes present at the facility in quantities equal to or greater than the applicable threshold amount. Each facility must also submit an inventory form estimating the maximum amount of hazardous chemicals present during the preceding year, an estimate of the average daily amount of hazardous chemicals at the facility, and the location of these chemicals within the facility.

In addition to the MSDS or list of chemicals, facilities are also required to submit a hazardous chemical inventory form to the state emergency response commission, the local emergency planning commission, and the local fire department by March 1st of each year.

The inventory consists of two tiers:

- **Tier One**—all facilities must estimate the maximum amount of hazardous chemicals present at the facility during the preceding year, the average daily amount, and the location of such chemicals within the facility. The information need not be given on a chemical-by-chemical basis, but rather may be aggregated into one of five categories.

- **Tier Two**—Upon request by either the state commission or local committee, the facility must provide detailed chemical-specific information with respect to where and how each chemical is stored within the facility.

Both Tier One and Tier Two forms must be certified by a supervisory person responsible for gathering the information provided on the form.

Through the local emergency planning committee, members of the public may make a written request for information submitted pursuant to §311–312.

Failure to comply with the reporting requirements of §311–312 may result in civil penalties of anywhere from $10,000 to $25,000 per violation. Each day the violation continues will be considered a separate violation.

Routine Releases

Facilities that have ten or more full-time employees and that manufacture, process, or otherwise use "hazardous" chemicals must generally make an annual report to the EPA and the state with regard to their releases of toxic chemicals and also with regard to the presence of toxic chemicals in the products they distribute. These annual reports must be made on the EPA's Form R (Toxic Chemical Release Inventory Reporting Form) by July 1st of each year with regard to toxic chemical releases that occurred during the preceding calendar year.

Violations are punishable by civil penalties of up to $25,000 per day.

Air Contaminant Standards

Between 1971 and 1988, the U.S. DOL established permissible exposure limits (PEL) with regard to approximately 400 toxic materials and harmful or hazardous physical agents. The PEL is the anticipated continuous long-term (working life) exposure level to which an individual can safely be subjected without adverse health consequences. In early 1989, the DOL adopted new air contaminant standards incorporating additional exposure concepts.

All air contaminants have time weighted average PEL's, whereby exposure is measured on an eight-hour day, forty-hour week. In addition, some air contaminants are now given "ceiling" exposure limits which must not be exceeded at any time during the working shift.

The new standards also recognized "skin designation" chemicals and other harmful physical agents which can be absorbed through the skin. To help protect against such absorption, employers are required to provide gloves, special clothing, goggles, etc., as well as to modify equipment, engineering controls, and/or work practices to protect employees.

There are three primary ways in which employers can comply with the air contaminant standards:

- Engineering controls can be utilized to avoid or control excessive exposure. This would include isolating or separating the hazardous process from the remainder of the facility, ventilating, using nontoxic substitute chemicals, and implementing other equipment modifications.

- Work practices and/or administrative controls can be altered to improve maintenance, materials handling, transfer, and other processing procedures. This would also include enhanced training, improved detection, and personal hygiene.

- Approved personal protective equipment—such as gloves, boots, eye protective devices, respirators, and other types of clothing—can be utilized.

The above hierarchy must also be followed when undertaking protective measures. Consequently, an employer must, to the extent feasible, undertake all engineering controls and administrative measures to correct the problem before personal protective measures can be implemented.

In 1990, the Michigan Department of Public Health adopted a final standard incorporating the entire federal Air Contaminant Standard. Although the Michigan standard applies to a small number of materials and agents not covered by the federal standard, for all practical purposes the MIOSHA standards are identical to OSHA's air contaminant standards.

Employee Medical Records and Exposure Studies

Medical records, whether prepared in-house by the employer's medical expert or by an outside contractor, must be retained by an employer for the duration of the employee's employment plus at least thirty years. Employee exposure records must also be retained for at least thirty years. Upon being hired, and at least annually thereafter, employers are required to notify employees as to the existence, availability, and location of these records, and the employee's rights to have access to his/her records.

Upon request, employees are entitled to review and have copies of their medical and/or exposure records made. A designated employee representative is also entitled to employee exposure records, but must have the employee's written authorization for access to the employee's medical records.

Guidelines for Avoiding Workplace Violence

Workplace violence is increasing. As employers change their corporate cultures and demand more of their employees (be it real or perceived) and things continue to change in the workplace, one can assume that violence will increase. It must be treated like a controllable health hazard. A proactive approach is required. Proper care, procedures, and appropriate steps can minimize and/or prevent workplace violence. The key is accepting the reality that it exists, recognizing the advanced symptoms that usually occur prior to a violent act, and then effectively dealing with the problem in a humane but firm fashion.

New Employees

Investigate a job applicant's background to determine whether he/she is fit for the job. Take careful and accurate written notes documenting the investigation process, including the names and titles of people contacted and their relationship to the applicant and the dates of all conversations.

See Chapter 2 for information on the proper use of job application forms, appropriate job interviewing techniques, the importance of contacting references and prior employers, as well as doing criminal records checks. Carrying out these practices can help reduce your potential liability for violence in the workplace, as can conducting drug and alcohol testing, and aptitude, personality, and honesty testing.

Mental Disability and Psychological Testing

While the ADA and MPWDCRA forbid an employer from inquiring about an applicant's medical condition, including mental stability, until a job offer is made, the employer may inquire into whether the applicant can perform the essential functions of the job, and may use post-offer screening tests to identify potentially violent employees. However, the use of such tests raises privacy issues as well as ADA and MPWDCRA issues resulting from the use of psychological testing. Employers should insure that the reason for the test is justified and that the test itself is conducted in a reasonable matter.

Retaining Current Employees

1. Maintain honest, accurate performance evaluations. Educate supervisors on the importance of providing truthful, accurate performance evaluations. Do not allow per-

formance reviews to be prepared by supervisors who hold biases toward certain employees.

2. Emphasize to supervisors the importance of remaining sensitive and alert to situations where an employee's performance, attendance, attitude, or behavior inexplicably undergoes dramatic changes over a short period of time.

3. Promptly investigate employees whose fitness for the job is called into question.

Threat Assessment and Response Team

Consider establishing a Threat Assessment/Response Team comprised of human resources personnel, legal counsel, line management, security personnel, a mental health consultant, and any other individuals you feel would be appropriate under the circumstances present in your workplace. This Team would be responsible for investigating any threats of violence, and assessing both the risks posed and the alternative appropriate responses.

In addition, the Threat Assessment/Response Team may be assigned to develop a general plan to reduce the possibility of workplace violence and to develop a plan to deal with workplace violence if it occurs. For example, such a Team might review security policies; implement security measures reducing access to the workplace; develop escape routes, publicize their locations, and ensure that they remain accessible; and educate employees and supervisors. If, in spite of such efforts, violence nonetheless occurs, then the Team might have authority to identify and assign responsibilities to employees and supervisors on the scene, notify the authorities, deal with the media, and/or conduct an initial investigation of the incident.

Educate Employees to Contact Human Resources

1. Inform all employees to contact human resources personnel or other designated management of any threats or questionable behavior by coworkers, regardless of how serious they believe the threats to be.

2. Discuss the issues raised in the investigation with the potentially dangerous employee. Take accurate written notes regarding the meeting. Avoid claims of false imprisonment by first determining that probable cause exists to interrogate the potentially violent individual and record that the interrogation/interview is reasonable in terms of its length, tenor, and restraints.

Take Immediate Action Once a Problem Comes to Light

1. Interview the informant and others involved. Preserve the confidentiality of these employees. Do not disclose their home phone numbers and addresses to anyone in-

volved. Perhaps mask the identify of specific informants by interviewing everyone in an group (i.e., a department of work area).

2. Discuss the issues raised in the investigation with the potentially dangerous employee. Take accurate written notes regarding the meeting.

3. If the potentially dangerous employee is targeting a particular employee, consider whether the harasser can be moved to a work area where he/she will not have contact with the targeted employee.

4. If the potentially dangerous employee is targeting a particular employee, warn the potential victim and advise him/her to seek some means of protection to ensure their safety outside of the workplace.

5. Place the potentially dangerous employee on suspension, or administrative or sick leave, pending the conclusion of the investigation.

6. Attempt to obtain voluntary, uncoerced consent before searching an employee's person or personal effects for a weapon or other evidence believed to be present in the workplace. In the absence of consent, consider whether the search is nonetheless justified by your compelling interest in protecting the safety of others in the existence of emergency circumstances. Also consider, in general, implementing a pre-announced search policy that would generally justify searches of company-owned lockers or desks.

7. Seek a restraining order or an injunction prohibiting harassment or stalking.

Michigan Stalker Statutes

Effective January 1, 1993 Michigan has legislation on the books designed to prevent and restrain stalking or aggravated stalking. See MCL §600.2950(a) which allows for a civil action to obtain an injunction against an individual who is engaging in activity prohibited by §411(h) or §411(I) of the Michigan Penal Code. We believe an "individual" would also include a corporation for purposes of this Statute. The Court's order would list the type of conduct restrained or enjoined, the length of the injunction, and possible implications for violating that order which would include imprisonment and fine of not more than $500.

Section 2954 allows a victim to file a civil action against anyone who violates the criminal stalking and harassment statutes. Remedies include damages they incur plus exemplary damages, costs, and attorney fees. To file a lawsuit, the defendant need not already have been established as having engaged in criminal acts in violation of the criminal statutes.

Sections 411(h) and 411(I) of the Michigan Criminal Code deal with stalking and aggravated stalking respectively. "Harassment" means conduct directed toward a victim and includes but is not limited to repeated or continued unconsented contact that would cause a reasonable individual to suffer emotional distress and that actually causes the victim to suffer emotional distress.

"Unconsented contact" means, among other things, following or approaching within the sight of the victim or individual, appearing at his or her workplace, or entering or remaining on property owned, leased, or occupied by that individual and the like.

"Emotional distress" means significant mental suffering or distress that may, but does not necessarily require medical or other professional treatment or counseling.

"Stalking" means a course of conduct which causes a reasonable person to feel terrorized, frightened, intimidated, threatened, harassed, or molested, that actually causes the victim to feel terrorized, frightened, intimidated, threatened, harassed, or molested.

"Course of conduct" means a pattern of conduct composed of a series of two or more separate discontinuous acts evidencing a continuity of purpose.

"Victim" means an individual who is the target of a willful course of conduct involving repeated or continued harassment.

Stalking is a misdemeanor punishable by imprisonment of not more than one year, a fine of not more than $1,000, or both. Probation can be up to five years and the court can impose numerous conditions to the probation, such as refraining from stalking or contact with the victim, psychiatric evaluation, etc.

Once you get a restraining order, extend it to the victim or threatened individual and his or her family. Send the order to local police departments that have jurisdiction over the relevant geographic area so as to inform them of the situation and get their help.

If the Investigation Reveals Discharge Is Appropriate

1. Discharge the employee.
2. Alert all security personnel of the personal danger.
3. Contact law enforcement.
4. Get security to escort the former employee until he/she leaves the premises.
5. If a particular worker is targeted by the harasser, alert that employee and consider providing special security measures for him/her until the threat subsides.
6. Consider obtaining a restraining order injunction prohibiting the employee from returning to or near the workplace, etc.

SAMPLE LOCKOUT/TAGOUT PROCEDURE

The following simple lockout procedure from 29 CFR 1910.147 App A, is provided to assist employers in developing their procedures so they meet the requirements of this standard. When the energy isolating devices are not lockable, tagout may be used, provided the employer complies with the provisions of the standard which require additional training and more rigorous periodic inspections. When tagout is used and the energy isolating devices are lockable, the employer must provide full employee protection (see paragraph (c)(3)) and additional training and more rigorous periodic inspections are required. For more complex systems, more comprehensive procedures may need to be developed, documented, and utilized.

Lockout Procedure

Lockout Procedure for

_____

(Name of Company for single procedure or identification of equipment if multiple procedures are used).

Purpose

This procedure establishes the minimum requirements for the lockout of energy isolating devices whenever maintenance or servicing is done on machines or equipment. It shall be used to ensure that the machine or equipment is stopped, isolated from all potentially hazardous energy sources and locked out before employees perform any servicing or maintenance where the unexpected energization or start-up of the machine or equipment or release of stored energy could cause injury.

Compliance With This Program

All employees are required to comply with the restrictions and limitations imposed upon them during the use of lockout. The authorized employees are required to perform the lockout in accordance with this procedure. All employees, upon observing a machine or piece of equipment which is locked out to perform servicing or maintenance shall not attempt to start, energize, or use that machine or equipment.

_____

(Type of compliance enforcement to be taken for violation of the above).

Sequence of Lockout

(1) Notify all affected employees that servicing or maintenance is required on a machine or equipment and that the machine or equipment must be shut down and locked out to perform the servicing or maintenance.

_____

(Name(s)/Job Title(s) of affected employees and how to notify).

(2) The authorized employee shall refer to the company procedure to identify the type and magnitude of the energy that the machine or equipment utilizes, shall understand the hazards of the energy, and shall know the methods to control the energy.

_____

(Type(s) and magnitude(s) of energy, its hazards and the methods to control the energy).

(3) If the machine or equipment is operating, shut it down by the normal stopping procedure (depress the stop button, open switch, close valve, etc.).

_____

(Type(s) and location(s) of machine or equipment operating controls).

(4) De-activate the energy isolating device(s) so that the machine or equipment is isolated from the energy source(s).

_____

(Type(s) and location(s) of energy isolating devices).

(5) Lock out the energy isolating device(s) with assigned individual lock(s).

(6) Stored or residual energy (such as that in capacitors, springs, elevated machine members, rotating flywheels, hydraulic systems, and air, gas, steam, or water pressure, etc.) must be dissipated or restrained by methods such as grounding, repositioning, blocking, bleeding down, etc.

_____

(Type(s) of stored energy - methods to dissipate or restrain).

(7) Ensure that the equipment is disconnected from the energy source(s) by first checking that no personnel are exposed, then verify the isolation of the equipment by operating the push button or other normal operating control(s) or by testing to make certain the equipment will not operate.

Caution: Return operating control(s) to neutral or "off" position after verifying the isolation of the equipment.

_____

(Method of verifying the isolation of the equipment).

(8) The machine or equipment is now locked out.

"Restoring Equipment to Service." When the servicing or maintenance is completed and the machine or equipment is ready to return to normal operating condition, the following steps shall be taken.

(1) Check the machine or equipment and the immediate area around the machine to ensure that nonessential items have been removed and that the machine or equipment components are operationally intact.

(2) Check the work area to ensure that all employees have been safely positioned or removed from the area.

(3) Verify that the controls are in neutral.

(4) Remove the lockout devices and reenergize the machine or equipment. Note: The removal of some forms of blocking may require reenergization of the machine before safe removal.

(5) Notify affected employees that the servicing or maintenance is completed and the machine or equipment is ready for used.

Employment Law Contact Information—Federal

To purchase required posters for the workplace:
    Michigan Chamber Services, Inc.
    600 South Walnut Street
    Lansing, MI 48933
    TEL: (800) 748-0344
    FAX: (517) 371-7228
    WEB: **www.michamber.com**

For information on Federal Wage and Hour Law:
    U. S. Department of Labor—Detroit District Office
    Wage Hour Division
    211 West Fort Street, Room 1317
    Detroit, MI 48226
    TEL: (313) 226-7447
    FAX: (313) 226-3072
    WEB: **www.dol.gov/esa/whd/**

For information on Federal Equal Employment Opportunity Law:
    Equal Employment Opportunity Commission—Detroit District Office
    477 Michigan Avenue, Room 1540
    Detroit, MI 48226
    TEL: (313) 226-4600
    WEB: **www.eeoc.gov/**

To Report New Employees (Multi-State Employers):
    Send notification to:
    Department of Health and Human Services
    Administration for Children and Families
    Office of Child Support Enforcement
    Multistate Employer Notification
    P.O. Box 509
    Randallstown, MD 21133
    FAX: (410) 277-9325

For Information on Safety and Health Regulation:

Lansing Area Office	Region 5 Office
U.S. Department of Labor	230 S. Dearborn, Room 3244
OSHA	Chicago, IL 60604
801 S. Waverly Road, Suite 306	TEL: (312) 353-2220
Lansing, MI 48917	FAX: (312) 353-7774
TEL: (517) 377-1892	
FAX: (517) 377-1616	

Employment Law Contact Information—Michigan

To purchase required posters for the workplace:
Michigan Chamber Services, Inc.
600 South Walnut Street
Lansing, MI 48933
TEL: (800) 748-0344
FAX: (517) 371-7228
WEB: www.michamber.com

For information on Michigan Wage and Hour Law:
Michigan Department of Labor & Economic Growth
Wage & Hour Division
7150 Harris Drive
P.O. Box 30476
Lansing, MI 48909-7976
TEL: (517) 322-1825
FAX: (517) 322-6352
WHINFO@MICHIGAN.GOV

Livonia Office:
33523 West 8 Mile Rd., B1
Livonia, MI 48152
TEL: (313) 456-4906

Upper Peninsula Office:
TEL: (906) 482-3602

To Report New Employees:
Michigan New Hire Operations Center
P.O. Box 85010
Lansing, MI 48908-5010
FAX: (517) 318-1659

For MIOSHA Training and Compliance Information:
Michigan Department of Labor & Economic Growth
Michigan Occupational Safety & Health Administration
P.O. Box 30643
7150 Harris Drive
Lansing MI 48909-8143
TEL: (800) 866-4674

Appendix

INDEX OF FORMS
EMPLOYMENT LAW HANDBOOK

1. **Federal W-4 Form**
2. **State W-4 Form**
3. **New Hire Reporting Form**
4. **Multi-State New Hire Reporting Form**
5. **I-9 (Employment Eligibility Verification) and Instructions**
6. **Employment Application (sample)**
7. **Unemployment Quarterly Tax Report**
8. **Wage Detail Report**
9. **Reimbursing Employer's Quarterly Payroll Report**

All additional forms and documents are available at www.hrmichigan.com. You receive a complimentary subscription to the site with the purchase of this guide. Please call (888) 763-0514 ext 204 with any questions.

Form W-4 (2008)

Purpose. Complete Form W-4 so that your employer can withhold the correct federal income tax from your pay. Consider completing a new Form W-4 each year and when your personal or financial situation changes.

Exemption from withholding. If you are exempt, complete **only** lines 1, 2, 3, 4, and 7 and sign the form to validate it. Your exemption for 2008 expires February 16, 2009. See Pub. 505, Tax Withholding and Estimated Tax.

Note. You cannot claim exemption from withholding if (a) your income exceeds $900 and includes more than $300 of unearned income (for example, interest and dividends) and (b) another person can claim you as a dependent on their tax return.

Basic instructions. If you are not exempt, complete the **Personal Allowances Worksheet** below. The worksheets on page 2 adjust your withholding allowances based on itemized deductions, certain credits, adjustments to income, or two-earner/multiple job situations. Complete all worksheets that apply. However, you may claim fewer (or zero) allowances.

Head of household. Generally, you may claim head of household filing status on your tax return only if you are unmarried and pay more than 50% of the costs of keeping up a home for yourself and your dependent(s) or other qualifying individuals. See Pub. 501, Exemptions, Standard Deduction, and Filing Information, for information.

Tax credits. You can take projected tax credits into account in figuring your allowable number of withholding allowances. Credits for child or dependent care expenses and the child tax credit may be claimed using the **Personal Allowances Worksheet** below. See Pub. 919, How Do I Adjust My Tax Withholding, for information on converting your other credits into withholding allowances.

Nonwage income. If you have a large amount of nonwage income, such as interest or dividends, consider making estimated tax payments using Form 1040-ES, Estimated Tax for Individuals. Otherwise, you may owe additional tax. If you have pension or annuity income, see Pub. 919 to find out if you should adjust your withholding on Form W-4 or W-4P.

Two earners or multiple jobs. If you have a working spouse or more than one job, figure the total number of allowances you are entitled to claim on all jobs using worksheets from only one Form W-4. Your withholding usually will be most accurate when all allowances are claimed on the Form W-4 for the highest paying job and zero allowances are claimed on the others. See Pub. 919 for details.

Nonresident alien. If you are a nonresident alien, see the Instructions for Form 8233 before completing this Form W-4.

Check your withholding. After your Form W-4 takes effect, use Pub. 919 to see how the dollar amount you are having withheld compares to your projected total tax for 2008. See Pub. 919, especially if your earnings exceed $130,000 (Single) or $180,000 (Married).

Personal Allowances Worksheet (Keep for your records.)

- **A** Enter "1" for **yourself** if no one else can claim you as a dependent . . . . **A** _____
- **B** Enter "1" if:
  - You are single and have only one job; or
  - You are married, have only one job, and your spouse does not work; or
  - Your wages from a second job or your spouse's wages (or the total of both) are $1,500 or less.

  B _____
- **C** Enter "1" for your **spouse.** But, you may choose to enter "-0-" if you are married and have either a working spouse or more than one job. (Entering "-0-" may help you avoid having too little tax withheld.) . . . **C** _____
- **D** Enter number of **dependents** (other than your spouse or yourself) you will claim on your tax return . . . **D** _____
- **E** Enter "1" if you will file as **head of household** on your tax return (see conditions under **Head of household** above) . **E** _____
- **F** Enter "1" if you have at least $1,500 of **child or dependent care expenses** for which you plan to claim a credit . . **F** _____
  (**Note. Do not** include child support payments. See Pub. 503, Child and Dependent Care Expenses, for details.)
- **G** **Child Tax Credit** (including additional child tax credit). See Pub. 972, Child Tax Credit, for more information.
  - If your total income will be less than $58,000 ($86,000 if married), enter "2" for each eligible child.
  - If your total income will be between $58,000 and $84,000 ($86,000 and $119,000 if married), enter "1" for each eligible child plus "1" **additional** if you have 4 or more eligible children.

  G _____
- **H** Add lines A through G and enter total here. (**Note.** This may be different from the number of exemptions you claim on your tax return.) ▶ **H** _____

For accuracy, complete all worksheets that apply.
- If you plan to **itemize or claim adjustments to income** and want to reduce your withholding, see the **Deductions and Adjustments Worksheet** on page 2.
- If you have **more than one job** or are **married and you and your spouse both work** and the combined earnings from all jobs exceed $40,000 ($25,000 if married), see the **Two-Earners/Multiple Jobs Worksheet** on page 2 to avoid having too little tax withheld.
- If **neither** of the above situations applies, **stop here** and enter the number from line H on line 5 of Form W-4 below.

------------------------- Cut here and give Form W-4 to your employer. Keep the top part for your records. -------------------------

Form **W-4**
Department of the Treasury
Internal Revenue Service

Employee's Withholding Allowance Certificate

▶ Whether you are entitled to claim a certain number of allowances or exemption from withholding is subject to review by the IRS. Your employer may be required to send a copy of this form to the IRS.

OMB No. 1545-0074

2008

1 Type or print your first name and middle initial.	Last name	2 Your social security number
Home address (number and street or rural route)	3 ☐ Single ☐ Married ☐ Married, but withhold at higher Single rate. **Note.** If married, but legally separated, or spouse is a nonresident alien, check the "Single" box.	
City or town, state, and ZIP code	4 If your last name differs from that shown on your social security card, check here. You must call 1-800-772-1213 for a replacement card. ▶ ☐	

- **5** Total number of allowances you are claiming (from line **H** above **or** from the applicable worksheet on page 2) . . **5** _____
- **6** Additional amount, if any, you want withheld from each paycheck . . . . **6** $_____
- **7** I claim exemption from withholding for 2008, and I certify that I meet **both** of the following conditions for exemption.
  - Last year I had a right to a refund of **all** federal income tax withheld because I had **no** tax liability **and**
  - This year I expect a refund of **all** federal income tax withheld because I expect to have **no** tax liability.

  If you meet both conditions, write "Exempt" here . . . . ▶ **7** _____

Under penalties of perjury, I declare that I have examined this certificate and to the best of my knowledge and belief, it is true, correct, and complete.

Employee's signature
(Form is not valid unless you sign it.) ▶   **Date** ▶

8 Employer's name and address (Employer: Complete lines 8 and 10 only if sending to the IRS.)	9 Office code (optional)	10 Employer identification number (EIN)

For Privacy Act and Paperwork Reduction Act Notice, see page 2.   Cat. No. 10220Q   Form **W-4** (2008)

Form W-4 (2008) Page **2**

Deductions and Adjustments Worksheet

Note. Use this worksheet *only* if you plan to itemize deductions, claim certain credits, or claim adjustments to income on your 2008 tax return.

1. Enter an estimate of your 2008 itemized deductions. These include qualifying home mortgage interest, charitable contributions, state and local taxes, medical expenses in excess of 7.5% of your income, and miscellaneous deductions. (For 2008, you may have to reduce your itemized deductions if your income is over $159,950 ($79,975 if married filing separately). See *Worksheet 2* in Pub. 919 for details.) . . **1** $ _____

2. Enter:
   - $10,900 if married filing jointly or qualifying widow(er)
   - $ 8,000 if head of household
   - $ 5,450 if single or married filing separately

   . . . . . . **2** $ _____

3. **Subtract** line 2 from line 1. If zero or less, enter "-0-" . . . . **3** $ _____
4. Enter an estimate of your 2008 adjustments to income, including alimony, deductible IRA contributions, and student loan interest **4** $ _____
5. **Add** lines 3 and 4 and enter the total. (Include any amount for credits from *Worksheet 8* in Pub. 919) . **5** $ _____
6. Enter an estimate of your 2008 nonwage income (such as dividends or interest) . . . . **6** $ _____
7. **Subtract** line 6 from line 5. If zero or less, enter "-0-" . . . . **7** $ _____
8. **Divide** the amount on line 7 by $3,500 and enter the result here. Drop any fraction . . . . . . **8** _____
9. Enter the number from the **Personal Allowances Worksheet**, line H, page 1 . . . . **9** _____
10. **Add** lines 8 and 9 and enter the total here. If you plan to use the **Two-Earners/Multiple Jobs Worksheet**, also enter this total on line 1 below. Otherwise, **stop here** and enter this total on Form W-4, line 5, page 1 **10** _____

Two-Earners/Multiple Jobs Worksheet (See *Two earners or multiple jobs* on page 1.)

Note. Use this worksheet *only* if the instructions under line H on page 1 direct you here.

1. Enter the number from line H, page 1 (or from line 10 above if you used the **Deductions and Adjustments Worksheet**) **1** _____
2. Find the number in **Table 1** below that applies to the **LOWEST** paying job and enter it here. **However,** if you are married filing jointly and wages from the highest paying job are $50,000 or less, do not enter more than "3." . . . . . . **2** _____
3. If line 1 is **more than or equal to** line 2, subtract line 2 from line 1. Enter the result here (if zero, enter "-0-") and on Form W-4, line 5, page 1. **Do not** use the rest of this worksheet . . . . **3** _____

Note. If line 1 is *less than* line 2, enter "-0-" on Form W-4, line 5, page 1. Complete lines 4–9 below to calculate the additional withholding amount necessary to avoid a year-end tax bill.

4. Enter the number from line 2 of this worksheet . . . . **4** _____
5. Enter the number from line 1 of this worksheet . . . . **5** _____
6. **Subtract** line 5 from line 4 . . . . **6** _____
7. Find the amount in **Table 2** below that applies to the **HIGHEST** paying job and enter it here . . . **7** $ _____
8. **Multiply** line 7 by line 6 and enter the result here. This is the additional annual withholding needed . . **8** $ _____
9. Divide line 8 by the number of pay periods remaining in 2008. For example, divide by 26 if you are paid every two weeks and you complete this form in December 2007. Enter the result here and on Form W-4, line 6, page 1. This is the additional amount to be withheld from each paycheck . . . . **9** $ _____

Table 1

Married Filing Jointly		All Others	
If wages from **LOWEST** paying job are—	Enter on line 2 above	If wages from **LOWEST** paying job are—	Enter on line 2 above
$0 - $4,500	0	$0 - $6,500	0
4,501 - 10,000	1	6,501 - 12,000	1
10,001 - 18,000	2	12,001 - 20,000	2
18,001 - 22,000	3	20,001 - 27,000	3
22,001 - 27,000	4	27,001 - 35,000	4
27,001 - 33,000	5	35,001 - 50,000	5
33,001 - 40,000	6	50,001 - 65,000	6
40,001 - 50,000	7	65,001 - 80,000	7
50,001 - 55,000	8	80,001 - 95,000	8
55,001 - 60,000	9	95,001 - 120,000	9
60,001 - 65,000	10	120,001 and over	10
65,001 - 75,000	11		
75,001 - 100,000	12		
100,001 - 110,000	13		
110,001 - 120,000	14		
120,001 and over	15		

Table 2

Married Filing Jointly		All Others	
If wages from **HIGHEST** paying job are—	Enter on line 7 above	If wages from **HIGHEST** paying job are—	Enter on line 7 above
$0 - $65,000	$530	$0 - $35,000	$530
65,001 - 120,000	880	35,001 - 80,000	880
120,001 - 180,000	980	80,001 - 150,000	980
180,001 - 310,000	1,160	150,001 - 340,000	1,160
310,001 and over	1,230	340,001 and over	1,230

Privacy Act and Paperwork Reduction Act Notice. We ask for the information on this form to carry out the Internal Revenue laws of the United States. The Internal Revenue Code requires this information under sections 3402(f)(2)(A) and 6109 and their regulations. Failure to provide a properly completed form will result in your being treated as a single person who claims no withholding allowances; providing fraudulent information may also subject you to penalties. Routine uses of this information include giving it to the Department of Justice for civil and criminal litigation, to cities, states, and the District of Columbia for use in administering their tax laws, and using it in the National Directory of New Hires. We may also disclose this information to other countries under a tax treaty, to federal and state agencies to enforce federal nontax criminal laws, or to federal law enforcement and intelligence agencies to combat terrorism.

You are not required to provide the information requested on a form that is subject to the Paperwork Reduction Act unless the form displays a valid OMB control number. Books or records relating to a form or its instructions must be retained as long as their contents may become material in the administration of any Internal Revenue law. Generally, tax returns and return information are confidential, as required by Code section 6103.

The average time and expenses required to complete and file this form will vary depending on individual circumstances. For estimated averages, see the instructions for your income tax return.

If you have suggestions for making this form simpler, we would be happy to hear from you. See the instructions for your income tax return.

MI-W4
(Rev. 8-08)

EMPLOYEE'S MICHIGAN WITHHOLDING EXEMPTION CERTIFICATE
STATE OF MICHIGAN - DEPARTMENT OF TREASURY

This certificate is for Michigan income tax withholding purposes only. You must file a revised form within 10 days if your exemptions decrease or your residency status changes from nonresident to resident. Read instructions below before completing this form.

Issued under P.A. 281 of 1967.

▶ 1. Social Security Number

▶ 2. Date of Birth

▶ 3. Type or Print Your First Name, Middle Initial and Last Name

4. Driver License Number

Home Address (No., Street, P.O. Box or Rural Route)

▶ 5. Are you a new employee?
☐ Yes   If Yes, enter date of hire . . . .
☐ No

City or Town | State | ZIP Code

6. Enter the number of personal and dependent exemptions you are claiming .... ▶ 6. ☐

7. Additional amount you want deducted from each pay
   (if employer agrees) .... 7. $ _____ .00

8. I claim exemption from withholding because (does not apply to nonresident members of flow-through entities - see instructions):
   a. ☐ A Michigan income tax liability is not expected this year.
   b. ☐ Wages are exempt from withholding. Explain: _____
   c. ☐ Permanent home (domicile) is located in the following Renaissance Zone: _____

EMPLOYEE:
If you fail or refuse to file this form, your employer must withhold Michigan income tax from your wages without allowance for any exemptions. Keep a copy of this form for your records.

Under penalty of perjury, I certify that the number of withholding exemptions claimed on this certificate does not exceed the number to which I am entitled. If claiming exemption from withholding, I certify that I anticipate that I will not incur a Michigan income tax liability for this year.

9. Employee's Signature | ▶ Date

INSTRUCTIONS TO EMPLOYER:
Employers must report all new hires to the State of Michigan. Keep a copy of this certificate with your records. If the employee claims 10 or more personal and dependent exemptions or claims a status exempting the employee from withholding, you must file their original MI-W4 form with the Michigan Department of Treasury. Mail to: New Hire Operations Center, P.O. Box 85010; Lansing, MI 48908-5010.

Employer: Complete lines 10 and 11 before sending to the Michigan Department of Treasury.
10. Employer's Name, Address, Phone No. and Name of Contact Person

▶ 11. Federal Employer Identification Number

INSTRUCTIONS TO EMPLOYEE

You must submit a Michigan withholding exemption certificate (form MI-W4) to your employer on or before the date that employment begins. If you fail or refuse to submit this certificate, your employer must withhold tax from your compensation without allowance for any exemptions. Your employer is required to notify the Michigan Department of Treasury if you have claimed 10 or more personal and dependent exemptions or claimed a status which exempts you from withholding.

You MUST file a new MI-W4 within 10 days if your residency status changes or if your exemptions decrease because: a) your spouse, for whom you have been claiming an exemption, is divorced or legally separated from you or claims his/her own exemption(s) on a separate certificate, or b) a dependent must be dropped for federal purposes.

Line 5: If you check "Yes," enter your date of hire (mo/day/year).

Line 6: Personal and dependent exemptions. The total number of exemptions you claim on the MI-W4 may not exceed the number of exemptions you are entitled to claim when you file your Michigan individual income tax return.

If you are married and you and your spouse are both employed, you both may not claim the same exemptions with each of your employers.

If you hold more than one job, you may not claim the same exemptions with more than one employer. If you claim the same exemptions at more than one job, your tax will be under withheld.

Line 7: You may designate additional withholding if you expect to owe more than the amount withheld.

Line 8: You may claim exemption from Michigan income tax withholding ONLY if you do not anticipate a Michigan income tax liability for the current year because all of the following exist: a) your employment is less than full time, b) your personal and dependent exemption allowance exceeds your annual compensation, c) you claimed exemption from federal withholding, d) you did not incur a Michigan income tax liability for the previous year. You may also claim exemption if your permanent home (domicile) is located in a Renaissance Zone. Members of flow-through entities may not claim exemption from nonresident flow-through withholding. For more information on Renaissance Zones call the Michigan Tele-Help System, 1-800-827-4000. Full-time students that do not satisfy all of the above requirements cannot claim exempt status.

Web Site
Visit the Treasury Web site at:
www.michigan.gov/businesstax

Michigan Department of Treasury
3281 (08-08)

STATE OF MICHIGAN
NEW HIRE REPORTING FORM

Federal legislation, effective October 1, 1997, requires all Michigan employers, both public and private, to report all newly hired, rehired, or returning to work employees to the State of Michigan. This form is recommended for use by all employers who do not report electronically.
*** Internet reporting is available online at: www.mi-newhire.com

This form may be photocopied as necessary.
Many employers preprint employer information on the form and have the employee complete the necessary information during the hiring process.

For optimum accuracy, please print neatly in capital letters and avoid contact with the edge of the box. The following will serve as an example:

A	B	C	D	E	F	G	H	I	J	K	L	M
N	O	P	Q	R	S	T	U	V	W	X	Y	Z

(Note: When reporting new hires with special exemptions, please use the MI-W4 to report.)

EMPLOYEE INFORMATION (Mandatory):

Social Security Number: ___-__-____

First Name: _____
M.I.: _

Last Name: _____

Address: _____

City: _____
State: __

Zip Code: _____-____

EMPLOYER INFORMATION (Mandatory):

Federal EIN: __-_____

Employer: _____

Address: _____

City: _____
State: __

Zip Code: _____-____

OPTIONAL EMPLOYEE INFORMATION:

Date of Hire: __-__-____

Date of Birth: __-__-____

Driver's License No.: _____

Reports must be submitted within 20 calendar days of date of hire

REPORTS WILL NOT BE PROCESSED IF MANDATORY INFORMATION IS MISSING

Send Reports To: Michigan New Hire Operations Center
P.O. Box 85010
Lansing, MI 48908-5010
Fax: 877-318-1659

Questions?
Call: 1-800-524-9846

20738

OMB Control No: 0970-0166
Expiration Date: 06/30/2010

MULTISTATE EMPLOYER NOTIFICATION FORM
FOR NEW HIRE (W4) REPORTING

This form is provided to employers who have employees in two or more states and wish to register to submit their new hire reports to one state or to make changes to their previous registration.

Federal law requires employers to provide to the State Directory of New Hires of the state in which a newly hired employee works, a report that contains the name, address, and Social Security number of the employee, and the name, address and Federal Employer Identification Number (FEIN) of the employer (42 USC 653A(b)(1)(A)).

If you are an employer with employees in two or more states AND you will transmit the required reports magnetically or electronically, Federal law allows you to comply with the new hire reporting requirement by exercising one of the following options (42 USC 653A(b)(1)(B)):

Option #1: Send the new hire reports to the State Directory of New Hires of the state in which each newly hired employee works.

OR

Option #2: Designate <u>one state</u> in which any employee works and transmit ALL new hire reports to the State Directory of New Hires of that state. You must notify the Secretary of the U.S. Department of Health and Human Services in writing of your choice to report to only one state and identify the chosen state (42 USC 653A(b)(1)(B)).

For Option #2: Complete this form to identify/register your entity as a multistate employer for new hire reporting.

If you are no longer a multistate employer –OR– you are a multistate employer but you no longer report to one state, check "No Longer a Multistate Employer" in the box below. Complete Items 1 – 5, provide your contact information in Item 10, and mail or fax this form to the address or fax number located on the last page.

☐ **No Longer a Multistate Employer – (If checked, complete Items 1 – 5 and Item 10 and return the form to the address or fax number located on the last page.)**

For assistance in completing this form, call the Multistate Employer Help Desk at 410-277-9470 (8:00 a.m. – 5:00 p.m. ET). If you wish to register electronically, go to: http://151.196.108.21/OCSE

---

1. **Print your company's Federal Employer Identification Number. This is the nine-digit number used by the IRS to identify your company.**

2. **Print today's date in MM/DD/YYYY format, e.g., 09/23/2007.**

   Federal Employer
   Identification Number (FEIN): _____   Date _____ / _____ / _____

3. **Print your company's name. This is the name associated with the FEIN in Item 1.**

   Employer Name: _____

OMB Control No: 0970-0166
Expiration Date: 06/30/2010

4. PRINT your company's address, including city, state, and zip code. This is the address associated with the FEIN in Item 1. If your company's FEIN address is a foreign address, PRINT the Country Name and the Country's Postal Code.

Employer Address: _____

_____

_____

City: _____ State: _____ Zip Code: _____

(For foreign addresses only) Country Name: _____ Country Postal Code: _____

5. Print your company's phone number, including area code. This is the phone number associated with the FEIN in Item 1.

Phone Number: (_____) _____ Ext. _____

6. Print the FEIN, name, state, and zip code of any subsidiary of your company that has its own FEIN and for which you will be reporting New Hire information.

<u>Subsidiary Information:</u> (Please list any additional subsidiaries on a separate sheet.)

FEIN: _____ FEIN: _____

Name: _____ Name: _____

State/Zip Code: _____ State/Zip Code: _____

FEIN: _____ FEIN: _____

Name: _____ Name: _____

State/Zip Code: _____ State/Zip Code: _____

7. Print the two-character abbreviation for the State or U.S. Territory to which your company has chosen to report new hire information. NOTE: The State that you designate must be a State in which you have one or more employees. Refer to the state listing shown in Item 9.

8. Enter the effective date (MM/DD/YYYY) on which your company will begin sending new hire (W-4) reports to the entry shown in Item 7.

Effective Date: ____/____/____

OMB Control No: 0970-0166
Expiration Date: 06/30/2010

9. Please circle the States or U.S. Territories in which your company has employees, other than the State or Territory selected as your reporting State in item 7. You must indicate at least one State in this list to register as a multistate employer.

DO NOT INCLUDE THE STATE CODE ENTERED IN ITEM 7

AK=Alaska	GA=Georgia	MA=Massachusetts	NE=Nebraska	PR=Puerto Rico	WA=Washington
AL=Alabama	GU=Guam	MD=Maryland	NH=New Hamp.	RI=Rhode Island	WI=Wisconsin
AR=Arkansas	HI=Hawaii	ME=Maine	NJ=New Jersey	SC=S. Carolina	WV=W. Virginia
AZ=Arizona	IA=Iowa	MI=Michigan	NM=New Mexico	SD=S. Dakota	WY=Wyoming
CA=California	ID=Idaho	MN=Minnesota	NV=Nevada	TN=Tennessee	
CO=Colorado	IL=Illinois	MO=Missouri	NY=New York	TX=Texas	
CT=Connecticut	IN=Indiana	MS=Mississippi	OH=Ohio	UT=Utah	
DC=Dist. of Col.	KS=Kansas	MT=Montana	OK=Oklahoma	VA=Virginia	
DE=Delaware	KY=Kentucky	NC=N. Carolina	OR=Oregon	VI=Virgin Islands	
FL=Florida	LA=Louisiana	ND=N. Dakota	PA=Pennsylvania	VT=Vermont	

10. Print your name, title, work phone number (if different from the company phone number entered in Item 5), work email address and work fax number. BE SURE TO SIGN THE FORM. The information in this form is used to acknowledge receipt of your notification and to contact you if any clarification is needed.

Contact Name: _____ Title _____

Phone: ( ) _____ Fax _____

Email: _____

Providing your email address will help us communicate with you more effectively in the future.

Signature of person
completing this form: _____

Send the completed form to:

**Department of Health and Human Services
Administration for Children and Families
Office of Child Support Enforcement
Multistate Employer Notification
PO Box 509
Randallstown, MD 21133**

Or fax the completed form to:

**Multistate Employer Notification
Fax 410-277-9325**

For assistance in completing this form, call the Multistate Employer Help Desk at 410-277-9470 (8:00 a.m. – 5:00 p.m. ET). For general child support information, visit OCSE's Employer Services website at: http://www.acf.hhs.gov/programs/cse/newhire/employer/home.htm

Please note: If your company experiences a merger, acquisition, or other change that may affect this reporting requirement, please send a revised form with the new information.

THE PAPERWORK REDUCTION ACT OF 1995
Public reporting burden for this collection of information is estimated to average 3 minutes per response, including the time for reviewing instructions, gathering and maintaining the data needed, and reviewing the collection of information.

An agency may not conduct or sponsor, and a person is not required to respond to, a collection of information unless it displays a currently valid OMB control number.

Department of Homeland Security
U.S. Citizenship and Immigration Services

OMB No. 1615-0047; Expires 06/30/09
Form I-9, Employment Eligibility Verification

Instructions
Please read all instructions carefully before completing this form.

Anti-Discrimination Notice. It is illegal to discriminate against any individual (other than an alien not authorized to work in the U.S.) in hiring, discharging, or recruiting or referring for a fee because of that individual's national origin or citizenship status. It is illegal to discriminate against work eligible individuals. Employers **CANNOT** specify which document(s) they will accept from an employee. The refusal to hire an individual because the documents presented have a future expiration date may also constitute illegal discrimination.

What Is the Purpose of This Form?

The purpose of this form is to document that each new employee (both citizen and non-citizen) hired after November 6, 1986 is authorized to work in the United States.

When Should the Form I-9 Be Used?

All employees, citizens and noncitizens, hired after November 6, 1986 and working in the United States must complete a Form I-9.

Filling Out the Form I-9

Section 1, Employee: This part of the form must be completed at the time of hire, which is the actual beginning of employment. Providing the Social Security number is voluntary, except for employees hired by employers participating in the USCIS Electronic Employment Eligibility Verification Program (E-Verify). **The employer is responsible for ensuring that Section 1 is timely and properly completed.**

Preparer/Translator Certification. The Preparer/Translator Certification must be completed if **Section 1** is prepared by a person other than the employee. A preparer/translator may be used only when the employee is unable to complete **Section 1** on his/her own. However, the employee must still sign **Section 1** personally.

Section 2, Employer: For the purpose of completing this form, the term "employer" means all employers including those recruiters and referrers for a fee who are agricultural associations, agricultural employers or farm labor contractors.

Employers must complete **Section 2** by examining evidence of identity and employment eligibility within three (3) business days of the date employment begins. If employees are authorized to work, but are unable to present the required document(s) within three business days, they must present a receipt for the application of the document(s) within three business days and the actual document(s) within ninety (90) days. However, if employers hire individuals for a duration of less than three business days, **Section 2** must be completed at the time employment begins. **Employers must record:**

1. Document title;
2. Issuing authority;
3. Document number;
4. Expiration date, if any; and
5. The date employment begins.

Employers must sign and date the certification. Employees must present original documents. Employers may, but are not required to, photocopy the document(s) presented. These photocopies may only be used for the verification process and must be retained with the Form I-9. **However, employers are still responsible for completing and retaining the Form I-9.**

Section 3, Updating and Reverification: Employers must complete **Section 3** when updating and/or reverifying the Form I-9. Employers must reverify employment eligibility of their employees on or before the expiration date recorded in **Section 1**. Employers **CANNOT** specify which document(s) they will accept from an employee.

A. If an employee's name has changed at the time this form is being updated/reverified, complete Block A.

B. If an employee is rehired within three (3) years of the date this form was originally completed and the employee is still eligible to be employed on the same basis as previously indicated on this form (updating), complete Block B and the signature block.

C. If an employee is rehired within three (3) years of the date this form was originally completed and the employee's work authorization has expired **or** if a current employee's work authorization is about to expire (reverification), complete Block B and:

1. Examine any document that reflects that the employee is authorized to work in the U.S. (see List A **or** C);
2. Record the document title, document number and expiration date (if any) in Block C, and
3. Complete the signature block.

Form I-9 (Rev. 06/05/07) N

What Is the Filing Fee?

There is no associated filing fee for completing the Form I-9. This form is not filed with USCIS or any government agency. The Form I-9 must be retained by the employer and made available for inspection by U.S. Government officials as specified in the Privacy Act Notice below.

USCIS Forms and Information

To order USCIS forms, call our toll-free number at **1-800-870-3676**. Individuals can also get USCIS forms and information on immigration laws, regulations and procedures by telephoning our National Customer Service Center at **1-800-375-5283** or visiting our internet website at **www.uscis.gov**.

Photocopying and Retaining the Form I-9

A blank Form I-9 may be reproduced, provided both sides are copied. The Instructions must be available to all employees completing this form. Employers must retain completed Forms I-9 for three (3) years after the date of hire or one (1) year after the date employment ends, whichever is later.

The Form I-9 may be signed and retained electronically, as authorized in Department of Homeland Security regulations at 8 CFR § 274a.2.

Privacy Act Notice

The authority for collecting this information is the Immigration Reform and Control Act of 1986, Pub. L. 99-603 (8 USC 1324a).

This information is for employers to verify the eligibility of individuals for employment to preclude the unlawful hiring, or recruiting or referring for a fee, of aliens who are not authorized to work in the United States.

This information will be used by employers as a record of their basis for determining eligibility of an employee to work in the United States. The form will be kept by the employer and made available for inspection by officials of U.S. Immigration and Customs Enforcement, Department of Labor and Office of Special Counsel for Immigration Related Unfair Employment Practices.

Submission of the information required in this form is voluntary. However, an individual may not begin employment unless this form is completed, since employers are subject to civil or criminal penalties if they do not comply with the Immigration Reform and Control Act of 1986.

Paperwork Reduction Act

We try to create forms and instructions that are accurate, can be easily understood and which impose the least possible burden on you to provide us with information. Often this is difficult because some immigration laws are very complex. Accordingly, the reporting burden for this collection of information is computed as follows: **1)** learning about this form, and completing the form, 9 minutes; **2)** assembling and filing (recordkeeping) the form, 3 minutes, for an average of 12 minutes per response. If you have comments regarding the accuracy of this burden estimate, or suggestions for making this form simpler, you can write to: U.S. Citizenship and Immigration Services, Regulatory Management Division, 111 Massachusetts Avenue, N.W., 3rd Floor, Suite 3008, Washington, DC 20529. OMB No. 1615-0047.

Department of Homeland Security
U.S. Citizenship and Immigration Services

OMB No. 1615-0047; Expires 06/30/09

Form I-9, Employment Eligibility Verification

Please read instructions carefully before completing this form. The instructions must be available during completion of this form.

ANTI-DISCRIMINATION NOTICE: It is illegal to discriminate against work eligible individuals. Employers CANNOT specify which document(s) they will accept from an employee. The refusal to hire an individual because the documents have a future expiration date may also constitute illegal discrimination.

Section 1. Employee Information and Verification. To be completed and signed by employee at the time employment begins.

Print Name: Last	First	Middle Initial	Maiden Name
Address (Street Name and Number)		Apt. #	Date of Birth (month/day/year)
City	State	Zip Code	Social Security #

I am aware that federal law provides for imprisonment and/or fines for false statements or use of false documents in connection with the completion of this form.

I attest, under penalty of perjury, that I am (check one of the following):
☐ A citizen or national of the United States
☐ A lawful permanent resident (Alien #) A _____
☐ An alien authorized to work until _____
(Alien # or Admission #) _____

Employee's Signature _____   Date (month/day/year) _____

Preparer and/or Translator Certification. *(To be completed and signed if Section 1 is prepared by a person other than the employee.)* I attest, under penalty of perjury, that I have assisted in the completion of this form and that to the best of my knowledge the information is true and correct.

Preparer's/Translator's Signature	Print Name
Address *(Street Name and Number, City, State, Zip Code)*	Date *(month/day/year)*

Section 2. Employer Review and Verification. To be completed and signed by employer. Examine one document from List A OR examine one document from List B and one from List C, as listed on the reverse of this form, and record the title, number and expiration date, if any, of the document(s).

List A	OR	List B	AND	List C
Document title: _____		_____		_____
Issuing authority: _____		_____		_____
Document #: _____		_____		_____
Expiration Date (if any): _____		_____		_____
Document #: _____				
Expiration Date (if any): _____				

CERTIFICATION - I attest, under penalty of perjury, that I have examined the document(s) presented by the above-named employee, that the above-listed document(s) appear to be genuine and to relate to the employee named, that the employee began employment on *(month/day/year)* _____ and that to the best of my knowledge the employee is eligible to work in the United States. (State employment agencies may omit the date the employee began employment.)

Signature of Employer or Authorized Representative	Print Name	Title
Business or Organization Name and Address *(Street Name and Number, City, State, Zip Code)*		Date *(month/day/year)*

Section 3. Updating and Reverification. To be completed and signed by employer.

A. New Name *(if applicable)*	B. Date of Rehire *(month/day/year) (if applicable)*

C. If employee's previous grant of work authorization has expired, provide the information below for the document that establishes current employment eligibility.

Document Title: _____	Document #: _____	Expiration Date (if any): _____

I attest, under penalty of perjury, that to the best of my knowledge, this employee is eligible to work in the United States, and if the employee presented document(s), the document(s) I have examined appear to be genuine and to relate to the individual.

Signature of Employer or Authorized Representative	Date *(month/day/year)*

Form I-9 (Rev. 06/05/07) N

LISTS OF ACCEPTABLE DOCUMENTS

LIST A Documents that Establish Both Identity and Employment Eligibility	LIST B Documents that Establish Identity	LIST C Documents that Establish Employment Eligibility
OR		AND
1. U.S. Passport (unexpired or expired)	1. Driver's license or ID card issued by a state or outlying possession of the United States provided it contains a photograph or information such as name, date of birth, gender, height, eye color and address	1. U.S. Social Security card issued by the Social Security Administration *(other than a card stating it is not valid for employment)*
2. Permanent Resident Card or Alien Registration Receipt Card (Form I-551)	2. ID card issued by federal, state or local government agencies or entities, provided it contains a photograph or information such as name, date of birth, gender, height, eye color and address	2. Certification of Birth Abroad issued by the Department of State *(Form FS-545 or Form DS-1350)*
3. An unexpired foreign passport with a temporary I-551 stamp	3. School ID card with a photograph	3. Original or certified copy of a birth certificate issued by a state, county, municipal authority or outlying possession of the United States bearing an official seal
4. An unexpired Employment Authorization Document that contains a photograph (Form I-766, I-688, I-688A, I-688B)	4. Voter's registration card	4. Native American tribal document
	5. U.S. Military card or draft record	5. U.S. Citizen ID Card *(Form I-197)*
5. An unexpired foreign passport with an unexpired Arrival-Departure Record, Form I-94, bearing the same name as the passport and containing an endorsement of the alien's nonimmigrant status, if that status authorizes the alien to work for the employer	6. Military dependent's ID card	6. ID Card for use of Resident Citizen in the United States *(Form I-179)*
	7. U.S. Coast Guard Merchant Mariner Card	
	8. Native American tribal document	7. Unexpired employment authorization document issued by DHS *(other than those listed under List A)*
	9. Driver's license issued by a Canadian government authority	
	For persons under age 18 who are unable to present a document listed above:	
	10. School record or report card	
	11. Clinic, doctor or hospital record	
	12. Day-care or nursery school record	

Illustrations of many of these documents appear in Part 8 of the Handbook for Employers (M-274)

SAMPLE

Employment Application

An Equal Opportunity Employer

A person with a disability or handicap requiring accommodation for completing the application process should notify _____ as soon as possible

Filing this application does not imply that the applicant will be employed, but rather only that the applicant will be considered in competition with other applicants.

_____ (hereafter "Company") is an Equal Opportunity Employer. It is the Company's policy to afford equal employment opportunity regardless of race, religion, color, national origin, sex, age, marital status, height, weight, disability, or veteran status. Michigan law requires that a person with a disability or handicap requiring accommodation for employment must notify the employer in writing within 182 days after the need is known.

PERSONAL INFORMATION

_____
Date of Application

_____
Name (first, middle, last)

_____
Present Address (street, city, state, zip code)

_____
Home Telephone or Number You Can be Reached at   Business Telephone

_____
Position Desired   Salary/Hourly Rate Desired   Date Available

1. Are you at least 18 years old?   ☐ Yes ☐ No

2. Work Permit No. _____ (if under 18)

3. Have you ever been convicted of a crime (including misdemeanors)?   ☐ Yes ☐ No

   Are there any felony charges pending against you?   ☐ Yes ☐ No
   (A "Yes" answer to either question will not automatically disqualify you).

   Explain: _____
   _____

4. Have you previously been employed by the Company?   ☐ Yes ☐ No
   If yes, when: _____
   Under what name: _____

5. Have you submitted an application to the Company before?   ☐ Yes ☐ No
   If yes, when: _____
   Under what name: _____

6. List any/all relatives currently employed at the Company.
   _____
   _____

Complete the following only if the position requires a driver's license:

Driver's License Number: _____

Has your driver's license ever been revoked, suspended, restricted?   ☐ Yes ☐ No
If yes, for what reason and for how long? _____
_____

List any moving violations during the last three (3) years: _____
_____
_____

EDUCATIONAL HISTORY

Circle last grade completed: 1   2   3   4   5   6   7   8   9   10   11   12

Name of High School: _____

GED: _____   State: _____

Schools (include trade schools) attended other than high school	Location (City and State)	Course or Major Studied	Dates Attended	Degree

EMPLOYMENT HISTORY

List below, beginning with the most recent, **_all_** present and past employment (use a separate sheet of paper if necessary)

Company Name	Company Address	Phone Number
Position Held/Job Title		Dates of Employment
Name and Title of Immediate Supervisor		
Reason for Leaving		Hourly Wage/Salary
Brief Description of Duties		

Company Name	Company Address	Phone Number
Position Held/Job Title		Dates of Employment
Name and Title of Immediate Supervisor		
Reason for Leaving		Hourly Wage/Salary
Brief Description of Duties		

Company Name	Company Address	Phone Number
Position Held/Job Title		Dates of Employment
Name and Title of Immediate Supervisor		
Reason for Leaving		Hourly Wage/Salary
Brief Description of Duties		

In case of emergency, contact:

_____
Name

_____
Address

_____
Telephone

I certify that all of the information furnished on this Application is true, complete and correct. I understand and agree that any falsification, misrepresentation or omission of fact, either on this Application or during the pre-hire process, will be reason for (1) my not being offered employment, or (2) dismissal at any time from the service of _____, if employed.

I understand that consideration for employment at _____, is conditional upon a review of my qualifications, work history, references, etc. I authorize _____, to request and obtain verification that the information given by me on this Application is true, accurate and complete. I understand that such verification may include, but may not be limited to background information pertinent to the position for which I have applied, verification of education, verification of employment history, investigation of criminal history, etc. I therefore authorize my current and all previous employers to cooperate with _____, and to release, on a confidential basis, any information they may have concerning me, including information in my personnel record or otherwise known to them, to _____, in connection with my application for employment with _____. I specifically release from liability any current or former employer(s), its agents, representatives, employees, officers, directors, etc., for or on account of their providing/disclosing such information to _____

I understand and agree that my employment and compensation is for no definite period and may, regardless of the time and manner of payment of my wages and salary, be terminated at any time by me or the Company, with or without cause, and with or without any previous notice. I also understand and agree that the Company has the right to unilaterally modify and/or terminate any policies, practices, procedures and standards it has adopted or implemented, to the extent not prohibited by law. I acknowledge that no Company employee nor representative, other than the President, has either the power or authority to enter into any agreement for employment for any specified period of time, or to make any representations or agreements contrary to any of the foregoing, unless that agreement is in writing and is signed by the President. I understand that any prior representations, promises, contracts or statements made by or on behalf of the Company are expressly superseded by the foregoing.

The Immigration Reform and Control Act of 1986 states that employers must require all persons hired to submit documents to the employer showing their identity and their right to be lawfully employed in the United States. It also requires that the employee complete and sign a government form to this effect. I understand that if hired by _____, I will timely furnish documents for inspection that verify my identity and that I am legally permitted to work in the United States. Furthermore, I understand that my employment will be terminated if I fail to timely provide the necessary documents.

Dated: _____

_____
Signature

_____
(Applicant's name – printed)

UIA 1020
(Rev. 6-08)

State of Michigan
Department of Labor & Economic Growth
UNEMPLOYMENT INSURANCE AGENCY
Tax Office – Suite 11-500
3024 W. Grand Boulevard – Detroit, Michigan 48202
www.michigan.gov/uia

Authorized by
MCL 421.1, et seq.

EMPLOYER'S QUARTERLY TAX REPORT

Employer Name & Address: **Mail To:**

Do Not Make Address Corrections On This Form.
If the pre-printed address is not correct, please call (800) 638-3994 (in Michigan) or (313) 456-2180 to obtain Form UIA 1025, *Employer Request for Address/Name Change.*

INSTRUCTIONS: This report is due on the 25th of the month following the end of the calendar quarter and can be filed on-line through B2G On-Line Services at www.michigan.gov/uia. See reverse side for detailed instructions, Statement of Authority, reporting requirements, and interest and penalty charges. Employers without a UIA account number: Note special instructions on reverse side.

CHECKS SHOULD BE MADE PAYABLE TO: State of Michigan – Unemployment Insurance Agency
(Write your 7-digit UIA Employer AccountNumber on the front of the check.)

To insure proper processing of this report, type/print characters in ink within the boxes as shown. | 0 1 2 3 4 5 6 7 8 9 | Check box, if final report.
*See reverse side for instructions

1. UIA Employer Account Number
2. Taxable Wage Limit
3. Quarter Ending Date
4. Federal Emp. I.D. Number

5. Gross Wages $
6. Excess Wages $
7. Taxable Wages $
8. Tax Rate
9. Tax Due $
10. Prior Account Balance As of
11. Amount Enclosed $

12. Provide the *number* of all *full-time* and *part-time workers* who worked during or received pay for the pay period which includes the 12th of the month.
1st Month
2nd Month
3rd Month

YOUR CERTIFICATION: I declare that I have examined this report, and to the best of my knowledge and belief, it is true, correct and complete.

Signature

Title   *Date*

MAKE A COPY FOR YOUR RECORDS   TELEPHONE (   )   -

For UIA Use Only. Do Not Write Below Line.
$

10200806

UIA 1020
(Rev. 6-08)
Reverse Side

QUARTERLY TAX REPORT & LINE-BY-LINE INSTRUCTIONS

REVIEW ALL PRE-PRINTED DATA FOR ACCURACY. If correction is necessary, or you are reporting a change of address, enter corrections on UIA 1025, *Employer Request for Address Change*.

DETAILED INSTRUCTIONS FOR COMPLETING UIA 1020

*Check box to indicate final report and receive UIA 1772 to inactivate, discontinue or report the sale or transfer of a business.

Line 1: If your UIA account number is not pre-printed, enter it here. New employers, see "SPECIAL INSTRUCTIONS FOR NEW EMPLOYERS" BELOW.

Line 2: This is the current amount of each employee's yearly wages that is considered taxable for unemployment tax purposes.

Line 3: Correct quarter ending dates are 03/31, 06/30, 09/30 and 12/31, plus the appropriate year. Month must be 2 digits, as shown.

Line 4: If your Federal Employer Identification Number (FEIN) is not pre-printed here, it is not part of your UIA record, and we cannot certify to the IRS the amount of unemployment tax you have paid to the State of Michigan. Make sure your FEIN is entered in this space.

Line 5: Enter total wages paid in quarter, including cash value of all compensation paid in any medium other than cash, such as meals, lodging and rent. Only cash wages should be reported for agricultural or domestic services.

NOTE: All compensation (remuneration) earned by an individual for personal services is wages, unless services performed are specifically excluded from coverage by law.

Line 6: Determine how much of each employee's wages reported on Line 5 is in excess of the taxable wage limit shown. Wages paid to an individual by a single employing unit, which exceed the taxable wage limit for that year, are not taxable.

For example: An employee is paid $3,250 per quarter, and the taxable wage limit for that year is $9,000. Quarterly wages are reported as follows:

Wages	1st Qtr.	2nd Qtr.	3rd Qtr.	4th Qtr.	TOTAL
Gross	$3,250	$3,250	$3,250	$3,250	$13,000
Excess	0	0	$750	$3,250	$ 4,000
Taxable	$3,250	$3,250	$2,500	0	$ 9,000

SUCCESSOR EMPLOYERS may use an employee's wages previously reported by a predecessor employer when determining excess wages within the same calendar year.

MULTI-STATE EMPLOYERS whose employees work in two or more states in one year, should use all of an individual's wages previously reported in another state when determining excess wages reportable to UIA in the calendar year.

Line 7: Subtract Line 6 from Line 5.

Line 8: Tax rate will be indicated on pre-printed reports. A "T" preceding your tax rate indicates a temporary rate. This rate is assigned until there is sufficient information to compute a permanent tax rate for the rate year.

Line 9: Multiply Line 7 by Line 8.

Line 10: Your account balance, if any, will be pre-printed. Date shown is date your account was last updated prior to mailing. "BALANCE DUE" indicates an amount owed, including penalties and interest; "CREDIT" indicates an amount overpaid.

Line 11: Enter amount of the payment being submitted. If no tax is due or no remittance is being made, enter 0. **MAKE CHECKS PAYABLE TO STATE OF MICHIGAN, UNEMPLOYMENT COMPENSATION, AND WRITE YOUR UIA ACCOUNT NUMBER ON THE FACE OF THE CHECK.**

Line 12: Include in the count all workers (full or part-time) who worked during or received pay (subject to Unemployment Insurance wages) for the payroll period which includes the 12th of the month. Do this for each month of the quarter for which you are filing. Include those workers who are on leave without pay. Workers are to be included even if they earned wages in excess of the taxable wage limit.

AUTHORITY – Every contributing employer is required to submit a quarterly report and any payment due on or before the 25th day of the month following the end of the calendar quarter as provided by Section 13 of the Michigan Employment Security Act (MCL 421.13). By statute, timeliness is determined by the UIA receipt date, not the date of mailing. Reports must be filed and taxes due should be paid promptly even if appeals are pending involving liability or tax rate issues.

REPORTING REQUIREMENTS – SUBMISSION OF THIS FORM IS MANDATORY. You must file a report for each calendar quarter even if you have no covered workers, no wages to report, no tax due, you are making only a partial payment or you are not remitting the payment due. Failure to file a report for each quarter may result in the assignment of a maximum tax rate. Each quarterly report filed should include only the wages paid in the quarterly period reported. A separate report must be filed for each employer or legal entity in order to ascertain the proper liability and to establish accurate experience accounting records. (The correction of a previously filed report must be made on Form UIA 1021, *Amended Quarterly Tax Report*.) Do not adjust wages on a current report to compensate for a prior error since such corrections can adversely affect your tax rate. Call (800)-638-3994 to obtain forms. Outside Michigan call (313) 456-2180.

INTEREST – Interest accrues at the rate of 1% per month (computed on a daily basis) on all taxes remaining unpaid after the due date as provided by Section 15(a) of the MES Act. Failure to pay can also result in the filing of a Tax Lien for unpaid taxes as provided in Section 15(e) of the MES Act, and adversely affect your tax rate in future years. Section 15(i) provides that your tax liability can be estimated if you fail to file your report.

PENALTY CHARGES – Penalty charges amounting to 10% of the taxes due on each report are assessed for late quarterly reports as provided in Section 54(c) of the MES Act. The penalty, however, cannot be less than $5.00 or greater than $25.00. In cases of negligence, willful neglect or fraud, the Act provides for more severe penalties.

YOU MUST FILE THIS REPORT EVEN IF YOU ARE UNABLE TO PAY OR HAVE NO PAYROLL FOR THE QUARTER.
KEEP A COPY FOR YOUR RECORDS.

Send correspondence with requests, protests or questions separately to:
Unemployment Insurance Agency
P.O. Box 8068
Royal Oak, Michigan 48068-8068

If you are having difficulty resolving a problem with your account, contact the UIA Tax Office at (313) 456-2180.

SPECIAL INSTRUCTIONS FOR NEW EMPLOYERS

IF YOU HAVE RECENTLY FILED FORM 518, *REGISTRATION FOR MICHIGAN BUSINESS TAXES*, AND HAVE NOT YET RECEIVED YOUR UIA ACCOUNT NUMBER, call **Team Support at (313) 456-2180** to request your account number. If we are able to provide your account number, enter it in the space provided on the form and complete report using line-by-line instructions. Mail completed report with payment to the post office box listed on the front of this form. If an account number has not yet been assigned, send a copy of your Registration Report (518), with your Quarterly Tax Report (UIA 1020). **Include your Federal Employer Identification Number (FEIN) and mark the registration report "DUPLICATE."** MAIL AS DIRECTED BELOW. **IF YOU HAVE NOT COMPLETED FORM 518** *REGISTRATION REPORT*, **YOU MUST SUBMIT THE REPORT WITH YOUR UIA 1020** *QUARTERLY REPORT*. Include your FEIN. To obtain forms, call Team Support at the number listed above or in Michigan call (800)-638-3994.

Mail completed reports without payments to:
Unemployment Insurance Agency
Tax Office, Suite 11-500
3024 W. Grand Boulevard
Detroit, Michigan 48202

MAIL COMPLETED REPORTS WITH PAYMENTS TO:
Unemployment Insurance Agency
P.O. Box 33598
Detroit, Michigan 48232-5598

NOTE: If your business has more than one location or type of business activity in Michigan, you may be instructed to file a Multiple Worksite Report (BLS 3020) each quarter.

DLEG is an Equal Opportunity Employer/Program.

A 1017 (Rev. 1-06)

Wage Detail Report
STATE OF MICHIGAN, DEPARTMENT OF LABOR & ECONOMIC GROWTH
UNEMPLOYMENT INSURANCE AGENCY
See reverse side for detailed instructions and penalty provisions.

Authorized by MCL 421.1, et seq.

CA ELITE

PICA ELITE

BY USING "ALIGNMENT BOXES" TYPED & LINE PRINTED DATA WILL FALL WITHIN ALL FIELDS

Report Quarter Ending:

Return by:

Mail original form to: *(Do not mail a copy)*

UIA Wage Record Unit
P.O. Box 9052
Detroit, MI 48202-9052
1-313-456-2760
(TTY customers use 1-866-366-0004)

FEIN

UIA Account Number

Multi-Unit

Please Type Or Print All Information

STATUS	DELETE (X)	SOCIAL SECURITY NUMBER	EMPLOYEE NAME LAST NAME	FIRST NAME	GROSS WAGES PAID THIS QUARTER
					$
					$
					$
					$
					$
					$
					$
					$
					$
					$
					$
					$
					$
					$
					$
					$
					$
					$
					$
					$

I declare that I have examined this report and to the best of my knowledge and belief, it is correct and complete.

TOTAL $

(Last page only)

Signature: Date:

PAGE   OF

Title: Telephone:

UIA 1017 (Rev. 1-06)
Reverse side

INSTRUCTIONS FOR COMPLETING WAGE DETAIL REPORT
(THIS FORM MUST BE TYPED OR PRINTED)

(NOTE: Employers reporting quarterly wage detail information using magnetic tape or computer printouts should not complete this form.)

STATUS	DELETE (X)	SOCIAL SECURITY NUMBER	EMPLOYEE NAME LAST NAME	FIRST NAME	GROSS WAGES PAID THIS QUARTER	
	X	123-45-6789	PUBLIC	JOHN	$	
		444-44-4444	ANTHONY	WAYNE	$ 13620	00
F		555-55-5555	GREEN	RALPH	$ 12345	00
		777-77-7777	PUBLIC	QUINCY	$ 12987	00

PREPRINTED FORM

1. Review each Social Security Number and employee name for correctness.
2. Enter the Social Security Number and name of any unlisted employee to whom you paid wages during the quarter. Wages cannot be processed without a Social Security Number.
3. If the Social Security Number or name is incorrect, or you wish to delete a name, place an "X" in the **Delete** column. Do not enter the wages. (See the sample at the top of this page.) **IF WAGES ARE REPORTED FOR THE QUARTER, THE EMPLOYEE NAME CANNOT BE DELETED.**

BLANK FORM

1. At the top of each page, in the space provided, enter the employer name, address, the 10-digit UIA Employer Account Number (including the 3-digit Multi Unit Number), Federal Employer Identification Number (FEIN) and quarter ending date, e.g., 06/30/2004.
2. Enter the Social Security Number, name, and gross quarterly wages paid for all employees.

STATUS

Leave blank unless you are a **family-owned business** and more than 50% of the business is owned by the employee, their spouse, child, or parent (if employee is under the age of 18 at the time the work was performed). If so, place an **"F"** in this column as shown in the above sample. Otherwise, this field is reserved for other future uses. Refer to Section 46(g) of the MES Act.

GROSS WAGES

Enter a zero (0) for each employee who was not paid any wages during the quarter. This ensures that the employee will be included on future reports.

Enter the **Total** on the bottom of the LAST PAGE ONLY. The total shown on the last page of this report **MUST** equal the Gross Quarterly Wages reported on your Employer's Quarterly Tax Report (Form UIA 1020) for the same quarter.

WAGES TO BE REPORTED

Wage detail information must be provided for every covered employee to whom wages were paid during the calendar quarter. Do not report wages that were earned but not actually paid during the calendar quarter. Also, do not report wages of a worker whose services are excluded from coverage under Section 43 of the Michigan Employment Security (MES) Act. When reporting gross wages, enter the total amount of wages paid to each employee during the calendar quarter.

Include wages paid either in cash or in a medium other than cash such as the cash equivalent of meals furnished on the employer's premises, and the cash equivalent of lodging provided by the employer as a condition of employment. Also included as wages are commissions and bonuses, awards and prizes, vacation and holiday pay, sick pay when paid to liquidate a worker's balance of sick pay at the time of separation from employment, tips actually reported by the worker to the employer, and the cash value of a cafeteria plan, if the employee has the option under the plan to choose cash. **Do not include** as wages such payments as severance pay, profit-sharing, sick pay paid under an employer plan on account of sickness, contributions to a retirement plan, discounts on purchases from the employer, or reimbursements to employees of expenses incurred on behalf of the employer.

Refer to Section 44 of the MES Act for more information.

PENALTY INFORMATION

Effective with the third quarter of 1995, any employer (or agent) failing to submit, when due, any Wage Detail Report, required by Section 54(2) of the MES Act, is subject to a penalty of $25.00 for each untimely report.

TO CORRECT PRIOR REPORTS

Please submit an Amended Wage Detail Report (Form UIA 1019). To obtain Form UIA 1019, contact the Wage Record Unit at 1-313-456-2760 (TTY customer use 1-866-366-0004) or visit our website at www.michigan.gov/uia.

CHANGE OF BUSINESS LOCATION OR MAILING ADDRESS

Please submit an Employer Request for Address/Name Change (Form UIA 1025). To obtain this form, contact the UIA Tax Office at 1-313-456-2180 (TTY customers use 1-866-366-0004).

DLEG IS AN EQUAL OPPORTUNITY EMPLOYER AND COMPLIES WITH THE AMERICANS WITH DISABILITIES ACT.

UIA 1020-R
(Rev. 2-07)

State of Michigan
Department of Labor & Economic Growth
UNEMPLOYMENT INSURANCE AGENCY
Tax Office – Suite 11-500
3024 W. Grand Boulevard – Detroit, Michigan 48202
Phone: (313) 456-2180 FAX: (313) 456-2130
www.michigan.gov/uia

Authorized by
MCL 421.1, et seq.

REIMBURSING EMPLOYER'S QUARTERLY PAYROLL REPORT

Employer Name & Address

Mail To:

Unemployment Insurance Agency
Tax Office
PO Box 33598
Detroit, MI 48232-5598

DO NOT MAKE ADDRESS CORRECTIONS ON THIS FORM.
If the pre-printed address is not correct, please call (800) 638-3994 (in Michigan) or (313) 456-2180 to obtain Form UIA 1025, *Employer Request for Address/Name Change.*

INSTRUCTIONS: This report is due on the 25th of the month following the end of the calendar quarter. See reverse side for detailed instructions.

To insure proper processing of this report, type/print characters in ink within the boxes as shown.	0	1	2	3	4	5	6	7	8	9

1. UIA Account Number
2. Federal Emp. I.D. Number
3. Quarter Ending Date
4. Gross Wages $
5. Provide the number of all full-time and part-time workers who worked during, or received pay for the pay period, which includes the 12th of the month

   1st Month
   2nd Month
   3rd Month

YOUR CERTIFICATION: I declare that I have examined this report, and to the best of my knowledge and belief, it is true, correct and complete.

Signature: Date:

Title: Telephone (   )   -

MAKE A COPY FOR YOUR RECORDS

For UIA Use Only. Do Not Write Below Line.

1020R0702

UIA 1020-R
(Rev. 2-07)
Reverse Side

REIMBURSING EMPLOYER'S QUARTERLY PAYROLL REPORT LINE-BY-LINE INSTRUCTIONS

REVIEW ALL PRE-PRINTED DATA FOR ACCURACY. If correction is necessary, or you are reporting a change of address, enter corrections on Form UIA 1025, *Employer Request for Address Change*.

DETAILED INSTRUCTIONS FOR COMPLETING UIA 1020-R

Line 1: Use this form only when you have been assigned a Reimbursing UIA Account Number. Your UIA account number starts with 08 and is the first seven digits of the account number.

Line 2: If your Federal Employer Identification Number (FEIN) is not pre-printed here, enter it here.

Line 3: Correct quarter ending dates are 03/31, 06/30, 09/30 and 12/31, plus the appropriate year. Month must be two digits, as shown.

Line 4: Enter total wages paid in the quarter (dollars and cents), including cash value of all compensation paid in any medium other than cash, such as meals, lodging and rent. Only cash wages should be reported for agricultural and domestic services. Do not include elected officials or voluntary fire fighters. If you have further questions, please call the Reimbursing Unit. The figure you enter should match what you report on Form UIA 1017, *Wage Detail Report*.

Line 5: Include in the count all workers (full-time or part-time) who worked during, or received pay (subject to unemployment insurance wages) for the payroll period that includes the 12th of the month. Do this for each month of the quarter for which your are filing. Include those workers who are on leave with or without pay. List one digit per box. For example **239** employees for the first month would be reported as

1st Month			2	3	9

AUTHORITY: Effective with the 2nd quarter of 2005, every reimbursing employer is required to submit a quarterly payroll report on or before the 25th day of the month following the end of the calendar quarter as provided by Section 13 of the Michigan Employment Security (MES) Act (MCL 421.13). By statute, timeliness is determined by the Unemployment Insurance Agency's (UIA) receipt date, not the date of mailing. Reports must be filed promptly, even if an appeal involving liability issues is pending.

REPORTING REQUIREMENTS – SUBMISSION OF THIS FORM IS MANDATORY:
You must file a report for each calendar quarter even if you have no covered workers or no wages to report. Failure to file a report for each quarter will result in a penalty charge being assessed. Each quarterly report filed should include only the wages paid in the quarterly period reported. A separate report must be filed for each employer or legal entity in order to obtain the needed information. Correction of a previously filed report must be made on Form UIA 1021-R, *Amended Reimbursing Employer's Quarterly Payroll Report*. Do not adjust wages on a current report to compensate for a prior error.

Form UIA 1020-R replaces DLEG Form 3104. However, for employers with multiple worksites, please continue to file Form BLS 3020, *Multiple Work Site Form*. Contact the Bureau of Labor Market and Statistical Initiatives, Quarterly Census of Employment and Wages Section, at 313-456-3071, regarding Form BLS 3020.

PENALTY CHARGES: Penalties are $10.00 for each report received after the due date as provided in Section 54(c) of the MES Act. In cases of negligence, willful neglect, or fraud, the Act provides for more severe penalties.

YOU MUST FILE THIS REPORT EVEN IF YOU HAVE NO PAYROLL FOR THIS QUARTER. KEEP A COPY FOR YOUR RECORDS.

MAILING INSTRUCTIONS

Mail completed Form UIA 1020-R to:

Unemployment Insurance Agency
PO Box 33598
Detroit, Michigan 48232-5598

FURTHER INFORMATION

UIA forms mentioned here are on our website:
www.michigan.gov/uia

For assistance regarding your reimbursing account, please contact the UIA Tax Office Reimbursing Unit at 313-456-2080.

SPECIAL INSTRUCTIONS FOR NEW REIMBURSING EMPLOYERS

You must register with the MI Dept. of Treasury and the Unemployment Insurance Agency (UIA) using Form 518, *Registration for Michigan Taxes*. Form 518 is available at www.michigan.gov/treasury or www.michigan.gov/uia. You may also register directly with our Agency online at www.michigan.gov/uia. If you are requesting reimbursing payment status at the time of registration, you must also provide a copy of your IRS 501(c)(3) exemption letter and be sure to provide an estimated total calendar year gross payroll when you register. **Failure to provide a copy of the IRS 501(c)(3) exemption letter and the annual gross payroll amount on your registration, will delay your registration with the UIA.** You may fax your IRS 501(c)(3) exemption letter to the Reimbursing Unit at 313-456-2132. Call the Reimbursing Unit at 313-456-2080 for questions regarding registration.

If you have not received a UIA account number prior to submitting Form UIA 1020-R, YOU MUST EITHER CONTACT THE REIMBURSING UNIT OR SUBMIT A COMPLETED COPY OF FORM 518 AND YOUR IRS 501(c)(3) EXEMPTION LETTER ALONG WITH FORM UIA 1020-R. Because you have no UIA account number, mail the required forms directly to the Reimbursing Unit at:

Unemployment Insurance Agency
Tax Office, Suite 11-500
3024 W. Grand Blvd.
Detroit, MI 48202

DLEG is an Equal Opportunity Employer and complies with the Americans with Disabilities Act.

Index

ADA .... *See* Americans with Disabilities Act
ADEA .... See Age Discrimination in Employment Act
ADR .... *See* Alternative Dispute Resolution
affirmative action 95
   employer's self-analysis 106
   plan obligations 21
   plans 100
   record retention 113
Age Discrimination in Employment Act 51, 52
AIDS issues 91
alcohol
   coverage under ADA and MPWDCRA 81
Alternative Dispute Resolution 5, 70
   drafting or adopting an enforceable procedure 73
   employment discrimination 70
Americans with Disabilities Act 77
   able to perform essential functions 81
   conflicts with other federal laws 92
   disability, definition of 78
   discriminatory acts 82
   drug and alcohol use 81
   employers subject to 77
   individuals protected by 78
   medical exams 83
   notification 92
   qualified for the position 81
   reasonable accommodation 84
   remedies under 93
   safety of self or others 90
   undue hardship 88
aptitude, personality and honesty testing 15
audits
   confidentiality 40
   danger of 43
   Human Resources 38
   Preventive Legal 38
   process 40
benefits 165
   avoiding liability 189
   cafeteria plans 177
      benefit types 179
      legal operating rules 180

>   nondiscrimination rules 183
>   flexible spending accounts 181
>   retirement plans 173
>   annuity requirements 176
>   governing rules 174
>   qualification of 177
>   vesting 176

BFOQ .... See bona fide occupational qualification
Bioterrorism Response Act of 2002 352
bona fide occupational qualification 49
Bullard-Plawecki Employee Right to Know Act 68
CCPA .... *See* Consumer Credit Protection Act
COBRA .... See Consolidated Omnibus Budget Reconciliation Act
collective bargaining 288
communicable diseases 91
concealed weapons law 350
Consolidated Omnibus Budget Reconciliation Act 184
>   coverage length 187
>   extended coverage option 186
>   notification obligations 185
>   penalties 188
>   types of benefits 187

Consumer Credit Protection Act 341
>   definition of earnings 341
>   restrictions on garnishments 342

criminal records checks 12
defamation 317
>   defenses to a claim 318
>   elements of a claim 318
>   in written information 322
>   types of 318
>   when communicating to outside parties 321
>   when investigation an employee 319
>   when terminating an employee 320

disability
>   definition of 78

discharge 365
discipline 365
>   employee representation in 290

discrimination 45, 46
>   adverse impact 49
>   age *51*
>   Alternative Dispute Resolution 70
>   avoiding liability 51, 55
>   BFOQ 49

disability 77
disparate treatment 47
Genetic Information Non-Discrimination Act 54
intentional 48
marital status 50
pregnancy 54
recordkeeping 66
retaliation 50
safety of self or others 90
Title VII 51
drug and alcohol testing 14
drugs
coverage under ADA and MPWDCRA 81
duty to the victim 23
earnings, definition of 341
Elliott-Larsen Civil Rights Act 46
adverse impact discrimination 49
avoiding discrimination liability 51
BFOQ 49
disparate treatment discrimination 47
intentional discrimination 48
marital status discrimination 50
retaliation prohibitions 50
e-mail monitoring 328
emergency safety standards 410
Employee Free Choice Act 291
Employee Retirement Income Security Act 165
accrual 169
agency responsibility 165
definitions 165
enforcement 172
fiduciary resonsibilities 170
jurisdiction 173
minimum funding 169
participation 168
preemption 173
reporting and disclosure 167
vesting 168
employee right-to-know 68
employees, types of
at-will 27
employment status 27
independent contractors 30
just-cause 28
leased or temporary 35

- mixed status ... 36
- satisfaction ... 28
- term contract ... 29

ergonomics ... 402
ERISA ... *See* Employee Retirement Income Security Act
Fair Credit Reporting Act ... 13
Fair Labor Standards Act ... 129
- administrative exemption ... 143
- employers subject to ... 129
- enforcement of ... 147
- executive exemption ... 142
- minimum wage under ... 137
- outside sales representative exemption ... 145
- overtime under ... 139
- professional exemption ... 143
- recordkeeping requirements ... 132
- regular rate of pay ... 139

Family and Medical Leave Act ... 3, 241
- Americans with Disabilities Act ... 261
- birth or adoption of a child ... 248
- collective bargaining agreements ... 262
- continuation of benefits during leave ... 253
- covered service members ... 248
- duration and conditions questions ... 251
- eligibility ... 243, 244
- employee requirements ... 259
- employers covered by ... 241
- equivalent position ... 256
- interplay with other laws ... 260
- key employees ... 257
- pay during leave ... 252
- posting and notice requirements ... 257
- remedies ... 260
- restoration of benefits ... 256
- return-to-work rights ... 255
- serious health condition of a parent, spouse, or child ... 247
- serious health condition of employee ... 244
- U.S.Constitution ... 260
- Uniformed Services Employment and Reemployment Rights Act ... 262
- workers' compensation ... 260

FCRA ... *See* Fair Credit Reporting Act
Federal Child Labor Laws ... 160
fiduciary ... 166
flexible spending accounts ... 178, 181
- coverage period ... 182

    healthcare, special rules 182
    use-it-or-lose-it rule 181
FMLA ....*See* Family and Medical Leave Act, *See* Family and Medical Leave Act
food handling safety 91
FSA .... *See* flexible spending accounts
garnishments 341
    definition of earnings 341
    enforcement of 343
    for family support 342
    Michigan provisions for 343
    multiple 343
    penalties for violating 344
    restrictions on 342
Genetic Information Non-Discrimination Act 3, 54
genetic testing 82
GINA .... *See* Genetic Information Non-Discrimination Act
Glossary of Acronyms and Abbreviations xxi
harassment 57
    avoiding lawsuits 66
    favoritism 59
    hostile environment 58
    investigations 64
    racial 62
    same sex 60
    sexual 57
hazard communication 435
    employee training 439
    Hazard Communication Standard
        checklist 452
        compliance guidelines 442
        violations of 442
    hazard determination 436
    Material Safety Data Sheets 437
    written program 437
hazardous materials
    air contaminant standards 456
    chemical contamination plans 453
    determination 436
    employee training 439
    handling 433
    labeling of 437
    medical records, employee 457
HCS .... *See* Hazard Communication Standard
Health Insurance Portability and Accountability Act 205, 239
    accelerated life insurance payments 205

disclosure requirements 205
enrollment periods 202
frequently asked questions... 200
limits on evidence of insurability... 203
long-term care 204
medical savings accounts... 204
pre-existing condition limits 195
prior coverage 198
types of creditable coverage... 199
health issues .... *See* safety and health issues
HIPAA .... See Health Insurance Portability and Accountability Act
hiring
    INS verification... 115
    negligent.. 22
    noncompete agreements.. 348
    pitfalls to avoid 16
    reporting requirements 25
I-9 Form requirements
    new I-9 forms.. 117
I–9 Form requirements.. 115
Immigration Reform and Control Act.. 115
    antidiscrimination provisions of 118
    avoiding discrimination liability.. 118
    avoiding sanctions.. 117
    INS audits.. 118
    inspections
        during... 120
        preparing for.. 119
    penalties for violating 117
independent contractors 30
    IRS Revenue Ruling 87-41 31
inspections
    Immigration Reform and Control Act... 118
    safety... 417
interviews... 8
    lawful and unlawful inquiries 9
IRCA .... *See* Immigration Reform and Control Act
IRS Revenue Ruling 87-41 31
job application forms 7
lawsuits, employee
    alternative dispute resolution 5, 70
    avoiding discrimination liability... 51, 55
    benefit liability, avoiding... 189
    harassment lawsuits, avoiding 66
    insurance for.. 6

invasion of privacy claims, defenses to 312
preventive audits 6
reducing risks 37
layoffs 355
documenting decisions 358
reductions in force
avoiding liability 355
libel 318
Lockout/Tagout
sample procedure 462
standards 419
long-term care 204
marital status
discrimination 50
Material Safety Data Sheets 437
trade secrets 440
medical exams 83
medical records
exposure to hazardous materials 457
medical savings accounts 204
MESA .... *See* Michigan Employment Security Act
Michigan Employment Security Act 379
Michigan Minimum Wage Law 149
employers subject to 149
recordkeeping requirements 153
Michigan Occupational Safety and Health Act 407
education and training 417
emergency safety standards 410
employee obligations 409
employer appeals 432
employer obligations 408
General Duty Clause 408
general rights and duties 407
recordkeeping 411
safety standards 409
variances 410
violation citations 429
Michigan Persons With Disabilities Civil Rights Act 77
able to perform essential functions 81
conflicts with other federal laws 92
disability, definition of 78
discriminatory acts 82
drug and alcohol use 81
employers subject to 77
genetic testing 82

    individuals protected by 78
    medical exams 83
    notification 92
    qualified for the position 81
    reasonable accommodation 84
    remedies under 93
    safety of self or others 90
    undue hardship 88
Michigan Wage and Fringe Benefits Act 121
    employers subjet to 121
    enforcement of 127
    purpose of 121
    recordkeeping requirements 125
Michigan Youth Employment Standards Act 155
    employers subject to 155
    minimum wage under 156
    recordkeeping requirements 159
    work permits 158
military duty 3, 293
    Uniformed Services Employment and Reemployment Rights Act (USERRA) 293
MIOSH Act .... *See* Michigan Occupational Safety and Health Act
misrepresentations of fact 22
MMWL .... *See* Michigan Minimum Wage Law
monitoring of telephones and computers 327
MPWDCRA .... *See* Michigan Persons With Disabilities Civil Rights Act
MSDS .... *See* Material Safety Data Sheets
MWDCA .... *See* workers' compensation
MWFBA .... *See* Michigan Wage and Fringe Benefits Act
MYESA .... *See* Michigan Youth Employment Standards Act
National Institute for Occupational Safety and Health 398
National Labor Relations Act 275
    collective bargaining 288
    election cases 275
    Employee Free Choice Act 291
    employee participation committees 289
    unfair labor practice cases 285
National Labor Relations Board 275
NIOSH .... *See* National Institute for Occupational Safety and Health
NLRA .... *See* National Labor Relations Act
NLRB .... *See* National Labor Relations Board
noncompete agreements .... *See* noncompete covenants
noncompete covenants 344
    court handling of 347
    duration of 346
    enforcement under Michigan law 345

    existing employees 349
    geographic limitations 347
    requiring employees to sign 344
    restricted activities in 345
Occupational Safety and Health Act 396
    agencies created by 397
    citations 397
    employers subject to 399
    enforcement of 397
    ergonomics 402
    inspections 397
    state plans 403
    violation types 397
OSHA .... See Occupational Safety and Health Act
Patroit Act of 2001 352
payment of wages 122
pension plan 166
    accrual 169
    fiduciary 166
    fiduciary responsibilities 170
    participant 166
    participation 168
    vesting 168
personnel file 68
    privacy guidelines 313
    subpoena of 329
polygraphs
    disclosure of information 337
    during a test 337
    enforcement of FEPPA 333
    examiner qualifications 337
    exemptions under FEPPA 334
    Federal Employee Polygraph Protection Act 332
    non-application of FEPPA 334
    Polygraph Protection Act 330
    PPA penalties 331
    PPA remedies 332
    PPA testing requirements 331
    pretest conditions 336
    prohibited practices 330
    regulation of 330
posting requirements
    EEOC 85
    Michigan Department of Civil Rights 85, 92
    Michigan Right-to-Know 438

- MSDS, new or revised ... 439
- Polygraph Protection Act ... 333
- under FMLA ... 257
- pre-existing condition ... 195
- pregnancy ... 54
- privacy
  - appropriation ... 312
  - defamation ... 317
  - defenses to invasion of privacy claims ... 312
  - false light ... 312
  - intrusion ... 311
  - invasion of ... 311
  - personnel file guidelines ... 313
  - Privacy Protection Act ... 327
  - protecting employee privacy ... 315
  - public disclosure ... 312
  - searches ... 317
- proximate cause ... 24
- racial harassment ... 62
- recordkeeping
  - antidiscrimination ... 66
  - Michigan Occupational Safety and Health Act ... 411
  - new hire reporting requirements ... 25
  - obligations
    - all employers ... 67
    - OSHA subjects ... 68
  - personnel file ... 68, 313
- reductions in force
  - avoiding liability ... 355
- reference checks ... 11
- references
  - liability concerns ... 24
- releases ... 5
- retirement plans ... 173
  - annuity requirements ... 176
  - governing rules ... 174
  - qualification of ... 177
  - vesting ... 176
- safety and health issues ... 395
  - education and training ... 417
  - emergency safety standards ... 410
  - inspections ... 417
  - Michigan safety standards ... 409
- searches ... 317
- sexual harassment ... 57

designing a policy 60
policy, sample 61, 62
slander 318
Social Security Number Privacy Act 322
financial institutions 324
limited exceptions 324
public employers 323
stalker statutes 460
SUTA Dumping 393
termination 365
outplacement 4
releases 5
Title VII 51
Toussaint Doctrine 36
undue hardship
ADA definition of 88
MPWDCRA definition of 89
unemployment compensation 379
appeals 384
basic provisions 379
benefits, determining 384
claimants' eligibility requirements 383
claiming benefits 382
covered employment 380
filing requirements 382
hearings 379
hearings, recommendations 387
preparing a case 384
record-keeping requirements 382
seasonal workers 382
statutory amendments 391
unemployment insurance tax 381
workers' compensation, coordinating with 384
unfair labor practices 285
remedies against 288
Uniformed Services Employment and Reemployment Rights Act
how long do employees have rights under USERRA 295
notice to employer 297
who has rights under USERRA 293, 294
unions
collective bargaining 288
election objections 284
election petitions 275
elections 283
National Labor Relations Act 275

pre-election campaigns 279
pre-election hearings 276
unfair labor practice 285
voluntary election agreements 278
video surveillance 328
violence 458
employee education 459
employees, investigating 458
mental or psychological testing 458
stalker statutes 460
taking action 459
threat assessment/response team 459
WARN .... *See* Worker Adjustment and Retraining Notification Act
weapons 350
Weingarten rights 290
Whistleblowers' Protection Act 338
enforcement of 340
protected activities 338
proving violations of 339
remedies under 340
Worker Adjustment and Retraining Notification Act 360
employers subject to 360
enforcement and penalties 363
notification obligations 361
purchase and sale of business 363
workers' compensation
employers and employees covered 263, 264, 265
exclusive remedy provision 270
injuries and illnesses covered 265
insurance requirements 273
unemployment compensation, coordinating with 384
workers' compensation 263
disability benefits 269
disability under Michigan law 268
noncompensable injuries 267
off-premises injuries 267
on-premises injuries 266
Workplace Smoking Bans 325
workplace violence .... *See* violence
WPA .... *See* Whistleblowers' Protection Act

LALIB:177198.1\103109-00003